# Raves from Diane Phillips's Cooking Students!

"Diane Phillips is definitely the Diva of Do-Ahead! Her do-ahead recipes are perfect for any skill level, from novice cook to expert, or somewhere in between. As a working woman, I find that her do-ahead recipes have helped to make my dinner parties, as well as my everyday cooking, much easier."                    —Kristal Custer, Newburgh, Indiana

"Because of Diane's great do-ahead recipes, I'm able to enjoy my own dinner party, mingle with the guests, and still 'wow' them with the food. Thanks, Diane."
                    —Diane LaPlante, Sykesville, Maryland

"I love the prepare-ahead recipes. The Diva is divine!"
                    —Patricia Lewis, Santa Rosa, California

"I've been cooking for a long time, but what a treat it was meeting Diane. I'm so excited to try each and every one of her do-ahead dishes! She has made a lasting impression on my cooking career."                    —M. Stamas, Springbow, Ohio

"Diane's recipes are delicious and stress free! You can actually relax before your party because of her excellent do-ahead tips."        —Sheryin Lobo, San Diego, California

"I impressed my friends with Diane's Do-Ahead Buffet. They couldn't believe I could be at the party instead of in the kitchen."        —Carla den Dulk, Modesto, California

"The do-ahead aspect of Diane's recipes allows working couples to enjoy gourmet cooking."
                    —C. Kreul, Monticello, Indiana

"I love Diane's recipes. The ingredients are easily available, the directions easy to follow, and the results delicious."                    —Susan Goe, San Diego, California

"Thanks to Diane's Cranberry Chutney and Sweet Potato–Apple Gratin, I can now have yams and cranberries at my Thanksgiving table—something I have never liked. Her dishes are simple to make, but wonderful to look at, smell, and, of course, eat. Thanks, Diane."
                    —Sue Poeppelman, Hamilton, Ohio

"My wonderful mother-in-law, Marge, took Diane's Do-Ahead Thanksgiving class. We are visiting my in-laws for the week and are having the best time preparing everything together, not rushed, drinking wine and laughing while the kids play nearby. Diane's ears must be burning because we are singing her praises with every taste. I love to cook, and was raised by an amazing cook, but definitely *not* a do-aheader! It is soooo much nicer to not race the clock! Thank you, Diane, for setting the easy, relaxed tone for our holiday—and for holidays to come!"                                   —Maria Dean, Valencia, California

"Diane Phillips's idea of do-ahead cooking has made my holiday dinners and other dinner parties a pleasure and a success. Diane gives you a countdown way of preparing a special dinner party so you can make dishes several days in advance. Her recipes are time efficient, all ingredients are easily accessible, and the tastes are gourmet. Now I can entertain with pleasure (and less stress) and enjoy my guests rather than being a slave in the kitchen. For people who love to entertain and are short on time but have gourmet tastes, Diane's do-ahead approach is fantastic!"         —Cathryn Ross, Santa Rosa, California

"Diane was amazing and has saved me and my family from another disastrous, stress-filled holiday by providing easy, do-ahead, and delicious recipes for the holidays. All her recipes can be prepared ahead, before crunch time, giving the hostess the ability to sit down and actually enjoy the meal along with her guests."
                                                          —Teri Hensley, Loomis, California

"I have been fortunate to have attended four of Diane's cooking classes so far and have enjoyed each and every one of them. I am a wife and the mother of three children, ages four, two, and three months. Diane's do-ahead approach allows me to make delicious, healthy gourmet meals for my family that I would not otherwise have the time to make. Thanks, Diane, for making my life easier in the kitchen."
                                                     —Kelly Smith, West Lafayette, Indiana

"Truly inspirational! I was skeptical about do-ahead cooking—keeping the flavor and texture intact. Diane has mastered this art!"       —Mary Schmidt Krebs, San Diego, California

"The first class I attended was Diane's Do-Ahead Thanksgiving Dinner. It altered a 50-year tradition in our family for the better! Wait till you taste her mashed potatoes!"
                                                   —Shirley Lipscomb, Burlingame, California

# Perfect Party Food

All the recipes and tips you'll ever need
for stress-free entertaining

FROM THE DIVA OF DO-AHEAD

# DIANE PHILLIPS

The Harvard Common Press  ✳  Boston, Massachusetts

The Harvard Common Press
535 Albany Street
Boston, Massachusetts 02118
www.harvardcommonpress.com

Printed in China

*Library of Congress Cataloging-in-Publication Data*

Phillips, Diane.
    Perfect party food : all the recipes and tips you'll ever need for stress-free
entertaining from the diva of do-ahead / Diane Phillips.
        p. cm.
    ISBN 1-55832-259-0 (hardcover : alk. paper) — ISBN 1-55832-260-4
    (pbk. : alk. paper)
    1. Entertaining. 2. Make-ahead cookery.  I.Title.
    TX731.P43 2005
    642'.4—dc22
                                                          2005004949


    ISBN-13: 978-1-55832-259-2 (hardcover); 978-1-55832-260-8 (paperback)
        ISBN-10: 1-55832-259-0 (hardcover); 1-55832-260-4 (paperback)

Special bulk-order discounts are available on this and other
Harvard Common Press books. Companies and organizations may
purchase books for premiums or resale, or may arrange a custom edition,
by contacting the Marketing Director at the address above.

2  4  6  8  10  9  7  5  3  1

Book design by Wendy Palitz
Illustrations by Laura Tedeschi

To Ted Pierot—

your friendship is a great gift

# Acknowledgments

My life is a party! I am blessed to have family, friends, and colleagues who make my life rich beyond measure. When I began this book, I had no idea it would become this large or this comprehensive, and along the way there were many people who helped make this book into what it is today. First and foremost, my husband, Chuck, was a willing participant in all the recipe testing, and I couldn't imagine having a party without him by my side, not only for moral support, but also to enjoy the moment. Thanks, Dr. Chuck, it has been 33 years of constant fun. And thanks to our children, Carrie and Ryan, who have been party participants since they were old enough to walk and make an appearance at our parties. Thank you, Carrie, for helping me with the beverage chapter and for being such an encouragement when I feel overwhelmed, and for all you have taught me about entertaining with style. To our son, Ryan, who is an incredible sports writer, thanks for being so encouraging and for eating most everything that I cook.

My agent and friend, Susan Ginsburg, went above and beyond the call of duty, by selling this book and patiently waiting for it to become a reality. Thank you, Susan, for the gift of your friendship, your advice, and for taking my career and molding it—I am so grateful to have you in my life! My pals Lora Brody and Rick Rodgers have been two of the most generous people in the business; I live vicariously through your successes, and thank you both for your friendship and advice over the years—I'm truly blessed.

The students and the cooking schools where I teach are some of my most treasured relationships. I'm able to whisk into these kitchens and teach eager students all over the country. A special thank you to: Chan Patterson and the staffs at the Viking Culinary Arts Centers and Viking Home Chef; Bob Nemorovski and the family at Ramekins; Cynthia

Liu, Mia Chambers, and the staffs at Draegers; Doralece Dullaghan and the staffs at Sur La Table; Marilyn Markel and the staff at A Southern Season; Larry Oats and the staff at KitchenArt; Nancy Pigg, Lana Santavicca, Nancy Rau, and the Fricke family at CooksWares; Sue and Lynn Hoffman and the angels at the Kitchen Shoppe; and the staffs at Central Markets. A special thank you to Ron and Devora Eisenberg, Allison Sherwood, Erika D'Eugenio, Sarah Rose, Carly Gunderson, and the amazing staff at Great News! in San Diego for giving me a kitchen to call home—you all are the best and it's so nice to come home!

To my friends who have tasted, sampled, and requested recipes, thank you for your love and support. I know that this book is better because of all of you. To the Sunday night group: Jim and Cindy Schoeneck, Brian and Wendy Morgan, Bill and Paula Taylor, Nancy and Mike Garrett, Steve and Terry Carter, and Steve and Susan Goe, thanks for bringing the party to our house—what a pleasure it is to know you all and to share in your lives. Thanks also to the Lunch Bunch, my friends Nancy Stansbury and Linda Costello, and the friends and family who shared recipes and stories about their parties. A special thanks to Jan Stapp for organizing the shopping lists for my Web site and giving me great editorial advice and feedback for various parts of this book. My friend Nonnie Owens and I began cooking up parties together more than 30 years ago and we continue to share friendship and party planning advice with each other—thank you for your friendship, hospitality, and encouragement. Robin Cox is an author's dream when it comes to recipe testing, and the recipes in this book are better because of her.

Finally, this book would not have come about had it not been for my publisher, Bruce Shaw, and the vision of one incredible friend and editor, Pam Hoenig. Thanks, Bruce, for believing in the concept, and to Pam, I am so grateful for your questions, tenacity, and encouragement, and for shaping the book. Special thanks to executive editor Valerie Cimino for taking over the final edit, and to Deborah Kops, the copyeditor authors only dream about, thank you for making the recipes into tight, organized, and readable prose.

I'm grateful to you both for your eye for detail and your sense of humor! Thanks also to the entire team at The Harvard Common Press: Christine Alaimo, Liza Beth, Abby Collier, Christine Corcoran Cox, Virginia Downes, Amy Etcheson, Pat Jalbert-Levine, Skye Stewart, Julie Strane, Megan Weireter, and Betsy Young. Thanks for taking me into the marketplace and for all your hard work on my behalf!

Finally, to you, dear reader—thanks for buying this book—if you have questions or comments or want to chat, please feel free to visit my Web site at www.dianephillips.com.

# Contents

# How Did a Nice Girl Like Me Become the Diva of Do-Ahead?

**I got my start as the Diva of Do-Ahead** when I cooked Thanksgiving dinner for my family one year a long time ago. After I labored for 10 hours to make all the dishes on Thanksgiving Day, and then sat down to dinner, exhausted, my family inhaled the meal in 10 minutes! I was left sitting at the table, thinking that it would have been easier to order in. I said to myself, Here I am an experienced cooking teacher and cookbook author, and this meal has made me crazy.

I decided there had to be a better way to plan and execute my favorite holiday meal, so I devised the Do-Ahead Thanksgiving cooking class. I figured that if I had a problem with this dinner, chances were that other people did, too. Strange as it may sound, this is the meal that people of all ages, from newly married twentysomethings to seasoned kitchen veterans, have a hard time with. The reason: Mom always made everything. So I started by giving a small class in my home to friends, testing the waters with them. Their response was amazing, and I went on to sell out this class in cooking schools all over the country.

From the success of that class, using the same basic principles of breaking the recipes down into manageable do-ahead steps, I've created classes for teaching do-ahead Christmas, Easter, cocktail parties, bridal showers, brunches, picnics, barbecues, Super Bowl parties, and many other seasonal occasions.

As a traveling cooking teacher, I now have the privilege of touring the country and teaching thousands of students every year. By far the most popular classes are my do-ahead entertaining and do-ahead holiday classes. They always sell out, and are filled with kitchen novices and seasoned cooks alike. I call them my "Oprah classes" because they literally transform people's lives. I have come to realize that what my students want more than anything is a game plan to streamline their time in the kitchen but still allow them to serve delicious meals to their friends and family; so that is what I show them.

My favorite class to teach is still the Do-Ahead Thanksgiving class. The dishes are all variations on the traditional foods typically served at Thanksgiving dinner, but everything is prepared ahead except for roasting the turkey, which is done on Thanksgiving Day. I tell my students that they can wallpaper the downstairs bathroom or build a boat in the garage while the turkey is roasting—it is that simple. I get e-mails from students all over the country who are thrilled that they can enjoy their friends and family on this important holiday instead of stressing over last-minute potato mashing and gravy making.

But Thanksgiving isn't the only meal that you can do ahead. *Perfect Party Food* gives you almost unlimited choices and combinations of dishes that you can choose to prepare for a do-ahead party. Let's face it: Everyone wants to serve great food and drinks and also enjoy the party, instead of stressing over fussy food and complicated preparations. Entertaining can truly strike fear in the heart of even the most experienced cook, but take it from me: It doesn't have to be that way. Think of this book as *your* game plan for entertaining, to personalize in any way you choose. In the first chapter, Party Planning Basics, I will explain in detail everything that you will need for whatever type of entertaining you want to plan. You'll be a Do-Ahead Diva yourself in no time, so get ready to plan for the best parties you've ever thrown!

# Party Planning Basics

So you really want to give a great party but you're a little daunted at the prospect. Or maybe you're just in need of some fresh, sensational new recipes. Join the club! We all want to throw the best parties possible, but have a hard time figuring out how to do it without losing our sanity or going broke. Any cook worth his or her salt knows that in order to plan and pull off a successful party, you need to have a game plan that begins with the decision to throw a party and doesn't end until you return the last rented or borrowed item. Well, sit down, relax, and follow the directions below for throwing the easiest (for you) and most enjoyable (for you and everyone else) parties ever. Whether you're a novice or an experienced cook, you can do it with relative ease and a whole lot of panache.

*Perfect Party Food* is your resource for throwing every kind of party imaginable, from a casual, last-minute get-together with friends, to intimate and elegant holiday soirees, to huge, festive bashes. Whatever kind of party you want to give, *Perfect Party Food* has got you covered. This book is first and foremost a guide to real-world entertaining. You will be able to enjoy your own party without feeling so overwhelmed that you don't even have time to taste the food.

Let's get started: In this book "party" means serving buffet style, because once you exceed eight guests, seating at a single table becomes difficult and complicated for most people. A buffet gives you the huge advantage of putting the food out and allowing your guests to help themselves.

*Perfect Party Food* has nearly 500 recipes to choose from, starting with beverages and appetizers and continuing through main courses, salads, sides, breads, brunch entrées, desserts, and more. They are all simple and delicious, and there are lots and lots of choices to fit your preferences and lifestyle. Remember, this is *your* party—I'm just the coach.

I created all of these recipes first and foremost for great taste. Almost all are delicious whether they are served piping hot, at room temperature, or cold. Their quality does not suffer if they are not eaten right out of the oven. Occasionally, when something is best served hot, I recommend that you keep it in a slow cooker on the buffet table.

These are all accessible and approachable recipes; when you're giving a party, that is not the time to challenge your culinary skills with specially constructed foods or exotic ingredients that take you three days to find.

Each recipe will serve 10 to 12 guests nicely, giving you a solid base for multiplying upward according to your own particular party needs. Many of the recipes include a number of variations, so if you want to make the recipe again, but with a different accent, you can easily do that. Do you want to serve a Southwestern-flavored salad to go with your grilled flank steak? It's here. If you decide to go with an Asian-inspired flank steak, you will find a dozen delicious side dishes to serve with it. Your only dilemma will be choosing which one to make! I've also made loads of suggestions for pairing foods and have provided hundreds of tips for streamlining your preparation and storing and serving your food. Many recipes can do double duty as well. Herb-Roasted Tomatoes (page 127) or Roasted Wild Mushroom Salad (page 163) can be part of a bruschetta bar, but they can also become a sauce or garnish for chicken, beef, or seafood. Or they can be tossed with hot pasta for a quick side dish. You have the freedom to mix and match your favorite flavors and choose the recipes that will appeal to you and your guests.

With the exception of a few drinks, each recipe contains do-ahead components that can be made ahead and refrigerated or frozen, and many recipes can be completely cooked in advance. The recipes have clearly marked, well-defined points that tell you where you can stop and refrigerate or freeze something and for how long. Because each recipe has this unique feature, you will be able to create a party-planning calendar with your complete timetable on it, so that you will know what you need to do every step of the way. (Check out www.dianephillips.com for downloadable calendars and shopping lists.) The flexibility of these recipes gives you almost unlimited choices for adapting preparty preparations to your own personal party schedule and energy level. If you want to make and freeze the desserts two months ahead of time, go right ahead. If your main course can be made the day before, then reheated in the slow cooker or served at room temperature, it will give you more time to relax and enjoy your party.

*Perfect Party Food* gives you choices that will suit your schedule, budget, and ambition. There are even plenty of hints for store-bought items to fill in with if you don't want to do it all yourself. Don't feel guilty if you don't make everything yourself. You can decide if you want to make the bread or dessert for the party or order it from your favorite bakery, or if you want to roast 40 pounds of meat for your party or ask the grocer or butcher to do that for you, or if you want to spend several hours cleaning and arranging the veggies for the veggie tray or just order one premade. If any friends ask what they can bring, give them a simple recipe to make for your party. A lot of things *can* be done by someone else.

My cooking and entertaining philosophy is, "It shouldn't feel like a root canal," and for many home cooks, that's exactly what entertaining feels like when they are too overwhelmed and stressed. Think of me as an entertaining missionary. Instead of making elaborate dishes that require large blocks of time and last-minute fuss, let the Diva of Do-Ahead come into your kitchen and help you simplify everything, giving you the confidence that your next party will be the most relaxing and enjoyable event you've ever planned and hosted.

## Entertaining, Diva Style

Okay, you've decided you want to have a party. Now you need to decide what type of party it will be. Will you host a backyard barbecue, an informal dinner, a swanky cocktails-and-finger-food party, a Super Bowl party, or an informal brunch? How do you decide? Start by thinking about your own lifestyle. If you don't like getting dressed up and laboring over intricate menus, chances are you have a more casual style. If you love the adrenaline rush of creating an event, you might be the type of person who gives more elegant parties. I am somewhere in between. I love to have casual dinners, but I enjoy making pretty table arrangements and pulling out my china and crystal. No matter what you choose to serve and how you choose to serve it, rest assured that if you make your guests feel welcome, they will enjoy the party.

So first you need to define the occasion, and second, how you want to celebrate it. Is it just that it's high time to get together with friends, or are you celebrating something in particular, perhaps a birthday or an anniversary or a bridal shower? Or is it a holiday, such as Thanksgiving or New Year's? Next, what style of party do you want: casual, informal, elegant? And how many people do you want to invite (and have room for)? These are all important questions to ask yourself because the answers will really give shape to your party.

To point you in the right direction, I have defined five typical and distinct styles of entertaining that will help you plan for your party and create the ambiance you are looking for.

## Casual Entertaining, Diva Style

The first style of party is what I call the casual, barefoot get-together. Recipes throughout the book that would be appropriate to serve at such a party are designated with a special symbol . This type of party can be spur of the moment or you may have planned it weeks in advance. It just needs a phone call or an e-mail invitation (check out www.evite.com for e-mail invitations), preferably a week or so ahead of time. The food, atmosphere, and dress are casual—you probably won't find caviar or Champagne at this party, and the host and hostess may or may not be wearing shoes. This is a hang-loose, easy type of entertaining. You may be partying outside with barbecue or picnic types of dishes as the centerpiece, or eating hearty dishes and drinking mulled cider huddled by the fire on a cold winter night. Or maybe you're serving 3-foot-long sandwiches and potato chips while watching the Super Bowl or NCAA Final Four.

Even though this is an informal affair, make sure there are places for everyone to sit and eat. This is where planning how many people to invite is crucial. If you don't have enough seats, you'll need to borrow or

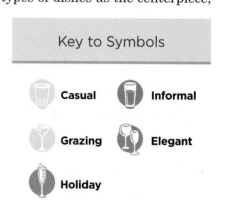

Key to Symbols

Casual     Informal

Grazing     Elegant

Holiday

rent them. And if you're planning an outdoor party, have a backup plan for setting up tables indoors in case the weather doesn't cooperate.

For these parties, prepared food from your local market may be used to supplement your homemade dishes. Or the food can be what I call "team cuisine"; you enlist your guests' help, asking each one to bring a dish or beverage. It's perfectly all right to use heavy-duty plastic or paper plates and heavy-duty plastic flatware for this kind of entertaining. The casual party is simple and fun—it's a matter of having a great time with your guests, rather than constructing an intricate menu. This party needs a main course, or if you are only serving salads, you'll need to have a game plan worked out to ensure that you have enough variety. You might have children at this type of party, so remember to think of at least two foods that are kid-friendly (carrot sticks and chicken in some form will work wonders). And don't forget to give the appetizers some thought. If you are serving a heavy dinner, go

### Casual Get-Together Menu Template for 12

**Wine, soft drinks, and beer**

**2 appetizers** (1 cold and 1 warm or at room temperature)

**1 entrée**

**1 salad**

**2 sides**

**Bread** (always optional, but a great stretcher when serving a crowd)

**1 dessert**

**Coffee station** (optional for lunch and brunch, essential with dinner)

### Casual Get-Together Décor

* **Tableware:** For utensils, plates, and cups, plastic is okay. Dress up utensils by wrapping them in pretty paper napkins and tying with ribbon, raffia, or twine. Please, no Styrofoam for hot beverages!

* **Table linens and napkins:** Paper is okay for everything.

* **Candles:** Place small votives on the tables or down the center of the main serving area.

* **Flowers:** Use small, low centerpieces. If there is a sports theme or the party is in celebration of an occasion, such as a birthday, then use appropriate items as centerpieces (for example, team logo items, balloons in team colors, a happy birthday banner as a runner down the center of the table, or happy birthday balloons).

light on the snacks; but if the main course is lighter, then you can serve something more substantial such as satay or cold shrimp for starters.

Decide what type of drinks you want to serve and get ready to set up a bar if appropriate. Or lug out some coolers if you need to. For this kind of meal, you could have the bar in the kitchen, where everyone will congregate, or you could set it up on your patio when the weather is mild.

## Informal Entertaining, Diva Style

The second category is the informal brunch, lunch, or dinner: You plan the date, time, and menu, but you want to keep it relaxed. These recipes are designated with a special symbol ⬛. You should give oral, written, or e-mail invitations at least 2 weeks before, and ask for an RSVP date of 7 to 10 days before the party.

This is a meal, not an appetizer party. You will plan for simple food and drink, and there will be a beginning and an end to the festivities (a brunch from 10:00 to 2:00, a lunch from 12:00 to 2:00, a dinner from 6:00 to 9:00). You can set up the dining table, a kitchen counter, or an outdoor table for your buffet service. Set up chairs for all your guests so that they can be seated when eating their main course. If the stairs in your home are close to the action, you can use them for seating as well—my husband and I sometimes do this when it's a huge party. If you don't have enough chairs, floor cushions will work, too. If you are renting tables or other items, don't forget to order them well in advance, and add them to the calendar for pickup or delivery and then return.

For this meal you'll want slam-dunk, do-ahead dishes, things that can be set out and eaten once everyone has assembled. To keep guests happy before the meal, have an appetizer platter and drinks that your guests can serve themselves. Wine, beer, and soft drinks would be perfect. If you're giving a brunch, I recommend an eye-opener such as Bloody Marys, Bellinis, or mimosas; if it's a themed dinner, then have a drink station with an appropriate drink for your guests to mix or pour ready-made from pitchers. It helps to set up a separate bar area for drinks, to ease traffic flow and encourage mingling.

## Informal Brunch Menu Template for 12

**Mimosas, Bloody Marys, or another eye-opener**

**1 savory egg dish**

**1 sweet brunch dish**

**1 vegetable or salad**

**Fresh fruit** (see Fruit Salads, page 168)

**1 dessert** (optional; if it's a wedding shower, try cupcakes or something in small bites, such as brownies)

**Coffee station**

## Informal Lunch Menu Template for 12

**Wine, beer, and soft drinks**

**2 small appetizers** to start off with, such as nuts, crudités, cheese and crackers, or warm olives

**1 grilled entrée** (optional)

**2 salads** (1 containing protein, 1 vegetable)

**Bread**

**1 dessert**

**Coffee station** (optional)

## Informal Dinner Menu Template for 12

**Wine, beer, and soft drinks**

**2 small appetizers**

**1 entrée**

**1 salad**

**2 side dishes** (1 could be an additional salad)

**Bread**

**1 dessert**

**Coffee station**

## Informal Entertaining Décor

✳ **Tableware:** Use stainless flatware, if possible, and ceramic or china plates; supplement with heavy plastic in coordinating colors if you don't have enough china. Use real glasses for drinks and ceramic for coffee.

✳ **Table linens:** Either cloth or paper is okay.

✳ **Candles:** Use votives on the serving tables, and pillar candles arranged with flowers in other spaces.

✳ **Flowers:** Scatter low arrangements around the entertaining space, not just on the food table. Small shallow bowls can be filled with small river rocks and just a few daisies or other inexpensive but interesting flowers. Try using fruits and vegetables instead of or in addition to flowers. Or arrange small bouquets of herbs in bud vases—nothing too complicated, just little accents. Small 2-inch pots of planted violas or other small flowers also make a nice addition to the table, depending upon the occasion and the time of year.

## Grazing Parties, Diva Style

Next is the grazing party, for which appropriate recipes are marked with a special symbol
. This is an entire meal of small bites or appetizers, and it can be dressed up or dressed
down, depending upon the occasion. For a dressed-up graze, think New Year's Eve, special
occasions, and the like. For one that is dressed down, think summer cocktails on the deck,
winter cocktails near a crackling fire, an open house, or a Super Bowl party. This type of
party is best accomplished with small tastes of food that are simple to pick up and eat,
rather than something that will need a knife and fork.

For a casual grazing party, you can phone or e-mail your invitations or send written
ones. For an elegant grazing party, a written invitation at least 2 to 3 weeks before the
party with an RSVP date of 10 days before is preferable. You need to make your guests
aware that you will be serving real food, not just chips and dip, so that they don't chow
down before arriving. Make sure you state times on the invitations: "Join us for cocktails
and hors d'oeuvres from 6:00 to 8:00 on Friday." That way, you have a beginning and an
end to the festivities.

Grazes are parties where everything is usually eaten while standing, so chairs for seating are not required. You may want to clear away furniture so there is more room for
people to stand and chat. Be sure to remove knickknacks from flat surfaces such as end
tables, so that there is a place for people to set their cups or plates. Also, leave lots of paper
cocktail napkins out on the tables throughout the house so that your guests can use them
for coasters.

Wine, beer, and soft drinks served in glassware are fine for a casual graze, while a formal grazing party requires a full bar with glass or crystal stemware, and a bartender if
you can swing it. Set up the bar away from the food, in a place that people can flow in and
out of easily.

For a casual graze, you decide whether or not you want a coffee station. You could simply ask people whether they want coffee, and then start brewing if they do. My rule for the
casual graze is coffee for evening affairs and none for daytime casual. For a formal graze,

### Basic Grazing Menu Template for 12

**3 spreads or dips with crudités, bread, crackers, or chips** (or 1 dip and 1 cheese platter)

**7 small bites**

**2 small dessert selections**

**Coffee station** (optional)

### Grazing Party Décor

❋ **Tableware:** For a casual grazing party, stainless or heavy-duty plastic cutlery is fine, and you may not need silverware at all. For formal grazing, I recommend china and silverware.

❋ **Table linens:** Paper napkins and tablecloths are fine for casual grazes. For more elegant parties, cloth tablecloths and paper or cloth napkins are best. With this type of entertaining your guests may put down their napkins and lose them, so it is a good idea to have extra paper cocktail napkins on hand.

❋ **Candles:** For a casual graze, votive candles are fine. If this is a Super Bowl party, daytime open house, or the like, then candles aren't necessary at all. For a formal graze, you want votives everywhere, and also pillar candles in arrangements of different heights. You want the lights low and the atmosphere to be sophisticated and sexy.

❋ **Flowers:** They are not necessary for a casual graze, but again, low arrangements are the key. If you are having a casual graze and want to decorate, low arrangements of vegetables and fruits will work well—think clusters of grapes, apples, pears, and oranges in a rustic basket or serving bowl. For the more elegant graze, you will want beautiful flowers in every room. This should be a gala event, so make the decorating a priority.

you will need a coffee station, which can be near the dessert table, if you have one. Desserts can also be added to the main buffet table, but I enjoy separating them from the other foods; that way, guests can pick up their dessert whenever they are ready. Make sure you have ceramic or china cups or mugs for coffee. If you can't make a dessert, then serve something such as chocolate-covered mints or other candies that can be picked up and eaten. No one has ever gone wrong with Hershey's Kisses!

## Elegant Entertaining, Diva Style

The next style is what I call the elegant dinner, marked by a special symbol 🍷. This is the knockout party, where your food and tables speak luxury and indulgence. This style requires a verbal or written invitation 4 to 6 weeks ahead of time, stating the time and place and also the dress (for example, formal, coat/no tie, jacket and tie, cocktail attire) with an RSVP deadline 2 to 3 weeks before the party. If people don't call you, then call them just to make sure they have received your invitation—this party is important, so make the follow-up calls, if necessary.

For this sort of entertaining, you'll need a stocked bar, plus wine, beer, and soft drinks, and I recommend a bartender if you can afford it. You will need a buffet set up for serving, and tables set around the house where your guests can eat their dinner. (Tables can be rented from party rental companies, or you can buy tables at wholesale clubs such as Costco or borrow from friends.) Your tables should have cloth table linens, as well as glass stemware, china, and stainless flatware. All of these can be rented if need be, but you can also find inexpensive linens, china, and flatware at discount stores.

You will need a coffee and dessert station, preferably on a separate table, although you could remove the dishes from the main buffet table while your guests are eating and set it up there.

## Elegant Party Menu Template for 12

**Full bar; wine with dinner**

**2 indulgent appetizers,** such as shrimp cocktail or a raw bar

**Cheese tray to serve 12** (4 cheeses with grapes and crackers)

**1 entrée**

**1 salad**

**2 or 3 side dishes**

**Bread** (optional—with 2 side dishes serve bread, with 3, omit)

**1 dessert**—something that makes a statement, such as a layered cake, trifle, cheesecake, or tart

**Coffee station**

## Elegant Entertaining Décor

* **Tableware:** Use stainless or sterling flatware, your best china or rented china, and crystal stemware or nice glassware.

* **Table linens:** Use cloth dinner table linens and napkins, and paper napkins for cocktails.

* **Candles:** Put a mix of different types of candles everywhere; candlelight will make this party very special and sexy.

* **Flowers:** Put small vases of flowers everywhere.

* **Tables:** Set up the dining room table with the food, then set up tables for dinner around the house. If this is impossible, then lap trays are imperative.

## Do-Ahead Holidays, Diva Style

Holiday dinners are in a class all by themselves—these are indicated with a special symbol —because they are fraught with anxiety: not only food-related anxiety (how will I keep everything hot and get it to the table at the same time?), but also family anxiety. The simple secret to success is to break down the dinner into manageable parts, then put it all together. These dinners should be served on your best china, with your nicest table linens—after all, this is your family or your dearest friends, so treat them like royalty! A lot of the rules for Elegant Entertaining apply here. It's fine to have guests bring a dish if you think you can't manage it all, but give them a recipe for something you want made, rather than that heart-shaped marshmallow and sweet potato casserole they always bring. One friend of mine asks her guests what it was their mom made for that special holiday meal, and then she makes it for them. The menu may become pretty eclectic, but it makes her guests feel at home.

I've listed various holiday meal suggestions on pages 666 to 668. If you are having a Thanksgiving dinner and will need a fresh turkey, order that at least 2 weeks before you plan to pick it up, and even sooner if possible. The same goes for large or specialty cuts of beef, lamb, pork, or ham. Luxuries such as lobsters, caviar, and other items that might need to be ordered online or by phone should be ordered well ahead of time. Check them off your shopping list, and add their delivery dates to your do-ahead calendar. Remember that if relatives with children are coming, they may need equipment such as high chairs and booster seats, so ask if they can bring these themselves. Also remember those who may be physically challenged. Older adults sometimes need a lot of help, so when it comes time to serve, have them go first, maybe with a young adult who can serve their food and help them find their place at the table. I always have parents go through the buffet line first to make up their small children's plates; that way the kids aren't taking food and then returning it to the serving plate (eww).

## Holiday Menu Template for 12

**Full bar; wine with dinner**

**2 small appetizers,** such as nuts, cheese and crackers, or crudités and dip

**1 entrée**

**1 salad**

**3 side dishes**

**Bread**

**1 dessert**—something lovely looking that makes a statement, such as a trifle

**Coffee station**

## Holiday Entertaining Décor

* **Tableware:** Use stainless or sterling flatware, your best china or rented china, and crystal stemware or nice glassware.

* **Table linens:** Use cloth dinner table linens and napkins, and paper napkins for cocktails.

* **Candles:** Put a mix of different types of candles everywhere; candlelight will make this party festive and special.

* **Flowers:** Put small vases of flowers everywhere.

* **Tables:** Set up the dining room table with the food, then set up tables for dinner around the house. If this is impossible, then lap trays are imperative.

# Diva Rescues

Over the years I have developed many techniques to call on when disaster strikes. These evolved out of my own experiences and from typical questions that my cooking students have asked during my classes. If you have a real dilemma that's not covered here, feel free to e-mail me at diane@dianephillips.com. One Thanksgiving I was answering e-mail until an hour before our own Thanksgiving dinner!

- No dessert? No problem: Serve liqueurs on the rocks with heavy cream, or pour liqueurs over vanilla ice cream.

- The roast has been in the oven for hours and is only just starting to cook, and dinner was supposed to be on the table by now. Don't panic! Serve the salad course, slice the roast into steaks, and grill them on the gas grill or on the stove top. No need to let anyone know this wasn't your plan all along, and if anyone does find out, you'll look like a genius.

- Okay, so you're serving a whole chicken, not a roast, and it hasn't cooked through. Cut the legs (but not the thighs) off of the chicken and raise the oven temperature to 450°F. Drizzle the chicken with olive oil or melted unsalted butter and blast it in the oven for 10 to 15 minutes, then check the thighs with an instant-read meat thermometer. They should register 170°F. Remove the chicken from the oven and allow to rest for 5 minutes before carving and serving.

- Dry chicken? Make a pan sauce with white wine and chicken broth to pour over it, or try one of the quick sauces in the sauce chapter (see pages 472 to 499).

- If extra people show up for the party, stretch the food. Make the simple rice pilaf recipe below, and then add more to the salad bowl—olives, roasted peppers, cheese cubes, cold

## DIVA'S RESCUE RICE PILAF

Serves 10 to 12 as a side dish

This basic pilaf can riff into all kinds of things—you can even add 1½ pounds of cooked seafood or chicken to make it another entrée.

**¼ cup (½ stick) unsalted butter**

**1 cup chopped onion**

**1 cup frozen defrosted spinach, squeezed dry, or corn kernels, or diced artichoke hearts**

**2 cups converted long-grain rice**

**5 cups chicken, vegetable, or seafood broth (depending on your entrée—avoid beef broth, which will overpower the vegetables)**

**½ cup freshly grated Parmesan cheese**

**Salt and pepper to taste**

**¼ cup chopped Italian parsley for garnish**

**1.** In a 4-quart saucepan over medium heat, melt 2 tablespoons of the butter, and sauté the onion and spinach until the onion begins to soften, 4 to 5 minutes. Add the rice and toss in the butter mixture to coat.

**2.** Add the broth and bring to a boil over high heat. Cover, reduce the heat to low, and simmer for 20 to 25 minutes, until the rice is tender and the liquid is absorbed.

✳ **DIVA DO-AHEAD:** At this point, you can let the rice sit, covered, at room temperature for up to 30 minutes. Or cool, cover, and refrigerate for up to 2 days, or freeze for up to 3 months. Defrost, then add 2 to 4 tablespoons of broth and reheat, covered, in the microwave. Proceed with the recipe.

**3.** Stir the remaining 2 tablespoons of butter and the Parmesan into the warm rice, season with salt and pepper, and serve, garnished with parsley.

chopped chicken, and chopped salami will stretch your salad and add color and texture. Next, if you're serving meat, cut all your entrée slices and chops in half, which will make 6 pork chops appear to be 12. Some people will take 2 halves, but not everyone. Finally, add ice cream to the dessert table if possible. Its richness will make your guests feel sated at the end of the night.

- Speaking of rice, if yours burns, scrape off the top layers, down to where the rice is glued to the pan, and transfer the loose rice to a microwavable bowl. Add a few tablespoons of liquid (stock or wine), cover, and microwave for a few minutes on High. Garnish with lots of chopped parsley, or stir in some toasted sliced almonds or dried fruit.

- Need to stretch the salad, and the bags of greens at the store are too pricey? Thinly slice some of your favorite vegetables or grate them in the food processor and add them to the salad; carrots, radishes, jicama, and other crisp veggies will add bulk and color. Toss in some finely chopped spinach and thinly sliced cabbage, too.

- Salty gravy or sauce? Cut up a raw potato and add it to the pan; the potato will absorb some of that salt (remove before serving). Or dilute with water, salt-free broth, or wine.

- If your avocados are still hard as a rock, pierce them with a sharp knife several times and heat in the microwave on 50 percent power for 20 seconds, then turn and microwave again for 20 seconds. Allow them to rest at room temperature for 1 hour.

- If your onions are sharp tasting and have a strong odor, add a small amount of sugar to the butter when you sauté them.

- You forgot to turn on the oven to bake the potatoes? Make Spicy Oven Steak Fries (page 252). They will be ready in half the time, and who doesn't love fries?

- Prefer a different potato rescue? Cube the potatoes and boil in chicken broth for 10 to 15 minutes, until just tender. Drain and toss with butter and chopped parsley and chives, or your favorite herbs. Or toss with a compound butter that will complement your main course. Or you can cube the potatoes, boil until tender, and then mash with your favorite herbs, butter, crumbled bacon, and chopped ham and/or cheese. Or stir in some blue cheese dressing for a real treat.

# Diva Master Checklist for Party Planning

## Right after the invitations are written:

✳ Write out a thorough and complete menu.

✳ Figure out your food quantities, based on your guest list, and adjust later if necessary depending on RSVPs. See the chart on page 24 for help with this.

✳ Make a shopping list of everything you will need to buy and add to your do-ahead calendar.

✳ Order any specialty food items that you will need. Insert their delivery dates in your do-ahead calendar.

✳ Order any tables, chairs, linens, china, flatware, or stemware that you will need and insert their delivery and return dates/times in your do-ahead calendar.

✳ Shop for nonperishable and nonfood related items now if you have enough space to store things, including candles, paper towels, napkins, toilet paper, guest hand towels, plastic utensils, zipper-top plastic bags, and trash bags; plus drinks, crackers, and other dry goods that can be stored without becoming stale. In addition, buy any items that can be frozen.

✳ Start your do-ahead recipe countdown on your calendar: Review the directions in the recipes you have chosen to determine which dishes can be made entirely or partially ahead of time and plot these on your calendar. Remember that you can start way ahead with the items that can be frozen. Be sure to include nonfood related tasks on the calendar, too (for example, rolling silverware in napkins and cleaning the serving dishes).

✳ Measure out coffee for your coffee pots, place the servings in zipper-top plastic bags, and freeze.

## 1 week before the party:

✳ Shop for all perishables; save any very perishable items, such as fresh vegetables and herbs and flowers for the tables, for the day before the party.

✳ Start your do-ahead dishes that can be refrigerated but not frozen.

✳ Wash and have ready all your serving pieces, bowls, and platters (cover them with a sheet or keep them in plastic bags so they remain dust-free).

✳ Make arrangements to board your pet.

✳ Decide what you will wear and clean it if necessary.

## 1 to 3 days before the party:

✳ Clean the house.

✳ Set up the tables and chairs, if possible, and cover them with sheets to protect them from dust, children, and animals. If you have a small space, you may have to wait until the day of the party.

✳ Place sticky notes on the tables, where appropriate, to indicate where each dish should be placed.

✳ Defrost any frozen items.

✻ Set up the bar if you have room. Again, depending on how much space you have, you may have to wait until the day of the party.

✻ Buy ice (both for drinks and to keep drinks cool) and store it in the freezer as you defrost food you will be serving at the party.

✻ Shop for salad greens and other highly perishable items, such as fresh flowers for the table.

✻ Arrange the flowers in vases.

✻ Get out your candles and make sure you have enough for each place you would like to use them.

## The day of the party:

✻ Take stock of what you have and figure out whether you will need to make one last run to the store. (Chances are you will.) You may use this time to buy ice, if you haven't already, and store it in coolers.

✻ Straighten up around the house, check bathrooms for cleanliness, and bedrooms as well if they will be used for coat storage.

✻ Board your pet. Now I know a lot of animal lovers will be angry at me for this, but if you have animals and you are having this many guests for a party, you need to make sure that the animals are out of sight. I was once at a party where the host's three large dogs ate the appetizers on the low coffee table, and what they didn't eat they knocked onto the floor with their wagging tails. This advice is all about making your guests comfortable—they may not love half-eaten canapés as much as you do, and many people are allergic to pets.

✻ If you're having an outdoor party, check the patio furniture to make sure it's clean. Tie down tablecloths with tape, and then anchor

them with something heavy to keep them in place.

✻ If you are grilling during the party, make sure the grill is clean.

✻ Arrange the food on platters, cover with plastic, and refrigerate all perishable food. (Food to be eaten at room temperature will need to be removed when specified in each recipe—sometimes 2 hours, sometimes 1 hour before serving.)

✻ Remove any food from its marinade, such as meat and poultry, and drain at least 2 hours before the party; keep refrigerated.

✻ Preheat the oven and bake anything that can be served at room temperature.

✻ Set up the bar and the coffee station if necessary.

✻ If you are using coolers, fill them with beer, soft drinks, and ice. Chill your wine on ice as well.

## 3 hours before the party:

✻ Take a shower or bath and relax. This is *very important.*

## 1½ hours before the party:

✻ Wear something over your nice clothes while you are getting the food ready so you'll avoid ruining that new outfit you've been saving for the party. I generally wear a huge oxford shirt that buttons down the front, and I whip that off when the first guest comes through the door.

✻ Begin to take out room-temperature food (see individual recipes for timing).

✻ Preheat the oven (if necessary), and heat any items that will be served warm.

## 30 minutes before the party:

* Sit down with your loved one, open a bottle of wine or try out that drink station, and toast each other before the party. Chances are you will be on the go until everyone is comfortably eating and drinking, so use this time to take a deep breath. I know you may be thinking that you won't have time for this, but make time! It's important to take that break, and if you've made everything ahead of time, you *will* be able to do it.

## Party time:

* After you take their coats, guide your guests to the drink station or bar and offer them something to drink along with some food.

* If you are serving appetizers, then dinner, allow an hour for the cocktails and appetizers. Use this time to warm up bread or any other items that need warming at the last minute.

* Allow an hour or so for dinner. Turn on the coffee while people are eating dinner. If you are serving a warm dessert, pop it into a warm, turned-off oven at the same time.

* Allow about 45 minutes for coffee and dessert.

* Make sure that you and your cohost, if you have one, mingle and chat with everyone!

## Post-party:

* It's better (really) to start the cleanup ASAP, after everyone has left. Trust me, you don't want to face everything in the morning. Put the dishes in the dishwasher, store or discard any uneaten food, store any leftover drinks, empty coolers, and empty trash. If the dishes won't all fit into the dishwasher, do one load of just dishes and assorted items and soak the serving dishes overnight. You can empty the dishwasher in the morning and reload.

* The next day, rearrange and/or store your tables, put away the dishes and coolers and any leftover drink supplies, and return any rented chairs or tables or other items.

---

- A Diva always remembers that everything tastes better with bacon. Overcooked green beans? Scatter crumbled bacon over the top and no one will care. Cooked bacon is available in vacuum packages in your grocery store; keep some in the pantry for just such emergencies.

- Do you need to perk up a bland sauce? Add sautéed or roasted garlic, hot sauce (such as Tabasco), or citrus juice or zest.

- Your chicken, roast, or fish is looking pretty boring? Cover it with a colorful sauce (such as Herb-Roasted Tomatoes on page 127 or Fiorentina Sauce on page 474), or garnish it with sliced lemons. You could also just lavish chopped parsley or other fresh herbs over everything.

- Do you need to fix a lumpy, too-thin, too-thick, or separated sauce? If it's lumpy, try straining it through a sieve and rewhisking it in the pan. If it's too thin, knead together 1 part all-purpose flour and 1 part unsalted butter, then whisk into your bubbling sauce a bit at a time until the sauce is the desired thickness. This is not a do-ahead trick; use this only at the last minute. If your sauce is too thick, add more liquid. If it has separated, cool the sauce, put it into a blender, dribble in cold liquid with the machine running, and then reheat over boiling water.

- Your bread dough didn't rise properly? Roll out the dough on a floured board and sprinkle with coarse salt and seeds (sesame, caraway, or poppy), embedding the seeds in both sides of the dough. Transfer to a baking sheet that has been sprinkled with a little oil to prevent sticking, and bake at 425°F for about 10 minutes, until the dough is golden brown. Slice with a pizza cutter and serve as crackers or flatbread.

- Does your layer cake look like Mt. Etna erupting? Scoop and serve the cake in bowls and call it trifle—your guests will think you're a star and everyone will love the dessert. And always have a jar of hot fudge or caramel sauce at the ready so you can drizzle that over whatever you are disguising.

- How do you perk up a bland dessert? Chocolate loves coffee (either powdered espresso or brewed coffee stirred in) or ground cinnamon. Other desserts can be jazzed up with the addition of citrus oil or zest.

- Need a few more sweet tricks? Add ground nuts or dried fruits to crumb crusts or crumble toppings along with other flavorings such as cinnamon, nutmeg, allspice, or citrus zest. Remember that sifted confectioners' sugar or cocoa powder will give your desserts a nice finish and that chopped nuts, chopped dried fruits, and flaked sweetened coconut can give your desserts a total redo. If your cake has a dent or huge crack in the center, fill that with fresh fruits or slather it with whipped cream.

# Setting Up the Tables

**To serve the food** on one large table (and this is the best way to do it if you are having a meal, such as dinner), arrange the plates at one end and the utensils at the other. If you put the utensils with the plates, it will be difficult for your guests to handle everything, and chances are that someone will forget to pick them up and will have to cut back in line. Place salt, pepper, and any condiments such as butter near the utensils or, even better, on another table that is within the line of traffic flow from the main buffet table. That way your guests will move away from the buffet and the line will move more quickly. Which brings me to another point: Make sure your main buffet table is set up in a location where traffic flow won't be a problem.

To set up the food on the main table, start with the entrée, then follow with vegetables, other side dishes, and salads. If you are serving two main courses, place them both where your guests will begin so they will know right away there is a choice. Be sure to have sauces next to the items that need to be sauced, rather than at the end of the table.

For a grazing party, you can set up one large table, or various smaller tables in one or more rooms. The choice is up to you. Either way, you will be setting out the food on the tables in a more or less random fashion, but be strategic: Separate cheesy items, alternate warm foods with cooler ones, and intersperse colorful foods with less colorful ones. Also, if you have two dips or spreads that will share crudités or crackers, keep them close together so your guests can partake of the dippers easily. Make sure you have small plates set out on the table so people can pick up more than one selection and move away from the table to mingle with the other guests. Arrange lots of napkins on the table, too. These basic rules all make for a more pleasant presentation. Think of this as "dressing" the table.

Of course, you will want to identify your foods so that your guests will know what they are eating. I have a friend who buys inexpensive 2-inch by 2-inch frames, prints the name of each dish on her computer, then inserts it into a frame. You could also write the names of the dishes by hand on pretty placecards.

Buffets are most successful if your food requires only a fork. This allows guests to move about and socialize while they eat. (Of course, you will always want to provide enough chairs for everyone to sit down.) However, a lot of wonderful food requires what I call "traction," or the need to eat it with a fork and knife. You will want to have portable TV tray tables on hand for this type of food, or you can set up small tables and chairs in various places in your house so that your guests will be comfortable while they are eating.

# Two Dozen Diva Tips for Stress-Free Entertaining

1. **Make a plan.** As I have said previously, define the occasion, the style, the number of guests, and the recipes you would like to serve.

2. **Don't deviate from the plan!** No matter how many suggestions you get from others, this is your plan. Stick to it so you don't lose your focus.

3. **Relax.** You won't have any fun if you are so stressed you can't think, and neither will your guests. If you're not confident that you can prepare all the food yourself, ask your guests to help out by bringing something. Or determine which parts of your menu can be bought ready-made from the supermarket, deli, or gourmet store so that you can reasonably accomplish the rest of the menu.

4. **Select appropriate recipes** and, if possible, give new recipes a trial run before the main event. If you absolutely must prepare a Moroccan feast, it might be a good idea to make the recipes well ahead of the party to see how they taste, as well as to figure out where you can streamline the recipes, whether any shortcut substitutions can be made, and which parts can be made ahead of time.

5. **Make lists!** You'll need a list of the dishes you want to prepare. Then check the yield on the recipes to see whether you'll need to double or triple them. Working from that, build a shopping list, making sure you include nonfood items such as paper towels, garbage bags, toilet paper, sterno, toothpicks, ice, candles, etc. Also list the types of serving dishes you will need and get these out two to three days before the party.

6. ***Don't lose the lists!*** If necessary, keep them on the computer, so you can print them out, over and over again. This is also a great way to keep track of your parties and remember what you have previously served to your guests. Some of my most anal-retentive friends actually have this done on spreadsheets, but that's way too much work, as far as I'm concerned.

7. Visualize the food and where you would like to place dishes, whether in the house or outside. Make sure the serving dishes will fit on the table you have selected—I can't tell you how many times a frustrated hostess has tried to wedge beautiful serving dishes onto a table, only to find that they won't all fit. Two days before the party, place a sticky note with the name of each dish in the spot where you want it to be served. That way, if people come early and ask whether they can help, you can tell them to place the dishes where the sticky notes are.

8. The best parties are those where you can do most of the preparation ahead of time, then pull things out of the refrigerator or oven just before serving. If you are not good at timing your dishes so they are all ready at the same moment, then serve a cold buffet. It's the easiest way to learn how to serve a number of dishes at once, and you can gain tremendous confidence from this kind of entertaining.

9. Keep cool, even if disaster strikes. The big Diva secret is that 90 percent of a successful party is the attitude of the host. Let's say your oven is only cooking at 250°F, the roast is still cold, and you promised dinner in an hour. Like any good Diva, use what you've got to make the best of a bad situation. Serve a cheese platter with crackers or go ahead and serve the salad course and lots of bread, and keep the wine flowing. While your guests are eating, sneak into the kitchen, cut the roast into ½-inch-thick slices, heat up the gas grill, and barbecue the steaks. No gas grill? Sear the slices in a hot grill pan or skillet on top of the stove, and then put them back in the low oven to roast. Never let on that the oven has been kicked and cried over—instead, make it sound like an adventure or a new way to serve the dinner.

10. Maintain a "loaves and fishes" mentality. People often don't RSVP (these are the people you don't invite back) and then show up anyway. You can stretch your buffet with more salad (always keep extra bagged greens in the fridge) and a cheese platter decorated with fresh fruits. You can also cook up a batch of rice simmered in chicken broth, then stir in frozen vegetables such as chopped spinach, snow

peas, or corn, a little butter, and a dash of Parmesan, and you've got an additional side dish.

11. Start the party with an empty dishwasher. Nothing is worse than having dirty dishes stacked in the sink; hide them in the dishwasher when you clear the table. Also, start with a fresh trash bag in the can so you won't have to empty it during the party. If you recycle, line a brown paper bag with a plastic bag (to prevent leakage) and use it to dispose of cans and bottles.

12. There is always someone who is allergic to something, so when your guests RSVP, ask them. Polite guests will tell you up front whether they can't eat something or are vegetarian.

13. Keep centerpieces simple—remember, your food is the real centerpiece. Small, short vases of flowers or herbs are a nice touch, or you can group fresh fruits and vegetables in a bowl to form a centerpiece.

14. Scented candles create a delicious aroma, but keep them away from the food so that they don't interfere with the main attraction. Use unscented votives on your table. Votive candles are preferable to tall tapers because you don't want guests lighting their sleeves on fire or knocking candles over as they reach for things.

15. Make the food stand out by arranging it at different heights. Use sturdy boxes or inverted bowls, cover them with a tablecloth, then a contrasting napkin, and set your food on top, giving the dishes height and interest.

16. Choose a color scheme. If you have cream-colored or white plates, then select something to work off that—primary colors like blue, red, or green look good all year long. Use the color you have chosen for your napkins, flowers, and candles in different shades, or mix and match different colors if you prefer. I generally use a white hotel type of tablecloth for my table, then decorate it with a contrasting runner (or three colored napkins arranged down the center of the table if I don't have a table runner), flowers, and candles.

# HOW MUCH FOOD WILL YOU NEED?

**The Diva says it's always better** to err on the high side; you may end up with leftovers, but believe me, that's much, much better than running out of food! The food estimates below are just that—estimates. I have been throwing parties for over 30 years, long enough to know that it's not an exact science. I've tried to make this as simple as possible, so that you can look at a recipe, then look at the chart, and know by how much you need to multiply the quantities in the list of ingredients. Your basic rule will be one serving of each dish per person. When multiplying, increase in full increments for entrées, sauces, desserts, and small bites, but only in half increments for salads, dips, bread, and sides.

In addition to consulting the table below, try to take into account the individuals you are inviting. If your friends love salad and don't eat as much bread, adjust the amounts accordingly. If you would like to increase the number of different recipes you make, rather than making larger amounts of the same dish, that is fine, too. This is all about giving you choices and having you decide what you want to serve. To estimate the quantities of beverages you will need, see page 37 in the beverage chapter.

## The Diva's Multiplication Table

| | Number of Guests | | | |
|---|---|---|---|---|
| | 12 | 24 | 36 | 48 |
| Entrée | 1x | 2x | 3x | 4x |
| Salad | 1x | 1.5x | 2x | 2.5x |
| Side dishes | 1x | 1.5x | 2x | 2.5x |
| Bread | 1x | 1.5x | 2x | 2.5x |
| Sauce | 1x | 2x | 3x | 4x |
| Dessert | 1x | 2x | 3x | 4x |
| Dips and spreads | 1x | 1.5x | 2x | 2.5x |
| Small bites | 1x | 2x | 3x | 4x |

17. When serving a more elegant meal, cloth napkins are a must, but paper napkins can be used for more casual entertaining.

18. If you can, set the table a day or two ahead of time and cover it with a sheet to protect it from dust, animals, and small children.

19. Roll the silverware in napkins as far in advance as possible. If you are using plastic utensils, you can do this well ahead of time and keep the rolled utensils stored in a zipper-top plastic bag. As an added decoration and to secure the napkin, tie it with ribbon, colored string, or raffia.

20. Two days before the party, check wineglasses and other partyware and run everything through the dishwasher; then store them under sheets so that they don't pick up dust.

21. Clean the bathroom ahead of time, then double-check it right before the party starts to make sure no one has left the sink dirty or towels unfolded. Have plenty of extra hand towels and extra toilet paper readily available so your guests can help themselves. I usually place a pretty basket of extras in the bathroom. Assign one of the kids or someone else to check the bathroom every 90 minutes or so to replenish towels and freshen it up a bit.

22. Always serve dessert at your parties. Whether you have a dramatic layer cake, homey cookies, or even just bowls of M&M's set out in various places, something sweet is a nice way to end a meal.

23. Small party favors can make a fun surprise for your guests. If you're giving a birthday party, you might want to have a goody bag for each guest to take home, just like at kids' parties. If you're hosting a holiday party, you could give seasonal foods (such as a jar of homemade cranberry sauce), small scented candles, or ornaments; or you could simply copy the recipes for the food served at the party onto sheets of colored paper and tie them with ribbons.

24. Polaroid snapshots are a great way to make an instant memory for your party. Photograph everyone as they come in the door (assign a friend or older child to

this). Then place all the photos in a small album to give to the guest of honor, or simply give them away as your guests leave. Or you could leave disposable cameras in strategic spots around the house so that your guests can take candid shots during the party.

Everyone tells you not to be nervous, but I think a few jitters are normal even for the most seasoned veteran. If you follow your plan, you will have everything done ahead of time, and you *will* have time to enjoy your guests and your party. Good luck!

## Ready and Waiting

I've always been an advocate of having the right equipment when starting any project, and the same holds true for entertaining. Here are a few of the items I wouldn't want to be without. I'm assuming that you already have kitchen basics, such as measuring cups and spoons, wooden spoons, and potholders.

*Food processor:* This versatile machine can do everything well, from kneading pie and bread dough to pureeing strawberries for margaritas.

*Hand or stand mixer:* I have had the same 5-quart KitchenAid stand mixer for more than 20 years; we call it Old Faithful at my house. This workhorse effortlessly whips cream for dessert and Make-Ahead Cheesy Mashed Potatoes (page 246) for dinner. If you don't have room for a stand mixer, KitchenAid and Cuisinart both make excellent hand mixers.

*Blender:* This is the tool you will need at the bar, not the food processor. So buy yourself a blender for those margaritas and daiquiris. You'll be glad you did!

*Heavy-duty roasting pan with a rack:* Large and functional, this pan can be used to roast your favorite meats and poultry or cook a double recipe of lasagna. It's also great to use as a bain-marie (water bath) for custards.

*12-inch stainless-steel skillet:* Nothing gives greater caramelization to chicken breasts, onions, or other sautéed items.

*3-quart saucier:* This saucepan is terrific for making sauces, as well as for reducing them. The rounded bottom makes it easy to whisk the contents. It's my choice for an all-purpose pan.

*Santoku:* I can't wield a 12-inch chef's knife to save my life, but this compact cross between a chef's knife and a cleaver has just the right weight and width to turn me into a Benihana chef. It is a great all-purpose knife that you can use for chopping vegetables or slicing meats, bread, or tomatoes. I recommend this to all my students who are just beginning a collection of knives. The Santoku comes in two sizes, 5 inch and 8 inch—make sure you try both to see which feels best in your hand before you buy.

*13 x 9-inch baking dish:* I still have the Pyrex dish I was given as a wedding shower gift many years ago, as well as several nice ceramic oven-to-table dishes. I have a silver holder for my Pyrex to dress it up for elegant occasions, as well as a wicker one that works well for picnics and less formal get-togethers.

*Silpat baking liners:* These silicone baking sheets are used to cover sheet pans and prevent cookies, biscuits, and other baked goods from getting burned. Because nothing sticks to them, they don't need to be buttered; cookies just slide right off.

*Sheet pans:* These are great cookie sheets and are terrific for reheating small bites before serving. Mine are always lined with silicone liners so I'm ready to rock and roll on any given day.

*Heat-proof spatulas:* Have you ever had a spatula melt in your caramel? The invention of heat-proof spatulas has taken care of that problem. In fact, I no longer use wooden cooking spoons. Tempered to 800°F, heat-proof spatulas can withstand almost any punishment you can give them.

*Whisks:* Everyone loves the balloon whisk because it looks formidable, but your best friend is the sauce whisk, used for mixing everything from salad dressings to gravies.

*Instant-read meat thermometer:* If you want to know whether the meat is done, this is the only true test. There are lots on the market, from the simple dial type to the digital read-out probe that beeps when the meat is at the programmed temperature.

**Swivel peeler:** Oxo brand makes one that is the Cadillac of peelers and costs less than $10. If you are still using the rusted one you got with your first apartment, make the switch. This peeler can peel vegetables and fruits in a snap, as well as make shavings of Parmesan and chocolate in a wink.

**Microplane grater:** This tool will help you zest citrus and grate fresh ginger, nutmeg, cinnamon, chocolate, and cheese. Best of all, it goes into the dishwasher.

**Tongs, slotted spoons, metal spatulas, and ladles:** You'll need to have these at hand, close to the stove.

**Offset spatulas:** These come in different lengths and are terrific for spreading everything from jam in a tart to icing on a cake, or even peanut butter on a sandwich.

**Pyrex mixing bowls:** They are great for mixing just about anything in quantity; you can also use them to melt butter or chocolate in the microwave.

**Slow cooker:** They're not much to look at, but they're beautiful for holding things at serving temperature or slowly simmering a main dish, saving valuable burner space on your stove top. I recommend the 5- to 6-quart size; if you are feeling flush, also get the mini 1½- to 2½-quart size, which is great for serving up hot dips and fondue.

**Thermal carafes or pump pots:** These are great for serving warm beverages. You may also want to invest in a coffee urn that serves 25 or more if you think you'll use it more than three times per year.

**Ice buckets or covered bowls:** You'll need these for keeping ice on hand for drinks.

**Nice to have:** two 9-inch round cake pans, muffin tins, a bundt or tube pan, an 8-quart stockpot, a 10-inch pie plate, and warming plates, a chafing dish, or a fondue pot.

## What's in the Do-Ahead Diva's Pantry

Keeping these items in my pantry helps me immeasurably when I want to throw a party, and they also help me decide what I want to make if unexpected company arrives. Sundried tomatoes can be tossed into a simple cream sauce for pasta; Italian tuna and artichoke hearts can be mixed with salad greens and turned into a main-course salad; coconut milk and peanut butter make a terrific Asian-inspired sauce for grilled chicken; rice and pasta can fill in as substantial side dishes. For those of you with limited storage space, I've starred what I think are nice to have, but not necessary, items.

Extra virgin olive oil

Good-quality all-purpose olive oil

Canola oil

Sun-dried tomatoes packed in oil*

Tuna packed in olive oil

Balsamic vinegar

Red wine vinegar

Rice vinegar

Dijon mustard

Best Foods or Hellmann's mayonnaise (low-fat is okay)

Prepared horseradish*

Ketchup

Tabasco, or your favorite hot sauce

Anchovy paste*

Canned green chiles*

Canned chipotle chiles in adobo sauce*

Chicken broth

Beef broth

Lobster stock base*

Canned chopped clams

Rice (converted and regular long-grain)

Pasta (different shapes)

Worcestershire sauce

Soy sauce

Toasted sesame oil

Hoisin sauce*

Fish sauce*

Coconut milk*

Peanut butter

Jam: Apricot and strawberry are my picks for spreading on cake layers or spooning into baked tart shells for an easy dessert.

Canned regular and marinated artichoke hearts

Canned plum tomatoes

Canned beans: black, white, and pinto

Pimento-stuffed olives

Capers*

Old Bay seasoning

Sea salt and coarse kosher salt

Peppercorns

Dried herbs and spices

Nonstick cooking spray: I like to have one plain and one with flour added for baking, such as Baker's Joy.

Semisweet chocolate chips

Unsweetened chocolate bars or cocoa powder

Store-bought hot fudge sauce and caramel sauce

Vanilla paste: You won't have to fiddle with vanilla beans anymore, and this doesn't evaporate when you heat it the way vanilla extract does (see Sources, page 669).

Cream sherry: I prefer the nutty flavor of cream sherry to dry sherry, but it's a personal choice; if you prefer the dry, then of course keep that in your pantry.

# Party
# Beverages

**When it came time to write about beverages** to serve at parties, I decided to consult with my daughter, Carrie (the Little Diva), who owns a PR firm and arranges events in New York City as part of her job. She is hip to what's happening in the world of drink-dom and I am quite happy to share this chapter with her, knowing she'll steer us all toward the best drinks to serve for swell parties.

The Little Diva says, "Some of my most vivid memories of childhood are of my parents entertaining in the 1970s. There were always wonderful smells coming from the kitchen. My father would mix up one of his signature cocktails, which usually sent my mother on the run for the fire extinguisher. The background music was lively, and people dressed up to come over and socialize. Back then you got the feeling that people channeled their creativity into entertaining. We seem to be busier now and, let's face it, most of us don't feel we have the time to slap together anything more inspired than a tray of cheese and crackers when our friends pop by. But all you need to do is whip up a couple of nibbles and dips (see the following two chapters) and a few delicious drinks, and you have a real party."

If you are giving a themed party, you might want to serve a drink to match; for example, a Mexican fiesta just screams for margaritas and Mexican beer. If you serve a featured beverage, though, make sure you also offer a nonalcoholic version, in addition to beer and wine. If you don't want to be responsible for the drinks, ask each of your guests to bring a bottle of wine or a six-pack of beer and make specific suggestions, such as "We're having a Mexican fiesta, can you bring a six-pack of Mexican beer or a lime and a bottle of tequila for margaritas?" Or, "We're having a pasta dinner, could you bring an Italian wine?" That way, your drinks will pair well with the food.

When it comes to drinks, the Diva still believes in do-ahead. We've chosen the drinks—alcoholic and nonalcoholic—in this chapter for three reasons: they can all be made ahead, they taste great, and they help make any party interesting and fun.

## Setting Up the Bar Area

Set up the bar away from the food table and make sure it's ready for the first guest who comes through your front door. It can be a table or counter, which you will probably want near the kitchen so ice and the sink are within easy work-

ing distance. If the weather is fine, move the bar outside; that gets everyone out of the kitchen and gives you room to put your last-minute Diva touches on the food. If drink mixing is required, set out a plate for people to use as a rest for the mixing spoon. If you are having a large party, I recommend pouring glasses of wine, sparkling water, and Champagne, and having those available as close to the door as possible. This helps cut down on the wait at the bar.

Search places such as Ikea for cheap and adorable tablecloths in fun prints. This way, if stains don't come out in the laundry, you won't be heartbroken. The bar is not the place

# SELECTING AND CHILLING THE BEER

**Beer is essential** for any well-stocked bar and is especially appreciated at picnics, tailgates, and outdoor parties. If you aren't a beer drinker, it's probably best to ask a knowledgeable friend or merchant for recommendations. Many regions are famous for their small microbreweries, and those beers are nice to include in your selection. You may want to have a range of different types of beers.

Below are the main choices:

- **Ale:** Dark, bitter, and high in alcohol content
- **Bitter:** Usually a product of the United Kingdom, this has a high alcohol content and, often, a bitter aftertaste
- **Lager:** A popular, all-around beer, not too dark or bitter
- **Light beer:** Fewer calories and lighter flavor
- **Malt liquor:** A high alcohol content and an unusual flavor
- **Stout:** Dark, bitter with a distinctive barley taste

Most beer has an expiration date on the bottle or can, and it should be stored in a cool, dry place. In case you are contemplating a keg instead of a selection of beer, it is equal to 15.5 gallons, or about 6½ cases of 12-ounce cans or bottles.

Beer tastes best when it's icy cold. Your refrigerator is probably bursting with food, so chill cans and bottles of beer, as well as water and soda, in your cooler. Place one layer of cans or bottles in the bottom of a cooler, cover it with chipped ice (it gets between the bottles and cans better than cubes), then repeat the layers until you've filled the cooler. Replace the cover on the cooler; the bottles and cans should be chilled within 90 minutes. A large cardboard box lined with a heavy-duty disposable plastic trash bag can be used to achieve the same purpose, but do this outside. There is always a possibility that the bag will leak, and it will be far easier to deal with on your patio than in your kitchen.

## SETTING UP THE DIVA DRINK PANTRY

**Here are a few essentials** that no drink-making Do-Ahead Diva would ever be without.

- **Superfine sugar:** The tiny size of these sugar granules means they dissolve quickly in liquid. Simple syrup (made from equal parts sugar and water) is made even simpler with superfine sugar.

- **Coarse kosher salt:** This coarse salt is excellent for rimming glasses for drinks like margaritas and Bloody Marys and is a whole lot less expensive than the stuff sold as margarita salt.

- **Wooden skewers:** Not only are long wooden skewers good for grilling, but they are also ideal for skewering olives, cocktail onions, and other garnishes for drinks. Most of the time you will be drinking out of deep glasses, and there is nothing less attractive than watching a guest stick a hand in the glass to get that last slippery olive.

- **Disposable ice cube bags:** These come 10 ice cube bags to a package, and each bag makes 24 cubes (see Sources, page 669). Just fill them and freeze, then empty into your ice bucket. With these in your pantry, you can make lots of flavored ice cubes (see page 64) without having to buy a stack of ice cube trays.

- **Cocktail mixes:** Smart Divas always have a bottle or two of ready-made Bloody Mary mix, margarita (sweet and sour) mix, and piña colada mix on hand for those spur of the moment parties.

for your grandmother's heirloom linens. (Discount stores are also great places for cheap and attractive glasses, pitchers, and bowls for nuts.)

You should invest in two watertight containers, one for ice and one for chilling wine. I like to buy galvanized metal garden buckets in different sizes because they look chic and don't leak. Put ice and tongs in the small ones for your guests to make their drinks. The large ones can be filled with ice for chilling beer, wine, and sodas. Remember that wine will be cold enough to drink after 30 to 40 minutes on ice; it will take almost 4 hours to chill in the fridge.

Any well-stocked bar should have the following ready to go for the party. Liquor is generally sold in ⅕-gallon bottles (fifths), or liters, half gallons, and gallons. You will need to decide how much of each you will eventually drink yourself (after the party) to determine how much to buy. If you think you'll drink more Scotch, vodka, or gin, buy the half-gallon or gallon size because it's more economical. And if you think you'll never use rye or Canadian whiskey, then don't buy it at all; chances are people who drink those will choose bourbon or Scotch instead. Depending on who's pouring, a fifth will yield about thirteen 2-ounce shots of liquor for mixed drinks. A shot glass measures 1½ ounces, but most bartenders overfill the shot glass.

Bourbon

Gin

Rum (light and dark)

Rye or Canadian whiskey

Scotch

Tequila

Vermouth (dry and sweet)

Vodka

Mixers should include:

7-Up or Sprite (diet and regular)

Club soda

Cola (diet and regular)

Ginger ale

Tonic water

Juices: orange, tomato, pineapple, cranberry, grapefruit

Ice (³/₄ pound per person)

Angostura bitters

Grenadine

Other stuff to have on hand:

Lemon, lime, and orange twists and wedges

Maraschino cherries

Olives

Pickled cocktail onions

Tabasco sauce

Worcestershire sauce

Coarse kosher salt, pepper, and superfine sugar

Cocktail napkins (2 to 3 per person)

You may also want to include a selection of liqueurs, such as Amaretto, Bailey's Irish Cream, Grand Marnier, crème de menthe, and Cognac; it's up to you.

## A Themed Drink Bar

Stock a bar with the ingredients for one type of drink so that it becomes a theme. For instance, you could have a mint julep bar or mimosa bar. This is a terrific way to get your guests involved when they first arrive, and it makes it easier for you. If you ask people what they want to drink, you will get a thousand different answers. But if you say, "Help yourself to a frozen margarita or Mexican beer at the bar," you've made it simpler for yourself and your guests. Have the recipe for the drink (both with alcohol and without) printed on a sturdy card and mounted in front of the glasses, ice, and ingredients. You can fill clean, empty wine bottles with infused syrups or other ingredients; just be sure to remove the wine labels and relabel the bottle with its new contents. Bowls or covered buckets of ice; garnishes such as olives, lime or lemon twists or wedges, or fresh fruit; and glasses in appropriate sizes should round out your bar.

# How Much Is Enough?

On the next page is a chart to help you figure quantities for your party beverages. It suggests a serving size, which you can multiply by the number of guests and by whatever you've determined will be the drink factor at your party. Remember that these are guess-

## Diva Drink-Making Do-Ahead

- Slice limes or lemons the day before, cover them with plastic, and refrigerate overnight. Take them out of the fridge an hour before the party.

- Skewer fruit or olive garnishes the day before, store them in zipper-top plastic bags, and set them out right before party time. (If you are serving martinis, try skewering two different types of stuffed olives and a cocktail onion for each cocktail.)

## Helpful Equivalents for Measuring

- One bottle of wine equals 750 milliliters (ml) or 25.4 fluid ounces, which yields about 5 servings per bottle. (Bartenders recommend ½ bottle per person.)

- A fifth of liquor equals about 750 ml or 25 fluid ounces, which yields almost thirteen 2-ounce shots or a little more than sixteen 1½-ounce shots.

- One liter of soda equals 33.8 fluid ounces, more than five 6-ounce servings.

timates, meaning average servings per person for a party. I usually figure on one drink per guest to get them started, and two more to drink with dinner. However, if you are throwing a fraternity toga party, you may want to increase the amounts, and if it's a ladies luncheon, you may want to decrease them a bit, though I know some bridge-playing dames who can drink the frat boys under the table. You will need about ¾ pound of ice per person—some for icing down drinks and some for mixed drinks.

## Estimating Beverage Servings Per Person

| Beverage | Serving Size |
|---|---|
| Predinner Champagne, wine, or wine punch | 4 ounces |
| Mixed drinks, cocktails | 8 ounces |
| Beer | One 12-ounce bottle or can |
| Dinner wine | 4 ounces |
| Dessert wine, sherry | 4 ounces |
| Nonalcoholic punch | 8 ounces |
| Soft drinks | 6 ounces |
| Bottled water (sparkling or still) | One 6-ounce bottle |
| Mixers | 6 ounces |
| Coffee | 8 ounces |
| Tea | 8 ounces |

Calculating total quantities for liquor is a bit tricky. Some caterers use a standard measure of a fifth of each liquor per 12 people, correcting for regional preferences. For example, if you live in the South, you'd have more bourbon than gin. In New York City, you'd have more vodka than bourbon, and in the Southwest, you'd have more tequila and vodka than Scotch. My suggestion is this: Start with a fifth of each of the liquors suggested on page 38 for a party for 12. After that, guesstimate how much more you will need: Will cocktails only be served for an hour? Will you be having a themed drink bar with only one or two kinds of drinks? If you are having a full bar, I recommend that you overstock a bit, just to be on the safe side. Unopened liquor and mixers cannot be returned to the store, but they keep for a long time in a cool, dry place, and chances are you will use them up soon enough.

## General Guidelines for Stocking Beverages for Your Party Bar

This is a general formula for stocking your bar. Remember to figure in the preferences of your geographical location and make adjustments.

| Beverage | Bar for 12 | For 48 | For Up to 100 |
| --- | --- | --- | --- |
| Vodka | 1 fifth | 3 fifths | 4 fifths |
| Rum | 1 fifth | 2 fifths | 2 fifths |
| Gin | 1 fifth | 2 fifths | 3 fifths |
| Scotch | 1 fifth | 2 fifths | 3 fifths |
| Bourbon | 1 fifth | 1 fifth | 1 fifth |
| Whiskey (optional) | 1 fifth | 1 fifth | 1 fifth |
| Wine | Six 750-ml bottles | Twelve 750-ml bottles | Eighteen 750-ml bottles |
| Beer | 1 or 2 cases | 3 to 4 cases | 6 cases |
| Soft drinks | Five 2-liter bottles | Twelve 2-liter bottles | Eighteen to twenty 2-liter bottles |
| Water | Three 2-liter bottles | Eight 2-liter bottles | Fifteen 2-liter bottles |

### The Diva Says:

I prefer to buy liters of soda and mixers because canned mixers and sodas can be wasteful; people often drink part of the can, then put it down. If you serve from liters, the drink can be properly iced in a glass and the remainder resealed in the bottle. I will serve cans if it's a beer and soda party in the backyard or a tailgate and I don't want to bother with a bar. If you're serving cans of soda, figure 1 ½ per person and recycle those cans!

# Choosing Wines

I do not claim to be a wine expert, but I do feel that since you are spending time and money to have the best party, why not take a little time and find the right wine to pair with your food? Not all food goes well with Chardonnay and Merlot! My first suggestion is to read the label on the bottle you're considering. It may say the wine is fruity, or tannic, or full-bodied. It may even give you some suggestions for pairing it with foods. If all else fails, below are some of my favorite picks for parties. But I would strongly recommend you ask the people at your local wine store for help. That's what they are there for. Also, remember

## Hiring a Bartender

There are pros and cons to hiring some-one to bartend at your party. The main advantage, of course, is that you and your significant other don't have to watch the bar. The cons are you have to pay well to get great bartenders, and they may pour more liberally than you would. For a party of more than 10 people where you will be serving a full bar, get a bartender; you can't pour drinks and have a relaxing party—it will drive you nuts. For most parties, where you'll serve only wine, beer, and soft drinks, you won't need a bartender. Your friends know the drill; they can serve themselves, and they tend to serve others, too.

A bartender/dishwasher can save your life, though. If you want to hire someone to do dishes after the party, so you don't have to, see whether he or she also pours drinks. If you are paying someone by the hour to do your dishes, why not spend a little extra and have that person set up the bar, serve, clear away, and clean up the bar, too? Or keep it in the family; when my children lived at home, they loved being the bartenders.

## Diva Bar Supplies

In addition to stocking your bar, I sug-gest you lay in a good supply of the following necessities for mixing, opening, and garnishing your libations:

- Bar towels
- Small bowl or bucket for discarded toothpicks, cocktail napkins, and other trash
- Can opener
- Cocktail shaker
- Shot glass
- Small Lucite cutting board
- Small paring knife for cutting fruits
- Long-handled spoon for stirring
- Strainer
- Wine bottle opener

some people will only drink white wine or red wine; balance the selections so you can have something for everyone.

- Chardonnay is a crisp white wine with fruity flavors; it pairs well with seafood, creamy pastas, and lightly sauced chicken dishes (think lemon or roasted chicken rather than tomato-sauced chicken).

- Pinot Grigio (the Italian name) or Pinot Gris (in French) is a white wine that is crisp and light, not heavy with oaky flavor like the Chardonnays. This slightly fruity wine is great for sipping before dinner and is also a nice table wine at lunch or brunch.

- Riesling is a sweeter white wine that pairs well with salty and smoky flavors such as ham, pâté, and cheeses. Asian foods and lightly sauced chicken and turkey are also complemented by this delicious wine.

- Merlot is a medium-bodied red wine with a jammy, berry flavor. It is a very popular drink before and with dinner.

- Cabernet Sauvignon is a full-bodied red wine that pairs well with roasted poultry, beef, or lamb; steak; pot roast; or sauced salmon. This bold wine has a spiciness that many people enjoy.

- Syrah is another spicy red wine, which has hints of herbs and spices; serve it with roasted lamb and poultry.

- Zinfandel has a peppery flavor that pairs well with tomato-sauced pastas, pizza, burgers, Latin or Mexican foods, and roasted and grilled meats.

- Pinot Noir often has the spicy flavors of cinnamon and berries, so serve this red wine with roasted or grilled turkey, beef, ham, or sausage. Chicken in a tomato or wine sauce would be delicious with Pinot Noir. Salmon in a robust sauce, such as a red wine sauce or heavier sauce, is also wonderful

> ## Party Glassware
> Please. Pretty please. We're begging you! *Do not* serve wine from plastic cups. Even nice wine seems cheap when you serve it in plastic or (God forbid) paper! For less than a dollar per glass you can serve your wine in a proper wineglass. Places like Kmart, Ikea, and dollar stores are great sources for inexpensive glass-ware. And don't throw away the boxes that the wineglasses came in. Once they are washed, put them back in their box and store them until the next party.

with Pinot Noir. A sparkling Pinot Noir is delicious with roasted turkey or ham for a holiday occasion.

The above descriptions of the most popular wines only scratch the surface. You should also consider Sauvignon Blanc, a deliciously crisp white wine; Voignier, which is a French grape that makes a delicious white wine; and Italian red wines such as Barolo and Barbaresco, which are deep and fragrant. For more information, I suggest you ask your wine merchant, or check out some wine merchants online.

# Coffee and After-Dinner Drinks

Always have coffee available for your guests; after eating a fabulous meal and drinking cocktails and wines, they will need a little caffeine to help them get home. Plan on 1½ cups of coffee per person. If you can buy yourself a coffee urn that serves 25 or more, that will save you from making 12 pots in your 4-cup Mr. Coffee machine. If you don't have a coffee urn, I suggest you make several pots of coffee and keep them warm in thermal carafes or pump pots. Thermal carafes are a terrific investment; they will keep your coffee hot for about 5 hours.

## Would You Like Your Cordial on the Rocks or over Ice Cream?

Sometimes I forgo a homemade dessert and set up the Diva's famous ice cream dessert bar with my guests' choice of after-dinner liqueur as the topping. There's nothing better than a little Bailey's dribbled over vanilla ice cream and topped with toasted almonds. Several days before the party, freeze ice cream scoops on sheet pans or in serving bowls. The day of your party, assemble some toasted nuts, coconut, and shaved chocolate in bowls, whip some cream, and stash it in the fridge. Ten minutes before serving, take out the ice cream and whipped cream, then let your guests indulge. Leftover maraschino cherries from the bar can be used as well!

I usually make one pot of decaffeinated coffee, so everyone has a choice. If I don't know whether decaf will be the favorite, I'll have a second pot measured and ready to brew, so that by the time the first round is served, the next pot of decaf is done. Measure out the coffee and store it in zipper-top plastic bags in the freezer, ready to brew when you need them.

A self-service coffee bar should include freshly brewed coffee in labeled pump pots or thermal carafes (decaf, regular, or flavored), plenty of cream or milk, sugar, sweetener, spoons, mugs or thermal cups, and napkins. After that, you can decide whether to include freshly whipped cream, shaved chocolate, cinnamon sugar, peppermint sticks, chocolate coffee spoons (simple to make or buy from mail order), flavored syrups like Torani, and after-dinner liqueurs of your choice to spike the coffee.

Remember to find a large jug for cream or milk; those tiny crystal creamers you got as a gift are gorgeous but totally impractical for your party. (I sometimes use a half-liter wine carafe for a creamer.) You can stand the creamer in a bowl of ice to keep it cold. I generally don't make tea in advance for a large party because it's simple enough to microwave hot water, pour it over tea bags, and brew tea for those who want it.

What about cordials or after-dinner liqueurs? Frankly, after eating and drinking all night, these almost seem anticlimactic, but they can be a lot of fun. Serve them from a tray, allowing guests to decide what they would like and whether they want their Kahlúa with cream or on the rocks.

# Mimosa

Serves 10

This lovely Champagne and orange juice drink can be made as a nonalcoholic version, too. It is a terrific starter for brunch or a ladies lunch and also lends itself to a serve-yourself bar. A fresh whole strawberry in the bottom of each glass is a beautiful garnish.

**1 gallon chilled orange juice**

**Three 750-ml bottles chilled Champagne**

Pour ½ cup orange juice into a wine-glass or Champagne flute. Top off with Champagne and serve.

## Diva Variations

**Virgin Mimosa:** Substitute 7-Up or another lemon-lime soda for the Champagne.

**Wine Mimosa:** Substitute white wine for the Champagne.

**Cantaloupe Mimosa:** Puree cantaloupe with orange juice and top it off with Champagne for a deliciously different mimosa. To make 10 mimosas, puree 3 cups of chopped cantaloupe (1 cantaloupe) with 1 cup of chilled orange juice. (You will need to do this in two batches.) Pour into a pitcher and chill for at least 2 hours. Fill each glass halfway with the chilled puree and top with Champagne.

# Vodka Slush

Serves 12

This simple cooler will refresh your guests on a hot summer night. The slush can be served as a drink or as an iced dessert with a bit of Champagne poured over it.

**Two 6-ounce cans frozen orange juice concentrate, defrosted**

**Two 12-ounce cans frozen lemonade concentrate, defrosted**

**One 6-ounce can frozen limeade concentrate, defrosted**

**3 cups water**

**1 fifth vodka**

**3 liters club soda**

**Fresh mint sprigs for garnish**

**1.** In a large bowl, combine the concentrates, water, and vodka, stirring to blend.

✳ **DIVA DO-AHEAD:** At this point, transfer to zipper-top plastic bags and freeze for at least 12 hours and up to 2 months.

**2.** When ready to serve, spoon ¾ cup of the mixture into an 8-ounce glass and pour in enough club soda to fill it. Garnish with mint and serve.

# Tequila Sunrise

Serves 12

This beautifully colored drink is a great choice for a serve-yourself bar and can also be made in a pitcher. Have the recipe printed on a card, the ingredients readily available, and be sure to have replenishments chilling nearby where your guests can help themselves.

**Ice cubes**

**1 gallon chilled fresh orange juice**

**1 fifth tequila**

**6 limes, cut into wedges**

**½ cup grenadine**

**1.** For each drink, fill an 8-ounce glass with ice cubes. Pour in ¾ cup of the orange juice and top with ¼ cup of tequila. Rub a lime wedge around the edge of the glass, add to the drink, and stir to blend.

**2.** Carefully pour 2 teaspoons of grenadine down the side of the glass. There are two schools of thought on stirring: Some people like the look of the red stripe in the glass, which resembles a red sun on the horizon (sunrise) and gradually gets mixed into the drink as it is sipped. Others like to stir in the grenadine.

## Diva Variation

**Diva Tequila Sunrise Pitchers:** You will need to make this in two pitchers to serve 12 people. Pour ¼ cup of grenadine into each pitcher. Add 4½ cups of orange juice, 1½ cups of tequila, and ½ cup of fresh lime juice, being careful not to stir too much.

✳ **DIVA DO-AHEAD:** At this point, cover and refrigerate for at least 4 hours and up to 4 days.

Just before serving, stir up the grenadine from the bottom, which will give the pitcher a rosy glow.

## Sunrise Cubes

A great way to flavor sunrises with grenadine is to make grenadine ice cubes. Blend 2 cups of grenadine with ½ cup of fresh lime juice and freeze in ice cube trays. Use the ice cubes instead of the syrup to flavor a pitcherful; they will melt slowly and will not dilute the mix.

# Martha's Pimm's Cup

Serves 10 to 12

➤ **From the Little Diva:** Several years ago, my boyfriend Eric's mother, Martha, introduced me to her favorite summertime drink, the Pimm's Cup. Pimm's No. 1 is a fruity, gin-based liquor from England. It is light and mild and makes for a splendidly refreshing cocktail, perfect for picnics, fancy lunches, and lazy afternoons. We usually make these by the glass, but in true Diva style we have modified this recipe so you can make pitchers of it ahead of time and let your guests serve themselves. Pimm's was originated in London by John Pimm, who mixed gin with lime juice and herbs. There are several different types of Pimm's, so look for No. 1 when you want to make the Pimm's Cup. I prefer to use diet ginger ale here because it is less sweet, but any ginger ale or lemon-lime soda will do.

**One 750-ml bottle Pimm's No. 1**

**1 orange, cut into 16 wedges**

**Ice cubes**

**10 to 12 maraschino cherries for garnish**

**1 European cucumber, cut into thin spears, for garnish**

**2 liters ginger ale**

**1 cup fresh strawberries (optional), hulled and quartered, and/or sliced lemons and limes**

**1.** Combine the Pimm's and orange wedges in a large serving pitcher.

✳ **DIVA DO-AHEAD:** At this point, you can cover and let stand at room temperature for 1 hour and up to 4 hours.

**2.** Fill each glass half full of ice and place a maraschino cherry and cucumber spear in each. Cover the ice with the Pimm's mixture and top off with ginger ale. Garnish with a piece of strawberry or a slice of citrus if desired.

# Little Diva's Favorite Bloody Mary

Serves 12

▶ **From the Little Diva:** For my money there is nothing that goes with Sunday brunch better than a Bloody Mary, and my boyfriend, Eric, makes the best. "Eric's Bloody" has become so popular among our friends that it is usually what we're asked to bring to parties and gatherings. So we keep a large Tupperware pitcher on hand for those occasions. The best way to serve these at a party is to have a Bloody Mary bar. Do yourself a favor and put down a trash bag, then a cheap (but chic) tablecloth wherever you set this up because we've found that when guests get creative, they also get messy! Fill a pitcher full of the basic "Bloody" mix and leave out some pint glasses and a good supply of ice. You should also put out lemon and lime slices, celery stalk stirrers, extra spices, sauces, and condiments to help people construct and embellish their brunch-time masterpieces.

In Colin Peter Field's book, *The Cocktails of the Ritz, Paris*, he tells the story of how the Bloody Mary came into existence. Ernest Hemingway's doctors had recommended that he not drink because of his failing health, and his wife, Mary, was a strict enforcer of the doctor's policy. The Ritz's head bartender devised a strong-tasting cocktail of tomato juice, vodka, and spices as a way to keep "Papa Hemingway" happy while hiding his habit from Mary.

## Gilding the Lily, Bloody Mary Style

Garnishing is one of the best ways to be creative with your Bloody Marys. A celery stalk keeps your Bloody from being totally pedestrian, but it's still not very exciting. Why not try jalapeño-stuffed olives, pickled asparagus or green beans, European cucumber spears, or zucchini spears? Our friend John Hollyer and his wife, Diane, brought us a jar of pickled okra for a Bloody Mary brunch, and these have now become a staple in our house. Or try a large cooked shrimp hung over the rim of the glass as they do at some Legal Seafood restaurants. Make sure to spear smaller garnishes with long wooden skewers, so your guests aren't fishing around in their glasses with their hands.

## Bloody Mary Cubes

Frozen tomato juice ice cubes are a great way to keep your Bloodys from becoming too diluted. Freeze tomato juice in ice cube trays, then serve them in a separate ice bucket. Or freeze Eric's Wasabi Mary mix (see right) in small ice cube trays and label the ice bucket "atomic"!

One 32-ounce bottle Clamato

One 64-ounce bottle V-8 vegetable juice or tomato juice (we like Sacramento)

¼ cup prepared horseradish

⅔ cup Worcestershire sauce

10 dashes of Tabasco sauce

1 tablespoon celery salt (the secret ingredient)

¼ teaspoon freshly ground black pepper (about 10 grinds of the pepper mill), plus extra for garnish

Juice of ½ lemon

Ice cubes

1 fifth vodka

Celery stalks for garnish

Lemon slices for garnish

**1.** In a 3- to 4-quart pitcher, stir together the Clamato, V-8, horseradish, Worcestershire, Tabasco, celery salt, pepper, and lemon juice.

✳ **DIVA DO-AHEAD:** Cover and refrigerate for at least 4 hours and up to 4 days.

**2.** For each drink, fill an 8-ounce glass with ice, pour in 2 ounces of vodka, and fill the glass with the Bloody Mary mix. Stir to blend. Garnish the drinks with a celery stalk, freshly ground black pepper, and lemon slices.

## Little Diva Variations

Play around with extra lemon and lime. And why stop at Tabasco? Try different hot pepper sauces or a Thai chili paste like sambal oelek for merciless heat or a chipotle hot sauce for a smoky kick. Rim the glasses with celery salt or a prepackaged Bloody Mary rimmer. We go to Nantucket every summer, so we love to add a few shots of Cioppino's Secret Sauce and Marinade to our Bloody Marys. It takes us right back to the island.

**Eric's Wasabi Mary:** This spicy add-in can turn your Bloody Mary into an atomic experience. Don't say we didn't warn you! In a small bowl, mix together 1¼ cups of Worcestershire sauce, 1½ teaspoons of wasabi paste diluted with 1 tablespoon of hot water (or 1½ teaspoons of wasabi powder diluted with water into a paste the consistency of pancake batter), 5 dashes of Tabasco sauce, and 5 dashes of Cholula or another Mexican hot sauce (the Tabasco adds heat, the other hot sauce adds flavor). Transfer the mixture to a squirt bottle. Hold your finger over the opening and shake vigorously for 10 seconds to dissolve the wasabi. Label the bottle, indicating its incendiary quality, and leave it with the Bloody Mary fixings.

✳ **DIVA DO-AHEAD:** This will keep in the refrigerator for up to 3 months.

**Oyster Shooters:** Measure 2 ounces of a premixed Bloody Mary (including the vodka) into a small glass and top with a raw oyster. Plan on 3 to 4 of these per person. This is only for oyster lovers.

# White Peach Sangria

Serves 10 to 12

▶ **From the Little Diva:** The summers are hot and humid in New York City. When my best friend, Laura, and I moved here, we would save our pennies and make a pilgrimage on hot summer nights to the Upper West Side to have sangria and guacamole. This is my version of the sangria we used to drink. In true Diva style, you can make it the night or the morning before you serve it.

One 750-ml bottle dry Riesling or Sauvignon Blanc

1½ cups white cranberry or white cranberry–peach cocktail

½ cup peach schnapps

Juice of 2 lemons

½ vanilla bean (optional), split lengthwise

1 tablespoon superfine sugar

1 lemon, cut into 1-inch-thick slices

1 orange, cut into 1-inch-thick slices

2 peaches, peeled, pitted, and cut into wedges

Ice cubes

1 to 2 pints fresh raspberries, blackberries, or hulled and sliced strawberries (optional) for garnish

**1.** In a gallon pitcher, combine the wine, cranberry juice, schnapps, and lemon juice. Add the seeds from the vanilla bean, if using, the sugar, and the lemon, orange, and peaches.

✱ **DIVA DO-AHEAD:** At this point, cover and refrigerate for at least 4 hours or overnight.

**2.** When ready to serve, fill 8-ounce glasses half full of ice cubes and pour the sangria over the ice. Serve immediately, garnished with some of the berries if desired.

## Punch Bowl Sangria

To serve sangria in a punch bowl, make an ice mold: Combine distilled water (to keep it clear) and berries and/or sliced or cut-up fruit in a fancy mold or a bundt pan and freeze. Run hot water over the bottom of the pan to loosen the ice block, place it in the punch bowl, and pour the sangria over it.

# Red, White, or Blush Sangria

Serves 10 to 12

Fruity and refreshing, this is our drink of choice before a Latin or Spanish meal. We like it ice cold in chilled wineglasses, without the usual addition of club soda, but if you have to stretch your wine dollar, fill double rocks glasses half full with sangria, then fill the rest of the way with club soda for a sparkly and light refresher. This master recipe works well for red, white, or blush wines, and you could serve a pitcher of each to your guests, if you'd like.

**1 cup superfine sugar**

**2½ cups hot water**

**2 limes, thinly sliced**

**2 oranges, thinly sliced**

**Ice cubes**

**1½ cups Triple Sec**

**Three 750-ml bottles red, white, or blush wine (such as Pinot Noir, Sauvignon Blanc, or white Zinfandel)**

**1 cup hulled and halved strawberries for garnish**

**1 cup fresh pineapple chunks for garnish**

**1.** Put the sugar in a medium-size heat-proof bowl and pour the water over it, stirring to dissolve. Add the limes and oranges.

✳ **DIVA DO-AHEAD:** At this point, cover and let sit at room temperature for at least 4 hours or refrigerate overnight.

**2.** Fill each of 3 pitchers with a tray of ice cubes (about 2 cups). Pour ¾ cup of the sugar syrup into each one and add some of the limes and oranges. Add ½ cup of the Triple Sec and 1 bottle of wine to each and stir gently.

**3.** Place a strawberry half and a pineapple chunk in each wineglass and pour in the sangria.

## A Quick Lemon Juice Fix

I am lucky enough to have lemons growing in my backyard that are thin skinned and filled with juice. Unfortunately, those found in the grocery store are usually not very juicy. One lemon usually yields about ½ cup of juice. If you need a lot of lemon juice, Minute Maid makes a frozen lemon juice in a bottle, which you can find at your supermarket in the case with the frozen juices. Defrost that in your fridge overnight (it will keep for about 6 months). This is a great solution if you live in a cold climate and the lemons are very expensive where you shop. Do not, however, buy that little plastic lemon in the produce section—it's nasty stuff.

# Mama D's Easy Margarita

Serves 12

▶ **From the Little Diva:** When I was younger, my parents entertained all the time. People would always rave about my mother's margaritas. She and my father would laugh to themselves that the recipe really couldn't have been easier. When I was in college, my friends and I called my mother to get her margarita recipe, which became known from then on as Mama D's Margaritas. Using the limeade can as a measure makes it really easy.

**Ice cubes**

**Two 12-ounce cans frozen limeade concentrate**

**2 concentrate cans gold tequila**

**1 concentrate can Triple Sec**

**1 concentrate can fresh lime juice (about 6 limes)**

**Lime wedges for garnish**

**Coarse kosher salt for the glasses**

**1.** Fill a blender container halfway with ice. Add half the limeade concentrate, tequila, Triple Sec, and lime juice and blend on high until the ice is crushed and the mixture is slushy, about 1 minute. Transfer to a zipper-top plastic bag. Repeat with the remaining ingredients.

✳ **DIVA DO-AHEAD:** At this point, freeze for about 6 hours or up to 6 months. Defrost before continuing with the recipe.

**2.** One hour before serving, transfer the margarita mixture to an iced pitcher and refrigerate.

**3.** When ready to serve, rub a lime wedge around the rim of each glass. Pour the salt into a small bowl. Dip the glass into the salt, and spoon in some of the margarita mixture. Serve up pronto!

## Diva Variations

**Berry Margarita:** To every recipe of Mama D's Easy Margarita, add 2 cups pureed and strained berries of your choice: strawberries, raspberries, blueberries, or blackberries.

**Watermelon Margarita:** To every recipe of Mama D's Easy Margarita, add 2 cups of seeded and pureed watermelon. Red watermelon will give you a delicate pink margarita, while yellow watermelon will give you an intense golden color.

**Virgin Margarita:** Make up 1 recipe Mama D's Easy Margarita, substituting one 12-ounce can of lemonade concentrate for the tequila and 1 cup of orange juice for the Triple Sec.

# Fresh Lime Margarita

Serves 12

▶ **From the Little Diva:** When I was growing up in San Diego, my parents would take us to Alfonso's, in La Jolla, for dinner. It has always been our favorite Mexican restaurant and they still have the world's best margarita. We've been going there for 30 years now, and Alfonso still won't tell us his margarita secrets. I have a feeling it has something to do with all that fresh lime juice and the addition of lemon, which complements the tequila.

**1 cup fresh lime juice (4 to 5 limes)**

**6 tablespoons fresh lemon juice**

**2 cups Triple Sec**

**2 cups white or silver tequila**

**3 cups ice cubes**

**1.** In a large pitcher, stir together the citrus juices, Triple Sec, and tequila.

**2.** Put 1½ cups of the ice in a blender and add half of the tequila mixture. Blend until slushy and transfer to a zipper-top plastic bag. Repeat with the remaining ice and tequila mixture.

✱ **DIVA DO-AHEAD:** At this point, refrigerate for at least 2 hours and up to 3 days.

**3.** Pour the margarita mix into a serving pitcher and serve over ice.

### The Little Diva Says:

Each lime will yield between 3 and 4 tablespoons of juice. If you are having a problem finding decent limes at a reasonable price, Key lime juice, available in many specialty stores, is a good alternative (see Sources, page 669).

### Diva Variations

**Margarita on the Rocks:** Rub a cut lime over the rim of a double rocks glass and dip the rim lightly in coarse kosher salt. Fill glass with ice and pour margarita to the top.

**Virgin Margarita:** Substitute 2 cups of fresh orange juice for the Triple Sec and 2 cups of club soda for the tequila.

### Keeping Up with Demand

Serving margaritas to the multitudes can be difficult if they are in a partying mood; in other words, you might run out. Keep a backup supply of margaritas made with a mix in the refrigerator and stir that with the slush remaining in the pitcher. For regular margaritas, mix together 1 cup of tequila, ⅓ cup of Triple Sec, and 3 cups of bottled margarita mix (I recommend Mr. & Mrs. T's).

✱ **DIVA DO-AHEAD:** At this point, you can cover and refrigerate for 5 days or freeze for several months.

For each serving, fill a glass halfway with the mixed margarita, then top with the slush and stir.

# Mojito

Serves 10

These Cuban cocktails seem to be all the rage, but crushing mint and trying to dissolve sugar in a cocktail glass were more than I wanted to deal with when throwing a party, so I decided to streamline the process by making a mint-infused simple syrup. You can have the ingredients ready for your guests to make their own; just provide a small recipe card at the bar to instruct them.

2 cups water

2 cups superfine sugar

2 cups packed fresh mint leaves, plus
　　1 bunch for garnish

Ice cubes

2½ cups light rum

½ cup fresh lime juice

About 2 liters club soda

Fresh mint sprigs for garnish

## Diva Variation

**Mojitos by the Pitcher:** If you would like to make these to have ready in a pitcher, fill a pitcher with the simple syrup, rum, and lime juice. Fill glasses with ice cubes, fill halfway with mojito mixture, then fill the rest of the way with club soda and garnish.

**1.** In a 2-quart saucepan, combine the water and sugar and bring to a boil, stirring until the sugar dissolves.

✳ **DIVA DO-AHEAD:** At this point, you can let cool, cover, and refrigerate for up to 4 months. Reheat before continuing.

Add the mint leaves and let steep for 1 hour.

**2.** Strain the syrup and discard the mint leaves.

✳ **DIVA DO-AHEAD:** At this point, you can let cool, cover, and refrigerate for up to 4 days.

**3.** When ready to serve, fill each glass with ice and add ¼ cup of rum, ¼ cup of mint syrup, 2 teaspoons of lime juice, and enough club soda to fill the glass. Garnish with mint sprigs and serve.

# Cosmopolitan Cocktail

Serves 12

The TV show *Sex and the City* changed the face of television, fashion, and drinking cocktails forever! Cosmopolitans became a standard pour among the hip set and sparked a renewed interest in martinis in all flavors, which explains all those new martini bars opening in cities across the country. Since this is so simple to make ahead for your party and have waiting at the drink station, plan to make a double batch; they go down easily. For more martini ideas, I recommend a good bartender's guide.

**2¼ cups lemon vodka**

**1½ cups Cointreau**

**1½ cups cranberry juice cocktail**

**½ cup fresh lime juice**

**Crushed ice**

**2 navel oranges, stripped of their zest in long, thin threads (a swivel peeler does a great job)**

**1.** In a pitcher, stir together the vodka, Cointreau, and cranberry and lime juices until blended.

✳ **DIVA DO-AHEAD:** At this point, cover and refrigerate for at least 4 hours and up to 2 days.

**2.** When ready to serve, pour the mixture into a cocktail shaker half filled with crushed ice and shake to blend. Strain into chilled glasses, garnish each one with a twist of orange zest, and serve.

## Diva Variations

**Champagne Cosmo:** Mix together the Cointreau and juices, and refrigerate until chilled. When ready to serve, blend in 2¼ cups of chilled Champagne.

**Cape Cod Cosmo:** When I was younger, the traditional Cape Codder—vodka, cranberry juice, and lime over ice—was a favorite of mine. For this cosmo twist, substitute orange vodka for the lemon and continue as directed. Pour over ice and serve, garnished with lime wedges and orange twists.

## Keeping It Clean

You don't want your new white carpet to look like a Jackson Pollock painting but you want to serve a drink that looks dangerously stain-producing? Don't use shallow martini glasses, which spill easily. Get creative and serve your cosmopolitan in a rocks glass with a slice of lemon at the bottom. If people are drinking plain martinis, serve them in frozen tall vodka glasses for a European touch. And only fill glasses half full with ice—they are less likely to overflow.

# Piña Colada

Serves 12

Any tropical vacation has to include at least one glass of this sinfully delicious drink, sipped poolside or underneath a cabana on the beach. There are lots of different recipes for piña colada, but the main ingredients are pineapple, coconut, and rum, three of my favorite flavors. I've given you variations for virgin, berry, and punch-bowl styles. If you are serving these in the backyard, I guarantee they will transport you to a tropical paradise. Serve them as a starter for a luau or tropical- or Asian-themed barbecue.

**10 cups pineapple-coconut juice or piña colada mix**

**2¼ cups white rum**

**1½ cups dark rum**

**Two 20-ounce cans pineapple chunks in heavy syrup, drained and frozen**

**3 cups ice cubes, plus extra for the glasses**

**Fresh pineapple spears or chunks, strawberries, or maraschino cherries (or a combination) for garnish**

**1.** In a large pitcher, combine juice and rums.

✳ **DIVA DO-AHEAD:** At this point, cover and refrigerate for at least 4 hours and up to 3 days, or freeze for up to 2 months. Defrost before continuing with the recipe.

**2.** Put ¼ cup of the frozen pineapple chunks and ¼ cup of the ice cubes in a blender. Add 4 cups of the rum and pineapple juice mixture and process for 1 minute, until smooth. Pour into 3 double rocks glasses, garnished with pineapple spears or skewers of pineapple chunks, strawberries, or maraschino cherries. Repeat 3 more times to make 12 drinks.

## Diva Variations

**Virgin Piña:** Omit the rum and blend the pineapple-coconut juice with the frozen pineapple and ice cubes.

**Berry Piña:** Substitute two 16-ounce bags of individually frozen strawberries for the pineapple chunks and blend as directed. Garnish with strawberry and pineapple skewers.

**Punch Bowl Piña:** Fill a fancy mold or bundt pan with pineapple juice and add the pineapple chunks, as well as any other complementary fruit, such as individually frozen strawberries or sliced oranges. Freeze the pan until firm, and unmold into the punch bowl. Mix the juice and rums and pour the mixture over the ice block. Or freeze an entire bundt pan full of pineapple-coconut juice and use that as your ice block. (Rum doesn't freeze solid, so don't add it to the ice block.) Blend the ice and pineapple chunks, stir in the rum, and pour it over the ice block.

**Chi Chi:** Substitute vodka for the rum.

# Daiquiri

Serves 12

The daiquiri is a tropical drink from the Caribbean, featuring rum, lime juice, and sugar. Daiquiris can morph into a rainbow of different colors and flavors, so we'll give you the basic recipe and you can take care of the rest using the Diva Variations. Make these up at least a day ahead of time, then whirl in the blender with ice, and you'll have nectar of the gods for your next party.

**3 cups light rum**

**One 12-ounce can frozen limeade concentrate, defrosted**

**Fresh pineapple chunks for garnish**

**Lime wedges for garnish**

**Maraschino cherries for garnish**

**Ice cubes**

**1.** In a pitcher, combine the rum and concentrate, stirring to blend.

✳ **DIVA DO-AHEAD:** At this point, cover and refrigerate for at least 4 hours or overnight, or freeze for up to 2 months.

**2.** Thread each of 12 skewers with a pineapple chunk, lime wedge, and cherry and set aside. Fill a blender container halfway with ice cubes and pour in the daiquiri mix to within 2 inches of the top. Blend on high speed until slushy, 1 to 2 minutes. Pour into chilled glasses and garnish each one with a fruit skewer.

## Diva Variations

**Mango Daiquiri:** Add 2 cups of peeled and chopped mango to the limeade and rum mixture.

**Strawberry Daiquiri:** Add 1 1/2 cups of strawberry puree (from about 1 1/2 pints of strawberries) to the limeade and rum mixture.

**Banana Daiquiri:** Add 4 peeled and sliced medium-size bananas to the limeade and rum mixture.

**Pineapple Daiquiri:** Add 2 cups of peeled, cored, and chopped fresh pineapple to the limeade and rum mixture.

**Watermelon Daiquiri:** Add 2 cups of watermelon puree to the limeade and rum mixture.

# Uncle Jeep's Sherbet Punch

Serves 10

Every year my friend Bobby has a Christmas party, which always lasts late into the night and ends with everyone in the living room looking at the Christmas tree. The fuel for his party is his Uncle Jeep's Sherbet Punch, and every Diva and Little Diva knows you need great punch for get-togethers of any kind.

---

**1 cup vodka**

**½ cup Triple Sec**

**Two 750-ml bottles chilled Champagne**

**3 liters chilled ginger ale**

**2 pints sherbet, any flavor**

---

In a large punch bowl, combine the vodka, Triple Sec, Champagne, and ginger ale. Scoop the sherbet into the punch bowl and serve.

### The Diva Says:

This tastes best cold, so it's a great excuse for making an ice ring for your punch bowl. Combine 6 cups of cranberry juice cocktail and 2 cups of water and pour into a bundt pan; add fruit if you wish. Freeze for several hours or overnight, until solid. Run hot water over the bottom of the pan to loosen the ice block and place in the punch bowl right before serving.

# Kir Royale

Serves 10

An apéritif from the 1940s and 1950s, this highly sophisticated drink is still in style. Make sure you use a dry white wine that doesn't have a lot of competing flavors, such as Sauvignon Blanc; otherwise, you'll only taste the wine and not the delightful crème de cassis. Crème de cassis is a liqueur made from black currants; it has a deep burgundy color and gives this drink a fabulous color, just right for the holidays.

---

**Two 750-ml bottles chilled dry white wine**

**¼ cup crème de cassis**

---

Pour ½ cup of wine into each wineglass. Slowly pour 1 teaspoon of crème de cassis into each glass. Serve immediately.

---

### Diva Bubbly Variation

Some bartending books say that a kir royale is only made with Champagne, but I was raised on the white wine version, which won't lose its fizz if it's left out on the bar station the way Champagne will. If you would like to use Champagne, simply substitute it for the white wine.

---

# Pear Bellini

Serves 12

A Sunday brunch calls for something bubbly, and although a mimosa is standard fare, it leaves little to the imagination. Delight your guests with bellinis made with pear nectar instead of the traditional peach. Bellinis are a Do-Ahead Diva's dream. Buy a bottle of pear nectar at the store and put it in an elegant glass pitcher—your guests will have visions of you lovingly juicing pears all morning for them. Pair that with an exotic-looking bottle of bubbly Italian Prosecco chilling on the bar station.

**1 quart chilled pear nectar (Looza is nice)**

**Two 750-ml bottles chilled Italian Prosecco (I recommend Rustico—it's cheap and widely available)**

Fill each Champagne flute or wineglass one-quarter full with pear nectar. Fill the rest of the way with Prosecco and serve.

## Opening Champagne Like a Pro

To successfully open a Champagne bottle and not have the cork go flying in someone's face, remove the wire around the cork, then place your palm over the cork. Turn the bottle, while holding the cork, to release it. It should pop right off with that classic "thump" instead of exploding and foaming over. Some experts recommend you hold the bottle at an angle, then twist the bottle, so the cork doesn't hit you in the eye. But I find I have better control over the bottle if I am holding it straight, with my head held at an angle.

### The Diva Says:

The beauty of Prosecco is that it's difficult to get a bad bottle, even in the lower price ranges, unlike domestic sparkling wine, where you tend to get what you pay for.

### Diva Variations

If you want to be extra swanky, put a thin half-slice of pear on the rim of each glass or float an edible flower (see page 591) in it.

Try this recipe using any blend of exotic fruit juices, traditional peach nectar, or just plain orange juice.

**Virgin Bellini:** Substitute 7-Up or another lemon-lime soda for the Prosecco.

# Sgroppino or "The Scorpion"

Serves 10

This is a version of a drink served in Italy after dinner. Traditionally, sgroppino is made with limoncello, an Italian lemon liqueur. However, when it's made with lemon sorbet there is nothing more refreshing and palate cleansing. Serve these make-ahead cocktails for people to enjoy while you are putting out dessert.

**1 pint lemon sorbet**

**1 to 1½ cups vodka**

**1.** Combine both ingredients in a blender and whir on high speed until fully blended and soupy.

❋ **DIVA DO-AHEAD:** At this point, you can cover and freeze for up to 2 months.

**2.** Pull the mixture out of the freezer 5 minutes before you want to serve. Pour into martini glasses or Champagne flutes.

### Diva Variation

Add a few fresh raspberries to each glass before pouring in the sgroppino, for a little treat at the bottom.

# Holiday Eggnog

Serves 12 to 14

Since there has been so much talk about the bacteria in raw eggs, my eggnog is cooked on the stove top long enough to eliminate any risk. You will need to make the base the day before so it is cooled and ready to go. Freshly grated nutmeg is essential for a great eggnog and so is good Kentucky bourbon. There are lots of people who prefer their eggnog with rum or brandy, but I'm betting that once you try this one, you won't go back! Leftover eggnog is terrific in pancake batter in place of milk and is delicious frozen as a dessert. It doesn't freeze rock-solid, making it more of a semifreddo; I like to garnish it with chocolate curls or chopped pistachios.

1 half-gallon whole milk

2 cups superfine sugar

12 large egg yolks

1 tablespoon vanilla paste (see Sources) or vanilla extract

3 cups heavy cream

2½ cups Kentucky bourbon

Freshly grated nutmeg for garnish

**1.** In a 4-quart saucepan over medium heat, warm the milk and sugar together, stirring until the sugar is dissolved and fine bubbles form along the side of the pan.

**2.** In a large bowl, beat the eggs, then gradually add a cup of the warm milk to the eggs, whisking until the milk is absorbed. Stir the egg-and-milk mixture into the saucepan, reduce the heat to low, and simmer until the mixture is thickened and coats the back of a spoon, 10 to 15 minutes. Remove from the heat and stir in the vanilla paste.

**3.** Strain the custard through a fine-mesh strainer into a bowl and place a piece of plastic wrap directly on the surface of the custard to keep a skin from forming.

**✳ DIVA DO-AHEAD:** At this point, cover and refrigerate for at least 8 hours and up to 3 days.

**4.** With an electric mixer, whip the heavy cream in a large bowl until stiff peaks form.

**5.** Remove the custard from the refrigerator and whisk in the bourbon and whipped cream. Pour into a chilled punch bowl, garnish liberally with nutmeg, and serve immediately.

## Keeping Eggnog Cold

It's hard to keep milk-based drinks cold, but you can make an ice mold in a bundt pan from the cooked custard for your eggnog. Make two batches of custard, one for your ice block and one for the nog. If you like, after you've poured the custard into the mold, drop in a few berries, then freeze. When ready to serve, run hot water over the bottom of the pan to loosen the ice mold and place in the punch bowl. Pour the eggnog over the mold and serve.

## Diva Variation

**Virgin Eggnog:** Omit the bourbon—what a shame!

# Mulled Wine

Serves 12

Warm spiced wine isn't served very often anymore. Although purists turn up their noses at this comforting drink, it actually brings out delicious flavors in the wine. I recommend using an Australian Shiraz or a Merlot and heating the wine in the slow cooker, so your guests can serve themselves. Orange slices make a lovely garnish and add a nice flavor, too.

**Three 750-ml bottles red wine**

**½ cup firmly packed dark brown sugar**

**½ teaspoon whole cloves**

**Three 4-inch cinnamon sticks**

**3 allspice berries**

**2 oranges, thinly sliced**

**1.** In a large Dutch oven over medium-low heat, combine the wine, brown sugar, cloves, cinnamon, and allspice, stirring to dissolve the sugar. Heat until very warm, but not boiling, about 15 minutes.

**2.** Remove from the heat and allow to steep for another 10 minutes. Fish out the spices with a small strainer and discard, or strain the wine into a refrigerator container.

✳ **DIVA DO-AHEAD:** At this point, you can store the wine in the refrigerator for up to 2 days.

**3.** When ready to serve, heat the wine in the slow cooker on Low, and float the orange slices on top.

### Slow Cooker Savvy
Combine the ingredients in a 5- to 6-quart slow cooker and heat on Low for 3 to 4 hours, until warmed through.

# Warm Spiced Cider

Serves 12

A favorite with young and old alike, this warm, fragrant cider is just the thing to start a fall or winter party. A splash of brandy is a nice touch for the grown-ups in the crowd.

2 quarts apple cider

1 teaspoon allspice berries

Two 4-inch cinnamon sticks

6 whole cloves

¼ teaspoon ground ginger

1 cup brandy or dark rum (optional)

**1.** In a large saucepan over low heat, combine the cider and spices and heat for 30 minutes. Strain the cider and discard the spices.

✳ **DIVA DO-AHEAD:** At this point, you can let cool, cover, and refrigerate for up to 3 days or freeze for up to 2 months.

**2.** Serve the cider warm, and add 2 tablespoons of brandy to each serving if desired.

The Diva Says:

If you are serving a crowd, double the recipe and use a coffee urn. Place the spices in the filter basket and perk the cider until warmed.

**Slow Cooker Savvy**

Combine the ingredients in a 5- to 6-quart slow cooker and heat on Low for 3 to 4 hours, until warmed through.

# Hot Chocolate for a Crowd

Serves 10

Keeping hot chocolate warm in the slow cooker makes this simple drink a crowd-pleaser for a casual evening or après-ski entertaining. Add a little Bailey's Irish Cream to the warm cocoa for a more adult drink.

1½ cups sugar

1¼ cups Dutch-process unsweetened cocoa powder

1 cup water

2 quarts whole milk

2 cups heavy cream

2 teaspoons vanilla extract

Miniature marshmallows for garnish

Whipped cream for garnish

**1.** In a 3-quart saucepan, heat the sugar, cocoa, and water together over medium heat, stirring, until the sugar and cocoa are dissolved. Gradually add the milk and cream and heat until almost boiling.

**2.** Remove from the heat and stir in the vanilla.

✳ **DIVA DO-AHEAD:** At this point you can cool the chocolate to room temperature and store in the refrigerator for up to 5 days. Reheat before serving.

**3.** Transfer the hot chocolate to a pump pot to keep warm or to a 5- to 6-quart slow cooker on Low. Ladle into heat-proof mugs and garnish with mini marshmallows and whipped cream.

## Diva Variations

**Peppermint Twist Hot Chocolate:** Use peppermint candy canes as stirrers.

**Wicked Hot Chocolate:** Jacques Torres, the incomparable French chocolatier, adds a touch of spice to his cocoa and calls it "wicked." You can create your own version by adding chili powder, ½ teaspoon at a time, and a few dashes of cayenne pepper. You'll find it really brings out the flavor of the chocolate.

**Irish Hot Chocolate:** Add 1 ounce of Bailey's Irish Cream to each serving.

**Italian Hot Chocolate:** Add 1 ounce of Frangelico hazelnut liqueur to each serving.

**Mexican Hot Chocolate:** Add 1 teaspoon of ground cinnamon and a pinch of cayenne pepper to the entire recipe.

# Old-Fashioned Lemonade

Serves 12

A great cooler for young and old alike, homemade lemonade knocks the powdered or frozen stuff out of the park. Make sure you garnish with plenty of lemon slices; the oil from the skin adds flavor to the finished drink.

**2 cups strained fresh lemon juice (about 4 lemons)**

**4 cups superfine sugar**

**8 cups water**

**Ice cubes**

**4 lemons, thinly sliced, for garnish**

**1.** In a large pitcher, combine the lemon juice and sugar, stirring until the sugar dissolves. Gradually stir in the water until blended.

✳ **DIVA DO-AHEAD:** At this point, cover and refrigerate until chilled or overnight.

**2.** Just before serving, add ice and lemon slices to the pitcher and serve.

## Diva Variations

**Punch Bowl Lemonade:** Fill a bundt pan with 2 cups of lemonade, 1 cup of fresh lemon juice, and 2 cups of water, add lemon slices, and freeze until firm. Unmold the ice block, place in a punch bowl, and pour the lemonade mixture over it. Make sure you do this 30 to 45 minutes before serving, so the ice block has a chance to chill the ingredients in the punch bowl and begins to melt.

**Strawberry Lemonade:** Add 4 cups of strained strawberry puree (from about 3 pints of strawberries) to the lemonade and stir to blend.

**Raspberry Lemonade:** Add 3 cups of strained raspberry puree (from about

3 pints of raspberries or one 16-ounce package frozen raspberries, defrosted) to the lemonade and stir to blend.

**Orange-Apricot Lemonade:** In a small saucepan, combine 8 dried apricots with $3/4$ cup of fresh orange juice. Bring to a boil, reduce the heat to low, and simmer until the apricots are almost dissolved, about 20 minutes. Push the mixture through a fine-mesh strainer and add to the lemonade.

**Arnold Palmer Ice Tea:** Brew 10 cups of tea and cool to room temperature. Fill glasses with ice and then fill halfway with cooled tea and halfway with lemonade. Garnish with lemon slices.

# Shirley's Old-Fashioned Ice Tea

Serves 12

On hot summer days in New Hampshire, my mother-in-law would make this ice tea, and I could never seem to drink enough of it. I think that the fresh lemons in the hot tea made the difference.

**1 gallon water**

**24 orange pekoe tea bags**

**2 cups sugar**

**4 lemons, cut in half and seeds removed, plus 1 lemon, thinly sliced, for garnish**

**Ice cubes**

**Fresh mint leaves for garnish**

**1.** Bring the water to a boil in a large non-reactive pot. Remove from the heat, add the tea bags, and steep for 5 minutes.

**2.** Remove the tea bags, add the sugar, and stir until dissolved. Squeeze the lemon halves into the tea, add the halves, and stir to blend. Allow to cool completely, then taste for sugar or lemon.

**3.** Remove the lemons and transfer the tea to a large pitcher.

✳ **DIVA DO-AHEAD:** At this point, cover and refrigerate until chilled or up to 5 days.

**4.** Serve the tea in ice-filled glasses, garnished with lemon slices and mint leaves.

## Diva Ice Cubes

Flavored ice cubes help keep the drink fresh as well as chilled. Freeze the base of your drink—for example, tomato juice for Bloody Marys—in ice cube trays or disposable ice cube bags, then serve them in a separate ice bucket for your guests to use. If you have leftover Bloody Mary mix, lemonade, or another drink, freeze it in ice cube trays, then store the ice in zipper-top plastic bags for your next party or tomorrow's cocktail hour. Or fill an ice cube tray with distilled water (it stays clear), add lime or lemon twists to give your drinks a little color, and freeze. Mint leaves in ice cubes are also a nice touch for Kentucky bourbon coolers, mojitos, lemonade, and ice tea.

## Diva Variation

**Mint Julep Ice Tea:** Add 1 cup of mint leaves to the boiling water along with the tea bags and steep. When ready to serve, fill each glass with ice, add 1½ ounces of bourbon, and fill the rest of the way with ice tea. Serve garnished with mint.

# Apricot Spice Peach Tea

Serves 12

This golden tea can be served hot or cold, depending upon the time of year and the type of party you're having. It's delightful hot for brunch or after dinner, and equally delicious cold at a picnic or barbecue.

**6 bags peach tea (I like Bigelow brand)**

**8 dried apricots, chopped**

**2 pieces crystallized ginger, cut into small pieces (see The Diva Says)**

**8 cups boiling water**

**2 cups cold water**

**Orange slices (optional) for garnish**

**Ice cubes if serving cold**

**1.** Put the tea bags, apricots, and ginger in a large bowl or saucepan. Pour the boiling water over and let steep for 5 to 7 minutes.

**2.** Strain the tea into a pitcher and add the cold water, stirring to blend.

✳ **DIVA DO-AHEAD:** At this point, you can store in the refrigerator for up to 5 days.

**3.** To serve warm, pour the tea into a slow cooker on Low and garnish with orange slices. To serve cold, fill 8-ounce glasses with ice cubes and pour the tea over the ice. Garnish with orange slices.

## The Diva Says:

To prevent the crystallized ginger from getting sticky, coat your knife with nonstick cooking spray before cutting.

# Chuck's Gourmet Dessert Coffee

Serves 12

In the 1970s my husband was famous for his flambéed dessert coffee. This version can be prepared without the flames and works well as a coffee bar for your guests.

**2 lemons, cut into wedges**

**½ cup sugar**

**2¼ cups Cointreau or Grand Marnier**

**8 cups hot brewed coffee**

**¾ cup Tia Maria or Kahlúa liqueur**

**3 cups heavy cream, whipped until stiff peaks form**

**½ cup dark crème de cacao**

**Shaved bittersweet or semisweet chocolate (optional, see The Diva Says)**

**1.** Rub the rim of each of 12 Irish coffee glasses with a lemon wedge. Place the sugar in a small bowl and dip the rim of the glass into the sugar.

**2.** Pour 1½ ounces (a shot glass) of Cointreau into each glass. Add ¾ cup of coffee and ½ ounce of Tia Maria. Top with whipped cream and a dash of crème de cacao. Garnish with shaved chocolate, if using, and serve.

✳ **DIVA DO-AHEAD:** Brew coffee up to 4 hours ahead of time and store in a pump pot.

**The Diva Says:**

To shave chocolate, use a microplane to grate the chocolate onto a plate or into a bowl, then transfer to a serving dish. If you don't have a microplane, a swivel vegetable peeler will do the job.

## Diva Coffee Bar

When serving coffee to your guests, it's always fun to add a little spice to the coffee bar. Make it as simple as adding Ghirardelli ground chocolate as a flavoring along with cream and sugar, or serve Chuck's Gourmet Dessert Coffee (above). You could also set out several of your favorite liqueurs for flavoring, including Amaretto, Bailey's Irish Cream, Drambuie, Frangelico, and/or Kahlúa. Another nice touch is sweetened and stiffly whipped heavy cream (either plain or flavored with a liqueur or chocolate) to serve in coffee instead of cream. Try serving raw sugar, rather than granulated, for a slightly different taste, and don't forget to include no-calorie sweeteners, too.

# Teddy's Perfect Iced Coffee

Serves 10

Our dear friend Teddy has practically been a member of the family for 15 years, and he lives on coffee. One winter I went to visit him in Florida, and he taught me how to keep iced coffee potent, even when it's sweltering outside.

**12 cups brewed coffee**

**1.** When the coffee has brewed, let it sit at room temperature to cool off for about 45 minutes.

✳ **DIVA DO-AHEAD:** Brew coffee up to 4 hours ahead of time.

**2.** Fill 4 ice cube trays with coffee and freeze until firm. Store the cubes in zipper-top plastic bags.

**3.** Refrigerate the remaining coffee in a pitcher.

**4.** When ready to serve, pour the cooled coffee over the coffee ice cubes and serve with sugar and your favorite creamer.

The Diva Says:

Any leftover coffee can be made into ice cubes. Try this with tea as well. Freeze brewed tea into ice cubes, and serve in lemonade or ice tea.

# Dips and Spreads

**When you are serving a large buffet,** you don't want your guests to load up on a lot of appetizers, which are meant only to take the edge off their hunger before the main event begins. Dips and spreads served with crackers and bread rounds or vegetables fit the bill to a T. When you plan your menu, try to balance a rich main course with lighter appetizers. If you are serving a roasted meat with all the trimmings, then offer some spicy nuts and a dip with vegetables for appetizers. If your main course is lighter, you may want to fill in with more substantial appetizers. Good choices would be a warm dip like The Crabbiest of Spreads (page 82) served with crackers, a dip with fresh vegetables, or a savory cheesecake or torte, along with a selection from the Small Bites chapter (pages 104 to 145). Remember that the idea is just to whet appetites, and not satisfy them.

# Crudités

Crudités are raw (or almost raw) cut-up vegetables served with a dip before dinner or as a snack. If you are in a hurry, check whether your grocer has already done some of the work for you by looking for baby carrots and cut-up vegetables in the produce section. Arranging crudités in a basket or on a large ceramic platter can be like flower arranging if you want to get that creative, or you can simply fan out leaves of endive, or choose two vegetables to arrange for a simpler platter. To keep the natural theme going, hollow out a vegetable such as a purple cabbage, a large bell pepper, or a large artichoke, and pour the dip into it; then arrange the dipping vegetables around it. Make the presentation even more attractive by using leaves from cabbage, decorative kale, or a bag of prepared field green salad for the base of the crudités arrangement. Try garnishing the platter with bouquets of fresh herbs, pea shoots, or broccoli sprouts. Edible flowers such as nasturtiums, daylilies, and violets also add a designer touch. Arrange all green vegetables with a white dip, or red, white, and green vegetables for an Italian-flavored dip. Remember, it's not the number of veggies in the basket, but the color, size, texture, and compatibility with the dip that are important. And don't forget to wash all vegetables in cold water before serving them. The following vegetables work well in crudités arrangements:

## KEEPING YOUR COOL

**Keeping a dip cold is simple** when you prepare for it: Try freezing a bread shell from a hollowed-out loaf for 24 hours, and then spooning in your dip (the less liquidy ones work best here). This will insulate the dip and keep it cold. Or maybe you would like to serve a dip in a hollowed-out vegetable, such as a purple cabbage or red, yellow, or green peppers. I have had great success freezing the scooped-out vegetables for 12 hours, then filling them with the dip right before the party begins. If you're not going the edible container route, freeze the serving bowl; metal bowls retain the cold much better than glass ones do.

*Artichokes:* Cut the top 1 inch off globe artichokes, remove the stem, and rub the stem end with a cut lemon. Steam in a steamer over boiling water until tender, 30 to 40 minutes (a knife inserted into the stem end will slide in easily). Remove the inside leaves and scrape out the

## Working Ahead

All of the dips and spreads in this chapter can be put together ahead of time—some can even be frozen, then defrosted overnight in the refrigerator. Look in each recipe for directions.

choke. Place on a platter with other vegetables and be sure to have a plate handy for the leftover leaves. Or steam baby artichokes for 15 to 20 minutes, quarter them lengthwise, and arrange on the platter.

*Asparagus:* Trim the tough bottoms, plunge into boiling salted water for 30 seconds, shock in ice water, pat dry, and refrigerate until ready to use. (I have some friends who serve pencil-thin spring asparagus raw.)

*Beans:* Trim the ends of tender green or yellow wax beans and pull off their tough strings. Then blanch in boiling salted water for 1 minute, shock in ice water, pat dry, and refrigerate until ready to use. Try presenting them standing upright in your arrangement by filling a hollowed-out bell pepper or positioning them among the other vegetables.

*Belgian endive:* Trim the bottom and separate the leaves. These make great "scoops" for lobster salad, shrimp salad, or chicken salad.

*Broccoli and cauliflower:* Some people like their broccoli and cauliflower raw, while others prefer them blanched for 1 minute in boiling salted water. Either method is fine; I find that blanched broccoli has a brighter green color. Broccoli and cauliflower should be separated into florets before blanching and serving. Cut the core from the cauliflower, then, with a sharp paring knife, cut the head into florets. Trim the broccoli stems, then cut the florets into bite-size pieces.

*Carrots:* Your grocer sells baby carrots in bags and I recommend using these to save time. If they look a little sad or dry, place them in a bowl of cold water in the refrigerator for 2 hours or overnight. Drain and pat dry before using. You can serve the carrots whole or cut them in half. These add color and crunch to your arrangement and, if you are serving children, you can count on these to be their vegetable of choice.

*Celery:* This is another item that your grocery may sell already cut up. Celery doesn't do well once it's cut, but you can soak the precut variety in cold water for a few hours to perk it up or buy hearts of celery. Trim these into 2-inch lengths, then cut each length into thin sticks. Store celery in resealable plastic bags for up to 36 hours to retain their crunch.

*Cucumbers:* I only buy European cucumbers, which have almost no seeds, meaning you get more usable cucumber for your dollar. You don't need to peel it, but do scrub the outside. Then trim the ends, slice into 2-inch lengths, and cut the lengths into quarters. Cut cucumbers can be stored, wrapped in paper towels (to absorb moisture) in resealable plastic bags, for up to 36 hours.

*Jicama:* Peel and cut into 3 x 1-inch lengths and store in resealable plastic bags for up to 48 hours.

*Mushrooms:* Clean raw button mushrooms and serve whole, halved, or quartered, depending upon their size. You can clean them up to 24 hours ahead and store them, wrapped in paper towels in resealable plastic bags.

*Peas:* Remove stems and tough strings from sugar snap peas and snow peas and blanch for 30 seconds in boiling salted water. Shock them in ice water to stop the cooking, pat dry, and refrigerate, wrapped in paper towels in resealable plastic bags for up to 24 hours. If the peas are especially tender (from your garden), then serve them raw.

*Peppers:* Green, yellow, orange, red, purple, and white bell peppers all add color and crunch to an arrangement. Cut peppers into strips about ¾ inch wide. Store, wrapped in paper towels in resealable plastic bags, for up to 24 hours.

*Radishes:* Red and white radishes need to be trimmed. Then cut them in half or serve them whole if they are small. You can clean and prepare the radishes the day before serving; keep them fresh in a bowl of cold water in the fridge until you are ready to use them, then pat dry and arrange.

## Bread, Chip, and Cracker Dippers

Nonveggie dippers include potato chips, tortilla chips, crackers, bagel chips, pita wedges, sliced baguettes, and bruschetta. Check the chip and cracker aisles at your grocery store and you will find everything you need. I recommend that you buy unflavored crackers or chips so that the flavor of the dip is what your guests will taste, not the flavor of the crackers.

*Tomatoes:* Tiny cherry tomatoes and pear-shaped orange and yellow tomatoes make great additions of color and taste to a crudités basket. You can leave on the stems or remove them; I leave the stems to give my guests something to hold onto when dipping.

*Zucchini and yellow squash:* Baby vegetables have become common in gourmet shops. I love to include whole baby zucchini, yellow squash, and pattypan squashes in my vegetable arrangements. If they are too costly, then use the larger varieties. Cut zucchini into 2-inch lengths, then cut those lengthwise into quarters for nice long dippers. Small yellow summer squash and crooknecks can be cut into ½-inch-thick rounds. The "crook" of the crookneck can be cut in half for dipping, too. Store squash, wrapped in paper towels in resealable plastic bags, for up to 36 hours.

# Smoky Blue Dip

Makes about 3 cups

This dip was served at Blue Smoke, an upscale barbecue restaurant in New York City, with homemade potato chips. I was so full from devouring this, I couldn't eat my plate of ribs! Delicious served with dippers such as vegetables, potato chips, and crackers, it's equally good over baked potatoes or stirred into warm orzo pasta.

**2 cups sour cream**

**½ cup mayonnaise**

**2 scallions (white and tender green parts), chopped**

**1 tablespoon Worcestershire sauce**

**1½ cups crumbled blue cheese (I like Maytag)**

**½ teaspoon freshly ground black pepper**

**4 shakes of Tabasco sauce**

**6 strips bacon, cooked until crisp, drained on paper towels, and crumbled**

**1.** In a medium-size bowl, stir together the sour cream, mayonnaise, scallions, Worcestershire, blue cheese, black pepper, and Tabasco until blended.

✳ **DIVA DO-AHEAD:** At this point, cover and refrigerate for at least 4 hours and up to 2 days to let the flavors develop.

**2.** Taste the dip for seasonings and adjust them before serving. Sprinkle the bacon over the dip and serve.

### Diva Variation

**Chipotle Blue Smoke Dip:** Substitute Chipotle Tabasco sauce for the regular Tabasco.

# Brewski Cheddar Dip

Makes about 3 cups

There is something so basic about beer and cheddar cheese, two strong flavors, that when blended together they make an awesome dip. Try this with pretzel sticks, veggies, and any kind of dipping chip.

**2 tablespoons unsalted butter**

**½ cup finely chopped onion**

**1 teaspoon fresh thyme leaves**

**½ cup dark beer**

**2 tablespoons Creole or another grainy mustard**

**6 shakes of Tabasco sauce**

**Two 3-ounce packages cream cheese, cut into small cubes and softened**

**5 cups thinly shredded sharp white cheddar**

**1.** Melt the butter in a 3-quart saucepan over medium heat and cook the onion and thyme, stirring, until golden but not brown, about 10 minutes. Add the beer, mustard, and Tabasco and bring to a boil.

**2.** Remove from the heat and add the cream cheese and cheddar cheese, stirring until the cheeses have melted. Taste and adjust the seasonings.

✳ **DIVA DO-AHEAD:** At this point you can let cool, cover, and refrigerate for up to 5 days.

**3.** Serve the dip warm in a fondue pot or small slow cooker on Low or serve it cold as a spread.

## Softening Cream Cheese and Butter

Softening cream cheese and butter is simple to do with your microwave oven. Unwrap the cheese or butter, and place on a microwavable plate or a paper towel. Microwave on High for 10 seconds; the cheese or butter may still feel a little firm, but by the time you have all your other ingredients ready, it will be perfect for blending. If it seems too hard, then 1 or 2 seconds more on High will do the trick. Be careful not to overdo it, though; you can melt the inside of the butter, while the outside still appears to be somewhat firm.

# Popeye's Dip

Makes 3 cups

Old Popeye the Sailor Man loved his spinach, and you will love serving this bright and festive dip to your friends. Flecked with colorful vegetables and flavored with tangy Parmesan cheese, it can be served hot or cold with fresh veggies and crackers.

**2 cups sour cream**

**½ cup mayonnaise**

**1 teaspoon anchovy paste**

**½ teaspoon Tabasco sauce**

**½ cup freshly grated Parmesan cheese**

**½ cup finely chopped shallots**

**2 cloves garlic, minced**

**¼ cup seeded and finely chopped red bell pepper**

**¼ cup seeded and finely chopped yellow bell pepper**

**One 10-ounce package fresh baby spinach, washed well, patted dry, and finely chopped**

**1½ teaspoons salt**

**½ teaspoon freshly ground black pepper**

**1.** In a large bowl, stir together the sour cream, mayonnaise, anchovy paste, Tabasco, and Parmesan until smooth. Stir in the shallots, garlic, bell peppers, and spinach, and then mix in the salt and black pepper.

✳ **DIVA DO-AHEAD:** At this point, cover and refrigerate for at least 4 hours and up to 2 days.

**2.** Stir the dip before serving with vegetables and crackers.

## Diva Variations

To serve warm, spoon the dip into a medium-size heavy saucepan over medium heat and stir until small bubbles form on the outside. Transfer to a fondue pot or a small slow cooker set on Low for dipping.

Or hollow out a round loaf of bread and pour in the unheated dip. Bake in a preheated 350°F oven until warm, 20 to 30 minutes. Serve immediately.

# Dried Herb Ranch Dip

Makes 3 cups

Everyone's favorite dip for vegetables comes from a little package on the grocer's shelf, but this dip can be made for half the price of the store-bought one and the kids at my house like it better. It's great to have on hand for spur-of-the-moment guests, so I usually have the dried herbs premixed. Then it takes just a few minutes to whip this together. If you can take a bit more time and have fresh herbs, then I recommend making the fresh herb version that follows, but if it is the dead of winter and the herbs are looking sad, this is the way to go. For a cheesy variation, stir in ½ cup of freshly grated Parmesan to either version.

**2 cups sour cream**

**½ cup milk**

**1 tablespoon buttermilk powder (look in the dry milk section of the grocery store, or see Sources)**

**1 tablespoon dried parsley**

**2 teaspoons dried chives**

**1 teaspoon dried oregano**

**½ teaspoon dried tarragon**

**1 teaspoon garlic salt**

**1 teaspoon lemon pepper**

**1.** In a medium-size bowl, whisk together the sour cream, milk, and buttermilk powder. Stir in the dried herbs, garlic salt, and lemon pepper.

✳ **DIVA DO-AHEAD:** At this point, cover and refrigerate for at least 2 hours and up to 4 days.

**2.** Stir the dip before serving with vegetables and crackers.

The Diva Says:
I also love this as a topping for baked potatoes or stirred into mashed potatoes.

# Fresh Herb Ranch Dip

Makes 3 cups

This herbaceous dip is a tasty choice for crudités, but it is also delicious spooned over baked potatoes, steamed vegetables, or grilled chicken or seafood.

**2 cups sour cream**

**½ cup buttermilk**

**3 tablespoons chopped fresh parsley**

**2 tablespoons snipped fresh chives**

**1 tablespoon chopped fresh oregano**

**1½ teaspoons chopped fresh tarragon**

**2 cloves garlic, mashed**

**1 teaspoon salt**

**½ teaspoon freshly ground black pepper**

**2 tablespoons grated lemon zest**

**1.** In a medium-size bowl, stir together the sour cream and buttermilk. Add the herbs, garlic, salt, pepper, and lemon zest and stir to blend.

✳ **DIVA DO-AHEAD:** At this point, cover and refrigerate for at least 4 hours and up to 5 days to let the flavors develop.

**2.** Stir the dip before serving with crudités.

# Creamy Cilantro Dip

Makes about 2½ cups

Creamy and gorgeous in color, this mixture is terrific with tortilla chips and vegetables.

**2 cups sour cream**

**½ cup chopped fresh cilantro**

**1 teaspoon ground cumin**

**1 clove garlic, minced**

**¼ cup freshly grated Parmesan cheese**

**1.** In a medium-size bowl, stir together all the ingredients.

✳ **DIVA DO-AHEAD:** At this point, cover and refrigerate for at least 6 and up to 24 hours to let the flavors develop.

**2.** Stir the dip before serving with tortilla chips and vegetables.

# Dillicious Dip

Makes about 2 cups

Another old favorite, this never ceases to amaze me when I bring it out at a party—people just love it. Serve this with your choice of crudités or over baked potatoes.

> 1 cup mayonnaise
>
> 1 cup sour cream
>
> 1 tablespoon dillweed
>
> 1 tablespoon dried minced onion
>
> 1 tablespoon dried parsley
>
> 2 teaspoons Spice Islands brand Beau Monde seasoning

**1.** In a medium-size bowl, whisk together the mayonnaise and sour cream. Fold in the seasonings until well blended.

✳ **DIVA DO-AHEAD:** At this point, cover and refrigerate for at least 4 hours and up to 2 days to let the flavors develop.

**2.** Stir the dip before serving with crudités.

# All New Dijon Dilly Dip

Makes about 2½ cups

This new millennium spin on Dillicious Dip takes advantage of the fact that fresh herbs are available almost year-round in the grocery store. Serve as a dip, or use as a sauce over baked potatoes, fish, or chicken.

> 1½ cups sour cream
>
> ½ cup mayonnaise
>
> ¼ cup Dijon mustard
>
> 2 scallions (white and tender green parts), chopped
>
> 3 tablespoons chopped fresh dill
>
> 3 tablespoons chopped fresh parsley
>
> 2 teaspoons grated lemon zest
>
> 1 teaspoon celery salt
>
> Salt and freshly ground black pepper to taste

**1.** In a medium-size bowl, stir together the sour cream, mayonnaise, and mustard until blended. Stir in the scallions, dill, parsley, lemon zest, and celery salt. Taste before adding salt and pepper.

✳ **DIVA DO-AHEAD:** At this point, cover and refrigerate for at least 6 hours or overnight to let the flavors develop.

**2.** Stir before serving with crudités.

# Sesame Seed Dip

Makes about 2 cups

A terrific dip for vegetables, this taste of Asia is also interesting when served with shrimp chips (look in the Asian section of your supermarket), shrimp, or bite-size pieces of chicken.

> 2 cups sour cream
>
> 1 teaspoon toasted sesame oil
>
> 1 tablespoon soy sauce
>
> 1 teaspoon peeled and grated fresh ginger
>
> 2 tablespoons sesame seeds, toasted (see page 83)

**1.** In a medium-size bowl, combine all the ingredients, except the sesame seeds, and whisk together until blended.

✳ **DIVA DO-AHEAD:** At this point, cover and refrigerate for at least 4 hours and up to 5 days to let the flavors develop.

**2.** Stir in the sesame seeds just before serving.

# Smoked Salmon Spread

Makes about 2 cups

This beautiful, creamy spread is studded with bits of smoky salmon, then rolled in spicy pecans. Serve on small slices of rye or pumpernickel or on water crackers.

> Two 8-ounce packages cream cheese, softened
>
> ½ pound smoked salmon, chopped
>
> 2 tablespoons chopped fresh dill
>
> 2 tablespoons finely chopped red onion
>
> 1 teaspoon prepared horseradish
>
> 1 teaspoon fresh lemon juice
>
> 1 cup Spicy Nuts (page 143) made with pecans, chopped

**1.** In a medium-size bowl, beat the cream cheese until smooth. Gradually fold in the salmon, dill, onion, horseradish, and lemon juice, stirring to blend. Place the mixture on a piece of plastic wrap and form into a log 1 inch in diameter.

**2.** Place the pecans on another sheet of plastic wrap and roll the log in the pecans until coated. Twist the plastic wrap to seal.

✳ **DIVA DO-AHEAD:** At this point, refrigerate for 6 hours or overnight, or freeze for up to 1 month. Defrost overnight in the refrigerator and bring to room temperature before serving.

# Mom's Top of the Stairs Clam Dip

Makes about 1½ cups

My mom and dad entertained a lot during the course of my childhood. This dip is a taste from those evenings when the lights were low, the women wore cocktail dresses, and everyone drank martinis and Manhattans. Mom would make the dip in the morning, promising my brothers and me that we could have a small bowl of it with some potato chips if we stayed upstairs during the party. (It's also good with Pita Chips, page 527.) Years later, my daughter is serving this dip to rave reviews!

**One 8-ounce package cream cheese, softened**

**One 8-ounce can chopped clams, drained and juice reserved**

**1 clove garlic, mashed**

**1 scallion (white and tender green parts), chopped**

**2 tablespoons mayonnaise**

**2 teaspoons Worcestershire sauce**

**1 teaspoon anchovy paste**

**Chopped fresh parsley for garnish**

**1.** In a medium-size bowl, beat together the cream cheese, 2 tablespoons of the reserved clam juice, and the garlic, scallion, mayonnaise, Worcestershire, and anchovy paste until smooth. Fold in the clams, stirring to blend.

**✳ DIVA DO-AHEAD:** At this point, cover and refrigerate for at least 3 and up to 8 hours to let the flavors develop.

**2.** Remove the dip from the refrigerator about 30 minutes before serving. If it is a bit stiff, thin it with a little more of the clam juice or some milk, and garnish with parsley.

# The Crabbiest of Spreads

Makes about 3 cups

This spread is more crab than spread—it includes a pound of lump crabmeat—but it's worth the splurge to hear your guests' oohs and ahhs. This is delicious served on European cucumber rounds, endive leaves, or crackers.

One 3-ounce package cream cheese, softened

½ cup mayonnaise

2 scallions (white and tender green parts), finely chopped

2 teaspoons prepared horseradish

2 teaspoons Worcestershire sauce

2 teaspoons Old Bay seasoning

1 to 2 teaspoons dry white wine or dry vermouth, as needed

1 pound lump crabmeat, picked over for shells and cartilage

¼ cup chopped fresh Italian parsley

¼ cup slivered almonds, toasted (right)

1. In a medium-size bowl, beat together the cream cheese, mayonnaise, scallions, horseradish, Worcestershire, Old Bay, and wine until smooth. Gradually fold in the crabmeat, being careful not to break up the lumps too much, but incorporating it into the cream cheese mixture. If the mixture is stiff, thin it with additional wine or some milk.

✳ **DIVA DO-AHEAD:** At this point, cover and refrigerate for at least 2 and up to 24 hours.

2. Garnish with the parsley and almonds and serve.

## Diva Variations

If you would like to serve the dip warm, heat it in a 2-quart saucepan over medium heat until small bubbles form around the side of the pan, about 15 minutes, stirring so it doesn't stick and cook. Transfer to a fondue pot or small slow cooker set on Low to keep warm on the table.

Or hollow out a round bread loaf, leaving a layer of bread about ³/₄ inch inside the crust. Pour the dip into the bread shell, place on a baking sheet, and bake at 350°F until the dip is bubbling, about 30 minutes. The bread should keep the dip warm for about 1½ hours. Use the bread you removed from inside the loaf for dippers.

# TOASTING NUTS AND SEEDS

**Toasted nuts add** a lovely crunch to so many recipes, whether they are folded right into a dip or sprinkled as a garnish. And your favorite mixed nuts, toasted and served warm, make a nice addition to the bar while people are waiting for dinner.

To toast a small quantity, pour the nuts into a dry nonstick skillet, and over medium-high heat, stir them constantly until they give off an aroma and turn golden brown. Remove them from the skillet to stop the cooking.

For larger quantities, preheat the oven to 350°F and line a baking sheet with parchment paper, aluminum foil, or a silicone liner. Spread out the nuts on the baking sheet, and bake for 5 minutes. Stir the nuts again and bake for another 5 to 7 minutes, just until the nuts are fragrant. They will continue to toast as they slowly cool right on the baking sheet. Cool the nuts completely and store, covered, at room temperature for 2 days, or transfer to a zipper-top plastic bag and refrigerate for up to 1 week or freeze for up to 6 months.

You can buy toasted sesame seeds in the Asian section of your grocer, but you can easily toast them yourself. Pour the seeds into a dry nonstick skillet and toast on medium-high heat, shaking the skillet back and forth to distribute the seeds. They will begin to give off an aroma before they turn golden. When you smell the seeds, remove the pan from the heat, continue to shake them for 1 or 2 minutes, and then remove them from the skillet so they stop cooking.

# Tapenade

Makes about 5 cups

This spicy relish can be served alongside seafood or poultry. It also makes a delicious topping for goat cheese to serve with crackers for an appetizer. A food processor makes this a snap to put together, but you can achieve the same results with a sharp knife and a cutting board.

**2 cups pimento-stuffed green olives, drained**

**1 cup Kalamata olives, drained and pitted**

**1 cup black olives, drained and pitted**

**½ cup capers, drained**

**1 tablespoon anchovy paste or 3 anchovy fillets, mashed**

**2 cloves garlic, peeled**

**Grated zest of 1 lemon**

**⅓ cup extra virgin olive oil**

**2 teaspoons red wine vinegar**

**¼ cup packed chopped fresh Italian parsley**

**Salt and freshly ground black pepper to taste**

**1.** Put the olives, capers, anchovy paste, and garlic in a food processor and pulse until finely chopped.

**2.** Transfer to a medium-size bowl. Add the remaining ingredients and stir to blend. Taste before adding salt and pepper.

✳ **DIVA DO-AHEAD:** At this point, cover and refrigerate for at least 2 hours and up to 1 month.

**3.** Serve this at room temperature.

# Chipotle Corn Dip

Makes about 6 cups

A colorful and delicious taste of the Southwest, this simple dip will be a hit at your next party. Surround it with yellow and blue corn tortilla chips as well as vegetable dippers, such as cucumber rounds, red and yellow bell pepper strips, and jicama and celery sticks.

**2 tablespoons unsalted butter**

**¼ cup finely chopped red onion**

**1 clove garlic, minced**

**½ teaspoon ground cumin**

**½ teaspoon chipotle chile powder**

**½ cup diced fresh tomato**

**2 cups frozen corn kernels, defrosted**

**1 cup sour cream**

**½ cup mayonnaise**

**1 cup finely shredded mild cheddar cheese**

**½ cup finely shredded Monterey Jack cheese**

**¼ cup chopped fresh cilantro**

**1.** Melt the butter in a medium-size skillet over medium-high heat and cook the onion, garlic, cumin, and chili powder, stirring, until you can smell the spices and the onion begins to soften, 2 to 3 minutes. Add the tomato and corn and toss once or twice to coat with the onion mixture. Transfer to a medium-size bowl and allow to cool.

**2.** Stir in the sour cream, mayonnaise, and cheeses.

❋ **DIVA DO-AHEAD:** At this point, cover and refrigerate for at least 4 hours or overnight to let the flavors develop.

**3.** Remove from the refrigerator, garnish with the cilantro, and serve with tortilla chips and fresh vegetables for dipping.

## Seedless Cukes

European or hothouse cucumbers are long and skinny, come wrapped in plastic, and have very few seeds. The nice thing about these cukes is that you can use virtually all of the cucumber, because the skin is delicious, too. A great alternative to crackers or bread, they provide additional color on your serving trays.

# Black Bean, Corn, and Salsa Dip 🫓🥤🍸

Makes 10 cups

Colorful and sassy, this dip tastes of the Southwest. It's simple to put together and is terrific with tortilla chips or served alongside a grilled entrée.

**Two 15-ounce cans black beans, drained and rinsed**

**1 cup peeled and chopped jicama (see The Diva Says, page 186)**

**¼ cup finely chopped scallions (white and tender green parts)**

**2 cups fresh or defrosted frozen corn kernels**

**½ cup seeded and finely chopped red bell pepper**

**1½ cups cherry tomatoes, cut in half**

**½ cup chopped ripe avocado**

**2 cloves garlic, minced**

**¼ cup seeded and finely chopped Anaheim chile**

**2 tablespoons chopped fresh cilantro**

**¼ cup fresh lime juice**

**¾ cup vegetable oil**

**1 teaspoon chipotle Tabasco sauce**

**1½ teaspoons salt**

**½ teaspoon freshly ground black pepper**

**1.** In a large bowl, mix the black beans, jicama, scallions, corn, red pepper, tomatoes, avocado, garlic, chile, and cilantro.

**2.** In a small bowl, whisk together the lime juice, oil, Tabasco, salt, and pepper. Pour over the vegetables and toss until blended.

✳ **DIVA DO-AHEAD:** At this point, cover and refrigerate for at least 2 hours or overnight to let the flavors develop.

**3.** Serve cold with tortilla chips.

## The Diva Says:

This dip keeps for 4 days in the refrigerator if you omit the avocado. The avocado tends to get mushy if it marinates in the dressing longer than 24 hours.

# Tostada Dip

Serves 10 to 12

Everyone should have at least one good recipe for a layered Mexican bean dip, and this is my favorite. It's quick and easy to put together on the spur of the moment, or you can refrigerate it a day ahead, then just pull it out of the fridge right before serving. Accompany with white, yellow, and blue corn tortilla chips.

**Two 15-ounce cans refried beans**

**2 cups Guacamole Olé (page 88; omit sour cream from recipe)**

**1½ cups sour cream**

**1 teaspoon chili powder**

**½ teaspoon ground cumin**

**2 cups shredded iceberg lettuce**

**6 scallions (white and tender green parts), chopped**

**20 cherry tomatoes, cut in half**

**½ cup black olives, drained, pitted, and sliced**

**½ cup pickled jalapeño peppers, drained and chopped**

**1 cup shredded Monterey Jack cheese**

**1 cup shredded mild cheddar cheese**

**Salsa for garnish (optional)**

**1.** In a 13 x 9-inch casserole dish or another serving dish, mash the refried beans and spread them out in an even layer. Spread the guacamole evenly over the beans.

**2.** Working quickly, in a small bowl, combine the sour cream, chili powder, and cumin and spread over the guacamole, sealing it completely.

**3.** Top the sour cream layer with the lettuce and continue layering with the scallions, tomatoes, olives, jalapeños, and cheeses.

✳ **DIVA DO-AHEAD:** At this point, you can cover and refrigerate overnight.

**4.** Tuck tortilla chips around the outside of the dish and garnish with salsa if desired.

## The Diva Says:

Sometimes avocados are rock hard in the grocery store when I want to make this dip, so I usually have a container of store-bought frozen guacamole on hand that I can soften up and use instead of the fresh. To liven up the frozen version, I usually add some minced garlic and fresh cilantro.

# Guacamole Olé

Makes about 4 cups

Guacamole should be made with Hass avocados, the ones with the dark, pebbly skin. An avocado is ripe when the flesh yields to pressure fairly easily, but you should still encounter a little resistance. Unripened avocados can be kept in a brown paper bag for a few days to hasten the ripening process—just don't forget they are in the bag! There are as many recipes for guacamole as there are cooks in the Southwest. This is one of my favorites because it can be made up ahead of time without the avocado discoloring. (One secret to helping keep the guacamole from turning brown is to press plastic wrap tightly against the dip when you place it in the refrigerator; it's the exposure to air that causes the avocado to darken.) Guacamole can be served at room temperature and should be made a few hours ahead of time so the flavors develop. If you like chunky guacamole, cut the avocado into ½-inch dice; otherwise, use a fork to mash it.

**2 large fully ripened avocados, peeled and pitted**

**½ cup diced fresh tomato**

**1 clove garlic, mashed**

**2 teaspoons fresh lime juice**

**1 scallion (white and tender green parts), chopped**

**1 tablespoon salsa of your choice**

**½ cup sour cream**

**1.** In a medium-size bowl, mash the avocado with a fork. Fold in the tomato, garlic, lime juice, scallion, and salsa, stirring to blend. Spread the sour cream over the top of the guacamole.

❋ **DIVA DO-AHEAD:** At this point, cover tightly with plastic wrap and refrigerate for at least 2 and up to 8 hours.

**2.** When ready to serve, stir the sour cream into the guacamole and serve with white, yellow, and blue corn tortilla chips for dipping.

## Keeping Your Avocado Green

To keep sliced avocado from discoloring, spray the cut surface with nonstick cooking spray; this will protect it from the air, which causes the discoloration. Or toss chopped avocado with a tablespoon or two of fresh lemon or lime juice or white vinegar. The acid will retard the discoloration. Make sure you keep cut avocados covered with plastic wrap while they are refrigerated.

# Roasted Garlic-Eggplant Dip

Makes about 3 cups

This smoky eggplant spread is a great dip for pita or crackers. I like to make it a few days ahead of time to let the flavors marry, then present the dip in a bowl, surrounded by pita wedges to resemble a flower.

**2 medium-size purple eggplants, cut in half lengthwise**

**¼ cup extra virgin olive oil**

**6 cloves garlic**

**6 scallions (white and tender green parts), chopped**

**½ cup tomato juice**

**2 teaspoons Tabasco sauce**

**½ cup chopped fresh Italian parsley**

**1 teaspoon salt**

**½ to ¾ teaspoon freshly ground black pepper, to your taste**

**½ cup plain yogurt**

**1.** Preheat the oven to 425°F and line a baking sheet with a silicone liner, parchment paper, or aluminum foil.

**2.** Brush the cut surfaces of the eggplants with the oil and place them, cut side down, on the baking sheet. Scatter the garlic on the baking sheet and drizzle the garlic and eggplant with the remaining oil. Roast until eggplant is tender when pierced with the tip of a sharp knife, about 25 minutes.

**3.** When cool enough to handle, scoop out the insides of the eggplants into a food processor. Squeeze the garlic cloves out of their skins into the food processor. Add the scallions, tomato juice, Tabasco, parsley, salt, and pepper and pulse 5 or 6 times, until smooth.

✳ **DIVA DO-AHEAD:** At this point, cover and refrigerate for at least 6 hours and up to 3 days to let the flavors develop.

**4.** When ready to serve, taste the dip for seasonings and adjust if necessary, top with the yogurt, and serve.

# Salsa Fresca

Makes 3 cups

Everyone has a favorite salsa, and this one is my choice for the winner's circle. Simple, a little spicy, and filled with chunky vegetables, it's terrific served with tortilla chips. Salsa is a great staple to have in your fridge to flavor chicken, beef, or shrimp in a simple sauté, to stir into cooked rice, or to add to sour cream for a quick dip. If you like a smooth salsa, process this in the food processor. Remember that the longer the salsa sits, the hotter it will become.

6 plum tomatoes, seeded and cut into ½-inch dice

1 teaspoon salt

2 tablespoons fresh lime juice

¼ cup finely chopped yellow onion

2 cloves garlic, minced

1 jalapeño pepper, seeded and finely chopped

2 tablespoons chopped fresh cilantro

1 teaspoon dried oregano (Mexican, if possible)

½ teaspoon ground cumin

**1.** Put the tomatoes in a colander, sprinkle them with the salt, and toss. Let drain for about 20 minutes.

**2.** In a medium-size bowl, combine the tomatoes with the remaining ingredients, stirring to blend.

✳ **DIVA DO-AHEAD:** At this point, cover and refrigerate for at least 4 hours and up to 1 week to let the flavors develop. Bring to room temperature before serving.

# Rosemary White Bean Spread

Makes 2 cups

This simple puree of white beans is flavored with rosemary and extra virgin olive oil. Serve it with pita wedges, toasted baguette slices, or cucumber slices.

Two 19-ounce cans cannellini beans or small white beans, drained and rinsed

¼ cup extra virgin olive oil, plus extra for drizzling

2 tablespoons red wine vinegar

2 tablespoons fresh rosemary leaves

2 teaspoons salt

1½ teaspoons freshly ground black pepper

⅓ cup chopped fresh Italian parsley

**1.** In a food processor, combine the beans, oil, vinegar, rosemary, salt, and pepper and process until smooth.

✳ **DIVA DO-AHEAD:** At this point, cover and refrigerate for at least 2 hours and up to 3 days to let the flavors develop. Bring to room temperature before serving.

**2.** When you are ready to serve, stir the dip, drizzle with extra virgin olive oil, and sprinkle with the parsley.

# Mock Boursin Cheese

Makes about 1½ cups

Boursin, that addictive, delicately flavored garlic and herb cheese, is no bargain at the grocery store. This version is a welcome alternative for your pocketbook. Serve with water crackers or stone-ground wheat crackers or spread on French bread and broil until golden. If there is any left over, try whipping it into potatoes.

Three 4-ounce packages whipped cream cheese, softened

½ teaspoon garlic salt

1 teaspoon chopped fresh chives

2 teaspoons chopped fresh Italian parsley

½ teaspoon dried thyme

½ teaspoon dried oregano

½ teaspoon freshly ground black pepper

**1.** In a medium-size bowl, beat the cream cheese until smooth, then add the remaining ingredients, stirring until they are incorporated.

**2.** Turn the cheese onto a large piece of plastic wrap and form into a ball, or transfer to small ramekins and cover with plastic wrap.

✳ **DIVA DO-AHEAD:** At this point, refrigerate for at least 12 hours and up to 3 days to let the flavors develop, or freeze for up to 6 weeks. Defrost in the refrigerator overnight and bring to room temperature before serving.

# Carrie's Chutney Cheese Ball

Makes about 2 cups

This is my daughter's favorite party spread. Cheddar cheese and curry combine for a delicious cheese ball that is covered with finely chopped chutney, scallions, and chopped peanuts. We like to serve this with Wheat Thins or other wheat crackers.

**One 8-ounce package cream cheese, softened**

**1⅓ cups finely shredded sharp cheddar cheese**

**2 teaspoons dry sherry**

**1 teaspoon curry powder**

**¾ cup Major Grey's chutney, finely chopped**

**2 scallions (white and tender green parts), finely chopped**

**½ cup chopped salted dry-roasted peanuts**

## Don't Be Out of Luck at a Potluck

If you ask your guests to bring food, don't have them bring the appetizers. Inevitably, the person bringing the first course is always late, and your guests are left waiting for something to accompany their drinks. Whether it's Spicy Nuts (page 143) or chips and dip, make something for your guests to eat when they arrive.

**1.** In a food processor, process the cream cheese, cheddar cheese, sherry, and curry powder together until smooth.

**2.** Remove from the food processor and place on a sheet of plastic wrap, forming it into a ball.

✳ **DIVA DO-AHEAD:** At this point, wrap it in plastic and refrigerate for at least 8 hours and up to 3 days to let the flavors develop, or freeze for up to 2 months. Defrost in the refrigerator overnight before continuing.

**3.** Remove the cheese ball from the refrigerator and place it in a serving dish. Spread the chutney over the cheese and garnish with the scallions and peanuts.

## The Diva Says:

The cheese mixture is great spread on celery sticks and garnished with a dollop of chutney and a sprinkling of peanuts.

# Cranberry-Walnut Cheese Ball

Makes about 2¼ cups

Dried cranberries add color and great flavor to this cheese spread. I like to serve it on apple slices (dipped in lemon water to keep them from turning brown) and wheat crackers.

½ cup unsweetened dried cranberries

2 tablespoons sherry or brandy

One 8-ounce package cream cheese, softened

1 cup finely shredded sharp white cheddar cheese

1 teaspoon Worcestershire sauce

½ cup chopped walnuts

1 cup chopped fresh Italian parsley

**1.** Soak the cranberries in the sherry for 10 minutes.

**2.** In a food processor or a medium-size bowl with an electric mixer, process or beat the cream cheese, cheddar, and Worcestershire together until smooth. Stir in the cranberries and sherry. Place the cheese on a piece of plastic wrap and form into a 1-inch log or a ball.

**3.** Combine the walnuts and parsley in a small bowl, pat over the cheese log (or ball), and roll the log in it until completely covered.

✳ **DIVA DO-AHEAD:** At this point, refrigerate for at least 4 hours and up to 1 week to let the flavors develop, or freeze for up to 6 weeks. Defrost in the refrigerator overnight and bring to room temperature before serving.

# Southwestern Cilantro Pesto Torte 🍸🍷🍶

Serves 12 to 16

This spicy version of a pesto torte is made with cilantro pesto and salsa fresca, creating a stunning spread for chips or crackers.

> **Two 8-ounce packages cream cheese, softened**
>
> **1 cup (2 sticks) unsalted butter, softened**
>
> **1 teaspoon garlic salt**
>
> **½ teaspoon chipotle Tabasco sauce**
>
> **2 cups Cilantro Pesto (page 472)**
>
> **1 cup Salsa Fresca (page 90)**
>
> **Bunches of fresh cilantro for garnish**

**1.** Line a 4-cup decorative mold with plastic wrap so it hangs over the sides by at least 4 inches.

**2.** In a large bowl with an electric mixer or in a food processor, cream or process together the cream cheese and butter until smooth. Add the garlic salt and Tabasco and mix until smooth.

**3.** Wet your hands with warm water, and pat a ½-inch layer of cream cheese into the bottom of the mold. Spread a ¾-inch layer of pesto over the cream cheese, then a ½-inch layer of cream cheese over the pesto. Continue to layer the pesto and cream cheese, ending with a layer of cream cheese. (You may have a little pesto left over, which you can freeze for another use.) Bring the plastic over the top of the mold.

✳ **DIVA DO-AHEAD:** At this point, refrigerate for at least 1 hour and up to 3 days to firm up the torte, or freeze for up to 6 weeks. Defrost in the refrigerator overnight before continuing.

**4.** When ready to serve, unmold the torte onto a serving plate and remove the plastic wrap. Drain the salsa of any excess liquid and spread over the torte. Garnish with sprigs of cilantro and surround with chips and crackers.

## Freezing Pesto

Pesto freezes beautifully, and will keep for up to 2 months. An easy way to freeze small portions is to line muffin cups with plastic wrap and fill each with ½ cup of pesto. Cover the tin with plastic and freeze until the pesto is firm. (It will not be rock hard.) Once the pesto is frozen, remove it from the muffin cups and transfer to zipper-top plastic bags. When you want to make pesto, remove a "puck" or two from the freezer and allow to thaw for about 30 minutes at room temperature. If you decide to freeze the pesto, you can forgo the step of pouring the oil over the top.

# Red, White, and Green Pesto Torte 🍸🍷🥂

Serves 12 to 16

Velvety layers of cream cheese interwoven with spicy green and red pestos make this spread a visual and sensory delight. Serve with sliced baguettes, cucumber rounds, Pita Chips (page 527), or water crackers.

**Two 8-ounce packages cream cheese, softened**

**1 pound (4 sticks) unsalted butter, softened**

**1 tablespoon Worcestershire sauce**

**1 tablespoon garlic salt**

**3½ cups Basil Pesto (page 97)**

**3½ to 4 cups Sun-Dried Tomato Pesto (page 97)**

**Fresh basil leaves for garnish**

**Oil-packed sun-dried tomatoes, drained and cut into strips, for garnish**

**1.** In a large bowl with an electric mixer, or in a food processor, cream or process together the cream cheese and butter. Add the Worcestershire and garlic salt and blend until smooth.

**2.** Line a 4- to 6-cup mold (or a loaf pan, soufflé dish, or lotus bowl) with plastic wrap, letting 4 inches hang over the edge. Wet your hands with warm water and pat a ½-inch layer of the cream cheese mixture into the bottom of the mold. Spread a ¾-inch layer of Basil Pesto over the cream cheese. Spread with another ½-inch layer of the cream cheese mixture. Cover with a ¾-inch layer of Sun-Dried Tomato Pesto. Continue to layer the cream cheese and pestos, ending with the cream cheese. Freeze any leftover pestos. Fold the plastic wrap over the top of the mold.

❋ **DIVA DO-AHEAD:** At this point, refrigerate for at least 1 hour and up to 2 days to firm up the torte, or freeze in a zipper-top plastic bag for up to 2 months. Defrost overnight in the refrigerator before continuing.

**3.** Unmold the torte onto a serving plate, peel off the plastic wrap, and decorate the top of the torte with basil leaves and sun-dried tomato strips.

## The Diva Says:

This elegant appetizer can be shaped into almost anything. At Christmastime, I have used a star-shaped baking dish for the mold, and for larger parties I have made several small tortes to place around the entertaining space. For an elegant decoration, cut sun-dried tomatoes into petals to form a flower head, and add a basil stem and leaves to complete it. If you like, you can also add pine nuts as the center of the flower. Or just use basil leaves for decoration.

# PUTTING ON THE RITZ WITH TORTES

**Layering creamy cheeses** and savory fillings in a mold creates a dramatic torte to serve with crackers, baguette slices, or cucumber slices. The beauty of these tortes is that they can be made at least 3 days ahead of time, and most of them can be frozen for up to 2 months. You can prepare one large dramatic torte or a few smaller ones, which can be placed around the entertaining space to create interest. Sometimes I'll put out two different tortes for different flavor combinations, say the Southwestern Cilantro Pesto Torte (page 94) and the Red, White, and Green Pesto Torte (page 95).

These are both impressive and have such intense flavors that people won't get stuck at one and hover over it. If you make smaller tortes, they can be included in a cheese tray or served to smaller groups. You'll find that it's a lot cheaper to make these yourself than to buy them ready-made at the grocer, and with the money you save, you can buy some nice wine to serve with them.

During testing we tried low-fat cream cheese, and it worked just fine, though it's a little softer than the full-fat cheese. I don't recommend using nonfat cream cheese.

## Diva Variations

Here's an almost no-prep variation that my editor Pam likes to make. Buy two 11-ounce packages of goat cheese and store-bought containers of basil pesto and sun-dried tomato pesto. Mash the goat cheese and press one-third of it into the bottom of your plastic wrap–lined mold. Top with a ³/₄-inch layer of one of the pestos and spread another third of the goat cheese evenly over that. Top with a ³/₄-inch layer of the other pesto and cover evenly with the remaining goat cheese. Refrigerate, unmold, and decorate as directed. You can also make this using just one type of pesto if you prefer.

## Basil Pesto

Makes about 3 ½ cups

> **2 cups fresh basil leaves**
>
> **1 cup freshly grated Parmesan cheese**
>
> **¼ cup pine nuts**
>
> **3 cloves garlic, peeled**
>
> **½ cup olive oil**

In a blender or food processor, process the basil, cheese, pine nuts, and garlic together until broken up. With the machine running, gradually add the oil and process until smooth. Scrape down the bowl, and process again for another 30 seconds.

✳ **DIVA DO-AHEAD:** At this point, you can pour the mixture into a jar, float ½ inch of olive oil on the top, and refrigerate for up to 5 days. Pour off the oil, and stir before using.

## Sun-Dried Tomato Pesto

Makes about 4 cups

> **1½ cups oil-packed sun-dried tomatoes**
>
> **6 medium-size cloves garlic, peeled**
>
> **1 cup packed fresh basil leaves**
>
> **1 cup freshly grated Parmesan cheese**
>
> **½ cup olive oil**
>
> **2 tablespoons balsamic vinegar**

In a food processor, combine the tomatoes, garlic, basil, and Parmesan and process for about 1 minute. With the machine running, gradually add the oil and vinegar and process until thoroughly incorporated. Scrape down the sides of the bowl and process for another 30 seconds.

✳ **DIVA DO-AHEAD:** At this point, you can pour the mixture into a jar and refrigerate for up to 7 days or freeze for up to 2 months.

# Creamy Southwestern Cheesecake 🍺 🍸 🍷

Makes one 9-inch cheesecake; serves 12 to 16

With its crunchy tortilla-chip crust, creamy Monterey Jack cheese, Anaheim chiles, cilantro, and chipotle-flavored sour cream topping, this cheesecake is sure to please all of your guests. Serve it with Black Bean, Corn, and Salsa Dip (page 86) or Mango Salsa (page 477) or your own favorite salsa on the side.

3 cups finely crushed tortilla chips

¼ cup (½ stick) butter, melted

½ to 1 teaspoon chili powder, to your taste

2 tablespoons butter

½ cup finely chopped red onion

One 4-ounce can diced green chiles, drained and rinsed

½ cup seeded and finely chopped yellow bell pepper

Two 8-ounce packages cream cheese, softened

2 cups sour cream

2 large eggs

2 cups finely shredded Monterey Jack cheese

¼ cup chopped fresh cilantro

¼ teaspoon chipotle chile powder

Salsa for serving

**1.** Put the crushed tortilla chips in a food processor. With the machine running, add the butter and chili powder and process until the ingredients are combined.

**2.** Line the inside of a 9-inch springform pan or a cake pan with aluminum foil and coat with nonstick cooking spray. Press the chip mixture into the bottom and set aside.

**3.** Preheat the oven to 350°F.

**4.** In a small skillet, melt the butter over medium heat and cook the onion, chiles, and yellow pepper, stirring, until softened, about 4 minutes. Let cool.

**5.** With an electric mixer, beat the cream cheese in a large bowl until smooth. Add

½ cup of the sour cream and the eggs, one at a time, and beat until smooth. Stir in the cheese, the sautéed mixture, and the cilantro until well blended. Pour evenly over the prepared crust and smooth the top with a rubber spatula. Bake for 45 minutes.

**6.** In a small bowl, stir the chipotle chile powder into the remaining 1½ cups of sour cream. When the cheesecake has baked for 45 minutes, remove it from the oven and increase the oven temperature to 425°F. Spread the sour cream over the top of the cheesecake and bake for another 5 minutes. Turn off the oven, leaving the door ajar, and leave the cheesecake in the oven for 30 minutes (this will help prevent cracks from forming).

**7.** Remove from the oven and let cool to room temperature.

**8.** Place a large serving plate over the pan and invert them. Remove the pan from the cheesecake and peel away the foil.

✳ **DIVA DO-AHEAD:** At this point, you can cover with plastic wrap and refrigerate for up to 3 days or freeze for up to 6 weeks. Defrost overnight in the refrigerator and bring to room temperature before serving.

**9.** Serve with the salsa on the side.

## A Fine Spread

The cooked cheesecakes and other spreads are best at room temperature because they need to loosen up a bit to be spreadable, and I have instructed you in each recipe on how to serve them.

**Savory cheesecakes** are stunning starters for your buffet dinner and can be made in an endless array of delightful flavors. You may make them in a 9-inch springform pan, for a large presentation, or in smaller pans to set out in different parts of the house for people to discover. Cheesecakes freeze beautifully and they actually improve with age in the refrigerator, so plan to make them at least the day before the party, or up to 3 days ahead. You can freeze them for up to 2 months; then defrost them overnight in the refrigerator and let them come to room temperature on the counter (at least 1 hour) before serving. Accompany with baguette slices and crackers.

Cracks in cheesecakes seem to happen with temperature variations in the oven. After my cheesecakes are baked, I leave them in the turned-off oven with the door ajar. This seems to inhibit the cracks, which tend to occur when you remove the cheesecake from the oven and let it cool at room temperature.

Another trick that I have learned over the years is to line the springform pan with aluminum foil and coat the foil with nonstick cooking spray. This helps remove the cheesecake from the springform pan easily. The foil comes right off the cheesecake for a great presentation, and you don't ruin the flat bottom of the springform by cutting the cheesecake on it.

# Chesapeake Bay Seafood Cheesecake

Makes one 9-inch cheesecake; serves 12 to 16

This seafood cheesecake is reminiscent of that old Eastern Shore classic, crab imperial, but in addition to the crab, it includes shrimp and clams. You could prepare it with only shrimp or crab, but I urge you to try this one because the variety of seafood is what makes it special.

### Crust

**2 cups crushed Ritz cracker crumbs**

**¼ cup (½ stick) butter, melted**

**1 teaspoon Old Bay seasoning**

**2 tablespoons chopped fresh Italian parsley**

**½ cup freshly grated Parmesan cheese**

### Filling

**2 tablespoons unsalted butter**

**¼ cup finely chopped shallots**

**2 cloves garlic, minced**

**Three 8-ounce packages cream cheese, softened**

**2 large eggs**

**1 cup mayonnaise**

**2 teaspoons Worcestershire sauce**

**2 teaspoons Old Bay seasoning**

**2 teaspoons dry sherry**

**¼ cup chopped fresh Italian parsley**

**1 cup lump crabmeat, picked over for shells and cartilage**

**1 cup chopped cooked shrimp**

**Two 6-ounce cans chopped clams, drained**

**Lemon wedges for garnish**

**Fresh parsley for garnish**

**1.** To make the crust, in a medium-size bowl, combine the cracker crumbs, melted butter, Old Bay, parsley, and Parmesan.

**2.** Line the inside of a 9-inch springform pan with aluminum foil and coat with nonstick cooking spray. Press the crust mixture into the bottom and set aside.

**3.** Preheat the oven to 325° F.

**4.** To make the filling, in a small skillet, melt the butter over medium heat and cook the shallots and garlic, stirring, until the shallots begin to soften. Set aside to cool.

**5.** With an electric mixer, beat the cream cheese in a large bowl until smooth. Add the eggs, one at a time, and then the mayonnaise, beating until light. Stir in the Worcestershire, Old Bay, sherry, and parsley. Fold in the seafood and garlic-shallot mixture, then turn the mixture into the prepared pan, smoothing the top with a rubber spatula.

**6.** Bake until a cake tester inserted into the middle comes out clean, 55 to 65 minutes. Turn off the oven and leave the oven door ajar for 30 minutes (this will help prevent cracks from forming).

**7.** Place a large serving plate over the pan and invert them. Remove the pan from the cheesecake and peel away the foil.

✳ **DIVA DO-AHEAD:** At this point, you can cover with plastic wrap and refrigerate for up to 3 days or freeze for up to 6 weeks. Defrost overnight in the refrigerator and bring to room temperature before serving.

**8.** Garnish with lemon wedges and fresh parsley and serve.

# Baked Brie with Apricots and Dried Cranberries 🍸🍷🍾

Serves 10 to 12

Crisp puff pastry enrobes creamy Brie covered with piquant apricots and Cognac-soaked cranberries. Serve with slices of baguette, cucumbers, or carrots.

**One 6- to 8-inch wheel Brie (with rind on)**

**1 sheet frozen puff pastry, defrosted and rolled out into a 15-inch square**

**1 cup apricot preserves**

**2 tablespoons Cognac**

**1 cup unsweetened dried cranberries**

**1 large egg beaten with 2 tablespoons milk, heavy cream, or water**

**1.** Place the Brie in the center of the puff pastry.

**2.** In a small bowl, combine the preserves, Cognac, and cranberries. Spread over the Brie. Bring the corners of the puff pastry toward the center of the Brie and twist together into a decorative knot.

✳ **DIVA DO-AHEAD:** At this point, cover or slip into a 2-gallon zipper-top plastic bag and refrigerate for at least 1 hour and up to 24 hours so the puff pastry will relax, or freeze for up to 6 weeks. Defrost overnight in the refrigerator before continuing.

**3.** Preheat the oven to 350°F and place the Brie on a cookie sheet lined with a silicone liner, parchment paper, or aluminum foil.

**4.** Brush with the egg wash. Bake until the crust is golden, 35 to 45 minutes. Remove from the oven and let it rest for 15 minutes before serving.

## Diva Variations

Substitute any of these toppings for the apricots and cranberries.

- 1 cup Basil Pesto, homemade (page 97) or store-bought

- 1 cup Sun-Dried Tomato Pesto, homemade (page 97) or store-bought

- 1 cup Wild Mushroom Spread (page 129)

- 1 cup raspberry jam thinned with Chambord or another brandy, and topped with slivered almonds

- 1 cup orange marmalade thinned with Grand Marnier

- 8 to 10 dried figs soaked in sherry (drain off the sherry after the figs have plumped), then coarsely chopped

- 8 to 10 dried apricots soaked in brandy (drain off the brandy after the apricots have plumped), then coarsely chopped

- 1 to 1½ cups Spicy Nuts (page 143) made with pecans, or Rosemary Walnuts (page 144)

# Marinated Goat Cheese

Serves 10 to 16

Smooth goat cheese has a subtle flavor, but when it's marinated in extra virgin olive oil and herbs, it becomes something very special for your buffet table. Serve with crackers or baguette slices.

**Two 11-ounce logs goat cheese**

**1 cup extra virgin olive oil**

**2 tablespoons fresh rosemary leaves, plus extra for garnish**

**1½ teaspoons salt**

**½ teaspoon freshly ground black pepper**

## Diva Variations

Other herbs also work well—try thyme, marjoram, or oregano.

Add 2 cloves chopped garlic to the marinade, but marinate the cheese for only 24 to 36 hours because the garlic will overpower the cheese if it marinates any longer.

**1.** Put the goat cheese into a zipper-top plastic bag. Add the oil, rosemary, salt, and pepper and shake the bag to distribute the contents.

**✳ DIVA DO-AHEAD:** At this point, seal the bag and refrigerate for at least 24 hours and up to 2 weeks. Remove from the refrigerator at least 1 hour before serving because the oil may solidify when it is refrigerated.

**2.** Drain off the oil and serve the cheese garnished with additional rosemary.

# Napa-Style Marinated Parmesan

Serves 10

This marinated cheese is a takeoff on Chef Michael Chiarello's "glop," which he sells through his company, Napa Style. I've toyed with his recipe and added some balsamic vinegar, which perks up the taste and flavor. Make sure you use a good quality extra virgin olive oil and balsamic vinegar—it makes a tremendous difference in the finished dish. Serve with baguette slices.

⅓ pound Parmesan cheese

⅓ pound Asiago cheese

3 cloves garlic, minced

2 teaspoons dried oregano

1 teaspoon freshly ground black pepper

½ teaspoon red pepper flakes

¾ cup extra virgin olive oil

¼ cup balsamic vinegar

**1.** Chop the cheeses into small chunks and place in a food processor. Pulse until they are the size of peas.

**2.** Transfer the cheeses to a medium-size bowl and add the garlic, oregano, black and red peppers, and oil, stirring to blend.

✳ **DIVA DO-AHEAD:** At this point, cover and let stand at room temperature for at least 4 hours or refrigerate for up to 1 week. Bring to room temperature before serving.

**3.** When ready to serve, add the vinegar and stir with a fork, so it blends with the oil. Transfer the cheese to a bowl and serve, surrounded by slices of baguette.

# Small Bites

**In this chapter you will find appetizers** and small first courses that can be picked up by hand or speared with a toothpick. A little more substantial than dips and spreads, they can be as simple as oysters and clams on the half shell with various dipping sauces or as sophisticated as Bacon-Wrapped Scallops (page 113). Ideally, these appetizers are consumed in one bite, with any shell or bone discarded on the plate.

Skewers of small pieces of food are usually part of a buffet table because they can be picked up and eaten while walking around. However, I can't tell you how many times I've seen someone pick up a skewer loaded with a whole meal on it and spend the entire party trying to get the food off the skewer; often it ended up on the floor. Make it easy on your guests and just put one biteful on a skewer. If they like it, they'll happily go back for more. This may feel like more work for you, but trust me, your guests will be delighted.

All of the warm small bites in this chapter will keep well and still taste great at room temperature for up to 2 hours.

# Diva Secrets for Almost Instant Nibbles

There are so many spur-of-the-moment hors d'oeuvres you can make for unexpected company that I thought I would offer up a few of my favorites.

- Chunks of Parmigiano-Reggiano cheese with aged balsamic vinegar poured over them. Serve with crusty bread.

- Cubes of cheddar and Monterey Jack cheeses tossed with your favorite vinaigrette and served with toothpicks

- Cherry tomatoes and cubes of Monterey Jack cheese or fresh mozzarella tossed with olive oil and chopped fresh herbs

- Bite-size pieces of smoked sausage or ham cubes, cubes of cheese, and pretzels, plus several different types of mustard for dipping (Diva's Mustard Magic: Combine ½ cup of Grey Poupon mustard with 2 tablespoons of honey, or with 2 teaspoons of chopped fresh tarragon, or with 1 teaspoon of Frank's RedHot Cayenne Pepper Sauce)

- Bite-size pieces of cooked chicken, turkey, smoked turkey, or ham, served with several different dips and sauces (barbecue, peanut, ranch, Caesar, pesto)

- Rolled-out pizza dough drizzled with extra virgin olive oil, sprinkled with rosemary and coarse salt, and baked for 10 to 15 minutes at 425°F. Cut into squares and serve with pesto for dipping.

- Two 7-ounce cans of Italian tuna packed in oil, drained and drizzled with balsamic vinegar. Serve with crackers or baguette slices.

- Edamame or soybeans. You can usually buy these frozen and cook them in boiling salted water for 8 to 10 minutes. Drain thoroughly, then sprinkle with kosher salt—and make sure you have a bowl for the empty pods.

- Large cooked shrimp wrapped with prosciutto and served on skewers

- Melon slices wrapped with prosciutto

- Large strawberries wrapped with prosciutto and drizzled with aged balsamic vinegar

- Hard-boiled eggs, peeled, quartered, topped with your favorite vinaigrette, ranch, or Caesar dressing, and served with toothpicks

- Tortilla chips topped with your favorite shredded cheese, baked at 350°F until the cheese melts, then dolloped with guacamole and sour cream and sprinkled with chopped tomatoes and scallions
- Endive leaves separated and topped with crumbled goat cheese and chopped oil-packed sun-dried tomatoes
- Endive leaves separated and topped with chicken, lobster, shrimp, or crab salad
- Cucumber rounds (cut ½ inch thick), each topped with a bit of scallion cream cheese, a piece of smoked salmon, and chopped fresh dill
- Cucumber rounds spread with garlic herb cheese and topped with chopped shrimp
- Cucumber rounds spread with goat cheese and dolloped with Tapenade, homemade (page 84) or store-bought

## THE CHEESE PLATTER

**Cheese in the fridge** is the entertainer's best friend. Add a few crackers, clusters of grapes, a couple of pears or apples, and you have a delectable platter for your buffet table.

Try to choose cheeses that will complement each other, rather than compete. Sharp cheddar and Roquefort, two very strong flavors, might be too much for your guests, but you can pair them if you also include mellower cheeses as well, like a creamy Brie or baby Swiss. Remember, you don't need too many cheeses on the platter; I think that confuses people. Four cheeses, with fruit and crackers, is a great start. A small torte or savory cheesecake is also nice—it breaks up the monotony and adds interest to the platter.

If your platter runs out, arrange another one, rather than having seven cheeses on a platter with two bites taken from each one. Or place one cheese platter on a table away from the buffet and one on the buffet table. If you can label the cheeses, your guests will appreciate it. Remember that some people are allergic to blue-veined cheeses, so place those away from the other cheeses on the platter, so that everyone can sample.

# Marinated Shrimp

Serves 8 to 10

Shrimp are an investment, and your guests will know that you have really splurged when they see this gorgeous presentation. They don't have to know that it takes only 3 minutes to put together, and then a few hours in the refrigerator.

½ cup olive oil

½ cup canola oil

⅓ cup rice vinegar

¼ cup fresh lemon juice

3 cloves garlic, minced

1½ teaspoons salt

½ teaspoon freshly ground black pepper

Pinch of cayenne pepper

1 tablespoon chopped fresh tarragon

1 tablespoon chopped fresh chives

½ cup chopped red onion

½ cup seeded and chopped green bell pepper

½ cup seeded and chopped red bell pepper

½ cup chopped fresh Italian parsley leaves

2 pounds large shrimp, cooked (see recipe, right) and peeled

**1.** In a large glass bowl, whisk together the oils, vinegar, lemon juice, garlic, salt, black pepper, cayenne, tarragon, and chives. Add the onion, bell peppers, and parsley, stirring to blend.

❋ **DIVA DO-AHEAD:** At this point, you can cover and refrigerate for up to 2 days.

**2.** Add the shrimp to the bowl and toss to coat well.

❋ **DIVA DO-AHEAD:** At this point, cover or transfer to a zipper-top plastic bag and refrigerate for at least 4 and up to 24 hours, but no longer, or the shrimp will start to get mushy.

**3.** To serve, drain the shrimp and serve them mounded on a large platter, accompanied by French bread and toothpicks for spearing the shrimp.

## Keeping Your Shrimp Cold

A great way to keep shrimp cold for dipping is to make an ice mold in the shape of the serving dish you will use. Take a zipper-top plastic bag and fill with some water (not too much, as you will want a place for the shrimp to sit). Place the bag in the serving bowl and adjust it so it forms to the contour of the serving bowl (you may need to weigh it down with something—I use bags of frozen veggies). Freeze the bag and the serving bowl together. When the water is frozen in the bag, remove it and fit it into the serving bowl. Place the shrimp on top of the ice, and you have a great way to keep your shrimp cold for the party.

# Boiled Shrimp

Serves 10 to 12

This simple cooking method is foolproof—the shrimp always come out tender and succulent. Overcooked shrimp are unappetizing, so follow these directions and you will be right on the money. Remember to buy enough; I recommend at least three shrimp per person (see What Size?, page 112). Leftovers, if there are any, can be thrown into a salad, pasta, soup, or gumbo.

4 cups water

2 tablespoons Old Bay seasoning

1 lemon, quartered

2 pounds large or extra-large shrimp (20/25 per pound), peeled and deveined

**1.** Combine the water and Old Bay in a 4-quart saucepan. Squeeze the lemons into the water and add the rinds. Bring to a boil. Add the shrimp, cover, and remove from the heat. Let the shrimp remain in the water for 15 minutes.

**2.** Drain the shrimp, allow them to cool slightly, and peel.

✳ **DIVA DO-AHEAD:** At this point, you can let cool completely, transfer to a zipper-top plastic bag, and refrigerate for up to 2 days.

## Shell On or Off?

Shrimp can be expensive for a large group, so try buying the shrimp raw and cooking them yourself. If you have time to peel and devein them, buy them raw with shells (the cheapest way to buy them). Starting on the underside, remove the feelers. Then pull off the top shell and either leave the tail on or discard it. Once the shell is removed, make a shallow cut with a sharp knife down the back of the shrimp and lift out the intestinal vein that runs down the back. Rinse the shrimp in cold water and keep refrigerated before cooking.

If you don't have time to peel, buy your shrimp already peeled and deveined (but still raw). If you buy frozen cooked shrimp, defrost them in a colander at room temperature for about 1 hour, toss them with a sprinkle of Old Bay seasoning and lemon juice, and refrigerate until ready to serve. Be sure to provide toothpicks when serving shrimp.

## How Much Sauce Is Enough?

Caterers usually figure 2 tablespoons of sauce per person, but people seem to like a lot of cocktail sauce with their shrimp. Two cups of sauce should feed 10 people nicely, but you may want to keep extra ingredients on hand just in case you need to whip up a new batch quickly.

# DIPPING SAUCES FOR SHRIMP

**Serving shrimp** on your buffet table will add a luxurious feel to your party. It tells your guests you care about them because you spent all this money for these gorgeous crustaceans. And for an accompaniment, you don't have to restrict yourself to cocktail sauce anymore. There are lots of wonderful dipping sauces that will complement cooked shrimp, and I recommend that you try a few new ones. It's always simple to make up your favorite cocktail sauce (people will expect it), but serve another on the side as well, and see what happens. I guarantee it will be gone, too!

## Old-Fashioned Shrimp Cocktail Sauce

*Makes 2 cups*

This crowd-pleaser has been around forever, and there are many variations. This one is pretty spicy, so if you like yours a little tamer, I suggest you reduce the amount of horse-radish and Tabasco.

**1½ cups ketchup**

**½ cup prepared chili sauce**

**2 tablespoons prepared horseradish**

**2 teaspoons fresh lemon juice**

**2 tablespoons Worcestershire sauce**

**¼ teaspoon Tabasco sauce**

**1 teaspoon salt**

**1 teaspoon sugar**

Combine all the ingredients in a medium-size bowl and stir until blended. Taste and adjust the seasonings as needed.

✳ **DIVA DO-AHEAD:** At this point, you can cover and refrigerate for up to 2 days.

Serve cold.

## Bloody Mary Shrimp Cocktail Sauce

*Makes 2 cups*

This is a spicy, relatively thin cocktail sauce, enhanced by celery salt and fresh onions. You could serve your shrimp hung over martini glasses with the sauce in the center; that way, you will have control over the amount of shrimp that people eat. Sometimes the shrimp are the first thing to go, and your late-arriving guests never see them!

**1½ cups Bloody Mary mix or spicy tomato juice**

**¼ cup ketchup**

**¼ cup vodka (optional)**

**2 teaspoons Worcestershire sauce**

**½ teaspoon Tabasco sauce**

**½ teaspoon celery seeds**

**½ teaspoon freshly ground black pepper**

**½ cup finely chopped celery**

**¼ cup finely chopped red onion**

Combine all the ingredients in a medium-size bowl and stir to blend.

**DIVA DO-AHEAD:** At this point, cover and refrigerate for at least 4 hours and up to 5 days to let the flavors develop.

Serve cold.

## Asian Dipping Sauce

Makes 2 cups

Smoky and sweet, this dip is sure to please. It's also a nice basting sauce for shrimp or chicken skewers. You can find hoisin sauce and chili oil in the Asian section of your grocery store.

- **1 teaspoon vegetable oil**
- **1 teaspoon chili oil, or more to taste**
- **2 cloves garlic, minced**
- **1 teaspoon peeled and grated fresh ginger**
- **½ cup hoisin sauce**
- **¼ cup soy sauce**
- **2 tablespoons rice vinegar**
- **2 tablespoons ketchup**
- **4 scallions (white and tender green parts), chopped, for garnish**

**1.** In a 2-quart saucepan, heat the vegetable oil over medium heat, add the chili oil, garlic, and ginger, and cook, stirring, until the garlic softens, about 1 minute. Reduce the heat to low, add the hoisin, soy sauce, rice vinegar, and ketchup, and stir until the mixture is smooth and begins to bubble.

**2.** Remove from the heat and allow to cool to room temperature.

**DIVA DO-AHEAD:** At this point, you can cover and refrigerate for up to 1 week. The sauce may congeal in the refrigerator, so warm it up or bring to room temperature before serving.

**3.** Sprinkle with the scallions and serve.

## Rémoulade Sauce

Makes about 2½ cups

In New Orleans they serve this delectable sauce with shrimp and crab. I love it mixed into a chicken salad or slathered on bread, which I grill and top with cold roast beef.

- **1½ cups mayonnaise**
- **½ cup Dijon or Creole mustard**
- **¼ cup ketchup**
- **2 tablespoons finely chopped cornichons or dill pickles**
- **1 tablespoon finely chopped shallots**
- **2 teaspoons prepared horseradish**
- **1 tablespoon finely chopped capers**
- **2 tablespoons chopped fresh Italian parsley**
- **1 teaspoon sweet paprika**

In a medium-size bowl, combine all the ingredients, stirring to blend.

**DIVA DO-AHEAD:** At this point, cover and refrigerate for at least 4 hours and up to 5 days to develop the flavors.

Serve cold.

## Spicy Peanut Sauce

Makes about 3 cups

The influence of Asian food has spread widely in this country; it is even evident on our buffet tables. Peanut sauce is delicious with shrimp, but it's also a wonderful dipping sauce for chicken, seafood, and beef on skewers.

**1 cup chicken broth**

**½ cup unsweetened coconut milk**

**1 cup smooth peanut butter**

**¼ cup firmly packed light brown sugar**

**¼ cup soy sauce**

**2 teaspoons peeled and grated fresh ginger**

**6 shakes of Tabasco sauce**

In a 2-quart saucepan, stir together all the ingredients and bring to a boil. Reduce the heat to medium-low and simmer for 10 minutes, stirring until smooth.

✳ **DIVA DO-AHEAD:** At this point, you can let cool, cover, and refrigerate for up to 5 days. Reheat, thinning with a little chicken broth if necessary, then let come to room temperature.

## The Diva Says:

Use regular peanut butter in this recipe; the natural-style peanut butters tend to get grainy, but regular peanut butter will give you a smooth sauce.

### What Size?

If you haven't had a lot of experience with shrimp, when you get to the store you may be unsure about the meaning of terms like "jumbo," "large," and "colossal." And then there are the numbers, such as 21/25 and U15. What does it all mean? The numbers are more important than the adjectives. They refer to how many of that particular size shrimp are in a pound, so 21/25, which are sold as jumbo, would mean there should be 21 to 25 in a pound. U15, or colossal, means there are under 15 in a pound. These numbers will help you figure out how many you need. I usually use large or extra-large shrimp for a presentation because I like everyone to have a nice serving, but I don't want to break the bank.

# Bacon-Wrapped Scallops

Serves 10

A classic appetizer, these scallops can be served on skewers as an hors d'oeuvre, or on a bed of sautéed corn and sugar snap peas for a main course. The beauty of this dish is that it can be made up ahead of time, then roasted or grilled at the last minute. The scallops are delicious warm or at room temperature, served with tartar sauce, hot sauce, or Rémoulade Sauce (page 111), and lemon wedges.

**12 strips bacon**

**½ cup firmly packed light brown sugar**

**1 tablespoon Old Bay seasoning**

**2 pounds sea scallops**

### Diva Variation

This treatment works well with shrimp, too. Substitute 2 pounds of jumbo shrimp for the scallops, twist the bacon around the shrimp, and secure with a toothpick. Broil for 2 to 3 minutes on each side, so the shrimp and bacon cook evenly. Serve with lemon wedges to squeeze over the shrimp, cocktail sauce, or Rémoulade Sauce (page 111).

**1.** In a large skillet, cook the bacon over medium heat just until it is softened. It will begin to turn opaque and render a lot of fat; do not let it begin to brown or crisp up at all. Remove it from the skillet and drain on paper towels. Cut each strip in half crosswise.

**2.** In a small bowl, combine the brown sugar and Old Bay and evenly sprinkle a little over each piece of bacon. Wrap a piece of bacon around each scallop, securing it with a long toothpick. Arrange them on a baking sheet lined with aluminum foil or a silicone liner.

**DIVA DO-AHEAD:** At this point, you can cover and refrigerate for up to 24 hours.

**3.** Preheat the broiler for 10 minutes. Broil the scallops for 3 minutes, turn them, and continue broiling until opaque and the bacon is crisp, another 2 minutes. Serve immediately.

# Mini–Crab Cakes

Serves 10 to 12

These little bites are so delicious, you won't be able to eat just one. Loaded with crab and spicy Old Bay seasoning, they are simple to make and can be prepared ahead of time. Then just pop them into a hot oven to warm up. Serve these with Rémoulade Sauce (page 111), Old-Fashioned Shrimp Cocktail Sauce (page 110), or Dilled Tartar Sauce (page 496) on the side.

**3 tablespoons mayonnaise**

**1 large egg**

**2 teaspoons Worcestershire sauce**

**1 teaspoon Dijon mustard**

**2 teaspoons minced fresh Italian parsley**

**1 tablespoon Old Bay seasoning**

**1 cup saltine cracker meal or plain dry bread crumbs**

**1 pound lump crabmeat, picked over for shells and cartilage**

**½ cup (1 stick) unsalted butter, melted**

**1.** In a large bowl, stir together the mayonnaise, egg, Worcestershire, mustard, parsley, Old Bay, and ¼ cup of the cracker meal. Stir in the crabmeat, being careful not to break it up. Form into 1-inch cakes about ½ inch thick. Dip the cakes into the remaining ¾ cup of cracker meal and place on a baking sheet lined with a silicone liner or aluminum foil.

❇ **DIVA DO-AHEAD:** At this point, cover and refrigerate for at least 1 hour to firm up and up to 24 hours. Bring to room temperature before continuing.

**2.** Preheat the oven to 375°F.

**3.** Brush the cakes with the melted butter and bake until golden brown, 12 to 15 minutes, turning once.

❇ **DIVA DO-AHEAD:** At this point, you can let cool, stack the cakes in plastic containers, separated by waxed or parchment paper, and refrigerate for up to 3 days or freeze for up to 1 month. Defrost overnight in the refrigerator, bring to room temperature, and reheat in a 350°F oven for 3 to 5 minutes.

# Crabby Stuffed Clams

Serves 10 to 12

These luscious morsels will be stars at your next party. Filled with luxurious lump crabmeat, each stuffed clam offers two bites of seafood heaven. The filling is also delicious mounded in Stuffed Mushrooms (page 139).

**2 tablespoons unsalted butter**

**1½ teaspoons Old Bay seasoning**

**¼ cup finely chopped shallots**

**⅓ cup mayonnaise**

**1 teaspoon Dijon mustard**

**½ pound lump crabmeat, picked over for shells and cartilage**

**24 littleneck clams, shucked and meat finely chopped (save the shells and scrub to remove any grit), or two 8-ounce cans chopped clams, drained**

**2 cups fresh French bread crumbs**

**Lemon wedges for garnish**

**Fresh parsley sprigs for garnish**

## Stuffed Clams

Stuffed clams are delicious little bites that can be served as a first course or on a buffet table. I recommend using little-neck clams because the shells are a nice size for a couple of bites of filling. If you can't get fresh clams in your area, use canned clams and store-bought clam-shells that can be baked in the oven. You can usually find the shells at a gourmet retailer, or see Sources. Once the clams have been baked, they are fine at room temperature for about an hour.

**1.** In a medium-size skillet over medium heat, melt the butter, add the Old Bay and shallot, and cook, stirring, for 2 minutes to blend the flavors and soften the shallots.

**2.** Transfer to a large bowl and stir in the mayonnaise, mustard, crabmeat, and clams until well blended. Add the bread crumbs and blend until well combined. Stuff the reserved clam shells or ovenproof store-bought shells with the mixture, and transfer to a baking sheet.

❋ **DIVA DO-AHEAD:** At this point, you can cover and refrigerate for up to 2 days.

**3.** Preheat the oven to 350°F. Bake the clams until heated through and browned on the top, 15 to 20 minutes. Transfer to a platter, garnish with lemon wedges and parsley sprigs, and serve warm or at room temperature.

# Sausage-Stuffed Clams

Serves 10 to 12

Spicy Italian sausage and spinach give these clams some pizzazz. Feel free to substitute hot sausage if you like your food spicy.

**1 pound Italian sweet sausage, casings removed**

**One 10-ounce bag fresh baby spinach**

**½ cup heavy cream**

**24 littleneck clams, shucked and meat finely chopped (save the shells and scrub to remove any grit), or two 8-ounce cans chopped clams, drained**

**1½ cups fresh French bread crumbs**

**½ cup freshly grated Romano cheese**

**1.** In a medium-size skillet over medium-high heat, cook the sausage, breaking it into small pieces, until no longer pink. Transfer to a medium-size bowl with a slotted spoon and remove all but 1 table-spoon of the fat from the skillet.

**2.** Add the spinach to the skillet and cook over medium heat until it begins to wilt, about 2 minutes. Add the cream and bring to a boil, scraping up any browned bits stuck to the bottom of the pan. Transfer to the bowl with the sausage. Add the clams and bread crumbs and stir until well blended. Stuff the reserved clamshells or ovenproof store-bought shells with the mixture, transfer to a baking sheet, and sprinkle the tops evenly with the cheese.

✳ **DIVA DO-AHEAD:** At this point, you can cover and refrigerate for up to 2 days.

**3.** Preheat the oven to 350°F. Bake the clams until heated through and the cheese is bubbling and beginning to turn golden, 15 to 20 minutes. Transfer to a platter and serve warm or at room temperature.

# Garlic-Stuffed Clams

Serves 10 to 12

These clams are reminiscent of the stuffed clams that were once standard fare at family-style Italian restaurants. Filled with a garlicky basil and bread crumb mixture, and topped with Parmesan cheese, they are a hit at any party.

½ cup (1 stick) unsalted butter

6 cloves garlic, minced

½ cup chopped fresh Italian parsley

¼ cup packed fresh basil leaves, cut into fine shreds

24 littleneck clams, shucked and meat finely chopped (save the shells and scrub to remove any grit), or two 8-ounce cans chopped clams, drained

2 cups fresh French bread crumbs

1 cup freshly grated Parmesan cheese

**1.** In a medium-size skillet over low heat, melt the butter, add the garlic, and cook until the butter is infused with the flavor of the garlic, about 5 minutes. Don't allow the garlic or butter to turn color at all; you want a slow infusion. Stir in the parsley and basil and set aside.

**2.** In a medium-size bowl, stir together the clams, bread crumbs, and Parmesan. Dribble in about half the butter mixture, until the crumbs appear moist but not soggy. Stuff the reserved clamshells or ovenproof store-bought shells with the mixture, transfer to a baking sheet, and drizzle each clam with a bit of the remaining garlic butter.

✳ **DIVA DO-AHEAD:** At this point, you can cover and refrigerate for up to 2 days.

**3.** Preheat the oven to 350°F. Bake the clams until heated through and the tops begin to turn golden, 15 to 20 minutes. Transfer to a platter and serve warm or at room temperature.

There is something very elegant and grown-up about serving raw clams and oysters on the half shell. That being said, some guests will not want to partake, so I recommend you do this only if you know your audience. If this is the first time you are having the boss over for dinner, skip the slurping of the clams and serve something more genteel. Keeping the seafood cold on ice is essential to keeping the seafood safe and your guests healthy. With that in mind, remember to have lots of chipped ice, and nestle the shells in the ice. Littleneck, cherrystone, and Puget Sound butter clams are great raw bar choices; you don't want to use soft-shell clams or quahogs. Some fishmongers will shuck the clams and oysters for you. (Be sure to bring them the serving platter so that they have a place to put the shellfish.) Otherwise, you will need an oyster knife and some thick gloves to shuck them yourself.

For determining serving sizes, I'd recommend 2 to 3 shells per person if you are serving other hors d'oeuvres, and 4 per person if this is the only starter. If you are having a huge buffet celebration and the raw bar will be a part of the buffet, I recommend that you place it on another table, away from the main buffet, as it will cause congestion around the table. Even though I am giving you a few sauces for this raw bar, I recommend that you have bowls of horseradish, lemon wedges, a pepper grinder, bottles of Tabasco, and Worcestershire sauce on hand for those who like to flavor their own. Bloody Mary Shrimp Cocktail Sauce (page 110) is also delicious with raw shellfish.

## Raw Bar Sauce

Makes about 1 cup

This resembles a standard cocktail sauce and is often served with clams on the half shell. Serve cold.

- ¼ cup ketchup
- ⅓ cup prepared horseradish
- 1 teaspoon Tabasco sauce, or more to your taste
- 2 teaspoons fresh lemon juice
- 2 teaspoons Worcestershire sauce
- ½ teaspoon salt

In a small bowl, stir together all the ingredients until blended.

✳ **DIVA DO-AHEAD:** At this point, cover and refrigerate for at least 1 hour and up to 1 week.

## Ginger-Chili Oyster Sauce

Makes about ½ cup

Hot and spicy, this Asian-inspired sauce is gorgeous spooned over clams and oysters.

- ¼ cup chopped shallots
- 2 tablespoons rice vinegar
- 2 teaspoons soy sauce
- ¼ teaspoon Asian chili-garlic sauce
- ¼ teaspoon peeled and grated fresh ginger

In a small bowl, stir all the ingredients together.

## Mignonette Sauce

Makes about ½ cup

Here is a classic vinegar and horseradish–based sauce. Serve this one on the side for guests to season their shellfish.

**½ teaspoon prepared horseradish**

**1 small shallot, finely chopped**

**¼ cup Champagne vinegar**

**¼ teaspoon salt**

**½ teaspoon coarsely ground black pepper**

**2 tablespoons chopped fresh Italian parsley**

**1.** In a small bowl, combine the horseradish, shallot, vinegar, salt, and pepper, stirring to blend.

✳ **DIVA DO-AHEAD:** Cover and refrigerate for at least 2 hours and up to 4 days.

**2.** Just before serving, stir in the parsley.

## Shucking with Success

To shuck clams, first scrub them under cold running water with a wire brush to remove any grit on the shells. If you're right-handed, put a heavy-duty work glove on your left hand and grab a clam. With the hinged end facing you, release the pressure at the back of the clam with the tip of a short knife. Lift the top of the shell and scrape the clam flesh to free it from the shell. You can refrigerate clams on the half shell for up to 8 hours.

To shuck oysters, you will need heavy-duty work gloves and an oyster knife. Scrub the oysters under cold water to remove any grit. Hold one in the palm of a gloved hand and insert the blade of the knife into the gap between the shell on the wide end, the one without the hinge. Twist the handle of the knife until the hinge pops and separates the shell. Make sure you slide the knife under the abductor muscle to separate the meat from the shell. The bottom shell is deep and best for serving oysters; discard the top shell. You can refrigerate oysters on the half shell for up to 8 hours.

## Serve It Forth!

Metal serving platters are terrific for serving raw shellfish because they will retain the cold—silver, pewter, and an aluminum-based alloy made by Wilton Armetale work really well. Line the bottom with plastic wrap, then pour chipped ice onto the platter. Many party stores have large disposable platters; I don't recommend these because they are not always strong enough to hold 50 oysters or clams. To make a do-it-yourself platter for a casual get-together, find a large shallow cardboard box, like a soda or beer case. Cover the outside of the case with contact paper, line the inside with heavy-duty aluminum foil, and load it with crushed ice. Set the shells into the crushed ice and serve.

# Easy Antipasto Platter

Serves 12 to 16

Antipasto in Italy is whatever the cook has on hand for a first course. It can be different salamis and cheeses with olives and roasted peppers, or fried zucchini flowers served with grilled marinated vegetables and crusty bread. Now that most grocers carry imported prosciutto, cheeses, and the like, it's easy to put together an antipasto platter in no time using store-bought ingredients.

One 10-ounce bag mixed field greens

½ pound very thinly sliced prosciutto di Parma

½ pound Italian breadsticks (without seeds)

¼ pound very thinly sliced soppressata, each slice cut into quarters

One ⅓-pound wedge aged provolone cheese, cut into ½-inch slices

One 6-ounce can imported Italian tuna packed in olive oil, drained

One 4-ounce jar giant pimento-stuffed green olives, drained

¼ pound Kalamata olives, drained

One 4-ounce jar marinated artichoke hearts, drained and cut in half

One 4-ounce jar roasted red peppers, drained and cut into thin strips

½ cup extra virgin olive oil

¼ cup balsamic vinegar

½ teaspoon salt

¼ teaspoon freshly ground black pepper

**1.** Line a large round or oval platter with the field greens.

**2.** Wind the prosciutto slices around the breadsticks and place them on the platter.

**3.** Arrange the soppressata and cheese slices in an alternating pattern so they overlap one another around the outside of the platter. Mound the tuna in the middle of the platter.

**4.** In a medium-size bowl, combine the olives, artichoke hearts, and roasted peppers. Whisk the oil, vinegar, salt, and pepper together and pour ¼ cup of it over the vegetables, tossing to coat. With a slotted spoon, arrange the vegetables around the tuna.

**5.** Serve the remaining dressing on the side or pour some over the tuna.

**❋ DIVA DO-AHEAD:** At this point, the entire platter can be covered and refrigerated for about 8 hours, although I recommend not winding the prosciutto around the breadsticks until just before serving because refrigeration tends to make them soggy.

# Warm Olives

Makes 3 cups

This mélange of olives is roasted in a hot oven, then served either warm or at room temperature. It can be a part of an antipasto platter or served alongside grilled entrées.

**3 cups assorted olives (cracked green, Kalamata, stuffed green, Niçoise—your choice), drained**

**¼ cup extra virgin olive oil**

**1 teaspoon freshly ground black pepper**

**2 teaspoons dried oregano, rosemary, or thyme, crumbled**

**6 cloves garlic, slivered**

**1.** Preheat the oven to 375°F. Line a baking sheet with a silicone liner or aluminum foil.

**2.** In a large bowl, combine all the ingredients until well blended. Transfer to the prepared sheet and bake until heated through, 15 to 20 minutes.

✴ **DIVA DO-AHEAD:** At this point, you can let cool, cover, and refrigerate for up to 1 week. Let come to room temperature before serving.

Serve warm or at room temperature.

## The Pits

I prefer to serve pitted olives, so that my guests don't have to deal with the pits and I don't find them ground into the carpet the next day. Most olives can be found with the pits already removed, but it's easy to do it yourself: Simply whack the olive with the flat part of a chef's knife and remove the pit after it pops to the surface.

# Marinated Bocconcini

Serves 10 to 12 as part of a platter

Small pieces of fresh mozzarella marinated in herbs, garlic, and extra virgin olive oil are a delicious addition to a buffet table or cheese tray. If you cannot find the tiny mozzarella balls called *bocconcini*, then use two large balls of fresh mozzarella and cut them into bite-size cubes.

**1 pound fresh mozzarella cheese (preferably the small balls)**

**1 cup extra virgin olive oil**

**2 teaspoons dried oregano**

**2 cloves garlic, minced**

**1 teaspoon salt**

**½ teaspoon freshly ground black pepper**

**1.** Put the mozzarella in a medium-size bowl, pour the oil over it, and sprinkle with the oregano, garlic, salt, and pepper. Stir to blend. Make sure that the cheese is submerged in the oil.

✳ **DIVA DO-AHEAD:** At this point, you can cover and refrigerate for up to 3 days. Allow to sit at room temperature for 2 hours before serving.

**2.** Stir the cheese to coat with the marinade and serve with toothpicks, or skewer 2 pieces onto each toothpick and arrange on a platter.

### Diva Variation

**Walk-About Caprese Salad:** Skewer a cherry tomato and a bocconcino onto a toothpick, separated by a square of torn fresh basil, and arrange on a platter. Drizzle with the oil and seasoning mixture and allow to sit at room temperature for 2 hours before serving. Try yellow, orange, and red pear-shaped tomatoes for color and interest.

## HOMEMADE ANTIPASTO

**The recipes listed in this section** are all delicious by themselves, but are a knockout served as part of a huge antipasto platter. The traditional formula for an antipasto is three meats and two cheeses, but I just make what I like. The beauty of it is that you can prepare as much as you want, fill in with store-bought items, then set it out and let people help themselves. The dishes can be prepared well in advance and don't need to be warmed up; just arrange them in bowls or on platters and you're good to go. *Buonissimo!*

- Warm Olives (page 121)
- Assorted sliced salamis
- Skewers of Marinated Bocconcini (page 121)
- Fresh Herb Tortellini-and-Olive Skewers (right)
- Rainbow Roasted Pepper Salad (page 124)
- Napa-Style Marinated Parmesan (page 103)
- Tarragon-Marinated Mushrooms (page 125)
- Steamed baby artichokes (see page 71)
- Grandma's Giardiniera (page 126)
- Roasted Wild Mushroom Salad (page 163)

# Fresh Herb Tortellini-and-Olive Skewers

Serves 10 to 12

These simple skewers are always a hit at our house. If you have a hard time finding white balsamic vinegar, check the Sources at the back of the book. Using dark balsamic turns the pasta a dark brown color that is unattractive.

**¾ pound fresh cheese tortellini made with egg pasta**

**½ cup extra virgin olive oil**

**¼ cup white balsamic vinegar or white wine vinegar**

**2 teaspoons chopped fresh rosemary, or 1 teaspoon dried**

**1 teaspoon chopped fresh oregano, or ½ teaspoon dried**

**½ teaspoon salt**

**¼ teaspoon freshly ground black pepper**

**1 clove garlic, minced**

**One 6-ounce jar large pimento-stuffed green olives, drained**

**¼ cup snipped fresh chives**

**Sprigs of fresh Italian parsley for garnish**

**1.** Bring a medium-size pot of salted water to a boil. Add the tortellini and cook for 1 minute. Drain and let cool.

**2.** In a small bowl, combine the oil, vinegar, rosemary, oregano, salt, pepper, and garlic, whisking until blended. Taste and adjust the seasonings.

**3.** Skewer one tortellini and one olive onto each toothpick and lay the toothpicks in a shallow dish or a 13 x 9-inch baking dish.

Pour the dressing over the tortellini and olives and turn so they are evenly coated.

✳ **DIVA DO-AHEAD:** At this point, cover and refrigerate for at least 2 and up to 24 hours to let the flavors develop, turning the toothpicks a few times. Bring to room temperature before continuing.

**4.** When ready to serve, arrange the tortellini and olives on a platter. Pour the remaining dressing over them and garnish with chives and parsley sprigs.

## Diva Variations

If you don't like olives, you can make the skewers with spinach pasta tortellini and egg pasta tortellini for color and interest. You will need to cook the spinach pasta separately from the egg pasta and double the marinade. You can also substitute any of the following for the olives:

- Cherry tomatoes
- ½-inch pieces cooked chicken
- ½-inch pieces salami
- Quartered store-bought marinated artichoke bottoms

# Rainbow Roasted Pepper Salad

Serves 10 to 12

This taste of my childhood makes me smile every time I prepare it because it reminds me of Grandma's house and the smells that I loved. Peppers are easy to roast, but if you don't have time, you can buy them in jars and toss them with the dressing. Colored peppers are expensive, but they add flavor to this dish, so I recommend that you use at least one or two yellow or orange ones in addition to the red and green.

Roasted pepper salad is great on a bruschetta bar; just cut the roasted peppers into bite-size pieces for easy handling. You can also use peppers to top a pizza, toss into pasta salads, or include in a filling for panini or other sandwiches.

4 large red bell peppers

2 large green bell peppers

2 large yellow bell peppers

1 large orange bell pepper

¾ cup olive oil (not extra virgin)

¼ to ⅓ cup balsamic vinegar, to your taste

1 teaspoon salt

½ teaspoon freshly ground black pepper

4 medium-size cloves garlic, each cut into 4 or 5 slivers

**1.** Line a baking sheet with aluminum foil and preheat the broiler.

**2.** Wash the peppers and remove any stickers that may be on them. Place them on their sides on the baking sheet and broil, turning to char them evenly on all sides.

**3.** When the peppers are blackened, turn off the broiler, close the oven door, and allow them to rest in the oven for 45 minutes to 1 hour. The steam formed will help you remove the skins more easily.

**4.** Remove the peppers from the oven and, when they are cool enough to handle, remove the skins and cut out the core and seeds. Slice into strips and put in a medium-size bowl. Stir the oil, vinegar, salt, pepper, and garlic into the peppers.

**DIVA DO-AHEAD:** At this point, cover and let marinate at room temperature for at least 2 and up to 8 hours.

**5.** Taste for seasonings by dipping a piece of crusty bread into the sauce and sampling it. Adjust as necessary.

**DIVA DO-AHEAD:** At this point, you can cover and refrigerate for up to 5 days. Bring to room temperature and discard the garlic before serving.

# Tarragon-Marinated Mushrooms

Serves 10 to 12

These aromatic mushrooms are always a big hit on the buffet table or served with assorted antipasti. Toss leftovers into salads or sandwiches, or use as a garnish.

⅔ cup red wine vinegar

¼ cup olive oil

¼ cup canola oil

1 clove garlic, mashed

1 tablespoon sugar

1 teaspoon salt

2 tablespoons chopped fresh tarragon, or 2 teaspoons dried

4 shakes of Tabasco sauce

1 bay leaf

2 teaspoons chopped fresh marjoram, or ¾ teaspoon dried

1 medium-size red onion, sliced ½ inch thick and separated into rings

1½ pounds small button mushrooms (if the mushrooms are large, cut in half or quarters to make them bite-size)

**1.** In a medium-size bowl, whisk together the vinegar, oils, garlic, sugar, salt, tarragon, Tabasco, bay leaf, and marjoram.

**2.** Put the onion and mushrooms in a large zipper-top plastic bag and pour the dressing over. Seal the bag and turn several times so everything gets coated.

✳ **DIVA DO-AHEAD:** At this point, refrigerate for at least 4 hours or overnight.

**3.** Drain the mushrooms and serve with toothpicks, garnished with some of the smaller onion rings.

## The Diva Says:

No time to make your own marinade? For 1 pound of mushrooms, use 1½ cups of bottled dressing, such as red wine vinaigrette, Caesar, or balsamic vinaigrette. An hour (but no more than 2) in a prepackaged vinaigrette is enough time to flavor the mushrooms without giving them that processed tang.

### Diva Variations

Substitute white balsamic vinegar for the red wine vinegar and substitute 2 teaspoons of chopped fresh oregano for the tarragon and marjoram.

Substitute rice vinegar for the red wine vinegar and substitute ¼ cup of packed fresh basil leaves, chopped, for the tarragon and marjoram.

Substitute ½ cup of rice vinegar and ¼ cup of soy sauce for the red wine vinegar. Omit the tarragon, bay leaf, and marjoram and add 1 teaspoon of peeled and grated fresh ginger. Substitute 6 scallions (white and tender green parts), chopped, for the red onion.

# Grandma's Giardiniera

Serves 12 to 16

This colorful jumble of pickled vegetables is a real eye-opener, with its variety of textures and flavors. Serve it with crusty bread as part of an antipasto platter.

½ cup olive oil

4 cloves garlic, minced

2 cups canned tomato puree

1 tablespoon firmly packed light brown sugar

2 teaspoons Worcestershire sauce

¼ cup ketchup

¼ cup balsamic vinegar

1 teaspoon salt

½ teaspoon freshly ground black pepper

Two 10-ounce jars Italian marinated vegetables (sold as giardiniera), drained

One 7-ounce jar pepperoncini (hot Italian peppers), drained

½ pound small button mushrooms

One 4-ounce jar pickled cocktail onions, drained

One 4-ounce jar jumbo pimento-stuffed green olives, drained

One 12-ounce jar baby kosher dill pickles, drained

Two 4-ounce jars marinated artichoke hearts, drained

½ cup coarsely chopped Italian parsley for garnish

**1.** In a 5-quart saucepan, heat the oil over medium heat and cook the garlic, stirring, until it softens, about 1 minute. Add the tomato puree, brown sugar, Worcestershire, ketchup, vinegar, salt, and pepper and bring to a boil. Reduce the heat to medium-low and simmer for about 10 minutes. Taste and adjust the seasonings.

**2.** Add the marinated vegetables, pepperoncini, mushrooms, onions, olives, pickles, and artichokes and simmer until the cauliflower in the pickled vegetables is tender when pierced with the sharp tip of a knife, another 10 minutes. Remove the pan from the heat and let cool.

✳ **DIVA DO-AHEAD:** At this point, you can transfer to a glass bowl, cover, and refrigerate for up to 2 weeks.

**3.** Serve the vegetables cold or at room temperature, garnished with the parsley.

# Bruschetta Bar

Serves 12

This is a great way to get your guests involved with the food. Set out a large basket filled with toasted bread rounds and place three bowls of toppings around it for spooning over the breads. If you would like to serve the bread spread with a topping and pass them on a tray, top the bread about 1 hour before serving.

## Bruschetta Toasts

Slice Italian or French bread about ½ inch thick. Place in a single layer on a baking sheet and toast in a preheated 375°F oven until dry, 5 to 7 minutes. Remove from the oven and rub one side of each slice with a garlic clove, if you'd like. You can store the bread at room temperature in zipper-top plastic bags for up to 24 hours.

## Artichoke Topping

Makes 2 cups

**Two 6-ounce jars marinated artichokes, drained and coarsely chopped**

**¼ cup olive oil**

**2 teaspoons red wine vinegar**

**¼ cup pine nuts**

**½ cup freshly grated Parmesan cheese**

**¼ cup chopped fresh Italian parsley**

In a medium-size bowl, combine all the ingredients.

✳ **DIVA DO-AHEAD:** At this point, you can cover and refrigerate for up to 4 days. Bring to room temperature before serving.

## Herb-Roasted Tomatoes

Makes about 4 cups

In Italy, they roast tomatoes in the oven when tomatoes are not at their peak. The roasting intensifies the flavor of the tomatoes, and sweetens them. I like to keep some in the freezer just in case I need a spur-of-the-moment pasta sauce or snack (like bruschetta). To turn these into a bruschetta topping, coarsely chop the tomatoes and stir in 1 cup of diced fresh mozzarella cubes and ¼ cup finely sliced fresh basil.

**Two 28-ounce cans peeled whole tomatoes, drained and juice reserved**

**½ cup extra virgin olive oil**

**2 teaspoons dried basil**

**1 teaspoon fresh rosemary leaves, crushed**

**½ cup chopped red onion**

**6 cloves garlic, coarsely chopped**

**1½ teaspoons salt**

**½ teaspoon freshly ground black pepper**

1. Preheat the oven to 350°F. Line a jelly roll pan with a silicone liner or aluminum foil.

2. Cut the tomatoes in half and put in a large glass bowl. Stir in the olive oil, basil, rosemary, onion, garlic, salt, and pepper, being careful not to tear the tomatoes. Pour onto the prepared pan, spreading it out in a single layer. Bake until the tomato liquid is absorbed and the tomatoes have firmed up and turned a deep red color, 1 to 1½ hours, checking to make sure that the tomatoes and garlic don't brown.

3. Transfer the tomato mixture to a clean glass bowl and let it mellow at room temperature for about 6 hours.

※ **DIVA DO-AHEAD:** At this point, you can cover and refrigerate for up to 4 days or freeze for up to 3 months. Defrost in the refrigerator overnight and bring to room temperature before continuing.

### Other Diva Ideas for Bruschetta Toppings

- Napa-Style Marinated Parmesan (page 103)
- Roasted Garlic-Eggplant Dip (page 89)
- Tapenade (page 84)

# Oven-Roasted Caponata
Makes about 3 cups

This piquant relish is terrific on bruschetta, or you can serve it as a side sauce for meats, poultry, or seafood. It's also great stirred into pasta and served with a generous shaving of Parmigiano-Reggiano or Pecorino Romano cheese. Olives and capers don't freeze particularly well, so I don't advise freezing this.

2 medium-size purple eggplants (about 1½ pounds), ends trimmed and cut in half lengthwise

¼ cup extra virgin olive oil

6 cloves garlic

½ cup coarsely chopped onion

½ cup coarsely chopped celery

1 teaspoon salt

½ teaspoon freshly ground black pepper

Pinch of red pepper flakes (optional)

¼ cup Balsamic Vinegar Syrup (page 480), or 2 tablespoons each balsamic vinegar and firmly packed light brown sugar

One 15.5-ounce can crushed tomatoes

2 teaspoons chopped fresh basil

½ cup drained and chopped pitted green olives

¼ cup drained and chopped capers

½ cup chopped fresh Italian parsley

**1.** Preheat the oven to 400°F and line a baking sheet with a silicone liner or aluminum foil.

**2.** Drizzle the cut sides of the eggplant with a little olive oil, and lay, cut side down, on the baking sheet. Place the garlic on the baking sheet and drizzle with some of the oil, reserving the remainder for the next step. Bake the garlic and eggplant until the eggplant is tender, 25 to 30 minutes; a knife should pierce the skin easily, with no resistance. Remove from the oven and allow to cool. Then peel off the skin of the eggplant and coarsely chop the flesh.

**3.** In a large skillet, heat the remaining olive oil over medium heat and add the eggplant. Squeeze the garlic from its skin into the skillet and cook the mixture, stirring, for 1 to 2 minutes, tossing to coat with the oil. Add the onion, celery, salt, black pepper, and red pepper flakes if using and cook, stirring, until the onion and celery begin to soften a bit, 3 to 4 minutes. Add the balsamic syrup, tomatoes, and basil and simmer the mixture for 20 minutes, stirring occasionally.

**4.** Remove from the heat and stir in the olives, capers, and parsley. Allow the caponata to cool to room temperature, then taste and adjust the seasonings.

✳ **DIVA DO-AHEAD:** At this point, you can cover and refrigerate for up to 1 week. Bring to room temperature before serving.

# Wild Mushroom Spread
Makes about 2 cups

Roasting the mushrooms at a high temperature intensifies their flavor in this savory spread.

> 2 pounds assorted fresh wild mushrooms, such as shiitake, oyster, porcini, portobello, or cremini, stems removed or trimmed and caps halved or quartered, depending upon their size
>
> ⅓ cup extra virgin olive oil
>
> 3 tablespoons balsamic vinegar
>
> 1½ teaspoons salt
>
> 1½ teaspoons freshly ground black pepper
>
> 2 cloves garlic, minced
>
> 1 tablespoon chopped fresh rosemary

**1.** Preheat the oven to 400°F. Put the mushrooms on a baking sheet lined with a silicone liner or aluminum foil.

**2.** In a small bowl, combine the remaining ingredients. Pour over the mushrooms, toss to coat well, and roast for 20 minutes. Let cool, then, using a slotted spoon, transfer the mushrooms to a food processor and pulse a few times to chop coarsely.

✳ **DIVA DO-AHEAD:** At this point, you can cover and refrigerate for up to 3 days. Bring to room temperature before serving.

# Pigs in a Blanket

Serves 12 to 16

A taste from childhood, when Mom would wrap hot dogs in Pillsbury crescent rolls, these little piggies are a bit more sophisticated, but just as much fun. There are lots of variations on the theme, and they can all be made ahead of time, frozen, and popped into the oven for a quick warm-up before serving. If children will be attending your get-together, you may want to omit the mustard.

---

**One 17.5-ounce package Pepperidge Farm puff pastry, defrosted and each sheet rolled out into a 12 x 16-inch rectangle**

**¼ cup Sweet Hot Mustard, homemade (recipe follows) or store-bought**

**One 1-pound package cocktail franks or mini–smoked sausage**

---

**1.** Line a baking sheet with a silicone liner, aluminum foil, or parchment paper.

**2.** Cut the puff pastry into 2 x 1-inch strips. Spread a thin layer of mustard in the center of the pastry, lay a frank across the pastry, and roll it up so that each end is sticking out of the pastry. Place on the prepared baking sheet and roll up the remaining franks, setting them 1 inch apart on the baking sheet.

✳ **DIVA DO-AHEAD:** At this point, you can cover and refrigerate for up to 24 hours or freeze on the baking sheet, then transfer to zipper-top plastic bags and freeze for up to 6 weeks.

**3.** Preheat the oven to 400°F. If necessary, line a baking sheet and place the pigs on

it. Bake until the pastry is golden brown, 7 to 10 minutes, or 10 to 12 minutes if frozen. Remove from the baking sheets and serve immediately.

✳ **DIVA DO-AHEAD:** You can also cook the pigs the night before or earlier in the day, let cool completely, transfer to plastic bags, refrigerate, then reheat in a 300°F oven when ready to serve.

## Diva Variation

If you would like to use a different mustard, feel free to substitute to your heart's content—yellow, Dijon, whole-grain, Creole, horseradish, honey, or one that contains herbs such as tarragon and dill.

## How Many Piggies Are Enough?

There are about 36 cocktail franks in a 1-pound package, but this does vary quite a bit. I always figure on 2 per person when I'm serving them with something else before dinner and 3 per person if I'm not. If this is the only kid-friendly food on the table, 4 per child should be enough.

## Sweet Hot Mustard

Makes about 2½ cups

This spicy hot mustard is simple to make. It is delicious spread on salmon before grilling or roasting and makes a nice dipping sauce for cheese, ham, cooked poultry, or pretzels.

⅔ cup Colman's dry mustard

1 cup rice vinegar

3 eggs

1¼ cups sugar

1. In a small saucepan, whisk together the mustard and vinegar over medium heat.

2. When the mixture is warm, remove from the stove and whisk in the eggs and sugar. Return to the heat, and cook, whisking constantly, until the mustard is thickened and smooth, about 5 minutes. Don't let the mustard boil; you just want it to be very hot and thickened. Remove from the heat and cool to room temperature.

✳ **DIVA DO-AHEAD:** At this point, you can store the mustard, covered, in the refrigerator for up to 2 weeks.

## Cheesy Piggies

Serves 12 to 16

What's not to like about cheese-encrusted cocktail franks? Use your favorite cheese as you would flour for rolling out the puff pastry. If you like sharp cheddar, as I do, you can "kick it up a notch" by sprinkling a little chili powder over the pastry.

2 cups finely shredded cheddar cheese

One 17.5-ounce package Pepperidge Farm puff pastry, defrosted

1 teaspoon chili powder (optional)

¼ cup yellow mustard (optional)

One 1-pound package cocktail franks or mini–smoked sausages

1. Line a baking sheet with a silicone liner, aluminum foil, or parchment paper.

2. Sprinkle ½ cup of the cheese over your work surface and lay a sheet of the puff pastry over the cheese. If you like, sprinkle ¼ teaspoon of the chili powder on one side of the pastry and another ¼ teaspoon on the other. Begin to roll out the puff pastry, sprinkling the work surface with another ½ cup of the cheese when you turn the pastry over. Roll the pastry into a 16 x 12-inch rectangle, then cut into 2 x 1-inch strips. Brush a thin layer of mustard down

the center of each strip, if using. Lay a frank across the dough on top of the mustard and roll up the pastry so the ends of the frank are sticking out. Place on the prepared baking sheet and repeat with the remaining franks, setting them 1 inch apart on the baking sheet, until you run out of pastry strips. Then roll out and cut the second pastry sheet in the same manner as the first and roll up the remaining franks.

✳ **DIVA DO-AHEAD:** At this point, you can cover and refrigerate for up to 24 hours or freeze on the baking sheets, then transfer to zipper-top plastic bags and keep frozen for up to 6 weeks.

**3.** Preheat the oven to 400°F. If necessary, line a baking sheet and place the pigs on it. Bake until the pastry is golden brown, 7 to 10 minutes, or 10 to 12 minutes if frozen. Serve hot.

# Whole Hog Sausage Rolls

Serves 10 to 12

This is a great way to serve sausage rolls to a crowd, with just a little bit of effort. Be sure to cook the sausages and cool them before you roll them in the puff pastry. That way, any excess fat will have drained off during their precooking and the pastry will not be soggy. The master recipe will take you through the steps for wrapping and rolling the sausage. It is followed by a list of variations that suggest flavorings to complement a variety of sausages you can use, from sweet Italian ones to spicy andouille sausage.

Two ½-pound sausages of your choice, about 1 inch thick

One 17.5-ounce package Pepperidge Farm puff pastry, defrosted and each sheet rolled into a 12-inch square

1 large egg beaten with 1 tablespoon water

**1.** Preheat the oven to 400°F. Place the sausage on an aluminum foil–lined baking sheet and bake for 20 minutes, pricking the skin halfway through the baking to allow the fat to drain off. When cooked through, let cool.

✳ **DIVA DO-AHEAD:** At this point, you can cover and refrigerate for up to 2 days.

**2.** Lay a sausage in the middle of each puff pastry square and roll the puff pastry around the sausage, sealing the edges with the egg wash (I like to twist the ends closed and brush them with the egg wash).

✳ **DIVA DO-AHEAD:** At this point, you can cover and refrigerate for up to 12 hours.

**3.** Preheat the oven to 400°F. Line a clean baking sheet with aluminum foil, a silicone liner, or parchment paper. Place the sausage rolls, seam side down, on the sheet and brush with the remaining egg wash. Make a few slits in the pastry to allow steam to escape. Bake until the pastry is golden, 20 to 25 minutes.

**4.** Let rest for 3 minutes, then cut the roll with a serrated knife into ½-inch-thick slices. Serve with toothpicks and mustard for dipping.

## All Puffed Up

While testing recipes for this book, I found many ways to use puff pastry, which is available in your grocer's freezer case near the breads and frozen piecrusts. Pepperidge Farm is the brand that is most widely available. The package comes with two sheets, which can be rolled into endless variations, from savory little bites before dinner to delectable after-dinner treats. The pastry takes about 20 minutes to thaw on the counter, then you are literally ready to roll.

Silicone liners, or Silpats, are a lifesaver when you are making puff pastry hors d'oeuvres because they keep the pastry from sticking to the baking sheets. If you don't have any, aluminum foil and parchment paper both work well.

## Diva Variations

I like to tailor the flavorings I use in the roll to the type of sausage I'm wrapping. Here are some of my favorite combinations using different sausages.

**Chicken apple sausage:** Brush the surface of the rolled-out pastry with ⅓ cup of apple butter mixed with 1 tablespoon of whole-grain mustard.

**Smoked sausage, such as kielbasa:** Brush the surface of the rolled-out pastry with honey mustard (see ham recipe variation, page 450) or whole-grain mustard.

**Sweet Italian sausage:** Roll out the pastry on a work surface sprinkled with 2 tablespoons of dried Italian herbs and ⅓ cup of freshly grated Parmesan cheese.

**Lamb sausage:** Roll out the pastry on a work surface sprinkled with 2 tablespoons of crumbled dried rosemary, and spread the surface of the pastry with Dijon mustard.

**Andouille sausage:** Roll out the pastry on a work surface sprinkled with finely shredded cheddar cheese, and spread the surface of the pastry with Creole mustard.

**Bratwurst:** Brush the surface of the rolled-out pastry with whole-grain mustard.

**Sweet Italian turkey sausage:** Brush the surface of the rolled-out pastry with Basil Pesto, homemade (page 97) or store-bought.

# Crabby Bites

Serves 12 to 16

These little puffs filled with lump crabmeat will be gone in no time, so plan to make plenty to have on hand. You can bake them directly from the freezer.

---

**One 17.5-ounce package Pepperidge Farm puff pastry, defrosted**

**1 recipe The Crabbiest of Spreads (page 82)**

**1 large egg mixed with 2 tablespoons water**

---

**1.** Roll out each of the puff pastry sheets into a 16-inch square. Cut each square into 2-inch squares. Place a square into one well of a muffin tin and spoon 1 teaspoon of the crab mixture into the center of the dough. Draw up the corners of the dough toward the center and twist together to seal. Brush with a bit of the egg wash. (If you are freezing the pastries, don't brush with the egg wash.) Repeat until you have used up all the pastry.

✳ **DIVA DO-AHEAD:** At this point, you can cover and refrigerate for up to 8 hours or freeze in the tins, then transfer to zipper-top plastic bags and keep frozen for up to 5 weeks.

**2.** Preheat the oven to 400°F. Bake until golden brown, 12 to 14 minutes. If the pastries are frozen, place them on a baking sheet lined with a silicone liner, parchment paper, or aluminum foil, brush with the egg wash, and bake for 15 to 17 minutes.

## Diva Variation

If you don't have enough muffin tins, you can make these into turnovers. Place the filling in the center of the square, then fold the dough over into a triangular shape and crimp the edges together all the way around. Brush with the egg wash before baking.

# Prosciutto Pinwheels

Serves 12 to 16

Pinwheels are the easiest appetizers to keep on hand because they can be frozen until you are ready to bake them. Just take them out while the oven is preheating, cut, and bake while still frozen. Here the pastry is rolled in grated Parmesan to give it a delightfully nutty flavor, but see the Diva Variations that follow for more suggestions.

**1 cup freshly grated Parmesan cheese**

**One 17.5-ounce package Pepperidge Farm frozen puff pastry sheets, defrosted**

**¼ cup Dijon mustard**

**⅓ pound very thinly sliced prosciutto**

**1.** Sprinkle half of the cheese over your work surface and roll out a sheet of puff pastry into a 12 x 16-inch rectangle. Repeat with the remaining cheese and puff pastry sheet. Spread each rectangle with half the mustard and lay half the prosciutto over each pastry sheet, covering it. Roll up each pastry sheet from the long side and seal the edges.

✳ **DIVA DO-AHEAD:** At this point, you can cover and refrigerate for up to 2 days or freeze for up to 2 months.

**2.** Preheat the oven to 400°F. Cut the rolls into ½-inch-thick slices and place on a baking sheet lined with a silicone liner, parchment paper, or aluminum foil.

**3.** Bake the pinwheels until golden brown, 10 to 12 minutes, or 15 to 17 minutes if frozen. Serve hot.

## Diva Variations

Here are some of my favorite combinations of pinwheels.

**Ham and Cheddar Pinwheels:** Substitute thinly sliced boiled ham for the prosciutto and finely shredded cheddar cheese for the Parmesan.

**Cheesy Pesto Pinwheels:** Mix ½ cup of Basil Pesto (page 97), Sun-Dried Tomato Pesto (page 97), or Cilantro Pesto (page 472), with two 3-ounce packages of cream cheese (store-bought pesto is okay). Spread over the rolled-out dough, roll up, and freeze. Cut into 1-inch-thick rounds and bake as directed.

**Ham 'n' Swiss Pinwheels:** Use finely shredded Swiss cheese for the work surface, then paint the pastry with the mustard of your choice. Lay ¼ pound thinly sliced Black Forest ham over each sheet, roll up, and freeze. Cut into 1-inch-thick rounds and bake as directed.

**Goat Cheese and Olive Pinwheels:** Spread a thin layer of softened goat cheese over each piece of rolled-out dough, then spread with 2 to 4 tablespoons of Tapenade, homemade (page 84) or store-bought, roll up, and freeze. Cut into 1-inch-thick rounds and bake as directed.

**Scallion and Parmesan Pinwheels:** Spread 2 to 4 tablespoons of mayonnaise over each piece of rolled-out dough. Sprinkle with chopped scallions and ¼ cup of freshly grated Parmesan cheese, then roll up and freeze. Cut into 1-inch-thick rounds and bake as directed.

**Try these ideas**, following the instructions for rolling out the puff pastry on page 134:

- Place a ½-inch cube of cream cheese or goat cheese in each puff pastry square and cover with 1 teaspoon of Sun-Dried Tomato Pesto (page 97), Basil Pesto (page 97), or Cilantro Pesto (page 472).

- Place a ½-inch cube of cream cheese in each puff pastry square and cover with 1 teaspoon of Salsa Fresca (page 90).

- Fill each puff pastry square with 1 teaspoon of Ratatouille (page 265) and sprinkle with crumbled feta cheese.

- Fill each puff pastry square with 1 tablespoon of goat cheese and 1 teaspoon Tapenade, homemade (page 84) or store-bought.

- Fill each puff pastry square with some crumbled cooked meatball (pages 409 to 414) or leftover meatloaf. Top with a little sauce of your choice and a sprinkling of the cheese of your choice.

# Cheesy Sticks

Serves 10 to 12

Thin strips of puff pastry can be rolled in cheese and herbs to make your own heavenly bites. They are great to serve with antipasti or as a fun alternative to bread. Let your imagination run wild with different combinations (see the Diva Variations that follow for suggestions). I recommend dried herbs over fresh here because they pack a punch, whereas fresh herbs have a subtler flavor that doesn't translate as well. This is purely a personal choice, though, so feel free to use fresh herbs if you wish.

**1 cup grated or finely shredded cheese of your choice**

**¼ cup dried herbs of your choice**

**One 17.5-ounce package Pepperidge Farm puff pastry, defrosted**

**1.** Sprinkle half of the cheese and herbs onto the work surface and roll out one sheet of the puff pastry over the cheese and herbs, turning frequently to distribute them all over the pastry until it is a 16 x 13-inch rectangle. Repeat with the other sheet of dough and the remaining cheese and herbs.

✳ **DIVA DO-AHEAD:** At this point, you can cover and refrigerate for up to 36 hours or freeze, then stack them and store in 2-gallon zipper-top plastic bags for up to 6 weeks. Defrost before proceeding with the recipe.

**2.** Cut each rectangle in half crosswise, then cut into 1-inch-wide strips. Twist the strips and lay on a baking sheet lined with a silicone liner, parchment paper, or aluminum foil.

✳ **DIVA DO-AHEAD:** At this point, you can cover and refrigerate for up to 36 hours or freeze, then transfer to a zipper-top plastic bag and keep frozen for up to 6 weeks. Place on a prepared baking sheet and defrost before continuing.

**3.** Preheat the oven to 400°F. Bake the cheese sticks until golden brown and crisp, 15 to 17 minutes.

✳ **DIVA DO-AHEAD:** At this point, you can let cool, transfer to a zipper-top plastic bag, and freeze for up to 1 month. Defrost and rewarm in a 400°F oven for 5 minutes.

## Diva Variations

You can have a lot of fun with this recipe. Since each pastry sheet will make quite a few sticks, try making two different types.

**Italiano Sticks:** Roll the pastry in freshly grated Parmesan cheese and oregano.

**All-American Sticks:** Roll the pastry in finely shredded mild cheddar cheese and crumbled bacon bits.

**Paris Bistro Sticks:** Roll the pastry in dried *herbes de Provence* or *fines herbes* and finely shredded Swiss cheese.

**Tex Mex Sticks:** Roll the pastry in ½ to 1 teaspoon of chili powder and finely shredded Monterey Jack cheese.

**Dilly Sticks:** Roll the pastry in dillweed and finely shredded white cheddar cheese.

**Chivey Sticks:** Roll the pastry in freeze-dried chives and freshly grated Parmesan cheese.

**El Greco Sticks:** Roll the pastry in Cavender's Greek seasoning.

**Seedy Sticks:** Omit the cheese and dried herbs, and roll the pastry in a blend of 1 tablespoon each of garlic salt, poppy seeds, sesame seeds, and caraway seeds (you should have ¼ cup total). Or just use the garlic salt with only one kind of seed if you prefer.

# Puffed Mushroom Delights

Serves 12 to 16

Spoonfuls of savory roasted mushroom spread are dropped into squares of puff pastry, which are baked until golden.

One 17.5-ounce package Pepperidge Farm puff pastry, defrosted

1 recipe Wild Mushroom Spread (page 129), drained of any juices

1 large egg beaten with 2 tablespoons water

**1.** Roll out each puff pastry sheet into a 16-inch square. Cut each square into 2-inch squares. Place a square into one well of a muffin tin and spoon 1 teaspoon of the mushroom spread into the center of the dough. Draw up the corners of the dough toward the center and twist together to seal it. Brush with a bit of the egg wash. (If you are freezing the pastries, don't brush with the egg wash.) Repeat until you have used up all the pastry.

## Getting the Best Mushrooms

Turn them over and make sure they are sealed all the way around; if they are starting to separate and you can see the gills, they have been in the store too long and will be dry and tough.

✳ **DIVA DO-AHEAD:** At this point, you can cover and refrigerate for up to 8 hours or freeze in the tins, then transfer to a zipper-top plastic bag and keep frozen for 5 weeks.

**2.** Preheat the oven to 400°F. Bake until golden brown, 12 to 14 minutes. If the pastries are frozen, place on a baking sheet lined with a silicone liner, parchment paper, or aluminum foil, brush with the egg wash, and bake for 15 to 17 minutes.

## Diva Variation

If you don't have enough muffin tins, you can also make these into turnovers. Place the filling in the center of the square, then fold the dough over into a triangular shape and crimp the edges together all the way around. Brush with the egg wash before baking.

# Stuffed Mushrooms

Serves 10

Stuffed mushrooms come in so many flavors and are the perfect one-bite pick-up on a buffet table. I usually figure on 2 mushrooms per person if I'm serving other small bites, and 3 if they are the only starter. Once they are broiled, they can be refrigerated and quickly reheated in the oven just before serving. These do require a little work, but the work is simple.

I don't like to freeze these because the mushrooms become a little soggy. Also, make sure your mushrooms are bite size. Supermarkets sell large mushrooms for stuffing, but they can actually be cumbersome for your guests.

**2 tablespoons olive oil**

**1 pound button mushrooms (about 1 inch in diameter), stems removed**

**1 cup filling of your choice (see recipes that follow)**

**1.** Heat the oil in a sauté pan over medium heat and add the mushrooms so they fit in a single layer. You may have to do this in batches. Cook until they soften and give off some of their liquid. Transfer to paper towels to drain and cool.

✳ **DIVA DO-AHEAD:** At this point, you can store in a zipper-top plastic bag and refrigerate for up to 12 hours.

**2.** When the mushrooms are cool, stuff them with filling.

✳ **DIVA DO-AHEAD:** At this point, you can cover and refrigerate for up to 8 hours.

Arrange the stuffed mushrooms on a rack in a baking dish.

**3.** When ready to serve, preheat the broiler and broil until the filling is bubbling. Serve immediately.

## Diva Variations

The possibilities are nearly endless. Here are some of my favorites. You need about 2 cups of filling to stuff 1 pound of small mushrooms.

• The Crabbiest of Spreads (page 82)

• Mock Boursin Cheese (page 91)

• Feta and Spinach Mushroom Filling (page 140)

• Cheddar and Bacon Mushroom Filling (page 140)

• ½ cup pizza sauce, topped with ¼ cup grated Pecorino Romano cheese

## Feta and Spinach Mushroom Filling

Makes 2½ cups

> ½ cup mayonnaise
>
> One 16-ounce package frozen spinach, defrosted and squeezed dry
>
> ⅛ teaspoon ground nutmeg
>
> ½ teaspoon garlic salt
>
> ¼ pound feta cheese, crumbled

In a small bowl, combine all of the ingredients.

❋ **DIVA DO-AHEAD:** At this point, you can cover and refrigerate for up to 4 days.

## Cheddar and Bacon Mushroom Filling

Makes about 2 cups

> One 3-ounce package cream cheese, softened
>
> ¼ cup mayonnaise
>
> 2 teaspoons finely chopped onion
>
> 1 cup finely shredded cheddar cheese
>
> 6 strips bacon, cooked until crisp, drained on paper towels, and crumbled

In a small bowl, beat together the cream cheese and mayonnaise until smooth. Add the onion, cheddar, and bacon and stir until blended.

❋ **DIVA DO-AHEAD:** At this point, you can cover and refrigerate for up to 3 days.

# Bacon-Wrapped Dates with Parmesan

Serves 10 to 12

My daughter, Carrie, gave me the idea for these delicious bites after eating them at a chic restaurant in Los Angeles. These are super simple to put together for unexpected company, or prepare the day before and then heat up before serving warm or at room temperature.

> 12 strips bacon, cut in half crosswise
>
> 24 pitted dates
>
> ¼ pound Parmigiano-Reggiano cheese, cut into small chunks

**1.** Cook the bacon in a large skillet over medium heat until it has rendered some fat and begins to turn translucent; don't let it brown at all. Remove from the pan and drain thoroughly on paper towels.

**2.** Make a slit in each date and stuff with a small piece of cheese. Wrap in a piece of bacon and secure with a toothpick if needed. Place the wrapped dates in a baking dish.

✳ **DIVA DO-AHEAD:** At this point, you can cover and refrigerate for up to 36 hours.

**3.** Preheat the oven to 375°F and bake the dates until the bacon is crisp, 10 to 12 minutes. Remove from the oven, drain the dates on paper towels, and set on a platter for serving. Thin shreds of any leftover Parmesan make an awesome garnish.

# Devilishly Good Deviled Eggs

Serves 10 to 12

There are many variations on the deviled egg, but my favorite is the classic deviled eggs with mayonnaise and prepared yellow mustard. I've given you lots of other ways to vary the recipe, and you may want to serve two different kinds on your buffet table. Whatever you choose, they will be gone before you know it. If you want to be fancy, use a star tip on a pastry bag to fill the eggs with a decorative flair. If you use a teaspoon, round the filling, then use the tines of a fork to mark a decorative pattern on the top. A melon baller or small ice cream scoop will also work. You can serve the deviled eggs on an egg plate, or you can nest them on a bed of field greens, chopped parsley, or shredded lettuce, which will keep them from slipping and sliding around.

**12 large hard-boiled eggs (see page 142)**

**½ to ¾ cup mayonnaise, as needed**

**2 teaspoons yellow mustard or another mustard of your choice**

**1 teaspoon salt**

**¼ teaspoon Tabasco sauce**

**Sweet paprika for sprinkling**

**1.** Cut the eggs in half lengthwise, carefully remove the yolks, and put them in a medium-size bowl. Set the whites aside.

**2.** Mash the yolks, then add ½ cup of the mayonnaise, the mustard, salt, and Tabasco and stir to blend. Taste and adjust the seasonings if necessary; add more of the mayonnaise if needed to get the consistency and flavor you want.

**3.** Fill each egg white with 1 tablespoon or so of the mixture so it is nicely rounded.

✳ **DIVA DO-AHEAD:** At this point, you can cover and refrigerate overnight.

**4.** Sprinkle with paprika before serving. Serve chilled.

## Diva Variations

**Raj Eggs:** Omit the mustard, Tabasco, and salt and add ½ teaspoon of curry powder and 1 tablespoon of finely chopped Major Grey's chutney. Garnish with finely chopped scallions instead of paprika.

**Dilly Eggs:** Add 2 teaspoons of finely chopped fresh dill.

**Béarnaise Eggs:** Add 2 teaspoons of finely chopped fresh tarragon.

**Chivey Eggs:** Add 2 teaspoons of finely chopped fresh chives

**Shrimply Deviled Eggs:** Add ½ cup of chopped cooked shrimp and 2 tablespoons of chopped fresh dill.

**Crabby Eggs:** Add ½ cup of picked-over lump crabmeat and garnish with Old Bay Seasoning instead of sweet paprika.

**Ham and Eggs:** Add ⅓ cup of finely ground smoked ham to the filling.

**Caviar Eggs:** Omit the paprika and top each egg with a tiny bit of caviar and a sprinkling of chopped red onion.

**Great Caesar's Eggs:** Omit the mustard and add 1 to 2 teaspoons of Worcestershire sauce and 2 to 3 tablespoons of freshly grated Parmesan cheese. Sprinkle with ground-up garlic croutons or more grated Parmesan instead of the paprika before serving.

**Southwestern Eggs:** Omit the mustard and add 2 tablespoons of finely chopped fresh cilantro and 1 to 2 tablespoons of salsa, to your taste. Top each deviled egg with a tiny dollop of sour cream and sprinkle with chili powder instead of paprika if desired.

## Perfect Hard-Boiled Eggs

Follow these directions and you'll never get that greenish cast on your hard-cooked yolks again. Put the raw eggs in a single layer in a saucepan with cold water to cover and place over high heat. When the water comes to a boil, turn off the heat and let the eggs sit in the water for 12 minutes. Remove from the water with tongs or a slotted spoon and plunge into ice water to stop the cooking process.

✳ **DIVA DO-AHEAD:** Once the eggs are cooked, they can be kept refrigerated in the shell for up to 1 week.

When the eggs are cool enough to handle, peel them under cold running water to remove the shells. In the case of hard-boiled eggs, by the way, older is better. Hard-cooked fresh eggs do not peel as well as eggs that are 7 to 10 days old.

## Keeping It Pretty

Food scientist Shirley Corriher recommends centering the egg yolks for the prettiest deviled eggs possible. Carefully turn the sealed egg carton of raw eggs on its side in the refrigerator the night before you intend to cook the eggs. The yolks should be centered once they are cooked. Another trick is to always turn the eggs in the carton so that they are large end down when you put them away.

# Spicy Nuts

Makes about 2 cups

These sweet and spicy nuts are so simple to make, and you can keep them in your freezer forever. I recommend using a nonstick skillet. You can multiply this recipe several times over and it's still fabulous. Just make sure your pan is large enough to handle all the nuts.

2 tablespoons (¼ stick) unsalted butter

3 tablespoons sugar

1 teaspoon seasoned salt

½ teaspoon Lawry's garlic salt

⅛ teaspoon cayenne pepper

2 cups pecan or walnut halves or whole almonds

**1.** Melt the butter in a large nonstick skillet over medium heat. Add 2 tablespoons of the sugar, the seasoned salt, the garlic salt, and the cayenne and stir until the spices give off some aroma, 1 to 2 minutes. Add the nuts and toss until well coated, about 4 minutes.

**2.** Remove from the heat and place the nuts in a glass bowl. Sprinkle the remaining 1 tablespoon of sugar over the nuts and toss until coated.

❋ **DIVA DO-AHEAD:** At this point, you can let cool and store in an airtight container at room temperature for up to 3 days, in the refrigerator for up to 2 weeks, or in the freezer indefinitely.

## The Diva Says:

If you would like to make nuts to toss into salads, chop them before cooking them in the butter and seasonings.

It's important to use dried spices with the nuts because they become fragrant in the butter and will adhere to the nuts.

# Rosemary Walnuts

Makes 2 cups

These savory walnuts are delicious as a starter before a holiday meal, or tossed into a field green salad. Be sure to make a double batch; you'll be eating these out of the pan!

**2 tablespoons (¼ stick) unsalted butter**

**2 teaspoons Lawry's garlic salt**

**1 teaspoon cayenne pepper**

**2 teaspoons dried rosemary, crumbled**

**2 cups walnut halves**

### Diva Variation

**Peppered Almonds:** Decrease the garlic salt to 1 teaspoon, decrease the cayenne to ½ teaspoon, omit the rosemary, add ½ teaspoon of coarsely ground black pepper, and substitute whole almonds for the walnuts.

**1.** Preheat the oven to 350°F and line a baking sheet with a silicone liner, parchment paper, or aluminum foil.

**2.** Melt the butter in a large nonstick skillet over medium heat, add the garlic salt, cayenne, and rosemary, and stir for 45 seconds to 1 minute. Stir in the walnuts and toss to coat.

**3.** Spread out the walnuts on the prepared sheet and bake until fragrant and toasted, 10 to 15 minutes. Remove from the sheet and let cool.

✳ **DIVA DO-AHEAD:** At this point, you can let cool and store in an airtight container at room temperature for up to 3 days, in the refrigerator for up to 2 weeks, or in the freezer for up to 6 months.

### The Diva Says:

Lawry's garlic salt contains coarsely granulated garlic and seems to have a truer garlic flavor than most other brands; it also contains dried parsley for color.

# Party Mix

Makes about 10 cups

You should always have a bowl of small snacks on hand for people to munch, whether you put them on the buffet table or around the entertaining areas of your home. There are lots of variations on the theme here, but this is our favorite. You should feel free to substitute your favorite cereals and crackers.

**One 14-ounce box Crispix cereal (or any of the Chex cereals)**

**2 cups mixed nuts**

**Two 8- to 10-ounce bags thin pretzel sticks**

**Two 5-ounce bags plain Pepperidge Farm Goldfish crackers**

**Two 3-ounce bags herbed croutons**

**1 cup (2 sticks) unsalted butter or margarine, melted**

**2 tablespoons Lawry's seasoned salt**

**1 tablespoon garlic salt**

**¼ cup Worcestershire sauce**

**6 shakes of Tabasco sauce**

**1.** Preheat the oven to 300°F.

**2.** Empty the cereal, nuts, pretzels, Goldfish, and croutons into a large ovenproof pan.

**3.** In a small bowl, combine the remaining ingredients, stirring to blend. Pour over the cereal mixture and, using a rubber spatula, carefully blend into the cereal until everything is coated, being careful not to break any of the cereal pieces or pretzels.

**4.** Bake until the mixture begins to dry out and turn golden, about 30 minutes, stirring every 10 to 15 minutes.

**5.** Remove from the oven and let cool.

✳ **DIVA DO-AHEAD:** At this point, you can transfer the mix to zipper-top plastic bags and store at room temperature for up to 1 week or freeze for up to 2 months.

# Party
# Salads

**Presenting salads on your party table** should be fun, and you should find interesting containers to display your bounty of garden goodies. With a few exceptions, salads should be served chilled or at room temperature, depending upon the preparation and ingredients. If you are serving it cold, keep the greens and dressings cold until you are ready to toss them. If a dish is better at room temperature and you've made it ahead of time, take it out of the refrigerator at least an hour and preferably 2 hours in advance so it can come to room temperature.

## How to Serve Your Salad

Be creative! In the summertime if you have a metal washtub, line it with clear contact paper or press-and-seal plastic wrap to protect it. Toss your salad in another container, so you don't tear the plastic wrap, then pile the tossed salad into the washtub.

Glass bowls are terrific; they are usually inexpensive, and they show off salads from all sides. A trifle bowl also makes a wonderful salad container.

Sometimes you need a huge container for a potato or pasta salad. Use a large lasagna pan, and line the inside with red leaf or other pretty lettuces; then pile in the salad. Finely shred some lettuce leaves and sprinkle on the top for a nice garnish.

Occasionally, I use soup tureens for serving salads; they work well because they are deep and hold a generous amount. You can also put a zipper-top plastic bag filled with ice in the bottom of a 6-quart stockpot, cover it with lettuce, and fill the pot with pasta or potato salad for a large outdoor party. Decorate the outside by folding a few red-and-white-checkered napkins into triangles, tying them to each other at the corners, and draping them around the top of the pot and over the handles.

For serving your salads, I recommend investing in nice salad servers; tong-like servers work really well for a buffet table because you can actually hold onto your plate and pick up the server in one hand. If you

### Keeping Your Salad Cold

To chill large salad bowls, fill zipper-top plastic bags with ice, then lay these in the salad bowl for 30 minutes before serving. Remove the bags when ready to serve.

have the typical fork and spoon salad servers for green salads, your guests will have a hard time picking up some salad while holding onto their plates (and wineglasses). For pasta, rice, and potato salads, large long-handled serving spoons work terrifically well. When setting out veggie condiments for a barbecue—lettuce, tomato, and onions—tongs work the best.

# What You'll Need

Salads require the best and freshest ingredients you can find, so shop carefully, inspect the produce for freshness, and make sure you buy ingredients as close to the day of your party as possible.

*Extra virgin olive oil:* Buy oil that will enhance your salad, not detract from its flavor. Extra virgin olive oil has its own flavor, so taste a few brands and buy one that you like. Some have a peppery aftertaste, others are smooth, but all have a deeper flavor and greener color than a filtered pure olive oil. I like the Colavita brand, which you can find in your supermarket. Il Molina and Monini brands may be available at your grocer as well; I recommend that you try to taste several and decide for yourself.

*Olive oil:* Filtered olive oil is golden in color and doesn't impart an overwhelming flavor to the finished dish. Use this olive oil when you want the flavor of the ingredients to shine through, but still want a hint of olive oil flavor. I recommend Bertolli Classico for regular use.

*Vegetable oil:* Vegetable oils that work nicely in salads include canola, safflower, and corn oils; use whichever you prefer.

*Balsamic vinegar:* This flavoring can make or break a salad dressing, so buy one that you like. The longer balsamic vinegar is aged, the thicker and sweeter it becomes, and hence the more expensive it is. Several brands available in the supermarket are nice to use in salads; I recommend 365 brand from Whole Foods. For a splurge, try Fini, which

**To make your own** fruit-flavored vinegar, pour 4 cups of distilled white vinegar into a glass or other nonreactive bowl and add 2 cups of cut-up fruit to the vinegar. Cover and let sit at room temperature for at least 12 hours. Strain the vinegar through a cheesecloth-lined strainer and store in a glass jar with an airtight cap. The vinegar will keep in a cool, dry pantry for about 6 months. (I don't recommend leaving any whole fruit in the vinegar because it will deteriorate, and you will run the very real risk of botulism.)

For herbed vinegars, use dried herbs and add 2 tablespoons to 4 cups of white vinegar. Strain before storing.

Suggested fruits:

- Raspberries (frozen unsweetened when fresh are too expensive)
- Blackberries
- Blueberries
- Peaches

Suggested herbs:

- Tarragon
- Oregano
- Basil
- Rosemary
- Red pepper flakes (1 teaspoon)
- Cumin seeds (2 tablespoons)

you can find in gourmet stores. As with the oils, I recommend that you taste it (if you can) before you buy.

*Other vinegars:* I recommend having on hand small bottles of red wine, rice, sherry, and white wine vinegars. Each will add a special flavor to your salad dressings. (To make your own flavored vinegars, see box above.)

*Mayonnaise:* I only use Hellman's/Best Foods mayonnaise at my house. It has a clean, fresh taste, which lets the flavors of the ingredients shine. Low-fat Hellmann's/Best Foods mayonnaise can be substituted in all the recipes, though it has a more pronounced lemon flavor than the regular mayonnaise.

***Mustard:*** Dijon mustard comes from Dijon, France, and contains white wine and herbs. It is tangy and adds a delicious piquant flavor to your salads. I like the Grey Poupon brand. Classic ballpark mustard is bright yellow in color, which comes from the addition of turmeric and the use of yellow mustard seeds. This mustard adds color and sharp flavor to dishes. Asian or Chinese mustard is a mixture of mustard powder and water and is very hot. German mustards are generally either mild or hot, no middle ground here. The whole mustard seed is used in German preparations, so the mustard is generally dark in color and may show some of the grainy texture of the mustard seeds. Honey mustard can be found on your grocer's shelves now, but I like to make my own by mixing 1 tablespoon of honey into ½ cup of Dijon mustard. Honey mustard and all the other mustard varieties will keep sealed in a jar in the refrigerator for up to 6 months. Having a selection of mustards on hand will allow you to tailor the flavor of your dressings.

***Salt:*** Many people like kosher salt, while others prefer sea salt, and I leave it to your personal preference. I prefer sea salt for its clean, salty flavor; kosher salt is less "salty" and you will need to use a bit more in your recipes.

***Pepper:*** Freshly ground black pepper adds real punch to a finished salad, so don't skimp on this terrific spice. Manufacturers are even selling peppercorns in small grinders on your grocer's shelf, so buy one and try it. You'll soon be moving on to varicolored peppercorns for added zip!

***Herbs and spices:*** My students are always asking me which I use, fresh or dried herbs. My answer is usually the "30-minute rule"—if the dish needs to simmer for more than 30 minutes, I use the dried version of an herb because it packs more punch and releases its potency over time. For salad dressings, the answer is a bit more fuzzy, but still important. If you want to store a dressing for more than 3 days, then use dried herbs, because they will keep longer (up to a week) once introduced to a liquid. If the dressing will be used within 3 days, use fresh.

Always buy whole dried herbs. The "rubbed" or ground versions contain less essential oils and will not release enough flavor into the finished dish.

*Garlic:* Fresh garlic is always the best choice for salads, but if you intend to store the salad or dressing longer than 3 days, use a granulated garlic product, either garlic salt or powder. I find that the Lawry's brand has a fresh taste and blends well with dressings. I don't recommend the chopped garlic in jars because it tends to have a strong, not-so-garlicky flavor. Invest in a garlic roller (a $5 tool that rolls the peel off the garlic). For chopping and mincing garlic, use a good chef's knife, a Santoku (a cross between a cleaver and a chef's knife), or a cleaver. Garlic intensifies in flavor the smaller it is chopped or minced, so if you want intense garlic flavor, finely chop or mince with a good knife or press the garlic through a press. If you want a hint of garlic in the salad, slice the garlic thickly and remove it before serving. Cooking garlic, either roasting it or slowly sautéing it in olive oil to flavor the oil, will also mellow its flavor.

*Shallots and onions:* Shallots are a delicious addition to salad dressings and add a garlicky onion flavor. Since they are fresh, they will only keep in dressings for about 3 days before they overwhelm the other flavors in the dressing and get soggy. If you want to make a dressing a week ahead of time with dried herbs and spices, omit the shallots and add them a day or two before serving.

*Red onions* are generally sweet and delicious thrown into salads, and I love the colorful contrast to the greens. *Sweet yellow onions*, such as Maui, Walla Walla, Vidalia, Mayan Sweets, and Texas Sweets, are my choice when I include yellow onion in salads. Plain old onions with brown skins don't have the same sugar content, so you will taste the strong raw onion flavor, rather than the sweet crispness characteristic of one of the sweeter varieties. *Scallions and chives* are all part of the spring onion family and provide a fresh, mild flavor in your salads. Try growing them in your garden or on a shelf in your kitchen window.

*Lettuce:* From iceberg to classy field greens, lettuce is the basis for many salads. To save time and energy, I recommend buying bagged salad. Sometimes it can be cheaper than buying heads and cleaning them yourself. If you decide that you want to buy head lettuce

# LETTUCES

**Going into your market** and choosing a lettuce may be almost as confusing as picking out the right wine; there is so much to choose from! Here is a quick buyer's guide to the greens aisle.

**Iceberg lettuce** gets a bad rap, but it's crisp and adds great crunch to salad. I like to use iceberg in salads that will have a heavier dressing, such as ranch or blue cheese, and also to fill out a salad made with tender, more flavorful greens, such as spinach.

**Romaine** is a long leaf lettuce that stands up to heavy or creamy dressings such as Caesar. A halved head of romaine can be sprinkled with extra virgin olive oil, salt, and pepper and broiled for a few minutes, until it begins to turn golden. Remove from the broiler, sprinkle with aged balsamic vinegar and shaved Parmigiano-Reggiano cheese, and serve.

**Red and green leaf lettuces** are soft, with a mild flavor. These can be used for tossing together a quick salad with an oil-based dressing.

**Watercress** has tough stalks that need to be removed. It has a spicy quality and perks up other greens in salad.

**Radicchio** is a tight head of purple and white leaves. It is strongly flavored and sometimes bitter; I like it best grilled, then added to salads, or finely chopped and added to red or green leaf lettuce for contrast.

**Baby spinach** is delicious in salads and can be used with warm or oil-based dressings. Serve it with dressings that will complement it rather than compete (no blue cheese or Caesar on these leaves, please).

**Endive** is usually cut up and used as an accent in salads. The tender inner leaves can also be used on an arranged salad plate.

**Arugula**, sometimes called "rocket," is added to salads as a peppery accent. In Italy they use this with radicchio and dress it with olive oil and Parmesan.

**Boston** and **Bibb lettuces** are two types of butter lettuce, which have soft, buttery leaves. They make an elegant addition to a salad or a good base for a chicken or seafood salad.

**Mesclun** is a French term for a selection of small-leaved lettuces, which may include baby spinach, baby red leaf, arugula, oak leaf varieties, frisée, and mâche. These lettuces are sold mixed together under the names "spring mix," "field greens," or "mesclun" and are used for classic mixed green salads.

or pick it from your garden, a salad spinner makes short work of cleaning and drying the lettuce.

*Tomatoes:* Tomatoes add color and sweet goodness to many salads; I recommend you spend a little extra money and buy vine-ripened ones. During the winter months in cold climates, the tomatoes are generally not very nice, but you can usually get cherry tomatoes, which are sweeter, or plum tomatoes, which are meatier and ripen faster than other types of tomatoes. In the summer, your tomato choices are endless, so use a palette of colors in your salads for the sake of presentation as well as taste.

*Cucumbers:* I use only European or hothouse cucumbers. These are the long, thin cucumbers that are wrapped in plastic in your supermarket. These cukes have more usable flesh than the large waxed variety, because they contain virtually no seeds, which is a big plus. The skin on the European cucumber is so tender that you need not peel it, either. If you are unable to get European cucumbers, buy small pickling cucumbers (such as Kirbys) or the thin Japanese cucumbers because they are mild in flavor, crisp, and sweet. None of those fat, waxed, flavorless cucumbers, please!

*Avocados:* I recommend the Hass variety of avocado, or similar varieties now coming on the market; they are the smaller avocados with a dark, pebbly skin. An avocado is ripe when it gives to slight pressure. If it is firm when you buy it, it will continue to ripen on the counter. Avocado flesh will turn brown when exposed to the air, but sprinkling it with an acid such as lemon or lime juice retards the discoloration. Add avocado to salads just before tossing to minimize the possibility of discoloration.

*Tuna:* I am a great fan of imported Italian tuna packed in olive oil because it has a deeper flavor than tuna packed in water. If you can't get tuna packed in olive oil, I recommend solid albacore packed in vegetable oil.

*Pastas:* Pasta salads are either really delicious or really mediocre. To lift yours out of the ordinary, use an imported dry Italian pasta and cook it just until it is *al dente* (check the package directions and taste the pasta during the last 3 minutes of cooking time). Don't rinse the pasta after draining, but rather toss with a few tablespoons of olive oil or the dressing that you will be using to help keep the pasta from sticking together. Fresh pastas make excellent pasta salads but only need to be cooked 1 to 2 minutes and drained thoroughly. Pasta shapes are important when making a pasta salad; be sure to use a shape that

will show off the ingredients in the salad, such as a shell-shaped pasta that will catch bits of vegetable and meat or fish in the pocket when the salad is tossed together. Once the salad is mixed, refrigerate it; 30 minutes before you are ready to serve it, remove it from the refrigerator and taste it. After refrigeration, the salad will absorb a lot of the seasonings and may need additional dressing or seasonings. Once you have made any adjustments, toss it again before serving.

*Potatoes:* I love potato salads, which I make with any variety of new potato or more mature red, white, or Yukon Gold. Each of these remains firm when boiled or steamed and will stay together when peeled and sliced; they don't fall apart the way a baking or russet potato will. The secret to a great potato salad is to boil or steam the potatoes, then let them cool completely before peeling and cutting them into small pieces; the cooling allows the potatoes to firm back up a bit. Also, tossing the potatoes with a little oil, vinegar, salt, and pepper allows them to absorb other seasonings better; then they are ready to be dressed with your favorite flavors.

*Rice:* I recommend using a long-grain rice, such as Uncle Ben's converted brand, jasmine, or basmati, and wild rice for salads. Short-grain rice and Arborio rice are too sticky to make a decent salad.

*Cheese:* Great cheese makes a great salad, so use imported Parmigiano-Reggiano, Maytag blue, Gorgonzola, French goat cheese, fresh mozzarella, feta, good quality cheddar, and smoked cheeses. Don't try to economize by using the store brand or a lesser cheese; it will only take away from the overall presentation and taste of the salad.

## Salad Dressings

Homemade salad dressings are a great way to make your salads special, and they take very little time to put together. Choose salads that pair well with main courses and that will complement or balance each other. If you are making a Southwestern main course, it might be a good idea to prepare a salad containing fruit to tone down the spice level. In the recipes that follow, I'll make suggestions for pairing salads with main courses for easy entertaining.

When mixing acidic salad dressings, I recommend using glass or stainless steel bowls, which will not react with acid. Aluminum bowls will react with the acid, and that's not a good thing. Blend the ingredients with a whisk to emulsify the dressing. Screw-top jars are great for storing dressings (that old Hellman's/Best Foods mayonnaise jar has a thousand uses). An immersion blender is also dandy for emulsifying dressings, to make them thick and creamy.

## THE DIVA'S 10-MINUTE COOKED CHICKEN

**Salads are a great way** to use leftover chicken, but sometimes you need to start from scratch. The Diva recommends the microwave for cooking moist and delicious chicken breasts, which you can cut up for salads. Place 6 skinless, boneless chicken breast halves in a microwavable dish that will hold them comfortably, spacing them about 1/4 inch apart. Sprinkle 1/4 cup of chicken broth, water, or wine over the breasts, and season with salt and pepper. Cover with plastic wrap, cut two vent holes into the plastic, and microwave on High for 5 to 6 minutes. Allow the chicken to rest (it will continue to cook) for 3 minutes. Slash at the thickest point to make sure the chicken is cooked through—if it is still a bit pink in the center, microwave on High for 1-minute intervals until done. Allow the chicken to cool before you cut it up. No time for cooking chicken? Most grocers carry cut-up cooked chicken breast meat in the deli case, and it can be your best friend when you are in a hurry.

# Layered Vegetable Salad with Creamy Dill and Chive Dressing

Serves 8 to 10

Layered and lovely, this can be made into a main-course salad by adding a layer of cooked chicken chunks, shrimp, crab, or leftover pulled pork.

Creamy Dill and Chive Dressing

**1 cup mayonnaise**

**½ cup milk**

**½ teaspoon lemon pepper**

**2 tablespoons dillweed**

**¼ cup chopped fresh chives**

**1 teaspoon salt**

**½ teaspoon freshly ground black pepper**

**1 teaspoon garlic salt**

Salad

**4 cups chopped salad greens (one 10-ounce bag)**

**1 large red bell pepper, seeded and cut into ½-inch-thick rings**

**4 hard-boiled eggs (see page 142), peeled and sliced**

**4 slices red onion, ½ inch thick, separated into rings**

**1 cup chopped celery**

**4 carrots, coarsely grated**

**One 6-ounce jar marinated artichoke hearts, drained and quartered**

**One 4.5-ounce can julienne beets, drained and patted dry, or 2 cups cherry tomatoes**

**¾ cup freshly grated Parmesan cheese**

**2 cups Garlic Croutons, homemade (page 219) or store-bought**

**1.** To make the dressing, in a small bowl, combine the dressing ingredients and stir to blend.

✳ **DIVA DO-AHEAD:** At this point, you can cover and refrigerate for up to 1 week.

**2.** To assemble the salad, in a large salad bowl, layer the lettuce, red pepper, eggs, red onion, celery, carrots, artichoke hearts, and beets. Spread the dressing over the top of the salad, sealing it, then sprinkle with the cheese.

✳ **DIVA DO-AHEAD:** At this point, cover and refrigerate for at least 4 hours or overnight.

**3.** Before serving, top with the croutons.

# Layered Vegetable Salad with Fresh Herb Dressing 🥤🥤

Serves 10 to 12

Another layered salad, this one has a delightful dressing and pairs well with grilled entrées on your buffet. I love to serve it in a large glass bowl to show off the beautiful colors of the ingredients. A food processor will help make quick work of slicing the vegetables.

### Salad

**Three 10-ounce bags mixed leaf lettuces**

**2 cups shredded carrots**

**1 European cucumber, cut into ¼-inch-thick rounds**

**1 medium-size red onion, cut ¼ inch thick and separated into rings**

**1½ cups finely chopped celery**

**1 bunch radishes, trimmed and sliced ¼ inch thick**

**2 cups frozen petite peas, defrosted**

**Two 4-ounce cans sliced black olives, drained**

**1 red bell pepper, seeded and sliced into ¼-inch-thick rings**

**1 yellow bell pepper, seeded and sliced into ¼-inch-thick rings**

### Fresh Herb Dressing

**2 cups mayonnaise**

**½ cup sour cream**

**2 tablespoons sugar**

**1 tablespoon fresh lemon juice**

**2 tablespoons chopped fresh Italian parsley**

**2 tablespoons chopped fresh basil**

**2 tablespoons chopped fresh tarragon**

**2 to 3 cups finely shredded sharp cheddar cheese, to your taste**

**1.** To assemble the salad, in a large glass salad bowl, layer the vegetables in the order listed.

**2.** To make the dressing, in a medium-size bowl, whisk together the dressing ingredients until well blended. Spread evenly over the top of the salad, sealing the edges, then sprinkle evenly with the cheese.

✳ **DIVA DO-AHEAD:** At this point, cover and refrigerate for at least 12 and up to 24 hours.

**3.** Remove from the refrigerator and toss salad before serving.

### Diva Variation

Add a layer of shredded cooked chicken or tuna, or 2 cups of cooked, drained, and cooled small cheese ravioli or tortellini.

# Mom's Mixed-Up Italian Salad 🥤🥤🍸

Serves 10 to 12

This colorful jumble of flavors and textures is simple to put together and you will get rave reviews. Serve with grilled meats or picnic food, or on a grazing table.

Garlic and Oregano Vinaigrette

**1½ cups olive oil**

**½ cup red wine vinegar**

**3 cloves garlic, minced**

**1 teaspoon salt**

**½ teaspoon freshly ground black pepper**

**2 teaspoons dried oregano**

**1 teaspoon dried marjoram**

Salad

**Two 6-ounce jars roasted red peppers, drained and cut into 1-inch pieces**

**Two 4-ounce cans pitted black olives, drained**

**One 6-ounce jar pimento-stuffed green olives, drained**

**One 4-ounce jar pepperoncini, drained**

**Two 8-ounce jars pickled Italian vegetables (sometimes called giardiniera), drained**

**Two 6-ounce jars marinated artichoke hearts, drained and quartered**

**½ pound salami or pepperoni, cut into ½-inch chunks**

**½ pound aged provolone cheese, cut into ½-inch chunks**

**½ pound button mushrooms, stems trimmed and halved**

**One 10-ounce package field greens**

**1.** To make the vinaigrette, in a medium-size bowl, whisk the vinaigrette ingredients until thickened.

✳ **DIVA DO-AHEAD:** At this point, you can cover and refrigerate for up to 1 week.

**2.** To assemble the salad, put all the salad ingredients, except the field greens, into a large glass salad bowl, pour the dressing over, and toss until everything is well coated.

✳ **DIVA DO-AHEAD:** At this point, cover and refrigerate for at least 24 hours and up to 2 days.

**3.** Drain the salad and serve on a platter lined with the field greens.

# Sugar Snap Pea, Corn, and Bacon Salad

Serves 10 to 12

A crunchy and colorful salad filled with vegetables, this is one recipe you'll be asked for time and again.

### Salad

¼ cup (½ stick) butter

1 cup finely chopped onion

1½ pounds sugar snap peas

4 cups fresh or defrosted frozen corn kernels

### Sweet Mustard Vinaigrette

¾ cup vegetable oil

½ cup rice vinegar

3 tablespoons firmly packed light brown sugar

2 tablespoons Dijon mustard

1 teaspoon salt

1 teaspoon freshly ground black pepper

12 strips bacon, cooked until crisp, drained on paper towels, and crumbled

¼ cup snipped fresh chives

**1.** To make the salad, in a large skillet over medium heat, melt the butter. Cook the onion, stirring, until it begins to caramelize, 10 to 15 minutes.

**2.** Add the peas and cook for another 2 minutes, tossing the peas in the butter-and-onion mixture. Transfer the mixture to a large salad bowl and let the peas cool.

**3.** Add the corn to the bowl and stir to blend.

**4.** To make the vinaigrette, in a medium-size bowl, whisk together the vinaigrette ingredients until thickened. Pour over the salad and toss to blend well.

✳ **DIVA DO-AHEAD:** Cover and refrigerate for at least 4 hours or overnight.

**5.** Remove from the refrigerator 30 minutes before serving and toss with the bacon and chives.

# Green Bean and Smoked Mozzarella Salad

Serves 10 to 12

A variation of this colorful salad combining green beans with smoked mozzarella and balsamic vinaigrette appeared in my book *The Soup Mix Gourmet* (The Harvard Common Press, 2001). The balsamic vinegar will turn the green beans dark once they are tossed with the vinaigrette, so it's important to do this just before serving.

### Rosemary Balsamic Vinaigrette

**1½ cups olive oil**

**¾ cup balsamic vinegar**

**2 tablespoons chopped fresh rosemary**

**2 cloves garlic, minced**

**1 teaspoon salt**

**½ teaspoon freshly ground black pepper**

### Salad

**2 pounds green beans, ends trimmed and cut into 1-inch pieces**

**½ teaspoon salt**

**½ teaspoon freshly ground black pepper**

**6 scallions (white and tender green parts), chopped**

**1½ cups smoked mozzarella cheese cut into matchsticks**

**1 cup pine nuts, toasted (see page 83)**

**¼ cup chopped fresh Italian parsley**

**1.** To make the vinaigrette, in a medium-size bowl, whisk the vinaigrette ingredients until thickened.

✳ **DIVA DO-AHEAD:** At this point, you can cover and refrigerate for up to 5 days. Bring to room temperature before using.

**2.** To begin the salad, cook the green beans in boiling water until crisp-tender, about 7 to 10 minutes. Drain and cool.

**3.** In a large salad bowl, combine the beans, salt, pepper, scallions, and cheese, tossing together until blended.

✳ **DIVA DO-AHEAD:** At this point, you can cover and refrigerate for up to 24 hours.

**4.** When ready to serve, pour the dressing over the beans and toss to coat. Add half the pine nuts and toss again. Serve garnished with the remaining pine nuts and the parsley.

# White Bean Salad with Rosemary-Garlic Oil

Serves 10

This delicious rosemary-flavored salad with tiny white beans pairs wonderfully with seafood, lamb, or chicken. I recommend cooking the white beans yourself, but in a pinch you can use canned (I recommend the Progresso brand), which you will need to drain and rinse.

**2 cups (1 pound) dried small white beans, picked over and rinsed**

**8 cups water**

**¾ cup extra virgin olive oil**

**3 tablespoons chopped fresh rosemary**

**Pinch of red pepper flakes**

**3 cloves garlic, minced**

**1½ teaspoons salt**

**¾ teaspoon freshly ground black pepper**

**½ cup red wine vinegar**

**½ cup finely chopped shallots**

**¼ cup finely chopped fresh Italian parsley**

**Cherry tomatoes for garnish**

**1.** Combine the beans and water in a 6-quart pot, bring to a boil, and continue boiling for 2 minutes. Remove from the heat and let stand for 1 hour.

**2.** Pour off the water and add 8 cups of fresh water. Bring to a boil, reduce the heat to medium, and simmer until the beans are tender, about 30 minutes. Drain well and transfer to a large bowl.

**3.** Heat the oil in a small saucepan over low heat, add the rosemary, red pepper flakes, and garlic, and cook, stirring, for 2 to 3 minutes; don't let the garlic brown. Remove the garlic oil from the heat and let cool to room temperature.

**4.** Pour some of the rosemary-garlic oil over the beans and toss together to coat the beans well. Season with the salt and pepper and stir in the vinegar, shallots, and half the parsley. Taste and adjust the seasonings if necessary, adding more oil, salt, and/or pepper.

✳ **DIVA DO-AHEAD:** At this point, you can cover and refrigerate for up to 2 days or leave at room temperature for up to 4 hours. Bring to room temperature before continuing.

**5.** Toss the salad, adding more rosemary-garlic oil if necessary. Just before serving, fold in the remaining parsley and garnish with the tomatoes.

# Roasted Wild Mushroom Salad 🍺🍷🥂

Serves 10 to 12

Earthy mushrooms intensify in flavor when they are roasted at a high temperature for a short period of time. Great in a salad, they are also delicious all by themselves and can be served alongside roasted meats as a condiment.

**2 pounds assorted fresh wild mushrooms, such as shiitake, oyster, porcini, portobello, and cremini, stems trimmed or removed and caps cut in half or quarters, depending upon their size**

**1 cup extra virgin olive oil**

**¼ cup balsamic vinegar**

**2 teaspoons salt**

**1 teaspoon freshly ground black pepper**

**3 cloves garlic, minced**

**2 tablespoons chopped fresh rosemary**

**Three 10-ounce bags mixed field greens**

**½ cup shaved Parmigiano-Reggiano cheese for garnish**

**1.** Preheat the oven to 425°F. Line a jelly roll pan with a silicone baking liner or aluminum foil.

**2.** Put the mushrooms in a large bowl. In a small bowl, whisk together the oil, vinegar, salt, pepper, garlic, and rosemary.

**3.** Pour ½ cup of the vinaigrette over the mushrooms, toss to coat, and spread out the mushrooms in a single layer on the baking sheet. Bake until fragrant and golden brown, about 20 minutes, and remove from the oven. Let cool for 10 minutes, then transfer to a clean bowl.

✳ **DIVA DO-AHEAD:** At this point, you can cover and refrigerate for up to 2 days. Reheat gently in a hot skillet before continuing.

**4.** When ready to serve, put the field greens in a large salad bowl and add the mushrooms (and their liquid) to the bowl. Add the remaining dressing to the salad and toss to coat. Garnish with the shavings of Parmigiano-Reggiano and serve immediately.

# Roasted Beet Salad

Serves 10 to 12

Beets are a neglected vegetable on the buffet table and it's a shame because they not only lend color to the table, but are also delicious and good for you, with lots of vitamins and minerals. Serve these marinated beets and shallots garnished with chives, or add them to a field green or an arugula salad garnished with goat cheese.

10 medium-size beets, scrubbed clean and ends trimmed  *5*

( 6 medium-size shallots, cut in half )

1¼ cups olive oil  *3/4 c.*

½ cup balsamic vinegar  *1/4 c.*

2 teaspoons salt  *1 t.*

1 teaspoon freshly ground black pepper  *1/2 t.*

( ¼ cup finely chopped fresh chives )

**1.** Preheat the oven to 400°F and line a baking sheet with a silicone liner, parchment paper, or aluminum foil.

**2.** Put the beets and shallots in a large bowl and pour ¼ cup of the oil over them, stirring to coat. Transfer to the prepared baking sheet and roast until the beets are tender when tested with a sharp knife, 40 to 50 minutes. Remove from the oven and let cool completely. Peel the beets, cut into bite-size pieces, and place in a salad bowl. Peel and coarsely chop the shallots and add them to the bowl.

✳ **DIVA DO-AHEAD:** At this point, you can cover and refrigerate for up to 3 days.

**3.** In a small bowl, whisk together the remaining 1 cup of oil, and the vinegar,

salt, and pepper until thickened. Pour over the beets and shallots.

✳ **DIVA DO-AHEAD:** At this point, cover and marinate at room temperature for up to 2 hours or in the refrigerator for up to 3 days. Bring to room temperature before continuing.

**4.** Garnish the beets with the chives and serve.

The Diva Says:

When peeling beets, wear rubber gloves because the beet juice will stain your hands.

## Diva Variations

Cut the roasted beets into ½-inch-thick slices, rather than bite-sized pieces, and arrange them attractively on a platter with the shallots. Then pour the dressing over and allow to marinate as directed. If you like, alternate slices of fresh fennel bulb with the beets.

No time to roast beets? Substitute four 14-ounce cans baby beets, drained, and ½ cup chopped shallots. Quarter the beets and toss with the shallots and dressing.

✳ **DIVA DO-AHEAD:** Cover and refrigerate for at least 2 hours and up to 3 days.

# Marinated Red Onions

Makes about 3 cups

A large bowl of marinated red onions on a buffet table is a terrific condiment to serve with grilled meats or chicken. The onions are also great with burgers at a barbecue or as an addition to a salad bar.

**2 large red onions, cut in half and thinly sliced into half-moons (about 3 cups)**

**¾ cup red wine vinegar**

**½ cup sugar**

**½ cup vegetable oil**

**Pinch of red pepper flakes**

**1 teaspoon dried oregano**

**1 teaspoon salt**

**½ teaspoon freshly ground black pepper**

**1.** Place the onions in a glass bowl.

**2.** In a medium-size bowl, whisk together the vinegar, sugar, oil, pepper flakes, oregano, salt, and pepper. Pour over the onions.

✳ **DIVA DO-AHEAD:** At this point, cover and refrigerate for at least 8 and up to 24 hours.

**3.** Drain the onions.

✳ **DIVA DO-AHEAD:** At this point, you can cover and refrigerate for up to 4 days.

Serve cold or at room temperature.

# Marinated Grilled Vegetable Salad

Serves 12

Marinated grilled vegetables are simple to prepare, and the best part is that you can grill them up to 2 days ahead of time, then marinate them until you are ready to serve. If you have a gas or charcoal grill, light it up and grill in the great outdoors, but you can also broil these in your oven and get a terrific result. The recipe is pretty loose regarding the choice of vegetables, which is really up to you. Just remember to grill similar vegetables together so that they cook for the same amount of time; otherwise, you'll be turning everything every few minutes. Serve this salad with pita, Bruschetta Toasts (page 127), or focaccia.

### Grilled Vegetables

1½ cups olive oil

1 tablespoon salt

2 teaspoons freshly ground black pepper

6 cloves garlic, minced

1 large purple eggplant, cut into ½-inch-thick slices

4 bell peppers in assorted colors, seeded and each cut into 4 wedges

3 medium-size zucchini, cut lengthwise into ½-inch-thick slices

3 medium-size yellow squash, cut into ¾-inch-thick rounds

2 medium-size red onions, sliced ¾ inch thick

2 fennel bulbs, feathery ends cut off, bulbs trimmed and cut into ¾-inch-thick slices

10 plum tomatoes, cut in half lengthwise

1 pound thick-stemmed asparagus (optional), thick bottoms trimmed

### Grilled Vegetable Marinade

1 cup olive oil

½ cup red wine vinegar

2 cloves garlic, minced

¼ cup thinly sliced fresh basil

1½ teaspoons salt

1 teaspoon freshly ground black pepper

½ cup chopped fresh Italian parsley

**1.** In a small bowl, combine the oil, salt, pepper, and garlic, stirring to blend.

**2.** Preheat a gas or charcoal grill. Brush the vegetables with the oil, and grill over high heat until the vegetables are tender but still crisp. Remove from the grill.

**3.** To make the marinade, in a medium-size bowl, whisk together the marinade ingredients.

**4.** In a large glass salad bowl or 13 x 9-inch baking dish, layer the vegetables, pouring some of the marinade over each layer and sprinkling with some of the parsley. When you are finished layering, pour any remaining marinade over the top and sprinkle with any remaining parsley.

✳ **DIVA DO-AHEAD:** At this point, cover and refrigerate for at least 3 hours and up to 2 days. Bring to room temperature before serving.

### The Diva Says:

To grill indoors in your broiler, preheat the broiler for 10 minutes. Line sheet pans with aluminum foil, place the vegetables on the pans, and brush with the seasoned oil. Broil 4 inches from the heat and turn when the vegetables begin to color. Continue to broil the vegetables until they are done and proceed as directed.

I find it easiest to leave the skin on the eggplant for grilling because it helps the eggplant retain its shape (otherwise, it may fall apart on the grill). If the skin is tough, I remove it after grilling.

# Marinated Orange Salad

Serves 10 to 12

Try this colorful salad on your buffet table for a change of pace. I like to use regular navel oranges and the new pink ones sold as Cara Cara here in California. If you can find blood oranges, they provide a beautiful contrast in the salad as well.

> 12 navel oranges (6 pink and 6 regular if possible)
>
> ½ cup extra virgin olive oil
>
> 3 tablespoons red wine vinegar
>
> 2 teaspoons dried oregano

**1.** Cut the ends off the oranges, then stand them on a cut end and, using a sharp knife, cut away the skin from the top to the bottom, totally removing the peel and white pith. Slice them ½ inch thick and arrange on a serving platter.

✳ **DIVA DO-AHEAD:** At this point, you can cover and refrigerate overnight.

**2.** In a small bowl, whisk together the oil, vinegar, and oregano until thickened. Pour over the oranges.

✳ **DIVA DO-AHEAD:** At this point, marinate for at least 2 and up to 6 hours at room temperature.

**3.** At least 30 minutes before serving, turn the oranges in the marinade, and drain off any excess. (When oranges are marinated they tend to give up some of their juice, and you don't want too much liquid.)

## Diva Variation

**Marinated Orange and Fennel Salad:** Another riff on this same idea is to trim 4 fennel bulbs and slice them very thinly (break out that mandoline, if you've got one), then alternate them with the orange slices. Sprinkle with the dressing and marinate as directed above.

# FRUIT SALADS

**Fresh fruit is a no-brainer** for salad. Just cut up the fruit and arrange it in a bowl, on a platter, or in a hollowed-out watermelon (see page 171). The possible combinations are endless, depending on which fruits are in season. Garnish the platters with wedges or slices of oranges, lemons, and/or limes and finely sliced mint leaves.

Fruit salads bring a sweet balance to the table, especially at a luncheon or brunch. During the summer, when fresh fruits are at their peak, a fruit salad is a great way to add color and a cooling flavor to your celebrations. When there isn't an abundance of fresh fruit, you can supplement with frozen fruits, such as peaches, mangoes, pineapple, strawberries, and blueberries. Just remember that frozen fruits tend to "drool" a bit, so make sure you defrost and drain them thoroughly before adding them to your bowl. You can also toss in some dried apricots, which will plump when mixed with the other fruit.

Cut-up fresh fruit can be stored, covered, in a bowl or in zipper-top plastic bags in your refrigerator overnight, so do this chore the day before the party. If you have fruits that will discolor when they are peeled and cut, such as peaches, apples, and pears, sprinkle them with a bit of lemon juice to retard discoloration, or sprinkle them with Fruit Fresh, a preservative that you can usually find in the baking aisle of your supermarket, with the pectin and canning supplies.

Fresh cut-up fruit is also sold in some produce departments. If you decide to buy some, add your own touches, such as fresh blueberries, raspberries, or peaches. If this is all too labor-intensive for you, you can always order a fruit platter from your local deli—it will come already cut up and garnished for you.

# Fruit and Gruyère Salad with Dijon-Honey Dressing

Serves 10 to 12

This delicious salad pairs Gruyère cheese, apples, and pears with a tangy dressing to give you a real showstopper for your buffet table. Make sure there is lots of crusty bread—it makes a great accompaniment.

## Dijon-Honey Dressing

**1 cup vegetable oil**

**½ cup rice vinegar**

**2 tablespoons Dijon mustard**

**2 teaspoons honey**

**1½ teaspoons salt**

**⅛ teaspoon cayenne pepper**

## Salad

**4 ripe pears, cored and cut into ½-inch-thick wedges**

**4 large Gala or another crisp eating apple, cored and cut into ½-inch-thick wedges**

**2 tablespoons fresh lemon juice**

**½ pound Gruyère cheese, cut into ½-inch-thick slices, then cut into 1-inch pieces**

**4 cups seedless red grapes, cut in half**

**1 cup pecan or walnut halves, toasted (see page 83), for garnish**

### Diva Variations

Other good choices for cheese in this salad are Monterey Jack, Brie (with the rind removed), sharp white cheddar, and crumbled blue cheese.

**1.** To make the dressing, in a medium-size bowl, whisk together the dressing ingredients until thickened.

✳ **DIVA DO-AHEAD:** At this point, you can cover and refrigerate for up to 1 week.

**2.** To assemble the salad, put the pears and apples in a large bowl and sprinkle with the lemon juice, tossing to coat. Arrange the pears and apples on a serving platter, alternating them with pieces of cheese, until the platter is filled. Scatter the grapes over the top.

✳ **DIVA DO-AHEAD:** At this point, you can cover and refrigerate for up to 24 hours.

**3.** When ready to serve, drizzle the dressing over the salad and sprinkle with the pecans.

# Spinach Salad with Strawberries and Raspberry Vinaigrette

Serves 10 to 12

An elegant and simple salad, this is delightful during the holidays because of its red and green color combination, but I love to serve it any time of the year. It's especially good as a basis for another salad, say Chicken Tortellini Salad with Artichokes and Snow Peas (page 205) or Curried Chicken Salad (page 207). If you aren't able to get great strawberries, substitute unsweetened dried cranberries, which are nice with spinach as well.

## Raspberry Vinaigrette

**1 cup raspberry vinegar**

**½ cup sugar**

**⅓ cup chopped red onion**

**2 teaspoons Dijon mustard**

**¼ cup poppy seeds**

**1 cup vegetable oil**

## Salad

**Four 10-ounce bags baby spinach**

**2 cups hulled and sliced fresh strawberries**

**1.** To make the vinaigrette, in a medium-size bowl, whisk the vinaigrette ingredients until thickened.

**✳ DIVA DO-AHEAD:** At this point, you can cover and refrigerate for up to 3 days.

**2.** When ready to serve, assemble the salad. Combine the spinach and strawberries in a large salad bowl and toss with some of the dressing, adding more to taste. Serve immediately.

# CARVING A WATERMELON CONTAINER

**A hollowed-out watermelon** makes a terrific container for displaying fruit. You can freeze the melon shell before filling it, which will keep the fruit cold for about 3 hours on the buffet table. To begin, slice off a piece from the bottom of the watermelon with a carving knife so that the shell will lie flat. If you like, draw a decorative cutting line all the way around the melon, about a third of the way down from the top. Next take a small paring knife to cut out the design, digging into the melon about 1½ to 2 inches. You should be able to loosen the top and lift it off. Or just cut off the top of the melon in a straight line. Using a melon baller or sharp knife, remove the flesh from the top and bottom of the melon, leaving about a 1-inch-thick shell in the bottom. Cut the flesh into bite-sized pieces and store in zipper-top plastic bags overnight. Put the melon shell in a 2-gallon zipper-top plastic bag, or if it won't fit, wrap it in aluminum foil and freeze or refrigerate.

When you are ready to serve the salad, mix the fruits together and pile them into the shell. Garnish with chopped fresh mint, citrus slices or wedges, and any other fruits that add color and interest. Kiwis, strawberries, or small Champagne grapes are nice. You can also toss the mixed fruit with Champagne; Prosecco; a sweet white wine, such as a Riesling; or a liqueur, like Grand Marnier or amaretto.

All of these are good choices for your watermelon container:

- **Berries** (all varieties, sliced or whole)
- **Seedless grapes**
- **Pitted cherries** (frozen and defrosted will work well here, too)
- **Kiwis**
- **Mangoes**
- **Papayas**
- **Pineapples**
- **Orange segments**
- **Red grapefruit segments**
- **Apples**
- **Pears** (including Asian pears)
- **Peaches** (peeled)
- **Nectarines** (peeled)
- **Apricots** (peeled fresh or dried)
- **Plums** (peeled)
- **Melons** (all varieties)

# Cranberry–Blue Cheese Field Greens Salad 🥛🍷🍶

Serves 10 to 12

Cranberries, blue cheese, and a simple dressing turn greens into a spectacular addition to any dinner party. Add some spicy pecans (see page 143) to take this over the top.

### Vinaigrette

**½ cup olive oil**

**½ cup canola oil**

**½ cup rice vinegar**

**1½ teaspoons salt**

**1 teaspoon freshly ground black pepper**

### Salad

**Four 10-ounce bags mixed field greens**

**1 cup unsweetened dried cranberries**

**¾ cup crumbled blue cheese**

**1.** To make the vinaigrette, in a medium-size bowl, whisk the vinaigrette ingredients until thickened.

✳ **DIVA DO-AHEAD:** At this point, you can cover and refrigerate for up to 2 weeks.

**2.** When ready to serve, assemble the salad. Put the greens in a large salad bowl and top with the cranberries and blue cheese. Pour some of the dressing over the salad and toss until coated. Add more dressing if needed and serve immediately.

## PACKAGED SALAD

**There are all kinds** of packaged salads in your supermarket. Some are blends, while others contain just one variety of lettuce. Here are some you might find in your produce section:

● American blend is usually iceberg lettuce with grated carrots, sliced radishes, and shredded red cabbage; this is what you see at salad bars.

● Italian blend is usually a tiny bit of arugula, romaine, and maybe some chopped radicchio.

● Lafayette or butter lettuce blend is a mix of butter lettuce and radicchio.

● European blend contains romaine, radicchio, endive, and leaf lettuces.

# Field Greens with Basil Vinaigrette 🥛🍷🥂

Serves 10

Field greens tossed with vinaigrette are like a strand of pearls with a little black dress, understated and classy, and they dress up the main course beautifully. This vinaigrette is flavored with fresh basil, but you can substitute fresh oregano or Italian parsley if you would like. The possibilities for garnishing this salad are endless: Try Marinated Red Onions (page 165); Spicy Nuts (page 143) made with pecans; crumbled goat, feta, or blue cheese; or shavings of Asiago or Parmesan cheese. This is your palette and you should paint it the way you want it!

### Basil Vinaigrette

**¾ cup extra virgin olive oil**

**⅓ cup balsamic vinegar**

**1½ teaspoons salt**

**½ teaspoon freshly ground black pepper**

**¼ cup finely chopped shallots**

**¼ cup thinly sliced fresh basil**

### Salad

**Two 10-ounce packages mixed field greens**

**1.** To make the vinaigrette, in a medium-size bowl, whisk the vinaigrette ingredients until thickened.

✳ **DIVA DO-AHEAD:** At this point, you can cover and refrigerate for up to 3 days; the taste will be fresher if you add the shallots and basil right before using, but the choice is yours. Bring to room temperature before using.

**2.** When ready to serve, assemble the salad. Put the greens in a large salad bowl. Toss with some of the vinaigrette, adding more to taste. Serve immediately.

## Getting Your Dressing Ready

Olive oil will solidify under refrigeration, so make sure you take the dressing out of the refrigerator 30 minutes before serving and reblend it before tossing with the salad ingredients. Some recipes in this chapter call for a blend of half olive oil and half vegetable oil, which will not solidify in the refrigerator.

# Ryan's Creamy Caesar Salad

Serves 10 to 12

I don't know anyone who doesn't like a Caesar salad. Even my finicky son loves Caesar, but his has to be creamy, without visible anchovies! This salad dressing is multipurpose and can be used to dress a pasta or potato salad, as well as romaine leaves.

Caesar salad is said to have originated about 20 miles from my house, at the Hotel Caesar in Tijuana, Baja California. Since it was invented all those years ago, it has morphed into an industry, with bottled dressings on every grocery shelf, and the salad on almost every restaurant menu. The original never had anchovies, but rather Worcestershire sauce, as the salty counterpart. I love the combination of the anchovy paste and Worcestershire to liven up this delicious dressing.

### Caesar Dressing

**1 cup mayonnaise**

**½ cup sour cream**

**½ cup freshly grated Parmesan cheese**

**2 teaspoons fresh lemon juice**

**1½ teaspoons anchovy paste**

**2 cloves garlic, minced**

**2 teaspoons Worcestershire sauce**

**1½ teaspoons freshly ground black pepper**

### Salad

**Four 10-ounce bags hearts of romaine, chopped**

**1 cup shredded Parmesan cheese**

**4 cups Garlic Croutons, homemade (page 219) or store-bought**

**1.** To make the dressing, in a medium-size bowl, whisk together the dressing ingredients until smooth.

✳ **DIVA DO-AHEAD:** At this point, cover and refrigerate for at least 4 hours and up to 5 days.

**2.** When ready to serve, assemble the salad. Put the romaine in a large salad bowl and toss with the dressing until evenly coated. Add the Parmesan and croutons and toss again until well coated. Serve immediately.

### Diva Variations

**Chicken Caesar:** Toss in 3 to 4 cups of cooked chicken in bite-size pieces.

**Shrimp Caesar:** Toss in 2 pounds of cooked, peeled, medium-size shrimp.

# Blue Cheese Caesar Salad

Serves 10 to 12

The latest evolution of the Caesar has been the introduction of blue cheese to the classic salad. I love this version with creamy Gorgonzola and toasted pecans instead of the Parmesan and croutons.

### Blue Cheese Caesar Dressing

½ cup fresh lemon juice

2 cloves garlic, minced

1 tablespoon Worcestershire sauce

1 teaspoon Dijon mustard

1½ teaspoons freshly ground black pepper

1⅓ cups olive oil

1½ cups crumbled Gorgonzola cheese

### Salad

Two 10-ounce bags red leaf lettuce mix

Two 10-ounce bags hearts of romaine

1½ cups pecan halves, toasted (see page 83)

**1.** To make the dressing, in a medium-size bowl, whisk together the lemon juice, garlic, Worcestershire, mustard, and pepper until blended. Gradually whisk in the oil until incorporated, then stir in the Gorgonzola.

✳ **DIVA DO-AHEAD:** At this point, you can cover and refrigerate for up to 3 days.

**2.** When ready to serve, assemble the salad. Place the lettuces in a large salad bowl, shake the dressing and pour half of it over the salad, and toss to blend. Add 1 cup of the pecans and more dressing if desired, and toss again. Garnish the salad with the remaining ½ cup of pecans and serve immediately.

# Caprese Salad

Serves 10 to 12

This vibrant salad of tomatoes in assorted colors, fresh mozzarella, and pungent basil is a beautiful addition to your buffet table. Serve this when tomatoes are at their peak in summer. Try to find red, orange, and yellow ones at your farmers' market, or maybe heirlooms, which also come in a variety of colors. And make sure you use a high quality extra virgin olive oil.

**6 large vine-ripened tomatoes in a variety of colors**

**2 bunches fresh basil (you will need about 40 leaves), thinly sliced**

**1½ to 2 pounds fresh mozzarella cheese, sliced ¼ inch thick**

**2 teaspoons salt**

**1 teaspoon freshly ground black pepper**

**1½ cups extra virgin olive oil**

### Diva Variations

When fresh basil isn't available, arrange the tomatoes and mozzarella and season with salt and pepper. Mix together ½ cup of pesto and 2 tablespoons of extra virgin olive oil and dress the salad with the pesto oil.

**Chicken Caprese Salad:** Slice 6 cooked boneless, skinless chicken breast halves thinly on an angle and arrange on the plate in layers with the tomatoes, mozzarella, and basil. Sprinkle the salad with ¼ cup of fresh lemon juice and then the olive oil before serving.

**1.** Arrange a tomato slice on the platter, sprinkle a few pieces of basil over the tomato, arrange a slice of mozzarella overlapping the tomato, and continue the arrangement, alternating the tomato and basil with the mozzarella, until the platter is filled.

✳ **DIVA DO-AHEAD:** At this point, you can cover and refrigerate for up to 8 hours.

**2.** One hour before serving, remove the platter from the refrigerator, sprinkle with the salt and pepper, and drizzle all over with the olive oil. Garnish with any additional basil leaves and serve at room temperature.

### The Diva Says:

Fresh mozzarella is easiest to cut when it is cold, so make sure you cut it right from the refrigerator.

# Nonna's Bread and Tomato Salad 🥛🥃🍷

Serves 12

Grandma Aleandra Pasquini was an amazing cook and, even though tomatoes were not my favorite as a child, she could always get me to eat this brilliant red, white, and green salad. This is a great way to use up stale bread and a bumper crop of vine-ripened tomatoes.

## Basil and Parsley Vinaigrette

**1 cup olive oil**

**⅓ cup red wine vinegar**

**1½ teaspoons salt**

**1 teaspoon freshly ground black pepper**

**½ cup thinly sliced fresh basil leaves**

**¼ cup finely chopped fresh Italian parsley**

**¼ cup finely chopped red onion**

## Salad

**8 large vine-ripened tomatoes, seeded, chopped, and drained in a colander for 30 minutes**

**6 cups day-old Italian bread, cut into ½-inch cubes**

**1.** To make the vinaigrette, in a medium-size bowl, whisk together the vinaigrette ingredients until thickened.

❋ **DIVA DO-AHEAD:** At this point, you can cover tightly and refrigerate for up to 3 days.

**2.** To make the salad, put the tomatoes and bread in a large salad bowl and drizzle with the vinaigrette, tossing to coat well. Let the salad sit for at least 1 hour to absorb the dressing before serving at room temperature.

# Tomato, Olive, and Feta Salad

Serves 10 to 12

Tomatoes and cucumbers are a match made in salad heaven, and this combination pairs them with salty olives and feta cheese. The salad is great served with grilled entrées, or as an addition to a salad buffet.

## Dill and Garlic Dressing

½ cup vegetable oil

½ cup olive oil

½ cup red wine vinegar

2 teaspoons sugar

2 cloves garlic, minced

2 tablespoons dillweed

2 teaspoons dried oregano

1 teaspoon freshly ground black pepper

## Salad

6 medium-size vine-ripened tomatoes, seeded and chopped

2 European cucumbers, cut into ½-inch dice

1½ cups Kalamata olives, drained, pitted, and coarsely chopped

1 cup crumbled feta cheese

1 cup finely chopped red onion

¼ cup chopped fresh dill for garnish (optional)

**1.** To make the dressing, in a medium-size bowl, whisk together the dressing ingredients until thickened.

❋ **DIVA DO-AHEAD:** At this point, you can cover and refrigerate for up to 1 week.

**2.** To assemble the salad, combine the salad ingredients in a large salad bowl. Pour the dressing over the vegetables and toss gently to coat well.

❋ **DIVA DO-AHEAD:** At this point, cover and refrigerate for at least 4 hours and up to 8 hours.

**3.** Remove from the refrigerator 30 minutes before serving, drain off any excess dressing, and serve, garnished with the dill if using.

### Diva Variation

**Tomato, Olive, and Feta Pasta Salad:** Toss this salad with 1 pound of cooked fusilli (corkscrew pasta) and serve as a pasta salad.

# Diane's Original Chopped Salad

Serves 12

I don't know whether this is even close to the original recipe from Los Angeles, but we all love the flavors in this simple salad at my house. I've usually got the ingredients on hand and can toss it together when unexpected company stops in. The cut-up meats and veggies can be prepped several days ahead of time. It's great as a side salad or as a whole meal.

Dressing

**1 cup olive oil**

**½ cup white wine vinegar**

**1½ teaspoons salt**

**1 teaspoon freshly ground black pepper**

**1 teaspoon sugar**

**2 cloves garlic, minced**

Salad

**Four 10-ounce bags American salad blend (iceberg, carrots, red cabbage) or your choice of lettuces**

**¼ pound thinly sliced Genoa salami or pepperoni, cut into matchsticks**

**2 cups diced cooked chicken (½-inch dice)**

**1½ cups shredded Monterey Jack or mozzarella cheese**

**½ cup sliced black olives, drained**

**1 European cucumber, cut in half and sliced into ½-inch-thick half-moons**

**2 cups cherry tomatoes**

**6 scallions (white and tender green parts), chopped**

**1.** To make the dressing, in a small bowl, whisk together the dressing ingredients until thickened.

✳ **DIVA DO-AHEAD:** At this point, you can cover and refrigerate for up to 3 days.

**2.** When ready to serve, assemble the salad. Combine the ingredients in a large salad bowl and toss with some of the dressing to coat. Add additional dressing as desired, toss the salad again, and serve immediately.

The Diva Says:

Although many foodies frown upon iceberg lettuce, I like the crunch it gives to certain salads. You can certainly substitute your favorite greens in this salad; romaine would be nice.

# Asian Chopped Salad with Hoisin-Ginger Dressing

Serves 12

A dressing of hoisin and rice vinegar turns these ingredients into an Oriental meal or side salad for the buffet table.

### Hoisin-Ginger Dressing

**1 cup vegetable oil**

**⅓ cup hoisin sauce (in the Asian section of your supermarket)**

**½ cup rice vinegar**

**2 tablespoons soy sauce**

**2 teaspoons peeled and grated fresh ginger**

**2 cloves garlic, minced**

### Salad

**Two 10-ounce bags baby spinach**

**Two 10-ounce bags hearts of romaine**

**4 medium-size carrots, coarsely grated**

**6 scallions (white and tender green parts), chopped**

**3 cups thin strips of cooked chicken, turkey, or duck**

**One 29-ounce can mandarin orange segments, drained**

**2 cups chopped cashews**

**1.** To make the dressing, in a medium-size bowl, whisk together the dressing ingredients until smooth.

✳ **DIVA DO-AHEAD:** At this point, you can cover and refrigerate for up to 3 days.

**2.** When ready to serve, assemble the salad. Combine the spinach, romaine, carrots, scallions, chicken, and orange segments in a large salad bowl. Toss with some of the dressing, adding more if necessary. Sprinkle with the cashews and serve immediately.

## Chopped Salads

In the '80s, chopped salad was the darling of the Hollywood crowd, who, of course, wanted their dressing on the side. The original has been lost in the many variations, and now there are all manner of chopped salads—basically, whatever you want to chop up and toss together. Many of these salads are my personal favorites for serving to family and friends because they combine so many wonderful ingredients and each bite has a new taste, texture, and crunch. If you would like to serve them without the meat, please feel free to do so.

Chopped salads can be prepped up to 24 hours ahead of time, and the vegetables and meat stored separately in zipper-top plastic bags or storage containers. Just before serving, toss everything into your salad bowl and mix together. Some of the dressings can be prepared days in advance and refrigerated as well.

# Crab Louis Chopped Salad

Serves 10

Luxurious lump crabmeat is pricey, but this salad, a takeoff on the classic Crab Louis, is a great way to stretch a pound of crab into a salad to serve as a main course. This makes a great summer meal and can be used for a ladies' luncheon or as part of a picnic or tailgate. I like to use sturdy greens here, such as romaine or iceberg, rather than baby lettuces or field greens.

**2 packages American salad blend or your choice of salad greens**

**1 European cucumber, cut into ½-inch dice**

**4 ribs celery, finely chopped**

**¼ cup chopped fresh chives**

**2 cups cherry or pear tomatoes, varicolored if possible**

**One 16-ounce package frozen white corn, defrosted and drained**

**1 pound lump crabmeat, picked over for shells and cartilage**

**1½ cups mayonnaise**

**½ cup ketchup**

**3 scallions (white part only), finely chopped**

**2 tablespoons sweet pickle relish**

**4 pimento-stuffed green olives, finely chopped**

**1 tablespoon finely chopped fresh Italian parsley**

**6 hard-boiled eggs, peeled and sliced, for garnish**

**1.** In a large salad bowl, layer the salad greens, cucumber, celery, chives, tomatoes, corn, and crabmeat.

✳ **DIVA DO-AHEAD:** At this point, you can cover and refrigerate for up to 24 hours.

**2.** In a medium-size bowl, combine the mayonnaise, ketchup, scallions, relish, olives, and parsley, stirring to blend.

✳ **DIVA DO-AHEAD:** At this point, cover and refrigerate for at least 4 hours and up to 1 week.

**3.** When ready to serve, toss the salad with about half of the dressing and arrange the hard-boiled eggs around the top of the salad. Dot the eggs with dressing and serve immediately.

## The Diva Says:

Some Louis dressings are pureed for a less chunky version. If you like yours smooth, process all the ingredients in a food processor.

# Tossed Cobb Salad

Serves 12

Cobb salads have been around since the 1930s, when the Brown Derby Restaurant in Hollywood began serving them. The original included diced chicken, bacon, avocado, hard-boiled eggs, tomatoes, and crumbled blue cheese, artfully arranged on a bed of lettuce. This chopped version has all the ingredients, but it's much easier to prepare and serve. The dressing is terrific on other greens and on potato salads and pasta salads.

### Dressing

1½ cups vegetable oil

⅔ cup red wine vinegar

1 teaspoon sugar

2 tablespoons fresh lemon juice

1½ teaspoons salt

2 teaspoons Worcestershire sauce

2 teaspoons Dijon mustard

2 cloves garlic, minced

1 teaspoon freshly ground black pepper

### Salad

Four 10-ounce bags salad greens (mix it up here with romaine, American salad blend, and field greens)

2 cups cherry tomatoes (varicolored varieties would be terrific)

3 cups diced or julienned cooked chicken breast (½-inch dice or matchsticks)

1 pound sliced bacon, cooked until crisp, drained on paper towels, and crumbled

2 ripe Hass avocados, peeled, pitted, and diced

6 hard-boiled eggs, peeled and diced

1½ cups crumbled Maytag or another blue cheese

**1.** In a medium-size bowl, whisk together the dressing ingredients until thickened.

❋ **DIVA DO-AHEAD:** At this point, you can cover and refrigerate for up to 3 days.

**2.** When ready to serve, assemble the salad. Combine the lettuce, tomatoes, chicken, bacon, avocado, eggs, and 1 cup of the blue cheese in a large salad bowl. Pour ⅔ cup of the dressing over the salad and toss to coat well. Taste, adding more dressing if needed. Garnish with the remaining ½ cup of blue cheese and serve immediately.

### Diva Variation

**Steak Chopped Cobb:** If you have leftover steak or roast beef, cut it into matchsticks and substitute for the chicken.

# Chopped Mediterranean Salad with Chicken, Olives, and Feta 🥤🥤

Serves 12

A little bit of everything from the Mediterranean goes into this tasty salad. Garnish it with torn pieces of pita instead of the usual croutons.

Dressing

1⅓ cups olive oil

⅓ cup red wine vinegar

2 tablespoons fresh lemon juice

3 cloves garlic, minced

¼ cup finely chopped fresh oregano

2 tablespoons chopped fresh rosemary

1½ teaspoons salt

1 teaspoon freshly ground black pepper

Salad

Four 10-ounce bags romaine or American salad blend

2 cups cherry tomatoes, cut in half

½ cup diced red onion

1 European cucumber, diced

1 medium-size yellow bell pepper, seeded and diced

1 medium-size red bell pepper, seeded and diced

1½ cups Kalamata olives, drained, pitted, and chopped

3 cups diced cooked chicken (½-inch dice)

1¼ cups crumbled feta cheese

Six 6-inch pita rounds, torn into 1-inch pieces

**1.** To make the dressing, in a medium-size bowl, whisk together the dressing ingredients until thickened.

✳ **DIVA DO-AHEAD:** At this point, you can cover and refrigerate for up to 3 days.

**2.** When ready to serve, assemble the salad. Combine the lettuce, tomatoes, onion, cucumber, bell peppers, olives, and chicken in a large salad bowl. Toss with some of the dressing and add the feta. Toss again, adding more dressing if needed. Garnish with the torn pita and serve immediately.

## Diva Variation

This salad is also delicious if you substitute 2 pounds of medium-size cooked shrimp for the chicken, or one 1-pound flank steak, grilled (see page 391) and cut into thin slices.

# Chopped Salad à la Française

Serves 12

This is my version of a chopped Salade Niçoise, the classic French main-course salad. This salad is great picnic fare, especially when packed into a hollowed-out round sourdough or French bread. For a not-so-Niçoise salad, you could substitute 3 cups of shredded cooked chicken for the tuna.

Dijon-Shallot Vinaigrette

**1½ cups olive oil**

**⅔ cup red wine vinegar**

**¼ cup finely chopped shallots**

**2 tablespoons Dijon mustard**

**2 cloves garlic, minced**

**1½ teaspoons salt**

**1 teaspoon freshly ground black pepper**

Salad

**6 medium-size red potatoes, scrubbed, steamed or boiled until a knife inserted into the center goes in easily, drained, and cooled completely**

**½ cup finely chopped fresh chives**

**1 pound green beans, ends trimmed, cut into 1-inch pieces, cooked in boiling salted water until crisp-tender, and drained**

**Three 10-ounce bags mixed field greens**

**3 cups cherry tomatoes**

**½ cup capers, drained**

**Two 6-ounce cans tuna packed in olive oil, drained**

**6 hard-boiled eggs, peeled and sliced, for garnish**

**1.** In a medium-size bowl, whisk the vinaigrette ingredients until thickened.

✳ **DIVA DO-AHEAD:** At this point, you can cover and refrigerate for up to 3 days.

**2.** To make the salad, cut the potatoes into ½-inch dice, put in a medium-size bowl, and add ¼ cup of the chives. Sprinkle with ¼ cup of the vinaigrette and toss to coat.

✳ **DIVA DO-AHEAD:** At this point, cover and refrigerate for at least 2 and up to 24 hours.

**3.** Put the beans and the remaining ¼ cup of chives in a small bowl and toss with 3 to 4 tablespoons of the vinaigrette.

✳ **DIVA DO-AHEAD:** At this point, cover and refrigerate for at least 2 and up to 24 hours.

**4.** When ready to serve, combine the greens, tomatoes, capers, and tuna in a large salad bowl. Add about ½ cup of the vinaigrette and toss to combine. Add the potatoes, beans, and ¼ cup or more vinaigrette and toss to coat evenly. Garnish with the eggs, drizzle with remaining vinaigrette, and serve immediately.

# Southwestern Chopped Salad

Serves 12

If you like taco salad, you will love this steak and vegetable salad with a southwestern flair. Serve it as a main dish or on the side at your next party, or use the dressing to toss with greens for a Mexican fiesta.

### Bloody Mary Dressing

**1 cup vegetable oil**

**½ cup rice vinegar**

**¼ cup Bloody Mary mix or spicy tomato juice**

**½ teaspoon ground cumin**

**¼ teaspoon chipotle Tabasco sauce**

**2 cloves garlic, minced**

**1 teaspoon salt**

**½ teaspoon freshly ground black pepper**

**2 tablespoons firmly packed light brown sugar**

### Salad

**Four 10-ounce bags hearts of romaine lettuce**

**2 cups cherry tomatoes, cut in half**

**1½ cups shredded Monterey Jack cheese**

**1½ cups shredded mild cheddar cheese**

**½ cup diced red onion**

**1½ cups fresh or defrosted frozen corn kernels**

**1 medium-size green bell pepper, seeded and diced**

**1 medium-size red bell pepper, seeded and diced**

**1 cup peeled and finely diced jicama (see The Diva Says on page 186)**

**One 1-pound flank steak, trimmed of any fat, grilled (see page 391), and thinly sliced**

**3 cups crushed corn tortilla chips (try a combination of yellow, white, and blue chips)**

**¼ cup chopped fresh cilantro**

**2 cups Guacamole Olé (page 88; omit sour cream from the recipe) for garnish**

**1 cup sour cream for garnish**

**1.** To make the dressing, in a medium-size bowl, whisk together the dressing ingredients until well blended.

✳ **DIVA DO-AHEAD:** At this point, you can cover and refrigerate for up to 3 days; shake vigorously before using.

**2.** When ready to serve, assemble the salad. Combine the lettuce, tomatoes, cheeses, onion, corn, bell peppers, jicama, and flank steak in a large salad bowl. Pour over some of the dressing and toss to coat well. Add the chips and cilantro and toss again with more dressing if needed. Garnish with dollops of guacamole and sour cream, or serve them on the side.

Jicama is a root vegetable with a crisp texture and an almost apple-like taste. If you are unable to find it, use 1 large Granny Smith apple, cored, peeled, thinly sliced, and tossed with 1 or 2 tablespoons of fresh lemon or lime juice to prevent discoloration.

# Shirley's Classic Coleslaw

Serves 12

My mother-in-law served coleslaw with almost every meal and she taught me how to make it. This recipe is terrific as a side dish at a picnic or barbecue—try any or all of the variations.

### Slaw

**12 cups cored and thinly sliced green cabbage (2 heads)**

**2 cups cored and thinly sliced red cabbage (½ head)**

**3 cups shredded carrots (6 medium-size)**

### Dressing

**2 cups mayonnaise**

**¼ cup distilled white vinegar**

**3 tablespoons sugar**

**3 tablespoons milk, or as needed**

**1.** To make the slaw, in a large salad bowl, combine the cabbages and carrots.

**2.** To make the dressing, in a medium-size bowl, whisk together the dressing ingredients until smooth. Taste the vinegar and sugar and adjust if necessary. Pour over the slaw and toss to combine well.

✳ **DIVA DO-AHEAD:** At this point, cover and refrigerate for at least 2 and up to 8 hours.

### Diva Variations

If you'd like to omit the red cabbage, substitute additional carrots or green cabbage.

**Poppy Seed Coleslaw:** Right before serving, stir in ⅓ cup of poppy seeds.

**Raspberry–Poppy Seed Coleslaw:** Substitute ¼ cup of raspberry vinegar for the white vinegar and stir in ⅓ cup of poppy seeds right before serving.

**Nutty Blue Cheese Coleslaw:** Add 1 cup of crumbled blue cheese to the dressing and, just before serving, stir in 1 cup of chopped Spicy Nuts (page 143) or plain pecans.

# Pacific Rim Slaw ⬚ ⬚

Serves 10 to 12

Everyone has a recipe for a great coleslaw, but sometimes you need a change; this slaw, made with Napa cabbage, red cabbage, carrots, apples, and pea pods, is just the ticket to serve with grilled meats, chicken, or seafood. The dressing is also delicious on sturdy greens such as romaine and spinach. The food processor makes quick work of slicing the cabbage and carrots. If you like, substitute grated Asian pears for the apples.

Dressing

½ cup soy sauce

1 cup rice vinegar

1¼ cups canola oil

2 cloves garlic, minced

2 teaspoons peeled and grated fresh ginger

½ cup firmly packed light brown sugar

¼ cup toasted sesame oil

Slaw

4 cups cored and thinly sliced Napa cabbage (1 large head)

2 cups cored and thinly sliced red cabbage (½ head)

2 cups coarsely grated carrots (4 medium-size)

1 cup coarsely grated sweet apples (2 medium-size; I like Galas, which hold their shape)

1 cup snow peas, cut in half on the diagonal

¼ cup sesame seeds, toasted (see page 83)

**1.** To make the dressing, in a medium-size bowl, whisk together the dressing ingredients until thickened.

✳ **DIVA DO-AHEAD:** At this point, you can cover and refrigerate for up to 5 days.

**2.** To assemble the salad, put the vegetables in a large salad bowl and toss with enough dressing to coat the salad.

✳ **DIVA DO-AHEAD:** At this point, you can cover and refrigerate for up to 4 hours.

**3.** When ready to serve, taste the salad and toss with more dressing if desired. Toss with some of the sesame seeds and sprinkle the rest on top.

# POTATO AND PASTA SALAD QUICK FIXES

**Potatoes and pasta** lend themselves to great spur-of-the-moment interpretations if you have the pantry ingredients on hand.

Six pounds of potatoes, cooked, cooled, and cut into ½-inch pieces will serve about 12 people as a side dish, about ½ cup of salad per person. If you'd like to err on the high side, go with 8 pounds of potatoes.

One pound of dry pasta, cooked, provides eight ¾-cup servings for a main course, or twelve ½-cup servings for a side dish, so plan accordingly.

Add any of the following vegetables to potatoes or pasta, chopped, diced, or otherwise cut up:

- Scallions
- Cucumber, seeded and peeled
- Tomatoes, seeded
- Red onion
- Shallots
- Asparagus, blanched in boiling salted water for 1 minute, then shocked in cold water
- Jarred marinated or plain artichoke hearts
- Olives: green-pimento stuffed, black, or Kalamata
- Sweet or dill pickles
- Oil-packed sun-dried tomatoes
- Hard-boiled eggs
- Bell peppers: red, yellow, or green
- Chile peppers, seeded
- Chopped fresh herbs
- Roasted Wild Mushroom Salad (page 163)

Then add the dressing:

- **Basil** (see page 173), **Balsamic** (page 213), or **Dijon-Tarragon Vinaigrette** (page 212)
- **Caesar Dressing** (see page 174) **or Blue Cheese Caesar Dressing** (see page 175)
- **Creamy Dill and Chive Dressing** (see page 157)
- **Sun-dried tomato mayonnaise** (see page 495)
- **Ranch Hand Special Dressing** (page 216)
- **Pesto Mayonnaise** (page 218)
- **Pesto Vinaigrette** (page 215)

# Baked Potato Salad

Serves 10

Although you don't bake the potatoes, the resulting salad is like a well-dressed baked potato, coated in sour cream and studded with chopped scallions and bacon bits. Serve this to the meat-and-potatoes crowd at your next barbecue—they will swoon!

**6 pounds medium-size red, Yukon Gold, new white, or fingerling potatoes**

**3 tablespoons olive oil**

**2 tablespoons white wine vinegar**

**2 teaspoons salt**

**1½ teaspoons freshly ground black pepper**

**2 cups sour cream**

**2 tablespoons Dijon mustard**

**8 scallions (white and tender green parts), finely chopped**

**12 strips bacon, cooked until crisp, drained on paper towels, and crumbled**

**1.** Cook the potatoes in a large pot of boiling salted water to cover until just tender, about 25 minutes. Drain, let cool a bit, and refrigerate until cold.

**2.** Peel the potatoes, cut into bite-size pieces, and transfer them to a large salad bowl. Toss with the oil, vinegar, salt, and pepper.

❋ **DIVA DO-AHEAD:** At this point, you can cover and refrigerate for up to 12 hours.

**3.** In a small bowl, whisk together the sour cream and Dijon. Stir half the dressing into the potatoes, sprinkle with the scallions, and stir gently to blend.

❋ **DIVA DO-AHEAD:** At this point, cover the potatoes and the remaining dressing and refrigerate for at least 4 and up to 12 hours.

**4.** One hour before serving, remove the salad from the refrigerator, taste, and add more dressing, tossing gently. Add the bacon and toss again. Refrigerate until serving time.

## Picking Your Potato

It's hard to choose when you go to the grocery store and see so many varieties of potatoes now available. For salads, choose red, new white, or Yukon Gold potatoes. Newer varieties include purple potatoes, which I find lacking in the flavor department for salads. Fingerling potatoes are another nice choice; they make great potato salad, but are very expensive. If you are serving 12 people, you are better off buying Yukon Golds or red potatoes. For a more economical use of fingerlings, include them as part of a roasted root vegetable medley.

# Mom's Potato Salad

Serves 12

My mom's potato salad was the typical salad with chopped hard-cooked egg, celery, onion, sweet pickle, and a mayonnaise dressing. This recipe still brings me back to a simpler time of backyard get-togethers. I love to serve it not only with picnic fare, but also with roasted meats and, even better, with boiled Maine lobsters!

**6 pounds red potatoes**

**6 ribs celery, finely chopped**

**½ cup finely chopped red onion, or 6 scallions (white and tender green parts), finely chopped**

**½ cup chopped sweet pickles**

**6 hard-boiled eggs, peeled and sliced**

**¼ cup finely chopped fresh Italian parsley**

**½ cup finely chopped European cucumber**

**¼ cup olive oil**

**2 tablespoons fresh lemon juice**

**1½ teaspoons salt**

**1 teaspoon freshly ground black pepper**

**2 cups mayonnaise**

**1 tablespoon prepared yellow mustard**

**1 tablespoon sweet pickle juice**

**1 to 2 tablespoons milk, as needed, to thin the dressing**

**1 teaspoon sweet paprika**

**1.** Cook the potatoes in a large pot of boiling salted water to cover until just tender, about 25 minutes. Drain, let cool a bit, and refrigerate until cold.

**2.** Peel the potatoes, cut into bite-size pieces, and transfer them to a large salad bowl. Add the celery, onion, pickles, about two-thirds of the eggs, the parsley, and cucumber. Sprinkle with the oil, lemon juice, salt, and pepper and toss to blend.

❋ **DIVA DO-AHEAD:** At this point, you can cover and refrigerate for up to 8 hours.

**3.** In a medium-size bowl, combine the mayonnaise, mustard, pickle juice, and milk, whisking to blend until smooth. Pour half the dressing over the potatoes and stir gently to coat.

❋ **DIVA DO-AHEAD:** At this point, cover and refrigerate the salad, the remaining dressing, and the remaining eggs for at least 4 hours or overnight.

**4.** One hour before serving, taste the salad and add additional dressing, tossing gently to coat. Cover the top of the salad with the remaining sliced eggs, sprinkle with the paprika, and refrigerate until just before serving.

# MYTHS ABOUT MAYO

**My friends at Hellman's/Best Foods** say that after 60 years of research, they have proved that commercially prepared mayonnaise doesn't cause food-borne illness. Forget all the old cautions about getting sick at the picnic from the potato salad—today's commercial mayonnaise is prepared with enough vinegar, lemon juice, and salt to create an environment in which bacteria won't grow. The mayonnaise available today also contains pasteurized eggs, which have been heated to destroy any bacteria. According to our friends at Best Foods, "From a food safety standpoint, commercial mayonnaise and mayonnaise-type dressings are perfectly stable when stored at room temperature after opening. Quality, not safety, is the only reason the labels on these products suggest they be refrigerated after opening. Refrigeration ensures that the commercial mayonnaise keeps its fresh flavor for a longer period of time."

Here are a few important tips for keeping your food safe.

1. Keep hot foods hot and cold foods cold, which means:

- Refrigerate leftovers within 2 hours.

- Keep all perishables cold until serving time.

- Don't mix hot foods into cold foods—cool everything to the same temperature before mixing them together.

- Make sure that foods (particularly meats, chicken, and pork) are cooked through to avoid any bacteria growth.

2. Avoid cross contamination, which means:

- Wash your hands, utensils, plates, and cutting boards after contact with raw poultry, meat, or fish.

- Wash your hands frequently when handling food; if you have handled raw poultry, meat, or fish, make sure you wash all your dish and hand towels thoroughly.

# Julia's Debatable French Potato Salad 🥤🥤

Serves 10 to 12

After Julia Child entered my life as the French Chef on public television, I was never the same. She introduced me to the possibilities that food had to offer in terms of texture, taste, aroma, and pure joy. This potato salad sparked a nasty debate between my mother, the quintessential Italian home cook, and me. I could not wait to make this French recipe, but my mother swore it was Italian. She insisted that it was really her mother's potato salad, but when the dish was complete, she realized that Grandmother never put vinegar in her salad, just great quality olive oil, scallions, and fresh basil. This is my version of Julia's classic, which includes a little bit of Grandma's recipe. It's delicious served with roasted meats and poultry, as well as with burgers on the grill.

**6 pounds Yukon Gold or red potatoes**

**6 scallions (white and tender green parts), finely chopped**

**¼ cup chopped fresh Italian parsley**

**¼ cup packed fresh basil leaves, thinly sliced**

**3 cloves garlic, cut in half**

**1 cup extra virgin olive oil**

**⅓ cup red wine vinegar**

**1½ teaspoons salt**

**1 teaspoon freshly ground black pepper**

**1.** Cook the potatoes in a large pot of boiling salted water to cover until just tender, about 25 minutes. Drain, let cool a bit, and refrigerate until cold.

**2.** Peel the potatoes, cut into bite-size pieces, and transfer them to a large salad bowl. Add the scallions, 2 tablespoons of the parsley, all but 1 tablespoon of the basil, and the garlic and toss gently to combine.

**3.** In a medium-size bowl, whisk together the oil, vinegar, salt, and pepper until blended. Pour half over the potatoes and stir gently to mix.

❋ **DIVA DO-AHEAD:** At this point, you can cover and refrigerate the salad and remaining dressing for up to 24 hours or leave at room temperature for up to 4 hours.

**4.** One hour before serving, toss the salad with additional dressing, remove the garlic cloves, and garnish with the remaining 2 tablespoons of parsley and 1 tablespoon of basil.

# Dilly Red Potato Salad

Serves 10 to 12

There is something so comforting about eating potato salad—it just transports you to picnics and barbecues from warm summers past. But you can make potato salads all year long and enjoy them even in the dead of winter. This simple salad made with red potatoes is flavored with dill, which is particularly delicious with potatoes. Make sure you let the potatoes cool completely before cutting them; that way they won't disintegrate when you mix them with the dressing ingredients.

**6 pounds medium-size red, Yukon Gold, new white, or fingerling potatoes**

**6 ribs celery, finely chopped**

**8 scallions (white and tender green parts), finely chopped**

**3 tablespoons distilled white vinegar**

**3 tablespoons olive oil**

**2 teaspoons salt**

**1 teaspoon freshly ground black pepper**

**2 cups mayonnaise**

**½ cup sour cream**

**¼ cup milk**

**Finely grated zest of 1 lemon**

**¼ to ⅓ cup finely chopped fresh dill, to your taste**

**1 teaspoon sweet paprika**

**1.** Cook the potatoes in a large pot of boiling salted water to cover until just tender, about 25 minutes. Drain the potatoes, let cool a bit, and refrigerate until cold.

**2.** Peel the potatoes, cut them into bite-size pieces, and transfer them to a large salad bowl. Add the celery and scallions, sprinkle with the vinegar, oil, 1 teaspoon of the salt, and ½ teaspoon of the pepper, and toss to coat the potatoes.

✳ **DIVA DO-AHEAD:** At this point, you can cover and refrigerate overnight.

**3.** In a medium-size bowl, whisk together the remaining 1 teaspoon of salt and ½ teaspoon of pepper, and the mayonnaise, sour cream, milk, lemon zest, dill, and ½ teaspoon of the paprika.

**4.** Toss the potatoes with half the dressing, stirring gently to coat.

✳ **DIVA DO-AHEAD:** At this point, cover and refrigerate for 4 to 12 hours before serving.

**5.** Thirty minutes before serving, toss the salad again, adding more dressing if needed. Sprinkle with the remaining ½ teaspoon of paprika and serve.

# German-Style Warm Potato Salad with Bacon and Caraway 🍷🥛

Serves 10 to 12

This potato salad has all the traditional elements of a German-style potato salad, along with the addition of caraway seeds for crunch and interest.

**12 strips bacon, cut into ¼-inch-wide matchsticks**

**1 cup chopped onions**

**2 tablespoons light brown sugar**

**2 tablespoons Dijon mustard**

**⅓ cup cider vinegar**

**½ cup chicken broth**

**6 pounds small red potatoes**

**1 teaspoon salt**

**1½ teaspoons freshly ground black pepper**

**2 tablespoons caraway seeds**

**½ cup chopped fresh Italian parsley for garnish**

## Peeling Potatoes

Whether or not you peel the potatoes is up to you. Sometimes I leave the skins on if they are clean and pretty, but if they are spotted or unattractive, I'll take them off. Also, remember who's coming for dinner, and whether you are entertaining with or without shoes on—peeled potatoes can be more formal, suitable for the shoes-on crowd, while unpeeled is very casual and chic.

**1.** In a large skillet over medium-high heat, cook the bacon until crisp and drain on paper towels. Remove all but 3 table-spoons of the fat from the skillet, add the onions, and cook, stirring, until translucent, about 5 minutes. Add the brown sugar and mustard and bring to a boil, stirring. Add the vinegar and return to a boil. Add the broth, return to a boil, reduce the heat to medium, and simmer for 5 minutes, stirring.

✳ **DIVA DO-AHEAD:** At this point, you can let cool, cover, and refrigerate the dressing and bacon (separately) for up to 3 days; reheat the dressing before continuing.

**2.** Cook the potatoes in a large pot of boiling salted water to cover until just tender, about 25 minutes. Drain and, using oven mitts, cut the hot potatoes into bite-size pieces. Transfer them to a serving bowl and sprinkle with the salt and pepper. Crumble the bacon and add to the potatoes, then sprinkle potatoes with the caraway seeds. Pour over the hot dressing, stirring gently to coat the potatoes, sprinkle with the parsley, and serve warm or at room temperature.

# Black Bean and Chicken Tostada Salad 🥤🥤

Serves 10 to 12

The vibrant colors, textures, and flavors of the Southwest make this salad a great choice to serve with grilled steaks or as a main-course salad for a picnic.

Salad

**Two 15-ounce cans black beans, rinsed and drained**

**2 cups peeled and chopped jicama (see The Diva Says, page 186)**

**6 scallions (white and tender green parts), chopped**

**3 cups fresh or defrosted frozen corn kernels**

**1 medium-size red bell pepper, seeded and finely chopped**

**3 cups cubed cooked chicken (see page 156) or turkey (1/2-inch cubes)**

Salsa Dressing

**2 cups seeded and chopped fresh tomatoes (plum tomatoes are a good choice year-round)**

**1 large ripe Hass avocado, peeled, pitted, and cut into 1/2-inch dice**

**1/2 cup chopped red onion**

**1/4 cup seeded and chopped Anaheim chile**

**1/4 cup finely chopped fresh cilantro**

**2 cloves garlic, minced**

**3/4 cup vegetable oil**

**1/3 cup fresh lime juice**

**1 1/2 teaspoons salt**

**1/2 teaspoon ground cumin**

**1/2 teaspoon freshly ground black pepper**

**4 cups crushed tortilla chips (try a combination of yellow, white, and blue) for garnish**

**1.** To assemble the salad, in a large bowl, combine the black beans, jicama, scallions, corn, bell pepper, and chicken.

✳ **DIVA DO-AHEAD:** At this point, you can cover and refrigerate for up to 24 hours.

**2.** To make the dressing, in a medium-size bowl, combine the tomatoes, avocado, red onion, chile, cilantro, and garlic. Add the oil, lime juice, salt, cumin, and black pepper and toss to combine.

✳ **DIVA DO-AHEAD:** At this point, cover and refrigerate for at least 2 and up to 24 hours.

**3.** When ready to serve, pour the salsa dressing over the salad and stir to combine well. Garnish with the crushed tortillas and serve immediately.

# Midwest Wild Rice Salad

Serves 10 to 12

This recipe was given to me by a student in one of my classes in the Midwest, where wild rice is a very popular addition to the dinner table. The salad is studded with colorful vegetables, and the crunchy wild rice pairs well with the light curry dressing.

### Dressing

**1 cup vegetable oil**

**½ cup distilled white vinegar**

**¼ cup sugar**

**1 teaspoon curry powder**

**1 clove garlic, mashed**

### Salad

**4 cups cooked long-grain white rice, cooled**

**1 cup cooked wild rice, cooled**

**2 cups frozen corn kernels, defrosted**

**1 medium-size red bell pepper, seeded and chopped**

**4 scallions (white and tender green parts), chopped**

**1.** To make the dressing, in a medium-size bowl, whisk together the dressing ingredients until thickened.

✳ **DIVA DO-AHEAD:** At this point, you can cover and refrigerate for up to 3 days.

**2.** To make the salad, combine the rices, corn, bell pepper, and half of the scallions in a large salad bowl. Pour in some of the dressing, and toss to coat, adding more if necessary.

✳ **DIVA DO-AHEAD:** At this point, cover and refrigerate the salad and remaining dressing for at least 1 hour and up to 24 hours.

**3.** Remove the salad from the refrigerator 30 minutes before serving, toss with additional dressing if needed, and garnish with the remaining scallions.

# Smoked Chicken, Mango, and Wild Rice Salad

Serves 10 to 12

Smoked chicken and crunchy wild rice, accented with pieces of sweet mango, make for a terrific salad to serve as part of a picnic dinner or tailgate party. Ask your deli person to slice off a chunk of smoked chicken or turkey so that you can dice it into bite-size pieces. Cooked wild rice keeps in the freezer for about 6 months, so cook it when you have the time, then freeze it for emergency salad making.

Mango-Cilantro Dressing

**1¼ cups vegetable oil**

**¼ cup white wine vinegar**

**¼ cup fresh lemon juice**

**1 cup finely diced ripe mango**

**½ cup chopped fresh cilantro**

**1½ teaspoons salt**

**1 teaspoon freshly ground black pepper**

**2 cloves garlic, chopped**

Salad

**8 cups cooked wild rice, cooled**

**6 scallions (white and tender green parts), chopped**

**1½ cups golden raisins**

**6 cups smoked chicken or turkey cut into ½-inch dice**

**1.** To make the dressing, in a medium-size bowl, combine the dressing ingredients and stir until blended.

**2.** To assemble the salad, combine the ingredients in a large salad bowl. Pour all but ¼ cup of the dressing over the salad and toss to coat.

✱ **DIVA DO-AHEAD:** At this point, you can cover and refrigerate the salad and remaining dressing for up to 3 days.

**3.** Thirty minutes before serving, remove the salad from the refrigerator and toss with the remaining dressing. Serve at room temperature.

# Cold Sesame Noodle Salad with Spicy Peanut Dressing

Serves 10 to 12

I love the complexity that simple Asian ingredients give to dishes, and the combination of sesame oil and peanuts in this salad dressing takes this cooling salad to my top ten list of favorites. Feel free to add your own touches to the basic salad, using leftover cooked chicken or shrimp, and vegetables that will pair well with the salad. This is great served with satay or grilled fish, chicken, pork, or beef.

1 pound linguine, cooked in boiling salted water until *al dente* and drained

¼ cup toasted sesame oil

2 tablespoons vegetable oil

2 cloves garlic, minced

2 teaspoons peeled and grated fresh ginger

¼ cup soy sauce

¼ cup creamy peanut butter (don't use natural)

¼ cup rice vinegar

2 teaspoons light brown sugar

1 cup snow peas, strings removed

6 scallions (white and tender green parts), thinly sliced on the diagonal

4 medium-size carrots, cut into matchsticks (about 2 cups)

¼ cup chopped unsalted dry-roasted peanuts

2 tablespoons sesame seeds, toasted (see page 83)

**1.** Toss the pasta with 1 or 2 tablespoons of the sesame oil.

✳ **DIVA DO-AHEAD:** At this point, you can cover and refrigerate for up to 8 hours.

**2.** In a blender or food processor, process together the remaining sesame oil and the vegetable oil, garlic, ginger, soy sauce, peanut butter, vinegar, and brown sugar until smooth. Taste for soy sauce and sugar.

✳ **DIVA DO-AHEAD:** At this point, you can cover and refrigerate for up to 3 days. Let come to room temperature and rewhisk to blend before continuing.

**3.** Microwave the snow peas on High or plunge into boiling water for 1 minute. Shock in ice water, pat dry, and cut in half on the diagonal. Add the snow peas, scallions, carrots, 2 tablespoons of the peanuts, and 1 tablespoon of the sesame seeds to the linguine. Pour half of the dressing over the salad and toss to coat.

**✳ DIVA DO-AHEAD:** At this point, cover and refrigerate the salad and remaining dressing for at least 6 and up to 24 hours.

**4.** One hour before serving, remove the salad from the refrigerator and toss with more dressing if needed. Garnish with the remaining 2 tablespoons of peanuts and 1 tablespoon of sesame seeds.

# Old-Fashioned Picnic Macaroni Salad 🥤 🥛

Serves 10 to 12

Sometimes, with all the hype about designer pasta and baby vegetables, it's nice to have something simple that you remember from childhood cookouts and picnics. This is the macaroni salad that your mom made or maybe a variation on the theme. But now it's yours: If you want it chunky, chop the veggies coarsely; if you like it more refined, chop them finely.

---

1 pound elbow macaroni, cooked in boiling salted water until *al dente* and drained

2 tablespoons olive oil

1 teaspoon salt

1 teaspoon freshly ground black pepper

½ cup chopped red onion or scallions

1½ cups chopped celery

½ cup chopped sweet pickles (about 6 small pickles)

1 medium-size red or yellow bell pepper, seeded and chopped

1½ cups mayonnaise

2 tablespoons milk

1 tablespoon prepared yellow mustard

2 teaspoons celery seeds

2 teaspoons sweet paprika

---

**1.** In a large salad bowl, toss together the warm pasta, oil, salt, and pepper and allow to cool, then add the onion, celery, pickles, and bell pepper and toss to blend.

**2.** In a small bowl, stir together the mayonnaise, milk, mustard, and celery seeds. Pour half over the salad and toss to coat.

**✳ DIVA DO-AHEAD:** At this point, cover and refrigerate the salad and the remaining dressing for at least 4 hours and up to 2 days.

**3.** One hour before serving, remove the salad from the refrigerator, add more dressing if needed, and taste for salt and pepper. Sprinkle with the paprika, cover, and refrigerate until ready to serve.

### Diva Variations

Try adding any of these to the salad:

- 2 cups frozen peas, defrosted

- 2 cups smoked turkey or ham cut into ½-inch chunks

- 2 cups cherry tomatoes, whole or cut in half

- 2 cups pimento-stuffed green olives, drained and chopped

- 2 cups ranch dressing, homemade (page 216) or store-bought, in place of the mustard and mayonnaise combination; omit the celery seeds

- 6 hard-boiled eggs (see page 142), sliced

## KEEPING SALADS COOL

**To keep your salads cool,** it's a good idea to pack them in ice in a cooler if you are taking them to someone else's home. Don't have a cooler, or yours is too small? If you have a box that your salad bowl will fit in, line it with heavy-duty aluminum foil, then fill with plastic bags filled with ice. Set the bowl in the ice and cover with a bath towel—that way it will keep the cold under the towel. When you are done, empty the ice and use the box to transport your salad bowl home.

If you are serving the salad at home, place the serving bowl on a larger tray and surround the bowl with ice packs (or small zipper-top plastic bags filled with ice). Cover the packs with cloth napkins that match your party décor. The ice packs will keep your salad cool well into the party. You can also put the salad bowl in the freezer for a half hour or so before placing the finished salad in it, or lay bags of ice in the salad bowl 30 minutes before serving.

# Garden Pasta Salad with Tomatoes, Basil, and Brie

Serves 10 to 12

This elegant but simple salad is right at home on the picnic table, as well as at an elegant dinner party. If you cannot find vine-ripened tomatoes, buy cherry tomatoes and cut them in half (no need to remove the seeds). The tomatoes should be sweet and red all the way through. Once you have made this recipe, you'll want to try using different varieties and colors for taste and interest, such as yellow, orange, and heirloom striped tomatoes.

**6 cups seeded and chopped tomatoes (about 6 medium-size to large vine-ripened tomatoes), or 6 cups cherry tomatoes, cut in half**

**1 cup firmly packed fresh basil leaves**

**4 cloves garlic, minced**

**½ cup extra virgin olive oil**

**½ cup plus 2 tablespoons olive oil**

**2 teaspoons salt**

**1 teaspoon freshly ground black pepper**

**Two 9-ounce packages fresh fettuccine, cut in half, cooked in boiling salted water until *al dente*, and drained**

**8 ounces Brie cheese, rind removed, cut into ½-inch-thick slices, then into 1-inch squares**

**½ cup chopped fresh Italian parsley**

**1.** In a glass salad bowl, combine the tomatoes, basil, garlic, extra virgin olive oil, ½ cup of the olive oil, the salt, and the pepper, stirring to blend.

✳ **DIVA DO-AHEAD:** Cover the bowl and let stand at room temperature for up to 6 hours.

**2.** Thirty minutes before serving, cook the fettuccine and toss with the remaining 2 tablespoons of olive oil. Toss with the tomato mixture until blended. Taste the pasta for salt and pepper. Garnish with the Brie and parsley and serve.

## While You Were Sleeping

Starchy salads containing potatoes, pasta, or rice all absorb their dressings when they are refrigerated. That is why I instruct you to toss them once before refrigerating, then to add additional dressing before serving. The salads will dry out while they are resting and will need more dressing to refresh their flavor.

# Dilly Pasta Salad with Feta, Peppers, and Olives 🥤⚫

Serves 10 to 12

Unlike the deli salad that comes out of a big plastic carton, this pasta salad has a terrific fresh flavor, with lots of vegetables and *al dente* pasta. For added pizzazz, you might want to use one of the new flavored feta cheeses. To make a main-course salad, add 3 cups of leftover chicken, lamb, beef, or shrimp.

## Dressing

**1½ cups olive oil**

**⅔ cup white wine vinegar**

**4 cloves garlic, minced**

**2 tablespoons dillweed**

**1 teaspoon sugar**

**1½ teaspoons salt**

**1 teaspoon freshly ground black pepper**

## Salad

**1 pound dried pasta, preferably shell or corkscrew, cooked in boiling salted water until *al dente*, drained, and cooled**

**2 tablespoons olive oil**

**1 medium-size yellow bell pepper, seeded and finely chopped**

**1 medium-size red bell pepper, seeded and finely chopped**

**1 European cucumber, cut into ½-inch dice**

**1 cup Kalamata olives, drained, pitted, and sliced**

**½ cup finely chopped red onion**

**1½ cups crumbled feta cheese**

**1.** To make the dressing, in a medium-size bowl, whisk together the dressing ingredients until thickened.

✳ **DIVA DO-AHEAD:** At this point, you can cover and refrigerate for up to 1 week.

**2.** To assemble the salad, combine the ingredients in a large salad bowl, tossing to blend.

✳ **DIVA DO-AHEAD:** At this point, you can cover and refrigerate for up to 2 days.

**3.** Pour ½ cup of the dressing over the salad and toss to coat.

✳ **DIVA DO-AHEAD:** At this point, cover and refrigerate for at least 4 hours and up to 2 days.

**4.** Thirty minutes before serving, remove the salad from the refrigerator. Toss with additional dressing and taste and adjust the seasonings as needed.

# Creamy Salmon and Dill Pasta Salad

Serves 10 to 12

Studded with nuggets of salmon and flavored with dill and lemon, this gorgeous salad is one of my favorites for bringing to a potluck supper or serving to friends as part of a summertime dinner.

## Dressing

**1½ cups mayonnaise**

**¼ cup milk**

**Grated zest of 1 lemon**

**2 tablespoons dillweed**

**1½ teaspoons salt**

**1 teaspoon freshly ground black pepper**

## Salad

**1 pound fusilli (corkscrew) or small shell pasta, cooked in boiling water until *al dente* and drained**

**6 ribs celery, finely chopped**

**½ cup finely chopped red onion**

**1 medium-size red pepper, seeded and cut into ½-inch dice**

**4 cups flaked cooked salmon fillet**

## Diva Variations

**Creamy Shrimp and Dill Pasta Salad:** For the salmon, substitute 2 pounds of medium-size shrimp, cooked in boiling water until just pink, drained, and peeled.

**1.** To make the dressing, in a medium-size bowl, whisk together the dressing ingredients until blended.

❋ **DIVA DO-AHEAD:** At this point, you can cover and refrigerate for up to 4 days.

**2.** To assemble the salad, combine the warm pasta with about ¼ cup of the dressing in a large salad bowl and toss to coat. Refrigerate until cooled completely.

**3.** Add the celery, onion, bell pepper, and salmon to the pasta, toss, add some more dressing, and toss again so everything is lightly coated.

❋ **DIVA DO-AHEAD:** At this point, cover and refrigerate the salad and remaining dressing for at least 12 hours and up to 2 days.

**4.** Two hours before serving, toss the salad with additional dressing and refrigerate until serving time.

# Shrimp, Sun-Dried Tomato, and Orzo Salad 🍹🍸🍷

Serves 10 to 12

You will love serving this beautiful, tasty salad, flavored with basil and red wine vinegar, alongside grilled entrées in summer or as a main-course salad with tossed greens. Orzo is a small, rice-shaped dried pasta that you can find in the pasta section of your grocery store.

½ cup extra virgin olive oil

2 cloves garlic, minced

½ cup finely chopped red onion

½ cup oil-packed sun-dried tomatoes, drained and cut into matchsticks

¼ cup chopped fresh basil

¾ pound medium-size shrimp, cooked in boiling water just until pink, drained, and peeled

1 pound orzo, cooked in boiling salted water until *al dente* and drained

¼ cup red wine vinegar

1 teaspoon salt

½ teaspoon freshly ground black pepper

¼ cup chopped fresh Italian parsley

### Diva Variations

This salad is terrific prepared with left-over cooked chicken or fish instead of the shrimp.

**1.** In a small skillet, heat the oil over medium heat, then add the garlic, onion, tomatoes, and basil and cook, stirring, for 2 minutes. Remove from the heat, add the shrimp, tossing to coat it with the oil, and allow to cool to room temperature.

**2.** Put the orzo in a large salad bowl, add the shrimp mixture, and toss to coat the pasta. Add the vinegar, salt, pepper, and parsley, stirring to blend. Taste for salt and pepper.

✳ **DIVA DO-AHEAD:** At this point, you can cover and refrigerate for up to 2 days.

**3.** Remove the salad from the refrigerator 30 minutes before serving.

# Chicken Tortellini Salad with Artichokes and Snow Peas

Serves 10 to 12

I love to serve this unusual pasta salad on a bed of Spinach Salad with Strawberries and Raspberry Vinaigrette (page 170).

1 cup snow peas, strings removed

Three 10-ounce packages fresh cheese
  tortellini, cooked for 3 minutes in
  boiling salted water and drained
  thoroughly

2 tablespoons olive oil

3 cups bite-size pieces of cooked chicken

6 scallions (white and tender green parts),
  thinly sliced

1 cup chopped celery

1 European cucumber, cut into ½-inch dice

2 cups seedless red grapes

½ cup golden raisins, chopped

Two 6-ounce jars marinated artichokes,
  drained, reserving the marinade, and
  chopped

1½ cups mayonnaise

½ cup freshly grated Parmesan cheese

¼ cup fresh lemon juice

1 recipe Spinach Salad with Strawberries
  and Raspberry Vinaigrette (page 170)

**1.** Microwave the snow peas on High or plunge into boiling water for 1 minute. Shock in ice water, pat dry, and cut in half on the diagonal.

**2.** Put the hot tortellini in a large salad bowl and toss with the oil to help keep the pasta from sticking together. Allow to cool slightly.

**3.** Add the chicken, scallions, snow peas, celery, cucumber, grapes, raisins, and artichokes to the pasta and toss to blend.

**4.** In a medium-size bowl, whisk together the mayonnaise, Parmesan, lemon juice, and ¼ to ½ cup of the reserved artichoke marinade, to your taste, until blended. Pour some of the dressing over the salad and stir to blend.

✳ **DIVA DO-AHEAD:** At this point, you can cover and refrigerate for up to 2 days. Remove from the refrigerator 30 minutes before serving.

 **5.** Just before serving, toss the remaining dressing with the salad and serve over the spinach salad.

# Crunchy Asian Salad with Candied Almonds 🗑 🍶

Serves 10

This is the perfect salad for the ladies who lunch or for a casual picnic dinner. It's so simple to put together. The candied almonds add crunch, and the curry-infused dressing is a welcome change from the more usual mayonnaise-based dressings for chicken salads.

### Candied Almonds

½ cup sugar

1½ cups sliced almonds

### Dressing

⅓ cup sugar

½ cup vegetable oil

½ cup red wine vinegar

2 teaspoons fresh lemon juice

1 teaspoon Worcestershire sauce

½ teaspoon garlic salt

½ teaspoon dry mustard

1 teaspoon curry powder

### Salad

Four 10-ounce bags red leaf or butter lettuce or American salad blend

4 cups cubed cooked chicken or turkey (½-inch cubes)

Two 11-ounce cans mandarin orange sections, drained

6 scallions (white and tender green parts), thinly sliced on the diagonal

**1.** To make the candied almonds, in a medium-size nonstick skillet, heat the sugar over medium-high heat until it begins to melt. Add the almonds and stir constantly until they are golden and coated with the sugar. Transfer to a plate and let cool completely. Break them apart when they are cool.

✳ **DIVA DO-AHEAD:** At this point, you can store in a zipper-top plastic bag in the freezer for up to 6 months.

**2.** To make the dressing, in a small bowl, whisk the dressing ingredients together until thickened.

✳ **DIVA DO-AHEAD:** At this point, you can cover and refrigerate for up to 1 week.

**3.** When you're ready to serve, assemble the salad. Combine the lettuce, chicken, oranges, and scallions in a large salad bowl. Pour the dressing over the salad and toss until everything is coated evenly. Sprinkle with the almonds and toss again. Serve immediately.

# Curried Chicken Salad

Serves 12

This combination of curried chicken and spinach salad tossed with a soy dressing is a delightful pairing and would be terrific to take to a picnic.

### Chicken Salad

**4 cups cubed cooked chicken (½-inch cubes)**

**1 cup chopped celery**

**2 red apples, cored, peeled, and cut into ½-inch dice**

**1 cup salted dry-roasted peanuts**

**1 cup golden raisins**

**1 cup chopped fresh or canned pineapple**

**1 cup seeded and chopped cantaloupe**

### Chicken Salad Dressing

**⅔ cup mayonnaise**

**⅓ cup sour cream**

**2 tablespoons chopped Major Grey's chutney**

**1 to 1½ teaspoons curry powder, to your taste**

### Spinach Salad Dressing

**1 cup vegetable oil**

**¼ cup soy sauce**

**½ cup rice vinegar**

**⅓ cup sugar**

**¼ teaspoon peeled and grated fresh ginger**

**1 clove garlic, minced**

### Spinach Salad

**Four 10-ounce bags baby spinach**

**½ cup thinly sliced red onion, separated into rings**

**Two 11-ounce cans mandarin oranges, drained**

**12 strips bacon, cooked until crisp, drained on paper towels, and crumbled, for garnish**

**1.** Combine the chicken salad ingredients in a large salad bowl.

**2.** To make the chicken salad dressing, in a small bowl, stir the ingredients together until blended. Add to the chicken mixture and toss to coat.

✳ **DIVA DO-AHEAD:** At this point, cover and refrigerate for at least 2 and up to 12 hours.

**3.** To make the spinach salad dressing, whisk together the ingredients in a small bowl until blended.

✳ **DIVA DO-AHEAD:** At this point, you can cover and refrigerate for up to 3 days.

**4.** To serve, assemble the spinach salad. In a large salad bowl, combine the spinach, onion, and oranges. Toss with the spinach salad dressing, place the chicken salad on top, and garnish with the bacon.

# New-Fashioned Chicken Waldorf Salad

Serves 10 to 12

This salad is a blast from the past, but with a total redo. Instead of the boring mayonnaise dressing, we are gilding this chicken-and-apple salad with an apple cider dressing accented with celery seeds, and adding spicy pecans to the mix as well. So instead of that ice-cream scoop lump of ho-hum chicken salad, you'll have a colorful jumble of greens, chicken, apples, and nuts.

### Apple Cider Dressing

1⅓ cups vegetable oil

½ cup apple juice or cider

2 tablespoons fresh lemon juice

1½ teaspoons salt

1 teaspoon celery seeds

¼ teaspoon dry mustard

Pinch of cayenne pepper

### Salad

4 cups bite-size pieces of cooked chicken

4 ribs celery, finely chopped

⅔ cup golden raisins

¼ cup finely chopped red onion

4 large apples, cored and cut into ½-inch dice

Two 10-ounce packages mixed field greens

1½ cups Spicy Nuts (page 143) made with pecans, chopped

**1.** To make the dressing, in a medium-size bowl, whisk the dressing ingredients until blended.

✳ **DIVA DO-AHEAD:** At this point, you can cover and refrigerate for up to 3 days.

**2.** To assemble the salad, in a large bowl, combine the chicken, celery, raisins, onion, and apples, then toss with about ¼ cup of the dressing.

✳ **DIVA DO-AHEAD:** At this point, you can cover and refrigerate overnight.

**3.** When ready to serve, put the greens into a large salad bowl and add the chicken mixture and 1 cup of the pecans. Toss with some of the dressing until everything is coated. Add more dressing if needed and garnish with the remaining ½ cup of pecans. Serve immediately.

# The Diva's Shrimp Salad

Serves 10 to 12

Shrimp salad is so versatile. You can serve it stuffed into tomatoes or avocado halves, make tea sandwiches with it, or serve it on a bed of field greens. This salad has my favorite flavors, shrimp and dill, combined with a bit of lemon zest; it is actually better after it has been refrigerated overnight. I like to cook my own shrimp, but if you don't have time, you can buy cooked shrimp (see The Skinny on Shrimp, page 210).

**2½ pounds medium-size shrimp, peeled and deveined**

**2 quarts water**

**1 tablespoon Old Bay seasoning**

**2 lemons**

**1½ cups finely chopped celery**

**1¾ cups mayonnaise**

**¼ cup chopped fresh dill, or 4 teaspoons dillweed**

**½ teaspoon freshly ground black pepper**

**¼ cup finely chopped fresh chives**

**1 teaspoon sweet paprika (optional) for garnish**

**1.** In a 4-quart saucepan, combine the shrimp, water, and Old Bay, stirring to distribute the Old Bay.

**2.** Grate the zest of 1 lemon and set aside.

**3.** Cut both lemons into quarters and squeeze their juice into the shrimp water.

Add the lemon rinds to the water and bring to a boil. Remove from the heat, cover, and let sit until the shrimp turn pink, about 10 minutes. Drain the shrimp and let cool.

✳ **DIVA DO-AHEAD:** At this point, cover and refrigerate until chilled, about 4 hours, or up to 2 days.

**4.** In a large bowl, stir together the celery, mayonnaise, dill, pepper, and reserved lemon zest until blended. Add the shrimp and toss until they are evenly coated.

✳ **DIVA DO-AHEAD:** At this point, you can cover and refrigerate for up to 2 hours or overnight.

**5.** When you are ready to serve the salad, toss half of the chives into the salad and serve garnished with the remaining chives and the paprika if using.

# Shrimp and Sweet Corn Rémoulade

Serves 10 to 12

Make this luscious salad the night before you plan to serve it so that the flavors will marry. Serve it on a bed of field greens dressed in a light vinaigrette for a nice light lunch entrée, along with some Basic Dinner Rolls (page 525), or bring it to a picnic or barbecue and serve it with crispy Pita Chips (page 527).

2 pounds cooked large shrimp, cooled and cut in half; or 1 pound shrimp and 1 pound crabmeat

2 cups chopped celery

3 cups fresh corn kernels cut from the cob or frozen corn, defrosted

2 cups Rémoulade Sauce (page 111)

Field greens for serving

## The Skinny on Shrimp

The cooked shrimp at your grocer have probably been frozen after they were cooked, then defrosted at the store, so you may not get the best-tasting product. To give these shrimp a little boost, I recommend you sprinkle them with some Old Bay seasoning and refrigerate them for an hour or so. This will perk them up and you'll have a tastier salad.

**1.** Stir all the ingredients together in a large bowl, except for the field greens.

✳ **DIVA DO-AHEAD:** At this point, you can cover and refrigerate for up to 8 hours.

**2.** Place the greens on a serving dish and mound the salad on top.

# Red Wine Citrus Vinaigrette

Makes about 2½ cups

This beautifully colored salad dressing is wonderful on field greens with orange or red grapefruit segments and a few toasted pine nuts tossed in.

1½ cups olive oil

½ cup red wine

½ cup fresh orange juice

3 tablespoons fresh lemon juice

2 tablespoons minced fresh sage

1½ teaspoons finely grated orange zest

1½ teaspoons salt

1 teaspoon freshly ground black pepper

2 cloves garlic, minced

In a medium-size bowl, whisk together the ingredients until blended.

✳ **DIVA DO-AHEAD:** At this point, you can cover and refrigerate for up to 3 days.

# Red Pepper Feta Vinaigrette

Makes 2½ cups

Vibrant red peppers and salty feta combine for a dressing that will catch the eye as well as the taste buds of your dinner companions. Try this dressing over sturdy greens like romaine, or as a dressing for a pasta salad.

6 jarred roasted red peppers, drained

3 cloves garlic, peeled

20 fresh basil leaves

2 tablespoons fresh oregano leaves

⅓ cup red wine vinegar

2 tablespoons fresh lemon juice

1 teaspoon salt

1 teaspoon freshly ground black pepper

1¼ cups olive oil

1 cup crumbled feta cheese

**1.** In a food processor or blender, combine the red peppers, garlic, basil, oregano, vinegar, lemon juice, salt, and black pepper and process or blend until smooth.

**2.** With the machine running, gradually add the oil and process until the dressing thickens. Stir in the feta.

✳ **DIVA DO-AHEAD:** At this point, you can cover and refrigerate for up to 3 days.

# Cabernet Vinaigrette

Makes 3 cups

Full-bodied Cabernet and balsamic vinegar give this dressing its assertive personality. Toss with sturdy greens and serve alongside roast beef or grilled steak.

1½ cups olive oil

½ cup canola oil

½ cup balsamic vinegar

¼ cup Cabernet Sauvignon or another full-bodied red wine

½ cup finely chopped shallots

¼ cup thinly sliced fresh herb of your choice, such as tarragon, oregano, basil, Italian parsley, thyme, marjoram, or rosemary

2 cloves garlic, mashed into a paste

2 teaspoons salt

1 teaspoon freshly ground black pepper

In a medium-size bowl, whisk together the oils, vinegar, and wine. Add the shallots, herb, garlic, salt, and pepper and whisk until blended.

✳ **DIVA DO-AHEAD:** At this point, you can cover and refrigerate for up to 3 days.

# Dijon-Tarragon Vinaigrette

Makes about 3 cups

This dressing is terrific over field greens; the tarragon gives it an unusual flavor, and the Dijon spices it up. If you are unable to find fresh tarragon, use a generous 1 tablespoon of dried instead.

1 cup olive oil

⅔ cup vegetable oil

½ cup white wine vinegar

½ cup finely chopped shallots

¼ cup Dijon mustard

¼ cup finely chopped fresh tarragon

1 teaspoon sugar

2 cloves garlic, minced

1½ teaspoons salt

1 teaspoon freshly ground black pepper

In a medium-size bowl, whisk together all the ingredients until thickened.

✳ **DIVA DO-AHEAD:** At this point, you can cover and refrigerate for up to 3 days.

# Balsamic Vinaigrette

Makes about 2¼ cups

You can add herbs to this basic dressing to customize its flavor.

**1½ cups olive oil**

**⅔ cup balsamic vinegar**

**2 cloves garlic, minced**

**1½ teaspoons salt**

**1 teaspoon freshly ground black pepper**

Whisk the ingredients together in a medium-size bowl until thickened.

✳ **DIVA DO-AHEAD:** At this point, you can cover and refrigerate for up to 3 days.

## Classic Dressings for a Crowd

These are the building blocks of any green salad. Two to 3 cups of dressing will dress four to six 10-ounce bags of packaged salad. Some people like their salads with a lot of dressing, while others like a little. I'm somewhere on the lighter side, but I want the dressing to coat everything. For most salads, you will probably have a little dressing left over, which you can refrigerate and use another time.

# Rice Vinegar Vinaigrette

Makes 2½ cups

This is my all-purpose standby dressing, which I keep in the fridge and then add to when I want to jazz it up.

**1½ cups vegetable oil**

**¾ cup rice vinegar**

**2 teaspoons salt**

**1 teaspoon freshly ground black pepper**

**1 teaspoon garlic powder**

In a medium-size bowl, whisk together the ingredients until thickened.

✳ **DIVA DO-AHEAD:** At this point, you can cover and refrigerate for up to 2 weeks.

## Diva Variations

This simple dressing lends itself to a variety of additions, such as:

- ¼ to ⅓ cup prepared basil pesto

- ¼ cup oil-packed sun-dried tomatoes, drained and cut into matchsticks

- ¾ cup crumbled blue cheese

- 2 tablespoons mango nectar and 1 teaspoon seeded and minced jalapeño

- Herbs of your choice, such as basil, rosemary, oregano, dill, or thyme

# Creole Vinaigrette

Makes about 1½ cups

As Chef Emeril would say, this is one kicked-up dressing, so serve it with sturdy mixed greens, slices of apple, and maybe a creamy soft cheese such as Brie cut into small pieces. Creole mustard is spicy whole-grain mustard sold in the mustard section of your supermarket.

**1 cup vegetable oil**

**⅓ cup red wine vinegar**

**¼ cup Creole mustard**

**¼ cup finely chopped shallots**

**2 cloves garlic, minced**

**1½ teaspoons salt**

**⅛ teaspoon Tabasco sauce**

In a medium-size bowl, whisk together all the ingredients until blended.

❋ **DIVA DO-AHEAD:** At this point, you can cover and refrigerate for up to 3 days.

# Sherry Vinaigrette

Makes 3¼ cups

Sherry vinegar is tart and adds an unusual flavor to vinaigrette. Toss this with sturdy greens or cooked and cooled potatoes.

**2⅓ cups olive oil**

**⅔ cup sherry vinegar**

**¼ cup Dijon mustard**

**1½ teaspoons salt**

**1 teaspoon freshly ground black pepper**

In a medium-size bowl, whisk together the ingredients until blended.

❋ **DIVA DO-AHEAD:** At this point, you can cover and refrigerate for up to 1 week.

## Diva Dressing Fixes

When I'm in a hurry, here are some bottled dressings I like to use for almost instant potato or pasta salad:

- Marzetti's or Marie's Fresh Blue Cheese Dressing
- Marzetti's or Marie's Fresh Ranch Style Dressing
- Hidden Valley Ranch Salad Dressing
- Newman's Own Balsamic Vinaigrette
- Newman's Own Caesar Dressing

# Pesto Vinaigrette

Makes about 1³/₄ cups

This vibrant showstopper perks up any buffet salad, and you can use leftover frozen pesto or prepared pesto from the grocery store to make it. The vinaigrette is also delicious tossed into pasta or potato salads.

> 1 cup Sun-Dried Tomato, Basil, or Cilantro Pesto, homemade (page 97 or 427) or store-bought
> ½ cup vegetable oil
> ¼ cup rice vinegar

In a medium-size bowl, whisk together the ingredients until blended.

✳ **DIVA DO-AHEAD:** At this point, you can cover and refrigerate for up to 1 week.

# Old-Fashioned Blue Cheese Dressing

Makes about 3 cups

I grew up on blue cheese dressing, and this one is simple and yet so delicious. I like to serve it on wedges of iceberg lettuce and top it with some crumbled bacon. This also makes a great dip for veggies.

> 1½ cups mayonnaise
> 1 cup sour cream
> 2 teaspoons Worcestershire sauce
> 1 teaspoon dry mustard
> 1 teaspoon freshly ground black pepper
> 1 teaspoon garlic powder
> 6 to 8 ounces blue cheese, to your taste, crumbled

**1.** In a medium-size bowl, stir together the mayonnaise, sour cream, Worcestershire, dry mustard, pepper, and garlic powder.

**2.** Fold in the blue cheese and stir until blended.

✳ **DIVA DO-AHEAD:** At this point, cover and refrigerate for at least 24 hours to let the flavors develop and up to 5 days.

# Ranch Hand Special Dressing

Makes about 3 cups

Ranch style dressing is found on every grocer's shelf in the country, but it's so simple to make at home. I like to use buttermilk in mine for a tangy flavor, but you can substitute milk for it in this recipe. Terrific on greens, it's also delicious over cucumbers and sliced tomatoes, in potato and pasta salads, and tossed with green beans.

1¾ cups mayonnaise

1 cup buttermilk, or substitute 1 cup whole milk mixed with 2 tablespoons fresh lemon juice

1 teaspoon dried chives

1 tablespoon dried parsley

½ teaspoon garlic salt

½ teaspoon dried tarragon

½ teaspoon dried oregano

½ teaspoon dried basil

½ teaspoon lemon pepper seasoning

In a medium-size bowl, whisk together the ingredients until blended.

**DIVA DO-AHEAD:** At this point, you can cover and refrigerate for up to 1 week. Shake well or whisk before using.

# Herb Garden Ranch Hand Special Dressing

Makes about 3 cups

If you would prefer to use fresh herbs in your ranch dressing, you will only be able to prepare it 2 days ahead of time because the herbs will make the dressing watery, and they will begin to disintegrate.

2 cups mayonnaise

1 cup buttermilk, or substitute 1 cup whole milk mixed with 2 tablespoons fresh lemon juice

2 cloves garlic, minced

2 tablespoons chopped fresh parsley

2 teaspoons chopped fresh chives

1½ teaspoons chopped fresh tarragon

1½ teaspoons chopped fresh basil

1½ teaspoons chopped fresh oregano

1 teaspoon salt

1 teaspoon pepper

1 teaspoon finely grated lemon zest

In a medium-size bowl, whisk together the mayonnaise and buttermilk, then add the garlic, herbs, salt, and lemon pepper and stir until blended.

**DIVA DO-AHEAD:** At this point, you can cover and refrigerate for up to 2 days. Shake well or whisk before using.

# Tarragon Caesar Dressing

Makes about 2½ cups

Marrying tarragon and anchovy paste may not seem like a good idea, but I urge you to try this deliciously different and beautifully colored Caesar. Toss it with romaine, or spoon it over chicken or shrimp. You can even use it as a dip for endive leaves.

2 cups mayonnaise

¼ cup fresh lemon juice

¼ cup coarsely chopped fresh parsley

¼ cup chopped fresh chives

2 tablespoons chopped fresh tarragon leaves

2 teaspoons anchovy paste

1 teaspoon freshly ground black pepper

Combine all the ingredients in a food processor and process until smooth and thick.

✳ **DIVA DO-AHEAD:** At this point, you can cover and refrigerate for up to 3 days.

# Sweet Tomato Dressing

Makes about 2 cups

This sweet and tart dressing is reminiscent of that bottled stuff from the '50s, but with a lot more character and pizzazz. Serve over spinach with crumbled crisp bacon and sliced mushrooms for a change of pace.

1½ cups vegetable oil

⅔ cup sugar

½ cup ketchup

½ cup red wine vinegar

½ cup finely chopped red onion

1 teaspoon Worcestershire sauce

1 teaspoon freshly ground black pepper

½ teaspoon dry mustard

In a medium-size bowl, whisk together the ingredients until blended.

✳ **DIVA DO-AHEAD:** At this point, you can cover and refrigerate for up to 4 days. Let come to room temperature and whisk before using.

# Pesto Mayonnaise

Makes about 3 cups

This delicately colored green mayonnaise is terrific on salads made with potatoes, pasta, or chicken. It's even delicious as a spread on crusty bread for sandwiches. Because there is a lot of oil in the pesto, I use low-fat mayonnaise in this recipe, which works very well.

**2 cups low-fat mayonnaise**

**1 cup Basil Pesto, homemade (page 97) or store-bought**

In a medium-size bowl, whisk together the mayonnaise and pesto until smooth.

✳ **DIVA DO-AHEAD:** At this point, you can cover and refrigerate for up to 3 days.

# Cheese Tuiles

Makes about twelve 3-inch rounds

These mounds of shredded cheese are baked and then shaped over a rolling pin while still hot or left in their flat shape. You'll love serving these crispy and delicious treats as a topping on your buffet salads, or as a nibble before dinner.

**3 cups shredded Parmigiano-Reggiano cheese**

**1.** Preheat the oven to 375°F and line 3 jelly roll pans with silicone liners, aluminum foil, or parchment paper.

**2.** Place ¼ cup of cheese on one of the prepared pans and spread it into a 3-inch circle. Repeat this process, spacing the circles about 1 inch apart, until all the cheese is used up.

**3.** Bake until the cheese melts and begins to turn brown, 5 to 6 minutes. Remove from the oven, allow the tuile to firm up for 30 to 45 seconds, then remove from the sheet with a metal spatula, and drape over a rolling pin to give it a curve. (If you don't want to shape them, remove the tuiles from the baking sheets and allow to cool on a plate.) Let cool completely.

✳ **DIVA DO-AHEAD:** At this point, you can store in an airtight container or a zipper-top plastic bag at room temperature for up to 2 days.

# Garlic Croutons

Makes about 4 cups

Homemade croutons are not only delicious, but they also help you recycle day-old baguettes or other breads that may otherwise end up in the trash. I have found that croutons made with dried herbs fare much better than those made with fresh. The herbs are optional, for added interest; if you are making croutons for a Caesar salad, just use the oil, garlic salt, and pepper.

½ to ¾ cup extra virgin olive oil

1 teaspoon garlic salt

1 teaspoon freshly ground black pepper

2 teaspoons dried herbs, such as oregano, rosemary, basil, marjoram, thyme, sage, or a combination

4 cups cubed leftover bread (½-inch cubes)

**1.** Preheat the oven to 350°F and line a baking sheet with a silicone liner, aluminum foil, or parchment paper.

**2.** In a large bowl, whisk together the oil, garlic salt, pepper, and optional herbs. Add the bread cubes and toss.

**3.** Spread the bread over the prepared baking sheet and bake for 5 minutes. Turn the cubes, bake for another 5 minutes, and turn the cubes again. Cook until they are dry and begin to turn golden, another 5 minutes.

**4.** Remove the croutons from the oven and let cool completely.

✳ **DIVA DO-AHEAD:** At this point, you can store in an airtight container or a zipper-top plastic bag at room temperature for up to 5 days or freeze for up to 6 months.

# On the
# Side

**The challenge of presenting attractive** and appropriate side dishes for your parties can seem like an overwhelming task, but it's really like putting together an outfit. You need a little color, a lot of taste, and something to catch the eye. For example, bright Green Beans with Sherried Onion and Mushroom Sauce (page 230) served alongside Honey-Thyme Carrots (page 236) or Eggplant Rollatini (page 239) is visually appealing and offers your guests a delicious choice of side dishes. Potatoes demand colorful company, so go with a dish with red tomato color that will complement the potatoes, or a spinach dish that will add pizzazz.

When planning your side dishes, try to complement the flavors of your entrée and salad choices. If you are serving a rather spicy or full-flavored entrée (think Cajun, Spanish, Southwestern, or Asian, or just a simple roast beef) your choices for sides and salads should not be overpowering so that your main course will be the star, and the side dishes will play supporting roles. For example, if you are serving Roast Beef Tenderloin (page 385), it should be the focal point of your meal. Cranberry–Blue Cheese Field Greens Salad (page 172), Roasted Wild Mushroom Salad (page 163), or Field Greens with Basil Vinaigrette (page 173) would complement the roast well. Other sides for this dinner might include a make-ahead mashed potato choice, Spinach Parmesan Casserole (page 257), and Honey-Thyme Carrots (page 236). None of these will overwhelm the flavor of the meat or disturb the balance of the meal, and each will give the table color as well. On the other hand, if you are serving grilled chicken, choose some punchy sides with a lot of flavor and color, such as Roasted Spicy Asian Sweet Potatoes (page 261).

The recipes in this chapter can be made ahead of time and reheated just before serving or else served at room temperature, so that you can sail through your party rather than sweating a lot of last-minute cooking. Flip through these pages for delicious new ways to cook vegetables and side dishes for a crowd without breaking your back or the bank. There are also a few nice fruit selections, some scrumptious stuffings, and a savory bread pudding to serve as alternatives to potatoes, pasta, or rice.

# The Easy Entertainer's Guide to Veggies for Side Dishes

**Bell peppers:** Green, yellow, and red peppers are available year-round; the red and yellow ones impart a sweetness to many dishes. Look for peppers that are tight, meaning the flesh doesn't feel wrinkled or shriveled. Remove the seeds and core, then slice or chop as directed.

**Broccoli:** When choosing broccoli at the store, make sure that the florets are tight. If they are big and fat, they will fall off the stalk when they are cooked.

**Carrots:** So-called baby carrots have taken over in the produce section. The baby carrots sold in huge bags are really big carrots cut smaller; true baby carrots are too expensive to make for a crowd, but they are lovely to serve as a garnish on your buffet platters. The less expensive ones, made from mature carrots, are terrific raw or cooked and add color and flavor to roasted vegetables and braises.

**Corn:** Corn on the cob for a crowd is difficult because you'll need several pots of boiling water going at the same time to cook them all. Frozen corn is a better use of your time and money, so I include dishes that are made with corn kernels instead.

**Eggplant:** I love small, mild Japanese eggplant for stuffing and sautéing, but for serving a crowd, large purple eggplants are the way to go. Make sure that the skin is unblemished and tight, with a deep purple color. I generally don't salt and drain eggplant; I've found that it doesn't make enough of a difference in the finished dish to warrant that extra step. If I am grilling eggplant, I leave the skin on so the eggplant doesn't fall apart. If you aren't fond of the skin, peel it off after it's cooked.

**Green beans:** Choose green beans without blemishes and snap off the tough ends. For a buffet, it might be advisable to cut the green beans into 1-inch (bite-size) pieces. Whole green beans are dramatic but cumbersome when eaten while standing.

**Mushrooms:** *Portobellos* are the large, brown mushrooms that you can grill or sauté. If you want to remove the gills (the spongy black stuff underneath the cap) to prevent the finished dish from turning black, you can scrape them away carefully with a spoon. If you are grilling the caps, I'd suggest you leave the gills because the cooked mushroom will be dark brown anyway, and they will be more flavorful.

*Small white button mushrooms* can be sautéed or roasted. Because of their pale color, they are excellent in creamy sauces.

Brown *cremini mushrooms* are a little more intense in flavor than button mushrooms. They are terrific in sauces or sautés, and also benefit from roasting. Portobellos are actually overgrown creminis.

*Shiitake mushrooms* are still more intensely flavored than creminis. They, too, are delicious sautéed or roasted. Discard the stems, which are sometimes very tough, and cook the caps.

**Onions:** *Sweet onions*—such as Walla Walla, Vidalia, Maui, and Texas Sweet—have a higher sugar content than the brown-skinned onions you will find in your grocer's bin. They are also more expensive, but the difference in taste is worth the price, in my opinion. *Red onions* are always available and they can be substituted for sweet onions.

**Potatoes:** *Russet* baking potatoes are terrific for oven fries, mashed potatoes, and baked stuffed potatoes. *New red* or *white* potatoes and *Yukon Golds* are delicious roasted and steamed, and they can be used for mashed potatoes as well. Other varieties, such as *fingerling* and various heirloom potatoes, are delicious and cute, but far too expensive to cook for large groups.

**Spinach:** Prepping fresh spinach to feed a crowd is unwieldy and time-consuming, so feel free to substitute frozen where appropriate. I think frozen vegetables work best in a dish where the other flavors will predominate. The best way to press all the moisture out of frozen spinach is to pass it through a ricer; if you don't have one, press it in a sieve until it is dry.

**Summer squash:** *Zucchini* is a great vegetable to use in sautés and casseroles; it's inexpensive and provides a vibrant green color and some moisture. Zucchini now comes in a yellow variety as well, which I think has a somewhat milder flavor. *Yellow squash* is delicate and benefits from sautéing, or it can be folded into a casserole.

***Sweet potatoes:*** Sweet potatoes benefit from roasting rather than boiling because the slow cooking helps bring out the natural sugar in the potato.

***Tomatoes:*** Varicolored tomatoes make a great visual statement on the buffet table, but I would only use them when you know they are truly vine-ripened—taste before beauty! *Cherry* tomatoes seem to be pretty good year-round, so I would recommend using those in recipes that call for ripe tomatoes when you're entertaining out of season. Canned plum tomatoes can be used in the winter for sauces and stews.

# Roasted Asparagus

Serves 10

I love thick-stemmed asparagus for its deep flavor, but you may prefer the pencil-thin variety. Roasting asparagus is simple; you can do it the day before, then toss it in some warm olive oil and serve it. If you love to squeeze lemon juice over your asparagus, do it right before serving; otherwise, it will turn the vegetable an unattractive shade of army green.

When trimming the asparagus, cut or snap the stem where it begins to be tender, so you don't waste too much of it. I recommend peeling the stalks on fat asparagus with a swivel vegetable peeler as well. It takes a few extra minutes, but the asparagus will look positively transcendent on the serving dish.

---

**2 pounds asparagus, trimmed of tough stem ends and peeled if desired**

**¼ cup olive oil**

**1½ teaspoons salt**

**1 teaspoon freshly ground black pepper**

---

**1.** Preheat the oven to 400°F. Line a baking sheet with a silicone liner, aluminum foil, or parchment paper.

**2.** Arrange the asparagus in a single layer on the prepared sheet, sprinkle with the oil, salt, and pepper, then roll the asparagus in the mixture until coated. Bake until crisp-tender, 4 to 5 minutes (pencil-thin asparagus will take about 3 minutes, and thicker asparagus, a bit longer).

**3.** Remove from the oven.

✳ **DIVA DO-AHEAD:** At this point, you can let sit at room temperature for up to 2 hours or let cool, cover, and refrigerate overnight. Return to room temperature before serving or heat in a skillet with 2 tablespoons of olive oil.

Serve warm or at room temperature.

## Diva Garnishes for Asparagus

• Try a quick lemon-dill butter sauce: Melt ½ cup (1 stick) of unsalted butter in a small saucepan over medium-low heat, then stir in 2 tablespoons of fresh lemon juice and 2 tablespoons of fresh chopped dill. Keep warm until you are ready to drizzle it over the asparagus.

• Shavings of Parmigiano-Reggiano cheese make a wonderful garnish; the heat from the asparagus will melt the cheese a bit.

• Hollandaise Sauce (page 496), Béarnaise Sauce (page 497), and any of the compound butters (see pages 510 to 513) make excellent "dress-ups" for asparagus. Or you could serve the roasted asparagus at room temperature with béarnaise mayonnaise (see page 495).

# Cheesy Refried Bean Bake

Serves 10

This easy side dish flavored with chiles and topped with a golden crown of cheddar and pepper Jack cheeses is a winner, especially when served with grilled meats and poultry. You can layer it in your slow cooker if you'd like, and it only takes about 10 minutes to put together.

**2 tablespoons olive oil**

**1 cup chopped onions**

**1 teaspoon ground cumin**

**¼ cup seeded and finely chopped Anaheim chile pepper**

**Four 15.5-ounce cans refried beans**

**1½ cups sour cream (low-fat is okay)**

**1 cup shredded mild cheddar cheese**

**1 cup shredded pepper Jack cheese**

**¼ cup chopped fresh cilantro for garnish**

### Slow Cooker Savvy

Coat a 4- to 6-quart slow cooker with nonstick cooking spray. Follow the instructions through step 3. Spread out the mixture evenly in the slow cooker and top with the cheeses. Cover and cook on Low until the cheese is melted and the beans are heated through, about 3 hours. Garnish with the cilantro.

**1.** Coat a 13 x 9-inch baking dish with non-stick cooking spray.

**2.** In a medium-size skillet, heat the olive oil, then add the onions, cumin, and chile pepper and cook, stirring, for about 3 minutes. Remove from the heat.

**3.** In a large bowl, blend together the refried beans and sour cream. Add the onions and stir to blend.

**4.** Spread out the bean and onion mixture in the prepared dish and sprinkle evenly with both cheeses.

❋ **DIVA DO-AHEAD:** At this point, you can cover and refrigerate for up to 2 days. Bring to room temperature before continuing.

**5.** Preheat the oven to 350°F. Bake the casserole until the cheese is bubbling, about 30 minutes. Garnish with the cilantro.

# Barbecue Baked Beans

Serves 10

My dad was from Boston, and he loved traditional baked beans. They're too bland for my taste, so I've jazzed them up a bit. Since this recipe uses canned beans, you can have them on the table in a jiffy. This dish is great to take to a barbecue or potluck, and I know lots of people who serve these at Easter alongside scalloped potatoes and ham.

**8 strips bacon, cut into ½-inch dice**

**1½ cups finely chopped onions**

**Four 15.5-ounce cans plain baked beans**

**½ cup ketchup**

**½ cup bottled barbecue sauce**

**1 tablespoon prepared yellow mustard**

**2 tablespoons Worcestershire sauce**

**½ cup firmly packed dark brown sugar**

### Slow Cooker Savvy

Cook the bacon and onions, as directed, on the stove top. Then combine with the remaining ingredients in a 4- to 6-quart slow cooker, cover, and cook on Low for 3 to 4 hours.

In a 4-quart saucepan over medium heat, cook the bacon, stirring, until crisp. Remove all but 1 tablespoon of the bacon fat, add the onions, and cook, stirring, until softened and starting to turn golden. Add the beans, ketchup, barbecue sauce, mustard, Worcestershire, and brown sugar and stir to blend. Simmer over low heat, stirring frequently, for 45 minutes.

✳ **DIVA DO-AHEAD:** At this point, you can let cool, cover, and refrigerate for up to 2 days. Gently reheat before serving.

### Diva Baked Bean Add-Ins

• Brown 1½ pounds of ground beef until no longer pink, drain away the fat, and add it to the onions to give these beans more oomph.

• Add 1 pound of Polish sausage (kielbasa), cut into ½-inch-thick slices, to the onions.

# White Bean Rosemary Gratin

Serves 10

This luscious, creamy bean dish with a nice crunchy topping is delicious to serve with grilled or roasted meats and poultry alongside some crisp vegetables or salad. And it's a budget stretcher because it's relatively inexpensive. The recipe can be multiplied many times to feed a large crowd. This is very tasty made in the slow cooker.

¼ cup extra virgin olive oil

1 large onion, finely chopped

2 medium-size carrots, finely chopped

2 ribs celery, finely chopped

2 teaspoons chopped fresh rosemary, or ¾ teaspoon dried

3 cloves garlic, minced

One 15.5-ounce can chopped tomatoes with their juice

½ cup dry white wine

1½ teaspoons salt

1 teaspoon freshly ground black pepper

Four 15.5-ounce cans small white beans, drained and rinsed

½ cup fresh bread crumbs

½ cup freshly grated Parmesan cheese

**1.** In a 5-quart sauté pan, heat 2 tablespoons of the olive oil over medium-high heat. Add the onion, carrots, celery, and rosemary and cook, stirring, until the vegetables are softened, about 3 minutes. Add the garlic and cook, stirring, for another 2 minutes. Add the tomatoes, wine, salt, and pepper and cook until some of the liquid in the pan has evaporated, about 5 minutes. Add the beans, reduce the heat to medium-low, and simmer for 15 minutes. Taste and adjust the salt and pepper as needed. Transfer the mixture to a 3-quart gratin or 13 x 9-inch baking dish.

**2.** In a small bowl, stir together the bread crumbs and cheese, add the remaining 2 tablespoons of olive oil, and stir to blend.

✳ **DIVA DO-AHEAD:** At this point, you can store the bread crumb mixture in a zipper-top plastic bag. Let the beans cool and cover. Refrigerate both for up to 2 days. Bring the beans to room temperature before continuing.

**3.** Preheat the oven to 350°F. Sprinkle the bread crumb mixture evenly over the beans and bake until bubbling and golden brown, 20 to 25 minutes. Let rest 5 to 10 minutes before serving.

## Slow Cooker Savvy

Follow as directed through step 1, transferring the mixture to a 5- to 6-quart slow cooker instead. Sprinkle with the bread crumb mixture, cover, and cook on Low until heated through, 3 to 4 hours.

# Green Beans with Sherried Onion and Mushroom Sauce 🥃🍷🍸

Serves 10

With its creamy sherry-spiked mushroom sauce, this is my idea of the perfect side dish for Thanksgiving or another elegant dinner. It's a perfect companion for grilled chicken or roasted meats. The sauce alone is scrumptious over peas and can be mixed with leftover turkey for a creamy alternative to leftover turkey with gravy.

**3 tablespoons unsalted butter**

**1 cup small pearl onions, cut in half**

**½ pound mushrooms**

**2 tablespoons all-purpose flour**

**1 cup chicken broth**

**½ cup heavy cream**

**2 tablespoons cream sherry**

**Pinch of ground nutmeg**

**Salt and freshly ground black pepper to taste**

**8 cups water**

**2 pounds green beans, ends trimmed and cut into 1-inch lengths**

**1.** In a medium-size skillet over medium heat, melt the butter. Add the onions and cook, stirring, for 3 minutes. Add the mushrooms and cook, stirring a few times, until the liquid from the mushrooms has evaporated. Sprinkle the flour over the mushrooms and onions and stir until blended. Cook for 2 to 3 minutes, stirring, to make sure the vegetables don't stick to the bottom of the pan. Gradually stir in the broth and whisk until it comes to a boil. Add the cream and sherry and cook, stirring, until the sauce thickens. Add the nutmeg and season with salt and pepper.

❋ **DIVA DO-AHEAD:** At this point, you can let cool, cover, and refrigerate for up to 3 days. Reheat gently before continuing.

**2.** Bring the water to a boil in a large saucepan, add the green beans, and return the water to a boil. Cook the beans until crisp-tender, about 3 minutes. Drain the beans.

❋ **DIVA DO-AHEAD:** At this point, you can shock the beans under cold running water to cool them down. Drain, cover, and refrigerate overnight. Reheat, covered, in the microwave for 3 minutes or plunge into boiling water for 1 minute and drain before continuing.

**3.** To serve, place the warm green beans in a serving dish and pour the warm sauce over them.

# Peperonata

Serves 10

Growing up, I referred to this as "peppersonionsandtomatoes," all one word, but Grandma called it peperonata. It was one of my favorite *contorni*, or side dishes, that Grandma would make. The sweet peppers, onions, and tomatoes are cooked down together to make a delicious dish to serve on the side with Italian sausages, grilled chicken, seafood, or meats. It also makes a stunning addition to a foot-long sandwich with grilled chicken or steak. As a child, however, my favorite way to eat this was scooped out of the pan on a slice of Grandma's homemade bread—that was heaven.

**3 tablespoons olive oil**

**3 large sweet onions, thinly sliced**

**4 yellow bell peppers, seeded and thinly sliced into rings**

**4 red bell peppers, seeded and thinly sliced into rings**

**2 teaspoons salt**

**2 teaspoons sugar**

**1 teaspoon freshly ground black pepper**

**One 15.5-ounce can crushed tomatoes**

## Diva Variations

For spicy peperonata, substitute red pepper flakes for the black pepper.

Add 3 tablespoons of balsamic vinegar along with the tomatoes to give the peppers a piquant, delicious taste.

A sprinkling of grated Romano cheese over the peppers is also lovely.

**1.** In an extra-large skillet, heat the olive oil over medium-high heat, add the onions, and cook, stirring, until almost translucent, about 5 minutes. Add the peppers, salt, sugar, and black pepper and cook, stirring frequently, until the bell peppers and onions have reduced to about half their original volume, about 10 minutes.

**2.** Add the tomatoes and stir until combined. Continue to cook, stirring, until the liquid from the tomatoes begins to evaporate, another 10 minutes.

✳ **DIVA DO-AHEAD:** At this point, you can let cool, cover, and refrigerate for up to 3 days. Gently reheat before serving.

**3.** Serve hot or at room temperature.

# Roasted Brussels Sprouts with Pancetta

Serves 10

I have to admit that Brussels sprouts were not my favorite vegetable, at least not until I tested this recipe. When the Brussels sprouts are roasted, they develop a sweeter flavor, and the addition of a little pancetta makes everything taste better! This dish is perfect for Thanksgiving or Christmas dinner.

**3 pounds Brussels sprouts, trimmed of tough outer leaves and cut in half**

**4 cloves garlic, cut into slivers**

**½ cup olive oil**

**2 teaspoons salt**

**½ teaspoon freshly ground black pepper**

**½ teaspoon red pepper flakes (optional)**

**4 slices pancetta, finely diced**

**½ cup chopped shallots**

**1.** Preheat the oven to 400°F. Line a baking sheet with a silicone liner or aluminum foil.

**2.** Combine the Brussels sprouts, garlic, olive oil, salt, black pepper, and red pepper flakes, if using, in a large bowl and toss to coat the Brussels sprouts. Spread out in a single layer on the baking sheet and roast until tender, 25 to 35 minutes.

**3.** While the Brussels sprouts are roasting, cook the pancetta in a small skillet over high heat, stirring, until the fat is rendered and the pancetta becomes crispy. Add the shallots and cook, stirring, until almost golden brown, about 8 minutes. Remove the pan from the heat.

✳ **DIVA DO-AHEAD:** At this point, you can let cool, transfer the sprouts to an ovenproof dish, and top with the pancetta mixture. Cover and refrigerate overnight. Bring to room temperature, toss the pancetta mixture with the sprouts to coat, and reheat in a 350°F oven for 10 to 15 minutes before serving.

**4.** When the sprouts come out of the oven, transfer to a serving bowl and garnish with the pancetta-and-shallot mixture, tossing to coat. Serve warm or at room temperature.

# Red Cabbage and Apple Sauté

Serves 10

I love sweet-and-sour red cabbage with pork, especially when it includes apples. This sauté tastes best when made ahead of time.

2 tablespoons olive oil

1 medium-size red onion, thinly sliced and separated into rings

3 medium-size Granny Smith apples, peeled, cored, and sliced ¼ inch thick

¼ teaspoon ground allspice

½ cup firmly packed light brown sugar

2 medium-size heads red cabbage, cored and thinly sliced

2 tablespoons balsamic vinegar

**1.** In a 5-quart Dutch oven, heat the olive oil over medium heat, then add the onion, apples, allspice, and brown sugar, stir to blend, and cook, stirring, until the apples are softened and the onions begin to turn golden, about 8 minutes.

**2.** Add the cabbage and vinegar, stirring to blend. Cover and simmer for 30 minutes over medium heat, stirring every 10 minutes until the cabbage is tender. Taste and adjust the salt and pepper as needed.

✳ **DIVA DO-AHEAD:** At this point, you can let cool, cover, and refrigerate for up to 5 days. Reheat over medium heat before serving.

**3.** Serve warm or at room temperature.

### Slow Cooker Savvy

Sauté the onions and apples as instructed. Transfer to a 4- to 6-quart slow cooker and mix in the cabbage and vinegar. Cover and cook for 4 hours on Low, stirring occasionally. Season with salt and pepper.

# Martha's Hapukapsa

Serves 10

My friend Martha Mand shared this delicious Estonian sauerkraut and apple dish (pronounced hah-POO-kahp-sa) with me. I love to serve it with roast pork.

½ cup (1 stick) unsalted butter

2 large onions, coarsely chopped

6 cups finely shredded cabbage (about 1½ medium-size heads)

Three 15.5-ounce cans sauerkraut, rinsed, drained, and squeezed dry

2 medium-size apples, peeled, cored, and thinly sliced

¼ cup sugar

**1.** In an 8-quart stockpot over medium heat, melt 6 tablespoons (¾ stick) of the butter, then add the onions, stirring to coat. Cook, stirring, until translucent, 8 to 10 minutes. Add the cabbage, cover, and steam the cabbage for about 10 minutes.

**2.** Add the sauerkraut and mix thoroughly. Add the remaining 2 tablespoons of butter, cut into small pieces, along with the apples and sugar. Increase the heat to medium-high and cook, uncovered, stirring, until the vegetables reduce and begin to brown, about 30 minutes. Taste and adjust the salt and pepper as needed.

✳ **DIVA DO-AHEAD:** At this point, you can let cool, cover, and refrigerate for up to 3 days. Gently reheat over medium heat before serving.

## The Diva Says:

When removing the cover of your slow cooker to stir the contents, try to work quickly and re-cover, so you don't change the temperature in the slow cooker too dramatically. Some slow cookers will lose heat rapidly if you leave the cover off for 3 to 5 minutes.

### Slow Cooker Savvy

Combine all the ingredients in a 4-quart slow cooker, cover, and cook on Low for 4 hours, stirring every hour, until the cabbage and apples are tender. Remove the top from the slow cooker and cook for another hour, until the mixture is reduced and the liquid has evaporated. When the hapukapsa is ready, serve it from the slow cooker, keeping it on the Low or Warm setting.

# Braised Cabbage with Bacon and Caraway

Serves 10

Cabbage is one of those vegetables that most people eat raw, but it's delicious cooked as well. This recipe actually improves with age, so I usually make it the day before I intend to serve it. The food processor makes quick work of the onions and cabbage.

8 strips bacon, cut into 1-inch pieces

2 large sweet onions, thinly sliced and separated into rings

¼ cup firmly packed light brown sugar

1 tablespoon caraway seeds

1 teaspoon freshly ground black pepper

2 medium-size heads green cabbage, cored and thinly sliced

½ cup chicken broth

**1.** In a 5-quart Dutch oven over medium-high heat, cook the bacon until crisp. Remove all but 2 tablespoons of the bacon fat, add the onions, stirring to coat, and cook, stirring, until softened, about 3 minutes. Add the sugar, caraway, and pepper and continue to cook, stirring, until the onions begin to brown, another 5 minutes.

**2.** Add the cabbage and stir to combine. Add the broth, bring to a boil, reduce the heat, and simmer for 30 minutes, stirring every 5 minutes to prevent sticking. Taste and adjust the salt and pepper as needed.

✳ **DIVA DO-AHEAD:** At this point, you can let cool, cover, and refrigerate for up to 3 days. Reheat gently or place in the slow cooker on Low for 3 hours before serving.

## Slow Cooker Savvy

Prepare the dish through step 1. Stir in the cabbage and broth, then transfer the mixture to a 4-quart slow cooker, cover, and cook on High for 4 hours, stirring occasionally.

# Honey-Thyme Carrots

Serves 10

Baby carrots abound in the grocery store produce section; they are so convenient to use for dips, but are also yummy in this special side dish. Serve these with roasted meats or poultry. They're especially nice for the winter holidays.

¼ cup (½ stick) unsalted butter

½ cup chopped shallots

1½ pounds baby carrots

2 tablespoons honey

2 teaspoons dried thyme

⅓ cup chicken broth

1 cup heavy cream

⅛ teaspoon ground nutmeg

Salt and freshly ground black pepper to taste

**1.** In a large skillet, melt the butter over medium heat, then add the shallots and carrots and cook, stirring, until the shallots begin to soften, about 3 minutes.

Add the honey and thyme and stir until the honey has coated the vegetables. Gradually add the broth and simmer, uncovered, until evaporated by half, about 15 minutes.

**2.** Stir in the heavy cream and reduce the sauce by about half, another 10 minutes. Stir in the nutmeg and season with salt and pepper.

✳ **DIVA DO-AHEAD:** At this point, you can let cool, cover, and refrigerate for up to 2 days. Reheat over medium heat before serving, being careful not to burn the carrots, or microwave on 50 percent power for 5 to 6 minutes, until heated through.

# Breaded Roasted Cauliflower

Serves 10

Cauliflower is in that category of vegetables that people either love or hate. When I tested this recipe, I found that roasting the cauliflower gave it a sweet taste and took away the rather strong odor it normally has. The breading gave it a little kick as well. It's very good hot or at room temperature, served with roasted or grilled beef or poultry.

2 medium-size heads cauliflower

½ cup olive oil

1½ teaspoons salt

½ teaspoon freshly ground black pepper

1½ cups fine dry bread crumbs

¾ cup freshly grated Parmesan cheese

1½ teaspoons dried oregano

**1.** Line a baking sheet with a silicone liner or aluminum foil.

**2.** Trim the cauliflower and cut into 1-inch florets. Try to keep them about the same size so they will cook evenly. Put the cauliflower in a large bowl and toss with 6 tablespoons of the oil, the salt, and pepper.

**3.** In another large bowl, combine the bread crumbs, cheese, and oregano, stirring until blended. Toss the florets in the crumbs, a few at a time, stirring to coat evenly. Transfer to the prepared baking sheet and drizzle with the remaining 2 tablespoons of olive oil.

✳ **DIVA DO-AHEAD:** At this point, you can cover and leave at room temperature for up to 2 hours or refrigerate for 8 hours.

**4.** Preheat the oven to 375°F. Bake until tender when pierced with the tip of a knife, 10 to 15 minutes. Remove from the oven, transfer to a serving bowl, and serve warm or at room temperature.

# Perfect Corn on the Cob

Serves 10

I recommend serving corn on the cob only when it's at its peak in summer; the rest of the year it can be marginal at best. This will require you to have a few pots on the stove, but if you are grilling a main dish outside, you should have plenty of room on the stove top to make great corn on the cob. You can prepare it about 30 minutes in advance. Serve the corn with melted butter or a compound butter (pages 510 to 513) of your choice.

12 quarts water

2 tablespoons sugar

12 to 14 ears fresh corn, shucked, with silks removed

Bring 6 quarts of water and 1 tablespoon of sugar to a boil in each of 2 large pots. Add half the corn to each pot and return the water to a boil. Remove the pot from the heat.

✳ **DIVA DO-AHEAD:** The corn can sit in the water for up to 30 minutes before serving.

# Gulliver's Corn

Serves 10

Of all the dishes I prepare at Thanksgiving, this recipe is the most requested. I guess it proves that if you keep it simple, people will love it! The name comes from a restaurant here in California that used to serve this creamy dish, which I've tinkered with. It can be prepared in individual ramekins instead of a baking dish.

**6 tablespoons (¾ stick) unsalted butter, melted**

**⅔ cup freshly grated Parmesan cheese**

**1½ cups heavy cream**

**Two 16-ounce bags frozen white corn, defrosted**

**2 teaspoons salt**

**1 teaspoon sugar**

**3 tablespoons all-purpose flour**

**1.** Brush a 13 x 9-inch baking dish with some of the butter. Sprinkle ⅓ cup of the Parmesan over the bottom of the dish and tilt so the cheese is evenly distributed and adheres to the butter.

**2.** In a 4-quart saucepan, heat the cream until it begins to boil. Add the corn, salt, and sugar, and heat, stirring occasionally, until the mixture is almost at a boil.

**3.** In the meantime, make a paste out of the remaining melted butter and the flour. Stir it into the mixture in the saucepan and cook until thickened and the liquid comes to a boil. Remove the pan from the heat, transfer the mixture to the prepared dish, and sprinkle with the remaining ⅓ cup of cheese.

✳ **DIVA DO-AHEAD:** At this point, you can let cool, cover, and refrigerate for up to 3 days or freeze for up to 1 month. Bring to room temperature before continuing.

**4.** Preheat the oven to 350°F. Bake the corn dish until bubbling and golden brown, about 30 minutes.

## The Diet Diva Says:

If you would prefer to skip the cream, try whole milk; it's not as luxurious, but it does the job.

## Corn Rules from the Farm Stand

I am fortunate enough to live around the corner from the world famous Chino Vegetable Shop in Rancho Santa Fe, where Alice Waters would fly to buy her produce for Chez Panisse. The corn melts in your mouth and is worth waiting in line to buy. At the shop, they recommend that you never salt the water for the corn (the sugar is my trick). They also advise their customers not to boil the corn. (See the recipe on page 237).

# Summer Succotash

Serves 10

This brightly colored succotash is a little different because it is made with sugar snap peas. It is quick to put together and you can make it the day before, then reheat it just before serving. If you have leftover corn on the cob, this would be an excellent way to use it up.

2 tablespoons unsalted butter

2 tablespoons olive oil

½ cup finely chopped shallots

2 cups sugar snap peas, stems trimmed

4 cups fresh corn kernels cut from the cob or frozen corn, defrosted

1½ teaspoons salt

1 teaspoon freshly ground black pepper

1 cup cherry tomatoes (optional), cut in half

¼ cup chopped fresh Italian parsley

### Diva Variation

Substitute 2 cups of shelled fresh edamame or shelled and peeled fava beans for the sugar snap peas.

**1.** Heat the butter and oil together in a large skillet over medium heat. When the butter is melted, add the shallots and cook, stirring, until softened, about 3 minutes. Add the peas and cook, stirring, for another 3 minutes, coating them with the butter and oil. Add the corn, salt, and pepper and cook, stirring, until heated through.

❋ **DIVA DO-AHEAD:** At this point, you can let cool, cover, and refrigerate overnight. Gently reheat before continuing.

**2.** Just before serving, add the tomatoes and parsley to the pan and toss until heated through.

# Eggplant Rollatini

Serves 10

I love eggplant parmigiana but it's a lot of work and messy at that, with all the breading and frying. This side dish is similar, but you grill the eggplant, then fill it with a cheese-and-bread-crumb mixture, cover it with tomato sauce and cheese, and bake. Each little rollatini is an individual serving, so it's easy to serve.

- 2 large purple eggplants, ends trimmed and cut lengthwise into ½-inch-thick slices
- ½ cup olive oil
- 1½ teaspoons salt
- 1 teaspoon freshly ground black pepper
- 3 cups soft fresh bread crumbs
- 1½ cups freshly grated Parmesan cheese
- 3 large eggs
- ¼ cup chopped fresh Italian parsley
- 4 cups Quick Marinara (page 482)
- 1 pound fresh mozzarella cheese, cut into ½-inch cubes
- 1½ teaspoons dried oregano

**1.** Preheat the broiler and line a baking sheet with aluminum foil. Place as many eggplant slices on the sheet as will fit in a single layer.

**2.** In a small bowl, combine the oil, salt, and pepper. Brush the eggplant slices with the oil mixture, then broil the slices on one side until softened. Turn over, brush with more oil, and broil until the second side begins to turn golden brown. Repeat the procedure until all the eggplant slices are broiled.

✳ **DIVA DO-AHEAD:** At this point, you can refrigerate for up to 2 days. To store, lay the slices in a single layer in a 13 x 9-inch baking dish, cover with waxed paper or plastic wrap, and layer the remaining eggplant slices, separating the layers with waxed paper or plastic wrap. Then cover the entire dish. Before continuing, drain off any excess moisture that accumulated in the dish and if necessary pat the eggplant dry with paper towels.

**3.** In a large bowl, stir together the bread crumbs, Parmesan, eggs, and parsley until blended.

**4.** Pour ¾ cup of the marinara into a 13 x 9-inch baking dish.

**5.** Working on a flat surface, place a slice of eggplant with its browned side down. Spoon 2 tablespoons of filling across the center and place 2 or 3 cubes of mozzarella on top of that. Roll up the eggplant from a wide end and place in the baking dish. Repeat until you have used all the eggplant. (Since not all eggplants are created equal, you may have a little leftover filling or a few leftover eggplant slices; if you have leftover slices, you can save them for a veggie sandwich or cut them up and use in salad.)

**6.** Spread the remaining 3¼ cups of marinara sauce over the rollatini, top with the remaining mozzarella, and sprinkle with the oregano.

✳ **DIVA DO-AHEAD:** At this point, you can cover and refrigerate for up to 2 days or freeze for up to 1 month. Defrost and bring to room temperature before continuing.

**7.** Preheat the oven to 350°F. Bake the rollatini until the cheese is melted and bubbling and the rollatini are heated through, 35 to 45 minutes. Let rest for 5 to 10 minutes before serving.

# Smoky Ham and Fennel Gratin

Serves 10

Sweet fennel, Gruyère, and Black Forest ham make a terrific combination in this side dish. Serve it with grilled meats, chicken, or seafood, and your guests will want seconds.

6 fennel bulbs, trimmed of their stalks and sliced ½ inch thick

¼ pound thinly sliced Black Forest ham, cut into matchsticks

1½ cups heavy cream

1½ teaspoons salt

½ teaspoon freshly ground black pepper

1½ cups shredded Gruyère cheese

**1.** Coat a 13 x 9-inch baking dish with non-stick cooking spray.

**2.** Arrange the fennel slices in the prepared dish. Scatter the ham on top.

**3.** In a small bowl, whisk together the cream, salt, and pepper and pour over the fennel. Sprinkle the cheese over the top.

✳ **DIVA DO-AHEAD:** At this point, you can cover and refrigerate overnight. Bring to room temperature before continuing.

**4.** Preheat the oven to 400°F. Bake until golden brown and tender when pierced with a knife, about 20 minutes. Remove from the oven and let rest for 5 minutes before serving.

# Grilled Portobello Mushrooms

Serves 10

Large portobello mushrooms are becoming regular fare in most restaurants these days because of their meaty flavor. Serve these portobellos in place of meat for vegetarians, slice them on the diagonal and serve over steak or chicken, or make them into little pizzas and top with Quick Marinara or Pizza Sauce (page 482) and your choice of cheese. Grilled portobellos are also delicious in sandwiches on a kaiser roll or foccacia spread with garlic mayonnaise, with chopped fresh basil and/or sliced ripe tomato and chopped fresh parsley as the filling. This is the master recipe for grilling the mushrooms. Try all the variations for serving them at the end of the recipe.

**10 portobello mushrooms, brushed clean and stems removed**

**1½ cups olive oil**

**¼ cup red wine vinegar**

**4 cloves garlic, minced**

**1 tablespoon dried oregano**

**1½ teaspoons salt**

**½ teaspoon freshly ground black pepper**

**1.** Place the mushroom caps on a baking sheet lined with aluminum foil.

**2.** In a medium-size bowl, whisk together the olive oil, vinegar, garlic, oregano, salt, and pepper. Pour the marinade over the mushrooms and turn them once. Cover with plastic wrap and let stand at room temperature for 1 hour, turning the mushrooms several more times.

✳ **DIVA DO-AHEAD:** At this point, you can drain the mushrooms, reserving the marinade, place them in zipper-top plastic bags, and refrigerate for 2 days.

**3.** Build a hot charcoal fire or preheat a gas grill or the broiler for 10 minutes. Grill or broil the mushrooms until tender, brushing them with the reserved marinade, and turning once after 3 or 4 minutes. Remove the mushrooms from the grill or broiler.

✳ **DIVA DO-AHEAD:** At this point, you can keep them at room temperature for 4 hours or cover and refrigerate overnight. If chilled, rewarm in a low oven before serving.

## Diva Variations

**Portobello Pizzas:** Place the grilled mushrooms on a baking sheet lined with aluminum foil or a silicone liner, cap side up. Using 1 cup of Quick Marinara (page 482) and 1½ cups of shredded mozzarella cheese, spread each cap with a thin layer of sauce and top with some of the cheese. Sprinkle with some crumbled dried oregano. Broil for 5 to 10 minutes, until the cheese is melted and bubbling.

**Portobello Sandwiches:** Spread a split kaiser roll with some garlic mayonnaise (see page 495), then top with a single grilled portobello or some slices, then a slice of tomato, and finally 3 fresh basil leaves.

Sprinkle with salt and pepper, top with the other half of the roll, and slice in half.

✳ **DIVA DO-AHEAD:** At this point, you can cover and refrigerate for up to 4 hours before serving.

Serve at room temperature, in halves for a buffet lunch or light supper, or in quarters for appetizer portions.

**Portobello Slices:** Slice the grilled portobellos thinly on the diagonal and sprinkle with some extra virgin olive oil and chopped fresh parsley for garnish. Serve alongside or over grilled or broiled steak or over chicken or seafood.

# Brandied Triple Mushroom Sauté

Serves 10

This elegant side dish was inspired by a similar one that I watched Julia Child prepare during a class I was attending. Julia served hers in puff pastry, but this version goes from the skillet to a serving dish. Back when I took that class, the only mushrooms one could easily find in the grocery store were button mushrooms. Since then, there has been a flood of unusual mushrooms in local markets, so I urge you to experiment with the basic recipe and substitute your favorites. Serve these with grilled meats and poultry and as a topping for green beans, broccoli, or squash.

¼ cup (½ stick) unsalted butter

2 tablespoons olive oil

2 pounds mushrooms, such as button, cremini, shiitake, chanterelle, or oyster, trimmed of tough stems and quartered

2 teaspoons salt

1 teaspoon freshly ground black pepper

2 teaspoons chopped fresh thyme, or ¾ teaspoon dried

½ cup dry sherry

¼ cup brandy

**1.** In a large skillet, heat the butter and olive oil together over high heat. When the butter has melted, add the mushrooms, salt, pepper, and thyme and cook, stirring, until the liquid from the mushrooms evaporates and the mushrooms begin to turn golden brown, about 7 minutes. Add the sherry and cook until reduced by about half.

**2.** Take the skillet off the heat (to prevent a flare-up) and pour in the brandy. Return the skillet to the heat, reduce heat to medium, and cook until the brandy has reduced by half. Remove the pan from the heat and serve.

**✳ DIVA DO-AHEAD:** At this point, you can let cool, cover, and refrigerate for up to 2 days. Reheat gently before serving.

## Diva Variation

**Creamy Brandied Triple Mushroom Sauce:** For an amazing cream sauce to serve with vegetables, poultry, or seafood, add 2 cups of heavy cream after the brandy has reduced and bring to a boil. Continue boiling and reduce the sauce until it coats the back of a spoon, about 10 minutes.

**✳ DIVA DO-AHEAD:** At this point, you can let cool, cover, and refrigerate for up to 2 days.

# Perfectly Caramelized Onions

Serves 10

My mother always used to say that good food takes time, and that is definitely the case with these onions. It will require almost 40 minutes for them to cook down and become golden, so plan on reading a good book while you are stirring! Once you have made them, though, you can refrigerate or freeze them, then reheat on the stove top over low heat. Use a sweet onion for this; I look for Vidalia, Walla Walla, Texas or Mayan Sweets, or Texas 10/15 onions, which are planted on October 15. If they are not available, I recommend red onions or, failing that, yellow onions, but add a few more teaspoons of sugar to help the flavor along. Serve these with burgers and grilled meats and chicken or as a garnish for string beans or tossed greens.

¼ cup (½ stick) unsalted butter

2 tablespoons olive oil

8 large onions, cut in half and thinly sliced into half-moons

1½ teaspoons dried thyme

2 teaspoons salt

1 teaspoon freshly ground black pepper

2 tablespoons sugar

**1.** In a large sauté pan, heat the butter and oil together over medium-high heat. When the butter has melted, add the onions and stir to coat with the butter and oil. (There will be a mound of onions, but they will begin to cook down rather quickly.) After about 3 minutes, turn the onions, sprinkle with the thyme, salt, and pepper and continue to cook, stirring, for another 10 minutes, watching carefully so that the onions do not burn.

**2.** After 10 minutes, add the sugar and toss to coat the onions with the sugar. Reduce the heat to medium-low and cook, stirring, for 10 minutes. Reduce the heat to low and continue to cook until the onions are a beautiful light golden brown. Taste and adjust the salt and pepper.

✳ **DIVA DO-AHEAD:** At this point, you can let cool, cover, and refrigerate overnight.

**3.** Serve warm or at room temperature.

## The Diva Says:

During testing, I found that a wide pan, such as a large sauté pan, worked best for evaporating the liquid in the onions. A tall stockpot created more liquid and therefore the onions took more time to caramelize.

If you would like your onion slices thicker, slice them about ½ inch thick and proceed. Be aware, though, that the cooking time may increase by about 10 minutes. You can chop the onions instead of slicing them, depending on your preference.

### Diva Variation

If you like, you can top the onions with ½ to 1 cup of crumbled blue cheese, goat cheese, or feta cheese for garnish before serving.

### The Diva's 30-Minute Rule

If you are cooking something longer than 30 minutes, use a dried herb; fresh herbs will lose their flavor and shape in a long simmering preparation. You can also use dried herbs to begin with, then add the fresh during the last 15 minutes of cooking time to refresh the flavor of the dish.

# Balsamic Glazed Onions

Serves 10

The addition of balsamic vinegar makes these onions really special. Try them with grilled meats and poultry or as a garnish for salads.

¼ cup (½ stick) unsalted butter

2 tablespoons olive oil

8 to 10 large sweet or red onions, cut in half and thinly sliced into half-moons

2 teaspoons salt

1 teaspoon freshly ground black pepper

2 tablespoons sugar

¼ cup balsamic vinegar

¼ cup chopped fresh Italian parsley for garnish

**1.** In a large skillet heat the butter and oil together over medium-high heat. When the butter has melted, add the onions, salt, and pepper, stir to coat the onions, and cook, stirring to prevent burning, until they begin to turn translucent, about 20 minutes. Add the sugar and vinegar and cook, stirring a few times, until the onions have reduced and are glazed with the vinegar, 10 to 15 minutes. Cool onions to room temperature.

✳ **DIVA DO-AHEAD:** At this point, you can cover and refrigerate for up to 3 days. Return to room temperature before serving.

**2.** Serve the onions sprinkled with the parsley.

### The Butter-and-Oil Thing

The nutty flavor of butter is great with caramelized or glazed onions. But when heated to a high temperature, butter has a tendency to burn, so adding a little oil will help keep the butter from burning. If you would like to omit the butter, just use olive oil.

# Make-Ahead Cheesy Mashed Potatoes 🥛🍷🥄

Serves 10 to 12

The additions of cream cheese and sour cream make these potatoes puff up in the oven like a soufflé, which makes them even more delicious. Try some of the variations that follow.

**8 to 10 medium-size baking potatoes, peeled and cut into chunks**

**6 tablespoons (¾ stick) unsalted butter, softened**

**¾ cup freshly grated Parmesan cheese**

**1 cup sour cream**

**One 8-ounce package cream cheese, softened**

**⅓ cup chopped fresh chives (optional)**

**Salt and freshly ground black pepper to taste**

**1.** Boil the potatoes in salted water to cover until tender, and then drain.

**2.** Rub a 3-quart soufflé dish or 13 x 9-inch baking dish with 2 tablespoons of the butter. Sprinkle ¼ cup of the Parmesan into the dish, making sure it is evenly distributed.

**3.** Put the potatoes in a large bowl, add the sour cream, cream cheese, 2 tablespoons of the remaining butter, ¼ cup of the remaining Parmesan, and the chives, if using, and season with salt and pepper. Using an electric mixer, beat the potatoes until smooth. Transfer to the prepared dish, dot with the remaining 2 tablespoons of butter, and sprinkle with the remaining ¼ cup of cheese.

✳ **DIVA DO-AHEAD:** At this point, you can cover and refrigerate for 2 to 3 days or freeze for up to 1 month. Bring to room temperature before continuing.

**4.** Preheat the oven to 350°F. Bake the potatoes until golden, about 25 minutes. Serve hot.

## Picky Eater's Alert

It isn't easy being green. I have one child who doesn't like anything green in his potatoes; hence, the chives are left out of Make-Ahead Cheesy Mashed Potatoes to accommodate him. They are a great addition to the recipe, but fussy eaters are a reality and you are better off accommodating your family and friends rather than making them eat something they won't enjoy. At holiday time, I'll make one batch with chives and one batch without, so that everyone is happy.

## Slow Cooker Savvy

These potatoes can be heated in a 4-quart slow cooker if you have a removable ceramic insert. Butter the insert and dust it with the cheese as directed above. Follow the recipe through step 3 and fill the insert with the mashed potatoes. Cover and cook on Low for 4 to 6 hours, until heated through. An extra dusting of Parmesan and butter makes them look divine.

## The Diva Says:

When boiling potatoes, I use a pasta pot with the colander insert; that way I can remove the potatoes from the water and drain them over the stove before I put them in the bowl.

## Smooth, Not Gluey

Many people marvel at the fact that these potatoes are not gluey, even though they are mixed with an electric mixer. Because we are whipping in so many other ingredients, the starch in the potatoes seems to suspend itself in the butter, sour cream, and cream cheese so that when you bake the potatoes, they puff up and become light and fluffy. Do not, however, mix them in a food processor or with an immersion blender; if you do that, you absolutely will end up with glue. A ricer will also turn these into glue. Ricers are great for mashing potatoes and serving them immediately, but if the potatoes sit around for a while after being riced, the gluten begins to develop and their nice texture is gone with the wind.

## Diva Variations

**Blue Cheese Mashed Potatoes:** Substitute crumbled blue cheese for the Parmesan.

**Garlic-Herb Mashed Potatoes:** Substitute 1/2 pound of a garlic-and-herb cheese, such as Boursin, for the cream cheese.

**Horseradish Mashed Potatoes:** Before beating the potatoes, add 1/4 cup of prepared horseradish, or to taste, along with the other ingredients as directed in step 3. (These are fabulous with prime rib.)

**Garlic Mashed Potatoes:** Peel 5 cloves of garlic and add to the potatoes while they are boiling. Drain and mash them together with the other ingredients as directed in step 3 and proceed with the recipe.

**Bacon Cheddar Mashed Potatoes:** Substitute white cheddar cheese for the Parmesan and sprinkle the top with crumbled fried bacon (about 12 strips).

**Pesto Mashed Potatoes:** When you transfer the mashed potatoes to the baking dish, swirl 1/3 cup of prepared pesto through them (as you would chocolate in vanilla batter for a marble cake), then top with the remaining cheese and butter and proceed as directed.

**Goat Cheese Mashed Potatoes:** Omit the cream cheese and substitute one 11-ounce log of softened goat cheese, crumbled. The Parmesan is optional, but it gives the potatoes a nice lift.

# Neapolitan Potato Cake

Serves 12

In Naples, cooks are quite clever in the ways they transform leftover foods into masterpieces. This potato cake—a beautifully browned cake filled with prosciutto, Parmesan, and ricotta cheese—is a classic example. Serve this as a side dish for roasted or grilled meats, seafood, or poultry, or as a main course with salad for a luncheon.

**8 medium-size baking potatoes, peeled and cut into 1-inch chunks**

**¾ cup fresh bread crumbs**

**½ cup ricotta cheese**

**1⅔ cups freshly grated Parmesan cheese**

**1½ teaspoons salt**

**¾ teaspoon freshly ground black pepper**

**¼ cup (½ stick) unsalted butter, softened**

**¼ cup milk, or more as needed**

**½ cup chopped fresh Italian parsley**

**⅓ pound thinly sliced prosciutto, large pieces of fat removed and cut into matchsticks**

**1 pound fresh mozzarella cheese, sliced ¼ inch thick**

**3 cloves garlic, minced**

**2 tablespoons olive oil**

**1.** Boil the potatoes in salted water to cover until tender, and then drain.

**2.** Line the bottom and sides of a 10-inch springform pan with aluminum foil. Coat the foil with nonstick cooking spray and sprinkle ¼ cup of the bread crumbs into the bottom of the pan, tilting to coat it evenly.

**3.** Combine the potatoes, ricotta, 1 cup of the Parmesan, the salt, pepper, 2 tablespoons of the butter, the milk, and ¼ cup of the parsley in a large bowl. With an electric mixer, beat until smooth. Fold in the prosciutto, blending until well combined. Taste and add more salt and pepper if desired.

**4.** Spread half the potatoes in the prepared pan, cover with half of the mozzarella and ⅓ cup of the remaining Parmesan, then layer in the remaining potatoes and mozzarella.

**5.** In a medium-size bowl, combine the remaining ½ cup of bread crumbs, the garlic, the remaining ⅓ cup of Parmesan, the remaining ¼ cup of parsley, and the olive oil, tossing until the crumbs are evenly moistened. Sprinkle this mixture over the mozzarella and dot with the remaining 2 tablespoons of butter.

✳ **DIVA DO-AHEAD:** At this point, you can cover and refrigerate overnight. Bring to room temperature before continuing.

**6.** Preheat the oven to 375°F. Bake the potatoes until puffed and golden, 30 to 40 minutes.

✳ **DIVA DO-AHEAD:** At this point, you can let cool, cover, and freeze for up to 1 month. When ready to serve, defrost, then reheat, loosely covered with aluminum foil, in a 350°F oven for 20 to 25 minutes.

**7.** Let the hot potatoes rest for about 20 minutes. Put a serving plate over the springform pan, invert them, and remove the pan. Peel back the foil from the potato cake and serve in slices.

### Give It a Rest!

In many recipes you will be asked to let baked items rest before cutting into them. This resting time is important because it gives the dish a chance to finish cooking and set up. That way, when you cut into it, it won't break apart. We are all concerned about serving things hot, but for the most part, dishes that come straight from the oven are too hot for your guests to eat immediately.

The Diva Says:

If you don't have a springform pan, you can make this in a 13 x 9-inch baking dish or a 4-quart soufflé dish. You won't be able to unmold it for a spectacular presentation, but your guests will be able to spoon the cake out of the baking dish.

### Diva Variations

Try the following additions and substitutions to Neapolitan Potato Cake:

• Spread ½ cup of Sun-Dried Tomato Pesto (page 97) over the first layer of potatoes and proceed with the recipe.

• Spread ½ cup of Basil Pesto, homemade (page 97) or store-bought, over the first layer of potatoes.

• For a vegetarian cake, omit the prosciutto and spread 1½ cups of Herb-Roasted Tomatoes (page 127) over the first layer of potatoes.

• For a seafood cake, sprinkle ½ pound of lump crabmeat over the first layer of potatoes.

# Baked and Stuffed Spuds

Makes 16 stuffed halves; serves at least 10

Baked stuffed potatoes are so simple to prepare. Bake the potatoes the day before and prepare the filling; then stuff the potatoes the next day and bake until heated through.

The variations on pages 250 to 251 are a few of my favorite combinations; serve all of one kind, or mix and match. I find that most people will eat half a potato and be well satisfied, so this recipe will give you enough for one half per person plus a few extras.

**8 large russet baking potatoes, scrubbed and pricked with the point of a sharp knife in several places (yes, they will explode in the oven if you don't do this)**

**Olive oil for rubbing the potatoes**

**½ cup (1 stick) unsalted butter, softened**

**½ cup milk**

**½ cup sour cream**

**12 strips bacon, cooked until crisp, drained on paper towels, and crumbled**

**1½ to 2 cups shredded sharp white cheddar cheese, to your taste**

**½ cup chopped scallions (white and tender green parts)**

**2 teaspoons salt or to taste**

**1 teaspoon freshly ground black pepper or to taste**

**1.** Preheat the oven to 400°F. Rub the potatoes with some olive oil, and bake until soft when pinched with a pot holder, 60 to 70 minutes. Remove from the oven and let rest for about 10 minutes.

**2.** With a serrated knife, cut the potatoes in half lengthwise and, using a soup spoon, remove the flesh, leaving a ½-inch-thick shell.

**3.** Put the flesh in a large bowl, add the butter, milk, and sour cream, and, using an electric mixer, beat on low speed until creamy. Add the bacon, cheese, and scallions and stir until combined. Taste the potatoes and season with the salt and pepper. Refill the potato halves and place on a baking sheet.

✳ **DIVA DO-AHEAD:** At this point, you can cover and refrigerate for up to 24 hours. Bring to room temperature before continuing.

**4.** Preheat the oven to 350°F. Bake the stuffed potatoes until heated through, about 15 minutes. Serve immediately.

---

### Diva Variations

**Caramelized Onion and Gruyère Stuffed Spuds:** Bake the potatoes and transfer the flesh to the bowl. Add the butter, milk, and cream and mix as directed. Omit the bacon, cheddar cheese, and scallions and instead add ½ recipe Perfectly Caramelized Onions (page 244) and 1½ to 2 cups of shredded Gruyère cheese. Add the salt and pepper and continue with the recipe.

**Sour Cream and Scallion Stuffed Spuds:** Bake the potatoes and transfer the flesh to the bowl. Add the butter, omit the milk, increase the sour cream to 1 cup, and mix as directed. Add the scallions, omitting the bacon and cheddar cheese, and proceed as directed.

**Southwestern Stuffed Spuds:** Bake the potatoes and transfer the flesh to the bowl. Add the butter and sour cream, decrease the milk to ¼ cup, and mix as directed. For the bacon, cheddar, and scallions, substitute 1½ cups of shredded pepper Jack cheese (or 1 cup of mild cheddar and ½ to 1 cup of pepper Jack, if you prefer less heat), ½ cup of chunky salsa, drained, and ¼ cup of finely chopped fresh cilantro. Proceed as directed.

**Gorgonzola Stuffed Spuds:** Bake the potatoes and transfer the flesh to a bowl. Add the butter, milk, and sour cream and mix as directed. Omit the bacon, cheddar cheese, and scallions, add 2 cups of crumbled Gorgonzola cheese, and proceed as directed.

**Shallot, Sherry, and Mushroom Stuffed Spuds:** Bake the potatoes and transfer the flesh to a bowl. Add the butter, milk, and sour cream and mix as directed. In a medium-size skillet over medium heat, melt 2 tablespoons of unsalted butter and cook $1/2$ cup of chopped shallots, stirring, until softened, about 3 minutes. Add 1 pound of thinly sliced mushrooms, 1 teaspoon of salt, and $1/2$ teaspoon of freshly ground black pepper and cook, stirring a few times, until the mushrooms begin to color and the liquid in the pan is evaporated. Add 2 tablespoons of sherry and cook until it is almost entirely evaporated. Let cool, then add three-quarters of the mushroom mixture to the potatoes and blend. Restuff the potatoes and top each with some of the remaining mushrooms. Bake as directed.

**Sausage and Mozzarella Stuffed Spuds:** Bake the potatoes and transfer the flesh to a bowl. Add the butter, milk, and sour cream and mix as directed. Omit the bacon, cheddar, and scallions. Cook and crumble $3/4$ pound of sweet Italian sausage and add to the potatoes, along with $1 1/2$ to 2 cups of shredded mozzarella cheese, and, if you like, $1/2$ cup of finely chopped oil-packed sun-dried tomatoes. Proceed as directed.

**Ham and Cheddar Stuffed Spuds:** Bake the potatoes and transfer the flesh to a bowl. Add the butter, milk, and sour cream and mix as directed. Omit the bacon. Add the cheddar, scallions, and 2 cups of ground or finely chopped smoked ham and proceed as directed.

**Goat Cheese Stuffed Spuds:** Bake the potatoes and transfer the flesh to a bowl. Add the butter and milk, omit the sour cream, and mix as directed. Add the scallions and omit the cheese and bacon. Add two 11-ounce packages of softened goat cheese, crumbled, and proceed as directed.

**Broccoli Cheddar Stuffed Spuds:** Bake the potatoes and transfer the flesh to a bowl. Add the butter, milk, and sour cream and mix as directed. Omit the bacon and add 2 cups of steamed broccoli florets, coarsely chopped, folding them in gently. Add half the cheddar and restuff the potatoes. Sprinkle the tops with the remaining cheddar and proceed as directed.

**Horseradish Stuffed Spuds:** Bake the potatoes and transfer the flesh to a bowl. Add the butter, milk, and sour cream and mix as directed. Omit the bacon and cheddar, reserve the scallions for garnish, and add 3 to 4 tablespoons of prepared horseradish, to your taste. Proceed as directed. Garnish the baked potatoes with the chopped scallions.

# Spicy Oven Steak Fries

Serves 10

These steak fries are everything you'd want them to be: salty, crispy, and delicious, and without all the mess of frying. I usually make a ton of these because they disappear quickly. Whatever is left is terrific stirred into scrambled eggs the next morning. The silicone baking liners help make cleanup a snap. I recommend using russets for this dish because they crisp nicely on the outside and become tender on the inside when roasted at a high temperature. You will be tossing them in seasoned oil, which prevents the normal discoloration that happens when you cut potatoes. So you can prepare the potatoes ahead, then pop them into the oven right before serving. The paprika helps give these a beautiful golden color. Kosher salt or coarse sea salt gives them a nice, last-minute finish.

½ cup olive oil

2 teaspoons table salt

1 teaspoon freshly ground black pepper

2 teaspoons sweet paprika

6 large russet baking potatoes, scrubbed and cut into ½-inch wedges

2 teaspoons kosher salt or coarse sea salt for garnish (optional)

**1.** Line a baking sheet with a silicone liner or aluminum foil.

**2.** In a large bowl, stir together the oil, table salt, pepper, and paprika. Stir in the potatoes and toss until well coated. Transfer to the prepared baking sheet.

❋ **DIVA DO-AHEAD:** At this point, you can transfer the potatoes to a zipper-top plastic bag and refrigerate for up to 8 hours. Bring to room temperature before continuing.

**3.** Preheat the oven to 400°F. Bake the potatoes until golden brown, 45 to 55 minutes, turning once at 25 minutes. Transfer to a serving dish, sprinkle with kosher salt if desired, and serve.

## Should You Prechill and Peel Those Spuds?

Whether you peel potatoes for fries is really up to you. If the peel on the potato looks nice and isn't spotted, then leave it on; if it's got a tinge of green, you will need to peel it because that color is the sign of a toxin in the skin that will make you sick. Get rid of the green, but not the potato; when the green is gone, so is the toxin.

Some culinary experts recommend starting with potatoes that have been stored overnight in the refrigerator for the best fries. I've tried it both ways and found the fries that started out cold had a somewhat crunchier crust, but it wasn't enough of a difference to warrant that extra step—especially if your fridge is already crowded.

# Cheesy Potato Gratin

Serves 10

I love potatoes and potato gratins in particular, with their creamy sauce and melted cheese topping. The nice thing about these gratins is that they can be assembled the day before; then they need just half an hour in the oven. The secret is to precook the potatoes in the sauce on top of the stove before baking them.

**4 pounds baking potatoes, peeled and thinly sliced (I use the slicing blade of a food processor)**

**1 medium-size sweet yellow onion (such as Vidalia, Maui, or Walla Walla), thinly sliced**

**1 cup heavy cream**

**1²⁄₃ cups whole milk**

**1½ teaspoons salt**

**½ teaspoon freshly ground black pepper**

**4 shakes of Tabasco sauce**

**2 cups shredded Gruyère cheese**

**½ cup freshly grated Parmesan cheese**

**1.** Put the potatoes and onion in a large sauté pan. Add the cream, milk, salt, pepper, and Tabasco and bring to a boil. Reduce the heat to medium and simmer just until the potatoes are tender, 6 to 8 minutes; they will not be cooked through and should still hold their shape.

**2.** Coat a 13 x 9-inch baking dish with nonstick cooking spray. Transfer half the potatoes and onion to the baking dish along with some of the sauce, and sprinkle with half the Gruyère. Cover with the remaining potatoes and sauce and sprinkle with the remaining Gruyère and the Parmesan.

**✳ DIVA DO-AHEAD:** At this point, you can cover and refrigerate overnight. Bring to room temperature before continuing.

**3.** Preheat the oven to 375°F. Bake the potatoes, covered with aluminum foil, for 20 minutes, then remove the foil and bake until the potatoes are tender and the cheese is golden brown, another 10 to 15 minutes. Let rest for 10 to 15 minutes before serving.

---

### Diva Gratin Heaven

There are so many ways to embellish this basic gratin. Follow the instructions for simmering the potatoes, but substitute any of the following for the Gruyère and Parmesan:

- 1½ to 2 cups crumbled blue cheese

- Two 3.5-ounce packages Boursin cheese, crumbled

- 2 cups shredded fontina cheese or half fontina and half Munster

- 2 cups shredded smoked Gouda cheese

- 2 cups shredded sharp white cheddar cheese

- 2 cups shredded pepper Jack cheese

---

# Roasted Potatoes

Serves 10

These potatoes are simple yet incredibly delicious with sautéed chicken or grilled beef or poultry or as part of a roasted vegetable platter. The leftovers are great for making potato salad or for tossing into soups. Try the basic recipe first, then all the variations.

**4 pounds 1-inch red or white new potatoes, cut in half or quartered**

**⅓ cup olive oil**

**2 teaspoons salt**

**1 teaspoon freshly ground black pepper**

**1.** Preheat the oven to 400°F. Line a baking sheet with a silicone liner or aluminum foil.

**2.** Put the potatoes in a large bowl, add the oil, salt, and pepper, and stir to coat the potatoes. Spread out the potatoes on the baking sheet in a single layer and bake until fork-tender, 45 to 55 minutes, turning the potatoes twice during the roasting time to ensure even browning.

**3.** Serve the potatoes immediately or at room temperature.

✳ **DIVA DO-AHEAD:** If you would like to roast these the day before, roast for 40 minutes, let cool, cover, and refrigerate. Bring to room temperature and then warm in a preheated 350°F oven until heated through, about 15 minutes. You can also roast the potatoes completely earlier in the day, transfer to a serving dish, and let sit on your counter until ready to serve, or roast completely the day before, refrigerate overnight, and simply let them come to room temperature before serving.

## Diva Variations

**Tuscan Roasted Potatoes:** Follow the basic recipe, but add 8 cloves of garlic, cut in half, and 3 tablespoons of chopped fresh rosemary to the bowl with the seasoned oil and potatoes and stir to distribute evenly. Continue as directed; just before serving, squeeze lemon wedges over the potatoes.

**Dijon Provençal Roasted Potatoes:** Follow the basic recipe, adding 4 cloves of garlic, minced; 1/4 cup of Dijon mustard; and 1 tablespoon of dried *herbes de Provence* to the bowl with the seasoned oil and potatoes and stirring to distribute evenly.

**Chili Roasted Potatoes:** Follow the basic recipe, adding 1 tablespoon of chili powder, 1 teaspoon of garlic salt, 1 teaspoon of sugar, and 2 teaspoons of sweet paprika to the bowl with the seasoned oil and potatoes and stirring to distribute evenly. When ready to serve, garnish with 1/4 to 1/2 cup of chopped fresh cilantro, if desired.

**Southwestern Roasted Potatoes and Corn:** Follow the basic recipe, adding 2 teaspoons of ground cumin, 1/2 teaspoon of chili powder, 1 cup of chopped red onion, and 2 cups of corn kernels, cut fresh from the cob or frozen (defrosted) to the bowl with the seasoned oil and potatoes and stirring to distribute evenly. Roast at 350°F for 1 hour. Garnish with 1/4 cup of chopped fresh cilantro before serving.

**Soy-Ginger Roasted Potatoes:** Follow the basic recipe, adding 2 teaspoons of peeled and grated fresh ginger; 4 cloves of garlic, minced; and 1/4 cup of light soy sauce to the bowl with the seasoned oil and potatoes and stirring to distribute evenly. Right before serving, drizzle the potatoes with 2 teaspoons of toasted sesame oil and sprinkle with 2 tablespoons of sesame seeds and 6 scallions (white and tender green parts), chopped.

# Breaded Roasted Potatoes Pizzaiola

Serves 10

I love these potatoes, which my cousin Maura serves. I found a way to streamline them a bit, and I've been serving them to rave reviews in my buffet classes. They're terrific for taking along to a potluck or barbecue.

**6 medium-size red potatoes**

**2 teaspoons salt**

**1 teaspoon freshly ground black pepper**

**¼ cup plus 2 tablespoons olive oil**

**⅔ cup fine dry bread crumbs**

**⅔ cup freshly grated Parmesan cheese**

**2 to 3 large ripe tomatoes, thinly sliced**

**1 large red onion, thinly sliced and separated into rings**

**2 teaspoons dried oregano**

**1.** Coat a 13 x 9-inch casserole dish with olive oil or nonstick cooking spray.

**2.** Cut the potatoes into ½-inch-thick wedges and put in a large bowl. Sprinkle with the salt and pepper, add ¼ cup of the olive oil, and toss to coat.

**3.** In another large bowl, combine the bread crumbs and cheese, then toss the potatoes in the crumb mixture until well coated. Transfer to the prepared dish.

✳ **DIVA DO-AHEAD:** At this point, you can cover and refrigerate overnight.

**4.** Preheat the oven to 400°F.

**5.** Top the potatoes with the sliced tomatoes and onion rings. Sprinkle evenly with oregano and the remaining 2 tablespoons of olive oil. Bake, uncovered, for 15 minutes, reduce the oven temperature to 350°F, and continue baking until the potatoes are browned and tender, about another 50 minutes. Remove from the oven and let rest for 10 minutes before serving.

## Roasted Vegetables

Roasting vegetables is simple, and the flavors intensify with the high heat. You can roast almost any vegetable with a drizzle of olive oil and a sprinkling of salt and pepper. Add your own choice of dried or chopped fresh herbs to complement the dish. Once the vegetable is roasted, it can be refrigerated for up to 1 day, then reheated in a hot skillet or in a preheated 350°F oven. Most roasted vegetables are delicious at room temperature as well, so you can roast them earlier in the day, transfer them to a serving platter, and cover. Then just keep them out on the counter until you are ready to serve them.

# Spinach Parmesan Casserole 🍺🍷🍸

Serves 10

Creamed spinach is one of my favorite sides when I eat at a steak house. Here I have transformed it into a simple casserole, which makes a tasty accompaniment for roast beef. Serve it for a special dinner, and for a large crowd, keep it warm in the slow cooker.

¼ cup (½ stick) unsalted butter

¼ cup chopped shallots

¼ cup all-purpose flour

2 cups whole or 2% milk

1½ teaspoons salt

½ teaspoon freshly ground black pepper

⅛ teaspoon ground nutmeg

Three 16-ounce packages frozen chopped spinach, defrosted and squeezed dry

½ cup freshly grated Parmesan cheese

½ cup fresh bread crumbs

**1.** Coat a 3-quart gratin dish with nonstick cooking spray.

**2.** In a 4-quart saucepan over medium heat, melt the butter, then add the shallots and cook, stirring, until softened. Add the flour and whisk until smooth and white bubbles begin to form on the surface. Continue to whisk for 2 more minutes, then gradually add the milk, bringing the mixture to a boil. Reduce the heat to medium and add the salt, pepper, nutmeg, and spinach, stirring to blend. Transfer the mixture to the prepared baking dish. In a small bowl, combine the cheese and bread crumbs.

✳ **DIVA DO-AHEAD:** At this point, you can store the bread crumb mixture in a zipper-top plastic bag; let the spinach cool and then cover. Refrigerate both for up to 3 days or freeze for up to 1 month. Bring the spinach to room temperature before continuing.

**3.** Preheat the oven to 350°F. Sprinkle the bread crumb mixture evenly over the top of the spinach. Bake until the spinach is bubbling and the topping is golden brown, about 20 minutes.

## Slow Cooker Savvy

Follow the directions through step 2, transferring the mixture instead to a 5-quart slow cooker. Top with the bread crumbs, cover, and cook on Low until heated through, about 3 hours.

# Roasted Butternut Squash

Serves 10

This recipe comes from the Italian region of Umbria, where my grandparents were born. The squash is simply roasted with sage and oil, which intensifies its flavor and makes it wonderfully sweet on the inside and crisp on the outside. Leftovers make a dynamite base for butternut squash soup.

**2 medium-size butternut squash, peeled, seeded, quartered, and cut into ½-inch-thick pieces**

**⅔ cup olive oil**

**1 tablespoon dried sage, crumbled**

**1½ teaspoons salt**

**1 teaspoon freshly ground black pepper**

## Vegetable Versus Machine

When peeling butternut squash, make sure you dispose of the peelings in the garbage and not your disposal. The peel is so tough it will clog your disposal, and you don't need that headache when you are preparing a big meal!

**1.** Preheat the oven to 375°F. Line a baking sheet with a silicone liner or aluminum foil.

**2.** Put the squash on the prepared sheet, drizzle with the oil, and sprinkle with the sage, salt, and pepper. Using your hands, toss the squash so it is evenly coated with the seasoned oil. Roast until tender when pierced with a fork, 30 to 35 minutes, turning several times during the cooking time.

✳ **DIVA DO-AHEAD:** At this point, you can let cool, cover, and refrigerate overnight. Bring to room temperature, then reheat in a 350°F oven for 10 minutes.

**3.** Serve hot.

# Yellow Squash and Spinach Casserole 🥛🍷🍶

Serves 10

This creamy casserole studded with chunks of yellow squash and bits of green spinach is gorgeous on a buffet table alongside grilled or roasted meats, poultry, or seafood.

2 tablespoons unsalted butter

2 tablespoons olive oil

½ cup chopped onion

6 cups cut-up yellow squash (1-inch pieces; about 8 to 10 small squash)

Two 16-ounce packages frozen chopped spinach, defrosted and squeezed dry

1½ teaspoons salt

1 teaspoon freshly ground black pepper

⅛ teaspoon ground nutmeg

3 tablespoons all-purpose flour

2 cups whole or 2% milk

Two 3.5-ounce packages Boursin cheese, crumbled

**1.** Coat a 13 x 9-inch baking dish with nonstick cooking spray.

**2.** In a large skillet, heat the butter and oil together over medium-high heat. When the butter is melted, add the onion and cook, stirring, until softened, about 3 minutes. Add the squash and cook another 3 minutes, stirring a few times. Stir in the spinach, salt, pepper, and nutmeg and cook, stirring, until the mixture begins to lose some of its moisture, about 5 minutes. Stir the flour into the squash mixture and cook until absorbed, another 2 minutes. Add the milk and stir until the mixture comes to a boil. Add the cheese and stir until it has melted. Transfer to the prepared dish.

✳ **DIVA DO-AHEAD:** At this point, you can let cool, cover, and refrigerate for up to 2 days. Bring to room temperature before continuing.

**3.** Preheat the oven to 350°F. Bake the casserole until the top is golden brown, about 20 minutes. Let rest 5 to 10 minutes before serving.

# Zucchini Parmesan

Serves 10

Grated zucchini and rice bake together in a rich and cheesy cream sauce. The dish is perfect alongside grilled or roasted meats, poultry, and seafood.

3 tablespoons unsalted butter

½ cup finely chopped onion

2 cloves garlic, minced

4 cups shredded zucchini (about 2½ pounds)

1½ teaspoons salt

½ teaspoon freshly ground black pepper

4 shakes of Tabasco sauce

2 tablespoons all-purpose flour

1 cup chicken broth

1½ cups heavy cream

¾ cup converted long-grain rice

¾ cup freshly grated Parmesan cheese

**1.** In a large skillet over medium heat, melt the butter, then add the onion and garlic and cook, stirring, until softened, 2 to 3 minutes. Add the zucchini and cook until it is no longer giving off moisture, 4 to 6 minutes. Season with the salt, pepper, and Tabasco. Sprinkle with the flour and cook, stirring, for 2 minutes. Gradually stir in the broth and heavy cream, stirring until the mixture is smooth and comes to a boil.

✳ **DIVA DO-AHEAD:** At this point, you can let cool, cover, and refrigerate for 2 days. Let come to room temperature before continuing.

**2.** Preheat the oven to 400°F. Coat a 13 x 9-inch baking dish with nonstick cooking spray.

**3.** Stir the rice into the zucchini mixture, pour into the prepared dish, and sprinkle with the cheese. Bake until the rice is tender and the cheese is golden, 25 to 35 minutes. Let rest for 5 to 10 minutes before serving.

## The Diva Says:

If you'd like to prepare this well in advance of your party, the baked casserole can be frozen after baking. Cook the casserole for 20 minutes; it will still be a bit runny in spots. Remove from the oven, allow to cool to room temperature, cover, and freeze for up to 1 month. Defrost and bring to room temperature. Bake at 350°F, covered, until the rice has absorbed all the liquid, 15 to 20 minutes. If you want a golden brown top, run the casserole under the broiler for a few minutes or uncover it during the last 5 minutes of cooking time.

# Roasted Spicy Asian Sweet Potatoes

Serves 10

When I lived in Japan, my favorite street food was the roasted yams sold by vendors. A far cry from the sweet potatoes we serve here in the States, slathered with marshmallows and other sweet things, those were sweet and smoky at the same time. This simple recipe gives sweet potatoes a little Asian spice. They are terrific served with Thanksgiving turkey or with other poultry or pork.

**6 large sweet potatoes, peeled and cut into 1-inch chunks**

**1 cup (2 sticks) unsalted butter, melted**

**⅔ cup firmly packed light brown sugar**

**2 tablespoons fresh lemon juice**

**2 teaspoons Chinese 5-spice powder**

**½ teaspoon ground ginger**

## Is It a Yam, Ma'am?

Yams are native to Africa and Asia and we seldom see them in our grocery stores. Their flesh is yellow in color and a bit starchier than the sweet potatoes we have in the States. When someone offers you yams at dinner, chances are they're sweet potatoes.

**1.** Coat a 13 x 9-inch baking dish with non-stick cooking spray.

**2.** Put the potatoes in the prepared dish. In a medium-size bowl, stir together the remaining ingredients until blended. Pour the butter mixture over the potatoes and turn to coat them evenly.

✳ **DIVA DO-AHEAD:** At this point, you can cover and refrigerate for up to 2 days. Bring to room temperature before continuing.

**3.** Preheat the oven to 375°F. Bake until tender when pierced with a knife, 45 to 55 minutes. Remove from the oven and serve hot or at room temperature.

### Diva Variation

Substitute two 32-ounce cans sweet potatoes, drained, for the fresh potatoes and reduce the baking time to 15 to 20 minutes, until heated through.

# Sweet Potato–Apple Gratin

Serves 8

Tart Granny Smiths and sherry-spiked sweet potatoes are a perfect combination for this delicious side dish, which is terrific with poultry or pork. I have taught this dish in my Do-Ahead Thanksgiving classes for more than 20 years, and it is even a hit with people who don't like sweet potatoes!

**Two 32-ounce cans sweet potatoes, drained (see The Diva Says)**

**½ cup (1 stick) unsalted butter, melted**

**⅔ cup firmly packed light brown sugar**

**⅔ cup dark corn syrup**

**3 tablespoons cream sherry**

**1½ teaspoons ground cinnamon**

**⅛ teaspoon ground nutmeg**

**4 medium-size Granny Smith or other tart apples, peeled, cored, and sliced ¼ inch thick (see The Diva Says)**

**1.** Put the sweet potatoes in a large bowl. With an electric mixer, beat until smooth. Add ¼ cup (½ stick) of the butter, the brown sugar, corn syrup, sherry, cinnamon, and nutmeg and blend until creamy.

**2.** Spread half the sweet potato mixture in a 10- to 12-inch pie plate 2 inches deep, or a 13 x 9-inch baking dish. Arrange half the apple slices over the yam layer and brush with some of the remaining butter. The butter will seal the apples and prevent discoloration. Spread the remaining sweet potato mixture over the apples and arrange the remaining apples on top in an attractive pattern. Brush with the remaining butter, covering the apples completely.

✳ **DIVA DO-AHEAD:** At this point, you can cover and refrigerate for up to 4 days or freeze for up to 1 month. Defrost and bring to room temperature before continuing.

**3.** Preheat the oven to 350°F. Bake the dish, uncovered, until the apples are golden brown, 30 to 40 minutes.

## The Diva Says:

If you would prefer to use fresh sweet potatoes, bake 8 medium-size sweet potatoes (remember to poke holes in them) at 425°F until tender when squeezed with an oven mitt, 50 to 60 minutes. When cool enough to handle, cut in half and scoop out the flesh. Proceed as directed.

If you want to peel your apples in advance, here's a way to keep them from discoloring: Add 2 tablespoons of fresh lemon juice to 2 quarts of water and toss the apples into the water as you slice them. Drain and pat dry when you're ready to proceed.

# Stuffed Tomatoes

Makes 16; serves at least 10

Stuffed with herbed bread crumbs and cheese, these tomatoes are a terrific side dish for grilled meats, fish, and poultry. The tomatoes can be prepared ahead of time and then baked before serving, or they can be baked and served later at room temperature.

½ cup olive oil

8 medium-size vine-ripened tomatoes, about 3 inches in diameter

2 teaspoons salt

1½ teaspoons freshly ground black pepper

2 cups fresh bread crumbs

⅔ cup freshly grated Parmesan cheese

3 cloves garlic, minced

¼ cup fresh basil leaves, finely chopped (see The Diva Says)

**1.** Brush a 13 x 9-inch baking dish with some of the olive oil.

**2.** Cut the tomatoes in half, gently squeeze to drain the juice, and remove the seeds with a small paring knife. Turn cut side down onto paper towels to drain, then place in the prepared dish and sprinkle with some of the salt and pepper.

**3.** In a medium-size bowl, stir together the bread crumbs, cheese, garlic, basil, and the remaining salt and pepper. Add about 3 tablespoons of the remaining oil to give the stuffing some moisture.

✳ **DIVA DO-AHEAD:** At this point, the stuffing and tomatoes can be refrigerated separately for up to 8 hours.

**4.** Preheat the oven to 375°F. Mound the stuffing on top of the tomatoes and drizzle with the remaining oil. Bake the tomatoes until tender, 20 to 25 minutes. Remove from the oven and serve warm or at room temperature.

## The Diva Says:

To chop basil finely, bunch the leaves together in a tight ball and finely chop with a chef's knife or cleaver, so that the basil is almost shredded.

### Diva Variations

**Southwestern Tomatoes:** Substitute chopped fresh cilantro for the basil and Monterey Jack cheese for the Parmesan.

**Tomatoes à la Française:** Substitute 2 teaspoons of dried *herbes de Provence* for the fresh basil.

**Athenian Tomatoes:** Substitute chopped fresh oregano for the basil and feta cheese for the Parmesan.

**Swiss Tomatoes:** Substitute finely shredded Gruyère or Emmenthaler cheese for the Parmesan.

# Easy Cheesy Tomatoes

Serves 10

Divas are always looking for colorful, easy side dishes, and these tomatoes are a trick to keep up your sleeve. You can vary the cheese to suit the entrée, but the basic recipe is the same.

**8 small vine-ripened tomatoes, about 2 inches in diameter**

**¼ cup olive oil**

**1½ teaspoons salt**

**¾ teaspoon freshly ground black pepper**

**1½ cups grated cheese, such as Parmesan, white cheddar, fontina, Gruyère, smoked Gouda, smoked mozzarella, or pepper Jack**

**1.** Preheat the broiler. Line a baking sheet with a silicone liner or aluminum foil.

**2.** Cut the tomatoes in half, gently squeeze to drain the juice, and remove the seeds with a small paring knife. Place cut side down on paper towels to drain.

✳ **DIVA DO-AHEAD:** At this point, you can cover and refrigerate for up to 24 hours.

**3.** Arrange the drained tomatoes on the prepared sheet cut side up. Sprinkle evenly with the olive oil, salt, and pepper. Sprinkle the cheese evenly over the top and broil until the cheese is bubbling, 5 to 6 minutes. Remove from the pan and serve warm or at room temperature.

# Roasted Roots

Serves 10

Simple roasted root vegetables make a colorful and delicious side dish. The high oven temperature caramelizes the sugars in the vegetables, making them crisp on the outside and sweet inside. You can change the herbs to suit your fancy; I like thyme, but rosemary, oregano, *herbes de Provence*, and others are fine. Try to cut the vegetables so they are uniform in size—that will ensure they will all be done at the same time.

3 pounds mixed root vegetables, such as white and sweet potatoes, beets, parsnips, turnips, and shallots, peeled and cut into 1½-inch pieces

½ cup olive oil

2 teaspoons salt, plus extra for final seasoning

1 teaspoon freshly ground black pepper

2 teaspoons dried thyme

**1.** Preheat the oven to 400°F. Line a baking sheet with a silicone liner or aluminum foil.

**2.** In a large bowl, toss the vegetables with the oil, salt, pepper, and thyme until coated. Spread on the prepared sheet in a single layer and roast until tender when pierced with the tip of a sharp knife, 40 to 55 minutes.

❋ **DIVA DO-AHEAD:** At this point, you can let cool, cover, and refrigerate overnight. Rewarm quickly on the stove top in a hot sauté pan before continuing.

**3.** Sprinkle the vegetables with more salt, if desired, and serve warm.

# Ratatouille

Serves 10

Ratatouille is a French dish made with eggplant, zucchini, onions, and peppers held together with a bit of tomato and flavored with *herbes de Provence*. A great make-ahead dish, it can be served either hot or cold. It is delicious served with grilled meats, poultry, and seafood, and it's also wonderful dolloped on baguette slices and offered as an appetizer.

¼ cup extra virgin olive oil

2 medium-size red onions, thinly sliced and separated into rings

2 cloves garlic, minced

1 large green bell pepper, seeded and thinly sliced into rings

1 large red bell pepper, seeded and thinly sliced into rings

3 medium-size zucchini, ends trimmed and cut into ½-inch-thick slices

1 medium-size purple eggplant, ends trimmed, peeled, and cut into ½-inch chunks

2 teaspoons salt

1 teaspoon freshly ground black pepper

2 teaspoons dried *herbes de Provence*

One 15.5-ounce can crushed tomatoes

½ cup chopped fresh Italian parsley for garnish (optional)

1. In a 5-quart Dutch oven, heat the olive oil over medium-high heat, then add the onions and cook, stirring, until softened, about 3 minutes. Add the garlic and cook, stirring, for another minute. Add the bell peppers and cook, stirring, until they begin to soften, about 5 minutes. Add the zucchini, eggplant, salt, pepper, and *herbes de Provence* and cook, stirring frequently, until the liquid in the bottom of the pan begins to evaporate, about 15 minutes.

2. Add the tomatoes, reduce the heat to medium, and simmer until the liquid is just about evaporated and the vegetables are tender, another 15 minutes. Taste and adjust the salt and pepper as needed.

✳ **DIVA DO-AHEAD:** At this point, you can let cool, cover, and refrigerate for up to 3 days.

3. Garnish with the parsley, if using. Serve the ratatouille warm, at room temperature, or cold.

### Diva Variation

Ratatouille is terrific with a little bit of melted cheese over the top. I like to use Brie, Parmesan, Munster, or Italian fontina. Sprinkle the cheese over the top, then slide the dish under the broiler for a few minutes.

# Grilled Vegetables

Serves 10

Grilled vegetables are light and add a huge dash of color to the buffet table. I like to arrange them together on a large platter, but you may prefer to arrange like vegetables on smaller individual platters. Sprinkle them with vinaigrette or some good quality extra virgin olive oil. Grilled vegetables are also nice in a large sandwich, which can be prepared ahead, then sliced before serving. Grill similar vegetables together so that they cook evenly, and remember to cut them uniformly to ensure even cooking as well. You will need a vegetable basket or rack so the vegetables don't fall through the grill grate. Or you can place them on lined baking sheets and broil them instead.

½ cup olive oil

2 teaspoons salt

1 teaspoon freshly ground black pepper

2 pounds vegetables, prepared for grilling (see box, right)

**1.** Build a hot charcoal fire or preheat the grill or broiler for 10 minutes. Line a baking sheet with aluminum foil if you are broiling. If using a grill, place a vegetable basket on the grate to preheat.

**2.** In a small bowl, combine the olive oil, salt, and pepper, stirring to blend. Brush the vegetables on both sides with the oil and lay in the grill basket or on the sheet pan. Grill or broil until soft and caramelized, 3 to 4 minutes per side (see The Diva Says). Remove vegetables from the grill or broiler and cool to room temperature.

✳ **DIVA DO-AHEAD:** At this point, you can cover and refrigerate overnight. Let come to room temperature before serving.

## The Diva Says:

Not all grills and broilers are the same, so it may take more or less time for your vegetables to cook. Make sure you watch them and turn them when they begin to turn golden brown.

### Veggie Skewers

When making veggie skewers, thread similar items on each skewer and brush with seasoned olive oil. Grill for about 5 minutes, turning once.

## VEGETABLES FOR GRILLING

- **Corn:** Pull back husk and remove the silk from the corn. Brush with the oil and reposition husk around the ear.

- **Eggplant:** Trim the stem ends, then cut crosswise or lengthwise into ¹/₂-inch-thick slices.

- **Mushrooms:** Mushrooms do best when skewered; leave a ¹/₂-inch space between them.

- **Onions:** Cut into ³/₄-inch-thick slices.

- **Peppers or chiles:** Remove core and seeds, cut in half lengthwise, then halve again, so you have 4 pieces.

- **Radicchio and endive:** These are delicious when grilled, but they will break the bank for a buffet, so I recommend that you only prepare them for a small group. Cut the endive in half lengthwise and the radicchio into quarters.

- **Tomatoes:** Plum or other vine-ripened tomatoes should be cut in half crosswise and cored before grilling.

- **Zucchini or summer squash:** Trim the ends, then cut lengthwise into ¹/₂-inch-thick slices.

# Broiled Citrus

Serves 10

Old-fashioned but never out of style, this simple dish can be broiled ahead of time and then served at room temperature. Try to find varieties of citrus in different colors; ruby red grapefruit, blood oranges, and navel oranges really make a statement. Or you can buy your fruit already sectioned in the produce department of your grocer.

**6 navel oranges, peeled and sectioned (see The Diva Says)**

**6 ruby red grapefruit, peeled and sectioned (see The Diva Says)**

**½ cup firmly packed dark brown sugar**

**2 tablespoons orange liqueur, such as Grand Marnier**

**1.** Preheat broiler for 10 minutes. Arrange the fruit in a 13 x 9-inch baking dish.

**2.** In a small bowl, combine the brown sugar and liqueur and pour over the fruit.

**3.** Broil the fruit until the sugar caramelizes and begins to bubble, 6 to 8 minutes. Remove from the broiler.

✳ **DIVA DO-AHEAD:** At this point, you can let cool, cover, and refrigerate for up to 2 days. Let come to room temperature before serving.

## The Diva Says:

To section citrus fruit, first cut off the top and bottom, then stand the fruit on the cutting board. Starting at the top, cut along the curve of the fruit with a sharp knife, removing the peel and white pith. Continue to cut the peel away until the fruit is naked. Cut the sections from the fruit by cutting close to a section, then lifting it out of the fruit.

# Brandied Peaches

Serves 10

These gorgeous peach halves are fragrant with cloves and brandy, which makes them perfect to serve with poultry or pork. Use them to garnish platters of turkey or pork roast or serve as a side dish for Thanksgiving dinner. Because the peaches are cooked in the syrup, you don't need overripe peaches for this dish. Frozen summer peaches will be fine here, too.

**8 large peaches, peeled, cut in half, and pitted**

**2 cups water**

**1½ cups sugar**

**2 tablespoons fresh lemon juice**

**12 cloves**

**½ cup brandy**

**1.** Put the peaches in an 8-quart saucepan. Add the remaining ingredients, stir to dissolve the sugar, and bring to a boil. Reduce the heat to medium-low and simmer for 5 minutes. Remove from the heat. Let the peaches cool in their syrup, then remove the cloves.

✳ **DIVA DO-AHEAD:** At this point, you can cover and refrigerate for up to 5 days.

**2.** To serve, drain the peaches and serve cold or at room temperature, topping each with a little bit of the syrup.

# Baked Rhubarb

Serves 10 to 12

This glorious, ruby-colored sauce is terrific spooned over ice cream or pound cake, but it's also a colorful addition to the buffet table as an accompaniment to pork or turkey. Make this any time of the year using frozen rhubarb; however, there is nothing better than those tart, freshly harvested stalks of rhubarb in season.

**5 cups rhubarb stalks, cut into 1-inch pieces**

**1½ cups sugar**

**½ teaspoon ground cinnamon**

### Slow Cooker Savvy

Combine all the ingredients in the slow cooker and cook on Low until the rhubarb is tender, 4 to 5 hours.

**1.** Preheat the oven to 350°F.

**2.** In a 13 x 9-inch baking dish, combine the rhubarb, sugar, and cinnamon. Bake, stirring several times, until tender and bubbling, 35 to 45 minutes.

✳ **DIVA DO-AHEAD:** At this point, you can let cool, cover, and refrigerate for up to 5 days.

**3.** Serve warm or cold.

# Baked Penne alla Carbonara

Serves 10 as a side dish

Classic pasta alla carbonara cannot be made ahead of time, but this creamy casserole, studded with bacon and cheese, is a great substitute for your buffet table. Serve as a main dish or as a side dish with grilled or roasted meats or poultry.

½ cup (1 stick) unsalted butter

½ cup chopped shallots

1 teaspoon chopped fresh thyme

¼ cup all-purpose flour

1½ cups heavy cream

½ cup chicken broth

1½ cups freshly grated Parmesan cheese

½ to 1½ teaspoons freshly ground black pepper, to taste

Salt (optional) to taste

1 pound penne pasta, cooked according to the package directions until *al dente* and drained

2 tablespoons olive oil

12 strips bacon, cut into ½-inch pieces, cooked until crisp, and drained on paper towels

½ pound fresh mozzarella cheese, cut into ½-inch cubes

**1.** In a 3-quart saucepan over medium heat, melt the butter, add the shallots and thyme, and cook, stirring, until softened, about 3 minutes. Whisk in the flour and cook, stirring constantly, until the flour is cooked, but hasn't turned color, 3 to 4 minutes. Stir in the cream and broth and bring to a boil, whisking constantly. Stir in 1 cup of the Parmesan and season with pepper and with salt if desired.

**2.** Coat a 13 x 9-inch baking pan with non-stick cooking spray and sprinkle ¼ cup of the remaining Parmesan over the bottom. In a large bowl, toss the hot penne with the olive oil.

**3.** Stir the sauce into the penne, then stir in the bacon and mozzarella. Transfer to the prepared pan and sprinkle with the remaining ¼ cup of Parmesan.

✳ **DIVA DO-AHEAD:** At this point, you can cover and refrigerate overnight. Bring to room temperature before continuing.

**4.** Preheat the oven to 350°F. Bake the penne until golden brown, about 30 minutes. Let rest for about 5 minutes before serving.

# Spinach and Ricotta Stuffed Shells 🥛🍷🍸

Serves 10 to 12 as a side dish

Filled with spinach and creamy ricotta and covered with a marinara sauce, these shells are just the ticket to serve with grilled salmon, steak, or chicken. They are also great as a main course.

> One 12-ounce package large pasta shells, cooked in boiling salted water for 5 minutes and drained
>
> 1 tablespoon olive oil, as needed
>
> 1 tablespoon unsalted butter
>
> ½ cup finely chopped onion
>
> One 16-ounce package frozen chopped spinach, defrosted and squeezed dry
>
> ⅛ teaspoon ground nutmeg
>
> 1 teaspoon salt
>
> ½ teaspoon freshly ground black pepper
>
> 1 cup ricotta cheese
>
> 1 large egg, beaten
>
> 1 cup freshly grated Romano cheese
>
> 1½ to 2 cups Quick Marinara (page 482)
>
> ½ cup shredded mozzarella cheese

1. Toss the hot shells with the olive oil to prevent sticking and set aside.

2. In a medium-size skillet, melt the butter over medium heat, add the onion, and cook, stirring, until softened, 4 to 5 minutes. Add the spinach, nutmeg, salt, and pepper and cook until the spinach is heated through and there is no longer any liquid in the bottom of the pan, about 3 minutes.

3. In a large bowl, stir together the ricotta, eggs, and 1 cup of the Romano cheese. Stir in the spinach mixture until thoroughly blended.

4. Coat the bottom of a 13 x 9-inch baking pan with nonstick cooking spray and spread 1 cup of the marinara sauce over the bottom.

5. Stuff each of the shells with 2 to 3 tablespoons of the ricotta-spinach mixture and set in the pan, filling side up. Cover shells with the remaining sauce and sprinkle with the remaining ½ cup of Romano and the mozzarella.

✳ **DIVA DO-AHEAD:** At this point, you can cover and refrigerate for up to 2 days or freeze for up to 2 months. Defrost and let come to room temperature before continuing.

6. Preheat the oven to 350°F. Bake the shells until heated through and the cheese is golden brown, 30 to 40 minutes.

# Apricot Noodle Kugel

Serves 10 to 12 as a side dish

Noodle kugel is a traditional dish made at Jewish holidays. This one is simple to prepare and, with its orange and apricot flavoring, will add a touch of sweetness to any meal. Kugel is delicious warm or at room temperature.

1½ cups cottage cheese (low-fat is okay)

1½ cups sour cream (low-fat is okay)

2 large eggs

⅔ cup sugar

½ cup (1 stick) unsalted butter, melted

½ teaspoon orange oil, or 1 teaspoon orange extract

Grated zest of 1 orange

1 cup chopped dried apricots

1 pound wide egg noodles, cooked according to the package directions until *al dente* and drained

⅔ cup sliced almonds

**1.** Coat a 13 x 9-inch baking dish with nonstick cooking spray.

**2.** In a food processor or blender, combine the cottage cheese, sour cream, eggs, ⅓ cup of the sugar, 2 tablespoons of the butter, and the orange oil and zest and process or blend until smooth. Transfer to a large bowl and stir in the apricots and noodles, then transfer to the prepared pan. Sprinkle the top evenly with the almonds and the remaining ⅓ cup of sugar and drizzle with the remaining 6 tablespoons of melted butter.

❋ **DIVA DO-AHEAD:** At this point, you can cover and refrigerate for up to 3 days. Bring to room temperature before continuing.

**3.** Preheat the oven to 350°F. Bake the kugel until golden brown, 40 to 50 minutes. Let rest for 10 minutes before serving.

## A Pasta Tip from the Pros

Most restaurants partially cook your pasta earlier in the day. They keep pots of water boiling on the stove during dinner, and immerse your pasta for a minute or two to rewarm and finish cooking it. To precook pasta, cook until it's about 3 minutes away from being done. Drain and keep it refrigerated or at room temperature. Don't coat it with oil or butter; it will loosen during its second cooking. Just before you are ready to serve, have a pot of water boiling on the stove. Add the partially cooked pasta, stirring to break it up. Boil for 1 or 2 minutes, or until it is *al dente*. Drain again, transfer to a serving dish, and stir in the sauce.

# Orzo

Serves 10 to 12 as a side dish

Orzo is a rice-shaped pasta that will serve a multitude. You can prepare the orzo the day before, then fold in the ingredients you wish to add to it. I recommend reheating it in the microwave or over low heat in a saucepan with a little added broth. If you would like to flavor your orzo while it is boiling, use broth; if you want it plain, use water.

**4 quarts water or broth**

**2 teaspoons salt**

**One 1-pound package orzo**

**2 tablespoons olive oil**

**Salt and freshly ground black pepper to taste**

**1.** In a 5-quart saucepan, bring the water and salt to a boil. (If you use broth, omit the salt.) Add the orzo and boil until tender, 8 to 9 minutes.

**2.** Drain, toss with the olive oil to prevent sticking, and season with salt and pepper if desired.

## Diva Variations

**Mushroom Orzo:** Melt 2 tablespoons of unsalted butter in a large skillet over medium-high heat. Add 1 pound of mushrooms, sliced ½ inch thick, and 1 teaspoon of dried thyme. Cook, stirring a few times, until the mushrooms are golden brown, 10 to 15 minutes.

✳ **DIVA DO-AHEAD:** At this point, you can let cool, cover, and refrigerate for up to 3 days or freeze for up to 2 months. Defrost and reheat before continuing.

Fold the warm mushrooms into 1 pound of orzo, cooked as directed, and serve.

**Pesto Orzo:** After the orzo is cooked, swirl in ½ cup of pesto of your choice, homemade (page 97, 472, or 473) or store-bought, and serve.

**Orzo Alfredo:** In a large serving bowl, mix together ¼ cup (½ stick) of unsalted butter, melted; ½ cup of heavy cream; and 1 cup of freshly grated Parmesan cheese. Stir in 1 pound of cooked orzo until blended. Season with freshly ground black pepper to taste, garnish with another ½ cup of grated Parmesan, and serve.

# Couscous

Serves 10 to 12 as a side dish

Couscous is a small pasta grain that can be served at room temperature, which makes it a perfect side dish for do-ahead entertaining. Prepare it early in the day if you like. You can flavor the couscous with your choice of vegetables, dried fruits, and spices. I'm particularly fond of finely chopped vegetables in my couscous, and I boil it in chicken broth rather than water to give it additional flavor.

**2 cups chicken broth**

**2 tablespoons olive oil**

**2 cups couscous**

**½ cup finely chopped zucchini**

**½ cup finely chopped red onion**

**¼ cup seeded and finely chopped red bell pepper**

**Salt and freshly ground black pepper to taste**

**1.** In a 2½-quart saucepan, bring the broth and oil to a boil, then stir in the couscous. Remove from the heat and let stand until the broth is absorbed, 5 to 7 minutes.

**2.** Fluff the couscous with a fork and fold in the zucchini, onion, and bell pepper. Season with salt and black pepper. Serve warm or at room temperature.

# Rice Pilaf

Serves 12

Rice pilaf is made by sautéing rice in oil or butter, then cooking it in stock. This gives you options for flavoring the pilaf with chicken, beef, or vegetable broth. Sautéed vegetables can be folded into the pilaf at the end of the cooking time for added interest. Rice pilaf can be made the day before, then reheated in the microwave for 5 minutes before serving.

**3 tablespoons unsalted butter**

**1 cup finely chopped onion**

**2 cups converted long-grain rice**

**5 cups chicken, beef, or vegetable broth**

**Salt and freshly ground black pepper to taste**

**1.** In a 4-quart saucepan, melt the butter over medium heat, add the onion, and cook, stirring, until softened, about 3 minutes. Add the rice and cook, stirring, until the rice begins to absorb some of the butter, about 2 minutes. Slowly stir in the broth and bring to a boil. Reduce the heat to low and simmer until the liquid is absorbed and the rice is tender, 25 to 30 minutes.

✳ **DIVA DO-AHEAD:** At this point, you can let cool, cover, and refrigerate overnight or freeze for up to 2 months. Defrost and reheat in the microwave.

**2.** Season the pilaf with salt and pepper and serve.

### Diva Variations

Stir in one of the following when cooking the onion:

- 1½ teaspoons dried thyme
- 1 teaspoon curry powder
- 2 ounces dried porcini mushrooms
- ½ cup oil-packed sun-dried tomatoes, drained and cut into matchsticks

# SOUP MIX PILAF

Serves 10 to 12 as a side dish

When I was writing my cookbook *The Soup Mix Gourmet* (The Harvard Common Press, 2001), I discovered that soup mixes add just the right flavor for a terrific pilaf. This is the master recipe.

**2 tablespoons unsalted butter**

**1 cup finely chopped onion**

**2 cups converted long-grain rice**

**1 envelope dry soup mix of your choice (see my suggestions below)**

**5 cups water**

**Salt and freshly ground black pepper to taste**

**1.** In a 5-quart saucepan, melt the butter over medium heat, add the onion, and cook, stirring, until softened, about 3 minutes. Add the rice and soup mix and cook, stirring, until the rice absorbs some of the butter and the soup mix begins to dissolve, about 3 minutes. Slowly add the water and bring to a boil, stirring. Reduce the heat to medium-low, cover, and simmer until the liquid is absorbed and the rice is tender, 25 to 30 minutes.

✳ **DIVA DO-AHEAD:** At this point, you can let cool, cover, and refrigerate overnight or freeze for up to 2 months. Defrost and reheat in the microwave before serving.

**2.** Season the pilaf with salt and pepper and serve.

### Diva Variations

My favorite dry soup mixes for this pilaf are Lipton's Onion, Beefy Onion, Golden Onion, Ranch, and Herb and Garlic; and Knorr's Cream of Leek, Cream of Spinach, Tomato Basil, and Vegetable.

# Pilaf Milanese

Serves 12 as a side dish

This variation of the classic risotto of Milan is a lot simpler to make because it doesn't need to be stirred, and the rice doesn't congeal when it's left out at room temperature.

¼ cup (½ stick) unsalted butter

1 cup finely chopped onion

⅛ teaspoon saffron threads (see The Diva Says)

2 cups converted long-grain rice

4 cups chicken, beef, or vegetable broth

1 cup whole or 2% milk

1 cup freshly grated Parmesan cheese

Salt and freshly ground black pepper to taste

## A Note about Rice

All the recipes in this chapter were tested with Uncle Ben's converted rice, which you can find in grocery stores everywhere. Make sure you buy the regular converted rice, and not the instant. Converted rice is long-grain rice that has been parboiled, and so it is ready in 20 minutes.

**1.** In a 4-quart saucepan, melt the butter over medium heat. Add the onion and saffron threads and cook, stirring, until the onion is softened, about 3 minutes. Add the rice and cook for another 2 minutes, stirring frequently. Slowly add the broth and milk and bring to a boil. Reduce the heat to medium-low and simmer until the rice is tender and the liquid is absorbed, 25 to 30 minutes.

❉ **DIVA DO-AHEAD:** At this point, you can let cool, cover, and refrigerate overnight or freeze for up to 2 months. Defrost and reheat in the microwave.

**2.** Stir in the cheese, season with salt and pepper, and serve.

## The Diva Says:

If saffron is out of your price range, substitute ¼ teaspoon of sweet paprika, which will give your dish a nice golden color but a different flavor, or you can omit a spice altogether.

# Florentine Rice Casserole

Serves 10 to 12 as a side dish

This casserole is not only visually appealing, but it's also a great way to eat your spinach!

2 tablespoons unsalted butter

1 tablespoon olive oil

1 cup finely chopped onion

2 cloves garlic, minced

Two 10-ounce packages frozen chopped spinach, defrosted and squeezed dry

1 teaspoon salt

½ teaspoon freshly ground black pepper

⅛ teaspoon freshly ground nutmeg

3 tablespoons all-purpose flour

5 cups whole or 2% milk

2 cups converted long-grain rice

1 cup freshly grated Parmesan cheese

1 cup finely shredded Swiss cheese

**1.** In a large skillet, heat the butter and oil over medium heat until the butter is melted. Add the onion and garlic and cook, stirring, until softened, about 3 minutes. Add the spinach, salt, pepper, and nutmeg and cook, stirring, until combined, 3 to 4 minutes. Sprinkle the spinach with the flour and cook for 2 minutes, scraping the bottom of the pan to prevent the flour from sticking. Slowly add the milk and stir until the mixture comes to a boil.

✳ **DIVA DO-AHEAD:** At this point, you can let cool, cover, and refrigerate for up to 3 days.

**2.** Preheat the oven to 375°F. Coat a 13 x 9-inch baking dish with nonstick cooking spray.

**3.** Stir the rice and ½ cup of the Parmesan into the spinach mixture and transfer to the prepared dish. Sprinkle the top with the remaining ½ cup of Parmesan and the Swiss cheese and bake until the rice is tender, the liquid is absorbed, and the cheese is melted, 35 to 40 minutes.

✳ **DIVA DO-AHEAD:** At this point you can let cool, cover, and freeze for up to 1 month. Defrost and bring to room temperature before continuing.

**4.** Let rest for 10 minutes before serving.

## Grating Your Own Nutmeg

Invest in fresh nutmeg and grate it yourself—the difference in flavor from the preground stuff in your grocery store is like night and day. A microplane grater (see Sources, page 669) is a terrific kitchen tool; you can grate nutmeg, cinnamon sticks, fresh ginger, citrus zest, and small amounts of hard cheeses like Parmigiano-Reggiano.

# Wild Mushroom Rice

Serves 10 to 12 as a side dish

This is a twist on an old potluck standby, but it's made with a variety of mushrooms to make it a little more interesting. Serve this with roast beef or poultry.

2 tablespoons unsalted butter

2 tablespoons olive oil

½ cup chopped shallots

½ pound shiitake mushrooms, stems removed and caps sliced ½ inch thick

½ pound cremini mushrooms, sliced ½ inch thick

3 portobello mushrooms, stems removed, gills scraped from underneath the cap, and coarsely chopped

1½ teaspoons dried thyme or rosemary

2 cups converted long-grain rice

5 cups chicken or beef broth

½ cup chopped fresh Italian parsley for garnish

**1.** Coat a 3-quart casserole dish with non-stick cooking spray.

**2.** In a large skillet, heat the butter and oil over medium heat until the butter melts. Add the shallots and cook, stirring, until softened, about 3 minutes. Add the mushrooms and thyme and cook until the mushrooms begin to turn golden brown, 7 to 8 minutes. Add the rice and broth, stirring up any browned bits stuck on the bottom of the pan. Transfer to the prepared dish and cover with aluminum foil.

✳ **DIVA DO-AHEAD:** At this point, you can let cool, cover, and refrigerate overnight. Bring to room temperature before continuing.

**3.** Preheat the oven to 350°F. Bake for 20 minutes, then remove the foil and bake until the liquid is absorbed and the rice is tender, another 15 to 20 minutes.

**4.** Let the rice rest for 10 minutes. Serve warm, garnished with the parsley.

# Fruit and Rice Medley

Serves 10 to 12 as a side dish

Savory rice and dried fruit make a terrific combination to serve with roasted or grilled entrées.

**2 tablespoons unsalted butter**

**½ cup finely chopped onion**

**½ cup finely chopped dried apricots**

**½ cup unsweetened dried cranberries**

**1 teaspoon dried thyme**

**Grated zest of ½ orange**

**2 cups converted long-grain rice**

**5 ¼ cups chicken broth**

**¼ cup chopped fresh Italian parsley**

**½ cup slivered almonds, toasted (see page 83)**

---

### Slicing without Sticking

To chop apricots or other dried fruit, spray your knife (or a pair of kitchen shears) with nonstick cooking spray; that should keep the fruit from sticking to the blades.

---

**1.** In a 4-quart saucepan, melt the butter over medium heat. Add the onion, apricots, cranberries, thyme, and orange zest and cook, stirring, until the onion is softened, about 3 minutes. Add the rice and cook, stirring, for another 2 minutes. Slowly add the broth and bring to a boil. Reduce the heat to low, cover, and simmer until the liquid is absorbed and the rice is tender, about 25 minutes.

✴ **DIVA DO-AHEAD:** At this point, you can let cool, cover, and refrigerate overnight. Reheat in the microwave before serving.

**2.** Stir the parsley and almonds into the hot rice and serve.

# Low Country Red Rice

Serves 10 to 12 as a side dish

This beautifully colored rice is a staple in Charleston, South Carolina, restaurants and home kitchens. Like many recipes that are handed down, there are many versions, but this one combines the best of the ones I have tried. In the South they use a spicy Cajun cured pork called tasso as the base for this dish; if you can't find it, substitute Italian capocollo or Cajun andouille sausage.

2 tablespoons olive oil

1 cup finely diced tasso

2 cups finely chopped onions

1 cup seeded and finely chopped red bell pepper

One 6-ounce can tomato paste

3 cups chicken broth

1 tablespoon sugar

½ teaspoon freshly ground black pepper

2 cups converted long-grain rice

**1.** In a 4-quart saucepan, heat the oil over medium heat, then add the tasso and cook, stirring, until it softens, about 2 minutes. Add the onions and bell pepper and cook, stirring, until softened, about 4 minutes. Add the tomato paste, broth, sugar, and black pepper, stirring to blend. Bring to a boil, reduce the heat to medium, and simmer for 10 minutes.

**2.** Add the rice, cover, and reduce the heat to low. Simmer until the liquid is absorbed and the rice is tender, about 30 minutes.

✳ **DIVA DO-AHEAD:** At this point, you can let cool, cover, and refrigerate overnight. Reheat in the microwave before serving.

# Cranberry Wild Rice

Serves 10 to 12 as a side dish

This combination of nutty wild rice and dried cranberries is a terrific side dish with roasted pork or poultry, or you can use it to stuff a crown roast of pork.

- ½ cup (1 stick) unsalted butter
- ½ cup finely chopped shallots
- 1 clove garlic, minced
- 1 teaspoon dried thyme
- ½ teaspoon dried sage
- 1 cup unsweetened dried cranberries
- 1½ teaspoons salt
- ½ teaspoon freshly ground black pepper
- ¼ cup chicken broth
- 2 cups wild rice, cooked according to the package directions

**1.** Coat a 3-quart casserole dish with non-stick cooking spray.

**2.** In a large skillet over medium heat, melt the butter. Add the shallots, garlic, thyme, and sage and cook, stirring, until fragrant and the onion is softened, about 4 minutes. Add the cranberries, salt, pepper, and broth and bring to a boil. Stir in the wild rice. Transfer to the prepared dish and cover with aluminum foil.

✳ **DIVA DO-AHEAD:** At this point, you can refrigerate for up to 3 days. Bring to room temperature before continuing.

**3.** Bake until heated through, about 20 minutes.

# Savory Bread Pudding

Serves 8 to 10

Savory bread puddings are a great alternative to potatoes when serving a buffet and, better yet, they can be assembled a day in advance, then baked just before serving.

- 3 tablespoons unsalted butter
- 1 tablespoon olive oil
- 2 large onions, thinly sliced
- 1 tablespoon sugar
- 2 teaspoons dried thyme
- 1½ teaspoons salt
- ½ teaspoon freshly ground black pepper
- 3 cloves garlic, mashed

- 5 large eggs
- 2 cups heavy cream
- 5 shakes of Tabasco sauce
- 1 teaspoon Worcestershire sauce
- 6 cups white bread cubes with crusts removed
- ¼ cup chopped fresh parsley
- ½ cup freshly grated Parmesan cheese

**1.** Coat a 13 x 9-inch baking dish with non-stick cooking spray.

**2.** In a large skillet, heat the butter with the oil over medium heat until the butter melts and the foam subsides. Add the onions, stir to coat with the butter, and cook until they begin to turn translucent. Sprinkle with the sugar, thyme, salt, pepper, and garlic and cook, stirring, until the onions become golden. Remove from the skillet.

✳ **DIVA DO-AHEAD:** At this point, you can let cool, cover, and refrigerate for up to 2 days or freeze for up to 2 weeks.

**3.** In a large bowl, whisk together the eggs, cream, Tabasco, and Worcestershire. Stir in the bread, onion mixture, and parsley. Pour into the prepared dish and sprinkle the top evenly with the cheese.

✳ **DIVA DO-AHEAD:** At this point, cover and refrigerate for at least 4 and up to 24 hours. Bring to room temperature before continuing.

**4.** Preheat the oven to 350°F. Bake the pudding until golden brown and bubbling, 45 to 55 minutes. Let rest for 5 minutes before serving.

✳ **DIVA DO-AHEAD:** At this point, you can let cool, cover, and freeze for up to 1 month. Defrost overnight in the refrigerator, then bake in a 325°F oven, covered with aluminum foil, for 30 minutes.

## Diva Variations

**Italian Bread Pudding:** Sauté ½ pound of cremini mushrooms, sliced, with the onions, then add ½ cup of oil-packed sun-dried tomatoes, drained and chopped, and ¼ cup of chopped fresh basil.

**Santa Fe Bread Pudding:** Omit the thyme and add one 4-ounce can of diced green chiles, drained and rinsed, and ¼ cup of chunky salsa to the egg mixture, and substitute Monterey Jack, pepper Jack, or mild cheddar cheese for the Parmesan. Serve with sour cream on the side.

**Blue Heaven Pudding:** Substitute 1 cup of crumbled Maytag or another blue cheese for the Parmesan, but stir it into the bread-and-egg mixture, so there are nuggets of blue cheese in the pudding.

**French Onion Bread Pudding:** Add 1 cup of chopped Gruyère cheese (½-inch chunks) to the bread-and-egg mixture and substitute additional Gruyère for the Parmesan topping.

# Prosciutto and Cornbread Stuffing

Serves 12

Another gift from my grandmother, this savory side can be stuffed into pork chops or poultry or served on its own. This recipe is always a winner when I serve it at parties—people love the savory bits of prosciutto mingled with the cornbread. Have your butcher give you a chunk or thick slices of prosciutto for you to dice, so you have nice little nuggets throughout the stuffing. I don't think this stuffing freezes well enough so that you can make it weeks in advance and store in the freezer, but if you have leftovers, they will keep, frozen in zipper-top plastic bags, for about 4 weeks. Defrost and reheat in a 350°F oven.

½ cup (1 stick) unsalted butter

1 cup finely chopped onion

⅓ pound prosciutto, diced

2 teaspoons dried sage

1 to 1½ cups chicken broth, as needed

Salt and freshly ground black pepper to taste

1 recipe Southern Cornbread (page 518), cooled and crumbled

½ cup chopped fresh Italian parsley

**1.** In a large skillet over medium heat, melt the butter, then add the onion, prosciutto, and sage and cook, stirring, until the onion is translucent. Add 1 cup of broth and season with salt and pepper if needed. The mixture should be highly seasoned.

**2.** Coat a 13 x 9-inch baking dish with nonstick cooking spray.

**3.** Crumble the cornbread into a large bowl and pour the broth mixture over it, stirring to blend. The stuffing should be slightly moist, but not wet; add more broth if it seems too dry. Stir in the parsley, then transfer to the prepared dish.

✳ **DIVA DO-AHEAD:** At this point, you can cover and refrigerate for up to 2 days. Bring to room temperature before continuing.

**4.** Preheat the oven to 350°F. Bake the stuffing until the top is golden brown, 30 to 40 minutes. Let rest for 5 to 10 minutes before serving.

# Classic Thanksgiving Stuffing

Serves 10 (enough to stuff a 14- to 18-pound bird)

This is the stuffing that is served at my house on Thanksgiving, and I have taught it at countless Do-Ahead Thanksgiving classes. For a large crowd, you may want to bake the stuffing in greased loaf pans, then cut it into ½-inch-thick slices for serving on a platter. Otherwise, you can bake the stuffing in a decorative casserole dish—a 13 x 9-inch one is great because you can cut the stuffing into squares. Be sure to make enough because people always want seconds.

1 cup (2 sticks) plus 3 tablespoons unsalted butter

2 cups chopped celery

2 cups chopped onions

1 teaspoon crushed dried sage or 1 tablespoon chopped fresh sage

1 teaspoon crushed dried thyme or 1 tablespoon chopped fresh thyme

1 tablespoon salt

½ teaspoon freshly ground black pepper

1½ cups chicken broth

4 quarts dry bread cubes (see The Diva Says)

2 large eggs, beaten

**1.** In a large skillet over low heat, melt all of the butter and set 3 tablespoons aside. Cook the celery and onions in the remaining butter until softened, about 3 minutes. Add the sage, thyme, salt, and pepper and cook, stirring, until the vegetables are translucent, another 5 to 6 minutes. Taste the broth and make sure it is highly seasoned because it will lose some of its potency when mixed with the bread. Pour over the vegetables and bring to a boil.

❋ **DIVA DO-AHEAD:** At this point, you can let cool, cover, and refrigerate for up to 2 days or freeze for up to 2 months.

**2.** Grease three 8-inch loaf pans or one 13 x 9-inch baking dish. Have the bread cubes ready in a large bowl and pour the broth mixture over them. Stir in the eggs until blended. If you prefer a wetter stuffing, add a few more tablespoons of broth. Transfer the mixture to the prepared baking pans.

✳ **DIVA DO-AHEAD:** At this point, you can cover and refrigerate for up to 8 hours.

**3.** Preheat the oven to 325°F. Brush the top of the stuffing with the reserved 3 tablespoons of melted butter and bake until golden brown, 35 to 45 minutes.

✳ **DIVA DO-AHEAD:** At this point, you can let cool, cover, and refrigerate for up to 2 days. If you would like to freeze the stuffing, cook it for just 25 minutes, then cool, cover, and freeze for up to 2 months. Defrost overnight in the refrigerator and set on the counter for 30 minutes to come to room temperature. Cover with aluminum foil and bake at 325°F until heated through, about 30 minutes.

**4.** Remove the stuffing from the oven and let rest 10 minutes before serving. If baked in loaf pans, remove from the pans and slice with a serrated knife that has been sprayed with nonstick cooking spray.

## The Diva Says:

To make your own dry bread cubes, remove the crust if it's brittle or dense and cut the bread into cubes. Lay them on a baking sheet and bake in a 300°F oven for 20 minutes, until dry. If time is of the essence, you can buy plain dry bread cubes in your supermarket. (They also come seasoned, but I recommend getting the plain ones and adding the seasonings suggested in the recipe.)

## Diva Variations

This is a basic stuffing, but there are almost unlimited ways in which you can jazz it up. Try throwing any of the following into the skillet while you are sautéing the onion and celery:

- 1 pound sliced mushrooms
- ½ pound frozen crawfish tails, defrosted and peeled
- ½ cup chopped dried apricots
- ½ cup unsweetened dried cranberries
- 1 dozen oysters, shucked and chopped
- 1 cup pecan halves

## Wet or Dry?

If you like a crispy stuffing, do not drown your bread cubes in liquid, and bake the stuffing in a baking dish. If you like it moist, stuff it in the cavity of the turkey before roasting, or add more liquid to the stuffing and bake it in a dish.

# Poultry

**Here in the United States, chicken is on the table** at least twice a week. Whether it's in a casserole, roasted to perfection, cooked on a rotisserie at the deli, or the colonel's secret recipe, almost everyone loves chicken. So serving chicken to your friends and family for a celebration is a sure bet. For entertaining, I like to cook with boneless, as it is neater and the pieces are easier to serve. If I'm making Oven-Fried Chicken (page 317), I'll use chicken pieces with the bone in because there is something about eating chicken with your hands at a picnic or backyard party that turns everyone into a child. Remember that if you are serving bone-in chicken, you'll need to provide plates for the leftover bones. Roasted chicken is great to serve for gatherings, as well. Cut it into small serving pieces with a cleaver, sharp knife, or poultry shears.

Turkey is another poultry choice for entertaining. Whether it's the Thanksgiving bird or the breast pounded into cutlets, turkey is economical and delicious. Goose and duck are impressive, but they don't serve very many people, and you will need at least two ovens to cook the number of birds it would take to serve 10 to 12 people. For that reason, I suggest you save the goose and duck for smaller, less ambitious entertaining.

Harmful bacteria can grow in raw poultry, but if you are careful when handling it there is no need to be fearful. Make sure you wash your hands with hot soapy water after handling raw poultry, and wipe down your counters with an antibacterial spray. Plastic cutting boards are considered much safer than wood for cutting raw poultry. They can be cleaned more thoroughly in hot soapy water or put through the dishwasher to sanitize them. Make sure you cook poultry to 170°F, then remove it from the oven, cover it with aluminum foil, and let it rest for 10 minutes. This will allow the final internal temperature to rise to 180°F, which is safe for poultry, and at the same time allow the chicken to reabsorb some of its juices.

## The Equipment You Need

- Poultry shears are invaluable for cutting away excess fat or cutting chicken into parts. I recommend the Joyce Chen brand with the red handles.

- A Santoku (a cross between a cleaver and a chef's knife) is perfect for cutting through the backbone of poultry to split it.

- Plastic cutting boards are terrific for easy cleanup.

- A heavy-duty roasting pan with a rack is essential for roasting turkeys and chickens evenly.

- A fat separator will take the aggravation out of trying to remove the fat from the pan juices.

## Chicken

**Whole broiler-fryer** chickens come in 2½- to 3½-pound sizes and are sold with the neck and giblets, so make sure you remove those from the cavity; use them for making broth if you'd like. These chickens can be cut in half or quarters for grilling or broiling, or into pieces for frying. It's worth your while to become comfortable with cutting a whole chicken into serving pieces because it's much cheaper to buy one whole than in parts. The cut-up chicken at the supermarket is usually from a broiler-fryer and is likely to include 2 breast halves, 2 thighs, 2 drumsticks, and 2 wings.

*Roasters* are larger meaty chickens ranging from 4 to 6 pounds. These will also include the neck and giblets, which you should remove. Use these chickens only for roasting whole; if you cut them up, the pieces will be too big to grill, broil, or fry properly.

*Leg quarters* are the drumstick and thigh, still attached, and are all dark meat. For easier serving, you'll want to cut the drumstick and thigh apart. The thigh is the part of the leg above the knee joint and is sold bone-in or boneless, while the drumstick, always bone-in, is the part below the joint, and is delicious roasted, braised, or fried.

*Breasts* come whole and cut in half, bone-in or boneless, with the skin or skinless. When grilling or broiling boneless breasts, I'll sometimes leave the skin on to keep the meat moist; if I'm sautéing, I'll remove it. Markets are now featuring breasts that have been pounded thin for quick sautés; it's actually simple (and cheaper) to pound the breasts yourself, but if time is of the essence, you can buy them already pounded.

A *tender* is the little flap of meat attached to the bottom of the breast; it has a tendon running the length of the meat. Remove the tender from each breast half, then take a sharp knife and peel the tendon away from the meat. I usually freeze the tenders for skewers and stir-fries, but you can also buy them in large quantities at your grocer in the frozen food section, with the tendon removed, or in the meat section, with the tendon still in. Use these to make your favorite skewers or Baked Buffalo Wings (page 295).

*Chicken wings* are great little bites for parties, and everyone seems to love them. I am particularly fond of drumettes, which are the meatier first section of the wing and look like drumsticks. Unlike a drumstick, however, a drumette is all white meat. If you can only find whole wings (which are cheaper than drumettes), remove the wing tip and cut the wings in half before marinating and cooking.

**Chicken wings** are a great starter for a party, whether they're traditional Buffalo wings bathed in Frank's RedHot Cayenne Pepper Sauce, glazed Hawaiian style with teriyaki sauce (see page 311) or covered with your favorite barbecue sauce. This chapter contains some tried and true recipes for wings your guest will devour. I use only the little drumstick part of the wing (it's called a "drumette") because a complete chicken wing is harder to handle when you have a plate, and then you've got more bones to get rid of. The meaty little drumette is a more satisfying and tidy package, perfect for grazing.

If you would like to serve the marinade as a dipping sauce, I recommend that you make a separate batch reserved just for that purpose to avoid cross contamination. I generally use a 2-gallon zipper-top plastic bag to marinate the wings so I can turn them easily in the refrigerator. All of the marinades can be used for larger, meatier chicken parts if you would like to serve them as a main dish, though you'll have to bake them a bit longer. To make boneless "wings," buy chicken tenders and marinate them as directed in the recipe. You can then skewer the tenders and grill them (5 minutes total cooking time) or lay them on baking sheets and roast as you would the wings, though they will cook in half the time.

When serving wings, I generally have little moistened towelettes on the table to help people clean up—wings tend to be messy because they are finger foods. I also put out a plate for discarded bones.

## Turkey

Although we usually serve these large, flavorful birds to our family and friends at Thanksgiving and during the holidays, you can cook them year-round. Turkey is such a bargain, I believe it's the best meat to serve on the buffet table if you need to economize. A 12-pound turkey will serve 16 to 18 people and you may even have a few leftovers. It's also terrific on an appetizer buffet, served with small rolls for sandwiches, or as part of a taco/fajita bar.

Many food magazines and chefs have been touting the benefits of brining turkey (soaking it in salt and water) overnight. Since not everyone has the space to refrigerate a turkey soaking in water, I recommend that you buy either a kosher turkey or a Butterball-brand bird because they are already brined. If you aren't sure whether you will like the taste of a brined turkey, cook a kosher chicken and see whether you like the flavor and consistency of the meat. I find that by slow-roasting the turkey in a 325°F oven, it comes out juicy and tender without the brining.

For a special meal, buy a fresh turkey; I think you'll find the flavor superior to that of a frozen one. Plan on ¾ pound per person if you want enough leftovers for a meal the next day; if you want to share leftovers with your guests, plan on 1 pound per person. If you are a beginner, I recommend that you cook a turkey weighing 18 pounds or less. Larger ones cook unevenly, giving you well-done dark meat and dry white meat. If you need 24 pounds of turkey, make two 12-pound turkeys instead if you have the oven space.

Make sure you roast the turkey in a heavy-duty roasting pan with a rack. The rack is essential if you want to end up with caramelized drippings, the foundation of a tasty gravy. If the turkey is placed directly on the bottom of the roasting pan, it will steam in its juices.

Always use an instant-read meat thermometer when cooking turkey. Those little plastic pop-up thermometers that are inserted in some turkeys work on a moisture principle. They pop up when the moisture in the turkey is gone, but that's not what you want. The turkey should register 170° to 175°F on an instant-read meat thermometer when it's pushed into the thickest part of the thigh, and the juices should run clear when you insert the tip of a knife between the drumstick and the thigh. The turkey will need to rest for at least 30 to 45 minutes, tented with aluminum foil, before you carve it, which will give you time to reheat all your side dishes.

# Timing for Defrosting a Turkey in the Refrigerator

| Weight of Turkey | Defrosting Time |
|---|---|
| 4 to 8 pounds | 1 to 1½ days |
| 8 to 12 pounds | 1½ to 2 days |
| 12 to 16 pounds | 2 to 2½ days |
| 16 to 20 pounds | 2½ to 3 days |
| 20 to 24 pounds | 3 to 3½ days |

# Turkey Roasting Times

The following estimates are for roasting a turkey in a conventional oven preheated to 325°F.

| Weight of Turkey | Roasting Times | |
|---|---|---|
| | Unstuffed | Stuffed |
| 4 to 8 pounds | 1½ to 2 hours | 2½ to 3½ hours |
| 8 to 12 pounds | 2¾ to 3 hours | 3 to 3½ hours |
| 12 to 14 pounds | 3 to 3¾ hours | 3½ to 4 hours |
| 14 to 18 pounds | 3¾ to 4¼ hours | 4 to 4¼ hours |
| 18 to 20 pounds | 4¼ to 4½ hours | 4¼ to 4¾ hours |
| 20 to 24 pounds | 4½ to 5 hours | 4¾ to 5¼ hours |
| 24 to 30 pounds | 5 to 5¼ hours | 5¼ to 6¼ hours |

The stuffing should register 165°F on an instant-read meat thermometer and the turkey should register 170° to 175°F at the thickest part of the thigh.

## SERVING IT UP

**Slice the turkey** in the kitchen, then arrange it on a platter with the dark meat on one side and the lighter meat on the other. Or, if you want to make a statement, you can slice one side of the turkey and use the turkey half as part of your presentation on the platter. Although this isn't my favorite way to do it (there are always a couple of people who can't find the parts they are looking for), half a bird does make a statement.

To carve a turkey, remove the legs and, holding a leg by the end, slice down the length of the drumstick to remove the meat. Repeat with the other drumstick. Slice the thigh meat parallel to the bird until you have a few slices. Cut through each thigh joint, remove the thigh, and cut the meat from the bone.

Beginning at the top of the breast, cut along the breastbone and remove the entire breast half. Cut the meat against the grain into slices and arrange on a platter. Repeat with the other side.

# Honey Teriyaki Wings

Serves 10 to 12

Asian flavors make these little bites a hit at any party. The sesame seeds and scallions add a little color and crunch to the finished dish.

**3 pounds chicken wings or drumettes**

**2 tablespoons water**

**1 tablespoon cornstarch**

**¼ cup vegetable oil**

**2 cloves garlic, minced**

**1 teaspoon peeled and grated fresh ginger**

**⅓ cup ketchup**

**¾ cup soy sauce**

**1 cup honey**

**2 tablespoons sesame seeds, toasted (see page 83), for garnish**

**4 scallions (white and tender green parts), chopped, for garnish**

**1.** Put the wings in a 13 x 9-inch baking dish or 2-gallon zipper-top plastic bag. Stir the water and cornstarch together in a small bowl and set aside.

**2.** In a medium-size skillet, heat the oil over medium heat, add the garlic and ginger, and cook, stirring, until fragrant, about 1 minute. Reduce the heat to low, add the ketchup, soy sauce, and honey, and stir until blended. Add the cornstarch mixture and stir until the sauce comes to a boil. Remove from the heat and let cool, then pour half the sauce over the wings (it becomes the marinade) and refrigerate the other half. Turn the wings in the marinade to coat them well and cover the dish or seal the bag.

✳ **DIVA DO-AHEAD:** At this point, refrigerate for at least 4 hours or overnight.

**3.** Preheat the oven to 350°F and pour the wings and marinade onto a rimmed baking sheet lined with a silicone liner or aluminum foil. Bake until cooked through, 35 to 45 minutes, basting every 10 minutes with the reserved sauce.

✳ **DIVA DO-AHEAD:** At this point, you can let cool, cover, and refrigerate overnight, then reheat in a 325°F oven, covered with foil, for about 20 minutes.

**4.** Remove the wings from the oven, arrange on a serving platter, and sprinkle with sesame seeds and scallions.

# Baked Buffalo Wings

Serves 10 to 12

These spicy bites are a favorite bar food. At the Anchor Bar in Buffalo, New York, the origina-tor of Buffalo wings, the chicken is deep-fried, but I like baking them to bypass the greasy mess. The Anchor serves their wings with blue cheese dressing and celery sticks to cut the heat; I follow tradition there, but I place the wings on a bed of shredded cabbage and offer a side of melted butter mixed with more hot sauce for those who can't get enough heat!

**3 pounds chicken wings or drumettes**

**2 tablespoons olive oil**

**1½ teaspoons salt**

**½ teaspoon freshly ground black pepper**

**1 cup (2 sticks) unsalted butter, melted**

**½ cup or more Frank's RedHot Cayenne Pepper Sauce (traditional), or your favorite hot sauce**

### Slow Cooker Savvy

After the wings have baked, you can keep them warm on Low in a 5- to 6-quart slow cooker.

**1.** Preheat the oven to 375°F. Line a rimmed baking sheet with a silicone liner or aluminum foil.

**2.** In a large bowl, combine the wings, olive oil, salt, and pepper, tossing to coat the wings. Arrange them on the prepared sheet and bake for 10 minutes.

**3.** Combine the butter and hot sauce in a 2-cup measure. At the end of 10 minutes of baking time, turn the wings, pour half the butter mixture over them, and bake for another 10 minutes. Turn the wings again, brush with some more of the butter mix-ture, and bake until cooked through, about another 10 minutes.

✳ **DIVA DO-AHEAD:** At this point, you can let cool, cover, and refrigerate for up to 2 days, then reheat in a 350°F oven, covered with foil, for about 15 minutes.

**4.** Remove the wings from the oven and serve immediately, giving them a fresh baste of the butter sauce.

# Mediterranean Wings

Serves 10 to 12

Lemon, rosemary, and garlic flavor these terrific wings, which are garnished with crumbles of feta for a salty counterpart. Serve them at a picnic or for an appetizer buffet.

**3 pounds chicken wings or drumettes**

**½ cup olive oil**

**Grated zest of 2 lemons**

**½ cup fresh lemon juice (1 to 2 lemons)**

**1½ teaspoons salt**

**1 teaspoon freshly ground black pepper**

**2 tablespoons chopped fresh rosemary**

**6 cloves garlic, crushed**

**½ cup chopped fresh parsley for garnish**

**¾ cup crumbled feta cheese for garnish**

## Other Sauces Delicious with Wings

- **Jezebel Sauce** (page 476)
- **Pacific Rim Peanut Sauce** (page 481)
- **Hoisin-Orange Barbecue Sauce** (page 486)
- **Old-Fashioned Brown Sugar Barbecue Sauce** (page 485)
- **Maple-Chipotle Basting Sauce** (page 487)
- **Honey mustard glaze** (in Honey Mustard Glazed Ham, page 450)

**1.** Put the chicken in a large bowl or zipper-top plastic bag and add the oil, lemon zest and juice, salt, pepper, rosemary, and garlic. Toss to coat the chicken, then cover the bowl or seal the bag.

✳ **DIVA DO-AHEAD:** At this point, refrigerate for at least 6 hours and up to 2 days.

**2.** Preheat the oven to 375°F and line a rimmed baking sheet with a silicone liner or aluminum foil.

**3.** Drain the chicken, reserving the marinade, and arrange on the baking sheet. Pour some of the marinade over the chicken and bake until cooked through, 35 to 40 minutes, turning them once halfway through baking.

✳ **DIVA DO-AHEAD:** At this point, you can let cool, cover, and refrigerate for up to 2 days, then reheat in a 350°F oven, covered with foil, for about 15 minutes.

**4.** Remove the chicken from the oven, garnish with the parsley and feta, and serve.

# Chipotle Wings

Serves 10 to 12

These spicy numbers are marinated in a chile-spiked concoction that creates a smoky, sweet tang. Serve them at your next tailgate party and they will be gone in no time!

3 pounds chicken wings or drumettes

¾ cup rice vinegar

¼ cup canola oil

3 cloves garlic, peeled

2 canned chipotle chiles packed in adobo sauce, drained and 1 teaspoon of the sauce reserved

¼ cup packed fresh cilantro leaves, plus extra for garnish

½ cup coarsely chopped red onion, plus extra for garnish

¼ cup honey

1. Put the wings in a large bowl or zipper-top plastic bag.

2. In a food processor, combine the vinegar, oil, garlic, chiles, reserved adobo sauce, cilantro, onion, and honey and process until smooth. Pour over the chicken, toss to coat, and cover the bowl or seal the bag.

✳ **DIVA DO-AHEAD:** At this point, refrigerate for at least 2 hours or overnight.

3. Preheat the oven to 375°F. Line a rimmed baking sheet with a silicone liner or aluminum foil. Transfer the chicken and marinade to the baking sheet and roast until cooked through, 35 to 40 minutes, turning once to make sure the wings brown evenly.

✳ **DIVA DO-AHEAD:** At this point, you can let cool, cover, and refrigerate for up to 2 days, then reheat in a 350°F oven, covered with foil, for about 15 minutes.

4. Remove the wings from the oven, garnish with chopped cilantro and red onion, and serve.

# Sticky Barbecued Wings

Serves 10

This is the barbecued chicken from your childhood, only it's baked. The recipe is almost too simple, and it also adapts well to meatier chicken parts. It is messy, but, by God, it's good. Make sure you provide lots of napkins and moistened towelettes for sticky fingers and faces!

**3 pounds chicken wings or drumettes**

**¼ cup honey**

**2 cups bottled barbecue sauce (I like KC Masterpiece)**

**½ teaspoon chili powder**

**1 tablespoon fresh lemon juice**

**1.** Put the wings in a large bowl or 2-gallon zipper-top plastic bag.

**2.** In a medium-size bowl, whisk together the honey, barbecue sauce, chili powder, and lemon juice until smooth. Pour over the wings, toss to coat evenly, and cover the bowl or seal the bag.

✳ **DIVA DO-AHEAD:** At this point, refrigerate for at least 6 hours and up to 2 days.

**3.** Preheat the oven to 375°F. Line a baking sheet with a silicone liner or aluminum foil. Transfer the chicken and marinade to the baking sheet and bake until cooked through, 35 to 40 minutes, turning once to ensure even browning.

✳ **DIVA DO-AHEAD:** At this point, you can let cool, cover, and refrigerate for up to 2 days, then reheat in a 350°F oven, covered with foil, for about 15 minutes.

**4.** Remove from the oven and serve immediately.

## CHICKEN SKEWERS

**Chicken threaded onto skewers** can be a nice little bite before dinner, or they can be the main event; either way, they are delicious marinated, then broiled or grilled and served with a dipping sauce. For serving 10 to 12 as an appetizer, you will need 6 skinless boneless chicken breast halves, cut into either bite-size pieces or strips to thread onto skewers.

Try any of these marinades for chicken skewers:

● Rosemary and Lemon Marinade (page 309)

● Teriyaki Marinade (page 395)

● Margaritaville Marinade (page 310)

● Southwestern Marinade (page 395)

● Soy-Ginger Marinade (page 394)

● Marinade Provençal (page 394)

● Bloody Mary Marinade (page 396)

● Citrus-Rosemary Marinade (page 397)

● 2 cups store-bought basil or cilantro pesto mixed with 2 tablespoons of white wine vinegar

● Any of the marinades used for the chicken wing recipes on pages 294 to 297

# Chicken Stuffed with Prosciutto and Fontina

Serves 10 to 12

This is my version of Chicken Cordon Bleu, which pairs salty prosciutto and tangy fontina with the chicken for a more full-flavored rendition.

12 skinless, boneless chicken breast halves, tenders removed (use for another purpose)

1 teaspoon salt

½ teaspoon freshly ground black pepper

1 tablespoon thinly sliced fresh sage (about 3 leaves)

12 thin slices prosciutto (about ¼ pound)

12 thin slices fontina cheese (about ⅓ pound)

½ cup (1 stick) unsalted butter, melted

2 cloves garlic, minced

2 tablespoons finely chopped fresh parsley

2 cups plain dry bread crumbs

½ cup freshly grated Parmesan cheese

¼ cup olive oil

1 cup dry white wine

½ cup chicken broth

## Diva Variations

Replace the fontina with provolone, or replace the prosciutto and fontina with Black Forest ham and Brie.

**1.** Lay the chicken between sheets of waxed paper or plastic wrap. Using a meat mallet, the bottom of a wine bottle, or a rolling pin, pound to a uniform thickness, about ½ inch. Season evenly on both sides with the salt, pepper, and sage.

**2.** Place a breast half on a cutting board or flat surface, cut side up. Lay a slice of prosciutto on top, cutting it to fit (reserve all the prosciutto trimmings). Lay a slice of fontina over the prosciutto and cut it to fit as well. Roll up the chicken, tucking in the sides and forming a neat package. If the chicken seems secure, there is no need to use a toothpick, but if it won't fold over well, secure the bottom. Place the chicken, seam side down, on a plate and repeat until all the chicken is rolled.

**3.** Combine half of the melted butter, the garlic, and parsley in a shallow dish. In another dish, combine the bread crumbs and Parmesan cheese.

**4.** Dip each stuffed breast half into the butter, then roll in the crumbs, coating it evenly.

**DIVA DO-AHEAD:** At this point, cover and refrigerate for at least 1 hour or overnight, or freeze for up to 1 month. Defrost chicken before continuing.

**5.** Preheat the oven to 350°F. Thinly slice any leftover pieces of prosciutto. Combine the remaining ¼ cup of melted butter with the oil in a large skillet over medium-high heat and cook the prosciutto, stirring, until crispy. Remove from the pan and reserve for a garnish.

**6.** Cook the chicken in the butter-and-oil mixture until golden brown on each side.

Arrange in a single layer in a baking dish and bake until cooked through, 15 to 20 minutes. Meanwhile, pour the wine and broth into the skillet, bring to a boil, and reduce the mixture to about ½ cup, scraping all the browned bits off the bottom of the pan.

**7.** When the chicken is done, remove from the oven and cover with aluminum foil for about 5 minutes. Cut the chicken on the diagonal into ½-inch-thick slices, pour the sauce over the top or serve it on the side, and garnish the chicken with the crispy prosciutto. Serve immediately.

# Chicken Stuffed with Spinach and Feta

Serves 10 to 12

This beautifully colored chicken is filled with creamy feta and deep green spinach. It's delicious served cold for an elegant picnic or *al fresco* dinner, and it's very tasty when warm.

½ cup (1 stick) unsalted butter

½ cup finely chopped onion

Two 16-ounce packages frozen spinach, defrosted and squeezed dry

2 tablespoons chopped fresh dill

2 teaspoons salt

1½ teaspoons freshly ground black pepper

1½ cups crumbled feta cheese

12 skinless, boneless chicken breast halves, tenders removed (use for another purpose)

**1.** In a large skillet over medium heat, melt ¼ cup (½ stick) of the butter, then cook the onion, stirring, until almost translucent, 3 to 5 minutes. Add the spinach and dill and cook, stirring, until the spinach is dry, another 3 minutes. Season with 1 teaspoon each of the salt and pepper. Turn the spinach into a medium-size bowl, add the feta, and mix well.

✳ **DIVA DO-AHEAD:** At this point, you can cover and refrigerate overnight.

**2.** Lay the chicken between sheets of waxed paper or plastic wrap. Using a meat mallet, the bottom of a wine bottle, or a rolling pin, pound to a uniform thickness, about ½ inch. Season the chicken on both sides with the remaining 1 teaspoon of salt and ½ teaspoon of pepper.

**3.** Place a breast half on a cutting board or flat surface, cut side up. Mound about 2 tablespoons of the filling over the length of the chicken and roll up, folding in the sides. Secure with a toothpick if needed

and place, seam side down, on a plate. Repeat with the remaining chicken and filling.

✳ **DIVA DO-AHEAD:** At this point, cover and refrigerate for at least 1 hour or overnight, or freeze for up to 1 month. Defrost chicken before continuing.

**4.** Preheat the oven to 350°F. Melt the remaining ¼ cup (½ stick) of butter in a large skillet over medium-high heat and cook the chicken until golden brown on all sides. Arrange in a single layer in a baking dish.

✳ **DIVA DO-AHEAD:** At this point, you can cool to room temperature, cover, and refrigerate overnight. Bring to room temperature before proceeding with the recipe.

Bake the chicken until cooked through, 15 to 20 minutes.

**5.** Remove the chicken from the oven and cover with aluminum foil for about 5 minutes, then cut on the diagonal into ½-inch-thick slices and serve on a platter.

## Sauce with That?

A pan sauce can be made from the drippings in the skillet. Add a little white wine and chicken broth, bring to a boil, and reduce until it is almost syrup, scraping up any browned bits from the bottom of the pan. To thicken sauce like the pros do, throw in bits of cold butter and stir into the boiling sauce, whisking after each addition. This will emulsify the sauce, making it glossy as well as thick. Don't try this if you want to reheat the sauce, though; it's a last-minute trick.

## Stuffed Chicken Breasts

Stuffing chicken breasts is a bit of work, but it is the do-ahead party planner's best friend. The chicken can be stuffed the day before and refrigerated, or frozen for up to 1 month. The chicken is sautéed and then baked until golden brown. It looks fantastic on the serving plate, especially if you slice the chicken so that the filling shows. With a little sauce and a nice salad, you have a five-star dinner.

# Chicken with Rice and Crawfish Stuffing 🍺🍷🥂

Serves 10 to 12

This spicy combination gives you a luscious main course to serve for any type of occasion. Look for cooked crawfish tails in the frozen fish section of your supermarket. If you are unable to find them, use an equal amount of cooked shrimp or lump crabmeat instead.

½ cup (1 stick) unsalted butter

¼ cup chopped onion

¼ cup chopped celery

¼ cup seeded and chopped green bell pepper

2 cloves garlic, minced

2 tablespoons or more Creole Seasoning (recipe follows)

2 cups coarsely chopped cooked crawfish or shrimp

2 cups cooked converted long-grain rice, cooled

12 skinless, boneless chicken breast halves, tenders removed (use for another purpose)

2½ cups plain dry bread crumbs

¼ cup olive oil

## Making It Last

An old caterer's trick for stretching the quantity of chicken is to slice it; people generally eat half of what they normally would and you save money in the long run.

**1.** In a medium-size skillet over medium heat, melt 2 tablespoons of the butter and cook the onion, celery, bell pepper, garlic, and 1 tablespoon of the Creole Seasoning, stirring, until the vegetables begin to turn translucent, 4 to 5 minutes. Transfer to a bowl and let cool slightly. Stir in the crawfish and rice, blending well. Taste and add more Creole Seasoning, if desired.

✳ **DIVA DO-AHEAD:** At this point, you can cover and refrigerate overnight.

**2.** Place each chicken breast half between sheets of waxed paper or plastic wrap and, using a meat mallet, the bottom of a wine bottle, or a rolling pin, pound until uniform in thickness, about ½ inch. Season on both sides with a little of the Creole seasoning.

**3.** Place a chicken breast on a cutting board, cut side up. Cover its length with 2 tablespoons of the filling. Roll up the chicken, folding in the sides, and secure with a toothpick. Repeat with the remaining chicken and filling.

**4.** Melt the remaining 6 tablespoons of butter and transfer to a shallow dish. Put the bread crumbs in another shallow dish and stir in the remaining Creole seasoning. Dip each chicken breast into the butter, then roll in the crumbs to coat evenly. Reserve any remaining butter for sautéing.

✳ **DIVA DO-AHEAD:** At this point, cover and refrigerate chicken for at least 1 hour and up to 24 hours, or freeze for up to 1 month. Defrost before continuing.

**5.** Preheat the oven to 350°F. Add any remaining butter to the oil in a large skillet over medium-high heat. Cook the chicken until golden brown on all sides, then arrange in a single layer in a baking dish. Bake until cooked through, 15 to 20 minutes.

**6.** Remove the chicken from the oven and cover with aluminum foil for about 5 minutes. Cut on the diagonal into ½-inch-thick slices and serve on a platter.

## Creole Seasoning

Making your own Creole seasoning blend is as simple as stirring together pantry spices. There are lots of formulas, but this is my favorite. It's not too spicy and really brings out the flavors in the food, instead of overpowering it with heat.

¼ **cup salt**

**2 tablespoons sweet paprika**

**2 tablespoons onion powder**

**2 tablespoons garlic powder**

**2 teaspoons cayenne pepper**

**1 teaspoon freshly ground black pepper**

¼ **teaspoon ground white pepper**

**2 teaspoons dried whole thyme leaves**

**1 teaspoon dried whole oregano**

In a small glass bowl, whisk together the ingredients until blended. Store in an airtight container for up to 6 months.

# Tarragon-Sesame Chicken

Serves 10 to 12

This simple dish can be assembled 2 days ahead of time, then baked before serving. Or you can bake the chicken and serve it cold as part of a cold buffet. Soaking the chicken in buttermilk is almost like brining it to keep it moist and tender. Serve this dish over rice pilaf, mashed potatoes, or pasta and nap it with Creamy Mushroom Sauce (page 499) or serve it over sautéed spinach instead. For a cold version, serve over field greens dressed with your favorite vinaigrette or slice the chicken on the diagonal and serve over sliced tomatoes.

2 cups buttermilk

1 teaspoon sweet paprika

1 teaspoon salt

1 teaspoon freshly ground black pepper

12 skinless, boneless chicken breast halves, tenders removed (use for another purpose)

1 cup (2 sticks) unsalted butter, melted

2½ cups plain dry bread crumbs

1 tablespoon dried tarragon

¼ cup sesame seeds, toasted (see page 83)

**1.** In a 2-gallon zipper-top plastic bag, combine the buttermilk, paprika, salt, and pepper, and stir or shake until blended. Add the chicken and turn to coat evenly.

**✳ DIVA DO-AHEAD:** At this point, seal the bag and refrigerate for at least 6 hours or overnight.

**2.** Drain the chicken breasts and discard the marinade.

**3.** Brush two 13 x 9-inch baking dishes or one 17 x 11-inch baking sheet with some of the melted butter and transfer the rest to a shallow bowl. In another shallow bowl, combine the bread crumbs, tarragon, and sesame seeds, stirring to blend.

**4.** Dip the chicken into the melted butter, then the crumbs, making sure it is totally covered. Transfer the chicken to the prepared baking dish and drizzle the remaining melted butter over the top.

**✳ DIVA DO-AHEAD:** At this point, cover and refrigerate for at least 2 hours or overnight. Bring to room temperature before continuing.

**5.** Preheat the oven to 350°F. Bake the chicken until golden brown and cooked through, 20 to 30 minutes. Serve hot or cold.

# Chicken Breasts with Lemon and Capers

Serves 10 to 12

Piquant capers and lemon juice give this chicken dish a bright, vibrant flavor and color, which is why it is one of my favorite dishes for company. Serve with pasta and sautéed spinach or broccoli for an easy meal. Sautéing the chicken breasts ahead of time takes all the guesswork out of the timing, allowing you to enjoy your guests.

**12 skinless, boneless chicken breast halves, tenders removed (use for another purpose)**

**2 teaspoons salt**

**1 teaspoon freshly ground black pepper**

**2 tablespoons unsalted butter**

**2 tablespoons olive oil**

**2 tablespoons Madeira**

**½ cup fresh lemon juice**

**½ cup capers, drained and chopped if large (see The Diva Says)**

**1 lemon, thinly sliced and seeds removed**

**1.** Put the chicken breasts between sheets of waxed paper or plastic wrap and, using a meat mallet, the bottom of a wine bottle, or a rolling pin, pound to a uniform thickness, about ½ inch. Season on both sides with the salt and pepper.

**2.** In a large skillet, heat the butter and oil over medium-high heat until the butter is melted. Cook the chicken breasts, a few at a time, for 2 to 3 minutes per side until just barely cooked through. Put the chicken in two 13 x 9-inch baking dishes or on one 17 x 11-inch baking sheet.

✳ **DIVA DO-AHEAD:** At this point, cover and refrigerate overnight. Bring to room temperature before continuing.

**3.** Add the Madeira to the skillet and scrape up any browned bits that may be sticking to the bottom. Add the lemon juice and capers and simmer for about 1 minute, then let cool.

✳ **DIVA DO-AHEAD:** At this point, cover and refrigerate overnight. Reheat gently before continuing.

**4.** Preheat the oven to 350°F. Pour the warm sauce over the chicken, cover with aluminum foil, and bake until heated through, about 10 minutes. Scatter the lemon slices over the chicken and serve immediately.

## The Diva Says:

For this dish, I prefer small capers packed in brine, which I use whole. If you are only able to find large ones, chop them.

# 'Shroom-Stuffed Chicken Breasts

Serves 10 to 12

Roasted mushrooms combine to give this chicken dish a rustic, earthy quality, and the pan juices make a terrific sauce to pour over them. I don't recommend freezing these because the mushrooms become a little softer after they have been frozen.

1 pound assorted fresh wild mushrooms, such as shiitake, oyster, porcini, portobello, or cremini; cleaned, stems removed or trimmed, and cut in half or quarters, depending upon their size

½ cup extra virgin olive oil

¼ cup balsamic vinegar

1½ teaspoons salt

1½ teaspoons freshly ground black pepper

2 cloves garlic, minced

1 tablespoon chopped fresh rosemary

12 skinless, boneless chicken breast halves, tenders removed (use for another purpose)

¼ cup (½ stick) unsalted butter

½ cup heavy cream

**1.** Preheat the oven to 425°F. Line a jelly roll pan with a silicone liner or aluminum foil.

**2.** Put the mushrooms in a large bowl. In a small bowl, whisk together the oil, vinegar, ½ teaspoon of the salt, ½ teaspoon of the pepper, the garlic, and rosemary. Pour over the mushrooms, toss to coat, and spread over the baking sheet. Bake for 20 minutes. Let cool for 10 minutes, then drain the mushrooms, reserving the juices. Coarsely chop the mushrooms and set aside.

**3.** Put the chicken between sheets of waxed paper or plastic wrap and, using a meat mallet, the bottom of a wine bottle, or a rolling pin, pound to a uniform thickness, about ½ inch. Season on both sides with the remaining 1 teaspoon of salt and 1 teaspoon of pepper.

**4.** Place a chicken breast on a cutting board, cut side up. Cover its length with 2 tablespoons of the mushrooms. Roll the chicken up, folding in the sides, and secure with a toothpick.

✳ **DIVA DO-AHEAD:** At this point, cover and refrigerate for at least 1 hour or overnight. If you have any remaining mushrooms, save them to stir into the sauce.

**5.** Preheat the oven to 350°F. Melt the butter in a large skillet over medium-high heat and cook the chicken until golden brown on all sides. Arrange in a single layer in a baking dish and bake until cooked through, 15 to 20 minutes. Meanwhile, add the reserved mushroom juices to the skillet and cook until reduced by half, about 10 minutes. Stir in the cream and any leftover mushrooms and bring to a boil.

**6.** When the chicken is done, remove from the oven and cover with aluminum foil for about 5 minutes. Cut on the diagonal into ½-inch-thick slices and serve on a platter, topped with the sauce.

# Chicken with Eggplant and Gorgonzola

Serves 10 to 12

This elegant main course is a deliciously different entrée that will delight family and friends. To serve, arrange the warm chicken on a large platter and garnish with sprigs of fresh parsley or basil, or let cool to room temperature and serve over a bed of field greens.

½ cup extra virgin olive oil

2 teaspoons salt

2 teaspoons freshly ground black pepper

2 medium-size purple eggplants, cut into ½-inch-thick rounds

12 skinless, boneless chicken breast halves, tenders removed (use for another purpose)

¼ cup (½ stick) unsalted butter

½ cup port wine

¼ cup chicken broth

2 cups crumbled Gorgonzola cheese

**1.** In a small bowl, stir together the oil, 1 teaspoon of the salt, and 1 teaspoon of the pepper.

**2.** Build a hot charcoal fire or preheat the broiler or a gas grill for 10 minutes. If you are broiling, line a baking sheet with aluminum foil and arrange the eggplant slices on top. If you are broiling, brush the eggplant with some of the seasoned oil and broil until it begins to turn golden, about 5 minutes; turn, brush with more oil, and broil until softened, another 3 minutes more. Or grill the eggplants until soft, pliable, and golden, about 3 minutes per side. Remove from the broiler or grill and let cool.

**3.** Place the chicken breasts between sheets of waxed paper or plastic wrap and, using a meat mallet, the bottom of a wine bottle, or a rolling pin, pound to a uniform thickness, about ½ inch. Season on both sides with the remaining 1 teaspoon of salt and 1 teaspoon of pepper.

**4.** Melt the butter in a large skillet and add 1 tablespoon of the remaining seasoned oil. Cook the chicken until white on both sides (it will not be cooked through), adding more of the remaining seasoned oil if needed. Transfer to an oven-to-table baking dish.

**5.** Pour the port into the skillet and scrape up any browned bits stuck to the bottom. Add the broth and boil for 1 minute. Pour the sauce over the chicken, top each breast with a slice of eggplant, and cover the eggplant with Gorgonzola.

✳ **DIVA DO-AHEAD:** At this point, you can cover and refrigerate for up to 24 hours. Bring to room temperature before continuing.

**6.** Preheat the oven to 350°F. Bake until the cheese is melted and the chicken is cooked through, 15 to 20 minutes.

# Grilled Lemon-Rosemary Chicken Breasts 🥤🥤

Serves 10 to 12

This simple grilled chicken is delicious served on a bed of sliced tomatoes and cucumbers dressed with extra virgin olive oil and fresh lemon juice. Or you can grill the chicken ahead, let cool, and use it to make sandwiches on crusty rolls, slathered with roasted garlic mayonnaise (see page 495) and topped with lettuce and sliced tomato. Or slice the chicken on the diagonal and serve over Caesar salad or other dressed greens. It's also terrific cut up and added to pasta salad.

**¾ cup extra virgin olive oil**

**⅓ cup fresh lemon juice**

**2 tablespoons dried rosemary**

**1½ teaspoons salt**

**1 teaspoon freshly ground black pepper**

**4 cloves garlic, minced**

**12 skinless, boneless chicken breast halves, tenders removed (use for another purpose)**

## Diva Variation

Substitute dried oregano or marjoram for the rosemary.

## Grilling Chicken

To grill chicken without it drying out, I generally heat both sides of my gas grill, cook the first side of the chicken over high heat, then turn the grill down to low and grill the second side so the chicken will cook through more slowly.

**1.** In a zipper-top plastic bag, combine the oil, lemon juice, rosemary, salt, pepper, and garlic, shaking to blend. Add the chicken, turning to coat it, and seal.

✳ **DIVA DO-AHEAD:** At this point, refrigerate for at least 2 hours and up to 2 days. Bring to room temperature before continuing.

**2.** Build a hot charcoal fire or preheat a gas grill, a grill pan, or the broiler for 10 minutes. Remove the chicken from the marinade and grill or place on a baking sheet lined with aluminum foil and broil until cooked through, about 3 minutes per side.

✳ **DIVA DO-AHEAD:** At this point, you can let cool, cover, and refrigerate for up to 8 hours.

**3.** Serve cold or bring to room temperature before serving.

# Margaritaville Grilled Chicken Breasts 🥤🥛

Serves 10 to 12

This spicy chicken flavored with chipotle, tequila, and citrus is terrific served hot or cold. Serve it up sliced on the diagonal and arranged over a bed of chopped fresh cilantro or as part of a make-your-own-taco/fajita bar. Grill the chicken, slice thinly, keep warm on Low in a 4- to 5-quart slow cooker, and serve with flour tortillas, shredded Monterey Jack and cheddar cheeses, guacamole, salsa fresca, sour cream, chopped black olives, chopped tomatoes, shredded lettuce, pickled jalapeño peppers, and chopped red onions or scallions. The chicken also makes a great addition to salads.

### Margaritaville Marinade

¼ cup olive oil

½ cup orange juice

¼ cup fresh lime juice

¼ cup gold tequila

½ teaspoon ground cumin

1 canned chipotle chile in adobo sauce

¼ cup packed fresh cilantro, plus extra for garnish

12 skinless, boneless chicken breast halves, tenders removed (use for another purpose)

2 limes, thinly sliced, for garnish

1 or 2 oranges, thinly sliced and any seeds removed, for garnish

**1.** To make the marinade, in a food processor or blender, combine the oil, juices, tequila, cumin, chipotle, and cilantro and process until smooth.

**2.** Put the chicken in a zipper-top plastic bag, pour in the marinade, seal the bag, and turn the chicken to coat.

✳ **DIVA DO-AHEAD:** At this point, refrigerate for at least 4 hours or overnight. Bring to room temperature before continuing.

**3.** Build a hot charcoal fire or preheat a gas grill, grill pan, or the broiler for 10 minutes. Drain the chicken and pat dry. Grill or broil on a baking sheet lined with aluminum foil until cooked through and golden brown, about 3 minutes per side.

✳ **DIVA DO-AHEAD:** At this point, you can let cool, cover, and refrigerate for up to 2 days. To reheat, bake, covered, in a 400°F oven for 5 to 7 minutes.

**4.** Serve hot, cold, or at room temperature, garnished with chopped cilantro and lime and orange slices.

# Teriyaki-Style Chicken Breasts

Serves 10 to 12

These chicken breasts are terrific as an entrée served hot, cold, or at room temperature with mounds of rice and fruit salsa. Or serve them on the side on skewers (see Diva Variation). Leftovers are delicious in salads.

**10 to 12 skinless, boneless chicken breast halves, tenders removed (use for another purpose)**

**1 cup soy sauce**

**¼ cup rice wine or seasoned rice vinegar**

**¼ cup firmly packed light brown sugar**

**4 cloves garlic, minced**

**1 teaspoon peeled and grated fresh ginger**

**¼ cup vegetable oil**

**6 scallions (white and tender green parts), chopped**

**¼ cup sesame seeds, toasted (see page 83), for garnish**

## Diva Variation

**Teriyaki-Style Chicken Skewers:** Soak about 50 wooden skewers in water for 1 hour. Marinate about 3 pounds of chicken tenders in the teriyaki mixture, drain, and thread onto the skewers. Grill or broil until cooked through, turning once, about 5 minutes total.

**1.** Put the chicken breasts in a zipper-top plastic bag or 13 x 9-inch baking dish.

**2.** In a medium-size bowl, stir together the soy sauce, rice wine, brown sugar, garlic, ginger, oil, and half the scallions. Pour over the chicken and seal the bag or cover the dish.

✳ **DIVA DO-AHEAD:** At this point, refrigerate for at least 4 hours or overnight.

**3.** Build a hot charcoal fire or preheat a gas grill, the broiler, or a grill pan for 10 minutes. Drain the chicken and grill or place on a baking sheet lined with aluminum foil and broil until cooked through, 3 to 4 minutes per side.

✳ **DIVA DO-AHEAD:** At this point, you can let cool, cover, and refrigerate overnight.

**4.** Serve hot or at room temperature, or slice and serve cold, garnished with the sesame seeds and the remaining scallions.

# Breaded Chicken Cutlets Italian Style 🥤🥤🍷🍸

Serves 10 to 12

Chicken and turkey cutlets are a staple in my house. I love to use them for entertaining because they can be cooked ahead of time, then warmed up just before serving. They are delicious served all by themselves with a green salad, but you can also dress them up with everything from fruit salsa to marinara and Parmesan cheese for a tasty chicken Parmigiano. I like to remove the chicken tender, the flap underneath the breast, then flatten the chicken breasts between sheets of plastic or waxed paper. Freeze the chicken tenders to make into skewers or use in chicken pot pies. Chicken tenders can also be prepared this way, to be served as appetizers or as part of a buffet table presentation; you will need 2 pounds of chicken tenders for these recipes. If you are using turkey cutlets, substitute 12 turkey cutlets for the chicken breast halves. Serve these cutlets sliced with Quick Marinara (page 482) on the side for dipping as an appetizer or with Oven-Roasted Caponata (page 128) or over a salad as a main course.

**3 large eggs**

**2 tablespoons water**

**1½ teaspoons salt**

**1 teaspoon freshly ground black pepper**

**12 skinless, boneless chicken breasts, tenders removed**

**2 cups plain dry bread crumbs**

**2 cups freshly grated Parmesan cheese**

**2 teaspoons dried basil**

**¼ cup (½ stick) unsalted butter**

**¼ cup olive oil**

**1.** In a large bowl, beat together the eggs, water, salt, and pepper until blended.

**2.** Place the chicken between pieces of waxed paper or plastic wrap and, using a meat mallet, the bottom of a wine bottle, or a rolling pin, pound to a uniform thickness, about ¼ inch. Add to the egg mixture, turning to coat.

**3.** In a shallow dish, combine the bread crumbs, cheese, and basil until blended.

**4.** Dredge each chicken breast in the crumb mixture, turning to coat evenly. Lay the dipped chicken on a rimmed baking sheet lined with paper towels.

✳ **DIVA DO-AHEAD:** At this point, cover and refrigerate for at least 1 hour and up to 8 hours.

**5.** In a large skillet, heat the butter and oil over high heat until the butter is melted, then add the cutlets a few at time, taking care not to crowd them. Cook until golden, about 3 minutes, turn, and cook until the other side is golden, another 3 minutes.

✳ **DIVA DO-AHEAD:** At this point, you can let cool and refrigerate overnight, covered with plastic wrap and separated by paper towels (they absorb any moisture and keep the breading from getting soggy). Reheat chicken in a 325°F oven on a rimmed baking sheet lined with aluminum foil for about 10 minutes or bring to room temperature.

**6.** Serve hot or at room temperature.

## A Sticky Situation

Some fried cutlet recipes have you dip the chicken in flour, then egg, then crumbs, but the Diva likes to eliminate the flour step and just refrigerate the chicken for an hour before cooking. Chilling helps the bread crumbs stick to the chicken so they don't come off in the sauté pan.

## Diva Variations

**Chicken Parmigiano:** Prepare the chicken cutlets as directed, place in a single layer in two 13 x 9-inch baking dishes, and cover with Quick Marinara (page 482) and 2 cups of freshly grated Parmesan cheese.

✳ **DIVA DO-AHEAD:** At this point, you can cover and refrigerate overnight.

Bake in a preheated 350°F oven until the cheese is melted, 15 to 20 minutes. Serve sliced with pasta or orzo.

**Southwestern Chicken Cutlets:** Substitute fresh lime juice for the water and 1/2 teaspoon each of chili powder and ground cumin for the black pepper. Increase the bread crumbs to 4 cups, omit the Parmesan and basil, and add 1 tablespoon of chili

powder and 1/2 cup of finely chopped fresh cilantro to the crumbs. Proceed as directed. Serve the chicken sliced on a bed of chopped fresh cilantro with Chipotle Corn Dip (page 85) or Salsa Fresca (page 90) and Guacamole Olé (page 88) on the side.

**Provençal Chicken Cutlets:** Substitute Dijon mustard for the water. Increase the bread crumbs to 4 cups, omit the Parmesan, and substitute 1 1/2 teaspoons dried thyme and 1/2 teaspoon dried sage for the basil. Proceed as directed. Serve the chicken sliced on a bed of field greens with Tapenade (page 84), Oven-Roasted Caponata (page 128), or Artichoke Rémoulade Sauce (page 494) on the side.

**Asian-Style Chicken Cutlets:** Substitute ¼ cup of soy sauce and 4 shakes of Tabasco sauce for the water. Substitute 4 cups of panko crumbs (Japanese bread crumbs, sold in Asian markets) for the bread crumbs, omit the Parmesan, and substitute ½ cup of sesame seeds for the basil. Proceed as directed, cooking the cutlets in ½ cup of vegetable oil instead of the butter and oil mixture. Serve the chicken sliced on a bed of chopped Napa cabbage with Pacific Rim Peanut Sauce (page 481) or soy sauce drizzled over the top or with Mango Salsa (page 477) on the side.

**Los Cabos–Style Chicken Cutlets:** Substitute fresh lime juice for the water and 1 teaspoon of chili powder for the black pepper. Dredge the cutlets in 4 cups of crushed tortilla chips mixed with 1 teaspoon of chili powder instead of the bread crumbs. Proceed as directed. Garnish the chicken with chopped fresh cilantro and lime wedges.

**Eastern Shore–Style Chicken Cutlets:** Substitute 2 teaspoons of Old Bay seasoning for the salt and pepper. Dredge the chicken in a mixture of 2 cups of plain dry bread crumbs, 2 cups of fine yellow cornmeal, and 1 tablespoon of Old Bay seasoning. Proceed as directed. Garnish with lemon wedges and serve with Creamy Corn Sauce (page 344) or Artichoke Rémoulade Sauce (page 494). This treatment also works well with fish fillets.

**Tater-Style Chicken Cutlets:** Instead of bread crumbs, dredge the chicken in 4 cups of crushed potato chips. Proceed as directed. Garnish with chopped fresh parsley and serve with the barbecue sauce of your choice or Parsley Pesto (page 473) for dipping.

# Buffalo Chicken Cutlets for Sandwiches

Serves 10 to 12

When I teach my picnic and tailgate classes, this recipe is a favorite. After the chicken cutlets are cooked, they soak in a butter and hot sauce bath. Then they're tucked into sandwiches with blue cheese dressing and Bibb lettuce. You can make these up ahead of time and serve the cutlets cold in sandwiches or keep them warm in a slow cooker for your guests to serve themselves. Want to serve them without the rolls? Then slice the cutlets thinly and arrange on a bed of Nutty Blue Cheese Coleslaw (see page 186). These sandwiches are terrific for a Super Bowl party or a casual dinner with friends.

- **14 skinless, boneless chicken breast halves, tenders removed (use for another purpose)**
- **2 teaspoons salt**
- **1 teaspoon freshly ground black pepper**
- **¼ cup vegetable oil**
- **1 cup (2 sticks) unsalted butter**
- **½ cup Frank's RedHot Cayenne Pepper Sauce or your favorite hot sauce**
- **14 kaiser rolls**
- **1 recipe Old-Fashioned Blue Cheese Dressing (page 215) made with Maytag blue, or store-bought blue cheese dressing**
- **14 leaves Bibb lettuce**

## Diva Variation

**Grilled Buffalo Chicken Cutlets:** If you would prefer to grill the chicken, build a hot charcoal fire or preheat a gas grill for 10 minutes and grill the chicken for 3 minutes per side. Melt the butter in a large skillet and add the hot sauce. Transfer the grilled chicken to the skillet and heat in the sauce.

**1.** Put the chicken between sheets of plastic or waxed paper and, using a meat mallet, the bottom of a wine bottle, or a rolling pin, pound to a uniform thickness, about ½ inch. Sprinkle on both sides with the salt and pepper.

**2.** Heat 2 tablespoons of the oil in a large skillet over medium-high heat, and cook the chicken until golden brown on both sides, 2 to 3 minutes per side, adding the remaining oil to the pan as needed; transfer to a platter.

**3.** Heat the butter in the skillet until melted and add the hot sauce, stirring to blend. Return the chicken to the skillet and turn it in the butter mixture.

✳ **DIVA DO-AHEAD:** At this point, you can let cool, cover, and refrigerate for up to 2 days. Reheat over medium heat or in a slow cooker on Low for 2 hours before continuing.

**4.** To assemble the sandwiches, split the rolls and lay a chicken breast half on the bottom. Top with dressing and lettuce.

The Diva Says:
Crusty artisan breads don't work as well with this—I recommend a softer roll, such as a kaiser.

### Slow Cooker Savvy

Sauté the chicken breasts, melt the butter, and add the hot sauce. Pour the hot sauce mixture into a 4- to 5-quart slow cooker, add the chicken, cover, and cook on Low for 4 hours, turning the chicken every hour.

# Chicken Marsala

Serves 10

This elegant entrée comes together in minutes and can be held overnight, until you are ready to bake it. Serve it with Grilled Vegetables (page 266) and Pilaf Milanese (page 276).

12 skinless, boneless chicken breast halves, tenders removed (use for another purpose)

2 teaspoons salt

1½ teaspoons freshly ground black pepper

½ cup (1 stick) unsalted butter

½ cup Marsala

1 cup heavy cream

½ cup finely chopped shallots

1 pound cremini mushrooms, sliced ½ inch thick

12 thin slices Gruyère cheese

**1.** Place the chicken between pieces of waxed paper or plastic wrap and, using a meat mallet, the bottom of a wine bottle, or a rolling pin, pound to a uniform thickness, about ½ inch. Sprinkle on both sides with the salt and pepper.

**2.** Melt 2 tablespoons of the butter in a large skillet over medium-high heat. Cook the chicken breasts, in batches, until white on each side, 1 to 2 minutes; they will not be cooked through. Add more butter to the skillet as needed, but reserve 2 tablespoons to sauté the mushrooms.

Transfer the chicken to a large oven-to-table baking dish.

**3.** Add the Marsala to the pan, scrape up any browned bits stuck to the bottom, and bring to a boil. Add the cream, return to a boil, and continue boiling until the sauce is slightly thickened and will coat the back of a spoon, about 2 minutes. Set aside.

**4.** In another large skillet, melt the remaining 2 tablespoons or more of butter over medium-high heat and cook the shallots, stirring, until softened, 3 to 4 minutes. Add the mushrooms and cook, stirring, until the liquid in the pan has evaporated and the mushrooms turn golden brown, 5 to 7 minutes. Season with the remaining salt and pepper if desired and stir into the sauce. Pour the sauce over the chicken and cover each breast half with a slice of Gruyère.

✳ **DIVA DO-AHEAD:** At this point, you can cover and refrigerate for up to 24 hours. Bring to room temperature before continuing.

**5.** Preheat the oven to 375°F. Bake until the cheese is bubbling and the chicken is cooked through, about 20 minutes. Serve hot.

# Oven-Fried Chicken

Serves 10 to 12

Instead of using gallons of oil, you can get a good approximation of fried chicken by cooking it in a hot oven. This helps cut down on the fat in the dish, as well as saving you from the mess of frying the chicken. If you prefer to use boneless cuts of chicken, I have given you the cooking time for those at the end of the recipe. Serve this with potato salad and other picnic salads, or with Make-Ahead Cheesy Mashed Potatoes (page 246) and gravy.

**Two 2½- to 3-pound frying chickens, cut into serving pieces**

Buttermilk Soak

**3 cups buttermilk, or 3 cups whole or 2% milk mixed with 2 teaspoons fresh lemon juice**

**1½ teaspoons salt**

**1 teaspoon freshly ground black pepper**

**1 teaspoon sweet paprika**

**1½ teaspoons dried thyme, crumbled**

**1 teaspoon dried sage, crumbled**

Bread Crumb Dredge

**4 cups plain dry bread crumbs**

**1½ teaspoons salt**

**1 teaspoon freshly ground black pepper**

**1 teaspoon sweet paprika**

**1½ teaspoons dried thyme, crumbled**

**1 teaspoon dried sage, crumbled**

**1.** Rinse the chicken in cold water and cut away any excess fat. Drain in a colander.

**2.** To make the buttermilk soak, stir together the buttermilk soak ingredients in a large bowl. Add the chicken and stir to blend. The soak acts as a brine, helping the chicken stay juicy and tender.

✳ **DIVA DO-AHEAD:** At this point, cover and refrigerate for at least 4 and up to 36 hours.

**3.** Line a baking sheet with a silicone liner or aluminum foil. To make the bread crumb dredge, in a 13 x 9-inch baking dish, stir together the bread crumb dredge ingredients. Drain the chicken and roll in the crumbs to coat evenly. Place on the prepared baking sheet and coat the top of the chicken with nonstick cooking spray (this helps give the chicken a nice browned crust).

✳ **DIVA DO-AHEAD:** At this point, you can cover and refrigerate for up to 6 hours. Bring to room temperature before continuing.

**4.** Preheat the oven to 425°F. Bake the chicken until golden brown and cooked through, 30 to 40 minutes (boneless breasts will take about 15 minutes; boneless thighs, 20 to 25 minutes). Remove from the oven and let rest for 5 to 10 minutes before serving. You can also serve it at room temperature or cold.

# Crispy Fried Chicken

Serves 10 to 12

This method of frying and then baking the chicken ensures a crispier crust and less mess than traditional fried chicken. Soaking the chicken in the buttermilk helps keep it tender and juicy. You can even rewarm it in a 300°F oven for about 10 minutes to serve it hot. Accompany the hot chicken with mashed potatoes, gravy, and your favorite sides, such as coleslaw and green beans. If you are serving the chicken cold, put it on your buffet table with some salads, corn on the cob, sliced tomatoes, and fresh fruit in season.

**3 cups buttermilk, or 3 cups whole or 2% milk mixed with 2 teaspoons fresh lemon juice**

**1½ teaspoons salt**

**1 teaspoon freshly ground black pepper**

**Two 2½- to 3-pound frying chickens, cut into serving pieces**

**Canola oil for frying**

**2 cups all-purpose flour**

**1½ teaspoons sweet paprika**

**1 teaspoon dried thyme**

**1.** Pour the buttermilk, salt, and pepper into a zipper-top plastic bag or a large bowl and stir to blend. Add the chicken and turn to coat. Seal the bag or cover the bowl.

✳ **DIVA DO-AHEAD:** At this point, refrigerate for at least 6 hours or overnight.

**2.** Preheat the oven to 375°F. Heat 1 inch of oil in a large skillet over medium-high heat until it registers 350°F on a deep-fat thermometer. Place a rack on a rimmed baking sheet.

**3.** In a zipper-top plastic bag, combine the flour, paprika, and thyme. Drain the chicken, transfer to the flour mixture, a few pieces at a time, and dredge to coat completely and evenly with flour.

**4.** Fry the floured chicken in the hot oil, a few pieces at a time, until golden brown on all sides, 5 to 6 minutes. As they are finished, transfer to the rack.

**5.** When all the pieces are done, bake until golden and crispy and the juices run clear when the thighs or drumsticks are pierced with the tip of a knife, 15 to 20 minutes.

✳ **DIVA DO-AHEAD:** At this point, you can let cool, wrap in aluminum foil, and refrigerate overnight.

**6.** Serve warm, cold, or at room temperature.

## Keeping It Clean

When serving "hand" food, I recommend that you have individually wrapped moistened towelettes on the table for your guests to use if they get really messy.

# Lemon Chicken Oreganata

Serves 12

I love this colorful, lemony chicken for an *al fresco* dinner or as part of a Mediterranean buffet table.

---

**5 pounds mixed chicken parts (legs, thighs, breasts, and wings), or two 2½- to 3-pound fryers, cut into serving pieces**

**2 teaspoons salt**

**1 teaspoon freshly ground black pepper**

**1 teaspoon sweet paprika**

**1 cup olive oil**

**⅔ cup fresh lemon juice**

**2 tablespoons red wine vinegar**

**8 cloves garlic, minced**

**1 tablespoon dried oregano**

**2 lemons, thinly sliced and seeds removed, for garnish**

---

**1.** Preheat the broiler for 10 minutes. Line a rimmed baking sheet with aluminum foil and place a rack on it.

**2.** Rinse the chicken in cold water and drain in a colander and pat dry. Combine 1 teaspoon of the salt, ½ teaspoon of the pepper, and ½ teaspoon of the paprika and sprinkle over the chicken, tossing it in the colander to coat.

**3.** Place the chicken on the rack, skin side down, and broil until browned on that side, 5 to 7 minutes. Turn the chicken over and broil until the skin is crisp and golden brown, another 7 minutes. Remove the

pan from the oven, remove the rack from the sheet pan, and put the chicken directly on the sheet pan, skin side up. Turn off the broiler and preheat the oven to 400°F.

**4.** In a medium-size bowl, whisk together the remaining 1 teaspoon of salt, ½ teaspoon each of pepper and paprika, the oil, lemon juice, vinegar, garlic, and oregano until blended.

**5.** Pour the mixture over the chicken and return it to the oven. Bake until cooked through, 10 to 15 minutes, basting the chicken once or twice with the sauce.

✳ **DIVA DO-AHEAD:** At this point, you can pour off the sauce into a container, let the sauce and chicken cool, cover separately, and refrigerate for up to 2 days. Before serving, bring the chicken to room temperature or reheat, covered, in a 325°F oven for about 15 minutes. Meanwhile, reduce the sauce as described below.

**6.** Transfer the chicken to a serving dish, cover with foil to keep warm, and transfer the sauce to a saucepan. Bring to a boil and continue boiling on high heat until it reduces a bit, 5 to 7 minutes. Spoon the sauce over the chicken and serve, garnished with the lemon slices.

# Nonna's Chicken

Serves 10

My grandmother's chicken is legendary in the Paquini-Ciuffoli family. Each of her children and grandchildren makes a slightly different version and calls it Grandma's chicken. The original Umbrian recipe began with pancetta and cut-up chicken (or sometimes rabbit), and was flavored with rosemary, garlic, and red wine vinegar. My version is made with meaty chicken thighs, which absorb the flavors of balsamic vinegar and fresh rosemary. The beauty of this dish is that it should be made the day before to allow the flavors to mellow.

**12 skinless, boneless chicken thighs**

**2 teaspoons salt**

**1½ teaspoons freshly ground black pepper**

**8 strips bacon, cut into ½-inch pieces**

**8 cloves garlic, slivered**

**1 tablespoon chopped fresh rosemary**

**½ cup balsamic vinegar**

## Getting Rid of Garlic Smell

Getting the smell of garlic (or onion or fish) off your hands is always a nuisance. Try this: Wash your hands and, while they are soapy, rub them on stainless steel (I use my sink faucet). Rinse your hands and the smell should be gone.

**1.** Rinse the chicken well in cold water and drain in a colander and pat dry. Sprinkle the chicken with the salt and pepper and toss in the colander.

**2.** In a large skillet over high heat, cook the bacon until crisp. Remove all but 3 tablespoons of the bacon fat from the pan and add the chicken thighs, garlic, and rosemary and cook the chicken until browned, 3 to 4 minutes per side.

**3.** Add the vinegar and bring to a boil. Reduce the heat to low, cover, and simmer until the chicken is tender, 25 to 30 minutes, turning occasionally.

✳ **DIVA DO-AHEAD:** At this point, you can let cool, cover, and refrigerate overnight. Reheat gently over medium heat before serving.

## Slow Cooker Savvy

Prepare the chicken through the first part of step 3, when the vinegar starts to boil. At that point, transfer the contents of the pan to a 5- to 6-quart slow cooker, cover, and cook on Low for 4 hours.

# Chicken Cacciatore

Serves 10 to 12

In Italy, chicken cacciatore does not have a red sauce; in fact, it is very much like Nonna's Chicken (left). But here in the United States, it isn't chicken cacciatore if it isn't swimming in a red sauce. This version is lighter, but still flavorful and delicious to serve with pasta, potatoes, or polenta. A Do-Ahead Diva plus: The dish benefits from being made ahead of time, and you can even finish it in the slow cooker once everything is sautéed.

**12 skinless, boneless chicken thighs**

**2 teaspoons salt**

**1½ teaspoons freshly ground black pepper**

**2 tablespoons olive oil**

**2 medium-size onions, cut in half and thinly sliced into half-moons**

**4 cloves garlic, minced**

**1 pound cremini mushrooms, quartered**

**1 cup red wine**

**One 15.5-ounce can crushed plum tomatoes**

**1 cup chicken broth**

**2 teaspoons chopped fresh sage**

**½ cup chopped fresh parsley for garnish**

**1.** Rinse the chicken under cold running water and drain in a colander and pat dry. Sprinkle with the salt and pepper and toss to coat.

**2.** In a 5-quart Dutch oven, heat the oil over medium-high heat, then brown the chicken on all sides, a few pieces at a time, transferring them to a plate as they brown.

**3.** Add the onion and cook, stirring, until softened, about 2 minutes. Add the garlic and cook, stirring, for another 2 minutes. Add the mushrooms and cook until their liquid has evaporated and the vegetables begin to caramelize, 15 to 17 minutes. Add the wine and scrape up any browned bits stuck to the bottom. Add the tomatoes, broth, and sage and bring to a boil. Return the chicken to the pan, reduce the heat to medium-low, and simmer until tender, about 45 minutes.

**4.** Skim off any fat that may have accumulated on the top of the sauce, taste the sauce for salt and pepper, adding more if necessary, and stir in the parsley.

✳ **DIVA DO-AHEAD:** At this point, you can let cool, cover, and refrigerate for up to 2 days. Reheat over low heat before serving.

## Slow Cooker Savvy

After the tomato mixture comes to a boil in step 3, transfer the sauce and chicken to a 5- to 6-quart slow cooker, cover, and cook on Low for 4 hours.

# French Farmhouse Chicken

Serves 10 to 12

This delicious casserole of chicken and wine, similar to classic Coq au Vin, benefits from being made ahead of time and is a terrific main course for any occasion. Serve it with roasted potatoes, a crisp green salad, and lots of crusty bread to dip in the sauce.

2 tablespoons olive oil

¼ cup (½ stick) unsalted butter

½ pound pearl onions, peeled

1½ pounds small white mushrooms, trimmed and left whole

2 teaspoons salt

1½ teaspoons freshly ground black pepper

2 teaspoons dried thyme

6 skinless, boneless chicken thighs

6 skinless, boneless chicken breast halves

1 cup Burgundy or another full-bodied red wine

2 cups double-strength chicken broth, such as Campbell's condensed broth without the water added

2 tablespoons all-purpose flour

**1.** In a 5-quart Dutch oven, heat the oil with 1 tablespoon of the butter over medium-high heat until the butter melts. Add the onions and cook, stirring frequently, until golden brown, about 5 minutes. Add the mushrooms, season with some of the salt and pepper, and add the thyme. Cook, stirring, until the mushrooms begin to turn golden and the liquid in the pan has evaporated, about 5 minutes. Remove the onions and mushrooms from the pan and melt 2 more tablespoons of the remaining butter in the Dutch oven.

**2.** Rinse the chicken under cold running water and drain in a colander and pat dry. Season the chicken with the remaining salt and pepper and cook, in batches, in the hot butter until golden brown on all sides, about 5 minutes per side. Add the wine and bring to a boil, scraping up any browned bits stuck to the bottom of the pan. Add the broth, return the onions and mushrooms to the pan, and reduce the heat to medium-low. Simmer until the chicken is tender and the sauce is reduced, 30 to 45 minutes.

**DIVA DO-AHEAD:** At this point, you can let cool, cover, and refrigerate for up to 2 days. Gently reheat before continuing.

**3.** Remove the chicken and vegetables from the pan with a slotted spoon and bring the sauce to a boil. Make a paste from the remaining 1 tablespoon of butter and the flour and add it to the sauce, a bit at a time, stirring until the sauce is thickened. Taste the sauce and adjust the seasoning as needed. Pour the sauce over the chicken and vegetables and serve.

### Slow Cooker Savvy

Prepare the dish up to the point where the wine is added in step 3, then transfer the chicken, wine, and pan juices to a 5- to 6-quart slow cooker. Add the broth, onions, and mushrooms, cover, and cook on Low for 8 hours. Finish the sauce on the stove top as instructed in step 3.

# Spicy Asian Chicken with Lettuce Wraps

Serves 10 to 12

This simple dish is terrific served as part of an Asian buffet. The lettuce I recommend for it is iceberg, which my daughter, Carrie, refers to as "the polyester of vegetables." Many cooks would agree, but it's very useful here because it's strong enough to hold the chicken without falling apart. Bibb lettuce also works well, but it's a bit pricey. For a serve-yourself buffet, you can keep the chicken warm in a fondue pot or slow cooker so your guests can make their own wraps.

3 cloves garlic, peeled

1 quarter-size slice fresh ginger, peeled

Two 8-ounce cans water chestnuts, drained

6 skinless, boneless chicken breast halves, cut into 1-inch cubes

2 tablespoons cornstarch

2 tablespoons rice wine or seasoned rice vinegar

½ cup soy sauce

2 tablespoons vegetable oil

6 scallions (white and tender green parts), chopped

2 teaspoons toasted sesame oil

3 heads iceberg lettuce, cored, washed, spun dry, and leaves separated (see The Diva Says, page 324)

**1.** Put the garlic, ginger, and water chestnuts in a food processor and pulse until chopped. Transfer to a large bowl. Add the chicken to the food processor and pulse until finely chopped. Transfer to the bowl and add the cornstarch, rice wine, and the soy sauce. Stir to blend.

✳ **DIVA DO-AHEAD:** At this point, cover and refrigerate for at least 2 hours and up to 2 days.

**2.** In a large skillet or wok, heat the oil over high heat. Add the chicken mixture and stir-fry, breaking it up as you stir, about 4 minutes. When cooked through, transfer to a bowl and stir in the scallions and sesame oil.

✳ **DIVA DO-AHEAD:** At this point, the wraps can be cooled and refrigerated overnight. Reheat gently before serving to loosen the ingredients.

**3.** Place 2 tablespoons of the chicken mixture in a lettuce leaf and roll the lettuce around it. Repeat until you've used up all the filling. Place the rolls on a platter and serve at room temperature.

The Diva Says: You can wash and spin the lettuce dry the day before and keep refrigerated in a zipper-top plastic bag with a paper towel in it.

### Slow Cooker Savvy

To serve in a slow cooker, prepare the chicken through step 3, then transfer to a 4- to 5-quart slow cooker, cover, and keep warm on Low.

# King Ranch Casserole

Serves 12

This old potluck standby gets a makeover with a creamy cilantro sauce and the addition of corn and sautéed vegetables. Serve this with Marinated Orange Salad (page 167).

¼ cup (½ stick) unsalted butter

½ cup finely chopped onion

2 cloves garlic, minced

2 teaspoons seeded and finely chopped jalapeño pepper

2 cups fresh corn kernels cut from the cob or frozen corn, defrosted

1 teaspoon ground cumin

⅛ teaspoon chili powder

¼ cup all-purpose flour

4 cups chicken broth

1 cup whole or 2% milk

¼ cup chopped fresh cilantro, plus extra for garnish

2 cups sour cream (low-fat is okay)

6 cups diced cooked chicken (½-inch dice)

Twelve 6-inch corn tortillas, cut into 1-inch pieces

2 cups finely shredded mild cheddar cheese

1 cup finely shredded Monterey Jack cheese

**1.** In a 4-quart saucepan over medium heat, melt the butter, add the onion, garlic, and jalapeño, and cook, stirring, until the onion begins to soften, about 2 minutes. Add the corn, cumin, and chili powder and cook, stirring, until the corn is softened, another 4 to 5 minutes. Add the flour and stir until bubbles form on the surface. Cook for another 2 minutes, stirring, then stir in 3 cups of the broth and bring to a boil. Add the milk and cilantro, and continue to boil, stirring, until the sauce is thickened and coats the back of a spoon. Remove from the heat and transfer to a large bowl. Stir in the sour cream and chicken.

**2.** Coat a 13 x 9-inch baking dish with nonstick cooking spray. Spread a layer of the tortillas over the bottom and top with some of the chicken-and-sauce mixture. Sprinkle with some of each of the cheeses. Continue to layer in this way, ending with a layer of cheese. Pour the remaining 1 cup of broth over the top.

✳ **DIVA DO-AHEAD:** At this point, cover and refrigerate for at least 12 and up to 24 hours. Bring to room temperature before continuing.

**3.** Preheat the oven to 350°F. Cover the casserole with aluminum foil and bake for 30 minutes, then remove the foil and bake until the cheese is golden brown and the sauce is bubbling, another 15 minutes. Serve garnished with chopped cilantro if desired.

# Chicken Tetrazzini Casserole

Serves 12

This is an oldie that is still a great dish to serve to company with a salad and bread. I like to use fresh fettuccine noodles for this because they tend not to dry out during the baking process. If you use dry pasta, make sure you undercook it by 2 minutes.

½ cup (1 stick) unsalted butter

½ cup finely chopped shallots

1 pound white mushrooms, sliced ½ inch thick

Two 15.5-ounce cans artichoke hearts, drained and quartered

1½ teaspoons salt

1 teaspoon freshly ground black pepper

6 tablespoons all-purpose flour

3 cups chicken broth

1 cup heavy cream

¼ cup dry sherry

¼ teaspoon ground nutmeg

5 cups diced cooked chicken (½-inch dice)

1 cup freshly grated Parmesan cheese

1 pound fresh fettuccine, cooked until *al dente* and drained

**1.** In a large skillet over medium-high heat, melt the butter, then add the shallots and cook, stirring, until softened, about 2 minutes. Add the mushrooms and artichokes and season with some of the salt and pepper. Cook, stirring a few times, until the mushrooms begin to color and the liquid in the pan has evaporated, 5 to 8 minutes. Add the flour and cook, stirring, for 2 minutes. Gradually add the broth, stirring, until the mixture comes to a boil and thickens. Add the cream, sherry, nutmeg, chicken, and half the cheese, stirring until the cheese melts. Taste and add more salt and pepper if needed.

**2.** Coat a 13 x 9-inch baking dish with nonstick cooking spray.

**3.** Stir the fettuccine into the sauce and blend well. Transfer to the prepared baking dish and cover with the remaining cheese.

✳ **DIVA DO-AHEAD:** At this point, you can cover and refrigerate for up to 2 days. Bring to room temperature before continuing.

**4.** Preheat the oven to 350°F. Bake the casserole until bubbly and browned on top, 30 to 40 minutes. Remove from the oven and let rest for 5 minutes before serving.

# Creamy Chicken Dill Stew

Serves 10

This elegant entrée is terrific served over rice, mashed potatoes, or biscuits for brunch or a simple dinner. We've even dished this up for Super Bowl parties!

6 tablespoons (¾ stick) unsalted butter

½ cup finely chopped onion

1 cup finely chopped celery

6 tablespoons all-purpose flour

4 cups chicken broth

1 teaspoon salt

½ teaspoon freshly ground black pepper

2 cups diced carrots (½-inch dice)

1½ cups fresh corn kernels cut from the cob or frozen corn, defrosted

1½ cups frozen petite peas, defrosted

6 cups diced cooked chicken or turkey (½-inch dice)

2 tablespoons chopped fresh dill, or 2 teaspoons dillweed

1 cup heavy cream

## Diva Variation

**Creamy Chicken Dill Stew, a Little Less Fattening:** Substitute more broth for the heavy cream.

In a 5-quart Dutch oven over medium heat, melt the butter, then cook the onion and celery, stirring, until softened, about 3 minutes. Add the flour and whisk until smooth and white bubbles begin to form on the surface. Continue to whisk for 2 more minutes, then gradually add the broth and bring to a boil. Season with the salt and pepper. Add the carrots, lower the heat, and simmer for 5 minutes. Add the corn, peas, chicken, and dill and simmer for another 5 minutes. Stir in the cream, cook until heated through, and serve.

✳ **DIVA DO-AHEAD:** At this point, you can keep warm over low heat for up to 2 hours or let cool, cover, and refrigerate for up to 3 days; reheat gently before serving.

## Slow Cooker Savvy

After you have added the broth, bring the sauce to a boil, then transfer to a 5- to 6-quart slow cooker and add the salt, pepper, carrots, corn, peas, chicken, and dill. Cover and cook on Low for 4 hours, stirring in the cream in the last hour before serving.

# Southwestern Turkey Chili

Serves 10 to 12

I make this delicious "blond" chili when the turkey leftovers from the holidays are overtaking my fridge. It's terrific for a large gathering and tastes best when it's made a day or two ahead of time. Serve this with an assortment of condiments and a salad.

**¼ cup (½ stick) unsalted butter**

**2 tablespoons olive oil**

**1 cup chopped onion**

**2 Anaheim chiles, seeded and finely chopped**

**1 medium-size red bell pepper, seeded and chopped**

**3 cloves garlic, minced**

**2 teaspoons dried oregano**

**2 teaspoons ground coriander**

**½ teaspoon ground cumin**

**1 tablespoon chili powder**

**1 teaspoon salt**

**¼ cup fine cornmeal or masa harina (corn flour)**

**1 teaspoon sugar**

**4 cups chicken broth**

**3 cups fresh corn kernels cut from the cob or frozen corn, defrosted**

**Two 15.5-ounce cans black beans, rinsed and drained**

**4 cups shredded cooked turkey or chicken**

**¼ cup chopped fresh cilantro for garnish**

**1.** In an 8-quart stockpot, heat the butter and oil over medium heat until the butter melts. Add the onion, chiles, pepper, and garlic and cook, stirring, until softened, about 5 minutes. Add the oregano, coriander, cumin, chili powder, salt, cornmeal, and sugar and cook for 3 minutes, stirring constantly. Pour in the broth and stir until it comes to a boil and thickens.

**2.** Add the corn, black beans, and turkey, reduce the heat to medium-low, and simmer until the vegetables are tender, about 45 minutes. Taste and add more salt if needed.

✳ **DIVA DO-AHEAD:** At this point, you can let cool, cover, and refrigerate for up to 2 days or freeze for up to 6 weeks. Defrost and reheat before serving.

**3.** Garnish with the cilantro and serve.

## Slow Cooker Savvy

Prepare the chili through step 1. Transfer to a 5- to 6-quart slow cooker and stir in the corn, black beans, and turkey. Cover and cook on Low for 6 to 8 hours.

# Chicken Chili with Pinto Beans

Serves 10 to 12

Chili is a delicious make-ahead meal for a casual gathering, whether it's to trim the Christmas tree or relax by the fire with friends. Chili improves with age, so I recommend you prepare this the day before, then reheat it in the slow cooker or on top of the stove. Serve with an assortment of toppings: sour cream, black olives, grated cheeses, pickled jalapeño peppers, chopped tomatoes, tortilla chips, and chopped scallions. The heat index for this chili is a 5 on a scale of 10. You can adjust the amount of chili powder as you wish.

**3 tablespoons olive oil**

**1 cup chopped onion**

**1 Anaheim chile, seeded and finely chopped**

**3 cloves garlic, minced**

**1 tablespoon (or more) chili powder**

**1½ teaspoons salt**

**1 teaspoon dried oregano**

**1 teaspoon ground cumin**

**¼ cup fine cornmeal or masa harina (corn flour)**

**2 cups canned tomato puree**

**2 cups chicken broth**

**6 cups diced cooked chicken (½-inch dice)**

**Two 15.5-ounce cans pinto beans, rinsed and drained**

**1.** In a 5-quart Dutch oven, heat the oil over medium heat, add the onion, chile, and garlic, and cook, stirring, until the onion softens, about 2 minutes. Add the chili powder, salt, oregano, and cumin and cook, stirring, for 2 minutes to cook the spices. Add the cornmeal and stir until blended into the vegetables. Cook for about 2 minutes, being careful not to burn the spices. Gradually add the tomato puree and broth, stirring until the mixture boils and thickens.

**2.** Reduce the heat to medium-low, add the chicken, and simmer, partially covered, for 45 minutes, stirring occasionally.

**3.** Add the beans and simmer for another 15 minutes.

✴ **DIVA DO-AHEAD:** At this point, you can let cool, cover, and refrigerate for up to 2 days or freeze for 2 months. Defrost and reheat before serving.

## Slow Cooker Savvy

Follow the recipe through step 1, then transfer the thickened chili, chicken, and beans to a 5- to 6-quart slow cooker, cover, and cook on Low for 6 hours.

# Mom's Sunday Roast Chicken 🥃🍷🍾

Serves 10 to 12

Whenever I picture a typical family dinner, I envision the Norman Rockwell painting of a family sitting down to a roasted chicken (actually, I think it was a turkey, but you get the idea). Roast chicken can be a lifesaver for those who don't have a lot of culinary ability because it is almost foolproof to make and everyone loves it. Serve the chicken hot with Make-Ahead Cheesy Mashed Potatoes (page 246) and gravy for a special Sunday dinner.

**Two 4- to 5-pound roasting chickens**

**2 teaspoons salt**

**1½ teaspoons freshly ground black pepper**

**1 large onion, quartered**

**4 ribs celery, cut into 1-inch lengths**

**4 carrots, cut into 1-inch lengths**

**¼ cup (½ stick) unsalted butter, melted**

**1 teaspoon dried thyme**

**1 teaspoon dried sage**

**½ to 1 cup chicken broth**

**1.** Preheat the oven to 400°F.

**2.** Remove the neck and giblet sack from the chickens and rinse the chickens thoroughly under cold running water. Pat dry inside and out and cut away any excess fat from the skin. Sprinkle the cavities with the salt and pepper. Stuff each cavity with half the onion, celery, and carrots, then tie the legs together with cotton string. Place the chickens on a rack in a heavy-duty roasting pan, arranging them so they don't touch.

**3.** In a small bowl, stir together the melted butter, thyme, and sage and brush liberally all over the chickens. Pour ½ cup of broth into the bottom of the roasting pan.

**4.** Roast the chickens, basting occasionally with the pan juices and adding more broth if necessary, until an instant-read meat thermometer registers 170°F when pushed into the thickest part of the thigh and the juices run clear when you insert the tip of a knife between the drumstick and the thigh, about 1½ hours.

**5.** Remove the chickens from the rack, place on a cutting board, and tent loosely with aluminum foil.

**DIVA DO-AHEAD:** At this point, you can let cool, cut into serving pieces, cover, and refrigerate overnight. Serve cold, at room temperature, or reheat in a preheated 375°F oven, loosely covered with foil, until the skin is crispy and the meat is heated through, 10 to 15 minutes.

**6.** Let rest at least 10 minutes before carving into serving pieces. Discard any fat from the pan drippings and serve the juices over the chicken.

## Cutting Up a Roast Chicken

To serve roast chicken at a party, cut it into easy-to-handle pieces: 2 wings, 2 drumsticks, 2 thighs, and the breast cut into 4 equal pieces. Poultry shears will make quick work of the smaller bones, and you can use a good carving knife to separate the joints at the thigh, leg, and wing.

I don't recommend bringing the entire bird to the table and carving it there—the Diva has seen more carving-related disasters at the table than she cares to mention. Allow everyone to oooh and ahhh over the birds, then carve them in the kitchen.

### Diva Variations

**Roast Lemon Chicken:** Rub the chicken inside and out with a mixture of the grated zest of 2 lemons, juice of 4 lemons, 1 tablespoon of salt, 1½ teaspoons of freshly ground black pepper, and ¼ cup of olive oil. Omit the onion, celery, carrots, butter, thyme, sage, and broth. Stuff each cavity with a whole lemon and tie the legs together. Proceed as directed from step 4. Serve the chicken with lemon wedges and garnish with ½ cup of chopped fresh Italian parsley.

**Provençal Roast Chicken:** Rub the chickens inside and out with a mixture of the grated zest of 2 lemons, 2 tablespoons of fresh lemon juice, 2 teaspoons of salt, 1½ teaspoons of freshly ground black pepper, ¼ cup of Dijon mustard, ½ cup of extra virgin olive oil, and 1 tablespoon of dried

*herbes de Provence*. Stuff with the onion, celery, and carrots, omit the thyme and sage, and proceed as directed above.

**Balsamic-Glazed Roast Chicken:** Follow the directions for the basic recipe, but omit the chicken broth and baste every 15 minutes with balsamic vinegar—you will need about 1½ cups.

**Porcini Roast Chicken:** Follow the directions for the basic recipe, but before roasting, gently separate the skin from the meat of the chicken on the breast. Slip dried porcini mushrooms (about 4 ounces) under the skin and roast as directed. The porcini will become soft and infuse the chicken with a lovely, woodsy flavor. As an added treat, brush the roast chicken all over with a little white truffle oil before serving.

# Traditional Thanksgiving Turkey 🍷🍾

Serves 10 to 12

I have taught this method in my Do-ahead Thanksgiving classes for years. One year I actually prepared 52 Thanksgiving dinners before Thanksgiving Day. That was the year my children prepared the holiday dinner for me, and they have been repeating at least parts of that performance ever since.

**One 12- to 14-pound turkey**

**Salt and freshly ground black pepper to taste**

**1 onion, quartered**

**2 carrots, cut into 1-inch lengths**

**3 ribs celery, cut into 1-inch lengths**

**6 strips bacon**

**1.** Remove the neck and giblets from the turkey and set aside to make stock if you wish, or discard them. Rinse the turkey inside and out under cold running water and pat the outside and inside dry with paper towels. Sprinkle the cavity liberally with salt and pepper.

✳ **DIVA DO-AHEAD:** At this point, you can cover and refrigerate for up to 3 days. Dry the inside of the turkey again if you store it for any length of time and let come to room temperature before continuing.

**2.** Preheat the oven to 325°F. Put the onion, carrots, and celery inside the cavity and tie the legs together with cotton string. Transfer the turkey to a rack in a heavy-duty roasting pan. Drape the bacon over the turkey and roast for 1½ hours, then remove the bacon. Continue roasting until an instant-read meat thermometer inserted into the thickest part of the thigh (behind the drumstick) registers 170° to 175°F, another 1½ to 2¼ hours. If you would like to baste the turkey with pan drippings, start doing so after 2 hours of roasting time. If the turkey is browned to your liking before it reaches 170°F, loosely tent it with aluminum foil for the duration of the cooking time.

**3.** Remove the turkey from the oven, transfer to a cutting board, and cover with foil. Allow the turkey to rest for at least 30 minutes, then carve (see pages 290 to 293).

## Cutting the Fat

Pan drippings from a turkey can be very fatty. I recommend that you buy a fat separator and separate the fat from the drippings before making a gravy or sauce for the turkey.

## Diva Variations

**Maple-Glazed Turkey:** Follow the basic recipe as directed, but baste the turkey with ¼ cup of pure maple syrup during the last hour of cooking.

**Cider-Glazed Roast Turkey:** Omit the onion, carrots, celery, and bacon. Stuff the turkey with 6 cored and quartered Gala or Golden Delicious apples. In a 2-quart saucepan over medium heat, combine 2 cups of apple cider and ½ cup of firmly packed light brown sugar and stir until the cider is hot and the sugar dissolves. Let cool and refrigerate until ready to use. Brush the turkey liberally with the cider syrup before it goes into the oven. Roast the turkey as directed, basting with more of the syrup every half hour.

**Thyme-and-Sage-Rubbed Turkey:** Omit the bacon. Combine 1 cup (2 sticks) of unsalted butter, melted, and 2 tablespoons each of chopped fresh thyme and sage and brush it liberally over the turkey; keep the butter warm over very low heat. Roast the turkey as directed, basting every half hour with the herbed butter.

**Hoisin-Glazed Roasted Turkey:** In a large bowl, combine 2 cups of hoisin sauce, ½ cup of soy sauce, and ½ cup of rice wine or seasoned rice vinegar until smooth. Divide the sauce in half, refrigerating one half and painting the turkey liberally with the rest.

✳ **DIVA DO-AHEAD:** At this point, cover and refrigerate for at least 24 hours and up to 3 days. Bring to room temperature before continuing.

Substitute 6 scallions, chopped, for the onion and omit the celery and bacon. Stuff the turkey with the scallions and carrots and roast as directed, basting the turkey every half hour. Transfer the roasted turkey to a cutting board, drizzle with ¼ cup of toasted sesame oil, cover with aluminum foil, and let rest at least 30 minutes. Carve and serve with warm flour tortillas, more hoisin sauce, and chopped scallions, as you would Peking duck.

## Do-Ahead Turkey

Everyone asks me whether you can roast turkey ahead of time. You can roast a turkey the day before, allow it to cool, and slice the meat. Arrange the meat in a baking dish and pour ½ to 1 cup of chicken or turkey broth over the turkey. Cover with aluminum foil and refrigerate overnight.

On Thanksgiving Day, roast another turkey, as directed. When the turkey is roasted, remove it from the oven and let it rest. Have the baking dish with your do-ahead turkey at room temperature and bake at 350°F, covered with aluminum foil, for 20 to 30 minutes, until heated through. Carve the freshly roasted turkey and serve that first, then for second helpings, serve the other one.

# Fish and Shellfish

**Seafood is a classy choice for a party.** It shows that you thought about the menu and wanted to do something a little out of the ordinary. That being said, you will need to ask your guests whether they can eat seafood because some people are allergic to particular fish or shellfish, or simply make sure you have another selection available for those who can't eat seafood or aren't fond of it.

In addition to the health benefits of fish and shellfish, they cook quickly, so no matter what you are serving, the cooking time will be under 1 hour. Many of the dishes I've included can be prepped the day before, then cooked just before serving. Some of the meatier fish can be grilled the day before, then served at room temperature.

The rule of thumb for cooking fish fillets and steaks is 10 minutes of cooking time per inch of thickness. This can vary, depending upon the density of the flesh of the fish, but it is a good standard to go by. Sea bass is definitely an exception, though; it needs at least 15 minutes per inch to be cooked through and tender.

# Fish and Shellfish Picks for Entertaining

*Fillet of sole:* This thin and fast-cooking fish is very expensive by the pound, but one very thin fillet, when stuffed, makes a serving. I like to stuff them with crab or other ingredients, then bake them quickly in a hot oven, which leaves them juicy and tender.

*Halibut:* Halibut, I tell my students, "tastes like chicken." Buy halibut fillets for your dinners, rather than steaks, as they will make a more impressive presentation.

*Red snapper:* Red snapper is available throughout much of the United States; it's a flaky fish that takes well to baking and sautéing.

*Salmon:* Gorgeous, deep pink salmon is a favorite for dinner. Chances are your grocery store carries fresh salmon most of the week; if not, search out a good fish market and buy it there. If you can, have the skin taken off, because it makes for a nicer presentation. If the skin is left on, you can easily remove it once the salmon is cooked; it should peel right off. I recommend fillets rather than steaks so that you will not have to mess with both the bones and the skin. You can also buy a whole side of salmon. Because it is thick at the forward end of the fish and tends to get thinner toward the tail, I recommend that you fold the thinner part under the thick part, so that it will cook evenly. Or you can cut the thinner tail end off and cook it separately for a shorter amount of time.

*Sea bass:* Sea bass is a succulent fish that is a no-brainer in my book. Because its flesh is a bit thicker and its protein structure is a little different from other fish, it actually benefits from a longer cooking time and is almost impossible to overcook. For that reason, I recommend it to anyone who might have FOF (fear of fish).

*Tuna:* Tuna is not just from a can; you can buy fresh tuna at the fish market. Trying to replicate the seared ahi tuna you enjoyed in a restaurant isn't a great idea when you want to serve a crowd, but you can bake tuna and serve it with your favorite sauce, or toss it into salads. Once you've baked tuna, you may never go back to the stuff in the can.

*Clams:* Whole clams are simple to prepare, whether steamed with garlic, wine, and herbs or included in a paella. You can also shuck whole clams to stuff them or use in a clam pie. Canned clams are available in 8-ounce sizes if fresh clams aren't an option.

**Crab:** Lump crabmeat is succulent and oh so delicious, but it is a splurge, so only serve it to those you love and those who will appreciate your culinary generosity! I buy refrigerated pasteurized lump crabmeat, but you may live in an area where you can get lump crabmeat fresh all year long. Dungeness crabmeat is sold frozen and fresh in some areas. King crab legs are sold frozen; you will need to crack the legs to extract the meat. You'll find a number of crab recipes in other chapters—check the index.

**Lobster:** Lobster is another indulgence in the shellfish category. Expensive, luxuriously rich, and beautifully colored, there is nothing better to serve for a special dinner. Whether you are folding lobster into a salad to serve on crackers or endive leaves for an appetizer or into a sumptuous lobster pie, or perhaps steaming a large potful at a picnic, nothing beats lobster for the wow factor at a party. Some stores sell lobster meat already cooked and shelled (at a much higher price), or you can buy live lobsters and cook and shell them yourself. Lobster is also available pasteurized and chilled at some markets.

**Scallops:** Large sea scallops are about 2 inches in diameter, rich in taste, and pearly white; figure on serving 3 to 4 per person for an entrée, or one large scallop cut into quarters for an appetizer serving. They cook quickly and their texture makes them a nice addition to seafood casseroles and soups. "Wet" scallops have been treated with a preservative to prolong their shelf life in the market. Because they have been treated, they will retain water and if you are sautéing them, they may not brown at all. "Dry" scallops are sometimes called diver scallops; they have not been chemically treated, have a much truer flavor, and will brown if sautéed. They are also more expensive than wet scallops. Bay scallops are the tiny ones—they're deliciously sweet but easy to overcook.

**Shrimp:** See the notes on shrimp on pages 108, 109, and 112. For serving shrimp in casseroles, I recommend using the medium size, that way there will be lots of bite-size whole shrimp in the dish. For grilled, skewered, or sautéed shrimp, I recommend the jumbo size. However, the final choice is up to you and your pocketbook. It's cheaper to buy shrimp with the shell on and devein them yourself, but if time is of the essence, buy them already peeled and deveined. Some stores sell what they call "easy peel" shrimp; the back of the shrimp has been slit for you, so it's just a matter of removing the peel.

# Quick Simply Baked Fish

Serves 10

This dish is foolproof and your guests will love it. Use any firm-fleshed fish, such as halibut, sea bass, or salmon. Avoid tuna or swordfish because they are too strongly flavored to work well with this treatment.

½ cup (1 stick) unsalted butter, melted

3 cloves garlic, minced

2 teaspoons Old Bay seasoning

2 teaspoons fresh lemon juice

¼ cup olive oil

2½ pounds sea bass, salmon, or halibut fillets

1 cup fresh bread crumbs

1 cup freshly grated Parmesan cheese

3 lemons, cut into wedges

**1.** Combine the melted butter, garlic, Old Bay, lemon juice, and olive oil in a 2-cup measuring cup. Pour about ⅓ cup of the mixture into the bottom of a 13 x 9-inch baking dish or one that is large enough to hold the fish in a single layer. Dip the fish into the butter, turning to coat.

✳ **DIVA DO-AHEAD:** At this point, you can cover and refrigerate the fish and remaining flavored butter for up to 12 hours. Melt the butter before continuing.

**2.** Combine the bread crumbs and cheese on a large plate and dredge the fish in the mixture to get a coating ½ to ¾ inch thick. Pour any remaining butter over the bread crumb–coated fillets.

✳ **DIVA DO-AHEAD:** At this point, you can cover and refrigerate for up to 8 hours.

**3.** Preheat the oven to 400°F. Bake the fish until cooked through, 10 to 12 minutes; it's best to test with the tip of a knife at the thickest part. If you have particularly thick fish and it doesn't cook evenly, put it in the microwave for about 3 minutes to finish. It should be opaque and flake easily when prodded with the tip of the knife. Sea bass may require a slightly longer cooking time, perhaps as much as 10 more minutes. Serve the fish with lemon wedges.

# Pesto-Crusted Fish Fillets

Serves 10 to 12

This simple way of baking fish works well with halibut, salmon, and sea bass. Pesto-crusted fish is delicious hot, at room temperature, or cold. If you are serving it cold, let it cool to room temperature after cooking, then refrigerate it for up to 12 hours. Serve the fish on a bed of field greens, or on sliced tomatoes and fresh mozzarella, and garnish with chopped basil and pine nuts. Panko are Japanese bread crumbs. You will find them in the Asian section of your grocery store or in an Asian market. Regular dry bread crumbs can be used for this treatment as well, but panko are very crispy and I like the texture better.

**2½ pounds firm-fleshed fish fillets, any skin removed**

**1 cup Basil Pesto, homemade (page 97) or store-bought**

**1 cup panko (Japanese bread crumbs)**

**Sprigs fresh basil for garnish**

**1 cup pine nuts, toasted (see page 83), for garnish**

**1.** Put the fish on a rimmed baking sheet lined with a silicone liner or aluminum foil. Brush the top of the fish with a thin layer of the pesto.

❋ **DIVA DO-AHEAD:** At this point, cover and refrigerate for at least 1 hour and up to 24 hours.

**2.** Preheat the broiler for 10 minutes. Mix the remaining pesto with the panko and spread over the fish fillets. Broil until the crumbs are golden and the fish is just cooked through, 7 to 10 minutes.

**3.** Serve the fish on a platter, garnished with the basil sprigs and pine nuts.

# Lemon-Dill Baked Fish

Serves 10 to 12

This recipe was almost too easy to include, but keeping it simple is what makes great entertaining an attainable goal. Serve it hot, or at room temperature with butter sauce, or cold, garnished with fresh dill and lemon wedges.

1 cup (2 sticks) unsalted butter, melted

2 scallions (white part only), finely chopped

¼ cup finely chopped fresh dill

¼ cup fresh lemon juice

1 teaspoon sweet paprika

2½ pounds firm-fleshed fish fillets, such as salmon, halibut, or sea bass

1 tablespoon Old Bay seasoning

**1.** In a small bowl, stir together the melted butter, scallions, dill, lemon juice, and paprika.

✳ **DIVA DO-AHEAD:** At this point, you can cover and refrigerate for up to 4 days. Gently reheat before continuing.

## Old Bay Seasoning

Old Bay seasoning from the Chesapeake is a mélange of spices similar to Cajun seasoning that brings out the flavor in seafood. It's sold in the spice section of your supermarket or in the seafood section.

**2.** Preheat the oven to 400°F. Put the fish in a 13 x 9-inch baking dish in a single layer and sprinkle with the Old Bay. Spoon about half of the butter mixture over the fish and bake until just cooked through, 10 to 15 minutes.

✳ **DIVA DO-AHEAD:** If you would like to serve the fish chilled, let cool, cover, and refrigerate overnight.

**3.** Transfer the fish to a serving platter, pour the remaining warmed butter over the fish, and serve immediately or cool to room temperature.

## Diva Variation

This treatment works well with swordfish and tuna if you omit the dill and substitute oregano—the strong flavor of these fish will overpower the dill in the dish.

# Miso-Glazed Fish Fillets

Serves 10 to 12

I love to make this dish with salmon because the rich fish pairs well with the miso and soy glaze, but you can use cod, halibut, sea bass, tuna, or swordfish. The miso paste and soup mix are available in Asian markets.

½ cup white miso paste or 2 envelopes Kikkoman shiro miso soup mix

⅓ cup rice wine or seasoned rice vinegar

2 tablespoons sugar

¼ cup vegetable oil

¼ cup soy sauce

6 shakes of Tabasco sauce

2½ pounds salmon or other fish fillets, skin removed

Chopped scallions (white and tender green parts) for garnish

Toasted sesame seeds (see page 83) for garnish

1. In a medium-size bowl, whisk together the miso, rice wine, sugar, oil, soy sauce, and Tabasco until blended. Transfer to a zipper-top plastic bag, add the fish, seal, and turn over a couple of times to coat.

✳ **DIVA DO-AHEAD:** At this point, refrigerate for at least 6 hours or overnight, turning the bag two or three more times.

2. Build a hot charcoal fire or preheat a gas grill or the broiler for 10 minutes. Remove the fish from the marinade and grill or broil on a baking sheet lined with aluminum foil until just cooked through, 5 to 7 minutes per side.

3. Transfer the fish to a serving platter and serve warm, at room temperature, or chilled, garnished with chopped scallions and sesame seeds.

# Crab-Stuffed Fillet of Sole

Serves 10 to 12

This simple entrée will elicit oohs and ahs from your guests. Stuff the sole the day before, then bake it briefly when you're almost ready to serve. Roasted asparagus and a salad would be my choices for side dishes. Although I usually serve these stuffed sole fillets plain, Lobster Sauce or Creamy Corn Sauce (both page 344) would be wonderful spooned on top.

1 cup (2 sticks) unsalted butter

4 cloves garlic, minced

1 teaspoon sweet paprika

2 tablespoons fresh lemon juice

½ cup chopped fresh Italian parsley

½ pound lump crabmeat, picked over for cartilage and shells

1½ cups fresh white bread crumbs (buy a nice loaf that has some structure, such as Pepperidge Farm)

¼ cup mayonnaise

1 teaspoon dry sherry

½ teaspoon Worcestershire sauce

14 pieces fillet of sole

1 tablespoon Old Bay seasoning

4 lemons, cut into wedges, for garnish

Sprigs fresh parsley for garnish

**1.** In a medium-size skillet over low heat, melt the butter. Add the garlic and cook for 4 to 5 minutes to infuse the butter with the garlic flavor. Remove from the heat and pour into a glass measuring cup. Stir in the paprika, lemon juice, and parsley and set aside.

✻ **DIVA DO-AHEAD:** At this point, you can let cool, cover, and refrigerate for up to 2 weeks. Gently reheat before continuing.

**2.** In medium-size bowl, combine the crab, bread crumbs, mayonnaise, sherry, and Worcestershire, stirring to blend but being careful not to break up the crab too much. Stir in ¼ cup of the garlic butter.

✻ **DIVA DO-AHEAD:** At this point, you can cover and refrigerate for up to 2 days.

**3.** Drizzle 2 tablespoons of the garlic butter over the bottom of a 13 x 9-inch baking dish. Sprinkle the fillets with a bit of the Old Bay. Spoon about 2 tablespoons of crab stuffing in the center of the darker side of each fillet and roll up with the white side facing out. Place the fillets, seam side down, in the prepared baking dish. Pour the remaining garlic butter over the top of the fillets.

✻ **DIVA DO-AHEAD:** At this point, you can cover and refrigerate for up to 2 days. Bring to room temperature before continuing.

**4.** Preheat the oven to 350°F. Bake until the fish is just cooked through and beginning to turn opaque, about 15 minutes. Remove from the oven and serve garnished with lemon wedges and parsley sprigs.

## The Diva Says:

When serving fish fillets such as salmon and halibut, I figure on ¼ pound per person. When I cook fillet of sole, which is much thinner, I don't go by the pound, but rather by the piece. One good-sized fillet that weighs about 2 ounces should do nicely. You may want to buy a few extra to stuff (there will be enough stuffing) just in case everyone is really hungry. I'm recommending you buy 14 sole fillets to serve 10 to 12 people.

# Potato-Crusted Halibut

Serves 10 to 12

This dish is served in fancy restaurants, but it is really simple to make at home and it's a showstopper for a dinner party. I use defrosted frozen hash brown potatoes for the crust. They contain a bit of moisture, but because they are already cooked, they give the fish a golden color, and the fish doesn't overcook waiting for the potatoes to brown. Either the Lobster Sauce or Creamy Corn Sauce makes a delicious accompaniment.

**1 cup (2 sticks) unsalted butter, melted**

**1 teaspoon salt**

**½ teaspoon freshly ground black pepper**

**1 teaspoon sweet paprika**

**2 cloves garlic, minced**

**¼ cup finely chopped fresh Italian parsley**

**2 cups frozen shredded hash brown potatoes, defrosted**

**2½ pounds halibut fillets, any skin removed**

**Lobster Sauce or Creamy Corn Sauce (page 344; optional)**

**1.** Line a 15 x 12-inch rimmed baking sheet with a silicone liner or aluminum foil.

**2.** In a wide bowl, combine the melted butter, salt, pepper, paprika, garlic, and parsley, stirring to blend.

**3.** Put the potatoes in a medium-size bowl, drizzle with half the butter mixture, and toss to coat evenly.

**4.** Dip each fish fillet into the remaining butter mixture, then roll in the potatoes to coat evenly. Place the coated fillets on the prepared baking sheet and drizzle with any remaining butter.

✳ **DIVA DO-AHEAD:** At this point, you can cover and refrigerate for up to 24 hours. Bring to room temperature before continuing.

**5.** Preheat the oven to 375°F. Bake until the fish is just cooked through and the potatoes are golden brown, 15 to 20 minutes. Remove from the oven and serve immediately on a pool of the Lobster Sauce or Creamy Corn Sauce if using.

## Lobster Sauce

Makes about 3¾ cups

Luxurious and delicate, this sauce can be served over your favorite baked fish or stuffed sole fillets. Or you can add about ½ pound of cooked lobster chunks, crab, or shrimp to it and serve over rice for a delicious main dish. There is no lobster in the sauce, but it will have an intense lobster flavor if you use the lobster stock.

**¼ cup (½ stick) unsalted butter**

**¼ cup all-purpose flour**

**1½ cups chicken broth mixed with 1½ cups bottled clam juice, or 3 cups reconstituted lobster or seafood stock (see Sources, page 669)**

**2 tablespoons cream sherry**

**½ cup heavy cream**

In a 2-quart saucepan over medium heat, melt the butter, then whisk in the flour. When white bubbles form on the surface, cook for 2 to 3 more minutes, whisking constantly. Add the broth mixture and whisk until it all comes to a boil. Add the sherry and cream, reduce the heat to medium, and simmer for 1 minute.

✳ **DIVA DO-AHEAD:** At this point, you can let cool, cover, and refrigerate for up to 4 days. Reheat gently before using.

### The Diva Says:

Make sure you bring sauces to a boil after adding the liquid; otherwise, they will not thicken properly.

## Creamy Corn Sauce

Makes about 3¾ cups

This sauce spiked with Creole seasoning is another choice for saucing the halibut on page 345. You can also pour it over 2 pounds of medium-size uncooked shrimp, peeled and deveined, top with crushed potato chips, and bake the shrimp in a casserole dish for a delicious entrée.

**¼ cup (½ stick) unsalted butter**

**½ cup finely chopped sweet onion**

**2 tablespoons Creole Seasoning (page 303)**

**¼ cup all-purpose flour**

**3 cups chicken or vegetable broth**

**One 16-ounce bag frozen white corn, defrosted**

**½ cup heavy cream**

In a 2-quart saucepan over medium heat, melt the butter. Add the onion and Creole Seasoning and cook, stirring, until softened, 3 to 4 minutes. Add the flour and whisk until smooth and white bubbles begin to form on the surface. Continue to whisk for 2 or 3 more minutes, then gradually add the broth and whisk until the mixture comes to a boil. Add the corn and cream and heat until the sauce is warm, 3 to 4 minutes.

✳ **DIVA DO-AHEAD:** At this point you can let cool, cover, and refrigerate for up to 4 days. Reheat gently before serving.

# Crab-Stuffed Halibut

Serves 10 to 12

This elegant entrée is so simple to put together. To take it over the top, serve it in a pool of Lobster Sauce (left). The stuffing blends beautifully with the flaky halibut, but you could also use salmon fillets or fillet of sole. The stuffing is also dynamite as a filling for baked mushroom caps.

6 tablespoons (¾ stick) unsalted butter

3 tablespoons Old Bay seasoning

¼ cup finely chopped shallots

¼ cup seeded and finely chopped red bell pepper

1 teaspoon Dijon mustard

½ cup mayonnaise

1 tablespoon Worcestershire sauce

½ pound lump crabmeat, picked over for shells and cartilage

¼ cup freshly grated Parmesan cheese

¼ cup finely chopped fresh Italian parsley

¼ cup olive oil

2½ to 3 pounds halibut fillets, any skin removed

Lemon wedges for garnish

Sprigs fresh parsley for garnish

**1.** In a medium-size skillet over medium heat, melt 4 tablespoons of the butter. Add 1 tablespoon of the Old Bay, the shallots, and bell pepper and cook, stirring until the shallots and pepper are softened, about 3 minutes. Transfer to a medium-size bowl and stir in the mustard, mayonnaise, Worcestershire, crab, cheese, and parsley until blended, being careful not to break up the crabmeat too much.

❋ **DIVA DO-AHEAD:** At this point, you can cover and refrigerate for up to 2 days. Bring to room temperature before continuing.

**2.** In a small bowl, combine the olive oil with the remaining 2 tablespoons of Old Bay. Paint both sides of the fillets with the seasoned oil and place them in a 13 x 9-inch baking dish.

**3.** Melt the remaining 2 tablespoons of butter in a small skillet. Mound the crab mixture on top of the fish and drizzle with the melted butter.

❋ **DIVA DO-AHEAD:** At this point, you can cover and refrigerate for up to 8 hours. Bring to room temperature before continuing.

**4.** Preheat the oven to 375°F. Bake until the fish is cooked through and the stuffing is golden brown, 15 to 20 minutes.

**5.** Remove the fish from the oven, transfer it to a serving platter, and surround it with lemon wedges and parsley sprigs. Serve hot or at room temperature.

# Red Snapper Parisienne

Serves 10 to 12

A friend shared her memory of a dish she enjoyed in Paris, and I had to try my hand at replicating it. This is probably not exactly what she had, but it's a delicious do-ahead entrée for a special occasion. Serve it with roasted potatoes and a green salad.

2 tablespoons unsalted butter

½ cup finely chopped shallots

½ pound white button mushrooms, thinly sliced

1½ teaspoons dried thyme

1 teaspoon salt

½ teaspoon freshly ground black pepper

½ cup dry white wine or dry vermouth

½ cup bottled clam juice

One 15.5-ounce can chopped tomatoes, with their juice

1 bay leaf

2 cups heavy cream

3 tablespoons olive oil

2½ pounds red snapper or other flaky fish fillets, skin removed if necessary

Chopped fresh parsley for garnish

**1.** In a large skillet, melt the butter over medium heat, then cook the shallots, stirring, until softened, about 3 minutes. Add the mushrooms, thyme, salt, and pepper and cook, stirring, until mushrooms begin to turn golden, about 7 to 10 minutes.

**2.** Stir in the wine and clam juice, bring to a boil, and continue boiling to reduce the liquid to about ½ cup. Add the tomatoes and bay leaf and cook for another 5 minutes, until the tomato juice begins to evaporate. Add the cream, return to a boil, reduce the heat to medium, and simmer the sauce until it is thick enough to coat the back of a spoon, about 5 minutes. Remove the bay leaf.

❋ **DIVA DO-AHEAD:** At this point, you can let cool, cover, and refrigerate for up to 3 days.

**3.** Brush a 13 x 9-inch baking dish with 1 tablespoon of the oil and place the fish in the dish in a single layer. Drizzle the fillets with the remaining 2 tablespoons of oil. Spread the sauce over the fillets and cover the baking dish with aluminum foil.

❋ **DIVA DO-AHEAD:** At this point, you can refrigerate for up to 24 hours.

**4.** Preheat the oven to 375°F. Bake until the fish is just cooked through and the sauce is bubbling, about 20 minutes.

**5.** Remove the foil and serve hot from the dish, garnished with chopped parsley.

# Salmon Poached in the Microwave

Serves 10

This is absolutely the simplest way to prepare salmon, and you don't have to preheat your oven or buy a pan to poach the fish on the stove top. I often do this if I need cooked salmon for a recipe—it's quick and foolproof.

2½ pounds salmon fillets

1 tablespoon Old Bay seasoning

¼ cup dry white wine or water

2 tablespoons fresh lemon juice

**1.** Put the salmon in a 13 x 9-inch baking dish, sprinkle with the Old Bay, and pour the wine and lemon juice over it. Cover with plastic wrap, cut two vent holes in the wrap, and microwave on High for 7 to 8 minutes.

**2.** Remove from the microwave and let rest for 5 minutes. (The fish should be cooked through at this point, but your microwave may take a little longer, so slash the fish at the thickest point to make sure.) Carefully remove the plastic from the dish, then remove the fish from the broth. Gently remove any skin, if it was left on.

✳ **DIVA DO-AHEAD:** At this point, you can cover and refrigerate for up to 3 days.

Serve the fish warm or chilled.

## Stellar Sauces for Poached Salmon

- Artichoke Rémoulade Sauce (page 494)
- Dilled Tartar Sauce (see page 496)
- Mango Salsa (page 477)
- Balsamic Vinegar Syrup (page 480)
- Chipotle Corn Salsa (page 478)
- Parsley Pesto (page 473)
- Oven-Roasted Caponata (page 128)
- Cucumber Yogurt Sauce (page 492)
- Mustard Yogurt Sauce (page 493)

## Flour-Thickened Sauces

Have you ever made a sauce that tasted like raw flour? Chances are you didn't cook the flour completely before adding the liquid. Make sure you add the flour, whisking, and wait until white bubbles form on the surface. Then whisk the roux for 2 to 3 minutes to cook the flour and to form a bond with the fat in the pan. That way, once you add the liquid, you won't have lumps and, when reheated, the sauce will not separate.

# Maui Salmon Skewers with Pacific Rim Peanut Sauce

Serves 10 to 12

Although I like to serve this salmon on skewers, you can also marinate sides of salmon and grill them for a delicious entrée. This marinade also works well with shrimp. Marinate 2½ pounds of large shrimp, skewer them, and broil or grill until pink, about 2 minutes each side.

1 cup soy sauce

1 cup water

½ cup rice wine or seasoned rice vinegar

2 tablespoons sugar

3 tablespoons Asian chili-garlic sauce

1 cup packed fresh cilantro leaves, finely chopped

2 teaspoons fresh lemon juice

2 tablespoons seeded and finely chopped jalapeño pepper

One 1½-pound salmon fillet or 1½ pounds tuna steaks, sliced on a 45-degree angle ½ inch thick

1 recipe Pacific Rim Peanut Sauce (page 481)

**1.** In a large bowl, whisk together the soy sauce, water, rice wine, sugar, chili sauce, ½ cup of the cilantro, the lemon juice, and jalapeño until the sugar is dissolved and the mixture is blended. Add the salmon, turn to coat, and cover.

❋ **DIVA DO-AHEAD:** At this point, refrigerate for at least 2 and up to 8 hours.

**2.** Soak wooden skewers in water for 1 hour. Remove the salmon from the marinade, pat dry, and thread a slice of salmon onto each skewer.

❋ **DIVA DO-AHEAD:** At this point, you can cover and refrigerate for up to 6 hours.

**3.** Build a hot charcoal fire or preheat the broiler or a gas grill for 10 minutes. Grill the skewers, or broil on a baking sheet lined with aluminum foil, until cooked through, about 2 minutes per side.

❋ **DIVA DO-AHEAD:** At this point, you can let cool, cover, and refrigerate for up to 8 hours. Let come to room temperature before serving.

**4.** Serve the salmon garnished with the remaining ½ cup of cilantro and the peanut sauce.

The Diva Says: Rice wine, or mirin, is sweet and lends balance to marinades and sauces. If you are unable to find it, substitute seasoned rice vinegar, which has a lower acidity than regular vinegar and will give you a nice flavor.

Try skewering other types of firm-fleshed fish, either thinly sliced or cut into bite-sized pieces, and vary the marinade.

• Swordfish prepared with Soy-Ginger Marinade (page 394), Marinade Provençal (page 394), Mediterranean Marinade (page 396), or Garlic-Herb Marinade (page 393). Serve with freshly made marinade for dipping or another complementary sauce.

• Tuna with Soy-Ginger Marinade (page 394) or Mediterranean Marinade (page 396). Serve with wasabi mayonnaise (see page 495) or roasted garlic mayonnaise (see page 495) for dipping.

• Sea bass or halibut with Bloody Mary Marinade (page 396), Mediterranean Marinade (page 396), Garlic-Herb Marinade (page 393), Soy-Ginger Marinade (page 394), Marinade Provençal (page 394), or Citrus-Rosemary Marinade (page 397). Serve with Artichoke Rémoulade Sauce (page 494) or Dilled Tartar Sauce (see page 496).

• Sometimes a dipping sauce can be made from a combination of seeds such as toasted and black sesame seeds, or salt combined with freshly grated citrus zest and freshly ground pepper. These will perk up the flavor of the skewer, but not take away from the taste of the fish.

# Roasted Stuffed Salmon with Leeks and Dill

Serves 12 to 14

This delicately seasoned fish is a favorite in my buffet classes. Make sure you use fresh bread crumbs in this preparation. They crisp up in the oven, making a nice contrast with the fresh leeks, dill, and moist salmon. For this recipe, you will need a whole salmon, which weighs 7 to 8 pounds. Your fish market can cut and fillet it for you so that you have 2 sides. If you can, have them remove the skin, but if not, then remove the skin after the fish is cooked. It will just peel away from the flesh. One side of salmon should weigh 2 to 2$\frac{1}{2}$ pounds. Remember to fold up the thinner tail section so it will cook evenly with the rest of the fish. This is also a delicious way to prepare halibut.

2 sides of salmon, skin removed

2 teaspoons Old Bay seasoning

¼ cup olive oil

¼ cup (½ stick) unsalted butter

½ cup finely chopped leeks (white part only)

¼ cup chopped fresh dill, or 2 tablespoons dillweed

4 cups fresh bread crumbs

1 teaspoon salt

½ teaspoon freshly ground black pepper

Lemon wedges for garnish

Sprigs fresh dill for garnish

**1.** Wash the salmon and pat dry with paper towels. Mix together the Old Bay and 2 tablespoons of the olive oil in a small bowl and paint over the fish on both sides.

❋ **DIVA DO-AHEAD:** At this point, you can cover and refrigerate for up to 24 hours. Bring to room temperature before continuing.

**2.** In a small skillet over medium heat, melt the butter. Add the leeks and cook, stirring until softened, about 3 minutes. Add the dill and cook for another minute. Remove from the heat.

**3.** Put the bread crumbs in a large bowl, add the leeks, salt, and pepper, and stir to blend. Add more olive oil if the stuffing appears dry.

❋ **DIVA DO-AHEAD:** At this point, you can cover and refrigerate for up to 24 hours.

**4.** Place the salmon on a baking sheet or in a large roasting pan lined with a silicone liner or aluminum foil. Top each of the sides of salmon with an even layer of the stuffing.

❋ **DIVA DO-AHEAD:** At this point, you can cover and refrigerate for up to 12 hours.

**5.** Preheat the oven to 375°F. Drizzle the salmon with the remaining 2 tablespoons of olive oil and roast until just cooked through, 20 to 30 minutes.

**6.** Remove the fish from the oven and let rest for 5 to 10 minutes.

❋ **DIVA DO-AHEAD:** At this point, you can cover and refrigerate overnight.

**7.** Cut the salmon into serving pieces and arrange on a platter, garnished with lemon wedges and sprigs of dill. Serve warm, at room temperature, or chilled.

# Honey Mustard–Glazed Salmon

Serves 10 to 12

Sweet and hot are a delicious combination with salmon as well as sea bass, halibut, and snapper. You can either grill this on the barbecue or broil it indoors. I like to serve it with a nice baked pasta dish, roasted asparagus, and salad.

1½ cups Dijon mustard

⅔ cup honey

2 tablespoons fresh lemon juice

¼ cup chopped fresh dill

2½ pounds salmon fillets, any skin removed

**1.** In a medium-size bowl, stir together the mustard, honey, lemon juice, and dill until smooth. Divide the mixture between 2 bowls.

**2.** Put the salmon on a rimmed baking sheet and paint generously on both sides with the honey mustard in one of the bowls.

✳ **DIVA DO-AHEAD:** At this point, cover and refrigerate for at least 4 and up to 24 hours, along with the remaining honey mustard.

**3.** Build a hot charcoal fire or preheat the broiler or a grill for 10 minutes, then broil on a baking sheet lined with aluminum foil or grill until just cooked through, 10 to 20 minutes.

✳ **DIVA DO-AHEAD:** At this point, you can let cool, cover, and refrigerate overnight. Take it out of the refrigerator 30 minutes before serving. To reheat, place on a baking sheet, cover with foil, and bake at 350°F for 15 minutes, or until heated through.

**4.** Serve the salmon warm, at room temperature, or chilled with the remaining sauce on the side.

# Grandma's Baked Tuna in Olive Oil

Serves 10

This technique for cooking tuna ensures that it is tender and juicy, whether it is served warm, at room temperature, or chilled. Serve with Oven-Roasted Caponata (page 128), Tapenade (page 84), or your favorite sauce. It's also delicious served over a salad of field greens or Caesar salad.

**1 cup extra virgin olive oil**

**2 teaspoons salt**

**1 teaspoon freshly ground black pepper**

**3½ pounds tuna steaks**

### Diva Variation

For an extra kick of flavor, add ⅛ teaspoon of red pepper flakes and 1 teaspoon of dried oregano to the oil.

**1.** Combine the olive oil, salt, and pepper and pour into a zipper-top plastic bag or 13 x 9-inch baking dish. Add the tuna and turn to coat it, then seal the bag or cover the baking dish.

✳ **DIVA DO-AHEAD:** At this point, you can refrigerate for up to 24 hours.

**2.** Preheat the oven to 325°F. Remove the tuna from the refrigerator for 45 minutes, transfer to a baking dish if necessary, then bake uncovered in the oil until white and just cooked through, 55 to 65 minutes.

**3.** Let cool for about 15 minutes, then drain off the oil. Slice the tuna against the grain on an angle into ½-inch-thick slices.

✳ **DIVA DO-AHEAD:** At this point, you can cover and refrigerate overnight. Serve cold or at room temperature.

# Macadamia Nut–Crusted Sea Bass

Serves 10

Sea bass is a versatile fish to serve to your family and friends. Mild-flavored and easy to prepare, this recipe is terrific for a Pacific Rim–themed dinner, served with Pacific Rim Slaw (page 187), your favorite rice dish, and a fruit salsa. If you are unable to find sea bass, halibut or red snapper is a nice substitute. If you like, try this with slivered almonds or chopped pecans, cashews, or pistachios instead of the macadamias.

2 tablespoons olive oil

2 tablespoons soy sauce

2 tablespoons orange juice

2 tablespoons fresh lime juice

2 tablespoons honey

4 pounds sea bass or other firm, white-fleshed fish fillets

1½ cups finely chopped macadamia nuts

½ cup (1 stick) unsalted butter, melted

2 cloves garlic, chopped

¼ cup chopped fresh parsley

**1.** In a small bowl, whisk together the olive oil, soy sauce, citrus juices, and honey.

**2.** Put the sea bass in a zipper-top plastic bag or baking dish, pour the marinade over the fillets, turn them to coat, and seal the bag or cover the baking dish.

✳ **DIVA DO-AHEAD:** At this point, refrigerate for at least 4 hours or overnight, turning the fillets a few times.

**3.** Preheat the oven to 375°F. Remove the sea bass from the marinade and pat dry. Place on a baking sheet lined with a silicone liner or aluminum foil. Press the nuts evenly into the fish, covering them uniformly on both sides.

**4.** Stir the melted butter, garlic, and parsley together in a small bowl, then pour over the fish. Bake until the fish is just cooked through and the nuts are golden brown, 15 to 20 minutes. Serve immediately or at room temperature.

# Seafood Florentine

Serves 10 to 12

This elegant entrée is one of my favorites for special occasions. Served on a bed of spinach with a creamy seafood sauce on top, it looks and tastes luxurious.

¾ cup (1½ sticks) unsalted butter

1 cup finely chopped shallots

2 pounds fresh baby spinach, or two 16-ounce packages frozen spinach, defrosted and squeezed dry

1½ teaspoons salt

1 teaspoon freshly ground black pepper

¼ teaspoon ground nutmeg

2 pounds mixed fish and/or shellfish (see The Diva Says)

¼ cup all-purpose flour

1 cup seafood stock (see The Diva Says), milk, or bottled clam juice

½ cup dry white wine or dry vermouth

1½ cups heavy cream

1 cup finely shredded imported Swiss cheese

½ cup freshly grated Parmesan cheese

### Diva Variation

**Chicken Florentine:** Substitute 8 skinless, boneless chicken breast halves, cut into ½-inch chunks, for the seafood. Sauté the chicken as directed in the recipe, then substitute chicken broth for the seafood stock and proceed as directed.

**1.** In a large skillet, melt ¼ cup (½ stick) of the butter over medium heat, add ½ cup of the shallots, and cook, stirring, until softened, about 4 minutes. Add the spinach, salt, pepper, and nutmeg and cook, stirring, until the spinach is wilted and cooked through, another 3 minutes. Transfer to a 13 x 9-inch baking dish.

✳ **DIVA DO-AHEAD:** At this point, you can let cool, cover, and refrigerate overnight.

**2.** Clean out the skillet, melt another ¼ cup (½ stick) of the butter over medium heat, add the remaining ½ cup of shallots, and cook, stirring, until softened, about 4 minutes. Add the seafood and cook for 3 to 5 minutes. The shrimp should begin to turn pink while fish and scallops will begin to turn opaque.

**3.** Transfer the contents of the pan to a colander set over a bowl; drain, reserving the juices from the seafood.

**4.** In a 4-quart saucepan over medium heat, melt the remaining ¼ cup (½ stick) of butter, then add the flour and whisk until white bubbles form on the surface. Cook, whisking constantly, 2 to 3 minutes longer, then add the liquid from the sautéed seafood and the seafood stock, stirring until the mixture begins to boil. Add the wine and cream, remove from the heat, add the Swiss cheese, and stir until melted. Add the seafood, stir to combine, and pour over the spinach in the baking dish.

✳ **DIVA DO-AHEAD:** At this point, you can let cool, cover, and refrigerate for up to 2 days. Bring to room temperature before continuing.

**5.** Preheat the oven to 350°F. Sprinkle the casserole with the grated Parmesan, and bake uncovered until the sauce is bubbling and the cheese begins to turn golden, 30 to 40 minutes. Remove from the oven and serve immediately.

The Diva Says: For the mixed shellfish, I like to use shrimp, crab, lobster, and scallops, or any combination of the four. If you would prefer to make this with fish fillets, use firm-fleshed fish such as salmon, halibut, and sea bass and cut them into 1-inch pieces.

Seafood stock can be found in the bouillon section of most grocers or you can order it from one of the purveyors listed in Sources (page 669).

# Neptune's Ranch Casserole

Serves 12

One of my favorite casseroles for a party is King Ranch Casserole, a staple at potluck dinners throughout the Southwest. A mélange of corn tortillas, green chiles, creamy sauce, chicken, and cheese, it has to be made at least a day ahead of time, so it's the Diva's favorite choice for an easy, do-ahead entrée. One day I decided to make it with shrimp and it was so delicious that now I usually make this version instead of the chicken one. You can also try it with a combination of lump crabmeat and cooked halibut or another firm, white-fleshed fish.

¼ cup (½ stick) unsalted butter

½ cup finely chopped onion

2 tablespoons seeded and finely diced Anaheim chile

2 teaspoons ground cumin

⅛ teaspoon chili powder

¼ cup all-purpose flour

2½ cups whole or 2% milk

1 recipe Boiled Shrimp (page 109)

2 cups fresh corn kernels cut from the cob or frozen corn, defrosted

¼ cup store-bought medium-hot salsa

2 cups sour cream (low-fat is okay)

Salt and freshly ground black pepper to taste

Sixteen 6-inch soft corn tortillas, torn into pieces

1½ cups finely shredded mild cheddar cheese

1 cup finely shredded Monterey or pepper Jack cheese

1 cup chicken broth

½ cup chopped fresh cilantro for garnish

**1.** In a 3-quart saucepan, melt the butter over medium heat. Add the onion, chile, cumin, and chili powder and cook for 2 minutes, stirring, so that the spices don't burn. Add the flour and whisk until white bubbles form on the surface. Cook, whisking constantly, 2 to 3 minutes longer. Slowly add the milk, whisking until it comes to a boil. Add the shrimp, corn, salsa, and 1 cup of the sour cream, stirring to combine. Remove from the heat, and season with salt and pepper if needed.

**2.** Coat a 13 x 9-inch baking dish with nonstick cooking spray and spread a thin layer of the cream sauce, without any of the shrimp, over the bottom. Scatter half of the tortillas in the bottom of the pan and top with half of the shrimp and cream sauce, making sure you get about half of the shrimp. Cover with half of the remaining tortillas and top with the remaining shrimp and sauce. Cover with the remaining tortillas and the cheeses. Carefully pour the broth over the top; this will soften the tortillas, so they blend in with the sauce and shrimp.

❋ **DIVA DO-AHEAD:** At this point, cover and refrigerate at least overnight and up to 2 days. Bring to room temperature before continuing.

**3.** Preheat the oven to 350°F. Bake the casserole until the sauce is bubbling and the cheese is golden brown, 35 to 45 minutes.

**4.** Remove from the oven and serve warm, garnished with the cilantro and the remaining 1 cup of sour cream on the side.

# Cioppino (San Francisco Fisherman's Stew) 🍷 🥛

Serves 10 to 12

Cioppino was originally made from what was left of the catch of the day, but this stew calls for the best that is available for your guests. The tomato base can be made as many as 5 days in advance, while the seafood is added 30 minutes before serving. This is a delicious meal to serve on a buffet table with crusty sourdough bread and a mixed green salad. You can also serve the stew in hollowed-out small, round sourdough loaves instead of bowls.

½ cup olive oil

6 cloves garlic, minced

1 cup chopped onions

1 medium-size green bell pepper, seeded and coarsely chopped

Three 15.5-ounce cans Italian plum tomatoes, drained and chopped

One 6-ounce can tomato paste

2 cups dry white wine

2 tablespoons sugar

1 teaspoon freshly ground black pepper

2 tablespoons chopped fresh oregano

2 tablespoons chopped fresh basil

2 cooked crabs, cut into pieces and claws cracked

2 pounds sea bass or halibut fillets, cut into 1-inch chunks

4 lobster tails, split and cut into 1-inch chunks

¾ pound sea scallops, cut in half, or bay scallops, left whole

1½ pounds large shrimp, peeled and deveined

30 to 36 littleneck clams, scrubbed

Salt to taste

1 cup chopped fresh Italian parsley

**1.** In an 8-quart stockpot, heat the oil over medium heat, add the garlic, onion, and bell pepper and cook, stirring, until the onion is softened, 3 to 4 minutes. Add the tomatoes and tomato paste and stir until the tomato paste blends into the mixture. Add the wine, sugar, black pepper, and half the oregano and basil. Simmer, par-tially covered, for 20 minutes, stirring occasionally.

❋ **DIVA DO-AHEAD:** At this point, you can let cool, cover, and refrigerate for up to 5 days or freeze for up to 3 months. Defrost and bring the mixture to a slow simmer before continuing.

**2.** Add the crab and sea bass to the simmering tomato base and cook for 10

minutes. Add the lobster and simmer for 5 minutes. Add the scallops, shrimp, and clams, pushing the clams into the sauce. Cover and simmer until the shrimp turn pink and all the clams open, about 15 minutes. Discard any clams that do not open. Taste and add salt and more black pepper if needed. Sprinkle with remaining oregano and basil and the parsley. Serve the cioppino, making sure that your guests have a little bit of everything in their bowls.

## The Diva Says:

If you can't find freshly cooked crabs, I recommend you use frozen king crab or snow crab legs. Defrost them, slit them with kitchen shears for easy opening, then add to the stew. If you can't get crab legs, then additional shrimp or lump crabmeat can be added. Don't add lump crab until the last 2 minutes of cooking, so it doesn't break up.

### Slow Cooker Savvy

To keep this warm on the buffet table, transfer to a 6-quart slow cooker and keep on the lowest setting. (Some slow cookers now have a Warm setting, which will keep this at a constant temperature for 3 hours.)

# Seafood Gumbo

Serves 10

There are many recipes for gumbo; this one is simple, with some nice variations. I sometimes make gumbo with a combination of chicken and sausage (see below), or chicken, sausage, and shrimp. I am not a fan of okra in my gumbo, but if you like it, add 2 cups of sliced fresh okra along with the onion, celery, and bell pepper mixture. The beauty of any gumbo is that it gets better the longer the flavors have a chance to mingle and marry. So plan to make this the day before, then reheat it and serve it over rice. I love this for winter entertaining, whether it's for a football party or a casual get-together.

½ cup vegetable oil

½ cup all-purpose flour

2 cups chopped onions

2 cups chopped celery

2 cups seeded and chopped green bell peppers

4 cloves garlic, minced

1 tablespoon Creole Seasoning (page 303) or Old Bay seasoning

1½ pounds andouille sausage, cut into ½-inch dice

4 cups chicken broth

2 pounds medium-size shrimp, peeled and deveined

½ pound bay scallops

1 pound lump crabmeat, picked over for shells and cartilage

6 scallions (white and tender green parts), chopped, for garnish

Gumbo filé powder for serving

Assorted hot sauces, such as Frank's RedHot Cayenne Pepper Sauce and Tabasco, for serving

## Slow Cooker Savvy

You can keep the gumbo warm in a slow cooker on the lowest setting. A rice cooker will also keep your rice warm for up to 2 hours.

**1.** In an 8-quart stockpot over medium heat, heat the oil, then whisk in the flour and cook, stirring constantly, until golden brown. Add the onions, celery, bell peppers, garlic, and Creole Seasoning and cook, stirring, until the vegetables are crisp-tender, 6 to 8 minutes. Add the andouille and cook, stirring, for another 2 minutes. Gradually stir in the broth and bring to a boil. Reduce the heat to low and simmer, partially covered, for 45 minutes, stirring occasionally.

✳ **DIVA DO-AHEAD:** At this point, you can let cool, cover, and refrigerate for up to 2 days. Gently reheat the mixture to a simmer, whisking occasionally.

**2.** Add the shrimp, cover, and cook for 3 minutes. Add the scallops and crab, being careful not to break up the crab. Cover and simmer until the shrimp are pink and the scallops are tender, another 3 minutes.

**3.** Serve the gumbo over rice, garnished with the scallions, and offer the filé powder on the side, along with assorted hot sauces.

## Diva Variation

**Chicken and Sausage Gumbo:** Cut 6 skinless, boneless chicken breasts into ½-inch dice and sauté with the sausage; omit the seafood and skip step 2.

✳ **DIVA DO-AHEAD:** After step 1, you can let cool, cover, and freeze for up to 2 months. Reheat and serve.

# Seafood Lasagna

Serves 10 as a main dish

The sauces for this deliciously different lasagna can be prepared in advance. Then the dish can be assembled a day ahead and baked just before serving. The seafood cooking liquid in the cream sauce is optional. Since the seafood can be prepared up to 24 hours in advance, if you would like to make the cream sauce even earlier, just leave the cooking liquid out. Make this for your best friends—it's a splurge and they will love you for it.

### Tomato Sauce

**3 tablespoons olive oil**

**1 medium-size onion, chopped**

**4 cups canned whole plum tomatoes, with their juice**

**2 tablespoons chopped fresh basil**

**¼ cup chopped fresh Italian parsley**

**1½ teaspoons salt**

**½ teaspoon freshly ground black pepper**

### Seafood

**¼ cup (½ stick) unsalted butter**

**1 pound bay scallops**

**½ pound medium-size shrimp, peeled and deveined**

**½ pound lump crabmeat, picked over for shells and cartilage**

**2 tablespoons dry white wine or dry vermouth**

### Seafood Cream Sauce

**½ cup (1 stick) unsalted butter**

**½ cup all-purpose flour**

**3 cups whole or 2% milk**

**⅔ cup seafood cooking liquid, bottled clam juice, or milk (optional)**

**About ¾ cup heavy cream**

**Salt and white pepper to taste**

**Dash of ground nutmeg**

### Assembly

**1 pound no-boil lasagna noodles, handled according to the package directions, or four 12 x 8-inch fresh pasta sheets**

**1¼ cups freshly grated Parmigiano-Reggiano cheese**

**1.** To make the tomato sauce, in a 2½-quart saucepan, heat the oil over medium-high heat, then cook the onion, stirring, until translucent. Add the tomatoes, basil, parsley, salt, and pepper and cook until thickened, about 15 minutes. Remove from the heat.

✳ **DIVA DO-AHEAD:** At this point, you can let cool, cover, and refrigerate for up to 3 days or freeze for up to 2 months. Defrost the sauce before continuing.

**2.** To prepare the seafood, in a large skillet, melt the butter over medium heat. Add the scallops, shrimp, and crab and cook, stirring, until the shrimp are barely pink and the scallops are almost opaque all the way through. Add the wine and cook, stirring, for another minute. Drain, reserving the liquid.

✳ **DIVA DO-AHEAD:** At this point, you can cover and refrigerate the seafood and liquid separately for up to 24 hours.

**3.** To make the seafood cream sauce, in a 3-quart saucepan, melt the butter over medium heat. Whisk in the flour, and cook until smooth and thick. Gradually add the milk and reserved seafood cooking liquid, if using, stirring constantly with a whisk, until the sauce comes to a boil. Add up to ¾ cup heavy cream and let simmer, stirring a few times, until the sauce coats the back of a spoon. Season with salt, pepper, and nutmeg.

✳ **DIVA DO-AHEAD:** At this point, you can let cool, cover, and refrigerate for up to 3 days. Reheat before assembling the lasagna.

**4.** To assemble the lasagna, butter the bottom of a 13 x 9-inch baking dish generously. Spread a thin layer of tomato sauce over the bottom of the pan. Layer a quarter of the noodles (or 1 sheet of fresh pasta) over the tomato sauce. Top with all the seafood mixture. Spoon a third of the cream sauce evenly over the top of the seafood. Top with a third of the remaining noodles. Spoon half of the remaining cream sauce over the noodles and sprinkle with about ½ cup of the Parmigiano-Reggiano. Top with half of the remaining noodles, all of the remaining tomato sauce, and ¼ cup of the cheese. Add the remaining noodles in one layer, cover with the remaining cream sauce, and sprinkle evenly with the remaining ½ cup of cheese. Cover with aluminum foil.

✳ **DIVA DO-AHEAD:** At this point, you can refrigerate for up to 24 hours. Bring to room temperature before continuing.

**5.** Preheat the oven to 350°F. Bake the lasagna, covered, for 1 hour, then uncover and bake until the cheese is golden, another 10 to 15 minutes. Let rest for 10 to 15 minutes before serving.

## Diva Variation

This is delicious made with 1½ pounds of cooked salmon, flaked into nice chunks, instead of the crab, shrimp, and scallops.

# Diva Seafood Boil

Serves 12

There aren't many things that are as much fun as a seafood boil. What I love about them is that the ingredients depend totally on the cook's whim, and there are so many flavors mingling that they explode in your mouth. This is a great meal to serve as a patio or beach dinner. I like to start the boil on the stove top by getting the water and seasonings boiling, then I transfer it to the gas grill; that way, all the mess is outside. Traditional seafood boils usually have crab or crawfish as one of the shellfish selections; if they are not available where you live, just add more shrimp and clams. You will need a 16-quart pot or two 8-quart pots to make this. A large pasta pot with an insert is also a good choice. Set the table with butcher paper, supply picks and nutcrackers for digging into the shellfish, and have lots of finger bowls and paper towels available for wiping off hands and faces. Cooking and eating this is messy but very rewarding work!

**8 cups water**

**Four 12-ounce bottles beer (dark beer will give the boil a more pronounced beer flavor)**

**¼ to ⅓ cup Old Bay seasoning, or 1 package dry crab boil (see The Diva Says)**

**2 lemons, quartered and seeds removed**

**1½ pounds small red or white potatoes, cut in half**

**6 ears corn, shucked and cut in thirds or quarters (pieces should be about 2 inches long)**

**2 pounds smoked sausage, either the traditional andouille or your favorite kielbasa or another Polish sausage, cut into 1-inch chunks**

**6 live blue crabs, or 4 live Maine lobsters, or 4 pounds crawfish**

**4 pounds large shrimp**

**4 pounds littleneck or cherrystone clams, scrubbed**

**1.** In a 16-quart stockpot or lobster pot, combine the water, beer, Old Bay, and juice from the lemons. Add the lemon rinds to the pot and bring to a boil. Taste the boil for seasoning—it should be highly seasoned because the water and seasonings will lose some punch when you add the other ingredients.

**2.** Add the potatoes to the pot, cover, and simmer for 5 minutes.

**3.** Add the corn and sausage, cover, and simmer for another 3 minutes.

**4.** Add the crabs, lobster, or crawfish, cover, and simmer until they begin to turn red, about 5 minutes.

**5.** Add the shrimp and clams, cover, and simmer for another 3 minutes.

**6.** Remove the pot from the stove; let rest for 5 minutes to continue cooking the clams.

**7.** Uncover the pot and discard any clams that have not opened. Carefully lift out the seafood, using tongs and a slotted spoon, and transfer it to a large serving platter.

❋ **DIVA DO AHEAD:** At this point, you can cover the platter with foil to keep warm for up to 30 minutes.

**8.** With a slotted spoon, remove the sausage, potatoes, and corn and transfer to a large serving bowl or another platter.

❋ **DIVA DO AHEAD:** At this point, you can cover the bowl or platter with foil to keep warm for up to 30 minutes.

**9.** Serve the boil with melted butter, Rémoulade Sauce (page 111), distilled white vinegar, and hot sauce.

The Diva Says: Old Bay seasoning is my choice for this seafood boil because it's readily available and you can use it for other seafood dishes. There are lots of other seafood boil products on the market. I like the Zatarain brand, which is a powder, because it seems to have more of a punch.

Many people like to add artichokes to the boil along with the potatoes. If you would like to do this, you will need 6 large trimmed artichokes. Remove them from the boil after cooking, cut them in half, and remove the choke before serving. They're yummy with béarnaise mayonnaise (see page 495).

# Party Paella

Serves 10 to 12

Many people think of paella as a huge undertaking, but it's really a simple dish to put together. I love it because there is something in it for everyone. My version is not traditional. I've substituted long-grain rice for the more expensive Arborio, used boneless chicken rather than bone-in, and streamlined the base for the paella, called sofrito, so that you can make it several days ahead of time and have it ready and waiting for the final cooking. Saffron, the traditional seasoning for this delicious meal, is very expensive, but the flavor is worth it and you can find small quantities at gourmet retailers. Make sure you freeze any leftover saffron, because it will lose its punch if it's not used within 3 months.

2 tablespoons olive oil

1½ pounds smoked sausage (Polish sausage for a mild flavor; chorizo, linguiça, or andouille if you want it spicy), cut into ½-inch-thick rounds

3 cups chopped chicken breast (½-inch pieces, from about 3 breast halves)

1 cup finely chopped red onion

4 cloves garlic, cut into slivers

1 large red bell pepper, seeded and cut into ½-inch-wide strips

Two 15.5-ounce cans chopped tomatoes, with their juice

½ teaspoon saffron threads, crushed in your palm

1 teaspoon freshly ground black pepper

3 cups converted long-grain rice

6 cups chicken broth

1½ pounds jumbo shrimp

24 littleneck or cherrystone clams, scrubbed

2 cups fresh peas or frozen petite peas, defrosted

4 lemons, cut into wedges, for garnish

1 cup chopped fresh Italian parsley for garnish

## Diva Variation

Refrigerate any leftover paella and toss it with Sherry Vinaigrette (page 214) for a delicious salad the next day.

**1.** In an 8- to 10-quart stockpot, heat the oil over medium-high heat, add the sausage, and cook, stirring a few times, until browned. Add the chicken and cook, stirring a few times, until browned on all sides. Add the onion, garlic, and red pepper and cook, stirring, until softened, 3 to 4 minutes. Stir in the tomatoes, saffron, and black pepper, reduce the heat to medium, and cook down until the tomato juices are almost evaporated and the vegetables are very soft, 5 to 7 minutes.

✻ **DIVA DO-AHEAD:** At this point, you can let cool, cover, and refrigerate for up to 3 days. Gently reheat before continuing.

**2.** Bring the tomato mixture to a simmer and stir in the rice, coating it with the tomato mixture. Add the broth and bring to a boil. Cover, reduce the heat to medium, and simmer for 15 minutes.

**3.** Add the shrimp, clams, and peas, pushing down on the clams so they are underneath the rice mixture. Cover and simmer until the rice is tender, the clams are open, and the shrimp are pink, another 5 to 7 minutes. Discard any clams that haven't opened.

**4.** Transfer the paella to a serving platter and serve, garnished with lemon wedges and chopped parsley.

# Seafood Stuffed Shells

Serves 10 to 12 as a main dish

These creamy shells are filled with seafood and ricotta cheese and topped with a luxurious seafood-flavored cream sauce.

**Two 12-ounce packages large pasta shells, cooked in salted boiling water for 5 minutes and drained**

**2 to 3 tablespoons olive oil, as needed**

**5 tablespoons unsalted butter**

**3 tablespoons all-purpose flour**

**2 cups seafood stock (see The Diva Says), or 1 cup chicken broth and 1 cup bottled clam juice**

**½ cup heavy cream**

**½ pound shrimp, peeled, deveined, and chopped**

**1 pound lump crabmeat, picked over for shells and cartilage**

**2 tablespoons sherry**

**1½ cups ricotta cheese**

**⅛ teaspoon ground nutmeg**

**¼ cup chopped fresh Italian parsley**

**1.** Toss the hot shells with the olive oil and set aside.

**2.** Coat a 13 x 9-inch baking pan with non-stick cooking spray.

**3.** In a 2½-quart saucepan, melt 3 tablespoons of the butter over medium heat and whisk in the flour. When white bubbles form on the surface, cook for another 2 to 3 minutes, whisking. Whisk in the stock and bring to a boil. Remove from the heat and stir in the heavy cream. Spread ¾ cup of the sauce over the bottom of prepared pan.

**4.** In a large skillet over medium heat, melt the remaining 2 tablespoons of butter, then add the shrimp and cook until pink, turning them over several times. Add the crab and sherry and stir to blend. Transfer the seafood mixture and any liquid accumulated in the bottom of the pan to a large bowl. Stir in the ricotta, nutmeg, and parsley until blended. Stuff each of the shells with 2 to 3 tablespoons of the mixture. Set, filling side up, in the prepared pan and pour the remaining sauce over the top.

✳ **DIVA DO-AHEAD:** At this point, you can cover and refrigerate for up to 2 days. Bring to room temperature before continuing.

**5.** Preheat the oven to 350°F. Bake until the sauce is bubbling and the shells are heated through, 30 to 40 minutes.

The Diva Says: My favorite seafood stock is made with Superior Touch Better Than Bouillon Lobster Base. Look for it in the soup aisle with the bouillon cubes at your grocery store, or see Sources (page 669).

# New England Clam Pie

Serves 10

This delicious pie is reminiscent of clam chowder, thick with clams, potatoes, and a creamy sauce and topped with a bacon-studded biscuit crust. You can serve it in a 13 x 9-inch baking dish or two 9-inch round pie plates, 2 inches deep.

8 medium-size red potatoes, scrubbed, steamed or boiled until a knife inserted into the center goes in easily, drained, and cut into ½-inch pieces

6 tablespoons (¾ stick) unsalted butter

1 cup finely chopped onion

1 teaspoon dried thyme

5 tablespoons all-purpose flour

1 cup water

Two 8-ounce bottles clam juice

6 shakes of Tabasco sauce

2 cups fresh corn kernels cut from the cob or frozen corn, defrosted

3 dozen shucked hard-shelled clams, juice reserved and coarsely chopped, or four 8-ounce cans chopped clams, drained and juice reserved

2 cups whole or 2% milk

Salt and freshly ground black pepper to taste (optional)

Bacon Biscuit Crust (recipe follows)

½ cup (1 stick) unsalted butter, melted

**1.** In a 5-quart Dutch oven, melt the butter over medium heat, add the onion and thyme and cook, stirring, until the onion is softened, about 3 minutes. Add the flour and whisk until white bubbles form on the surface. Cook, whisking constantly, for 2 to 3 minutes longer. Gradually add the water and clam juice, whisking until the mixture comes to a boil. Add the cooked potatoes, the Tabasco, corn, and clams and cook for about 5 minutes. Add the milk, bring to a boil, and cook for another 10 minutes, stirring, so the filling doesn't stick to the bottom of the pan. Season with salt and pepper if needed.

☀ **DIVA DO-AHEAD:** At this point, you can let cool, cover, and refrigerate for up to 3 days.

**2.** Preheat the oven to 375°F. Pour the clam filling into a 13 x 9-inch baking dish or two 9-inch deep-dish pie plates and cover with the crust, sealing the edges by crimping them together with the tines of a fork. Brush the crust with the melted butter. Bake until the crust is puffed and golden brown, 20 to 25 minutes. Remove from the oven and serve.

# Bacon Biscuit Crust

Makes enough for one 13 x 9-inch or two 9-inch deep-dish pies

**12 slices bacon, cooked until crisp, drained on paper towels, and crumbled**

**2½ cups all-purpose flour, plus extra to roll out the dough**

**1 tablespoon baking powder**

**1 teaspoon salt**

**1½ cups heavy cream**

**1.** In a large bowl, stir together the bacon, flour, baking powder, and salt. Dribble in the cream a bit at a time, mixing until the dough begins to come together.

**2.** Turn out the dough onto a lightly floured board and roll into a 13 x 9-inch rectangle or two 10-inch round circles, ½ inch thick.

## Diva Variation

If you would like to make individual biscuits, roll or pat the dough to a thickness of ¾ inch, use a biscuit cutter to cut into 2-inch biscuits, and place on a baking sheet lined with parchment, aluminum foil, or a silicone liner. Brush with ½ cup (1 stick) butter, melted, and bake until golden brown, 9 to 12 minutes. Serve immediately.

# Steamed Lobsters

Serves 10 to 12

This is another summer favorite to serve with potato salad, corn on the cob, and cold wine or beer. Since it is definitely finger food, make sure you serve the lobsters outside, so that the mess is kept out of the house. I find that large pots kept simmering on a large outdoor barbecue accommodate the lobsters easily, but you can use your stove top as well. Five 1- to 1¼-pound lobsters will fit into a 10-quart lobster or stockpot. Once the lobsters are steamed, you can serve them immediately or chill and serve cold. I figure one lobster per person, then fill in with lots of delicious sides (see my recommendations below).

**Four 12-ounce bottles light beer, such as Corona (not an ale or a dark lager)**

**4 limes, quartered**

**Ten to twelve 1- to 1¼-pound live lobsters**

**1 pound (4 sticks) unsalted butter, melted**

**1.** Pour two bottles of beer into a 10-quart stockpot, squeeze 2 limes over the beer, cover the pot, and bring to a boil. Plunge 5 or 6 lobsters into the boiling water, cover the pot, and cook, until the lobsters are totally red and the shell softened, about 30 minutes. Repeat the procedure in another pot with the remaining beer, limes, and lobsters.

**2.** Remove the lobsters from the pots.

✳ **DIVA DO-AHEAD:** At this point, you can let cool, cover, and refrigerate overnight to serve chilled.

**3.** Serve immediately for hot lobster or serve chilled. Either way, provide nut-crackers, small seafood forks, and picks to dig out the meat from the shells and serve the melted butter for dipping.

## Suggested Salads and Sides for Lobster

- **Sugar Snap Pea and Bacon Salad** (page 160)
- **Layered Vegetable Salad with Fresh Herb Dressing** (page 158) **or Creamy Dill and Chive Dressing** (page 157)
- **Marinated Orange Salad** (page 167)
- **Caprese Salad** (page 176)
- **Shirley's Classic Coleslaw** (page 186)
- **Dilly Red Potato Salad** (page 193)
- **Mom's Potato Salad** (page 190)
- **Perfect Corn on the Cob** (page 237)
- **Roasted Asparagus** (page 226)
- **Summer Succotash** (page 239)
- **Stuffed Tomatoes** (page 263)

# Lobster Stew

Serves 10 to 12

Lobster is so expensive that serving it to a crowd might break the bank, but this simple stew has lots of other delicious flavors in it to stretch the lobster, making it a more affordable dish. The stew actually improves with age. Try serving it in hollowed-out small, round sourdough loaves on Christmas Eve or for an après-ski party—it's warm, luxurious, and comforting food for a cold winter's night.

**¼ cup (½ stick) unsalted butter**

**¼ cup all-purpose flour**

**2½ cups reconstituted lobster stock (see Sources, page 669), or 1¼ cups chicken broth mixed with 1¼ cups bottled clam juice**

**1½ cups heavy cream**

**¼ cup cream sherry**

**2 pounds small red potatoes, scrubbed, steamed or boiled until a knife inserted into the center goes in easily, drained, and cut into ½-inch pieces**

**4 cups fresh corn kernels cut from the cob or frozen corn, defrosted**

**1½ pounds cooked lobster meat, cut into small pieces**

**½ cup chopped fresh chives for garnish**

**1.** In a 4-quart saucepan over medium heat, melt the butter. Add the flour and whisk until white bubbles form on the surface. Cook, whisking constantly, for another 2 to 3 minutes. Slowly add the stock, whisking until the mixture is smooth and comes to a boil. Stir in the cream and sherry, add the potatoes, corn, and lobster, and bring to a simmer. Reduce the heat to medium-low, and keep warm until ready to serve.

❋ **DIVA DO-AHEAD:** At this point, you can let cool, cover, and refrigerate for up to 2 days. Reheat gently before continuing.

**2.** Serve garnished with the chopped chives.

# Shrimp and Lobster Rolls

Serves 10 to 12

This is perfect picnic or backyard party food, elegant but so simple. The salad can be made the day before, but I don't recommend stuffing the rolls until about 6 hours before serving. You can also stuff this filling into avocado halves or tomatoes for those friends who aren't eating bread these days. Instead of using just lobster for the filling, I've added shrimp, which will help keep the cost down, but by all means use only lobster, shrimp, or crab if that's your preference.

**1 pound cooked lobster meat, cut into ½-inch pieces**

**½ pound cooked shrimp, cut into ½-inch pieces (avoid baby shrimp, which don't have enough flavor)**

**1 cup finely chopped celery**

**1 cup mayonnaise**

**1 teaspoon fresh lemon juice**

**12 hot dog rolls**

**½ cup (1 stick) unsalted butter, melted**

**¼ cup chopped fresh chives**

The Diva Says: My feeling about salads is that the main ingredient—in this case, lobster—should be the star, not the mayonnaise. But that's a personal preference; if you love mayonnaise, then you should add as much as you like.

**1.** In a large bowl, combine the lobster, shrimp, and celery. Stir in the mayonnaise and lemon juice until well blended.

❋ **DIVA DO-AHEAD:** At this point, you can cover and refrigerate for up to 24 hours.

**2.** Preheat the broiler or a griddle. Brush the inside of the rolls with the melted butter (or the outside if you're using the buns that open at the top and have no crusts on the sides), and broil or grill on the buttered side until golden brown. Remove the rolls from the griddle and let cool slightly.

**3.** Stuff the buns with the lobster salad and sprinkle the top of the salad with chives.

❋ **DIVA DO-AHEAD:** At this point, you can wrap the buns in aluminum foil and refrigerate for up to 6 hours.

# Harborside Garlic Herbed Scallops

Serves 10 to 12

This recipe comes from an old Boston restaurant, where they served this as an appetizer while you were deciding what to order. I always thought it was the best part of the meal! Serve as an appetizer or as a main course over a bed of pasta or field greens.

**3 tablespoons olive oil**

**¼ cup dry sherry**

**¼ cup fresh lemon juice**

**3 cloves garlic, minced**

**1 teaspoon dried oregano**

**1½ teaspoons sweet paprika**

**2½ pounds sea scallops, quartered, or bay scallops, left whole**

**1 cup dry bread crumbs or panko (Japanese bread crumbs)**

**¼ cup freshly grated Parmesan cheese**

**6 tablespoons (¾ stick) unsalted butter, melted**

**Lemon wedges for garnish**

**Sprigs fresh oregano or parsley for garnish**

**1.** In a large bowl, whisk together the oil, sherry, lemon juice, garlic, oregano, and paprika until blended. Add the scallops and toss to coat. Transfer the scallops and marinade to a zipper-top plastic bag and seal.

✳ **DIVA DO-AHEAD:** Refrigerate for at least 6 hours or overnight, turning the bag several times.

**2.** Preheat the broiler. Line a rimmed baking sheet with aluminum foil or a silicone liner. Drain the scallops and arrange them on the prepared sheet.

**3.** In small bowl, combine the bread crumbs and cheese. Sprinkle evenly over the scallops and drizzle with the melted butter. Broil until the crumbs are browned and the scallops are cooked through (they should be opaque), about 5 minutes.

**4.** Carefully transfer the scallops to a serving platter and garnish with lemon wedges and oregano sprigs. Serve warm or at room temperature.

# Shrimp Jambalaya

Serves 12 to 14

Jambalaya makes me smile; it is spicy and soothing comfort food all at the same time. It also feeds an army without much work. You can have this on the table in less than an hour. Serve it with a salad and some bread, and you'll look like a genius! This actually keeps well in a covered pot, off the heat, for about 30 minutes. I like to serve it with an assortment of hot sauces.

2 tablespoons vegetable oil

1½ pounds andouille or Polish-style sausage, cut into ½-inch-thick rounds

1 cup chopped onions

1 cup seeded and chopped green bell peppers

1 cup chopped celery

3 cloves garlic, minced

½ teaspoon dried thyme

½ teaspoon dried oregano

½ teaspoon dried basil

½ teaspoon freshly ground black pepper

¼ teaspoon cayenne pepper

1 bay leaf

One 15.5-ounce can chopped tomatoes, with their juice

6 cups chicken broth

2 cups converted long-grain rice

1½ pounds medium-size shrimp, peeled and deveined

1½ cups chopped scallions (white and tender green parts) for garnish

**1.** In an 8-quart stockpot, heat the oil over medium-high heat, then cook the sausage until it begins to render some of its fat, about 5 minutes. Remove all but 2 table-spoons of the fat from the pan and add the onion, bell pepper, celery, garlic, thyme, oregano, basil, black pepper, cayenne, and bay leaf. Cook, stirring, until the vegetables are translucent, about 5 minutes. Stir in the tomatoes and cook until some of the liquid evaporates, about 4 minutes. Add the broth and bring to a boil.

❋ **DIVA DO-AHEAD:** At this point, you can let cool, cover, and refrigerate for up to 3 days. Gently reheat before continuing.

**2.** Stir in the rice and cook for 15 minutes over medium heat. Add the shrimp and cook until they turn pink, another 3 to 5 minutes. Serve immediately or turn off the heat, cover, and let stand for up to 30 minutes before serving.

**3.** Garnish the jambalaya with chopped scallions and serve with an assortment of hot sauces.

# Peel and Eat Shrimp

Serves 10 to 12

This is a meal to eat with your hands—perfect for an informal dinner with friends or family or a backyard picnic. Make sure you have lots of bowls for the shells, as well extra napkins and wet towels for wiping sticky fingers and faces. I like to serve these with cocktail sauce, melted butter, and Artichoke Rémoulade Sauce (page 494), so people can take their pick. Round out the menu with pasta or potato salad and mixed greens. The shrimp can be served hot or cold, depending upon your preference.

**Four 12-ounce bottles beer (I like to use a lighter beer, rather than ale or dark beer)**

**½ cup Old Bay seasoning**

**4 lemons, quartered**

**4 to 5 pounds large shrimp**

**1.** Pour the beer into a 10-quart stockpot. Add the Old Bay, squeeze the juice from the lemons into the pot, add the rinds, and stir to blend. Bring to a boil and add the shrimp. Cover the pot, return to a boil, and remove from the heat.

**2.** Let the shrimp sit in the beer for another 10 minutes. Drain the shrimp and serve.

✳ **DIVA DO-AHEAD:** At this point, you can let cool, place in zipper-top plastic bags, and refrigerate for up to 24 hours before serving cold.

# Garlic Prawns

Serves 10

This succulent dish of shrimp and garlic is delicious as an appetizer, but it's also wonderful as a main course for a buffet. You can serve it over pasta or all by itself with lots of crusty bread to dip into the sauce. I sometimes serve it in a hollowed-out long sourdough loaf, which I cut into ¼-inch-thick slices, so that everyone can grab a chunk of bread topped with shrimp. Another dramatic presentation is to roast a whole beef tenderloin, slice it, then distribute the prawns over the roast beef for an awesome surf and turf! This is also delicious made with half shrimp and half sea scallops, or half shrimp and half lump crabmeat.

> 1 cup (2 sticks) unsalted butter
>
> 8 cloves garlic, minced
>
> 1 tablespoon Old Bay seasoning
>
> 2 tablespoons fresh lemon juice
>
> ¼ cup cream sherry (see The Diva Says)
>
> ¼ cup chopped fresh parsley
>
> 2 pounds jumbo shrimp, peeled and deveined

**1.** In a large skillet, melt the butter over low heat, add the garlic, and cook until softened, about 10 minutes—but don't let the garlic brown.

**2.** Add the Old Bay and cook for another 2 minutes, stirring constantly so the garlic and spices don't burn. Add the lemon juice and sherry and bring to a boil. Reduce the heat to low, simmer for 1 minute, and remove from the heat.

✳ **DIVA DO-AHEAD:** At this point, you can let cool, cover, and refrigerate for up to a week. Reheat gently before continuing.

**3.** Add the parsley and shrimp to the garlic butter and toss together. Cook over medium heat until the shrimp turn completely pink. Serve immediately or at room temperature.

## The Diva Says:

Whether to use dry or cream sherry is purely a personal preference. Cream sherry has a sweeter and more full flavor than dry. Gallo makes a nice, reasonably priced sherry called Sheffield Cellars.

# Cajun Shrimp Barbecue

Serves 10

This spicy dish is terrific to serve over rice or pasta, or as an appetizer. You can make the seasoned butter ahead of time, then toss the shrimp with it just before serving. This may not be authentically Cajun, but I've had similar dishes in little bistros in the French Quarter of New Orleans. Make sure you have crusty French bread on hand to soak up the sauce.

1 cup (2 sticks) unsalted butter

¼ cup olive oil

8 cloves garlic, minced

2 teaspoons dried oregano

1 teaspoon dried thyme

½ teaspoon freshly ground black pepper

½ teaspoon cayenne pepper

1½ teaspoons sweet paprika

¼ cup Worcestershire sauce

½ cup fresh lemon juice

3 pounds large shrimp, peeled and deveined

½ cup chopped fresh parsley for garnish

1. In a large skillet, heat the butter with the oil over medium heat until the butter melts and cook the garlic, stirring, until softened, about 3 minutes. Add the oregano, thyme, black pepper, cayenne, and paprika and cook for another 2 minutes, stirring so the spices don't burn. Add the Worcestershire and lemon juice and simmer for 1 minute.

❋ **DIVA DO-AHEAD:** At this point, you can let cool, cover, and refrigerate for up to a week. Gently reheat before continuing.

2. Add the shrimp and cook, stirring, until they turn completely pink, about 8 minutes.

3. Serve garnished with the parsley. These shrimp are best served warm, but you can also serve them at room temperature.

# Athens Shrimp with Feta and Basil

Serves 10 to 12

This delicious, Mediterranean-inspired shrimp dish is so easy to put together. I serve it as a main course with orzo or rice, but you can also serve it with toothpicks as an appetizer.

**2 tablespoons olive oil**

**1 cup coarsely chopped onions**

**2 cloves garlic, minced**

**1 tablespoon chopped fresh oregano**

**1 tablespoon chopped fresh basil**

**½ cup dry white wine or dry vermouth**

**One 32-ounce can chopped tomatoes, with their juice**

**1 teaspoon sugar**

**1½ teaspoons salt**

**1 teaspoon freshly ground black pepper**

**2 pounds large shrimp, peeled and deveined**

**¾ pound feta cheese, crumbled**

**8 scallions (white and tender green parts), chopped, for garnish**

**½ cup chopped fresh Italian parsley**

**1.** In a large skillet, heat the oil over medium heat, add the onions and garlic, and cook, stirring, until softened, about 3 minutes. Add the oregano and basil and cook another minute. Add the wine, bring to a boil, and continue boiling for 2 min- utes. Add the tomatoes, sugar, salt, and pepper, reduce the heat to medium, and simmer until reduced and thickened, 20 to 30 minutes.

✳ **DIVA DO-AHEAD:** At this point, you can let cool, cover, and refrigerate for up to 5 days or freeze for 2 months. Defrost before continuing.

**2.** Arrange the shrimp in an ovenproof serving dish and top with the tomato sauce. Sprinkle the feta evenly on top.

✳ **DIVA DO-AHEAD:** At this point, you can cover and refrigerate for up to 2 days.

**3.** Preheat oven to 350°F. Bake until the shrimp are pink and cooked through and the cheese is melted, about 15 minutes.

**4.** Remove from the oven and serve warm, garnished with the scallions and parsley.

## Diva Variation

This treatment also works well with red snapper and halibut, but the fish will need about 5 more minutes in the oven.

# Buffalo Shrimp

Serves 10 to 12

This hot and spicy shrimp dish is a takeoff on Buffalo chicken wings. Serve them as a main course, on a bed of Nutty Blue Cheese Coleslaw (see page 186), or as an appetizer, either grilled on skewers or sautéed. If you are serving these as an appetizer, make sure you serve them on a platter, with a small bowl of Old-Fashioned Blue Cheese Dressing (page 215) for dipping and some celery sticks to cut the heat.

**1 cup (2 sticks) unsalted butter**

**¾ cup Frank's RedHot Cayenne Pepper Sauce**

**3 pounds jumbo shrimp, peeled and deveined, with tail section left on**

**1.** In a 2-quart saucepan over medium heat, slowly heat the butter and hot sauce together until the butter melts. Remove from the heat and let cool.

❋ **DIVA DO-AHEAD:** At this point, you can cover and refrigerate for up to a week. Gently reheat before continuing.

**2.** Soak wooden skewers in water for 1 hour. Divide the butter sauce between 2 bowls. Skewer the shrimp (4-inch skewers for 1 shrimp, 8-inch for 4 shrimp). Brush with some of the warm butter and discard any remaining butter.

❋ **DIVA DO-AHEAD:** At this point, you can cover and refrigerate for up to 24 hours.

**3.** Build a hot charcoal fire or preheat the broiler or a gas grill for 10 minutes and broil the shrimp on a baking sheet lined with aluminum foil or grill until pink, about 2 minutes per side, basting each cooked side with the warm butter in the second bowl.

**4.** Remove the skewers from the grill or broiler and remove the shrimp from the skewers. Serve immediately, and don't forget to provide toothpicks.

## Diva Variation

To do this really fast, melt the butter and hot sauce in a large skillet over medium heat, add the shrimp, and cook, stirring, until completely pink, about 5 minutes. Transfer the shrimp to a large platter and top with the sauce.

# Asian Chili Shrimp

Serves 10 to 12

The Diva loves these shrimp, with their sweet-hot, spicy flavor and quick-as-a-wink cooking time. For a main course, serve them on a bed of Pacific Rim Slaw (page 187) with sticky rice as an accompaniment. If you are serving them as an appetizer, offer a fresh batch of the marinade for dipping.

**2 tablespoons canola oil**

**2 teaspoons peeled and grated fresh ginger**

**3 cloves garlic, minced**

**1 teaspoon Asian garlic-chili oil (found in the Asian section at your grocer)**

**2 teaspoons sugar**

**2 tablespoons rice wine or seasoned rice vinegar**

**¼ cup soy sauce**

**¼ cup ketchup**

**2½ pounds large shrimp, peeled and deveined, with tail section left on**

**8 scallions (white and tender green parts), chopped, for garnish**

## Keeping It Safe and Tasty

When using a marinade with raw foods, I sometimes make a fresh batch to brush onto the food while it's grilling. This helps intensify and freshen the flavor of the finished dish.

**1.** In a large bowl, whisk together the canola oil, ginger, garlic, garlic-chili oil, sugar, rice wine, soy sauce, and ketchup until blended. Pour into a zipper-top plastic bag. Add the shrimp, seal, and turn the bag so that the shrimp are coated with the marinade.

✳ **DIVA DO-AHEAD:** Refrigerate for at least 6 and up to 24 hours, turning the bag several times.

**2.** Soak wooden skewers in water for 1 hour. Build a hot charcoal fire or preheat a gas grill or the broiler for 10 minutes.

**3.** Drain the shrimp and thread 4 onto each skewer, leaving space between them. Broil the shrimp on a baking sheet lined with aluminum foil or grill until pink and cooked through, 2 to 3 minutes per side.

✳ **DIVA DO-AHEAD:** At this point, you can let cool, arrange on a serving platter, cover, and refrigerate overnight. Remove from the refrigerator about 15 minutes before serving.

**4.** Serve warm or cold on a platter, garnished with the scallions.

# Southwestern Chili Shrimp

Serves 10 to 12

These shrimp, with their margarita flavor, will be a hit at any party.

2 tablespoons canola oil

¼ cup fresh lime juice

¼ cup orange juice

¼ cup gold tequila

2 teaspoons ground cumin

1 teaspoon pure ancho chile powder

2 cloves garlic, minced

¼ cup finely chopped fresh cilantro, plus extra for garnish

2½ pounds large shrimp, peeled and deveined, with tail section left on

4 limes, cut into wedges, for garnish

## Chili-Glazed Shrimp

The glazed spicy shrimp above and on page 378 are prepared in two dramatically different ways, one with an Asian flavor and the other with a Southwestern kick. They are a nice addition to an appetizer buffet or to serve as a main course. Terrific warm, they can also be served cold; just grill them the day before.

**1.** In a large bowl, whisk together the oil, citrus juices, tequila, cumin, chile powder, garlic, and cilantro until blended. Pour into a zipper-top plastic bag, add the shrimp, seal, and turn over to coat the shrimp.

✳ **DIVA DO-AHEAD:** Refrigerate for at least 6 and up to 24 hours.

**2.** Soak wooden skewers in water for 1 hour. Build a hot charcoal fire or preheat a gas grill or broiler for 10 minutes.

**3.** Drain the shrimp and thread 4 shrimp onto each skewer, leaving a little space between them. Grill the shrimp or broil on a baking sheet lined with aluminum foil until pink and cooked through, 2 to 3 minutes per side.

✳ **DIVA DO-AHEAD:** At this point, you can let cool, arrange on a serving platter, cover, and refrigerate overnight. Remove from the refrigerator about 15 minutes before serving.

**4.** Serve the shrimp warm or cold on a platter, garnished with lime wedges and chopped cilantro.

# Beef

**There aren't many entrées that can rival** the dramatic appearance of a freshly sliced roast brought to the table. This chapter will explore the best cuts of beef to serve to your company and the best ways to prepare them, with a minimum amount of last-minute fussing.

It's always difficult to judge just how many pounds of meat you will need for your company. My rule of thumb is ⅓ pound per person of a boneless piece of meat, and ½ pound per person for a bone-in cut. I always add another 1½ servings to each dinner, to make up for the person who takes 5 slices of beef tenderloin instead of 2!

## Cuts of Beef for Entertaining

*Beef tenderloin:* This is the whole piece from which filet mignon is cut. Possibly the easiest cut of meat to roast, it is very tender, but because it lacks fat, it needs to be marinated before roasting to give it a flavor boost. Beef tenderloin can be very expensive, but there is practically no waste on the roast. You are paying for usable beef, rather than a lot of fat and bone weight. Like pork tenderloin, this cut has a layer of silver skin under the fat, which will need to be trimmed away before roasting. This is my favorite choice for a large dinner party. It can be roasted ahead of time, and then served cold or at room temperature; or it can be roasted just before serving. Tenderloin steaks are terrific for skewering and grilling, too.

*Rolled rib roast* or *rib eye,* sometimes called a *Spencer roast:* This roast is nothing more than the standing rib roast that has been removed from the bone, rolled, and tied. This will give you a compact piece of meat to roast, without the bones, but it will be more expensive than the bone-in roast.

*New York strip, top loin,* or *strip roast:* This piece of meat is from the loin, which makes it a tender and elegant choice for a party entrée, with no bones to fuss with and a minimum amount of fat. New York strip steaks, from the same cut, are delicious grilled.

*Sirloin roast:* Not as tender as the roasts described above, but more economical, sirloin roasts can be braised or marinated and then roasted. The most popular cuts are sirloin tip or tri-tip (sometimes called triangle sirloin). Sirloin has a deep, beefy flavor, and when roasted or grilled, it will give you a satisfying entrée.

*Round roast:* Eye of the round is a boneless roast with almost no fat, which means it will need to be braised or roasted at a low temperature to ensure that it is tender. I find

## Where to Shop

Most of us don't have unlimited funds to spend on beef for our parties, so I recommend shopping at wholesale clubs like Costco. They sell whole beef tenderloin, rib eyes, standing rib roasts, sirloins, and New York strip roasts for a fraction of what they sell for in the supermarket. The meat is sold in vacuum-packed plastic (called Cryovac). You will have to wash the meat and trim it yourself.

## What's Your Grade?

Beef comes in grades: Prime is the highest grade, Choice is the next-highest, and Select is at the bottom of the scale. I recommend buying only Prime or Choice. Your market is required to label its meat grades on the package, so inspect them carefully. You will pay more for Prime or Choice, but the proof is in the taste and tenderness.

the eye of the round to be a nice substitute for whole roasted tenderloin if I need to economize. It can be sliced thin and served with your choice of sauce or gravy.

***Rump roast:*** Rump is a flavorful, boneless roast that needs special care so it doesn't dry out when cooked. Roast it at 325°F until medium-rare for sandwiches, or for roast beef to serve at a casual dinner party.

***Flank steak:*** Flank steaks are delicious when marinated, grilled, and sliced thinly across the grain. They have very little fat, making them a nice choice for those who are watching their red meat intake. You can also cut them across the grain while they are still raw, then marinate the slices and grill them on skewers.

***London broil:*** There are lots of cuts in your market that may be marked "London broil." Usually they are thick round steaks that need to be marinated for at least 12 hours before they are grilled and sliced thin. My favorite cut of London broil is actually a top sirloin because of its meaty flavor; it has more marbling than round steaks. Apply a dry rub to top sirloin and let it sit overnight, then rub with olive oil before grilling, or marinate it overnight and grill before serving.

Top sirloin and flank steak are both nice served warm, cold, or at room temperature, making them the Diva's favorites.

# Cutting Up Beef

I am a big advocate of carving a whole roast, steak, or other cut of meat in the kitchen, without a lot of fanfare. That way, if you make a mistake, you can cover it up with parsley or another garnish. Admittedly, a whole roast looks gorgeous coming out of the oven, but slicing it at the dinner table is a recipe for disaster—better to slice and arrange everything on a platter in the kitchen. If your significant other just has to carve at the table, make sure that he or she has the right utensils: a large meat fork, a sharpened carving knife, a platter, and a cutting board with grooves in it that will catch the juices from the roast once it is cut.

## Diva Doneness Test

I am a medium-rare girl, but many people prefer their meat rare or medium-well. The best way to gauge doneness is with an instant-read meat thermometer. I have tested all the recipes for a medium-rare to medium degree of doneness: The meat is still pink in the center, but it's not mooing at you. As I have said elsewhere, this is your party, so you decide whether you need to cook the meat a shorter or longer amount of time, but please, please, don't cook beef tenderloin to well done. Although it's an incredibly tender piece of meat, the longer you cook it, the tougher it will become.

# Roast Beef Tenderloin

Serves 12 to 14

Like other recipes in this book, this is a master recipe with many variations, depending on your choice of marinade. I love to serve beef tenderloin because there is almost no waste and it is always tender. It can also be roasted the day before the party, then served at room temperature with your choice of sauce. Some good choices are Do-Ahead Gravy (page 488), Parsley Pesto (page 473), Simple Au Jus (page 489), and Bourbon-Peppercorn Sauce for Beef (page 489). Many wholesale clubs like Costco sell whole beef tenderloins for about $50 and since one will serve about 12 to 14 people as a main course, it's really not as big a splurge as you might think, so don't rule it out altogether.

Because beef tenderloin has little or no fat, it needs a bit of help in the flavor department, which is why marinating is essential. I've included my favorite marinades on pages 393 to 397, but you can also dry rub the beef overnight with Grandma's Rub (page 398) if you like.

To trim the roast, remove the silver skin, a tendon sheath that surrounds the center portion of the meat. This is easily done with a sharp knife; cut close to the skin and peel it off the meat. Also remove any fat extending down the roast and connecting a thin strip of meat to the center portion. I prefer to cut off this thin strip of meat and freeze it for kabobs and stir-fries because it cooks much faster than the rest of the tenderloin. If you decide to roast this piece, remove it from the pan after it registers 130°F on an instant-read meat thermometer and cover it with aluminum foil.

The trimmed meat should weigh about 5 to 6 pounds. The tapered portion of the roast will cook more quickly than the center. To help prevent this, fold the tapered piece under itself, and it will cook to medium, not medium-rare. I like to include this portion for those who don't like their meat pink.

Roast your beef in a heavy-duty roasting pan, which will give you some caramelized drippings in the bottom. With the help of some wine or another liquid, you can turn these luscious drippings into a nice au jus (see page 489) or gravy. Tying the roast with cotton string every 1 1/2 inches will ensure that it cooks evenly and the meat stays compact for easy carving. You can ask your butcher to do this for you.

**One 5- to 6-pound trimmed beef tenderloin, tapered end tucked under and roast tied with cotton string every 1½ inches**

**2 cups marinade of your choice (pages 393 to 397)**

**1.** Put the tenderloin in a 2-gallon zipper-top plastic bag, pour in the marinade, and seal.

❋ **DIVA DO-AHEAD:** At this point, refrigerate for at least 24 and up to 36 hours. Bring to room temperature before continuing.

**2.** Preheat the oven to 400°F.

**3.** Drain the meat and pat it dry with paper towels. Place in a heavy-duty roasting pan and roast until an instant-read meat thermometer inserted in the thickest part registers 135°F, 45 to 55 minutes. (When taken out at this temperature, your roast will be medium-rare to medium when it finishes resting.)

**4.** Remove the meat from the oven, cover with aluminum foil, and let rest for at least 15 minutes.

❋ **DIVA DO-AHEAD:** At this point, you can let cool completely, cover, and refrigerate overnight. Bring to room temperature before continuing.

**5.** Clip the strings from the meat and slice thinly, arranging the slices on a platter according to their degree of doneness. Serve with the sauce of your choice.

# New York Strip Roast 🍷🥩

Serves 10

The New York strip is a beautiful piece of meat that will make a stunning main course for your party. The boneless meat is simple to carve and every piece is tender and succulent. Since this roast does have some fat on it, you don't need to marinate it, but it benefits from a dry rub a day before cooking. A sauce is nice to serve on the side; whether it's Simple Au Jus (page 489) or gravy or something more ambitious, such as Fiorentina Sauce (page 474), Balsamic Vinegar Syrup (page 480), Cabernet-Thyme Reduction Sauce (page 490), or Port Wine Sauce (page 492), each will give your roast nice pizzazz.

**One 7-pound trimmed New York strip roast**

**6 cloves garlic, minced**

**1 tablespoon salt**

**2 teaspoons coarsely ground black pepper**

**1 tablespoon dried thyme**

**2 tablespoons olive oil**

**1.** Pat the roast dry with paper towels and place on a large sheet of waxed paper or plastic wrap.

**2.** In a small bowl, blend together the garlic, salt, pepper, thyme, and oil until it forms a paste. Rub this into the roast, using the waxed paper or plastic wrap to catch anything that falls off; then wrap up the roast.

✳ **DIVA DO-AHEAD:** At this point, refrigerate for at least 1 hour and up to 24 hours. Bring to room temperature before continuing.

**3.** Preheat the oven to 400°F. Remove the covering, place the roast on a rack in a heavy-duty roasting pan, and roast for 15 minutes. Reduce the oven temperature to 325°F and continue roasting until an instant-read meat thermometer inserted into the thickest part of the meat registers 125°F, about another 45 minutes. (This will give you a medium-rare to medium roast—I think of it as the "something for everyone" roast.)

**4.** Remove the roast from the oven, cover with aluminum foil, and let rest for at least 20 minutes.

✳ **DIVA DO-AHEAD:** At this point, you can let cool completely, cover, and refrigerate overnight. Bring to room temperature before slicing.

Cut into ½-inch-thick slices and serve warm or at room temperature.

# Santa Maria Barbecue Tri-Tip Roast ⬛⬛⬛

Serves 10

A tri-tip roast is sometimes called a triangle sirloin. Your butcher can roll and tie two together for you to make this spicy and delicious taste of Santa Maria, a town near Santa Barbara, California. Traditionally, this dish is prepared over an outdoor grill, but you can achieve terrific results in your oven as well. The roast can be thinly sliced and served with refried beans, rice, tortillas, guacamole, and cheese for a fajita bar, or you can use it for sandwiches.

**Two 1- to 1½-pound tri-tip roasts, tied together**

**2 teaspoons sweet paprika**

**½ teaspoon chili powder**

**2 teaspoons firmly packed dark brown sugar**

**2 cloves garlic, minced**

**½ teaspoon dry mustard**

**1½ teaspoons salt**

**½ teaspoon freshly ground black pepper**

**1.** Pat roast dry with paper towels and lay on a piece of plastic wrap or waxed paper.

**2.** In a small bowl, combine the paprika, chili powder, brown sugar, garlic, dry mustard, salt, and pepper. Spread the rub all over the roast, using the plastic wrap to help roll it in the seasonings.

✳ **DIVA DO-AHEAD:** At this point, you can cover and refrigerate for up to 2 days.

**3.** Preheat the oven to 325°F.

**4.** Place the roast on a rack in a heavy-duty roasting pan and roast until an instant-read meat thermometer inserted into the thickest part registers 135°F, 35 to 40 minutes. The meat will be medium-rare. Remove from the oven, cover loosely with aluminum foil, and let rest for 15 minutes.

✳ **DIVA DO-AHEAD:** At this point, you can let the roast cool completely, cover, and refrigerate overnight. Bring to room temperature before continuing.

Slice the roast thinly on the diagonal and serve warm or at room temperature.

## Rubs and Marinades for Tri-Tip

Try these other tri-tip rubs and marinades: Grandma's Rub (page 398), All-Purpose Dry Rub for Pork or Beef (page 426), Old Bay seasoning, Garlic-Herb Marinade (page 393), Soy-Ginger Marinade (page 394), Carne Asada Marinade (page 397), and Cabernet Marinade (page 393).

# Beef Kabobs

Serves 10

For appetizers, serve kabobs on a bed of field greens or shredded lettuce, surrounding bowls of dipping sauces, on a large platter. Make sure you have a plate nearby for the discarded skewers.

To serve as a main course, mound rice on a large serving platter or casserole dish, remove the meat from the skewers, and arrange in rows across the rice. Or arrange the beef over grilled vegetables on a serving platter. If you are serving a summer supper, toss field greens and arrange the meat over the salad.

---

**3 pounds beef sirloin, trimmed of any fat and cut into 1-inch cubes**

**1½ to 2 cups marinade of your choice (see pages 393 to 397)**

---

**1.** Place the beef cubes in a zipper-top plastic bag, pour in the marinade, and seal.

✳ **DIVA DO-AHEAD:** At this point, refrigerate for at least 4 and up to 24 hours.

**2.** Soak wooden skewers in water for 1 hour. Drain the meat and discard the marinade.

**3.** Build a hot charcoal fire or preheat a gas grill or the broiler for 10 minutes. Thread the beef onto skewers, spacing the pieces ¼ inch apart for even cooking. If you're broiling, place the skewers on a broiler pan with a rack. Broil or grill for 5 to 8 minutes total for medium-rare to medium, turning once during the cooking.

**4.** Remove the beef from the skewers and serve immediately or at room temperature.

## Kabobs for a Crowd

You will need about 3½ pounds of meat to serve as a main course for 12 people, or 2 pounds of meat for skewered appetizers. Great choices for kabobs would be 1-inch pieces of top sirloin or thin slices of marinated flank steak. The flank steak is the way to go for one-bite satay-type appetizers, while the sirloin beef kabobs work best as an entrée to serve over a huge platter of grilled vegetables or pilaf.

If you are using wooden skewers for your satay or kabobs, make sure you soak them in water for at least half an hour, so they don't burn when you cook the meat. When serving kabobs as an entrée, I usually remove them from the skewers and lay the meat across the platter so they look as if they are still on the skewers. Satay can be left on the skewers, though I recommend that you put only one bite on each skewer; otherwise, your guests will spend the evening trying to get the meat off.

# Beef Satay

Serves 10

A traditional Indonesian satay consists of thinly sliced meat, fish, or poultry grilled on skewers and served with a peanut sauce. It has inspired many variations. You can make these delicious bites either on the grill or under your broiler. Choose a marinade and sauce that please you. My favorite sauce for this dish is Pacific Rim Peanut Sauce (page 481). To make it easier to slice the meat thinly, freeze it first for 45 minutes, so that it is firm.

**2 pounds flank steak, trimmed of any fat and silver skin and sliced against the grain into ⅛-inch-thick slices**

**1½ to 2 cups marinade of your choice (see pages 393 to 397)**

**1.** Put the steak in a zipper-top plastic bag, pour the marinade over, and seal.

✳ **DIVA DO-AHEAD:** At this point, refrigerate for at least 4 and up to 12 hours.

**2.** Soak wooden skewers in water for 1 hour. Drain the meat, discarding the marinade.

**3.** Build a hot charcoal fire or preheat a gas grill or the broiler for 10 minutes. Thread the beef onto skewers (use 1 slice per skewer). If broiling, place on a broiler pan with a rack. Broil or grill for 1 minute on each side. Serve immediately or at room temperature.

# Grilled or Broiled Flank Steak

Serves 10

Grilled flank steak is a total no-brainer as far as I'm concerned; it needs to marinate overnight, you can grill it ahead of time, then slice it right before serving for a delicious entrée. Whether you prepare your own marinade, use one of the recipes on pages 393 to 397, or pour a favorite store-bought brand, you need only add a couple of side dishes and presto! You have a wonderful meal anyone would be delighted to share.

---

**Three 1-pound flank steaks, trimmed of any fat and silver skin**

**1½ to 2 cups marinade of your choice (see pages 393 to 397)**

---

**1.** Put each steak into a zipper-top plastic bag. Divide the marinade evenly among the bags and seal.

❋ **DIVA DO-AHEAD:** At this point, refrigerate for at least 4 and up to 24 hours, turning the bags occasionally.

**2.** Drain steak and discard the marinade.

**3.** Build a hot charcoal fire or preheat a gas grill or broiler for 10 minutes. If broiling, place the steaks on a broiler pan with a rack. Broil or grill for 3 to 4 minutes per side for medium-rare to medium. Let rest for 10 minutes, then slice very thinly on the diagonal against the grain. Serve warm or at room temperature.

---

## Suggestions for Serving Flank Steak

Slice and garnish with: Balsamic Vinegar Syrup (page 480), Fiorentina Sauce (page 474), Perfectly Caramelized Onions (page 244), Roasted Wild Mushroom Salad (page 163), Herb-Roasted Tomatoes (page 127), or Bruschetta Salsa (page 476).

## The Taco/Fajita Bar

A terrific way to entertain is to set up a taco or fajita bar. Grill steak, slice it thin, and serve with warm flour tortillas, sautéed onions and green peppers, guacamole, sour cream, salsa fresca, shredded cheddar cheese, and refried beans. You can also do this with shredded or sliced grilled chicken or pulled roasted pork.

# Broiled or Grilled Top Sirloin

Serves 10 to 12

Sirloin is another excellent choice for a grilled entrée when you're entertaining because it marinates well, and you can prepare it ahead of time and serve it either warm or at room temperature. The steak goes well with Fiorentina Sauce (page 474) or Bruschetta Salsa (page 476); or choose another sauce that you like. Roasted Wild Mushroom Salad (page 163) and Perfectly Caramelized Onions (page 244) make nice garnishes. For a family-style platter, serve the sliced meat with roasted potatoes and sautéed or roasted mushrooms. Sliced tomatoes or a green salad will round out this meal.

**One 3- to 4-pound top sirloin, 1 inch thick**

**1½ to 2 cups marinade of your choice (see pages 393 to 397)**

**1.** Put the steak in a 2-gallon zipper-top plastic bag, pour over the marinade, and seal.

✳ **DIVA DO-AHEAD:** At this point, refrigerate steak for at least 4 and up to 24 hours, turning occasionally.

**2.** Drain steak and discard the marinade.

**3.** Build a hot charcoal fire or preheat a gas grill or the broiler for 10 minutes. If broiling, place the steak on a broiler pan with a rack. Broil or grill the steak for 4 to 5 minutes per side for medium-rare to medium. Let rest for 10 minutes, then thinly slice on the diagonal.

## The Diva Says:

The cut of meat sold as "London broil" is typically a thick round steak, which is fairly tough and needs to be marinated for at least 12 hours, then sliced very thinly after cooking.

## Grilled Steak

Steaks can be the star of a backyard cookout, but they can be served as the main course for an indoor party, too. My favorite steaks for entertaining are flank steak and top sirloin because they can be thinly sliced and yield a nice number of servings. In addition, these steaks can be marinated in advance and even grilled the day before serving, then brought to room temperature. That way, your main course is completed, except for the slicing, and you can concentrate your efforts on other parts of the meal.

# MARINADES AND CRUSTS

**Marinades are flavor enhancers** for beef, lamb, pork, poultry, and seafood. Soy-based marinades actually act as a brine for certain cuts of meat, helping them become tender and juicy when cooked. Other marinades contain acids, such as lemon juice or vinegar, which help break down the protein in the meat and make it more tender.

That being said, you can overdo a marinade; I recommend you marinate beef, lamb, or pork for only up to 24 hours and chicken and seafood for no more than 6 hours.

Crusts are patted onto the outside of the raw meat. They are seared onto the meat during the cooking process, so that when you taste the meat, you taste the crust.

## Garlic-Herb Marinade

Makes about 1½ cups (enough for 4 pounds of meat)

This soy-based marinade is great for roasts as well as steaks and kabobs. After a long soak in the marinade, the meat will be tender and juicy, no matter which cut of beef you try. This is also great with lamb and pork.

**½ cup olive oil**

**2 tablespoons red wine vinegar**

**½ cup soy sauce**

**4 cloves garlic, minced**

**2 teaspoons dried thyme**

**1 bay leaf**

**1 teaspoon freshly ground black pepper**

In a small glass bowl, whisk together all the ingredients.

❋ **DIVA DO-AHEAD:** At this point, you can cover and refrigerate for up to 5 days.

Soak the meat in the marinade for at least 8 and up to 36 hours.

## Cabernet Marinade

Makes about 2 cups (enough for 6 pounds of meat)

This rich marinade gets its character from the full-bodied flavor of Cabernet Sauvignon and a little sweetness from the honey, which helps create a bit of a caramelized crust on the meat. Try it with lamb or pork as well as beef.

**1 cup Cabernet Sauvignon**

**⅓ cup olive oil**

**2 tablespoons honey**

**2 teaspoons dried thyme**

**1½ teaspoons salt**

**1 teaspoon freshly ground black pepper**

In a medium-size glass bowl, whisk together all the ingredients.

❋ **DIVA DO-AHEAD:** At this point, you can cover and refrigerate for up to 5 days.

Soak the meat in the marinade for at least 8 and up to 36 hours.

## Soy-Ginger Marinade

Makes about 1½ cups (enough for 4 pounds of meat)

This taste of Asia is terrific for marinating beef tenderloin and other cuts of beef, lamb, pork, or poultry. If you would like to brush some on during the cooking process, make an extra batch to apply once the meat has seared on all sides.

- **⅔ cup soy sauce**
- **2 cloves garlic, minced**
- **1 tablespoon peeled and grated fresh ginger**
- **¼ cup firmly packed light brown sugar**
- **¼ cup rice wine or seasoned rice vinegar**
- **¼ cup vegetable oil**

In a small bowl, whisk together all of the ingredients.

✳ **DIVA DO-AHEAD:** At this point, you can cover and refrigerate for up to 5 days.

Soak the beef, lamb, or pork in the marinade for least 8 and up to 36 hours; marinate chicken or seafood for at least 30 minutes and up to 8 hours.

## Marinade Provençal

Makes about 2 cups (enough for 6 pounds of meat)

Featuring the flavors of southern France, this marinade will enhance beef, lamb, or poultry.

- **1 cup olive oil**
- **⅔ cup Dijon mustard**
- **4 cloves garlic, minced**
- **¼ cup white wine vinegar**
- **1 tablespoon dried *herbes de Provence***
- **1½ teaspoons salt**
- **1 teaspoon freshly ground black pepper**

In a medium-size bowl, whisk together all the ingredients.

✳ **DIVA DO-AHEAD:** At this point, you can cover and refrigerate for up to 5 days.

Soak beef or lamb in the marinade for at least 8 and up to 36 hours; marinate poultry or seafood for at least 2 and up to 8 hours.

## Teriyaki Marinade

Makes 2 cups (enough for 6 pounds of meat)

This soy, garlic, and ginger marinade gives beef, pork, poultry, and seafood a sweet and salty taste that is almost addictive. Use the marinade for foods that will be grilled directly on the rack or on skewers.

- **2 tablespoons vegetable oil**
- **3 cloves garlic, minced**
- **2 teaspoons peeled and grated fresh ginger**
- **1½ cups soy sauce**
- **⅓ cup firmly packed light brown sugar**
- **¼ cup rice wine or seasoned rice vinegar**
- **6 scallions (white and tender green parts), chopped**
- **3 tablespoons sesame seeds, toasted (see page 83)**
- **2 teaspoons toasted sesame oil**

**1.** In a 2-quart saucepan, heat the vegetable oil over medium heat; add the garlic and ginger and cook, stirring, for 2 minutes. Add the soy sauce, brown sugar, and rice wine and stir to dissolve the brown sugar. Bring to a boil and remove from the heat.

**2.** Stir in the scallions, sesame seeds, and sesame oil. Cool to room temperature.

✳ **DIVA DO-AHEAD:** At this point, you can cover and refrigerate for up to 3 days.

Soak beef and pork in the marinade for at least 2 and up to 8 hours; marinate poultry for at least 1 hour and up to 3 hours; marinate seafood for at least 30 minutes and up to 2 hours.

## Southwestern Marinade

Makes about 1½ cups (enough for 4 pounds of meat)

Flavored with cilantro, cumin, and a kick of chili powder, this marinade will perk up your carne asada (Mexican grilled or roasted meat) or beef tenderloin for a Southwestern fiesta. It's also terrific for marinating pork, poultry, or seafood that is to be roasted or grilled.

- **½ cup vegetable oil**
- **2 cloves garlic, minced**
- **⅓ cup finely chopped fresh cilantro**
- **1 teaspoon ground cumin**
- **½ teaspoon chili powder, or more to taste**
- **2 tablespoons red wine vinegar**
- **1 teaspoon salt**

In a small bowl, whisk together all of the ingredients.

✳ **DIVA DO-AHEAD:** At this point, you can cover and refrigerate for up to 5 days.

Soak beef and pork in the marinade for at least 4 and up to 24 hours; marinate poultry or seafood for at least 2 and up to 12 hours.

## Mediterranean Marinade

Makes 1²/₃ cups (enough for 4 pounds of meat)

This rosemary-scented marinade is a perfect choice for beef, lamb, pork, poultry, and seafood.

**1 cup extra virgin olive oil**

**½ cup fresh lemon juice**

**Grated zest of 2 lemons**

**2 tablespoons chopped fresh rosemary**

**1½ teaspoons salt**

**1 teaspoon freshly ground black pepper**

**3 cloves garlic, minced**

In a small bowl, whisk together all the ingredients until blended.

✳ **DIVA DO-AHEAD:** At this point, you can cover and refrigerate for up to 5 days.

Soak beef, pork, or lamb in the marinade for at least 4 and up to 24 hours; marinate chicken or seafood at least 1 hour and up to 4 hours.

## Bloody Mary Marinade

Makes about 4 cups (enough for 6 pounds of meat)

Great for steaks, pork, lamb, and chicken, this marinade has all the peppy flavors of that favorite eye-opening drink.

**2 cups Bloody Mary mix or spicy tomato juice**

**¼ cup olive oil**

**2 tablespoons Worcestershire sauce**

**¼ cup vodka**

**2 teaspoons celery salt**

**2 cloves garlic, minced**

**Pinch of cayenne pepper**

In a medium-size bowl, whisk together all the ingredients.

✳ **DIVA DO-AHEAD:** At this point, you can cover and refrigerate for up to 5 days.

Soak beef, pork, or lamb in the marinade for at least 4 and up to 48 hours; marinate chicken for at least 4 and up to 24 hours.

## Triple Pepper Marinade

Makes about 1³/₄ cups (enough for 4 to 5 pounds of meat)

This marinade is for those who can't get enough pepper. Use it on beef or lamb.

**½ cup olive oil**

**⅓ cup red wine vinegar**

**½ cup Worcestershire sauce**

**½ cup finely chopped onion**

**2 cloves garlic, minced**

**½ teaspoon freshly ground black pepper**

**¼ teaspoon freshly ground white pepper**

**Pinch of cayenne pepper**

In a small bowl, whisk together all the ingredients until blended.

**DIVA DO-AHEAD:** At this point, you can cover and refrigerate for up to 2 weeks; the peppery flavor will intensify the longer the marinade is stored.

Soak beef or lamb in the marinade for up to 2 hours, but no longer—this is potent.

## Carne Asada Marinade

Makes about 3 cups (enough for 6 pounds of meat)

When I asked the local butcher what he marinated his carne asada in, this was his simple answer. Use this to make fabulous beef, pork, or chicken.

**2 cups store-bought medium-hot salsa**
**½ cup olive oil**
**¼ cup fresh lime juice**
**1 teaspoon freshly ground black pepper**

Combine all the ingredients in a medium-size bowl and stir until blended.

**DIVA DO-AHEAD:** At this point, you can cover and refrigerate for up to 5 days.

Soak flank steak or sirloin cubes in the marinade for at least 2 and up to 24 hours; marinate pork tenderloin for at least 2 and up to 12 hours; and marinate chicken for at least 1 hour and up to 8 hours.

## Citrus-Rosemary Marinade

Makes about 1 cup (enough for 2 to 3 pounds of meat)

This tangy marinade will take you to the Mediterranean. It is terrific on beef kabobs, roasted lamb, or poultry; you may want to make extra to brush on while the meat is cooking.

**1 cup extra virgin olive oil**
**½ cup fresh lemon juice**
**Grated zest of 2 lemons**
**2 teaspoons salt**
**1½ teaspoons freshly ground black pepper**
**4 cloves garlic, minced**
**3 tablespoons chopped fresh rosemary**

In a small bowl, whisk together all of the ingredients.

**DIVA DO-AHEAD:** At this point, you can cover and refrigerate for up to 5 days.

Soak beef and lamb in the marinade for at least 4 and up to 24 hours; marinate chicken for at least 1 hour and up to 8 hours.

### Diva Marinade Shortcut

When grilling meat, if you don't have time to marinate it first, brush the meat with good quality olive oil and sprinkle with salt and pepper.

## Grandma's Rub

Makes ⅔ cup (enough for 3 pounds of meat)

In Umbria, the traditional way to grill or roast meat is to rub it with this moist garlic and spice rub at least 12 hours before cooking. The spices and garlic permeate the meat, and the resulting flavor is incredible. This is the way my grandmother Aleandra would season her meats. The rub is especially good on bone-in cuts like prime rib and rack of lamb, but it also does a fine job on beef tenderloin and pork loin.

**½ cup olive oil**

**6 cloves garlic, minced**

**2 tablespoons chopped fresh thyme, rosemary, or sage**

**1 tablespoon salt**

**2 teaspoons freshly ground black pepper**

**1.** In a small bowl, stir together all the ingredients until blended.

✳ **DIVA DO-AHEAD:** At this point, you can cover and refrigerate for up to 1 week.

**2.** Pierce the meat all over at 1-inch intervals with the tip of a sharp knife, then rub the mixture into the roast. Store in a zipper-top plastic bag and refrigerate for at least 12 hours and up to 2 days before grilling or roasting.

## Brandy Peppercorn Crust for Beef Tenderloin or Kabobs

Makes about 2 cups (enough for 6 pounds of meat)

This slather will give meat a similar flavor to steak au poivre and is terrific for beef tenderloin or kabobs.

**½ cup olive oil**

**¼ cup brandy**

**1½ teaspoons salt**

**2 cloves garlic, minced**

**1 tablespoon coarsely ground black pepper**

**1.** In a medium-size bowl, whisk together the oil, brandy, salt, and garlic.

✳ **DIVA DO-AHEAD:** At this point, you can cover and refrigerate for up to 5 days.

**2.** Soak beef tenderloin or another large cut in the marinade for at least 4 and up to 24 hours. If using for kabobs, marinate for at least 1 hour and up to 4 hours.

**3.** Drain the beef, pat dry with paper towels, and press the pepper into the meat so it forms a crust.

## Mustard-Horseradish Crust

Makes about 1¼ cups (enough for one 5- to 6-pound roast)

This tangy crust will bake to a golden brown on a beef tenderloin, New York strip roast, or pork loin. Marinate beef tenderloin in Garlic-Herb Marinade (page 393), then drain and coat it in the mustard crust. Other meats need only be slathered with the mustard crust mixture. Meat prepared this way is terrific roasted the day before you entertain, then served at room temperature, though it's still tasty when served warm.

**1 cup Dijon mustard**

**¼ cup prepared horseradish**

**2 tablespoons salt**

**1 tablespoon freshly ground black pepper**

In a small bowl, whisk together all the ingredients. Spread over the meat and roast.

✳ **DIVA DO-AHEAD:** After spreading the meat with the crust, refrigerate for up to 2 days before roasting.

## Garlic-Herb Crust

Makes ½ cup (enough for a 5- to 6-pound roast)

For this crust the garlic roasts on and in the meat, giving you a terrific entrée. Try this with beef tenderloin, New York strip roast, roasted chicken or turkey, or pork loin. Make sure you marinate beef tenderloin before crusting it with the mixture; other cuts of meat are fine with just the crust.

**10 cloves garlic, minced**

**¼ cup olive oil**

**2 tablespoons salt**

**1 tablespoon freshly ground black pepper**

**2 teaspoons sweet paprika**

**2 teaspoons dried thyme**

**1.** In a small bowl, mix together all the ingredients.

**2.** With the tip of a sharp knife, make slits about ½ inch deep and 1 inch apart all over the meat, then spread the garlic and herb mixture over the meat, pushing it into the slits.

✳ **DIVA DO-AHEAD:** After spreading the meat with the mixture, refrigerate for up to 2 days before roasting.

# The Very Best Brisket

Serves 10

Every traditional Jewish cook has a favorite recipe for brisket, a very flavorful but notoriously tough piece of meat unless handled correctly. Although I'm not Jewish, this is my rendition of this classic dish. I find that the dried apricots cut some of the strong beefy flavor and add a nice taste to the sauce, which is spooned over the meat.

1½ teaspoons salt

½ teaspoon freshly ground black pepper

4 cloves garlic, minced

One 4½- to 5-pound beef brisket, trimmed of excess fat

2 tablespoons olive oil

1½ cups chopped onions

4 medium-size carrots, chopped

2 teaspoons dried thyme

½ cup red wine

3 to 4 cups beef broth, as needed

1 cup dried apricots, cut in half

½ cup chopped fresh parsley for garnish

**1.** In a small bowl, combine the salt, pepper, and garlic until it forms a paste. Rub the paste all over the brisket. Heat the oil in a 5- to 6-quart Dutch oven over medium-high heat and brown the beef on all sides.

**2.** Remove the beef from the Dutch oven, add the onions, carrots, and thyme, and cook, stirring, until the onions become translucent, about 6 minutes. Add the wine and cook for about 2 minutes, until reduced somewhat.

**3.** Return the beef to the Dutch oven and add enough of the broth so it comes up about 1 inch around the beef, then add the apricots. Cover, reduce the heat to medium-low, and simmer until the meat is fork-tender, about 3 hours, turning it after each hour.

**4.** Remove the meat from the sauce and cover loosely with aluminum foil. Bring the sauce to a boil and continue boiling for 10 minutes, stirring, until reduced. Skim off any fat that may have accumulated on top of the sauce. Taste for salt and pepper, adding more if needed.

✳ **DIVA DO-AHEAD:** At this point, you can let the meat and sauce cool, cover, and refrigerate for up to 2 days. Rewarm over low heat before continuing.

**5.** Trim off the fat, then thinly slice the brisket against the grain. Arrange meat on a platter and spoon some of the sauce over the top. Sprinkle the platter with the parsley and serve the remaining sauce alongside.

**Slow Cooker Savvy**

If you would like to make this in your slow cooker, prepare the brisket on the stove top through step 2. Then place the browned beef, vegetables, beef broth, and apricots in a 5- to 6-quart slow cooker and cook on Low for 8 to 10 hours. To reduce the sauce, transfer to a sauce-pan and boil it for 10 minutes. To reheat the brisket if you have refrigerated it, you can slice it, then lay it in the slow cooker with the sauce and heat on Low for 2 to 4 hours.

# Pot Roast Italian Style

Serves 10 to 12

Classic comfort food, this delicious pot roast gets its flavor and character from simmering in a red wine and tomato sauce, which is also fabulous served over pasta, mashed potatoes, or polenta. I like to use an eye of the round roast because there is virtually no waste on it and it keeps its shape during the long simmering.

**3 cloves garlic, minced**

**2 teaspoons salt**

**1 teaspoon freshly ground black pepper**

**2 tablespoons olive oil**

**One 4-pound eye of the round roast**

**1 cup finely chopped onion**

**4 carrots, finely chopped**

**2 ribs celery, finely chopped**

**2 teaspoons dried rosemary**

**1 cup red wine**

**Two 15.75-ounce cans crushed plum tomatoes, with their juice**

**2 cups beef broth**

**1.** Sprinkle the garlic, salt, and pepper over the roast, rubbing them in.

**2.** Heat the oil in a 5- to 6-quart Dutch oven over medium-high heat, add the roast, and brown on all sides.

**3.** Remove the roast from the pan and add the onion, carrots, celery, and rosemary. Cook, stirring, until the vegetables are softened and the onion becomes translucent, 6 to 8 minutes. Stir in the wine and tomatoes, scraping up any browned bits from the bottom of the pan.

**4.** Return the roast to the pan and add the beef broth. Bring to a boil, reduce the heat to medium-low, and simmer until the meat is fork-tender, 2½ to 3 hours.

✻ **DIVA DO-AHEAD:** At this point, cool the meat and sauce to room temperature and refrigerate for up to 2 days, or freeze for up to 1 month. Defrost, skim off any fat that has accumulated on the top of the sauce, and continue with the recipe.

**5.** Remove the meat from the sauce, cover loosely with aluminum foil, and let rest for 15 minutes before carving. Meanwhile, bring the sauce to a boil and simmer for 10 minutes to concentrate its flavor. Skim off any accumulated fat on the top of the sauce.

**6.** Thinly slice the beef and arrange around the outside of a serving platter. Fill the center of the platter with mashed potatoes, pasta, or polenta, spoon some of the sauce over them, and spoon a bit over the meat. Serve the remaining sauce in a sauceboat or a small slow cooker to keep it warm. Or arrange the beef and fill the center of the platter with a green vegetable, such as sautéed spinach, green beans, or Roasted Asparagus (page 226). Spoon a bit of the sauce over the meat and serve the rest on the side. If the meat is at room temperature, serve all of the sauce on the side.

### Slow Cooker Savvy

Prepare the recipe as instructed through step 3. Place the roast, beef broth, and vegetables in a 5- to 6-quart slow cooker, cover, and cook on Low until the meat is tender, 7 to 8 hours. Pick up the recipe with step 5.

# Pot Roast Carne Asada Style

Serves 10 to 12

This south of the border pot roast is terrific for making into shredded beef for a taco bar or for serving with rice, beans, and tortillas for a Cinco de Mayo festival.

One 4-pound sirloin roast, trimmed of excess fat

2 teaspoons salt

1 teaspoon freshly ground black pepper

2 tablespoons olive oil

1 cup coarsely chopped onion

1 jalapeño pepper, seeded and finely chopped

1 teaspoon ground cumin

2 cups medium-hot salsa

1½ cups beef broth

**1.** Sprinkle the beef evenly with half the salt and pepper.

**2.** Heat the oil in a 5- to 6-quart Dutch oven over medium-high heat, add the beef, and brown on all sides. Remove the meat from the pan, add the onion, jalapeño, and cumin, and cook, stirring, until the onion and jalapeño are softened, about 3 minutes.

**3.** Return the meat to the pan and add the salsa and broth. Bring to a boil, scraping up any browned bits stuck to the bot-tom of the pan. Cover, reduce the heat to medium-low, and simmer, stirring occa-sionally, until the meat falls apart, 2½ to 3 hours.

**4.** Remove the meat from the pan and cover loosely with aluminum foil. Taste the sauce for salt and pepper and add more if necessary.

**5.** Shred the beef, removing any fat, and serve with the sauce on the side.

✳ **DIVA DO-AHEAD:** At this point, you can combine the beef and sauce, cover, and refrig-erate for up to 2 days; it actually tastes better when cooked in advance. You can also freeze it in its sauce for up to 1 month.

Gently reheat before serving.

## Slow Cooker Savvy

Prepare the recipe through step 2, then transfer everything, including the salsa and broth, to a 5- to 6-quart slow cooker. Cover and cook on Low until the meat shreds, 6 to 8 hours. Pick up the recipe with step 4.

# Braised Beef in Cabernet Sauvignon

Serves 10 to 12

This rich stew, fashioned after the classic Beef Bourguignon, cooks in a beefy red wine sauce. I recommend that you use an eye of the round roast, because it holds together through the long simmering and slices beautifully. I love to serve this with buttered noodles, mashed potatoes, or a potato gratin for a starch, some mixed greens or roasted asparagus for crunch, and crusty bread to soak up the delicious sauce.

**One 4- to 5-pound eye of the round roast**

**2 teaspoons salt**

**1 teaspoon freshly ground black pepper**

**2 tablespoons olive oil**

**1 cup finely chopped onion**

**2 cloves garlic, minced**

**1 teaspoon dried thyme**

**1 bay leaf**

**1½ cups Cabernet Sauvignon**

**Four 10.75-ounce cans Campbell's condensed beef broth**

**7 tablespoons unsalted butter, softened**

**½ pound small pearl onions, peeled (see The Diva Says)**

**1 pound cremini mushrooms, stems trimmed and quartered**

**3 tablespoons all-purpose flour**

**1.** Sprinkle the meat with half of the salt and pepper.

**2.** Heat the oil in a 5- to 6-quart Dutch oven over medium-high heat and brown the meat on all sides. Add the chopped onion, garlic, thyme, and bay leaf and cook for about 3 minutes, stirring to make sure that the garlic doesn't burn. Stir in the wine and broth and scrape up any browned bits from the bottom of the pan. Cover, reduce the heat to medium-low, and simmer until the meat is fork-tender, 2½ to 3 hours.

**3.** Meanwhile, melt 2 tablespoons of the butter in a large skillet over medium heat, add the pearl onions and sprinkle them with the remaining salt and pepper. Cook, stirring, until they begin to turn golden, about 10 minutes. Remove the onions from the pan. Melt 2 more tablespoons of the butter, add the mushrooms, and cook, stirring, until the liquid in the pan has evaporated and the mushrooms begin to turn golden, about 5 minutes. Return the onions to the pan and stir to blend with the mushrooms. Remove the pan from the heat and set aside while the beef cooks.

**4.** When the meat has become tender, remove it from the sauce, cover loosely with aluminum foil, and let rest for 15 minutes.

✳ **DIVA DO-AHEAD:** At this point, you can return the meat to the sauce and cool to room temperature. Cover and refrigerate for up to 2 days, or freeze for up to 1 month. Defrost, skim off any fat that has accumulated on the top of the sauce, and rewarm the meat and sauce. Remove the meat from the sauce and proceed with the recipe.

**5.** Skim off any fat from the top of the sauce. Blend the flour with the remaining 3 tablespoons of butter in a small dish. With the sauce simmering, whisk in the butter-and-flour mixture, a tablespoon at a time, to thicken the sauce. Add the mush-

rooms and onions and additional salt and pepper if necessary.

**6.** Slice the meat, remove the bay leaf from the sauce, and serve the meat topped with the sauce and vegetables.

The Diva Says: If you have trouble finding fresh pearl onions, frozen pearls should be available at your supermarket, and they are a reasonable substitute. Make sure you defrost and drain them thoroughly before using.

### Slow Cooker Savvy

Prepare the recipe as instructed through the first half of step 2, then transfer the browned meat to a 5- to 6-quart slow cooker, add the onion, garlic, thyme, bay leaf, wine, and broth and cook on Low until the meat is fork-tender, 6 to 8 hours. Pick up the recipe with step 3.

# Mamma Mia's Braciole

Serves 10

Braciole is an old Italian recipe for thinly sliced meat that is stuffed, sautéed, then braised in a tomato sauce, making it tender and oh so delicious. To serve, slice the braciole and arrange on a bed of polenta, mashed potatoes, or pasta, with any sauce on the side. You could also serve it on a bed of wilted greens, sautéed spinach, or field greens dressed with balsamic vinaigrette. Round steak can be found in your grocery store, sliced thin and ready to roll for this terrific party dish. It is almost fat free, so braising is the perfect way to tenderize and give it added flavor.

**12 thin slices round steak**

**2 teaspoons salt**

**1 teaspoon freshly ground black pepper**

**12 thin slices prosciutto di Parma**

**2 tablespoons unsalted butter**

**1 clove garlic, minced**

**Three 16-ounce packages frozen spinach, defrosted and squeezed dry**

**¼ teaspoon ground nutmeg**

**⅔ cup freshly grated Parmesan cheese**

**1½ cups soft bread crumbs**

**2 large eggs, beaten**

**2 tablespoons olive oil**

**1 cup finely chopped onion**

**4 medium-size carrots, finely chopped**

**2 ribs celery, finely chopped**

**2 teaspoons dried basil**

**½ cup red wine**

**Two 32-ounce cans crushed plum tomatoes**

**1.** Lay the beef on a piece of plastic wrap or waxed paper, cover with another sheet, and pound thin with a meat pounder, the bottom of a wine bottle, or a rolling pin. Sprinkle with some of the salt and pepper and lay a slice of prosciutto over each piece of beef.

**2.** In a large skillet over medium heat, melt the butter, then add the garlic and cook, stirring, for 1 minute. Add the spinach and nutmeg and cook, stirring, until the spinach is dry. Season with salt and pepper and transfer to a medium-size bowl. Add the cheese, bread crumbs, and eggs and stir to blend.

**3.** Spread 3 tablespoons of the filling over the prosciutto and roll up the beef. Secure with toothpicks or tie with cotton string. Repeat the procedure, using up the remaining beef, prosciutto, and filling.

**4.** In a 6-quart Dutch oven, heat the oil over medium-high heat. Add the beef rolls, a few at a time, and brown them on all sides, transferring them to a plate when they're done.

**5.** Add the onion, carrots, celery, and basil to the skillet and cook, stirring, until the vegetables are softened and the onion is translucent, about 6 minutes. Add the wine, tomatoes, and the remaining salt and pepper and scrape up any browned bits on the bottom of the pan. Gently add the meat to the pan, cover, reduce the heat to medium-low, and simmer until the meat is tender, about 2 hours.

✳ **DIVA DO-AHEAD:** At this point, you can let cool, cover, and refrigerate for up to 2 days or freeze for up to 2 months.

**6.** Remove the meat rolls from the sauce and cover loosely with aluminum foil to keep warm. Skim off any fat on the top of the sauce and season with additional salt and pepper if needed. Remove the toothpicks from the meat, slice each roll in half, and serve, topped with some of the sauce.

### Slow Cooker Savvy

Prepare the recipe as instructed through step 5. Transfer everything to a 5- to 6-quart slow cooker, including the meat rolls, cover, and cook on High for about 4 hours, or on Low for 6 to 7 hours, until the meat is tender.

### Diva Variations

Combine one 8-ounce package cream cheese with 1 cup store-bought basil or sun-dried tomato pesto. Spread over the pounded beef, roll up, and proceed as directed.

Lay strips of soppressata or Genoa salami over the pounded beef and arrange slices of hard-cooked eggs over that. Roll up and proceed as directed.

Lay thin slices of prosciutto over the pounded beef and arrange one stick of mozzarella string cheese over the prosciutto. Roll up and proceed as directed.

Combine 1 cup of homemade (page 84) or store-bought Tapenade, 1 cup of dry bread crumbs, and 1/2 cup of freshly grated Parmesan cheese. Spread over the pounded beef, roll up, and proceed as directed.

# Barbecued Sirloin Roast for Sandwiches

Serves 10

This is the recipe that I use to make barbecue beef sandwiches or French dip sandwiches for my family when we are watching football or college basketball games. I roast the beef the day before, then slow-cook it in homemade barbecue sauce, or au jus for French dips, for 4 hours, until the meat is melt-in-your-mouth tender. This also works well with grilled boneless chicken and pork. The chicken and pork become tender and actually shred like pulled pork.

---

2 tablespoons olive oil

1½ teaspoons salt

1 teaspoon freshly ground black pepper

4 cloves garlic, minced

One 4-pound sirloin tip, rump, or eye of
   round roast

1 recipe Old-Fashioned Brown Sugar
   Barbecue Sauce (page 485)

10 crusty rolls, split open

---

**1.** Preheat the oven to 325°F.

**2.** In a small bowl, combine the oil, salt, pepper, and garlic. Rub the garlic oil all over the roast and place in a heavy-duty roasting pan. Roast for 45 to 50 minutes, or until an instant-read meat thermometer inserted into the thickest part registers 145°F. Remove from the oven, cover loosely with aluminum foil, and let rest for at least 15 minutes.

✳ **DIVA DO-AHEAD:** At this point, you can cover and refrigerate for up to 2 days.

If you are continuing with the recipe, leave the oven on.

**3.** Preheat the oven to 325°F if you have turned it off. Thinly slice the roast and lay the slices in a baking dish. Pour the sauce over the slices, cover, and bake until tender, about 1½ hours. Or put the sliced beef and sauce in a slow cooker and cook on Low for 4 hours.

✳ **DIVA DO-AHEAD:** At this point, you can let cool, cover, and freeze for up to 1 month. Defrost and reheat before serving.

**4.** Serve on crusty rolls.

## Diva Variation

**French Dip Sandwiches:** Roast the meat, slice, and bake or slow-cook in 4 cups of beef broth and 1 teaspoon of dried thyme. To serve, dip the cut side of the rolls into the jus, then pile with the meat and spoon some jus on top. I like to serve additional jus in a small cup on each plate for further dipping.

# Mom's Italian Meatballs

Makes about 30 meatballs; serves 10 as main dish, 18 to 20 as a side dish

These meatballs can be cooked, then simmered in Mom's Sunday Sauce (page 483) or served alongside other Italian food on a buffet table.

2 pounds ground beef

1 cup finely chopped onion

1 clove garlic, minced

Grated zest of 1 lemon

1½ teaspoons salt

1 teaspoon freshly ground black pepper

¼ cup chopped fresh parsley

1½ cups soft bread crumbs

2 large eggs, beaten

Olive oil for frying

**1.** In a large bowl, combine the beef, onion, garlic, lemon zest, salt, pepper, parsley, bread crumbs, and eggs until blended. Form the mixture into small balls and set on a plate or baking sheet.

✳ **DIVA DO-AHEAD:** At this point, you can cover and refrigerate for up to 2 days.

**2.** In a large skillet, heat ½ inch of oil until a piece of bread dropped in it begins to float and bubble. Add the meatballs, a few at a time, being careful not to crowd them, and fry until browned on all sides and cooked through. Using a slotted spoon or tongs, remove the meatballs from the pan and drain on paper towels.

✳ **DIVA DO-AHEAD:** At this point, you can let cool, cover, and refrigerate for up to 2 days or freeze for up to 2 months. Defrost and reheat on a rack on a baking sheet in a 325°F oven for 10 minutes.

Serve immediately or keep warm in a pre-heated 250°F oven for up to 45 minutes.

# Grecian Meatballs with Red Wine Sauce

Makes about 30 meatballs; serves 10 as a main course, 15 to 18 as an appetizer

These spicy meatballs are terrific to serve for appetizers or on a buffet table with other Mediterranean specialties. The wine sauce complements the meatballs well, but they are also delicious in Quick Marinara (page 482).

### Meatballs

**1 pound ground beef**

**1 pound ground lamb**

**1 cup finely chopped onion**

**1½ cups soft bread crumbs**

**2 large eggs, well beaten**

**1 clove garlic, minced**

**1 tablespoon chopped fresh oregano, or 1 teaspoon dried**

**1½ teaspoons salt**

**½ teaspoon freshly ground black pepper**

**2 tablespoons chopped fresh parsley**

**2 tablespoons chopped fresh mint**

**1½ cups dry bread crumbs**

**Vegetable oil for frying**

### Red Wine Sauce

**3 tablespoons unsalted butter**

**½ cup finely chopped onion**

**3 tablespoons all-purpose flour**

**1½ cups red wine**

**⅔ cup beef broth**

**1 teaspoon salt**

**½ teaspoon freshly ground black pepper**

**1.** To make the meatballs, in a large bowl, blend together the beef, lamb, onion, soft bread crumbs, eggs, garlic, oregano, salt, pepper, parsley, and mint. Form into golf ball–sized balls, roll in the dry bread crumbs, and place on a baking sheet or plate.

✳ **DIVA DO-AHEAD:** At this point, cover and refrigerate for at least 1 hour and up to 24 hours to firm up.

**2.** In a large skillet, heat about ½ inch of oil until a piece of bread dropped in it begins to float and bubble. Add the meatballs, a few at a time, being careful not to crowd them, and fry until browned on all sides and cooked through. Using a slotted spoon or tongs, remove the meatballs from the pan and drain on paper towels.

✳ **DIVA DO-AHEAD:** At this point, you can let cool, cover, and refrigerate for up to 2 days or freeze for up to 2 months. Defrost and reheat on a rack on a baking sheet in a 325°F oven for 10 minutes before continuing. Or make the sauce and then reheat the meatballs gently in the sauce on the stove top. If necessary, you can keep the freshly cooked meatballs warm in a preheated 250°F oven for up to 45 minutes.

**3.** To make the sauce, in a 2-quart saucepan, melt the butter over medium heat. Add the onion and cook, stirring, until softened, about 3 minutes. Whisk in the flour and cook until white bubbles form on the surface. Cook, whisking constantly, 2 to 3 minutes longer, then whisk in the

wine and beef broth, and continue whisking until the mixture comes to a boil and thickens. Whisk in the salt and pepper.

✳ **DIVA DO-AHEAD:** At this point, you can let cool, cover, and refrigerate for up to 3 days or freeze for 1 month. Defrost before continuing.

**4.** To serve the meatballs in the sauce, reheat the sauce, add the meatballs, and simmer until heated through, about 20 minutes. Transfer to a slow cooker, fondue pot, or chafing dish and serve with toothpicks.

### Quick Trick for Meatballs

When forming meatballs, use an ice cream scoop to help give them shape. Also, wet your hands to keep the meat from sticking to them when rolling.

# MEATBALLS TO MEAT LOAF

**Meatballs make a great** addition to any party table, whether they are served as an appetizer or as part of the main course. Each of these meatball recipes also makes terrific meat loaf, which is a great entrée on the party table; just shape the meatball mixture into two 6-inch-long and 3-inch-wide loaves and bake on silicone- or aluminum foil–lined baking sheets at 350°F until cooked through or an instant-read meat thermometer inserted into the center reaches 160°F, 35 to 45 minutes. Let it rest for at least 15 minutes, then slice with a serrated knife.

Cold meat loaf is terrific for sandwiches at a picnic. Think Grecian meat loaf (see page 410) served with Cucumber Yogurt Sauce (page 492), Mom's Italian meat loaf (see page 409) with Caprese Salad (page 176), and Southwestern meat loaf (see page 413) with Chipotle Corn Salsa (page 478). Meat loaf can be cooked and refrigerated for up to 2 days or frozen for up to 1 month. To reheat defrosted meat loaf, wrap it in aluminum foil and bake at 325°F for 20 to 25 minutes.

To serve hot meat loaf, arrange the slices on a serving platter over a bed of field greens, mashed potatoes, or grilled vegetables. To serve it cold, arrange the meat loaf slices over sliced tomatoes or in the center of the plate, garnished with grilled or cooked fresh vegetables around the rim. You can serve a complementary sauce drizzled down the center of the slices or on the side. Ketchup is usually on the side at my house in addition to sauce, but you can choose whatever will make your guests happy.

Meatballs are becoming more readily available in the frozen food section of your grocery store, and you can certainly use those when time is not on your side. Make sure you serve these meatballs in some sort of sauce, which will help disguise their not-homemade flavor.

Meatballs can be served on a bed of field greens or decorative greens or, if you would like to serve them warm, consider a slow cooker, wide fondue pot, or chafing dish. Make sure you have toothpicks nearby and a plate for the discarded ones as well.

# Southwestern Meatballs

Makes about 30 meatballs; serves 15 to 18 as an appetizer

These spicy bites are made with ground turkey, pork sausage, and smoky chipotle chiles. Serve them as appetizers with Salsa Fresca (page 90), Cilantro Pesto (page 472), or Maple-Chipotle Basting Sauce (page 487) for dipping, or heat them in 4 cups of Ranchero Sauce (page 562) and keep them warm in the slow cooker on the buffet table.

**1 pound bulk mild pork sausage**

**1 pound ground turkey**

**2 large eggs, beaten**

**1½ cups torn soft corn tortillas, soaked in milk to cover for 15 minutes, drained, and squeezed dry**

**1 canned chipotle chile in adobo sauce, finely minced**

**1 cup finely chopped onion**

**1 clove garlic, minced**

**1 teaspoon ground cumin**

**1 teaspoon salt**

**½ teaspoon freshly ground black pepper**

**Vegetable oil for frying**

**1.** In a large bowl, combine the pork, turkey, eggs, tortillas, chile, onion, garlic, cumin, salt, and pepper until blended. Form into golf ball–size meatballs and set on a plate or a baking sheet.

**2.** In a large skillet, heat ½ inch of oil until a piece of tortilla floats and bubbles in the oil. Add the meatballs, a few at a time, being careful not to crowd them, and fry until browned on all sides and cooked through. Using a slotted spoon or tongs, remove from the pan and drain on paper towels.

✳ **DIVA DO-AHEAD:** At this point, you can let cool, cover, and refrigerate for up to 2 days or freeze for up to 2 months. Defrost and reheat on a rack on a baking sheet in a 325°F oven for 10 minutes.

**3.** Serve immediately or keep warm in a preheated 250°F oven for up to 1 hour.

# Swedish Meatballs

Makes 30 meatballs; serves 15 to 18 as an appetizer

Swedish meatballs got a bad rep in the '70s and '80s, when people would cover them with grape jelly and ketchup. Traditional Swedish meatballs are coated with a lovely creamy sauce that enhances the flavor of the meat rather than covering it up.

1 cup fresh bread crumbs

½ cup milk

1 pound lean ground beef

1 pound lean ground pork

1½ teaspoons salt

½ teaspoon freshly ground black pepper

⅛ teaspoon ground allspice

⅔ cup finely chopped sweet onion

2 large eggs

½ cup (1 stick) unsalted butter

Vegetable oil for frying

2 tablespoons all-purpose flour

2 cups beef broth

½ cup heavy cream

**1.** In a small bowl, soak the bread crumbs in the milk for 15 minutes and squeeze dry.

**2.** In a large bowl, stir together the soaked bread, beef, pork, salt, pepper, allspice, onion, and eggs until blended. Form into small balls the size of a walnut, and place on a plate or baking sheet.

✳ **DIVA DO-AHEAD:** At this point, you can cover and refrigerate for up to 2 days.

**3.** In a large skillet over medium-high heat, melt ¼ cup (½ stick) of the butter with enough vegetable oil to achieve a depth of ½ inch in the pan. When the foam subsides, add the meatballs a few at a time, being careful not to crowd them, and brown evenly on all sides until cooked through, 5 to 7 minutes total. Using a slotted spoon, transfer them to paper towels.

**4.** Pour off all the fat, and melt the remaining butter in the pan. Add the flour and whisk until white bubbles form on the surface. Cook, whisking constantly, 2 to 3 minutes longer, then gradually add the broth and bring to a boil. Taste for salt and pepper and add more if needed.

✳ **DIVA DO-AHEAD:** At this point, you can let the meatballs and sauce cool, cover, and refrigerate for up to 4 days, or freeze for up to 1 month. Defrost and reheat gently before continuing.

**5.** Add the cream to the sauce and bring to a simmer. Add the meatballs and heat through. Serve immediately in a chafing dish, slow cooker set on Low, or a fondue pot, and have lots of toothpicks on hand.

# Pastitsio ⬤⬤⬤

Serves 10 as a main course, 15 to 18 as a side dish

Pastitsio is a Greek macaroni and meat dish that is served at holiday times and on other festive occasions. Make sure you let the casserole rest for at least 20 to 30 minutes, until it is firmly set; then it can be cut into neat squares. Kefalotyri cheese (a Greek hard grating cheese with irregular holes, made from sheep and goat's milk) can be found in the imported cheese section of most grocery stores; if you can't find it, substitute Asiago, which has a similar flavor.

Meat Sauce

**2 tablespoons olive oil**

**2 pounds lean ground beef**

**1 large onion, finely chopped**

**1½ teaspoons salt**

**½ teaspoon freshly ground black pepper**

**¼ teaspoon ground nutmeg**

**¼ teaspoon ground cinnamon**

**2 cups canned tomato puree**

**1 cup grated kefalotyri or Asiago cheese**

Cream Sauce

**¼ cup (½ stick) unsalted butter**

**¼ cup all-purpose flour**

**2½ cups whole or 2% milk**

**2 teaspoons salt**

**1 teaspoon freshly ground black pepper**

**8 large eggs, beaten**

**1 cup grated kefalotyri, Asiago, or Parmesan cheese**

Assembly

**¼ cup (½ stick) unsalted butter, melted**

**2 pounds elbow macaroni, cooked according to the package directions until *al dente* and drained**

**1¼ cups freshly grated Parmesan cheese**

**1 teaspoon sweet paprika**

**1.** To make the meat sauce, in a 5-quart saucepan, heat the oil over medium-high heat. Brown the meat, breaking it up, until there is no more pink. Drain off any excess fat or water.

**2.** Add the onion, salt, pepper, nutmeg, and cinnamon and cook, stirring, until the onion is translucent, another 3 to 4 minutes. Add the tomato puree, reduce the heat to medium, and simmer until the juices are absorbed and the sauce is thick, about 20 minutes. Stir in the cheese.

**3.** To make the cream sauce, in a 3-quart saucepan, melt the butter over medium heat, add the flour, and whisk until white bubbles form on the surface. Cook for 2 to 3 more minutes, whisking constantly. Slowly add the milk, whisking until the sauce is smooth and comes to boil. Season with the salt and pepper, remove from the heat, and whisk in the eggs and cheese, stirring until the cheese is melted.

**4.** When you are ready to assemble the dish, stir the melted butter into the hot cooked macaroni and then add 1 cup of the cheese, stirring until it is almost melted.

**5.** Coat a 13 x 9-inch baking dish with nonstick cooking spray. Layer half of the cheesy macaroni in the bottom. Spread a third of the cream sauce over the macaroni. Spread all the meat sauce over the cream sauce, then spread half the remaining cream sauce over the meat sauce. Cover with the remaining macaroni, and spread with the remaining cream sauce. Sprinkle the top evenly with the remaining ¼ cup of cheese and the paprika.

**6.** Preheat the oven to 350°F. Bake the pastitsio until the cheese sauce is bubbling and the top is a deep golden brown, about 1 hour. Remove from the oven, cover with aluminum foil, and let rest until firmly set, 30 to 45 minutes. Cut into squares and serve.

# Ryan's Chili

Serves 10 to 12

My son, Ryan, is a sports fanatic, and our Sundays are sometimes spent in front of the TV watching endless football and college basketball games and eating his favorite chili. He likes it in a bowl, topped with cheddar cheese, or spooned over grilled hot dogs. Either way, the dish is a winner to serve a crowd at a picnic, tailgate, or Super Bowl party.

2½ pounds ground beef

1½ teaspoons chili powder

¼ teaspoon ground cumin

1½ teaspoons salt

Three 8-ounce cans tomato sauce

4 cups water

¼ cup yellow cornmeal

½ cup warm water

**1.** In 5- to 6-quart Dutch oven over medium-high heat, brown the ground beef until no longer pink, breaking up any clumps. Drain off any water or fat that accumulates in the bottom of the pan with a bulb baster. Add the chili powder, cumin, and salt and cook for 3 minutes, stirring, so the spices don't burn. Stir in the tomato sauce and the 4 cups of water and bring to a boil. Reduce the heat to medium-low and simmer for 30 minutes, stirring a few times so that the chili doesn't stick to the bottom of the pan.

**2.** In a small bowl, stir together the cornmeal and ½ cup of warm water. Stir the cornmeal slurry into the chili and simmer until thickened, about another 10 minutes. Taste for salt and pepper and add more if needed.

✳ **DIVA DO-AHEAD:** At this point, you can refrigerate the chili for up to 2 days or freeze for up to 2 months.

The Diva Says: If you like your chili hot, increase the chili powder to your preference, but make sure you cook it because this helps release the oils in the spices, developing the flavor.

## Slow Cooker Savvy

After you stir in the spices and cook for 3 minutes, transfer the mixture to a 5- to 6-quart slow cooker, stir in the tomatoes and water, cover, and cook on Low for 4 hours. Add the cornmeal slurry, cover, and cook for an additional hour, until the chili is thickened.

# Black Bean Sirloin Chili

Serves 10 to 12

This hearty chili is about a 7 out of a possible 10 on the heat meter, so you might want to tone it down by adjusting the cayenne pepper and chili powder to suit your taste. The sirloin cooks in the chili until it is falling apart, and the black beans add a nice texture and flavor to the mix. I like to serve this with Southwestern Cornbread (page 519) or tortillas, along with Guacamole Olé (page 88), grated cheddar and Monterey Jack cheeses, and Salsa Fresca (page 90).

¼ cup olive oil

2 pounds sirloin, trimmed of fat and cut into ½-inch pieces (if you like chunkier chili, cut into 1- to 1½-inch pieces)

2 cups chopped sweet onions

3 cloves garlic, minced

1 jalapeño pepper, seeded and finely chopped

3 tablespoons pure ancho chile powder

1 teaspoon ground cumin

1 teaspoon dried oregano

⅛ to ½ teaspoon cayenne pepper, to your taste

2 teaspoons salt

½ cup yellow cornmeal

One 12-ounce bottle beer

4 cups beef broth

Two 8-ounce cans tomato sauce

Two 15.75-ounce cans black beans, drained and rinsed

1 bunch fresh cilantro, chopped

2 cups chopped red onions for garnish

4 cups finely shredded mild cheddar and/ or Monterey Jack cheese for garnish

**1.** Heat 2 tablespoons of the oil in a 5- to 6-quart Dutch oven over medium-high heat and brown the meat on all sides. Remove the meat from the pan.

**2.** Heat the remaining 2 tablespoons of oil in the pot and add the sweet onions, garlic, jalapeño, ancho chile powder, cumin, oregano, cayenne, and salt and cook, stirring, until the onions begin to soften and the spices become aromatic, about 3 minutes. Whisk in the cornmeal and stir until the mixture begins to bubble. Gradually whisk in the beer, broth, and tomato sauce and bring to a boil. Stir in the meat and reduce the heat to medium-low. Cover and simmer until the meat is tender, about 1½ hours.

**3.** Fold in the beans and ¼ cup of the cilantro, taste the sauce for salt and pepper, and add more if needed. Simmer the chili for another 10 minutes.

✳ **DIVA DO-AHEAD:** At this point, you can let cool, cover, and refrigerate for up to 4 days or freeze for up to 2 months. Defrost and reheat on the stove top before continuing.

**4.** Serve the chili with the remaining cilantro, and offer the red onion and cheese in bowls on the side.

### Slow Cooker Savvy

Follow the recipe as instructed through step 2, then transfer to a 5- to 6-quart slow cooker. Cover and cook on Low for 7 to 8 hours. Add the beans and cilantro during the last hour of cooking. Pick up the recipe with step 4 above.

### Serving Chili

The Do-Ahead Diva loves a serve-yourself chili bar. Cook the chili ahead of time, then keep it warm in the slow cooker. Serve it with an assortment of condiments: shredded Monterey Jack and cheddar cheeses, chopped red onions or scallions, chopped fresh cilantro, chopped fresh tomatoes, chopped black olives, tortilla chips or small soft corn tortillas, and pickled jalapeño peppers for even more heat. If you are serving a crowd, bake some potatoes and keep those warm in a slow cooker. Have your guests each split a potato and ladle on the chili and fixings. Chili is one of those dishes that can be served as the main event or on the side with grilled burgers, steak, and hot dogs at a casual get-together.

# Pork

**Pork makes a lean and delicious entrée** to serve for parties. Whether you serve a roast ham with a beautiful glaze, a pork roast studded with garlic and herbs, marinated pork tenderloins, barbecued ribs, pulled pork, or a fresh ham, pork can be a delicious change of pace for your parties. Many of the recipes in this chapter can either be prepared ahead of time or else marinated so they are ready to go onto the grill or into the oven the day of your party.

# The Whole Hog

*Pork tenderloin:* This cut is the filet mignon of pork. Tender, and without any fat, it will need a marinade or brine to help keep it juicy during cooking. Most pork tenderloins weigh around 1 pound. The tenderloin has what is called a silver skin, a tendon sheath that can run the length of the meat, and you will need to trim and discard that. Simply run a thin, sharp knife underneath it, and separate it from the meat. If you don't trim the silver skin, it will cause the meat to buckle when it cooks and it won't cook evenly.

    *Pork loin:* Think of a bone-in pork chop: the smaller side of the chop is the tenderloin and the other side is the loin. When the bone is removed, the meat—both tenderloin and loin—is rolled and tied into one compact piece called a "whole" pork loin. Sometimes the tenderloin is removed, leaving only the loin, a solid piece of delicious eating. This loin can be roasted and served in any number of ways. I like to braise or brine it, then roast it with garlic and herbs. I trim the fat off the roast after it has finished cooking, not before, because the fat helps keep the meat moist while cooking.

**Pork shoulder:** There are two different cuts of pork shoulder available on the market: the Boston shoulder, which weighs about 6 pounds, and the picnic shoulder,

weighing in at about 4 pounds. Both are succulent pieces of meat with a lot of fat (great for keeping the meat moist), and they need to be braised or slow-roasted. I don't recommend the picnic shoulder for entertaining, though, because the meat-to-fat ratio is not dependable and you could end up with less usable meat than you want. Buy the Boston shoulder, also called pork butt or Boston butt, and roast it in a 300°F oven for 6 to 8 hours. The result will be delicious meat so tender it can be pulled apart into juicy shreds with a fork. This pulled pork can be used in everything from fajitas to barbecue sandwiches.

**Fully cooked ham:** A fully cooked ham is great for serving a lot of people at a party. Warm up the ham before serving and, if you like, add a glaze for visual interest and to provide a nice contrast to the smoky flavor. A fully cooked ham can come already spiral sliced (a bonus for those who don't want to carve it) or unsliced. The difference in price is huge: A 10-pound spiral-sliced ham can cost upward of $25, while the unsliced ham can cost around $8 to $10 for the same amount of meat. It's really up to you to decide which appeals more. Slicing the ham isn't a difficult job with a sharp carving knife; just follow the contours of the meat as you cut it off the bone.

**Fresh ham:** A fresh ham comes from the leg portion of the pig. This is actually my favorite cut of pork because the skin becomes crackly and crisp and the meat succulent and juicy when slow-roasted in the oven. A whole leg weighs 15 to 20 pounds, and you will need a large roasting pan as well as a large oven to handle it. We're talking about feeding the entire neighborhood here. A half fresh ham can be ordered from your butcher, boned, rolled, and tied. This way, you don't have to mess with a large piece of meat attached to an equally large bone. A half ham will feed 12 nicely, with some leftovers.

*Ribs:* Ribs are messy, finger-licking good food to serve for a casual backyard picnic. You can also cut them into individual portions to serve as finger food at indoor parties. Ribs can be cooked ahead of time, then warmed up in the oven or on the grill. I recommend buying baby back ribs, which are the smallest ribs. They require less work and can easily be cut into nice, small portions for appetizers after they are cooked. Spareribs are meatier than baby back ribs, so you will need to do more cutting to get the cooked ribs into manageable pieces. This is easily accomplished with a cleaver or another sharp knife. So-called country-style spareribs are really blade pork chops that have been split. They are delicious when braised, but I don't recommend them for entertaining a big group—they can be messy and you will need a lot of them. However, if you would like to cook a mix of pork ribs and other meats, the country-style ribs, braised in your favorite sauce, would work well.

*Pork chops:* I don't recommend serving chops for entertaining because it's so easy to overcook them. A crown roast of pork is an option, though; it is a rack of chops tied into a circle, which leaves the center open for stuffing. Although a crown roast is impressive, a whole pork loin is easier to prepare and serve and you'll get more servings out of it.

*Kabobs:* Pork satay, or skewers, is a delicious way to present pork when you are entertaining, whether you are serving the satay as an appetizer or entrée. Pork from the loin or tenderloin is the best choice for kabobs, and it should be brined or marinated before grilling or broiling. Pork kabobs can be served warm, at room temperature, or cold, with a complementary dipping sauce on the side.

*Suckling pig:* A suckling pig is a whole dressed pig that you can roast and then serve to your guests. This requires a huge oven space or a pit in the backyard built for just such a purpose.

# Baby Back Ribs

Serves 12

Baby back ribs are the upper ribs of the loin; they are more expensive than other pork ribs, but also more tender. Each slab of baby back ribs has about 16 ribs on it, so you will need 6 slabs to serve 12 people for a main course or 3 slabs for appetizers. The ribs cook very nicely in the oven. They can be fully baked, then cooled to room temperature and heated up in aluminum foil just before serving, though they're just as tasty at room temperature. If you want a grilled flavor, roast the ribs in the oven, then finish cooking them on the grill over indirect heat (see the variation at right).

After you dry rub your ribs, you can sauce them as they cook and serve with extra sauce on the side, or skip the sauce altogether. It's your choice. I like to offer some type of sauce for dipping, which I also brush on the ribs at the end of the baking time, and have included some of my favorites. Make sure you have bowls for the discarded bones and extra napkins and moistened cloths or individually wrapped towelettes for sticky hands and faces.

⅔ cup All-Purpose Dry Rub for Pork or Beef (page 426)

6 slabs baby back ribs

3 to 4 cups barbecue sauce of your choice, homemade (recipes follow) or store-bought

**1.** Sprinkle the rub over the ribs and wrap in plastic wrap.

✳ **DIVA DO-AHEAD:** At this point, refrigerate for at least 12 and up to 24 hours.

**2.** Preheat the oven to 325°F and line 3 baking sheets with silicone liners or aluminum foil. Unwrap the ribs and arrange on the baking sheets. Bake until cooked through and tender, about 1 hour. During the last 15 minutes of cooking, brush the ribs liberally on both sides with the sauce.

**3.** Remove the ribs from the oven, allow to rest for 5 minutes, and cut into individual portions, using a sharp knife to cut between the rib bones. Serve plain or with the remaining sauce warm on the side.

### Diva Variations

**Barbecued Ribs:** If you would like a smoky charcoal taste for your ribs, sprinkle them with your favorite rub or salt and pepper. Wrap them in aluminum foil, place on a baking sheet, and bake in a preheated 325°F oven for 2 hours. At the end of the cooking time, carefully unwrap the ribs, pouring off the juices that have accumulated in the foil.

✳ **DIVA DO-AHEAD:** At this point, you can let cool, cover, and refrigerate for up to 2 days.

Reheat over a hot charcoal fire for 10 minutes on each side, basting with the sauce of your choice. Cut the ribs into serving pieces and serve with additional sauce.

## SUGGESTIONS FOR DRY RUBBING, SAUCING, AND SERVING BABY BACK RIBS

- Rub with Cavender's Greek seasoning, then serve with **Lemon-Oregano Slather** (page 469).

- Prepare with **Garlic-Herb Crust** (page 399).

- Marinate in **Bloody Mary Marinade** (page 396), **then serve the cooked ribs with the boiled leftover marinade or prepare a fresh batch for dipping.**

- Rub with Old Bay seasoning, then **serve with any barbecue sauce.**

- **Rub with Creole Seasoning** (page 303), **then serve with Jezebel Sauce** (page 476) **or Honey Mustard–Apricot Sauce** (page 428).

- **Coat with Jerk Seasoning Rub** (page 427), **then serve with pureed Mango Salsa** (page 477).

- **Coat with Ancho Chile Rub** (page 426), **then serve with pureed Salsa Fresca** (page 90).

## All-Purpose Dry Rub for Pork or Beef

Makes about ⅔ cup (enough for 6 pounds of meat)

Make up a batch of this rub to keep in your pantry. Use it to rub pork, beef, and poultry before roasting or grilling. Store the rub in an airtight jar and give it as gifts to your friends who love the thrill of the grill.

½ cup firmly packed light brown sugar

2 tablespoons garlic salt

2 tablespoons celery salt

2 tablespoons onion salt

¼ cup sweet paprika

1 teaspoon freshly ground black pepper

2 teaspoons dry mustard

¼ teaspoon chili powder

In a small bowl, stir together the ingredients until blended.

✱ **DIVA DO-AHEAD:** Store in an airtight container indefinitely.

## Ancho Chile Rub

Makes about 1¼ cups (enough for 20 pounds of meat)

Spicy and nicely seasoned, this rub is terrific for Santa Maria barbecue, ribs, Boston butt, or poultry.

½ cup pure ancho chile powder

¼ cup ground cumin

2 tablespoons garlic salt

2 tablespoons onion salt

3 tablespoons dried oregano

Stir everything together in a small bowl.

✱ **DIVA DO-AHEAD:** At this point, you can cover and store at room temperature for up to 6 months.

### No-Brainers for Boston Butt, Shoulder, or Whole Fresh Ham Roasts

If you don't want to make your own rubs, here are some ready-made mixtures I can recommend:

- Cavender's Greek seasoning
- Lawry's seasoned salt
- Old Bay seasoning
- Gephardt's chili powder
- Ancho chile powder
- Lipton's Recipe Secrets Onion Soup Mix
- Knorr Tomato with Basil Soup Mix

# Jerk Seasoning Rub

Makes about ½ cup (enough for 8 pounds of meat)

This Jamaican spice blend is terrific to rub on pork, shrimp, or poultry before roasting or grilling. It has a bit of a kick, so serve meats treated with this rub with fruit salsa and cooling side dishes.

2 tablespoons onion salt

2 teaspoons dried thyme

2 teaspoons ground allspice

2 teaspoons freshly ground black pepper

2 teaspoons cayenne pepper (less if you don't like the heat)

2 teaspoons sugar

2 teaspoons garlic salt

1 teaspoon ground nutmeg

1 teaspoon ground cinnamon

Combine everything in a small bowl and stir to blend.

❋ **DIVA DO-AHEAD:** At this point, you can cover and store at room temperature for up to 6 months.

# Old-Fashioned Barbecue Sauce

Makes 4½ cups (enough for 4 to 6 pounds of meat)

This sauce is sweet, hot, and a little smoky. It's delicious brushed on ribs or used for a dipping sauce, and it's also great on chicken or beef.

2 tablespoons olive oil

1 cup finely chopped onion

3 cloves garlic, minced

¼ teaspoon chili powder

¼ teaspoon ground allspice

Three 8-ounce cans tomato sauce

1 cup ketchup

⅓ cup unsulfured molasses

⅓ cup prepared yellow mustard

In a 3-quart saucepan, heat the oil over medium heat, add the onion and garlic, and cook, stirring, for 2 minutes. Add the chili powder and allspice and cook, stirring, until the onion and garlic are softened, another 2 minutes. Add the tomato sauce, ketchup, molasses, and mustard, stirring to blend, and simmer until thickened and reduced a bit, 45 minutes to 1 hour.

❋ **DIVA DO-AHEAD:** At this point, you can let cool, cover, and refrigerate for up to 1 week. Reheat before serving.

# Hoisin Barbecue Sauce

Makes about 3 cups (enough for 6 pounds of meat)

Smoky hoisin is terrific on ribs, as well as chicken and beef. Baste ribs with the sauce during the last 15 minutes of cooking time or serve it on the side for dipping. Either way, it adds a nice flavor to the ribs.

2 tablespoons vegetable oil

3 cloves garlic, minced

1 teaspoon peeled and grated fresh ginger

1½ cups light soy sauce

1 cup hoisin sauce

½ cup ketchup

2 tablespoons honey

¼ cup rice wine or seasoned rice vinegar

2 teaspoons toasted sesame oil

2 tablespoons sesame seeds, toasted (see page 83), for garnish

1 cup chopped scallions (white and tender green parts) for garnish

**1.** In a 2½-quart saucepan, heat the oil over medium heat, add the garlic and ginger, and cook, stirring, until fragrant, about 1 minute. Stir in the soy sauce, hoisin, ketchup, honey, and rice wine and bring to a boil. Reduce the heat to medium-low and simmer for 10 minutes. Remove from the heat.

✳ **DIVA DO-AHEAD:** At this point, you can let cool, cover, and refrigerate for up to 1 week. Gently reheat before proceeding.

**2.** Stir in the sesame oil, then garnish the sauce (or basted ribs) with the sesame seeds and scallions.

# Honey Mustard–Apricot Sauce

Makes about 3 cups (enough for 6 pounds of meat)

This is a great sweet-tart dipping sauce for ribs and roasted pork, but it also works beautifully with shrimp skewers and chicken. Serve it warm or at room temperature.

2 teaspoons vegetable oil

1 clove garlic, minced

1 cup Dijon mustard

2 tablespoons honey

1 cup apricot jam

2 tablespoons white wine vinegar

In a 2-quart saucepan, heat the oil over medium heat, add the garlic, and cook, stirring, until softened but not browned, about 2 minutes. Stir in the mustard, honey, jam, and vinegar and simmer for 10 minutes.

✳ **DIVA DO-AHEAD:** At this point, you can let cool, cover, and refrigerate for up to 2 weeks. Gently reheat or bring to room temperature before serving, or serve cold.

## SERVING SUGGESTIONS FOR PORK SHOULDER

- Serve the shredded meat piled on a platter with rice, beans, warm flour tortillas, guacamole, sour cream, and salsa arranged around it for a carnitas taco bar.

- Serve the shredded meat on a platter with small rolls on the side, accompanied by an assortment of barbecue sauces and slaw.

- Chop the meat and serve on a platter, garnished with Perfectly Caramelized Onions (page 244) and accompanied by rolls.

- Chop the meat and serve with warm flour tortillas, hoisin sauce, thinly sliced cucumbers, and sliced scallions for Pork Peking.

- Make Cuban sandwiches: Pack the meat into Italian sandwich rolls and top with a little garlic mayonnaise and grated Swiss cheese. Wrap the sandwich in aluminum foil.

  ✳ **DIVA DO-AHEAD:** At this point, you can refrigerate for up to 24 hours. Heat in a preheated 350°F oven until the cheese is melted, about 20 minutes. These are great to take to a picnic or barbecue, where you can heat them on top of a covered grill for 15 to 20 minutes.

- Slice or chop the meat and serve on a bed of field greens drizzled with Balsamic Vinegar Syrup (page 480).

- Slice or chop the meat and serve with Martha's Hapukapsa (page 234).

- Slice or chop the meat and serve with Herb-Roasted Tomatoes (page 127) and polenta.

# Pam's Pork Peggy's Way

Serves 12

When I was just getting started on this book, my editor, Pam Hoenig, said I just had to include this recipe, which she learned from her neighbor Peggy Young. Pam makes this with a Boston butt, but it's also a great treatment for fresh ham. Super simple, inexpensive, and absolutely scrumptious, it is the Do-Ahead Diva's dream. Roast the pork the day before. Then chop or shred it like pulled pork and reheat it, covered or wrapped in aluminum foil, before serving. The leftovers are delicious when served smothered in barbecue sauce. Fresh ham has skin on it; you need to decide whether you want to roast the ham with the skin on so that you will have cracklings, or ask your butcher to remove it. Also, you may want the butcher to remove the bone and tie the roast for you.

---

¼ cup olive oil

10 cloves garlic, peeled

½ cup packed fresh oregano leaves

2 teaspoons salt

1 teaspoon freshly ground black pepper

One 6- to 8-pound leg of pork (fresh ham), Boston butt, or Boston shoulder roast

---

**1.** In a food processor or blender, combine the oil, garlic, oregano, salt, and pepper and process until smooth.

**2.** Stab the meat of the roast about ¾ inch deep (go through the skin) all over at ½-inch intervals. Rub the meat all over with the garlic oil mixture, trying to push it into the slits you have made.

✳ **DIVA DO-AHEAD:** At this point, you can cover tightly with plastic wrap and refrigerate for up to 2 days. Bring to room temperature before continuing.

**3.** Preheat the oven to 300°F. Place the roast in a heavy-duty roasting pan, fat side up, cover with aluminum foil, and roast until an instant-read meat thermometer inserted into the center reads 155°F and the meat is fork-tender (you should literally be able to twist the fork in the meat), 5 to 6 hours. Remove from the oven and let rest for at least 30 minutes.

**4.** Remove the foil, cut away the cracklings, and break up into pieces to serve on the side as a garnish. Then carve the meat into serving pieces or chop and shred it.

### Diva Pan Drippings

Roasted pork usually leaves deliciously flavored drippings in the bottom of the pan. Deglaze them with wine and chicken or beef broth for a delicious pan sauce.

**Jamaican Pork:** This delicious pork is flavored with orange juice and jerk seasoning to give it a taste of the islands. Serve this with piles of white rice and black beans. Omit the olive oil, garlic, oregano, salt, and pepper. Instead, marinate the meat in a mixture of 3 cups of orange juice, ½ cup of packed light brown sugar, 2 tablespoons of Jerk Seasoning Rub (page 427), and 1½ cups of light rum in the refrigerator for at least 12 and up to 36 hours, turning every so often to distribute the marinade evenly. Remove the pork from the bag, pat it dry, and roast as directed above. Roughly chop 2 bunches of fresh cilantro, pile on a platter, arrange the chopped or shredded pork over it, and garnish with 6 large navel oranges, skin and pith removed and sliced ½ inch thick.

**Roasted Chipotle Pork:** This is wonderful served for a fiesta with Black Bean, Corn, and Salsa Dip (page 86) and warm flour or corn tortillas. Increase the olive oil to ½ cup and omit the garlic, oregano, and black pepper. Combine the oil, salt, 3 canned chipotle peppers and about 3 tablespoons of the adobo sauce, 1 teaspoon ground cumin, 2 tablespoons rice vinegar, ½ cup orange juice, and the grated zest of 1 orange in a blender or food processor and process until smooth. Prepare the pork as directed in step 2 and rub with the chipotle mixture. Continue as directed above.

# Pulled Pork Barbecue

Serves 10

This isn't authentic pulled pork, but, being a Do-Ahead Diva, I love it for its ease of preparation and the fact it can be done a day or two ahead of time, then reheated for serving. You can use your favorite bottled barbecue sauce or one of the recipes in this book—it's really up to you. Bottled barbecue sauces can sometimes be a bit thick, however. If yours is, thin it with water, chicken broth, or apple juice, whichever you have on hand. For serving, I'd recommend a fresh batch of homemade barbecue sauce. Pile the meat on a platter and accompany it with the freshly made sauce, a huge bowl of slaw, and soft rolls.

**One 6- to 8-pound leg of pork, Boston butt, or Boston shoulder roast**

**Salt and freshly ground black pepper**

**3 to 4 cups barbecue sauce of your choice (see The Diva Says, page 432)**

**1.** Preheat the oven to 300°F. Season the pork evenly with salt and pepper, place in a heavy-duty roasting pan, fat side up, and roast for 3 hours.

**2.** At the end of 3 hours, slash the fat on the meat and brush the meat with some of the sauce. Continue to roast for another 2 to 3 hours, basting liberally every half hour with more barbecue sauce. Roast until an instant-read meat thermometer inserted into the center reads 155°F and the meat is fork-tender (meaning you can literally twist a fork in it).

**3.** Remove the roast from the oven and allow to rest, covered with aluminum foil, for at least 30 minutes.

**4.** Remove the foil, cut away the cracklings, and break them up into pieces to serve on the side as garnish. Carve the meat into serving pieces, or pull or shred it with a fork.

✳ **DIVA DO-AHEAD:** At this point, you can cover and refrigerate for up to 2 days. To reheat, wrap the meat in foil and bake at 325°F for 30 to 45 minutes.

**5.** Serve the pork on a platter, topped with additional warm barbecue sauce and accompanied with soft rolls and slaw.

## Diva Variation

**Coca-Cola Pork:** Many Southern cooks baste their pork with one or two cans of Coca-Cola during the roasting process, which results in a sweet pork with a crispy crust. If you do this, make sure you use regular Coke, not sugar-free. Some Southerners also add a little kick of cayenne pepper or Tabasco sauce to their Coke-basted pork.

## Slow Cooker Savvy

This dish is simple to prepare in the slow cooker, and the results are terrific. Season the pork, then brown it on all sides in a skillet over medium-high heat. Transfer to a 5- to 6-quart slow cooker, add 2 cups of barbecue sauce, and cook on Low until fork-tender, about 6 hours. Remove the pork from the slow cooker, cover with foil, and let rest for 15 minutes before carving. Remove all the fat from the pork and shred or pull the pork.

✳ **DIVA DO-AHEAD:** At this point, you can let cool, cover, and refrigerate for up to 2 days before continuing. Return the meat and sauce to the cooker and heat through on Low.

## The Diva Says:

You may love your pork drowned in sauce or you may prefer just to dab it on; it's really your choice. I sometimes roast the pork, refrigerate it, then reheat it in the slow cooker with lots of sauce, allowing my guests to serve themselves.

# Sugar and Spice Pork Loin Roast with Creamy Mustard Sauce

Serves 10 to 12

This roast is coated with brown sugar and aromatic spices and pairs beautifully with almost any kind of sauce, including the Creamy Mustard Sauce suggested here.

One 4-pound rolled boneless pork loin roast

½ cup firmly packed dark brown sugar

2 teaspoons freshly ground black pepper

1 tablespoon salt

1½ teaspoons ground cinnamon

½ teaspoon Chinese 5-spice powder

2 tablespoons olive oil

1 recipe Creamy Mustard Sauce (recipe follows)

**1.** Place the roast on a large piece of plastic wrap. In a small bowl, combine the brown sugar, pepper, salt, cinnamon, and 5-spice powder. Rub this all over the roast and wrap tightly in the plastic wrap.

✳ **DIVA DO-AHEAD:** At this point, refrigerate for at least 8 and up to 24 hours.

**2.** Preheat the oven to 325°F. Remove the roast from the refrigerator, remove the wrap, and pat any rub back onto the meat. Allow it to come to room temperature.

**3.** Heat the oil in a large ovenproof skillet over medium-high heat and brown the roast on all sides. Transfer the skillet to the oven and roast until an instant-read meat thermometer inserted into the center registers 155°F, about 1 hour.

**4.** Remove the meat from the oven and allow to rest, covered loosely with aluminum foil, for 15 to 20 minutes.

✳ **DIVA DO-AHEAD:** At this point, you can refrigerate overnight. To reheat, cover with foil and bake in a 325°F oven for 30 minutes.

**5.** Carve the roast into thin slices and serve with the sauce.

# Creamy Mustard Sauce

Makes 3 cups

This is delicious with roast pork, beef, or lamb. It is also fabulous poured into a fondue pot and used as a dipping sauce for pork, chicken, seafood, beef, or lamb skewers.

2 tablespoons unsalted butter

¼ cup finely chopped shallots

1 teaspoon chopped fresh sage

1 teaspoon chopped fresh thyme

2 tablespoons all-purpose flour

¼ cup Dijon mustard

2 tablespoons dry white wine or dry vermouth

1 cup beef broth

1½ cups heavy cream

Salt and freshly ground black pepper to taste

**1.** In a 2-quart saucepan, melt the butter over medium heat, add the shallots, sage, and thyme, and cook, stirring, until the shallots soften a bit, 2 to 3 minutes. Stir in the flour, whisking until white bubbles form on the surface. Continue to whisk for 2 minutes more, then gradually add the mustard, wine, and broth, stirring until the mixture comes to a boil.

**2.** Reduce the heat to low, stir in the cream, and continue stirring until the sauce is heated through and is smooth and thickened, about 5 to 10 minutes. Season with salt and pepper.

✳ **DIVA DO-AHEAD:** At this point, you can let cool, cover, and refrigerate for up to 1 week. Gently reheat before serving.

# Roasted Pork with Plum Bourbon Sauce

Serves 10

This delicious entrée is a terrific choice for a large dinner party because it can be roasted ahead of time, then refrigerated and reheated. The pork is very lean, so thin slices can be arranged on a platter and napped with the sauce. I like to serve this with roasted red potatoes and a nice mixed green salad.

**24 dried plums**

**1½ cups beef broth**

**One 4-pound rolled boneless pork loin roast**

**½ cup Dijon mustard**

**⅔ cup firmly packed dark brown sugar**

**1 tablespoon vegetable oil**

**⅓ cup bourbon**

**Salt and freshly ground black pepper to taste**

**1 teaspoon dried sage**

**1½ teaspoons dried thyme**

**1 tablespoon cornstarch**

**1 tablespoon water**

**¼ cup chopped fresh parsley**

**1.** Preheat the oven to 375°F. In a medium-size bowl, soak the plums in the broth for 30 minutes. Dry the outside of the roast with paper towels. Rub the meat all over with the mustard and roll it in the brown sugar, coating it evenly.

**2.** In a heavy 5- to 6-quart Dutch oven with a lid, heat the oil over medium-high heat, then brown the meat on all sides. Watch it—if the heat is too high, the sugar will burn, so take your time.

**3.** Remove from the heat and pour in the bourbon. Drain ½ cup of the broth that the plums are soaking in, and add to pot. Bring the mixture to a simmer, cover, transfer to the oven, and bake for 1 hour.

**4.** Remove the pot from the oven, turn the meat over, and add salt, pepper, sage, and thyme. Reduce the oven temperature to 350°F and bake for another 30 minutes. Add the plums and remaining broth and bake for another 10 minutes.

**5.** Remove from the oven, place the pork and plums on a platter and cover loosely with aluminum foil.

**6.** Strain the cooking liquid and remove as much fat as possible. Return the liquid to the pot and bring to a boil. Taste and correct the seasonings. Stir the cornstarch and water together in a small bowl and then stir the slurry into the liquid. Bring to a boil, reduce the heat to medium, and stir in the parsley and plums.

✳ **DIVA DO-AHEAD:** At this point, you can cover and refrigerate the meat in the sauce overnight or freeze for up to 1 month. Defrost, then reheat the meat wrapped in foil in a 325°F oven for 20 minutes and warm the sauce over low heat on the stove top.

**7.** Slice the meat thinly, transfer to a warm serving platter, and pour the sauce over.

# Cider-Glazed Pork and Apples

Serves 10

Pork is delicious with fruit, and apples are a perfect partner in this delicious cold-weather dish. It benefits from being made a day or two ahead so that the flavors can marry, and it can be cooked in the slow cooker after some prep work (see right), giving you lots of time to devote to other parts of the meal. I like to serve this with a savory bread pudding and a field greens salad.

2 tablespoons oil

One 4-pound rolled boneless pork loin roast

1½ teaspoons salt

1 teaspoon freshly ground black pepper

5 tablespoons unsalted butter, softened

2 large sweet onions, cut in half and thinly sliced into half-moons

6 medium-size Golden Delicious apples, peeled, cored, and cut into ½-inch wedges

¼ teaspoon ground nutmeg

⅛ teaspoon ground ginger

1 teaspoon dried thyme

⅓ cup firmly packed light brown sugar

1½ cups apple cider

½ cup beef broth

½ cup chicken broth

3 tablespoons all-purpose flour

**1.** Heat the oil in a 5-quart Dutch oven over medium-high heat and sprinkle the pork roast evenly with the salt and pepper. Brown on all sides in the hot oil and transfer to a plate.

**2.** Melt 2 tablespoons of the butter in the same pan, add the onions, apples, nutmeg, ginger, and thyme, and cook, stirring, until the onions are translucent and the apples begin to soften, about 6 minutes. Add the brown sugar, cider, and both broths, scraping up any browned bits stuck to the bottom of the pan.

**3.** Return the pork to the pan, cover, reduce the heat to medium-low, and simmer until the pork is tender, 3 to 4 hours.

✳ **DIVA DO-AHEAD:** At this point, you can let cool, cover, and refrigerate for up to 3 days. Gently reheat before continuing.

**4.** Remove the pork from the pan and cover with aluminum foil. Using a slotted spoon, remove the apples and onions from the sauce, reserving them. Mix the flour and remaining 3 tablespoons of softened butter together in a small bowl.

**5.** Bring the sauce to a boil and stir in the butter-and-flour mixture, a bit at a time, until the sauce is thickened to your taste. Taste the sauce for salt and pepper and add more if necessary. Return the apples and onions to the sauce.

**6.** Carve the pork into ½-inch-thick slices and serve, garnished with the sauce.

## Mixing Broths

Since it's difficult to find pork broth on the market, a combination of chicken and beef broths in equal proportions gives you a nice mild broth to use in pork braises.

## Slow Cooker Savvy

Prepare the pork on the stove top through step 2, then transfer everything to a 6-quart slow cooker. Cover and cook on Low for 8 to 9 hours.

# Tuscan Herbed Pork Loin

Serves 10 to 12

In Tuscany and throughout Umbria, this pork is sometimes roasted over an open fire on a rotisserie or in a wood-burning oven. You can get the same effect using your oven.

**¼ cup fresh rosemary leaves**

**2 tablespoons olive oil**

**6 cloves garlic, peeled**

**Grated zest of 1 lemon**

**1½ teaspoons salt**

**1 teaspoon freshly ground black pepper**

**One 4-pound rolled boneless pork loin roast**

**1.** In a food processor or blender, combine the rosemary, oil, garlic, lemon zest, salt, and pepper and process until the garlic is pureed.

**2.** Place the pork on a large sheet of plastic wrap and rub it all over with the rosemary mixture. Wrap tightly in the plastic wrap.

✳ **DIVA DO-AHEAD:** At this point, refrigerate for at least 12 and up to 24 hours. Bring to room temperature before continuing.

**3.** Preheat the oven to 325°F.

**4.** Preheat a large ovenproof skillet over medium-high heat and brown the roast all over. Transfer the skillet to the oven and roast the pork until an instant-read meat thermometer inserted into the center registers 155°F, about 1½ hours.

**5.** Remove from the oven, cover loosely with aluminum foil, and let rest for 20 to 25 minutes. Serve warm or at room temperature, thinly sliced and garnished with any pan juices.

## Making Gravy for the Tuscan Herbed Pork Loin

Deglaze the pan juices in the bottom of the skillet, with 1 cup of white wine and about 1½ cups of chicken broth to make a simple pan sauce. Pour the wine into the pan, set over high heat, and allow it to almost evaporate. Add the chicken broth and bring to a boil, scraping up any browned bits from the bottom of the pan. Boil the sauce for 5 to 10 minutes to reduce it. To thicken, whisk in bits of cold unsalted butter and continue whisking until the sauce is thickened and emulsified. Serve over the sliced pork. This type of pan sauce really lends itself to any interpretation; you can add fruit juice instead of wine, or a combination of beef and chicken broths for a stronger flavor.

## Pork Loin Glazes

Here are some tasty suggestions for glazing and serving with your pork loin (the glazes are easily adapted from the Glazed Ham on page 449):

- **Honey Mustard–Apricot Sauce** (page 428)
- **Old-Fashioned Barbecue Sauce** (page 427)
- **Cranberry-port glaze** (see page 451)
- **Honey mustard glaze** (see page 450)
- **Maple-orange glaze** (see page 453)
- **Apple cider glaze** (see page 453)
- **Brandied peach glaze** (see page 451)
- **Hot pineapple-mango glaze** (see page 453)

# Orange-Chipotle Pork Roast

Serves 10

Flavors of the Southwest infuse this beautifully glazed pork roast, which can be served warm, cold, or at room temperature. You can also use the glaze for ribs and chicken. Some people like a lot of heat in their food, while others like it a bit milder. Using 1 chipotle pepper gives you a nice rounded heat, while 2 kick it up quite a few notches.

**2 tablespoons olive oil**

**1½ cups finely chopped onions**

**2 cloves garlic, minced**

**1 or 2 canned chipotle chiles in adobo sauce, to your taste, finely chopped, with 1 teaspoon of sauce**

**1 cup orange marmalade**

**2 tablespoons fresh lime juice**

**2 tablespoons whole-grain mustard**

**One 4-pound rolled boneless pork loin roast**

**4 navel oranges, cut into wedges or sliced, for garnish**

**1.** Preheat the oven to 325°F. Line a roasting pan with a silicone liner or aluminum foil or coat it with nonstick cooking spray.

**2.** In a 2½-quart saucepan, heat the oil over medium heat, add the onion and garlic, and cook, stirring, until softened, about 3 minutes. Gradually stir in the chipotle peppers and sauce and cook, stirring, for another minute. Stir in the marmalade, lime juice, and mustard and bring to a boil. Remove from the heat.

✳ **DIVA DO-AHEAD:** At this point, you can let cool, cover, and refrigerate for up to 7 days. Gently reheat before continuing.

**3.** Place the roast in the roasting pan and pour half the sauce over it; keep the remaining sauce warm. Slice one of the oranges thinly and lay it over the meat. Roast, basting every half hour with the pan juices, until an instant-read meat thermometer inserted into the center registers 155°F, about 1½ hours.

**4.** Remove the pork from the oven, cover loosely with aluminum foil, and allow to rest for 20 minutes.

✳ **DIVA DO-AHEAD:** At this point, you can refrigerate the pork and reserved sauce overnight. To reheat, slice the meat, arrange on an ovenproof platter with the oranges, sprinkle the meat with 3 tablespoons of chicken broth, and cover with foil. Reheat in a preheated 325°F oven for 15 to 20 minutes. Gently reheat the sauce on the stove top.

**5.** Slice the meat thinly and arrange on a heated platter, surrounded with orange wedges or slices. Drizzle the meat with the reserved sauce or serve it separately.

# Balsamic-Glazed Pork Loin

Serves 10

For a Mediterranean feast, try this pork roast as the focus of your menu. It is delicious warm, at room temperature, or cold, and you can roast it up to 2 days ahead of time. Make sure you marinate the roast for at least 6 hours, and ideally 12 hours, to really infuse it with the flavor of the balsamic vinegar and herbs.

½ cup balsamic vinegar

¼ cup firmly packed light brown sugar

⅓ cup extra virgin olive oil

8 cloves garlic, minced

¼ cup chopped fresh rosemary

2 teaspoons salt

1 teaspoon freshly ground black pepper

One 4-pound rolled boneless pork loin roast

1 recipe Balsamic Vinegar Syrup (page 480)

Sprigs fresh rosemary for garnish

**1.** In a medium-size bowl, whisk together the vinegar, brown sugar, oil, garlic, rosemary, salt, and pepper until blended. Pour into a 2-gallon zipper-top plastic bag and add the pork roast. Squeeze the air out of the bag, seal, and smush the pork around to coat it completely with the glaze.

✳ **DIVA DO-AHEAD:** At this point, refrigerate, turning several times, for at least 6 and up to 12 hours.

**2.** Preheat the oven to 325°F. Remove the pork from the refrigerator and drain, discarding the marinade. Pat the meat dry with paper towels and let the pork come to room temperature.

**3.** Place the pork in a roasting pan and cook until an instant-read meat thermometer inserted into the center registers 155°F, about 1½ hours.

**4.** Remove from oven, cover loosely with aluminum foil, and let rest for 20 minutes.

✳ **DIVA DO-AHEAD:** At this point, you can refrigerate the pork for up to 2 days. Serve cold.

**5.** Carve the roast into thin slices and serve with the syrup on the side or spooned over the slices. Garnish with rosemary sprigs.

## Diva Fat-Free Tip

To remove small amounts of fat from sauces, skim a paper towel over the surface; it should pick up the fat and not the sauce.

# Braised Pork Loin with Sauerkraut and Onions

Serves 10

This is a great dish to serve for an Oktoberfest celebration or on any cold winter night you are in the mood to entertain. This dish is better if it's made a day or two ahead and reheated before serving. Accompany it with mashed potatoes and chunky applesauce.

2 tablespoons olive oil

One 4-pound rolled boneless pork loin roast

1½ teaspoons salt

1 teaspoon freshly ground black pepper

¼ cup (½ stick) unsalted butter

4 cups thinly sliced sweet onions

½ cup firmly packed light brown sugar

¼ cup Dijon mustard

Four 15.5-ounce cans sauerkraut, rinsed and drained

¾ cup chicken broth

¾ cup beef broth

2 teaspoons caraway seeds (optional)

**1.** Heat the oil in a 5-quart Dutch oven over medium-high heat and sprinkle the pork with the salt and pepper. Brown on all sides in the oil and transfer to a plate.

**2.** Melt the butter in the same pan over medium-high heat, add the onions, and cook, stirring, until softened, about 4 minutes. Add the brown sugar and cook, stirring, until the onions begin to caramelize, another 4 minutes. Add the mustard and sauerkraut and stir until well combined. Pour in the broths and bring to a boil, stirring to loosen any browned bits in the pan.

**3.** Return the meat to the pan, cover, and reduce the heat to medium-low. Simmer until the meat is tender, 3 to 4 hours. Add the caraway seeds, if using, during the last 45 minutes of cooking.

✳ **DIVA DO-AHEAD:** At this point, you can refrigerate for up to 2 days. Gently reheat the mixture before continuing.

**4.** Remove the meat from the pan and cover loosely with aluminum foil. Bring the sauerkraut mixture to a boil and reduce the liquid in the pan by half.

**5.** Cut the strings from the meat, carve the meat into ½-inch-thick slices, and serve with the sauerkraut mixture.

### Slow Cooker Savvy

Prepare the dish through step 2, then transfer to a 5-quart slow cooker, cover, and cook on Low for 8 to 9 hours. (Add the caraway seeds during the last 2 hours of cooking.)

# PORK TENDERLOIN

**Pork tenderloin,** or the filet mignon roast of the pork, needs to be marinated or brined before cooking since it has a tendency to dry out. Brine is a salt and water solution that can be flavored with sugar, herbs, and spices. The tenderloins are brined for 4 hours, drained, and patted dry. Then they can be rubbed and roasted to produce a tender and juicy main course or appetizer.

A pork tenderloin generally weighs around 1 pound, so 4 will serve a crowd of 10 to 12 nicely, with ³/₈ to ¹/₃ pound per person. Pork tenderloin is my cut of choice for skewers: for appetizer portions you will need 2 to 3 pounds of pork tenderloin for 10 to 12 people.

The preceding recipes for pork loin can also be used for pork tenderloin, but you will have to brine or marinate the tenderloins first (see the recipe below). For skewers, marinate the sliced meat, then thread onto the skewers. Once the meat is on the skewers, it can be refrigerated for up to 12 hours before grilling. I sometimes grill the meat and then rewarm it, covered in aluminum foil, just before serving. If you cook the skewers ahead of time, they will keep in the refrigerator for about 36 hours.

## All-Purpose Brine for Pork

Makes 4 ²/₃ cups (enough for 2 pork tenderloins or 2 to 2½ pounds of meat)

**¼ cup firmly packed light brown sugar**

**⅓ cup kosher or coarse salt**

**4 cups boiling water**

**1.** Stir the sugar and salt into the water until dissolved. Let cool to room temperature, then pour into a 2-gallon zipper-top plastic bag.

**2.** Remove the silver skin from the tenderloins (see page 421), add the tenderloins to the brine, and seal the bags.

✳ **DIVA DO-AHEAD:** At this point, refrigerate for at least 2 and up to 4 hours.

**3.** Remove the tenderloins from the brine, rinse with cold water, and pat dry before beginning the recipe.

# Shanghai Red Roasted Pork Tenderloin 🍺🥛🍸

Serves 10 to 12 as an appetizer

Asian spices and soy sauce serve as the brine for this pork tenderloin dish. You can marinate the pork overnight, then roast it early on the day you want to serve it. The meat stays moist because you roast it on a rack above simmering water. The outside of the pork will caramelize and the inside will be tender and juicy. I like to serve this warm, at room temperature, or cold, with the slices arranged on a platter, surrounded by sauces for dipping.

**Three 1-pound pork tenderloins, trimmed of silver skin (see page 421) and any fat**

**2 cloves garlic, minced**

**1 teaspoon peeled and grated fresh ginger**

**3 scallions (white and tender green parts), coarsely chopped**

**2 tablespoons firmly packed light brown sugar**

**2 tablespoons rice wine or seasoned rice vinegar**

**½ cup soy sauce**

**2 tablespoons hoisin sauce**

**¼ cup honey**

**¼ cup toasted sesame oil**

**2 cups water**

**1 recipe Chinese Hot Mustard Sauce (page 444)**

**1 recipe Sweet-and-Sour Dipping Sauce (page 444)**

**1.** Put the pork in a 2-gallon zipper-top plastic bag.

**2.** In a small bowl, stir together the garlic, ginger, scallions, brown sugar, rice wine, soy sauce, and hoisin sauce. Pour over the tenderloins and seal.

✳ **DIVA DO-AHEAD:** At this point, refrigerate for at least 8 and up to 24 hours.

**3.** Preheat the oven to 375°F. Drain the meat, discarding the marinade, and let come to room temperature.

**4.** Stir together the honey and sesame oil. Place the meat on a rack in a roasting pan and brush with some of the honey mixture. Pour the water into the bottom of the pan and roast for 20 minutes. Turn the meat and brush with more of the honey mixture. Roast for another 10 minutes, then turn again, brush with the remaining honey mixture, and add more water to the roasting pan if necessary. Continue roasting until an instant-read meat thermometer inserted into the thickest part of the meat registers 155°F, another 15 to 20 minutes.

**5.** Remove the meat from the rack, cover loosely with aluminum foil, and allow to rest for 10 to 15 minutes.

✳ **DIVA DO-AHEAD:** At this point, you can refrigerate for up to 24 hours. Serve cold or slice as directed below, cover with foil, and reheat in a preheated 325°F oven until warm, 10 to 15 minutes.

**6.** Cut the pork on an angle into ½-inch-thick slices and arrange on a platter. Serve the sauces in small lotus bowls on the serving platter and make sure you provide small spoons for serving.

## Chinese Hot Mustard Sauce

Makes ⅓ cup

A little of this hot sauce goes a long way, but it's a nice complement for Shanghai Red Roasted Pork Tenderloin.

> **2 tablespoons dry mustard**
> **¼ cup cold water**
> **1 teaspoon rice vinegar**
> **¼ teaspoon salt**

In a small bowl, whisk together all the ingredients until smooth and blended.

✳ **DIVA DO-AHEAD:** At this point, you can cover and refrigerate for up to 3 days; the mustard will get stronger the longer it sits.

## Sweet-and-Sour Dipping Sauce

Makes about 1¼ cups

This dipping sauce is great for chicken or pork skewers as well as slices of Shanghai Red Roasted Pork Tenderloin.

> **⅓ cup sugar**
> **⅓ cup rice vinegar**
> **¼ cup ketchup**
> **2 tablespoons soy sauce**
> **2½ tablespoons cornstarch mixed with 1 cup cold water**
> **2 tablespoons toasted sesame oil**

**1.** In a 2-quart saucepan, combine the sugar, vinegar, ketchup, soy sauce, and cornstarch slurry and bring to a boil.

✳ **DIVA DO-AHEAD:** At this point, you can let cool, cover, and refrigerate for up to 1 week. Reheat gently before continuing.

**2.** Remove from the heat and stir in the sesame oil. Serve the sauce warm or at room temperature.

# Braised Pork Osso Bucco Style

Serves 10

Veal osso bucco is a lovely classic Italian dish, but serving it to a large group is costly. Substituting pork makes it easy and economical to serve. I like to use cubed pork tenderloins in this recipe but you can also use loin or shoulder meat. After cutting the meat into cubes, you will brown them and then stew them in an aromatic vegetable and herb sauce. The flavor in this dish actually gets better if it's made a day or two ahead of time. Just reheat it and serve with your choice of polenta, rice, savory bread pudding, or pasta.

2 tablespoons unsalted butter

1 tablespoon olive oil

4 pounds pork tenderloin, trimmed of silver skin (see page 421) and any fat and cut into 1-inch cubes

1½ teaspoons salt

1 teaspoon freshly ground black pepper

1 cup finely chopped onions

1 cup finely chopped carrots

1 cup finely chopped celery

1 teaspoon dried sage

½ cup dry white wine or dry vermouth

½ cup chicken broth

½ cup beef broth

Two 15.5-ounce cans chopped plum tomatoes, with their juice

4 cloves garlic, minced

Grated zest of 1 lemon

Grated zest of 1 orange

½ cup finely chopped fresh parsley

**1.** In a 5-quart Dutch oven, heat the butter and the oil over medium-high heat until the butter melts. Sprinkle the pork with the salt and pepper, then brown the meat in several batches until nicely crusted on all sides, transferring them from the pan to a plate as they are cooked.

**2.** When all the meat is browned, add the onions, carrots, celery, and sage to the pan and cook, stirring, until they begin to soften and turn translucent, about 5 minutes. Add the wine and scrape up any browned bits from the bottom of the pan. Add both broths and the tomatoes and bring to a boil.

**3.** Return the pork to the pan, along with any juices that may have accumulated on the plate. Reduce the heat to medium-low, cover, and simmer until the pork is tender, about 2 hours.

**DIVA DO-AHEAD:** At this point, you can let cool, cover, and refrigerate for up to 3 days. Gently reheat before continuing.

**4.** In a small bowl, combine the garlic, citrus zests, and parsley. Remove any fat that may have accumulated on the top of the sauce, garnish with the garlic mixture, and serve.

# Fiesta Tamale Pie

Serves 10 to 12

This savory pie got a bad rap when it was served in school cafeterias, but it's really a delicious dish to make for company. The biscuits are simple to prepare, and you can have them ready to mix just before baking. If you decide not to make the biscuit topping, serve the tamale stew with corn tortillas and condiments; your guests can roll the stew in the tortillas. Anaheim chiles are mild in flavor, so if you aren't too crazy about spicy food, cut down on the amount of chili powder, rather than the Anaheim chile, which gives the dish a fresh taste and gentle heat.

Tamale Stew

**2 tablespoons vegetable oil**

**4 pounds pork tenderloin, boneless pork loin, or pork shoulder, trimmed of silver skin (see page 421) and any fat and cut into 1-inch chunks; or 8 cups leftover Pulled Pork Barbecue (page 431), trimmed of fat (see The Diva Says)**

**1½ teaspoons salt**

**1 teaspoon freshly ground black pepper**

**2 cups finely chopped onions**

**3 cloves garlic, minced**

**½ cup seeded and finely chopped Anaheim chiles**

**1 teaspoon ground cumin**

**2 teaspoons chili powder**

**Two 32-ounce cans chopped plum tomatoes, with their juice**

**2 tablespoons sugar**

**3 cups fresh corn kernels cut from the cob or frozen corn, defrosted**

**Three 15.5-ounce cans black beans, drained and rinsed**

### Cheesy Cornmeal Biscuit Topping

2 cups coarse yellow cornmeal

¼ cup sugar

2 cups all-purpose flour

1 tablespoon baking powder

¼ cup (½ stick) unsalted butter, melted

1¼ cups whole or 2% milk or evaporated skim milk

2 large eggs

2 cups finely shredded mild cheddar cheese

6 shakes of Tabasco sauce

**1.** To make the stew, heat the oil in a 5-quart Dutch oven over medium-high heat and sprinkle the pork with the salt and pepper. Working in batches, brown the meat on all sides, transferring the pieces to a plate as they are done.

**2.** When all of the pork is browned, combine the onions, garlic, chiles, cumin, and chili powder in the pan and cook, stirring, until the onion begins to turn translucent, about 4 minutes. Add the tomatoes, sugar, and the browned pork. Cover, reduce the heat to medium-low, and simmer until the meat is tender and falling apart, 2 to 3 hours. Add the corn and beans to the pan and simmer for another 20 minutes.

✳ **DIVA DO-AHEAD:** At this point, you can let cool, cover, and refrigerate for up to 3 days. Gently reheat before continuing.

**3.** Preheat the oven to 375°F.

**4.** To make the biscuit topping, in a large bowl, whisk together the cornmeal, sugar, flour, and baking powder to aerate them. Make a well in the center and blend in the melted butter, milk, eggs, 1½ cups of the cheese, and the Tabasco until combined.

**5.** Transfer the pork stew mixture to a 13 x 9-inch baking dish or leave it in the Dutch oven. Either drop ¼-cup portions of the biscuit mixture or spread the biscuit mixture over the top as you would a crust. Sprinkle with the remaining ½ cup of cheese and bake until the topping is cooked through and golden and the filling is bubbling. Remove from the oven and serve right from the dish.

The Diva Says: If using leftover cooked pulled pork, add it to the Dutch oven with the tomatoes and sugar. Simmer for 1 hour before adding the corn and beans, and proceed with the recipe.

### Slow Cooker Savvy

Prepare the stew on the stove top through step 2, then transfer the entire stew mixture, including the corn and beans, to a 5- to 6-quart slow cooker. Cover and cook on Low for 6 hours. Remove from the slow cooker and pick up the recipe with step 4.

# Honey-Ginger Pork Satay

Serves 10 to 12 as an appetizer

These spicy pork slices are marinated for at least 4 hours, then grilled on skewers and served with a peanut sauce for dipping. I like to serve them as appetizers along with spring rolls or lettuce wraps. Perfect for a tailgate party, they cook quickly on the grill.

⅔ cup soy sauce

¼ cup honey

1½ teaspoons ground coriander

1 teaspoon peeled and grated fresh ginger

2 cloves garlic, minced

3 tablespoons rice vinegar

4 scallions (white and tender green parts), minced

2 tablespoons toasted sesame oil

¼ teaspoon cayenne pepper

3 pounds pork tenderloin, trimmed of silver skin (see page 421) and any fat and cut into ½-inch-thick slices

1 recipe Pacific Rim Peanut Sauce (page 481)

**1.** In a medium-size bowl, whisk together the soy sauce, honey, coriander, ginger, garlic, vinegar, scallions, sesame oil, and cayenne until blended.

**2.** Put the pork in a 2-gallon zipper-top plastic bag and pour the marinade over it. Seal the bag and turn upside down a few times to coat the pork.

✳ **DIVA DO-AHEAD:** At this point, refrigerate for at least 4 and up to 8 hours.

**3.** Soak bamboo skewers in water for 1 hour.

**4.** Drain the pork, discarding the marinade, and pat dry with paper towels. Thread 1 or 2 pieces of meat onto each skewer.

✳ **DIVA DO-AHEAD:** At this point, you can arrange on a baking sheet, cover, and refrigerate for up to 12 hours.

**5.** Build a hot charcoal fire or preheat the gas grill or broiler for 10 minutes. Grill or broil the pork skewers until cooked through, about 2 minutes on one side and 1 minute on the other side.

**6.** Arrange the skewers on a serving platter, and serve warm or at room temperature with the sauce on the side for dipping.

## Great Marinades for Pork Satay

- **Garlic-Herb Marinade** (page 393)
- **Marinade Provençal** (page 394)
- **Southwestern Marinade** (page 395)
- **Teriyaki Marinade** (page 395)
- **Mediterranean Marinade** (page 396)
- **Bloody Mary Marinade** (page 396)

# Glazed Ham ⬛🍷🥂

Serves 10 to 12

Every year at Mom's house, she would spend what seemed like an eternity studding a ham with cloves and then garnishing with pineapple slices to make that picture-perfect ham you see in magazines. Unfortunately, the ham cooked for so long that all you tasted was the cloves and not the delectable smoked flavor of the meat. The secret to a great ham, which is already cooked when you buy it, is to bake it slowly in a 300°F oven, covered, for 2 to 3 hours to warm it through and then, for the last 30 minutes, turn up the heat and slather on the glaze. This will yield a gloriously crackly and attractive glaze that still lets the smoky character of the meat shine through. I long ago overdosed on the clove-and-pineapple combination and have since moved on to other flavors in my ham glazes, which I share on pages 450 to 453.

I recommend that you buy a spiral-sliced ham because it's already sliced and, when you pour on the glaze, it actually will flavor the meat to some degree because it will ooze down a bit in between the slices. If you don't buy an already sliced ham, it will be simple to carve before serving, so don't worry about that part. Hams are sold whole, and as halves in shank and butt portions. I think the butt portion is the most tender, but either one will make a fine main course when reheated and glazed.

I'm not fond of canned hams, or the hams that are shaped into a boneless ham-like form; the manufacturer usually adds a lot of water to the ham and rolls different cuts of the ham together to make this product. When shopping for a ham in the store, read the label; you are looking for something labeled "ham with natural juices." It shouldn't contain any water.

## How Much Glaze?

You will need 2 to 4 cups of glaze: two cups will give you a nice thin coat, while 4 cups gives you a barrier of glaze. Some glazes are more fluid than others and for those types you'll need more because, given the effects of gravity, they will slide off. But they do mingle with the pan juices to give you a nice sauce for pouring over the ham before serving.

## Save a Pan, Use a Bag

Oven baking bags work really well for cooking ham, sealing in the juices. It has gotten harder and harder to find the large size, however. If you're lucky enough to have some, seal the ham in a bag and bake as directed in the master recipe. Slit the bag open and proceed with the instructions for glazing.

**One 6- to 8-pound fully cooked, bone-in, spiral-sliced or unsliced ham**

**Glaze of your choice (see below)**

**1.** Preheat the oven to 300°F. Line a large roasting pan with a silicone liner or aluminum foil.

**2.** Remove the packaging from the ham and drain off any juices. Place the ham in the prepared pan, flat side down, and cover the ham and pan completely with foil. Bake until an instant-read meat thermometer inserted into the center registers 130°F, about 2½ hours. (Since the meat is already cooked, you only need to warm it up.)

**3.** Increase the oven temperature to 375°F and remove the aluminum foil from the pan. Pour the glaze over the ham and bake, uncovered, basting every 10 minutes with the pan juices, until the glaze is set, another 20 to 30 minutes.

**4.** Remove the ham from the oven, cover with foil, and allow to rest for 15 minutes before carving, if necessary. Brush the ham with some of the remaining glaze or surround with fruit and serve.

---

### Diva Variations

**Honey Mustard Glazed Ham:** In a medium-size bowl, combine 1½ cups of Dijon mustard, 1 cup of honey, ¼ cup of distilled white vinegar, and 2 teaspoons of dried tarragon.

✳ **DIVA DO-AHEAD:** At this point, you can cover and refrigerate for up to 1 week.

Bake the ham as directed in the recipe, raising the oven temperature and removing the foil when you are ready to glaze. Spread half the glaze over the ham and bake for 20 minutes, basting as directed in step 3. Ten minutes before the ham is done, if you wish, sprinkle ½ cup of firmly packed light brown sugar evenly over the ham and bake until it caramelizes and forms an attractive crust. (For a truly crackly glaze, substitute raw sugar, which has a larger crystal.) Remove the ham from the oven and serve the remaining glaze on the side.

**Crackly Honey-Cinnamon Glazed Ham:** In a medium-size bowl, combine 1½ cups of honey, ¼ cup of fresh lemon juice, and 1 teaspoon of ground cinnamon. Bake the ham as directed in the recipe, raising the oven temperature and removing the foil when you are ready to glaze. Brush the mixture evenly over the ham and bake for 20 minutes, basting as directed in step 3. Then press ½ cup of raw or firmly packed dark brown sugar evenly into the glaze all around and bake until the glaze sets and begins to caramelize, another 10 minutes.

**Traditional Pineapple Glazed Ham:** Canned pineapple actually works best for this, because the fresh is not always sweet and can be tough. In a medium-size bowl, combine one 15.5-ounce can of crushed pineapple in heavy syrup, 1 cup of firmly packed dark brown sugar, ¼ cup of Dijon mustard, and 1 teaspoon of ground cloves. Bake the ham as directed in the recipe, raising the oven temperature and removing the foil when you are ready to glaze. Pour the mixture evenly over the ham and bake for 15 minutes, basting as directed in step 3. Drape the drained slices from one 15.5-ounce can of sliced pineapple over the ham and bake for another 15 minutes. Serve garnished with the pineapple slices.

**Cranberry-Port Glazed Ham:** In a 3-quart saucepan, over medium heat, combine one 15.5-ounce can whole-berry cranberry sauce, 1 cup of orange marmalade, ¼ cup of orange juice, ¼ cup of port wine, ½ teaspoon of ground cinnamon, and ¼ teaspoon of ground ginger and heat until bubbling. Remove from the heat and let cool to room temperature.

✳ **DIVA DO-AHEAD:** At this point, you can cover and refrigerate for up to 3 weeks.

Bake the ham as directed in the recipe, raising the oven temperature and removing

## The Diva's Restaurant Look

After the ham has baked, spread a thin layer of Dijon mustard all over the ham, then press raw sugar into the Dijon mustard. (Depending upon the size of your ham, you will need about 1 to 1½ cups of sugar.) Using a crème brûlée torch, apply the flame to the sugar until it begins to caramelize and crackle, using long strokes with the torch, holding it about 8 inches from the surface of the ham to prevent burning. Display the ham for all to see, then carve it in the kitchen before serving.

the foil when you are ready to glaze. Pour the glaze evenly over the ham and bake for 30 minutes, basting as directed in step 3. Serve garnished with orange slices.

**Brandied Peach Glazed Ham:** This beautiful glaze can also be served as a sauce to accompany the ham if you'd like. The peaches need to soak in the brandy syrup for at least 24 hours. If nice fresh peaches are unavailable, I suggest substituting 8 cups (about two 16-ounce bags) of frozen sliced peaches, defrosted. In a 5-quart saucepan or Dutch oven, combine 1½ cups of brandy, 2 sticks of cinnamon, 1 teaspoon of ground ginger, 1 cup of firmly packed light brown sugar, and 2 tablespoons of vanilla extract and bring to a boil. Turn off the heat, allow the syrup to steep for 1 hour, and strain the spices out of the syrup. Put 8 large peeled, pitted, and quartered peaches in a 2-gallon zipper-top plastic bag, pour the syrup over the peaches, and seal the bag.

✳ **DIVA DO-AHEAD:** At this point, refrigerate for at least 24 hours and up to 3 days.

Drain the peaches, reserving the syrup. Put half the peaches in a food processor or blender and process until smooth. Stir in ½ cup of the brandy syrup and ⅓ cup of firmly packed light brown sugar. Bake the ham as directed in the recipe, raising the oven temperature and removing the foil when you are ready to glaze. Pour the glaze evenly over the ham and bake for 15 minutes, basting as directed in step 3. Arrange the remaining peaches in the bottom of the roasting pan and sprinkle the ham and peaches with ⅔ cup of firmly packed light brown sugar. Bake for another 15 minutes,

# SLAM DUNK SIMPLE GLAZES

**These glazes are beyond easy,** based on one or two ingredients that are probably in your pantry. For instructions on how to bake and glaze a ham, see the master recipe on page 449.

- 2 cans of Coca-Cola and ⅔ cup of firmly packed dark brown sugar. Blend together and glaze as directed. Add 2 tablespoons of Jerk Seasoning Rub (page 427) and ¼ cup of dark rum for a Caribbean flavor.

- 2 cans of root beer and ⅔ cup of firmly packed dark brown sugar. Blend together and glaze as directed. Add ½ cup of bourbon to the mix for an old Kentucky favorite!

- 1½ cups of apple jelly and ½ cup of Dijon mustard. Blend together and glaze as directed. Garnish the platter with baked apple slices, which can be strewn in the roasting pan to bake along with the ham.

- 1½ cups of currant jelly, ½ cup of crème de cassis, and ⅓ cup of firmly packed dark brown sugar. Heat together in a small saucepan and glaze as directed.

- 1½ cups of currant jelly and 1 cup of orange marmalade. Heat together in a small saucepan and glaze as directed. Garnish the platter with sliced oranges.

- 2 tablespoons of Chinese 5-spice powder, 2 cups of orange marmalade, and ¼ cup of rice vinegar. Heat together in a small saucepan and glaze as directed.

- 2 tablespoons of Jerk Seasoning Rub (page 427), 1 cup of firmly packed dark brown sugar, 2 tablespoons of dark rum (optional), and 1½ cups of mango nectar. Heat together in a small saucepan and glaze as directed.

- 2 tablespoons of pure ancho chile powder and 2 cans of Coca-Cola. Heat together in a small saucepan and glaze as directed.

then serve the ham, garnished with the peaches.

**Hot Pineapple-Mango Glazed Ham:**
Combine 2 cups of peeled, pitted, and diced ripe mangoes (3 large); one 15.5-ounce can of crushed pineapple, drained; 1 cup of firmly packed light brown sugar; 2 table-spoons of seeded and finely chopped jala-peños; and 2 tablespoons of fresh lime juice in a blender or food processor and process until smooth. Bake the ham as directed in the recipe, raising the oven temperature and removing the foil when you are ready to glaze. Pour the glaze evenly over the ham and bake for 30 minutes, basting as directed in step 3.

**Maple-Orange Glazed Ham:** Make sure you use pure maple syrup rather than the stuff sold in the log house in your grocery store. In a small saucepan, combine 1/2 cup of maple syrup, 1 cup of orange marma-lade, 1/3 cup of rice vinegar, and 1/2 cup of firmly packed dark brown sugar and bring to a boil, stirring until the sugar dissolves. Reduce the heat to low and simmer, stirring occasionally, until the glaze is thickened slightly, about 10 minutes. Bake the ham as directed in the recipe, raising the oven tem-perature and removing the foil when you are ready to glaze. Pour the glaze evenly over the ham and bake for 20 minutes, basting as directed in step 3. Garnish the ham with 4 peeled and thinly sliced navel oranges and bake for another 10 minutes.

**Pan Asian Glazed Ham:** This glaze also makes a nice dipping sauce for seafood, pork, chicken, lamb, and beef. In a medium-size saucepan, combine 2 cloves of garlic, minced; 1 teaspoon of peeled and grated fresh ginger; 1 cup of soy sauce; 1/2 cup of

rice wine or seasoned rice vinegar; 1/2 cup of firmly packed dark brown sugar; 1/2 cup of hoisin sauce; and 1/4 cup of ketchup and bring to a boil. Reduce the heat to medium-low and simmer, stirring occasionally, until slightly thickened, about 10 minutes.

✳ **DIVA DO-AHEAD:** At this point, you can let cool, cover, and refrigerate for up to 5 days. Bring to room temperature or reheat gently before using.

Bake the ham as directed in the recipe, rais-ing the oven temperature and removing the foil when you are ready to glaze. Pour the glaze evenly over the ham and bake, bast-ing as directed in step 3, for 30 minutes. Garnish the platter with sliced scallions and sprinkle toasted sesame seeds over the ham for a nice crunch.

**Apple Cider–Glazed Ham:** When I use this glaze, I like to bake the ham with apple slices and then serve the ham surrounded by the apples. They become caramelized and infused with the flavors of the ham and glaze. In a medium-size saucepan, combine 1 cup of apple jelly, 1 1/2 cups of unfiltered apple cider, 2 tablespoons of cider vinegar, 1/2 cup of firmly packed dark brown sugar, and 1/4 teaspoon of ground allspice and bring to a boil. Reduce the heat to medium-low and simmer for 10 minutes to blend the flavors.

✳ **DIVA DO-AHEAD:** At this point, you can let cool, cover, and refrigerate for up to 5 days.

Bake the ham as directed in the recipe, rais-ing the oven temperature and removing the foil when you are ready to glaze. Pour evenly over the ham and bake, basting as directed in step 3, for 30 minutes.

# Lamb

**Lamb is a juicy and succulent meat** that, when handled right, can be the star of your party. Many people say they don't like it because they remember their mom's Sunday lamb dinner being tough and fatty. Years have passed and the lamb that is available now is both lean and tender. The best cuts to serve for parties are a boned rolled leg of lamb (it takes all the guesswork out of carving); lamb racks (which are so simple, you'll be making them all the time, experimenting with the different crust options I give you); and kabobs, cut from the lamb leg or shoulder, which are marinated and grilled. Lamb, like beef tenderloin, can be expensive, so watch for sales. Most warehouse clubs, such as Costco and Sam's, sell lamb racks and lamb already boned and tied at reasonable prices.

*Lamb racks:* These generally weigh about 1 pound and come with 8 ribs attached. Make sure that the butcher has removed the chine or backbone; otherwise, the roast will be nearly impossible to carve. Try to remove as much of the fat as possible from the rack, so that the rub or crust will adhere, rather than running off during the cooking process. Lamb racks are terrific to do ahead; just roast or grill them beforehand to an internal temperature of 125°F (rare). Let them cool to room temperature, wrap in aluminum foil, and refrigerate for up to 24 hours. Then reheat the lamb right before serving in a preheated 325°F oven for 15 minutes; this will give you medium-rare lamb. Always allow the meat to rest, covered loosely with foil, before carving.

*Whole bone-in leg of lamb:* A whole leg makes an impressive dinner entrée and is easily roasted with a coating of your choice of flavors. Any leftovers are terrific served in pita with Cucumber Yogurt Sauce (page 492), or sautéed with peppers and onions, or tossed into a salad. Carving a leg of lamb is tricky, though, so if you don't feel comfortable carving, a boned leg of lamb is a good choice.

***Rolled leg of lamb:*** This is great for roasting ahead of time and can be served at room temperature with an appropriate sauce. Doing it ahead of time has the added benefit of allowing the smoke and odor of the lamb to dissipate. Lamb needs to be cooked at high heat to give it a nice crispy crust, often resulting in some smoke.

***Kabobs:*** You can also cook kabobs ahead of time. Allow them to cool and refrigerate for up to 2 days. When you're ready, bring them to room temperature, then heat them on the grill before serving, or serve them at room temperature. See the box on page 465 for more information about lamb kabobs.

# Rolled Boneless Leg of Lamb

Serves 10 to 14

I love to serve thinly sliced medium (pink in the center) roast leg of lamb on a platter, surrounded by roasted vegetables or beautiful spring greens dressed with a Dijon vinaigrette. Regardless of how you decide to serve this delectable cut of meat, remember that you can roast it the day before, then slice it on the day you wish to serve it. I recommend marinating leg of lamb; that will ensure it is tender and juicy when roasted. Unrolling a boneless roast and stuffing it is another option; this gives you a beautifully patterned roast that is flavorful inside and out.

**One 5- to 6-pound leg of lamb or 3- to 4½-pound boneless leg of lamb**

**2 cups marinade of your choice**

**¼ cup olive oil**

**1.** Have your butcher bone, if necessary, and butterfly the leg so it is a uniform thickness all over; this will help it cook more evenly.

**2.** Place the lamb in a large zipper-top plastic bag, pour over the marinade, seal, and shake a few times to coat with the marinade.

❋ **DIVA DO-AHEAD:** At this point, refrigerate for at least 12 and up to 36 hours, turning the bag a few times to keep the lamb evenly coated.

**3.** Preheat the oven to 400°F.

**4.** Drain the lamb, discarding the marinade, and pat dry with paper towels. Place the lamb on a cutting board, roll it up, and tie at 1-inch intervals with cotton string. Place on a rack in a roasting pan, brush with the olive oil, and roast for 15 minutes. Reduce the oven temperature to 350°F and roast until an instant-read meat thermometer inserted into the center registers 135°F, another 45 to 55 minutes.

**5.** Remove the lamb from the oven, transfer to a cutting board, and cover loosely with aluminum foil. Let rest for 15 to 20 minutes.

❋ **DIVA DO-AHEAD:** At this point, you can cover and refrigerate overnight. Let come to room temperature before serving.

**6.** Cut the strings, thinly slice the lamb, and arrange on a serving platter.

# FIVE FANTASTIC LAMB MARINADES

**These simple marinades** will give your roast lamb a knock-out flavor.

## Rosemary and Lemon Marinade

Makes about 1½ cups (enough for 4 pounds of meat)

Rosemary, lemon, and lamb are a match made in culinary heaven, and the marinade is also dandy made with oregano instead of rosemary. Try this for a Mediterranean-inspired party or a summertime al fresco dinner. The addition of vegetable oil helps keep the olive oil from solidifying in the refrigerator. This marinade also works well with chicken.

- **½ cup extra virgin olive oil**
- **½ cup fresh lemon juice**
- **⅓ cup vegetable oil**
- **¼ cup chopped fresh rosemary**
- **Grated zest of 2 lemons**
- **3 cloves garlic, minced**
- **1½ teaspoons salt**
- **1 teaspoon freshly ground black pepper**

In a small bowl, whisk together all the ingredients until blended.

✳ **DIVA DO-AHEAD:** At this point, you can cover and refrigerate for up to 1 week.

## Garlic-Thyme Marinade

Makes about 1½ cups (enough for 4 pounds of meat)

This is a great all-purpose marinade that you can use for lamb or poultry. The soy sauce and red wine vinegar give it some character, while garlic and thyme add spice to the mix.

- **½ cup extra virgin olive oil**
- **⅓ cup vegetable oil**
- **⅓ cup red wine vinegar**
- **¼ cup soy sauce**
- **6 cloves garlic, slivered**
- **2 teaspoons dried thyme**
- **1 teaspoon salt**
- **1 teaspoon freshly ground black pepper**

In a small bowl, whisk together all the ingredients.

✳ **DIVA DO-AHEAD:** At this point, you can cover and refrigerate for up to 1 week.

## Burgundy Marinade

Makes about 2 cups (enough for 6 pounds of meat)

This deep red marinade gives the lamb a rosy glow when it's roasted. The wine helps mellow the flavor of the lamb and makes it very tender.

- **1¼ cups Burgundy wine**
- **½ cup extra virgin olive oil**

⅓ cup vegetable oil

2 teaspoons dried thyme

1 teaspoon salt

1 teaspoon freshly ground black pepper

In a medium-size bowl, whisk together all the ingredients.

✳ **DIVA DO-AHEAD:** At this point, you can cover and refrigerate for up to 1 week.

## Ginger-Soy Marinade

Makes about 1¾ cups (enough for 4 to 5 pounds of meat)

This Asian-inspired marinade produces a deliciously tender and juicy lamb, which is terrific hot, cold, or at room temperature. Try serving it on a bed of Pacific Rim Slaw (page 187) with fried rice; it's a great casual dinner choice. Garnish the finished dish with 2 tablespoons of toasted sesame seeds (see page 83) and 3 chopped scallions.

1 cup soy sauce

¼ cup vegetable oil

¼ cup rice wine or seasoned rice vinegar

3 cloves garlic, minced

2 teaspoons peeled and grated fresh ginger

3 scallions (white and tender green parts), chopped

2 teaspoons toasted sesame oil

In a small bowl, combine all of the ingredients.

✳ **DIVA DO-AHEAD:** At this point, you can cover and refrigerate for up to 1 week.

## Kasbah Marinade

Makes about 1⅓ cups (enough for 4 pounds of meat)

This savory marinade with mint, apricots, cumin, and turmeric has the flavors of Morocco. Try it for a roasted rolled leg of lamb or kabobs.

⅔ cup olive oil

½ cup apricot nectar

4 cloves garlic, minced

1½ teaspoons ground cumin

½ teaspoon turmeric

Grated zest of 1 orange

¼ cup packed chopped fresh mint

Combine all the ingredients in a small bowl, and stir to blend.

✳ **DIVA DO-AHEAD:** At this point, you can cover and refrigerate for up to 5 days.

# Feta and Spinach Stuffed Leg of Lamb

Serves 10 to 12

The gorgeously green stuffing forms a lovely pattern when the meat is sliced. Mediterranean Marinade (page 396), Marinade Provençal (page 394), or Citrus-Rosemary Marinade (page 397) would work very nicely here. Make sure you let the lamb rest before slicing because it gives the stuffing a chance to firm up.

2 tablespoons unsalted butter

½ cup finely chopped onion

4 cloves garlic, minced

Two 16-ounce bags frozen chopped spinach, defrosted

⅛ teaspoon ground nutmeg

1 teaspoon salt

½ teaspoon freshly ground black pepper

1½ cups crumbled feta cheese

1½ to 2 cups marinade of your choice

One 5- to 6-pound leg of lamb, prepared through step 2 on page 457

¼ cup olive oil

**1.** In a medium-size skillet, melt the butter over medium heat, add the onion and garlic, and cook, stirring, until the onion is softened, about 3 minutes. Add the spinach, nutmeg, salt, and pepper and cook, stirring, until the spinach mixture is dry. Taste for salt and pepper and add more if necessary.

**2.** Transfer the stuffing to a bowl and allow to cool for 15 to 20 minutes. Add the feta and stir to combine.

✳ **DIVA DO-AHEAD:** At this point, you can cover and refrigerate for up to 2 days.

**3.** After marinating the lamb, drain it and pat dry. Place it on a work surface and spread evenly with the spinach stuffing. Roll the lamb into a tight roll and tie with cotton string at 1-inch intervals.

✳ **DIVA DO-AHEAD:** At this point, you can cover and refrigerate for up to 24 hours. Bring to room temperature before continuing.

**4.** Preheat the oven to 400°F.

**5.** Place the roast on a rack in a roasting pan, brush with the olive oil, and roast for 15 minutes. Reduce the oven temperature to 350°F and roast until an instant-read meat thermometer inserted into the center registers 135°F, another 45 to 55 minutes.

**6.** Remove the roast from the oven and transfer to a cutting board. Cover loosely with aluminum foil, and let rest for 15 to 20 minutes.

✳ **DIVA DO-AHEAD:** At this point, you can cover and refrigerate overnight. Let come to room temperature before serving.

**7.** Cut the strings, thinly slice the lamb, and arrange on a serving platter.

# Garlic and Herb Stuffed Leg of Lamb 🍶🍺🍷🥂

Serves 10 to 12

This rosemary-and-garlic stuffing is a perfect partner for roasted lamb dry rubbed with Grandma's Rub (page 398) or marinated in Garlic-Herb Marinade (page 393), Cabernet Marinade (page 393), Garlic-Thyme Marinade (page 458), Burgundy Marinade (page 458), or Kasbah Marinade (page 459).

**3 tablespoons unsalted butter**

**6 tablespoons olive oil**

**8 cloves garlic, slivered**

**¼ cup chopped fresh rosemary**

**3½ cups fresh bread crumbs**

**1½ to 2 cups marinade of your choice**

**One 5- to 6-pound leg of lamb, prepared through step 2 on page 457**

**⅓ to ½ cup Dijon mustard, as needed**

**1.** In a large skillet, heat the butter and 2 tablespoons of the oil over medium-low heat until the butter is melted. Cook the garlic, stirring, for about 6 minutes, being careful not to let it brown. Add the rosemary and cook, stirring, until fragrant, another 2 minutes. Add the bread crumbs and cook, stirring, until they begin to become crisp, about 3 minutes. Transfer the crumb mixture to a bowl and allow to cool.

✳ **DIVA DO-AHEAD:** At this point, you can cover and refrigerate for up to 5 days or freeze for up to 2 months. Defrost before continuing.

**2.** Remove the lamb from the marinade and pat dry. Put the lamb on a work surface and spread the mustard over the top.

Press the bread crumb mixture evenly into the mustard and roll up the lamb into a tight roll, tying it with cotton string at 1-inch intervals.

✳ **DIVA DO-AHEAD:** At this point, you can cover and refrigerate for up to 8 hours. Bring to room temperature before continuing

**3.** Preheat the oven to 400°F.

**4.** Place the roast on a rack in a roasting pan, brush with the remaining ¼ cup of olive oil, and roast for 15 minutes. Reduce the oven temperature to 350°F and roast until an instant-read meat thermometer inserted into the center registers 135°F, another 45 to 55 minutes.

**5.** Remove the roast from the oven. Transfer to a cutting board, cover loosely with aluminum foil, and let rest for 15 to 20 minutes.

✳ **DIVA DO-AHEAD:** At this point, you can cover and refrigerate overnight. Let come to room temperature before serving.

**6.** Cut the strings, thinly slice the lamb, and arrange on a serving platter.

---

## Great Marinades, Rubs, and Crusts for Leg of Lamb

- Garlic-Herb Marinade (page 393)
- Cabernet Marinade (page 393)
- Marinade Provençal (page 394)
- Southwestern Marinade (page 395)
- Mediterranean Marinade (page 396)
- Bloody Mary Marinade (page 396)
- Citrus-Rosemary Marinade (page 397)
- Grandma's Rub (page 398)
- Garlic-Herb Crust (page 399)

## Serving It Up

Many people don't like bloody rare meat; others dislike it well done. I find it is a nice touch to serve lamb or beef arranged according to its degree of doneness—beginning with rare and ending with medium to well-done slices. I also like to trim the fat from particularly fatty pieces of meat before placing them on the platter; it's definitely more attractive that way.

# Sun-Dried Tomato and Leek Stuffed Leg of Lamb

Serves 10 to 12

This aromatic and beautifully colored stuffing adds a nice flavor to the roasted leg of lamb, which you can marinate in Mediterranean Marinade (page 396) or Garlic-Herb Marinade (page 393). The roast slices beautifully, and the herbed garlic cheese melts over the slices when served warm or makes a nice surprise inside when served at room temperature.

**2 tablespoons unsalted butter**

**2 leeks (white part only), washed well and finely chopped**

**1 cup oil-packed sun-dried tomatoes, drained and finely chopped**

**1½ to 2 cups Mediterranean Marinade (page 396) or Garlic-Herb Marinade (page 393)**

**One 5- to 6-pound leg of lamb, prepared through step 2 on page 457**

**Two 3.5-ounce packages herbed garlic cheese, such as Boursin, softened**

**¼ cup chopped fresh basil**

**¼ cup olive oil**

**1.** In a medium-size skillet, melt the butter over medium heat. Add the leeks and cook, stirring, until softened, about 3 minutes. Add the tomatoes and cook, stirring, another minute to blend the flavors.

**2.** Drain the lamb, discarding the marinade, and pat dry. Lay the roast on a work surface and spread the garlic herb cheese evenly over the lamb. Press the leek-and-tomato mixture into the lamb and top with the basil leaves. Roll up the lamb into a tight roll and tie with cotton string at 1-inch intervals.

✳ **DIVA DO-AHEAD:** At this point, you can cover and refrigerate for up to 24 hours. Bring to room temperature before continuing.

**3.** Preheat the oven to 400°F.

**4.** Place the roast on a wire rack in a roasting pan, brush with the olive oil, and roast for 15 minutes. Reduce the oven temperature to 350°F and roast until an instant-read meat thermometer inserted into the center registers 135°F, another 45 to 55 minutes.

**5.** Remove the roast from the oven, transfer to a cutting board, cover loosely with aluminum foil, and let rest for 15 to 20 minutes.

✳ **DIVA DO-AHEAD:** At this point, you can cover and refrigerate overnight. Let come to room temperature before serving.

**6.** Cut the strings, slice the lamb thinly, and arrange on a serving platter.

# Pesto-Crusted and Stuffed Leg of Lamb

Serves 10 to 12

A gorgeously green crust and spiral swirl on the inside of this leg of lamb make it a beautiful centerpiece for any buffet dinner. I use the pesto as you would a dry rub and allow it to permeate the meat for up to 36 hours. This is best at room temperature, but it's also delicious warm or cold.

**One 5- to 6-pound leg of lamb**

**3 cups Basil or Sun-Dried Tomato Pesto, homemade (page 97) or store-bought, or Tapenade (page 84)**

**1.** Have your butcher bone and butterfly the leg so that it is a uniform thickness all over; this will help it cook more evenly.

**2.** Place the meat on a work surface and spread some of the pesto over the lamb. Roll up the lamb tightly and tie with cotton string at 1-inch intervals.

**3.** Brush some of the remaining pesto over the rolled lamb and cover tightly with plastic wrap.

❋ **DIVA DO-AHEAD:** At this point, refrigerate for at least 12 and up to 36 hours. Cover and refrigerate or freeze any leftover pesto as well. Defrost the pesto before continuing.

**4.** Preheat the oven to 400°F.

**5.** Remove the lamb from the refrigerator and let come to room temperature for 30 minutes. Brush the outside of the lamb with the remaining pesto.

**6.** Place the roast on a wire rack in a roasting pan and roast for 15 minutes. Reduce the oven temperature to 350°F and roast until an instant-read meat thermometer inserted into the center registers 135°F, another 45 to 55 minutes.

**7.** Remove the roast from the oven, transfer to a cutting board, cover loosely with aluminum foil, and let rest for 15 to 20 minutes.

❋ **DIVA DO-AHEAD:** At this point, you can cover and refrigerate overnight. Let come to room temperature, unless you prefer to serve cold.

**8.** Cut the strings, slice the lamb thinly, and arrange on a serving platter.

# LAMB KABOBS

**Lamb kabobs are a nice choice** for appetizers or entrées at parties. For 10 servings, cut 4 pounds of lamb shoulder or leg into 1-inch pieces, then marinate for at least 4 hours and up to 24 hours in any of the marinades on pages 393 to 397 or 458 to 459. If you are grilling on wooden skewers, soak them in water for at least 1 hour to prevent burning.

To grill kabobs, build a hot charcoal fire or preheat a gas grill, grill pan, or broiler for 10 minutes. Grill the kabobs for 3 to 4 minutes on each side for medium-rare. Remove from the heat and serve, or allow to cool to room temperature first. You can also refrigerate for up to 24 hours and bring to room temperature before serving, or reheat, covered with aluminum foil, in a preheated 350°F oven for 10 minutes.

For an appetizer, thread 2 small chunks of meat onto each skewer and grill to the desired degree of doneness, then serve on a bed of field greens or with pita bread quarters and one or more dipping sauces alongside to complement the flavor of the marinade you have used.

To serve kabobs for a main course, grill, then remove from the skewers and serve family style on top of a huge platter of roasted vegetables, pilaf, or a field green salad dressed with your favorite vinaigrette.

## The Diva Says:

I recommend removing the food from the skewers when serving kabobs as a main course for two reasons: If you have used metal skewers they will be red-hot and your guests shouldn't have to deal with them. Second, it's much easier for you to remove the food from the skewers than for your guests, who may have trouble wrestling with a skewer while balancing a plate of food.

# Roasted Rack of Lamb

Serves 10

Rack of lamb is terrific finger food and an elegant choice for that evening when you want to serve a luxurious meal. No one has to know that you've prepared it ahead of time. You can quickly reheat racks of lamb just before serving or just let them come to room temperature. Each rack of lamb usually has 8 ribs attached to it and weighs almost 1 pound. I usually figure on 3 ribs per person for a main course, so you will need at least 3 racks, and 4 if you are serving a hungry crowd. Rack of lamb is the loin of the lamb. It therefore doesn't need any marinating for tenderness, but it does benefit from a slather or rub on the outside to flavor the chops.

> **Three or four 8-rib racks of lamb, trimmed of excess fat and chine bone removed (have the butcher do this for you)**
>
> **1 cup rub of your choice (see below)**

**1.** Place the lamb racks on individual pieces of plastic wrap, spread the rub over the lamb on both sides, and wrap in the plastic wrap.

✳ **DIVA DO-AHEAD:** At this point, refrigerate for at least 4 and up to 24 hours.

**2.** Preheat the oven to 400°F.

**3.** Remove the lamb from the wrap, place in a roasting pan, fat side up, and roast until an instant-read meat thermometer inserted into the thickest part of the meat registers 135°F, 30 to 40 minutes.

✳ **DIVA DO-AHEAD:** If you want to prepare this earlier in the day or the day before, roast until the internal temperature reaches 125°F and remove from the oven. Let cool to room temperature, then wrap in foil and refrigerate for up to 24 hours. Reheat the lamb, tented with foil, in a preheated 350°F oven for 15 minutes. The internal temperature should be 135°F.

**4.** Remove the lamb from the oven, cover loosely with aluminum foil, and let rest for 10 minutes. Carve the lamb into chops and serve.

## Great Rubs for Rack of Lamb

- **Grandma's Rub** (page 398)
- **Santa Maria Tri-Tip Roast barbecue rub** (see page 388)
- **Garlic-Herb Crust** (page 399)
- **Mustard-Horseradish Crust** (page 399)

## Diva Variation

**Grilled Rack of Lamb:** Preheat your gas grill for 10 minutes or make a charcoal fire and push the coals to either side of the center once they are covered with a white ash. Prep the lamb as directed and grill the rack, fat side up, in the center of the grill for 15 minutes, then turn and grill until an instant-read meat thermometer inserted into the center registers 135°F, another 15 to 20 minutes. For a gas grill, place the rack, fat side up, on one side of the grill and grill for 10 minutes, then reduce the heat on that side of the grill to low, turn the meat, and grill until the meat reaches 135°F, another 20 to 25 minutes. Remove from the grill and allow to rest, loosely covered with foil, before carving.

## Handling Kitchen Odors

A sweet-smelling kitchen is only as far away as your spice cabinet. When you're cooking fish, lamb, or something else with a strong odor, take several cinnamon sticks and whole cloves, cut up a lemon or an orange, and put everything in a saucepan with about 1 cup of water. Bring the mixture to a boil, reduce the heat to medium, and simmer, being careful to add more water as it evaporates. The steam from this aromatic mixture will overpower most other odors.

## Great Dipping Sauces for Lamb Kabobs

- **Fiorentina Sauce** (page 474)
- **Oven-Roasted Caponata** (page 128, finely chopped)
- **Balsamic Vinegar Syrup** (page 480)
- **Parsley Pesto** (page 473)
- **Roasted garlic mayonnaise** (see page 495)
- **Cucumber Yogurt Sauce** (page 492)
- **Mustard Yogurt Sauce** (page 493)
- **Pacific Rim Peanut Sauce** (page 481)

# THREE SLATHERS AND ONE RUB FOR EWE

## Mint Chimichurri Slather

Makes about 1 ½ cups
(enough for 4 pounds of meat)

This spicy sauce is a terrific seasoning for rack of lamb and delicious to serve on the side as well. When I was a kid, my mom always served a glop of mint jelly with lamb—this is definitely an improvement!

**3 cloves garlic, peeled**

**1 cup packed fresh mint leaves**

**¼ cup packed fresh Italian parsley leaves**

**1½ teaspoons salt**

**½ teaspoon freshly ground black pepper**

**Pinch of cayenne pepper**

**2 teaspoons rice vinegar**

**½ to ⅔ cup olive oil**

**1.** Combine the garlic, mint, parsley, salt, pepper, and cayenne in a food processor and process until the herbs and garlic are chopped.

**2.** With the machine running, add the vinegar and ½ cup of the oil in a steady stream through the feed tube and process until smooth. If you would like to serve this as a sauce, add the additional oil; otherwise, remove it from the food processor and spread it on the lamb before roasting.

✳ **DIVA DO-AHEAD:** You can cover and refrigerate for up to 1 week or freeze for up to 1 month. Before storing, cover the top with 2 more tablespoons of olive oil. Stir the oil into the sauce before using.

## Mustard Slather

Makes about 1 ½ cups
(enough for 4 pounds of meat)

Dijon mustard makes an excellent seasoning for the outside of roasted lamb. This is also an excellent dipping sauce for grilled lamb kabobs.

**1 cup Dijon mustard**

**2 tablespoons fresh rosemary leaves**

**1½ teaspoons salt**

**1 teaspoon freshly ground black pepper**

**4 cloves garlic, peeled**

**¼ cup olive oil**

**1.** Combine the mustard, rosemary, salt, pepper, and garlic in a food processor and process until the garlic and rosemary are chopped.

**2.** While the machine is running, slowly add the oil through the feed tube until incorporated.

✳ **DIVA DO-AHEAD:** You can cover and refrigerate for up to 2 weeks.

## Lemon-Oregano Slather

Makes about ¾ cup
(enough for 2 pounds of meat)

This slather, fragrant with lemon zest, oregano, and garlic, perks up racks of lamb, roasted poultry, fish, or pork. Make sure you coat the lamb at least 4 hours and up to 24 hours before roasting.

**½ cup fresh oregano leaves**

**Grated zest of 3 lemons**

**6 cloves garlic, peeled**

**1½ teaspoons salt**

**½ teaspoon freshly ground black pepper**

**¼ cup olive oil**

**1.** In a food processor, combine the oregano, lemon zest, garlic, salt, and pepper and process until the garlic and oregano are chopped.

**2.** With the machine running, slowly add the oil through the feed tube as the sauce thickens.

✳ **DIVA DO-AHEAD:** You can cover and refrigerate for up to 5 days or freeze for up to 2 months.

## Garlic-Rosemary Rub

Makes ⅔ cup
(enough for 1½ to 2 pounds of meat)

This rub is held together with a little olive oil but is mostly a paste of garlic and rosemary, which seasons the meat before and during cooking. I like to rub the meat with this at least 12 hours in advance or the day before cooking to allow it to absorb the flavors.

**10 cloves garlic, peeled**

**¼ cup fresh rosemary leaves**

**3 to 4 tablespoons olive oil**

**2 teaspoons salt**

**1 teaspoon freshly ground black pepper**

**1.** Put the garlic and rosemary in a food processor and process until it forms a paste.

**2.** Add the oil, salt, and pepper and process until blended.

✳ **DIVA DO-AHEAD:** You can cover and refrigerate for up to 3 days or freeze for up to 1 month.

# Sauces

**When serving roasted or grilled meats,** it's always a good idea to accompany with a sauce, whether it's a fruit salsa for fish or poultry or a gravy for roast beef. Each of these recipes will help make your party a little more special with the addition of color, flavor, and texture. I'll help you along with suggestions for what to pair the sauces with and how to present the food in interesting ways.

Gravies and pourable sauces should be served in gravy boats or thermal servers with a lip for easy pouring. Present salsas and sauces in attractive serving dishes. Have spoons for serving and a plate underneath the dish to catch any drips or spills. Salsas should be served with a slotted spoon, since they will have some accumulated juices that could run into the other items on a dinner plate.

# Cilantro Pesto

Makes about 3 cups

Based on the flavors of the Southwest, cilantro pesto is terrific to stir into pasta or rice, or to spread on grilled meats, poultry, or fish after they come off the fire. For a great salad, whisk together ¼ cup of cilantro pesto and 2 tablespoons of fresh lime juice and toss with greens mixed with citrus. For a quick appetizer, spread the pesto over softened cream cheese and serve with crackers, or spread it over crusty bread and put it under a broiler until bubbly.

**2 cups tightly packed fresh cilantro leaves (you can include soft stems)**

**2 cloves garlic, peeled**

**½ cup pine nuts**

**1 teaspoon salt**

**½ teaspoon freshly ground black pepper**

**½ cup grated Monterey Jack or Parmesan cheese**

**⅓ to ½ cup olive oil, as needed, plus extra to float on top of the pesto**

**1.** Combine the cilantro, garlic, pine nuts, salt, pepper, and cheese in a food processor and pulse until the cilantro and garlic are broken up.

**2.** With the machine running, gradually pour in the oil through the feed tube until the mixture begins to come together. Taste the pesto for salt and pepper and add more if needed.

**3.** If not using immediately, transfer the pesto to a storage container and float a little oil over the top of it to prevent it from turning black.

✳ **DIVA DO-AHEAD:** At this point, you can cover and refrigerate for up to 5 days or freeze for up to 2 months.

# Parsley Pesto

Makes about 2 cups

Fragrant with parsley, basil, mint, and garlic, this spicy sauce will give plain old chicken or steak a new personality. It is also great to stir into cooled pasta for a unique pasta salad.

**1½ cups packed fresh Italian parsley leaves**

**½ cup packed fresh basil leaves**

**¼ cup packed fresh mint leaves**

**2 cloves garlic, peeled**

**2 teaspoons anchovy paste, or 2 anchovy fillets, mashed**

**1 teaspoon red wine vinegar**

**¾ cup olive oil, plus extra to float on top of the pesto**

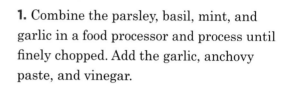

**1.** Combine the parsley, basil, mint, and garlic in a food processor and process until finely chopped. Add the garlic, anchovy paste, and vinegar.

**2.** With the machine running, gradually add the oil through the feed tube and process until the mixture begins to come together. Scrape down the bowl, process again, and transfer to a storage container if not using immediately. Float 1 or 2 tablespoons of oil over the top of the pesto to keep it from turning black.

✳ **DIVA DO-AHEAD:** At this point, you can cover and refrigerate for up to 4 days or freeze for up to 1 month.

### Diva Variation

**Parsley Pesto Dip:** This makes a particularly delicious dip for veggies. Mix ½ cup of pesto with 1 cup of mayonnaise and 1 cup of sour cream.

✳ **DIVA DO-AHEAD:** At this point, cover and refrigerate for at least 2 hours and up to 4 days.

# Fiorentina Sauce

Makes 2 cups

This vibrant green sauce, fragrant with garlic and parsley, is traditionally served in Florence over a grilled porterhouse steak (Bistecca Fiorentina), but it pairs equally well with grilled chicken, pork, or fish. It should be made a day ahead of time to let the flavors develop. This is where your extra virgin olive oil can make or break the dish; make sure you buy good quality oil that you have tasted and like; otherwise, you could be in for an ugly surprise.

1½ cups extra virgin olive oil

½ cup packed fresh Italian parsley leaves, chopped

4 cloves garlic, finely minced

1½ teaspoons salt

1 teaspoon freshly ground black pepper

**1.** Pour the oil into an airtight container. Stir in the parsley, garlic, salt, and pepper.

**❋ DIVA DO-AHEAD:** At this point, you can cover and refrigerate for up to 1 week.

**2.** Remove the flavored oil from the refrigerator at least 1 hour before you are ready to use it. Stir or shake to redistribute the parsley and seasonings. You can either spoon the sauce over the bottom of a serving platter and arrange the meats on top, adding an extra drizzle, or serve on the side as a condiment.

## The Diva Says:

This is a deliciously easy presentation when grilling flank steaks, which can be cooked the day before, then sliced cold. Pool the sauce on the platter as described above. Another delicious way to serve this is drizzled over a sliced roasted fillet of beef or New York strip steak. The color and flavor really make the beef sparkle.

# Artichoke and Caper Relish

Makes about 3 cups

Two of my favorite flavors are combined in this relish, which is super alongside grilled chicken or beef. It is also terrific as a topping for goat cheese to serve with crackers, or stirred into pasta for a cold pasta salad.

⅔ cup extra virgin olive oil

4 cloves garlic, minced

Pinch of red pepper flakes

⅓ cup red wine vinegar

1 teaspoon salt

½ teaspoon freshly ground black pepper

2 tablespoons chopped fresh oregano

¼ cup chopped fresh Italian parsley

Four 15.75-ounce cans marinated artichoke hearts, drained and cut in half

1 cup capers, drained and chopped if large

**1.** In a medium-size saucepan, heat the oil over medium heat, then add the garlic and red pepper flakes and cook, stirring, for 1 to 2 minutes, being careful not to burn the garlic or pepper. Remove from the heat, let cool, and strain the oil through a fine-mesh strainer. Add the vinegar, salt, pepper, oregano, and parsley and whisk together.

**2.** In a large bowl, combine the artichoke hearts and capers, then pour over the oil mixture and stir to blend.

✳ **DIVA DO-AHEAD:** At this point, you can let cool, cover, and refrigerate for up to 5 days.

**3.** Drain the relish before serving cold or at room temperature.

# Jezebel Sauce

Makes about 3 cups

This spicy, sweet sauce is native to the South, where it is served as a dipping sauce, but I love to use it as a glaze for ham. You can also dollop it over softened cream cheese and serve it with crackers.

> 1⅓ cups apricot preserves
> ⅔ cup apple jelly
> ⅓ cup prepared horseradish
> ¼ cup Colman's prepared English mustard

In a medium-size bowl, combine all the ingredients until blended.

✳ **DIVA DO-AHEAD:** At this point, you can cover and refrigerate for up to 1 month.

# Bruschetta Salsa

Makes 3 cups

This vibrant sauce adds zest to grilled poultry, seafood, or steak. Try it tossed into hot or cold pasta, spread on toasted baguette slices, or stirred into cooked rice. It keeps for about 8 hours; after that, the tomatoes will become a bit watery. If you are feeling particularly adventuresome, use varicolored tomatoes.

> 3 cups quartered cherry tomatoes (about 2 small baskets)
> ½ cup packed fresh basil leaves, thinly sliced
> ¼ cup extra virgin olive oil
> 3 cloves garlic, minced
> 1½ teaspoons salt
> ½ teaspoon freshly ground black pepper

In a medium-size bowl, gently toss together all the ingredients until blended.

✳ **DIVA DO-AHEAD:** At this point, you can cover and refrigerate for up to 8 hours or let sit at room temperature for up to 4 hours.

# Peach Salsa

Makes about 3 cups

Serve this with grilled pork or poultry or use as a dip or to glaze ham (see The Diva Says). The peaches will eventually cook in the acid and salt, so don't make it any more than 2 days ahead of time.

4 cups peeled, pitted, and finely chopped ripe peaches (about 5 medium-size peaches)

5 scallions (white and tender green parts), finely chopped

1 teaspoon salt

4 shakes of Tabasco sauce

2 tablespoons fresh lime juice

1 teaspoon seeded and finely chopped jalapeño pepper

¼ cup packed fresh cilantro leaves, finely chopped

In a large bowl, stir together all the ingredients until blended.

✳ **DIVA DO-AHEAD:** At this point, cover and refrigerate for at least 2 hours and up to 2 days.

The Diva Says:
To use the salsa as a glaze, puree half of it in a blender, then stir into the remaining salsa. When the ham is done, the chunks will be golden and the saucy part will stick to the meat.

# Mango Salsa

Makes 3 cups

A quick sauce to serve on the side with grilled meats, poultry, and seafood, this salsa is also delicious as a dip for tortilla chips. Or you can spread it over softened cream cheese and serve with crackers.

2 cups peeled and chopped ripe mango

1 clove garlic, minced

2 tablespoons seeded and minced jalapeño pepper

4 scallions (white and tender green parts), finely chopped

1 teaspoon salt

3 shakes of Tabasco sauce

2 tablespoons fresh lime juice

¼ cup finely chopped fresh cilantro

2 tablespoons finely chopped fresh Italian parsley

**1.** In a medium-size glass bowl, toss together all the ingredients until blended.

✳ **DIVA DO-AHEAD:** Cover and refrigerate for at least 2 hours and up to 2 days.

**2.** Drain the salsa before serving.

# Chipotle Corn Salsa

Makes about 3 cups

Smoky chipotle peppers and sweet corn are key flavors in this dynamite salsa, which is terrific served with tortilla chips or grilled poultry, meats, or seafood. The salsa will keep in the refrigerator for 2 days, but remember that the longer it sits, the hotter it gets.

**2 cups fresh corn kernels cut from the cob or frozen corn, defrosted**

**½ cup finely chopped red onion**

**1 cup cherry tomatoes, quartered**

**1 canned chipotle chile in adobo sauce, finely chopped**

**2 tablespoons fresh lime juice**

**1 clove garlic, minced**

**¼ cup packed fresh cilantro leaves, finely chopped**

**2 tablespoons canola oil**

**1 teaspoon salt**

**½ teaspoon freshly ground black pepper**

**1.** In a medium-size bowl, combine the corn, onion, and tomatoes.

**2.** In a small bowl, stir together the chile, lime juice, garlic, cilantro, oil, salt, and pepper. Pour over the corn mixture and toss to blend.

✳ **DIVA DO-AHEAD:** At this point, cover and refrigerate for at least 2 hours and up to 2 days.

**3.** Before serving, stir the salsa to reblend.

# Teriyaki Dipping Sauce

Makes about 3 cups

This is terrific as a dip for beef, chicken, pork, or seafood skewers.

**3 tablespoons cornstarch**

**3 tablespoons water**

**1½ cups soy sauce**

**½ cup granulated sugar**

**1 teaspoon Tabasco sauce**

**6 cloves garlic, minced**

**2 teaspoons peeled and grated fresh ginger**

**2 tablespoons light brown sugar**

**1 cup chicken broth**

**¼ cup pineapple juice**

**2 tablespoons sesame seeds, toasted (see page 83)**

**2 tablespoons toasted sesame oil**

**6 scallions (white and tender green parts), chopped**

**1.** In a small dish, stir the cornstarch and water together and set aside.

**2.** In a 2½-quart saucepan, combine the soy sauce, granulated sugar, Tabasco, garlic, ginger, brown sugar, chicken broth, and pineapple juice and bring to a boil. Reduce the heat to medium-low, add the cornstarch mixture, and stir until thickened.

**3.** Remove from the heat and stir in the sesame seeds, sesame oil, and scallions. Cool to room temperature.

✳ **DIVA DO-AHEAD:** At this point, you can cover and refrigerate for up to 10 days.

# Cranberry Chutney

Makes about 4½ cups

Sweet, savory, and tart all at the same time, this chutney is one of the most popular dishes in my Do-Ahead Thanksgiving classes. It is great with poultry and pork and terrific on a turkey sandwich the next day!

**One 16-ounce can peach halves packed in syrup, drained and syrup reserved**

**One 12-ounce package fresh or frozen cranberries**

**1½ cups sugar**

**1 medium-size onion, chopped**

**1 cup pecan halves**

**½ teaspoon ground cinnamon**

**¼ teaspoon ground ginger**

**1.** Coarsely chop the peaches.

**2.** Combine the cranberries, reserved peach syrup, sugar, and onion in a large saucepan over medium-high heat and cook until the cranberries begin to pop, about 10 minutes. Stir in the pecans, cinnamon, ginger, and peaches and cook 10 minutes longer.

**3.** Remove from the heat and let cool.

✳ **DIVA DO-AHEAD:** At this point, you can cover and refrigerate for up to 1 month or freeze for up to 3 months.

Serve the chutney cold, warm, or at room temperature.

# Balsamic Vinegar Syrup

Makes about 1½ cups

In this old restaurant trick, inexpensive balsamic vinegar is boiled down with brown sugar to produce a reasonable substitute for the very expensive balsamic vinegar sold in gourmet stores. The glaze can be used in vinaigrettes and drizzled over meats and poultry, as well as over Parmigiano-Reggiano cheese for a tasty appetizer.

2 cups balsamic vinegar

1 cup firmly packed light brown sugar

**1.** In a 2-quart saucepan over medium heat, stir together the vinegar and brown sugar until the sugar dissolves. Bring to a boil, reduce the heat to medium-low, and simmer, stirring frequently, until mixture is reduced by about a third and begins to look thick and syrupy, about 20 minutes.

**2.** Remove from the heat and let cool.

❋ **DIVA DO-AHEAD:** At this point, you can cover and refrigerate for up to 3 months. Reheat gently before serving warm or at room temperature.

# Pacific Rim Peanut Sauce

Makes about 3 cups

This Asian sauce makes a terrific dip for satay, Thai spring rolls, or cold seafood. It's also delicious to serve alongside grilled pork or poultry.

1½ cups creamy peanut butter (don't use natural, which becomes grainy)

½ cup canned unsweetened coconut milk

¼ cup rice wine

2 cloves garlic, minced

1 teaspoon peeled and grated fresh ginger

2 tablespoons light soy sauce

2 tablespoons toasted sesame oil

4 shakes of Tabasco sauce

6 scallions (white and tender green parts), chopped, for garnish

½ cup chopped dry-roasted peanuts for garnish

**1.** In a food processor or blender, combine the peanut butter, coconut milk, rice wine, garlic, ginger, soy sauce, sesame oil, and Tabasco and process until smooth.

❋ **DIVA DO-AHEAD:** At this point, you can cover and refrigerate for up to 2 weeks. Bring to room temperature before serving.

**2.** Transfer to a serving bowl and garnish with the scallions and peanuts.

### Diva Variation

**Really Quick Peanut Sauce:** I usually have a package of Taste of Thai dry peanut sauce in the pantry for emergency use. The manufacturer's instructions say to dilute it with milk or water, but I add a 16-ounce can of unsweetened coconut milk and a little sesame oil. It's pretty tasty. Make sure you garnish the sauce with the scallions and peanuts if you have them on hand.

# Quick Marinara

Makes 3 cups

Here is another quick sauce that can be a lifesaver if you stash some in the freezer; enjoy it over pasta, meat, poultry, or fish.

2 tablespoons extra virgin olive oil

½ cup finely chopped onion

Two 15.5-ounce cans chopped tomatoes, with their juices

1½ teaspoons salt

½ teaspoon freshly ground black pepper

1 teaspoon sugar

In a 2-quart saucepan, heat the oil over medium heat, then add the onion and cook, stirring, until it begins to turn translucent, about 3 minutes. Add the tomatoes, salt, pepper, and sugar and simmer, stirring occasionally, until reduced and thickened, 30 to 45 minutes.

✳ **DIVA DO-AHEAD:** At this point, you can let cool, cover, and refrigerate for up to 4 days or freeze for up to 3 months.

# Pizza Sauce

Makes 5 to 6 cups

Traditional pizza sauce consists of crushed tomatoes, a little salt, pepper, and olive oil. This one includes a generous amount of garlic and oregano to give the pizza a nice flavor boost from the sauce. It can also be served over grilled meats, chicken, and seafood to give them a Mediterranean flair.

2 tablespoons olive oil

1 large onion, chopped

2 cloves garlic, crushed

Two 28-ounce cans crushed tomatoes

¼ cup chopped fresh Italian parsley

2 teaspoons dried oregano, crushed

1½ teaspoons salt

½ teaspoon freshly ground black pepper

1 tablespoon sugar

In a medium-size saucepan, heat the oil over medium heat, then add the onion and garlic and cook, stirring, until translucent, about 4 minutes. Add the remaining ingredients and cook, uncovered, for about 30 minutes, stirring frequently.

✳ **DIVA DO-AHEAD:** At this point, you can let cool, cover, and refrigerate for up to 5 days or freeze for up to 4 months.

# Mom's Sunday Sauce

Makes 16 cups; serves 12 to 14

Every Sunday, Italian mammas make their Sunday sauce, the one they will use during the week to serve to their families. Sunday sauce is a great one-pot meal for entertaining. It can be made ahead and stored in the freezer. Serve the meats as the main course and toss the sauce with pasta. All you need to round out this menu is a huge salad, some bread, and a lemon ice for dessert—*mamma mia*!

¼ cup olive oil

1½ cups finely chopped onions

4 cloves garlic, minced

2 teaspoons dried basil

1 pound lean pork, trimmed of any excess fat and cut into ½-inch pieces

2 pounds Italian sweet sausages

One 3-pound eye of the round roast, trimmed of excess fat

Four 32-ounce cans crushed plum tomatoes

½ cup red wine

¼ cup sugar

1½ teaspoons salt

1 teaspoon freshly ground black pepper

½ cup finely chopped fresh Italian parsley

### Slow Cooker Savvy

Proceed through step 1, and then transfer all the ingredients, except the parsley, to a 7- to 8-quart slow cooker. Cook on High for 8 to 9 hours. Pick up the recipe with step 3 and simmer the sauce and parsley on the stove top for 10 minutes.

**1.** In a 10-quart stockpot or large roasting pan, heat the oil over medium-high heat, add the onions and cook, stirring, until softened, 2 to 3 minutes. Add the garlic and basil and cook, stirring, for another minute. Add the pork and brown on all sides. With tongs, remove the pork from the pan and set aside. Next, brown the sausages on all sides, then transfer to the plate. Add the roast to the pan, and brown it on all sides. Remove from the pan and add the tomatoes and wine, stirring up the browned bits stuck to the bottom of the pan.

**2.** Return the meats to the pan and add the sugar, salt, and pepper. Reduce the heat to medium-low, cover, and simmer until the meats are fork-tender, about 3 hours, stirring occasionally so the sauce and meats don't stick to the bottom.

**3.** Transfer the meat to a plate and taste the sauce for salt and pepper. Stir in the parsley and simmer the sauce for another 10 minutes.

**DIVA DO-AHEAD:** At this point, you can let everything cool, cover, and refrigerate the sauce for up to 1 week and the meats for up to 4 days or freeze the meat and the sauce together for up to 3 months. Defrost and reheat gently before continuing.

**4.** Slice the meat and the sausages. Toss some of the sauce with 2 pounds cooked pasta and serve alongside the sliced meats.

# Kentucky Bourbon Barbecue Sauce

Makes about 4½ cups

The sweet, smoky flavor of bourbon enhances this sauce, which is terrific on steaks, pork, or poultry. You can also add this to three 15.5-ounce cans of plain baked beans for a quick side dish to serve at a backyard picnic.

> **2 tablespoons canola oil**
>
> **1 cup finely chopped red onion**
>
> **1 teaspoon salt**
>
> **⅛ teaspoon cayenne pepper**
>
> **1 teaspoon beef bouillon base or soup base, or 1 beef bouillon cube**
>
> **¼ cup Kentucky bourbon**
>
> **Four 8-ounce cans tomato sauce**

**1.** In a 4-quart saucepan, heat the oil over medium heat, then add the onion and cook, stirring, until onion is softened, about 3 minutes.

**2.** Remove the pan from the heat (to prevent a flare-up) and add the salt, cayenne, beef base, and bourbon, stirring to dissolve the beef base. Stir in the tomato sauce and simmer until thickened slightly, about 40 minutes. Taste for salt and pepper.

**DIVA DO-AHEAD:** At this point, you can let cool, cover, and refrigerate for up to 5 days or freeze for up to 2 months. Reheat gently on the stove top.

# Old-Fashioned Brown Sugar Barbecue Sauce

Makes about 4½ cups

Smooth, slightly sweet, and spiked with Tabasco, this sauce is so much better than the old bottled barbecue sauce you may have had as a kid. Brush this on poultry, pork, or beef brisket when grilling. Or slice cooked roast beef and simmer it in the sauce, either on the stove top or in a slow cooker for a great barbecue beef sandwich. This is also a terrific sauce for leftover pork shoulder roast. Just heat the pulled pork shoulder in the sauce and serve on crusty rolls with some creamy coleslaw on the side—life doesn't get much better than that!

**2 tablespoons canola oil**

**1 cup finely chopped onion**

**2 cloves garlic, minced**

**¼ cup firmly packed light brown sugar**

**2 tablespoons Dijon mustard**

**3 tablespoons Worcestershire sauce**

**6 shakes of Tabasco sauce**

**Two 15.75-ounce cans tomato puree**

In a 4-quart saucepan, heat the oil over medium heat, add the onion, and cook, stirring, until softened, about 3 minutes. Add the garlic and cook, stirring, for another 2 minutes. Add the brown sugar, mustard, Worcestershire, and Tabasco and cook for 1 minute to dissolve the sugar. Stir in the tomato puree and simmer until the sauce is thickened slightly, about 40 minutes.

✳ **DIVA DO-AHEAD:** At this point, you can let cool, cover, and refrigerate for up to 5 days or freeze for up to 2 months.

## Sauce on the Side

Barbecue sauces are used to enhance grilled or roasted main courses. Since these sauces are usually thick and have some sugar in them, they work best when brushed on during the last 10 to 20 minutes of cooking time (the last 10 minutes on the grill, 20 minutes in the oven). If you wish to serve some sauce on the side, make sure you set it aside before you cook the meat or make another batch, because the brushing sauce may become contaminated from the raw meat.

### Diva Variation

**Old-Fashioned Maple Barbecue Sauce:** Substitute pure maple syrup for the brown sugar.

# Hoisin-Orange Barbecue Sauce

Makes about 3½ cups

This Asian-inspired sauce is luscious for dipping satay or shrimp skewers, or for brushing on poultry, beef, lamb, pork, or salmon. You'll find hoisin sauce, which is used like ketchup in China, in your grocer's Asian food section. I recommend an imported brand, such as Lee Kum Kee.

2 tablespoons canola oil

2 cloves garlic, minced

2 teaspoons peeled and grated fresh ginger

Grated zest of 1 orange

½ cup hoisin sauce

1 cup soy sauce

½ cup fresh orange juice

1 cup ketchup

½ cup chicken broth

1 teaspoon toasted sesame oil

6 scallions (white and tender green parts), thinly sliced on the diagonal, for garnish

½ cup sesame seeds, toasted (see page 83), for garnish

**1.** In a wide-bottomed saucepan or wok, heat the canola oil over medium heat. Add the garlic, ginger, and orange zest and stir-fry until fragrant, about 1 minute. Add the hoisin, soy sauce, orange juice, ketchup, and broth and bring to a boil. Reduce the heat to medium-low and simmer for 15 minutes.

**2.** Stir in the sesame oil and remove from the heat.

✳ **DIVA DO-AHEAD:** At this point, you can let cool, cover, and refrigerate for up to 5 days or freeze for up to 2 months. Reheat gently before continuing.

**3.** Garnish the finished sauce with the scallions and sesame seeds just before serving.

## The Diva Says:

Sesame oil intensifies in flavor if heated, so make sure you stir it in after the sauce is finished cooking.

# Texas-Style Barbecue Sauce

Makes about 3 cups

There are many versions of Texas barbecue sauce; this one is bold and spicy, without being overpowering. Brush it on beef, pork, or poultry to give it a rustic, outdoor campfire taste.

2 tablespoons canola oil

1 cup chopped onion

4 cloves garlic, minced

1 teaspoon ground cumin

1 teaspoon pure chipotle powder

Four 8-ounce cans tomato sauce

2 tablespoons tequila

½ cup chopped fresh cilantro

In a 4-quart saucepan, heat the oil, then add the onion and cook, stirring, until softened, about 3 minutes. Add the garlic, cumin, and chipotle powder and cook for another minute, stirring, so the spices don't burn. Stir in the tomato sauce and tequila and simmer until the sauce thickens a bit, about 30 minutes. Remove from the heat and stir in the cilantro.

✳ **DIVA DO-AHEAD:** At this point, you can let cool, cover, and refrigerate for up to 5 days or freeze for up to 2 months.

# Maple-Chipotle Basting Sauce

Makes about 2½ cups

Sweet maple syrup and smoky hot chipotle team up to make a terrific basting sauce for poultry or pork. The sauce is also delicious served as a dip for satay.

2 tablespoons canola oil

½ cup finely chopped onion

2 canned chipotle chiles packed in adobo sauce, drained and finely chopped

½ cup pure maple syrup

1 cup bottled chili sauce

1 cup chicken broth

In a 2-quart saucepan, heat the oil over medium heat, then add the onion and chiles and cook, stirring, until the onion begins to soften, about 3 minutes. Add the maple syrup, chili sauce, and broth and bring to a boil. Reduce the heat to medium-low and simmer until thickened, about 30 minutes.

✳ **DIVA DO-AHEAD:** At this point, you can let cool, cover, and refrigerate for up to 5 days or freeze for up to 1 month.

# Do-Ahead Gravy

Makes about 4 cups

The last-minute whisking and stirring usually required to make a gravy can frazzle even the most seasoned kitchen veteran. This is the magic trick to give you perfect gravy every time. If you have a family of gravy lovers, double or triple the recipe.

> 6 tablespoons (¾ stick) unsalted butter or margarine
>
> 6 tablespoons all-purpose flour
>
> 4 cups chicken, turkey, or beef broth
>
> Salt and freshly ground black pepper to taste

**1.** In a medium-size saucepan over medium-high heat, melt the butter, then whisk in the flour until incorporated and white bubbles begin to form on the surface. Cook, whisking constantly, 2 to 3 minutes longer. Gradually add the broth, whisking constantly until the gravy is thickened and comes to a boil.

**2.** Remove from the heat and season with salt and pepper.

✳ **DIVA DO-AHEAD:** At this point, you can let cool, cover, and refrigerate for 3 to 4 days or freeze for up to 2 months. Defrost if necessary and gently reheat before continuing.

**3.** When you are ready to serve the gravy, stir in any pan drippings or deglaze the roasting pan with the gravy, scraping up any bits stuck to the bottom, and heat through.

## When You're Hot, You're Hot

Keeping sauces hot is always the dilemma of the Do-Ahead Diva. A small slow cooker is a great investment for keeping gravy or sauce hot on the buffet table for those second and third helpings. If you don't own one, you can use a thermal carafe or a fondue pot. Another technique is to pour boiling water into your gravy boat 15 minutes before serving. When you are ready to serve, drain the water from the boat and add the hot gravy. That should keep it hot for the first round of servings. Keep extra gravy hot on the stove top over low heat and replenish the gravy boat when it is low.

# Simple Au Jus

Makes about 4 cups

With those wonderful meat juices in the bottom of the roasting pan, you can make a simple sauce in no time. If you like your sauce thicker, remember to use a beurre manié (see page 491) to thicken it.

> **Drippings from the pan**
>
> **4 cups broth (chicken, beef, lamb, or pork)**
>
> **Salt and freshly ground black pepper to taste**

Skim off the fat from the drippings in the pan. If your roasting pan can't be used on the stove top, transfer the drippings to a saucepan. Otherwise, add the broth to the pan, bring to a boil, and continue boiling until reduced, about 10 minutes. Season with salt and pepper and serve immediately.

**DIVA DO-AHEAD:** At this point, you can keep the sauce warm for up to 1 hour over low heat.

# Bourbon-Peppercorn Sauce for Beef

Makes about 3 cups

This mellow spiced sauce is awesome served with grilled or roasted beef, turning an otherwise plain entrée into a five-star dining experience. I like to serve the meat sliced, with a drizzle of the sauce down the center of the plate and the extra served on the side.

> **2 tablespoons unsalted butter**
>
> **½ cup finely chopped shallots**
>
> **1 tablespoon coarsely ground black pepper, or more to your taste**
>
> **⅓ cup bourbon**
>
> **2 cups beef broth**
>
> **1 cup heavy cream**
>
> **Salt to taste**

**1.** In a 2½-quart saucepan, melt the butter over medium heat, then add the shallots and pepper and cook, stirring, until the shallots are softened, about 3 minutes.

**2.** Remove from the heat (to avoid a flare-up) and add the bourbon. Return the pan to the heat and let the bourbon cook down for 1 minute. Add the broth and bring to a boil. Reduce the heat to medium-low and simmer for 15 minutes. Strain the sauce through a fine-mesh strainer and return it to the saucepan. Add the cream, bring to a simmer, add salt to taste, and serve.

✳ **DIVA DO-AHEAD:** At this point, you can let cool, cover, and refrigerate for up to 5 days or freeze for up to 1 month.

# Cabernet-Thyme Reduction Sauce

Makes about 3 cups

This rich sauce is just the right accompaniment for roast beef. I like to serve it with beef tenderloin at Christmastime, but it's also delicious spooned over steaks right off the grill in the summer.

½ cup (1 stick) unsalted butter, softened

⅔ cup chopped shallots

8 sprigs fresh thyme, or 1½ tablespoons dried

1½ cups Cabernet Sauvignon

Two 10.75-ounce cans condensed beef broth

¼ cup all-purpose flour

**1.** In a 2½-quart saucepan, melt ¼ cup (½ stick) of the butter over medium heat. Add the shallots and thyme and cook, stirring, until the shallots soften, 3 to 4 minutes. Pour in the Cabernet and broth and bring to a boil. Reduce the heat to medium and simmer until it begins to thicken, about 30 minutes. Strain through a fine-mesh strainer.

✳ **DIVA DO-AHEAD:** At this point, you can let cool, cover, and refrigerate for up to 5 days or freeze for up to 2 months. Defrost and reheat gently before continuing.

**2.** In a small bowl, blend together the flour and remaining ¼ cup (½ stick) of butter until it forms a smooth paste.

**3.** Bring the sauce to a boil, then add the flour mixture a tablespoon at a time, bringing the sauce to a boil after each addition. Add only enough of the flour mixture to get the sauce to the thickness you prefer. Remove from the heat and serve.

✳ **DIVA DO-AHEAD:** At this point, you can let cool, cover, and refrigerate for up to 5 days. Reheat gently.

The Diva Says:

Sometimes this sauce can have a pronounced wine flavor after boiling it down. To counteract this, I recommend you deglaze the roasting pan with the sauce—the drippings from your roast will round out all the flavors.

## BEURRE MANIÉ: A CHEF'S AND DIVA'S CULINARY SECRET

**Beurre manié** (pronounced burr mahn-YAY) is an uncooked butter-and-flour roux; the French term means, literally, "kneaded butter." I usually have some lurking in the back of the fridge to thicken sauces quickly for my guests. Sauces containing a beurre manié don't freeze well, but you can certainly freeze a sauce before adding the beurre manié, then add the beurre manié as you reheat the sauce. A sauce thickened with it has a glossy sheen that looks terrific on your finished dish.

To make a beurre manié, work together equal parts softened unsalted butter and all-purpose flour to form an uncooked roux.

✳ **DIVA DO-AHEAD:** This will keep, covered, in the refrigerator for up to 6 weeks. It's nice to have some extra on hand if you regularly make gravies, though it's very easy to throw together at the last minute.

# Port Wine Sauce

Makes 3 cups

This is a lovely sauce to serve over poultry or pork. You can add fruit as well; orange segments, cherries, dried plums, or apricots make nice additions. Although I don't thicken this sauce, you can use a beurre manié (see page 491) if you like.

> ¼ cup (½ stick) unsalted butter
>
> ½ cup chopped shallots
>
> 1½ cups port wine
>
> One 10.75-ounce can condensed chicken broth
>
> One 10.75-ounce can condensed beef broth
>
> Salt and freshly ground black pepper to taste

**1.** Melt the butter in a 2-quart saucepan over medium heat, then add the shallots and cook, stirring, until translucent, about 5 minutes. Add the port and both broths and simmer, uncovered, for 30 minutes.

**2.** Strain the sauce through a fine-mesh strainer and season with salt and pepper.

✳ **DIVA DO-AHEAD:** At this point, you can let cool, cover, and refrigerate for up to 5 days or freeze for up to 1 month.

# Cucumber Yogurt Sauce

Makes about 3 cups

This smooth and garlicky yogurt sauce is perfect served on the side with grilled lamb, poultry, or seafood. It makes a great sauce for grilled vegetables and can also be served with pita bread as an appetizer spread.

> 1 European cucumber, peeled, seeded, and finely chopped
>
> ½ teaspoon salt
>
> 2½ cups plain yogurt
>
> 2 cloves garlic, minced
>
> ¼ cup chopped fresh dill
>
> 2 teaspoons distilled white vinegar
>
> 2 tablespoons olive oil
>
> ½ teaspoon white pepper

**1.** Put the cucumber in a colander and toss with the salt. Drain for 30 minutes.

**2.** In a medium-size bowl, whisk together the yogurt, garlic, dill, vinegar, oil, and pepper until blended.

**3.** Fold cucumber into the yogurt mixture.

✳ **DIVA DO-AHEAD:** At this point, cover and refrigerate for at least 2 hours and up to 4 days.

**4.** Stir before serving cold.

# Mustard Yogurt Sauce

Makes about 3 cups

This tangy sauce is delicious for dipping cold seafood and crudités, and it is also wonderful served with grilled seafood, poultry, and meats.

> 2 cups plain yogurt
>
> 1 cup Dijon mustard
>
> 6 scallions (white and tender green parts), chopped
>
> 1 teaspoon white pepper

In a medium-size bowl, whisk together all the ingredients until blended.

✳ **DIVA DO-AHEAD:** At this point, cover and refrigerate for at least 2 hours and up to 3 days to let the flavors blend.

# Horseradish Sauce

Makes about 2⅓ cups

This tangy sauce is terrific served with roast beef or slathered on sandwiches. You can also stir a small amount into mashed potatoes for a terrific side dish.

> 1¾ cups sour cream
>
> ⅓ cup prepared horseradish
>
> 1 teaspoon salt
>
> ¼ teaspoon freshly ground black pepper
>
> 1 teaspoon Worcestershire sauce
>
> 2 teaspoons sugar
>
> ½ teaspoon dry mustard

In a medium-size bowl, whisk together all the ingredients until blended.

✳ **DIVA DO-AHEAD:** At this point, you can cover and refrigerate for up to 1 week. Serve cold.

# Blue Cheese Sauce

Makes 2 cups

This sauce, studded with chunks of blue cheese, is just the ticket to serve over steak or chicken. The sauce should be made at least a day ahead to let the flavors develop.

> 1½ cups crumbled blue cheese
>
> 1 cup mayonnaise (low-fat is okay)
>
> 1 cup sour cream (low-fat is okay)
>
> 2 teaspoons Worcestershire sauce
>
> 6 shakes of Tabasco sauce
>
> ½ teaspoon garlic salt

In a large bowl, whisk together all the ingredients.

✳ **DIVA DO-AHEAD:** At this point, cover and refrigerate for at least 6 hours and up to 5 days. Serve cold or at room temperature.

## How Low Can You Go?

Low-fat, nonfat, what's a diva to do? Nonfat products are like a blind date; you have high expectations, but they never quite measure up to your standards. You need to remember that when fat is removed from a product, something else needs to be added to give it flavor, and usually it's sugar and/or salt. I will use low-fat products, but the nonfat dairy products have a waxy consistency that I don't find appetizing at all.

# Artichoke Rémoulade Sauce

Makes about 4 cups

Traditional Creole rémoulade sauce is served over cold seafood. This one, enhanced with marinated artichoke hearts, makes a great sauce for cold cooked shrimp and warm crab cakes, and it is also terrific with grilled poultry and seafood. Creole mustard is found in the mustard section of your grocer; the Zatarain brand is sold nationwide.

> 3 cups mayonnaise
>
> ⅓ cup Creole or whole-grain mustard
>
> 2 cloves garlic, minced
>
> 2 teaspoons sweet paprika
>
> 6 shakes of Tabasco sauce
>
> 6 scallions (white and tender green parts), chopped
>
> Two 4-ounce jars marinated artichoke hearts, drained and finely chopped

In a medium-size bowl, stir together all the ingredients until blended.

✳ **DIVA DO-AHEAD:** At this point, cover and refrigerate for at least 4 hours and up to 10 days.

## GREAT DIVA TRICKS WITH MAYONNAISE

**Mayonnaise**, either regular or low-fat, is a great basis for making terrific sauces or spreads.

To 1 cup of mayonnaise, you can add the following:

- 1 or 2 canned chipotle chiles in adobo sauce, finely chopped or processed in the food processor. (Use in sandwiches or as a dip for chicken or seafood kabobs, slather it on corn on the cob, or add corn kernels and chopped scallions and you've got an appetizer dip.)

- 2 tablespoons basil, sun-dried tomato, or cilantro pesto, homemade or store-bought. (Use it as a sandwich spread or a dip for veggies or skewered chicken, seafood, pork, lamb, or beef.)

- 3 cloves roasted garlic. (Use on sandwiches or as a dipping sauce for skewered beef, lamb, chicken, or seafood.)

- 2 tablespoons fresh lemon juice and 1 teaspoon dried tarragon or 1 tablespoon chopped fresh tarragon for a béarnaise mayo sauce. (Serve it with veggies, cooked shrimp, or chicken and on sandwiches.)

- 1 tablespoon fresh lemon juice, 1 tablespoon Worcestershire sauce, and 2 tablespoons freshly grated Parmesan cheese for a Caesar spread. (Toss it with greens for a salad; use it as a dip for veggies, seafood, chicken, or beef; or spread it on sandwiches.)

- ¼ cup ketchup; 2 scallions (white and tender green parts), chopped; and 1 tablespoon sweet pickle relish for a quick Thousand Island dressing. (Toss with greens for a salad or use it as a sandwich spread or a dip for veggies.)

- 2 tablespoons soy sauce; 2 scallions (white and tender green parts), chopped; and 2 teaspoons toasted sesame oil. (Use as a dipping sauce for chicken or fish skewers.)

- 2 teaspoons curry powder and 2 tablespoons finely chopped mango chutney. (Toss with greens for a salad; spread on sandwiches; or use as a dip for veggies or pork, chicken, or shrimp skewers.)

- 1 to 2 teaspoons wasabi, to your taste. (Use as an appetizer dip, sandwich spread, or dipping sauce for skewers.)

# Old-Fashioned Tartar Sauce

Makes 4 cups

This delicious sauce is so much better than the prepared tartar sauce you buy at the supermarket.

> **3 cups mayonnaise**
>
> **8 pimento-stuffed green olives**
>
> **¼ cup capers, drained**
>
> **1 small dill pickle, quartered**
>
> **2 medium-size shallots, quartered**
>
> **Grated zest of 1 lemon**
>
> **4 shakes of Tabasco sauce**

Combine all the ingredients in a food processor and pulse until almost smooth (some people like chunks in their sauce, others don't—it's up to you).

✳ **DIVA DO-AHEAD:** At this point, cover and refrigerate for at least 2 hours and up to 5 days.

## Diva Variation

**Dilled Tartar Sauce:** Add 2 tablespoons of chopped fresh dill.

# Hollandaise Sauce

Makes 2 cups

Heavenly over vegetables, chicken, or seafood, hollandaise makes any meal a sophisticated and luxurious experience.

> **6 large egg yolks**
>
> **¼ cup fresh lemon juice**
>
> **1 teaspoon salt**
>
> **½ teaspoon freshly ground black pepper**
>
> **1 cup (2 sticks) unsalted butter, melted and kept warm**

**1.** In a blender or food processor, blend the egg yolks, 3 tablespoons of the lemon juice, and the salt and pepper until the mixture is well combined. Add more lemon juice if desired.

**2.** With the machine running, slowly pour in the hot butter through the top or feed tube and blend until the sauce is thickened. Serve warm.

✳ **DIVA DO-AHEAD:** At this point, you can keep the sauce warm for up to 1 hour in a thermal container.

# Béarnaise Sauce ▮▮▮

Makes 2½ cups

This sauce enhances a special meal when spooned over vegetables or served in a pool under chicken, beef, lamb, or seafood.

⅓ cup white wine

2 tablespoons dry white wine vinegar

¼ cup finely chopped shallots

2 tablespoons fresh tarragon leaves, plus extra for blending

½ teaspoon salt

⅛ teaspoon freshly ground black pepper

6 large egg yolks

1 cup (2 sticks) unsalted butter, melted and kept warm

**1.** In a small nonreactive saucepan, combine the wine, vinegar, shallots, tarragon, salt, and pepper and bring to a boil. Reduce heat to medium, and simmer until mixture has reduced to ¼ cup. Strain the liquid through a fine-mesh sieve.

**2.** In a blender or food processor, blend the egg yolks with the reduced liquid and 2 or 3 fresh tarragon leaves. With the machine running, slowly pour in the hot butter through the top or feed tube and blend until the mixture thickens. Serve warm.

✳ **DIVA DO-AHEAD:** At this point, you can keep the sauce warm for up to 1 hour in a thermal container.

# Gorgonzola Sauce ▮▮▮▮▮

Makes 3 cups

This savory sauce is delicious over pasta, gnocchi, roasted beef tenderloin, or grilled chicken.

2 tablespoons unsalted butter

1½ cups crumbled Gorgonzola cheese

2 cups heavy cream

½ teaspoon freshly ground black pepper

¼ cup chopped fresh chives (optional)

**1.** In a 2½-quart saucepan, melt the butter over medium heat, then add the Gorgonzola and cream, stirring until the cheese melts and the sauce begins to boil. Reduce the heat to medium-low and simmer for 10 minutes.

**2.** Remove from the heat and stir in the pepper and the chives if using.

✳ **DIVA DO-AHEAD:** At this point, you can let cool, cover, and refrigerate for up to 5 days.

Serve warm or at room temperature.

# Béchamel Sauce

Makes about 4 cups

Basic béchamel, or white sauce, can be turned into all types of other sauces with the addition of a few ingredients. Here is the master recipe for béchamel, which can be used in lasagna or served over vegetables, chicken, or fish.

---

**6 tablespoons (¾ stick) unsalted butter**

**6 tablespoons all-purpose flour**

**4 cups whole milk**

**1 teaspoon salt**

**½ teaspoon freshly ground black or white pepper**

---

In a 2-quart saucepan over medium heat, melt the butter. Add the flour and whisk until white bubbles form on the surface.

Cook, whisking constantly, 2 to 3 minutes longer. Gradually add the milk, whisking until blended and smooth. Bring to a boil, whisking constantly. Add the salt and pepper and remove from the heat.

✳ **DIVA DO-AHEAD:** At this point, you can let cool, transfer to a storage container, spread a thin film of milk over the top of the sauce to keep a skin from forming, and refrigerate for up to 4 days or freeze for up to 2 months. Defrost and reheat gently, whisking.

## Diva Variations

**Herbed Béchamel Sauce:** Add ¼ cup of finely chopped fresh herbs to the sauce after the milk comes to a boil. Basil, chives, parsley, tarragon, or dill would work well.

**Cheesy Creamy Sauce (Mornay):** Remove the sauce from the heat and whisk in 1½ to 2 cups of finely shredded, crumbled, or grated cheese. The heat from the sauce should melt the cheese. (If the cheese becomes stringy or grainy, which happens when the sauce is too hot, bring the sauce to a simmer and whisk in a few drops of white wine. Or strain out the strings with a sieve.) Cheeses that work well in this sauce include blue cheese (Gorgonzola and Maytag blue), cheddar (which does have a

tendency to get stringy in sauce, so wait a minute or so after removing the béchamel from the heat before stirring it in), Swiss, fontina, Parmesan, smoked gouda, Pecorino Romano, feta, Monterey or pepper Jack, mozzarella, and Asiago.

✳ **DIVA DO-AHEAD:** You can refrigerate for up to 4 days or freeze for up to 1 month.

**Broth-Based White Sauce (Velouté):** Substitute chicken, beef, or fish broth for 2 cups of the milk. This will give your sauce an additional flavor boost; serve it over vegetables, beef, poultry, or seafood.

✳ **DIVA DO-AHEAD:** Refrigerate for up to 4 days or freeze for up to 1 month.

# Creamy Mushroom Sauce

Makes about 6 cups

This creamy sauce can be served with chicken, seafood, vegetables, or beef. Just be sure to make the sauce with a broth that will complement the dish (chicken broth for a chicken dish, and beef broth for a beef dish). The sauce can be prepared up to 3 days ahead, and then gently reheated before serving. If you would like to leave out the cream, replace it with an additional cup of broth. Your sauce won't have the same rich flavor, but it will still be thick and cream-like.

½ cup (1 stick) unsalted butter

1 pound white button mushrooms, sliced

1 teaspoon salt

½ teaspoon freshly ground black pepper

½ cup all-purpose flour

4 cups broth (chicken, beef, vegetable, or seafood)

1 cup heavy cream

¼ cup chopped fresh parsley for garnish

**1.** In a large skillet, heat the butter, add the mushrooms, and sauté for 3 minutes, until the mushrooms begin to give off some liquid. Sprinkle with the salt and pepper and continue to sauté until the mushrooms begins to turn golden. Sprinkle the mushrooms with the flour, stir until it is absorbed, and cook for 2 minutes.

**2.** Gradually stir in the broth, catching any bits of flour that remain on the bottom of the pan, and stir until the mixture comes to a boil. Taste the sauce for salt and pepper, and adjust if needed.

✳ **DIVA DO-AHEAD:** At this point, you can cool the sauce and store it, covered, in the refrigerator for up to 3 days.

**3.** Add the cream and bring to a boil, stirring constantly. Remove from the heat, stir in the parsley, and serve.

# Warm Lemon Sauce

Makes 3 cups

This tart sauce is delicious over vanilla ice cream or pound cake. I have even filled a pastry shell with vanilla ice cream, then served this sauce over the top for a sophisticated dessert to end an Italian meal.

1 cup sugar

2 tablespoons cornstarch

1¾ cups water

¼ cup fresh lemon juice, or more to your taste

Grated zest of 2 lemons

3 tablespoons cold unsalted butter, cut into bits

**1.** In a 2-quart saucepan, whisk together the sugar, cornstarch, water, and lemon juice. Bring to a boil and continue boiling until the mixture becomes clear.

**2.** Remove from the heat, whisk in the zest and butter, and continue whisking until the butter melts. Taste and add more lemon juice if desired.

❋ **DIVA DO-AHEAD:** At this point, you can let cool, cover, and refrigerate for up to 1 week. Rewarm over low heat before using.

## The Diva Says:

If you would like your sauce to have a bit more color, add a drop of yellow food coloring when you stir in the zest and butter.

Lemons can sometimes feel hard to the touch; if that's the case, roll the lemon on your cutting board to break down some of the membranes before juicing it.

### Diva Variations

Flavor the sauce with 2 tablespoons of your favorite liqueur—amaretto, Chambord, Grand Marnier, or Triple Sec.

**Warm Key Lime Sauce:** Substitute Key lime juice, bottled or fresh, for the lemon juice, and the grated zest of 2 to 3 limes for the lemon zest.

# World's Best Hot Fudge Sauce

Makes about 3 cups

This is also the world's easiest hot fudge sauce.

> ½ cup (1 stick) unsalted butter
>
> 4 ounces unsweetened chocolate
>
> 1½ cups sugar
>
> 1 cup evaporated milk

In a 2-quart saucepan over low heat, melt the butter and chocolate together. Stir in the sugar and cook until it dissolves. Gradually pour in the evaporated milk and cook until the sauce is no longer grainy and has a glossy sheen, about 3 or 4 minutes.

✳ **DIVA DO-AHEAD:** At this point, you can let cool, cover, and refrigerate for up to 2 weeks or freeze for up to 6 months. Reheat over low heat on top of the stove or in the microwave before using.

## Diva Variations

Feel free to add your favorite flavor to this delicious sauce—Grand Marnier, amaretto, crème de menthe, Chambord, or Kahlúa.

# Toasted Pecan Sauce

Makes about 5 cups

This tawny-colored sauce is delicious served over ice cream, bread pudding, or cake or layered into parfaits. You can also keep this warm in a fondue pot on the buffet table for people to serve themselves.

> ½ cup (1 stick) unsalted butter
>
> 1 cup pecan halves
>
> 2 cups firmly packed light brown sugar
>
> 2 cups heavy cream

Melt the butter in a medium-size saucepan over medium-high heat. Add the pecans and toast, stirring, for about 3 minutes. Stir in the brown sugar and continue stirring until it dissolves. Add the cream and cook, stirring constantly, until the sauce boils.

✳ **DIVA DO-AHEAD:** At this point, you can let cool, cover, and refrigerate for up to 1 week. Reheat over medium heat or on 50 percent power in the microwave before serving.

# Butterscotch Sauce

Makes about 4 cups

This sauce is basically Toasted Pecan Sauce (page 501) without the pecans. It is delicious over ice cream or cake or served with Pumpkin Ice Cream Pie (page 620).

½ cup (1 stick) unsalted butter

2 cups firmly packed dark brown sugar

2 cups heavy cream

In a small saucepan over medium heat, melt the butter, then add the brown sugar, stirring until dissolved. Add the cream and stir until the sauce boils.

✳ **DIVA DO-AHEAD:** At this point, you can let cool, cover, and refrigerate for up to 2 weeks. Reheat over medium heat on the stove top or at 50 percent power in the microwave before using.

### Diva Variation

**Kentucky Bourbon Butterscotch Sauce:** Add ¼ cup of bourbon when you add the cream.

# Brown Sugar–Sour Cream Dip

Makes about 3 cups

This dip falls into the no-brainer category. There are only two ingredients, which are stirred together. The simplicity of this recipe belies its sophistication when served with pound cake or spooned over fresh fruit.

2 cups sour cream

1½ cups firmly packed light brown sugar

Whisk together the sour cream and brown sugar in a large bowl until blended.

✳ **DIVA DO-AHEAD:** At this point, cover and refrigerate for at least 4 hours and up to 1 week. Stir to reblend before using.

Serve the dip with whole strawberries, or other fruits on skewers for dipping. Or, layer the dip in parfait glasses with fruit.

# Quick Berry Sauce

Makes about 3 cups

This simple sauce is terrific over French toast, ice cream, and other desserts.

> 1 cup sugar
>
> 2 tablespoons cornstarch
>
> 1 cup water
>
> 2 tablespoons fresh lemon juice
>
> 2 cups blueberries, raspberries, sliced strawberries, or mixed berries

In a 2-quart saucepan, stir together the sugar and cornstarch and gradually whisk in the water. Bring to a boil, stirring constantly. Reduce the heat to medium-low and add the lemon juice and the berries, stirring to blend, and cook, stirring, for 3 minutes.

**DIVA DO-AHEAD:** At this point, you can let cool, cover, and refrigerate for up to 4 days.

Serve warm, at room temperature, or cold.

# Raspberry Sauce

Makes about 4 cups

Perfect for jazzing up pound cake or chocolate cake or drizzling over cheesecake, this sauce freezes beautifully, so you can have it on hand for spur-of-the-moment entertaining.

> Three 12-ounce packages individually frozen raspberries, defrosted
>
> 1 cup sugar
>
> 2 tablespoons fresh lemon juice

**1.** In a 2-quart saucepan, combine all the ingredients, bring to a boil, and cook, stirring, for about 2 minutes. Remove from the heat and let cool.

**2.** Press the mixture through a fine-mesh sieve, discarding the seeds.

**DIVA DO-AHEAD:** At this point, you can let cool, cover, and refrigerate for up to 1 week or freeze for up to 6 weeks.

Serve warm or cold.

## Diva Variations

Flavor the sauce with 2 tablespoons of your favorite liqueur—amaretto, Chambord, Grand Marnier, or Triple Sec.

**Really Quick Raspberry Sauce:** Heat 2 cups of seedless raspberry preserves with 2 teaspoons of fresh lemon juice until boiling. Serve warm or cold.

# Sweet and Savory Breads, Pizza, and Sandwiches

**Some breads are essential for entertaining.** Muffins or scones are great for brunch, while sliced breads are ideal for picnics and barbecues, to serve with the grilled star of the show. Soft or crusty rolls are terrific for sopping up juices from a gravy or pan sauce; they help balance the richness of the foods served and are the perfect tool to use as a "pusher" to help food onto a fork when knives are not available.

Sandwiches are also simple to prepare for entertaining. Whether they're made from thin flatbreads such as lavash, filled with savory goodies and cut into pinwheels, or are 3-foot-long Dagwood sandwiches that you cut into individual slices, they are invaluable for putting together a knockout buffet table.

Baking yeast breads isn't difficult, but it can take up blocks of time during the day, with its requisite rising and forming. Each bread in this chapter has do-ahead components, though, so that you can refrigerate or freeze the dough and break up the process into more manageable blocks of time. Baking bread, like cakes, is an exacting process, so make sure you follow the recipes and don't make substitutions unless they are suggested in the recipe.

Scones and muffins are simple to make and, even better, they can be made ahead and frozen so that you can have them on hand when you need them. Arranged attractively in a basket, muffins and scones also make a great show on the table.

You can generally keep most breads in the freezer for up to 6 weeks; after that they tend to lose some of their crispy crust and muffins tend to lose some moisture. I generally figure one roll or muffin per person, unless it's a bunch of hungry teenagers or men. With so many people on a low-carb diet these days, a little bread will probably go a long way.

Pizzas are terrific on the buffet table, as the star of the meal or served as a side dish or bread substitute. Most grocers sell fresh pizza dough in their bakery departments, or you can buy it frozen. There are also the preformed and baked pizza shells, such as Boboli, and pita bread makes a great base for pizzas, too.

Flavored butters are terrific for enhancing your breads, and they can also be stirred into vegetables or dolloped on grilled meats, fish, or poultry for an elegant finish. They can be frozen—another plus—so that you can have them on hand for those times when you need a little pizzazz on short notice.

# Nonna's Rustic Loaf

Makes 2 standard loaves

My grandmother baked her own bread every Friday, and her children and grandchildren would line up to get a loaf to take home. This bread is simple, dense, and absolutely delicious with unsalted butter or really good extra virgin olive oil. It makes terrific bruschetta and crostini when shaped into long free-form loaves, and it is a nice addition in a breadbasket along with other breads on your buffet table. You can also shape it into rolls or wonderful bread sticks flavored with garlic and cheese (see variations on page 508).

---

**1 package active dry yeast**

**1 teaspoon sugar**

**1 teaspoon salt**

**1½ teaspoons vegetable shortening (I prefer Crisco)**

**1¼ cups warm water (105°F)**

**3 cups unbleached all-purpose flour**

---

**1.** In a 2-cup measure, stir together the yeast, sugar, salt, shortening, and water. Allow to sit at room temperature until it bubbles, about 10 minutes.

**2.** Put flour in a large bowl and gradually add proofed yeast mixture, stirring with a wooden spoon until well combined. Transfer to a lightly floured work surface and knead until smooth and elastic, about 10 minutes, adding more flour as needed to keep dough from becoming sticky. (You can also do this in a stand mixer fitted with a dough hook.) Put dough in an oiled bowl, cover, and allow to rise in a warm, dry place (a warmed and turned-off oven is great) until doubled in bulk, about 45 minutes.

✳ **DIVA DO-AHEAD:** At this point, you can refrigerate in an oiled zipper-top plastic bag for up to 2 days or freeze for up to 2 months. Defrost before continuing.

**3.** Punch down the dough and cut into 2 equal pieces. Shape into long free-form loaves or loaf pan size. Slash the tops with a sharp knife in several places and transfer to loaf pans or a baking sheet lined with a silicone liner, parchment paper, or aluminum foil. Cover and let rise again until doubled in bulk, about 1½ hours.

**4.** Preheat the oven to 400°F. Bake the loaves for 10 minutes, then reduce the oven temperature to 375°F and bake until the crust is golden brown and the loaves sound hollow when tapped, another 40 to 50 minutes. Remove from the oven and let cool in the pans for about 20 minutes, then transfer to a rack and cool completely.

✳ **DIVA DO-AHEAD:** At this point, you can cover and freeze for up to 6 months.

## Diva Variations

**Cheesy Garlic Rolls or Bread Sticks:** Melt ¼ cup (½ stick) unsalted butter, then stir in ⅓ cup of extra virgin olive oil, ⅔ cup of grated Pecorino Romano cheese, 4 cloves garlic, minced, and 2 teaspoons of dried oregano. After the first rising, shape the dough into 2-inch rolls. Or to form into breadsticks: Take a 1-inch ball of dough and roll between your palms until it is 6 to 8 inches long. Brush the roll or breadstick with the butter and oil mixture. Place on a lined baking sheet 1 inch apart and bake at 375°F until golden brown, about 20 minutes. Serve the rolls warm, but allow the breadsticks to cool for 15 to 20 minutes.

**Pepperoni Pizza Bread:** Add ½ cup of finely diced pepperoni, ¼ cup of oil-packed sun-dried tomatoes, drained and finely chopped, ½ cup of freshly grated Parmesan cheese, and 2 teaspoons of dried oregano to the dough along with the yeast mixture.

# Romano Sausage Bread

Makes 1 large free-form loaf

This dense, flavorful bread is terrific to serve any time. Filled with Italian sausage and Romano cheese, it is almost a meal in itself and is especially nice with antipasti, Caprese Salad (page 176), or any pasta dish. It is best eaten warm.

1½ pounds Italian sausage (remove from the casings if you can't find bulk)

1 cup warm whole milk (105°F)

1 teaspoon sugar

2 packages active dry yeast

¼ cup olive oil

4 large eggs

4 cups unbleached all-purpose flour

2 cups grated Pecorino Romano cheese

**1.** Put the sausage in a medium-size skillet over medium-high heat and cook, breaking the meat up, until no longer pink. Remove from the pan and drain in a colander.

✳ **DIVA DO-AHEAD:** You can cover and refrigerate for up to 2 days.

**2.** In a 4-cup measure, combine the milk, sugar, and yeast and set aside while you assemble the other ingredients.

**3.** In a large bowl, combine the oil and eggs and beat until blended. Add the yeast mixture, then the flour and cheese, mixing until the dough pulls away from the side of the bowl. It will be sticky. Turn the dough into an oiled bowl, cover, and allow to rise in a warm, draft-free spot until doubled in bulk, about 1½ hours.

✳ **DIVA DO-AHEAD:** At this point, you can refrigerate overnight.

**4.** Punch down the dough and flatten it on a floured work surface until about 1 inch thick. Spread the sausage over the dough, then fold the dough over and knead it for a couple of turns, until it is no longer sticky. Shape into a long, 3-inch-wide loaf and place on a baking sheet lined with silicone, parchment paper, or aluminum foil or place in a 10-cup tube pan coated with nonstick cooking spray. Cover and allow the dough to rise again until doubled in bulk, about 1 hour.

✳ **DIVA DO-AHEAD:** At this point, you can freeze for up to 1 month. Defrost and proceed with the recipe.

## When You Freeze Unbaked Bread . . .

Make sure you indicate on the bag with an indelible marker the contents of the bag, the date, and where you need to pick up the recipe.

**5.** Preheat the oven to 375°F. At the end of the rising time, bake the bread until the crust sounds hollow when tapped, 30 to 40 minutes. Remove from the oven and cool slightly on a rack before slicing. If baked in a tube pan, cool in the pan for 15 minutes.

✳ **DIVA DO-AHEAD:** At this point, you can let cool completely, cover, and refrigerate overnight or freeze for up to 1 month. If you like, rewarm, wrapped in aluminum foil, in a 300°F oven for about 20 minutes.

## Diva Variation

This bread is terrific for shaping into rolls and bringing to a picnic or potluck dinner. After the first rise, shape the dough into 1-inch balls and place about ½ inch apart on a baking sheet lined with a silicone liner, aluminum foil, or parchment paper, cover, allow to rise again, and bake until golden brown, 20 to 25 minutes.

# COMPOUND BUTTERS

**A compound butter** is a mixture of butter and herbs that can be used as a simple sauce over meats, poultry, seafood, or vegetables, and to flavor store-bought bread for a homemade taste. (See Cool Things to Do with Store-Bought Bread on page 521.) Sweet compound butters are delicious to serve on bread and are a nice touch for a brunch buffet. Try Honey Butter with cornbread and Strawberry Butter with muffins or scones.

Shape each of the butters below into a log 1 inch in diameter. Wrap it in plastic wrap and store in the freezer. Then you can slice off what you need, and return the log to the freezer.

**✳ DIVA DO-AHEAD:** Compound butters will keep in the freezer for up to 4 months and in the refrigerator up to 1 week.

## Béarnaise Butter

Makes 1 cup

A dollop of this savory butter over a steak, chicken, seafood, or vegetables will give it the flavor of béarnaise sauce, without all the last-minute preparation.

**1 cup (2 sticks) unsalted butter, softened**

**2 cloves garlic, minced**

**2 teaspoons dried tarragon**

**2 tablespoons Dijon mustard**

**2 tablespoons Worcestershire sauce**

In a medium-size bowl, cream the butter together with the remaining ingredients. Shape and store as directed above.

## Blue Cheese Butter

Makes about 2¼ cups

Tangy blue cheese, butter, and a few other flavors combine to make this a dynamite topper for grilled steak, chicken, steamed potatoes, or grilled bread. I love the flavor of Maytag blue cheese, but you can substitute your favorite blue-veined cheese, such as Stilton, Gorgonzola, or Point Reyes.

**1 cup (2 sticks) unsalted butter, softened**

**2 teaspoons Worcestershire sauce**

**½ teaspoon freshly ground black pepper**

**4 shakes of Tabasco sauce**

**1¼ cups crumbled blue cheese**

In a medium-size bowl, cream together the butter, Worcestershire, pepper, Tabasco, and blue cheese. Shape and store as directed above.

## Chipotle-Lime-Cilantro Butter

Makes about 1¼ cups

A spicy taste of the Southwest, this butter is terrific on grilled fish, chicken, or meats. I love to stir it into rice or pasta for a simple side dish. You can also slather it on bread for a Southwestern accent. If you enjoy the heat, then increase the amount of chipotle powder.

**1 cup (2 sticks) unsalted butter, softened**

**½ teaspoon chipotle chile powder**

**2 tablespoons fresh lime juice**

**¼ cup chopped fresh cilantro**

In a medium-size bowl, cream together the butter, chipotle powder, lime juice, and cilantro until blended. Shape and store as directed on page 510.

## Sun-Dried Tomato Butter

Makes about 1⅓ cups

This red-hued butter is terrific for livening up chicken, seafood, veggies, and breads. Serve it on the side with your breadbasket; your guests will love the spicy flavor. I like to make this in the food processor so I can throw in all the ingredients and have them chopped in one step. If you don't have a food processor, then chop the tomatoes, garlic, basil, and parsley and mix them into the butter.

**1 cup (2 sticks) unsalted butter, softened**

**6 oil-packed sun-dried tomatoes, halved**

**2 cloves garlic, peeled**

**6 fresh basil leaves**

**¼ cup packed fresh Italian parsley leaves**

Put all the ingredients in a food processor and process until smooth. Shape and store as directed on page 510.

## Lemon-Dill-Chive Butter

Makes about 1½ cups

This attractive butter, flecked with green dill and chives, is a delicious topping for seafood or chicken. Swirl a bit of this through steamed rice, and you have an attractive and subtly flavored side dish.

**1 cup (2 sticks) unsalted butter, softened**

**2 tablespoons fresh lemon juice**

**1 teaspoon grated lemon zest**

**¼ cup chopped fresh dill**

**2 tablespoons snipped fresh chives**

In a medium-size bowl, cream together the butter, lemon juice and zest, dill, and chives until combined. Shape and store as directed on page 510.

## Basil Pesto Butter

Makes about 1 cup

This simple butter is terrific on seafood, chicken, and even grilled meats. I love to stir it into orzo pasta for a quick side dish and slather it on bread for a peppy counterpart to the main course.

**½ cup (1 stick) unsalted butter, softened**

**½ cup store-bought basil pesto**

In a small bowl, stir together the butter and pesto until blended. Shape and store as directed on page 510.

## Garlic-Parsley Butter

Makes about 1½ cups

This beautifully colored and tasty butter is terrific for dressing steamed red potatoes and other vegetables. It also adds flavor and zip to meats, poultry, seafood, pastas, rice, and breads.

**1 cup (2 sticks) unsalted butter, softened**

**4 cloves garlic, minced**

**½ cup chopped fresh Italian parsley**

**6 shakes of Tabasco sauce**

In a medium-size bowl, cream together the butter, garlic, parsley, and Tabasco until blended. Shape and store as directed on page 510.

## Roasted Garlic Butter

Makes about 1⅓ cups

This robust butter is delicious spread on steaks, chicken, and breads, or melted and tossed with pasta. It is the only compound butter that does not freeze well because the flavor of the roasted garlic will fade. It can be stored in the refrigerator for up to 1 week.

**1 cup (2 sticks) unsalted butter, softened**

**10 cloves garlic, roasted (see The Diva Says) and squeezed from their skins**

**¼ cup chopped fresh Italian parsley**

In a medium-size bowl, mash the butter into the garlic until the mixture is smooth. Add the parsley and continue to blend until well combined. Transfer to an airtight container—or place in the center of a sheet of plastic wrap, form into a log 1 inch in diameter, and wrap—and refrigerate.

### The Diva Says:

To roast garlic, preheat oven to 400°F. Remove the papery outsides of the garlic and cut off the top of the head to expose the cloves. Place on a piece of aluminum foil large enough to wrap around the garlic. Drizzle with olive oil, sprinkle with salt and pepper, and wrap in the foil. Bake until garlic is soft, about 30 minutes. Let cool for 15 minutes, then gently squeeze the garlic out of the skin. Roasted garlic can be stored in olive oil for up to 1 week in the refrigerator.

## Butter Provençal

Makes about 1⅛ cups

This is the spread to serve for that bistro dinner you want to have. Stir into steamed green beans or potatoes; cut off pieces and let them melt onto grilled meats, poultry, or seafood; or stir into rice or pasta.

**1 cup (2 sticks) unsalted butter, softened**

**2 teaspoons dried thyme**

**2 teaspoons dried rosemary, crumbled**

**2 teaspoons dried oregano**

**2 teaspoons dried basil**

**2 teaspoons grated lemon zest**

In a medium-size bowl, cream together all the ingredients until combined. Shape and store as directed on page 510.

## Romano Oregano Butter

Makes about 1¾ cups

Strong Romano cheese, spicy red pepper flakes, and pungent oregano combine to make this butter a perfect complement to chicken, vegetables, pastas, and breads. I love to spread this on bread and grill it until golden brown.

**1 cup (2 sticks) unsalted butter, softened**

**⅔ cup grated Pecorino Romano cheese**

**2 teaspoons dried oregano**

**¼ teaspoon red pepper flakes**

In a medium-size bowl, cream together all the ingredients until blended. Shape and store as directed on page 510.

## Rosemary, Thyme, and Sage Butter

Makes 1¼ cups

This fragrant butter is delicious slathered over turkey or chicken before roasting, or served on top of grilled steak or chicken, or spread on bread.

**1 cup (2 sticks) unsalted butter, softened**

**2 teaspoons chopped fresh rosemary**

**2 teaspoons chopped fresh thyme**

**2 teaspoons chopped fresh sage**

In a medium-size bowl, cream together all the ingredients until blended. Shape and store as directed on page 510.

## Honey Butter

Makes 1¼ cups

Slather this sweet butter over cornbread or scones still warm from the oven. Serve it in small crocks or ramekins on your buffet table.

**1 cup (2 sticks) unsalted butter, softened**

**¼ to ⅓ cup honey, to your taste**

In a medium-size bowl, cream together the butter and honey until smooth.

✳ **DIVA DO-AHEAD:** Cover and refrigerate for up to 2 weeks or freeze for up to 6 months.

## Strawberry Butter

Makes 1½ cups

Here, sweet berries and butter are mashed together, giving you a delectable spread for scones, biscuits, and cornbreads.

**1 cup (2 sticks) unsalted butter, softened**

**½ cup hulled and sliced fresh strawberries or frozen strawberries, defrosted**

Combine the butter and strawberries in a food processor and process until smooth.

✳ **DIVA DO-AHEAD:** At this point, you can cover and refrigerate for up to 5 days or freeze for up to 3 months. Soften the butter before serving.

### The Diva Says:

If you don't have a food processor, mash the berries with a fork, then stir in the butter until blended.

# Cousin Nella's Umbrian Easter Bread

Makes 1 loaf

When I visited my cousin Nella in the small Italian town of Gubbio, she served us this traditional bread, called *crescia,* which is usually enjoyed at Easter time. It is delicious served with antipasti or to accompany a main course. I recommend buying a block of Pecorino Romano and grating it fresh; it makes a world of difference in the final flavor of the bread.

**1 package active dry yeast**

**1 teaspoon sugar**

**1 teaspoon salt**

**⅔ cup warm whole milk (105°F)**

**8 large eggs**

**¾ cup vegetable shortening (I prefer Crisco)**

**6 shakes of Tabasco sauce**

**1⅓ cups grated Pecorino Romano cheese**

**3¼ cups unbleached all-purpose flour**

**1.** Coat a 10-cup tube pan with nonstick cooking spray and set it aside.

**2.** In a 4-cup measure, stir together the yeast, sugar, salt, and milk. Set aside until the mixture begins to bubble, about 10 minutes.

**3.** With an electric mixer, beat together the eggs, shortening, and Tabasco in a large bowl until light and fluffy and the shortening is incorporated into the eggs. Stir in the yeast mixture and continue to beat until thoroughly combined. Gradually add the flour and cheese and beat for 4 minutes. The dough will be sticky and loose. Transfer to the prepared pan, cover, and let rise in a warm, draft-free place until doubled in bulk, about 45 minutes.

**4.** Preheat the oven to 375°F. At the end of the rising, bake the bread until golden and a skewer inserted into the center comes out clean, 45 to 55 minutes. Cool completely and remove from the pan.

✳ **DIVA DO-AHEAD:** At this point, you can cover and refrigerate for up to 4 days or freeze for up to 6 weeks.

# Stuffing Bread

Makes 2 loaves or 24 to 36 rolls

Here are all the flavors of Thanksgiving dressing rolled up in one bread. This is a terrific choice for serving with chicken or egg salad or with turkey and cranberry sauce. Or you can just toast it and slather with cream cheese.

1¾ cups warm chicken broth (105°F)

1 package dry yeast

1 tablespoon sugar

¼ cup (½ stick) unsalted butter

½ cup finely chopped celery

½ cup finely chopped onion

½ teaspoon dried sage

½ teaspoon dried thyme

½ teaspoon salt

4½ to 5 cups unbleached all-purpose flour

**1.** Pour ¾ cup of the broth into a 2-cup measuring cup, sprinkle the yeast over it, and stir in the sugar. Set aside until the mixture begins to bubble, about 10 minutes.

**2.** In a medium-size skillet, melt 2 tablespoons of the butter over medium heat, then add the celery, onion, sage, thyme, and salt and cook, stirring, until the vegetables soften and the onion becomes translucent, 8 to 10 minutes.

**3.** Put 4½ cups of the flour in a large bowl, then stir in the vegetables. Add the yeast mixture and the remaining 1 cup of broth

and stir until the dough comes together. Transfer to a lightly floured work surface and knead, adding more flour if necessary, until the dough is smooth and elastic. (You can also do this in a stand mixer fitted with a dough hook.) Put the dough in a lightly oiled bowl, cover, and put in a warm, draft-free place until doubled in bulk, 45 minutes to 1 hour.

✳ **DIVA DO-AHEAD:** At this point, you can freeze for up to 1 month; defrost overnight in the refrigerator before continuing.

**4.** Turn out the dough onto a floured work surface and knead for about 5 minutes. Divide in half and shape into loaves, or roll into 1-inch balls to make rolls. Place the loaves into greased loaf pans, cover, and allow to rise until doubled in bulk, another 45 minutes. If you are making rolls, place ½ inch apart on a baking sheet lined with a silicone liner, aluminum foil, or parchment paper and cover with a towel until doubled in bulk, 30 to 40 minutes.

✳ **DIVA DO-AHEAD:** After this rising, you can freeze shaped dough for up to 1 month; defrost overnight in the refrigerator before continuing.

**5.** Preheat the oven to 375°F. Melt the remaining 2 tablespoons of butter. Brush the loaves or rolls with the butter and bake until they sound hollow when tapped, 30 to 40 minutes. Cool for 15 to 20 minutes, remove from the pans, and cool for another 10 minutes on a rack before slicing.

✳ **DIVA DO-AHEAD:** At this point, you can let cool, wrap, and freeze for up to 1 month.

---

## How Much Flour Is Enough?

Baking conditions will dictate how much flour you will need. If the flour has absorbed moisture from the air (which may happen on a humid day), you will need more. Always have a little more flour on hand than you think you need. Bread baking is a little science and a lot of instinct. You will know that the dough has reached the right consistency when it is no longer sticky and is smooth and elastic.

---

# Old-Fashioned California Cornbread 🥛🥛🍸

Makes about 24 squares

This slightly sweet, cake-like cornbread is delicious slathered with Honey Butter or Strawberry Butter (both page 514), and it is simple to put together.

> 4 cups Bisquick baking mix
>
> 1 cup cornmeal
>
> 1 cup sugar
>
> 2 tablespoons baking powder
>
> 4 large eggs
>
> 1 cup whole milk
>
> ½ cup (1 stick) unsalted butter, melted

**1.** Preheat the oven to 350°F. Coat a 13 x 9-inch baking pan with nonstick cooking spray.

**2.** In a large bowl, whisk together the Bisquick, cornmeal, sugar, and baking powder. Add the eggs, milk, and butter and stir to blend. Pour into the prepared pan and bake until golden and a skewer inserted into the center comes out with only a few crumbs clinging to it, 30 to 40 minutes.

**3.** Let the cornbread cool about 10 minutes before slicing. Serve warm.

✳ **DIVA DO-AHEAD:** The bread can be baked a day ahead of time and stored, covered, at room temperature or frozen for up to 6 weeks. Rewarm the bread in a 300°F oven for about 15 minutes if it has been frozen.

# Southern Cornbread

Makes 24 wedges or squares

This cornbread is not sweet, but it is wonderfully crispy on the outside, and you taste the cornmeal in every bite. In the South they use white cornmeal, but I prefer the color and texture that yellow cornmeal gives this bread. Serve it with chili, fried chicken, pork, or seafood. Southerners make this in cast-iron skillets. If you don't have one, two 9-inch round cake pans will do nicely, or you can use a 13 x 9-inch baking pan. The rounds are nice because they can be cut into wedges. You can also use this recipe to make 24 corn muffins or corn sticks.

½ cup (1 stick) unsalted butter, melted and cooled slightly

1½ cups unbleached all-purpose flour

2 cups yellow cornmeal

2 teaspoons sugar

2 teaspoons salt

1 tablespoon baking powder

2 large eggs

1¼ cups buttermilk

**1.** Preheat the oven to 400°F. Brush two 9-inch round cake pans or a 13 x 9-inch baking pan with 2 tablespoons of the melted butter.

**2.** In a large bowl, whisk together the flour, cornmeal, sugar, salt, and baking powder. In a large measuring cup, beat together the eggs, buttermilk, and remaining 6 tablespoons of melted butter. Gradually stir the liquid ingredients into the dry, then beat until smooth. Pour into the prepared pans and bake until golden and a skewer inserted into the center comes out clean and the top is golden brown, about 25 minutes for 9-inch rounds and 35 to 40 minutes for the larger pan.

**3.** Remove from the oven, let cool for 10 minutes before slicing, and serve warm.

**✳ DIVA DO-AHEAD:** The bread can be made a day ahead of time and stored, covered, at room temperature or frozen for up to 6 weeks. Rewarm the bread in a 300°F oven for about 15 minutes if it has been frozen.

## Making Corn Sticks

To make corn sticks from any of the cornbread recipes, coat 12 corn stick pans with nonstick cooking spray or melted butter. Pour the batter into the pans and bake until golden brown and crisp, about 20 minutes. Turn out of the pans immediately and serve.

# Southwestern Cornbread

Makes 24 squares or muffins

Filled with sweet corn, red peppers, and green chiles and spiked with a little chile powder, this bread is great to serve with a Southwestern buffet or any grilled menu.

**2 tablespoons unsalted butter**

**½ cup finely chopped onion**

**1 cup fresh corn kernels cut from the cob or frozen corn, defrosted**

**½ cup seeded and finely chopped red bell pepper**

**¼ cup (half a 4-ounce can) canned chopped green chiles (see The Diva Says), drained and rinsed**

**⅛ to ¼ teaspoon chipotle or another pure chile powder**

**2 cups yellow cornmeal**

**2 cups unbleached all-purpose flour**

**1 tablespoon baking powder**

**1 teaspoon baking soda**

**⅓ cup sugar**

**3 large eggs**

**2 cups whole milk**

**¼ cup (½ stick) unsalted butter, melted**

**2 cups finely shredded mild cheddar cheese**

**1.** Preheat the oven to 400°F. Coat a 13 x 9-inch baking pan or two 12-cup muffin tins with nonstick cooking spray.

**2.** Melt the butter in a small skillet over medium heat, then add the onion and corn and cook, stirring, until fragrant and softened slightly, about 2 minutes. Add the red bell pepper and cook, stirring, another 1 or 2 minutes. Stir in the chiles and chile powder and cook for 2 minutes, stirring constantly so the chile powder doesn't burn. Remove from the heat.

**3.** In a large bowl, whisk together the cornmeal, flour, baking powder, baking soda, and sugar. Make a well in the center of the dry ingredients and add the eggs, milk, melted butter, cheese, and the cooled vegetables, stirring with a wooden spoon to blend. Pour into the prepared pan(s) and bake until golden and a skewer inserted into the center comes out clean, 22 to 26 minutes for the bread, 12 to 15 minutes for the muffins. Let cool for 10 minutes before slicing or serving.

✳ **DIVA DO-AHEAD:** The baked bread can be made a day ahead of time and stored, covered, at room temperature or frozen for up to 6 weeks. Rewarm the bread in a 300°F oven for about 15 minutes if it has been frozen.

## The Diva Says:

Some people love a lot of heat and others, a bit less. With a whole can of green chiles you get about a 7 on the 10-point heat meter—half a can will give you a 4.

# Dilly Bread

Makes two 8-inch loaves or about 48 dinner rolls

Fragrant with dill and made moist because of the cottage cheese, this is a bread no one can resist. The recipe makes 2 standard-size loaves, or you can shape the dough into rolls and bake them in round cake pans.

1½ tablespoons active dry yeast

½ cup warm water (105°F)

2 tablespoons sugar

4½ cups unbleached all-purpose flour

½ teaspoon baking soda

2 teaspoons salt

1½ tablespoons dillweed

1 tablespoon dried minced onion

2 cups cottage cheese

¼ cup (½ stick) unsalted butter, melted

1 large egg

**1.** In a 2-cup measure, sprinkle the yeast over the water and stir in the sugar. Set aside until the mixture begins to bubble, about 10 minutes.

**2.** Stir together the flour, baking soda, salt, dillweed, and onion in a large bowl. Add the cottage cheese, 2 tablespoons of the butter, and the egg and stir to combine. Gradually add the yeast mixture and continue to stir until it forms a nice dough; it may be a bit sticky, which is fine. (You can also do this in a stand mixer fitted with a dough hook.) Transfer to an oiled bowl, cover, and allow to rise in a warm, draft-free place until doubled in bulk, about 1 hour.

**3.** At the end of the rising time, punch down the dough, shape into 2 loaves, and place in greased loaf pans. Or pinch off golf ball–sized pieces of the dough and shape into balls. Arrange the balls in 2 greased 9-inch round cake pans. Cover and let rise again until doubled in bulk, about another 45 minutes.

❋ **DIVA DO-AHEAD:** At this point, you can cover and freeze for up to 6 weeks; defrost overnight in the refrigerator before continuing.

**4.** Preheat the oven to 350°F. Brush the tops of the bread or rolls with the remaining 2 tablespoons of butter. Bake until browned and the loaf sounds hollow when tapped on the crust, 45 to 55 minutes, or until the rolls are golden brown, 20 to 25 minutes. Remove from the oven and allow to cool slightly before serving, or cool completely before storing.

❋ **DIVA DO-AHEAD:** At this point, you can cool to room temperature and store in zipper-top plastic bags in the refrigerator overnight or freeze for up to 6 weeks.

## COOL THINGS TO DO WITH STORE-BOUGHT BREAD

**There is nothing wrong** with store-bought bread, but you can make it special by slathering it with a homemade spread or brushing it with seasoned butter, and then heating it before serving. Try any or all of the compound butters on pages 510 to 514.

Refrigerated doughs and frozen bread doughs are a host's best friend. All the work has been done for you—you just have to heat and serve. Frozen bread doughs are especially nice because when they defrost, you can brush them with a melted compound butter or, for a sweet bread, cinnamon and sugar. Follow the manufacturer's directions for baking, but have fun creating new breads your own way.

Try slathering store-bought breads with any of these spreads and bake until hot and crispy or run sliced bread under the broiler.

- Pesto
- Garlic herb cheese spread, such as Boursin
- A mixture of one part port wine and sharp cheddar spread and one part softened unsalted butter
- Cream cheese mixed with chopped fresh chives, topped with chopped oil-packed sun-dried tomatoes
- Cream cheese mixed with Tapenade, homemade (page 84), or store-bought
- Herbed goat cheese
- A mixture of $1/4$ cup ($1/2$ stick) softened unsalted butter, 2 tablespoons of Dijon mustard, and 1 teaspoon of dried tarragon

# Stuffed Artichoke Bread

Serves 12

This cheesy loaf is studded with nuggets of artichokes and Kalamata olives, then topped with tomatoes. It's terrific to serve alongside grilled meats or to take to a tailgate buffet.

**1 long loaf French bread, about 3 inches in diameter, cut in half lengthwise**

**½ cup (1 stick) unsalted butter**

**6 cloves garlic, minced**

**Two 6-ounce jars marinated artichokes, drained, reserving the marinade, and coarsely chopped**

**2 cups sour cream (low-fat is okay)**

**1½ cups finely shredded Monterey Jack cheese**

**⅔ cup freshly grated Parmesan cheese**

**2 teaspoons lemon pepper seasoning**

**½ cup pitted Kalamata olives, drained and coarsely chopped**

**2 medium-size vine-ripened tomatoes, thinly sliced**

**1.** Hollow out the bread, leaving about ¾ inch around the inside of the bread. Tear the removed bread into small pieces.

**2.** In a large skillet, melt the butter over medium heat, add the garlic, and cook, stirring, until the garlic begins to smell fragrant. Add the bread pieces and toss to coat with the garlic butter. Remove from the heat.

**3.** In a large bowl, stir together the chopped artichokes, sour cream, Monterey Jack, ⅓ cup of the Parmesan, lemon pep-per, olives, and garlic bread cubes until combined.

✳ **DIVA DO-AHEAD:** At this point, you can cover and refrigerate for up to 2 days; wrap the bread halves in zipper-top plastic bags or aluminum foil and store at room temperature.

**4.** Preheat the oven to 350°F. Line a baking sheet with a silicone liner, aluminum foil, or parchment paper.

**5.** Stuff the bread with the artichoke-cheese mixture and top with the tomatoes. Sprinkle with some of the reserved artichoke marinade and the remaining ⅓ cup of Parmesan and bake until the cheese is golden and melted, about 30 minutes.

**6.** Remove the bread from the oven, and let rest for about 5 minutes. Cut into 1-inch-thick slices with a serrated knife.

## Diva Variations

**Stuffed Artichoke and Sun-Dried Tomato Bread:** Add ½ cup of chopped oil-packed sun-dried tomatoes, drained, to the filling, and omit the sliced tomatoes on the top.

**Southwestern Stuffed Bread:** Omit the artichokes and add one 4-ounce can of chopped green chiles, drained. Substitute cheddar cheese for the Parmesan and substitute Mission olives for the Kalamatas.

# Dijon, Bacon, and Swiss Bread

Serves 12

Take this bread to your friends' house when they ask you to make something. It's a real crowd-pleaser served with grilled or roasted meats or poultry, salads, or seafood.

½ cup (1 stick) unsalted butter, softened

¼ cup Dijon mustard

2 cloves garlic, minced

1 teaspoon dried tarragon

2 teaspoons poppy seeds

1 teaspoon sweet paprika

⅛ teaspoon cayenne pepper

1 long loaf Italian or French bread, about 3 inches wide, cut into ¾-inch-thick slices

14 slices Jarlsberg or Swiss cheese, cut the same size as the bread slices

6 strips bacon (turkey bacon is okay)

**1.** Cut a piece of aluminum foil twice as long as the bread.

**2.** Stir together the butter, mustard, garlic, tarragon, poppy seeds, paprika, and cayenne in a small bowl until blended. Spread over the bread slices and top each one with a slice of cheese. Reassemble the bread on the aluminum foil, and bring the foil three-quarters of the way up the bread to keep it together.

❋ **DIVA DO-AHEAD:** At this point, you can wrap the bread tightly in foil and refrigerate for up to 2 days or freeze for up to 1 month. Defrost, remove from the refrigerator 45 minutes before baking, and peel the foil a quarter of the way down the sides before continuing.

**3.** Preheat the oven to 375°F. Lay the bacon strips over the top of the loaf and bake until the bacon is browned and crisp, 25 to 35 minutes.

**4.** Remove the bacon from the top of the bread, chop it coarsely, and sprinkle over the bread before serving.

# Pesto Bread

Serves 12

Basil or sun-dried tomato pestos give this store-bought loaf a new look and jazzy flavor.

**½ cup store-bought sun-dried tomato or basil pesto**

**½ cup (1 stick) unsalted butter, softened**

**1 loaf Italian or French bread, cut into ¾-inch-thick slices**

**1.** Cut a piece of aluminum foil twice as long as the bread.

**2.** In a small bowl, cream together the pesto and butter until thoroughly combined. With a small spreading knife, spread some of the butter onto each slice of bread and reassemble the loaf on the aluminum foil.

✳ **DIVA DO-AHEAD:** At this point, you can refrigerate for up to 24 hours.

**3.** Preheat oven to 350°F. Place the loaf on a baking sheet and bake until heated through, 25 to 30 minutes. Serve hot.

### Diva Variation

**Broiled Pesto Bread:** Preheat the broiler. Slice the loaf in half lengthwise, place on a baking sheet lined with parchment paper, a silicone liner, or aluminum foil, and spread the pesto butter over each cut half. Broil the bread until golden brown, 4 to 5 minutes. Remove from the broiler, slice, and serve.

# Garlic-Parmesan Bread

Serves 12

This cheesy garlic bread is delicious served with Mediterranean entrées, or as a side dish with salads, soups, or grilled main courses.

**½ cup (1 stick) unsalted butter, softened**

**⅓ cup olive oil**

**3 cloves garlic, minced**

**1 teaspoon sweet paprika**

**1 teaspoon dried basil or oregano**

**½ cup freshly grated Parmesan cheese**

**1 long loaf French bread, cut into ¾-inch-thick slices**

**1.** Cut a piece of aluminum foil twice as long as the bread.

**2.** Stir the butter, oil, garlic, paprika, basil, and cheese together until blended.

✳ **DIVA DO-AHEAD:** At this point, you can cover and refrigerate for up to 1 week or freeze for up to 3 months.

**3.** Spread the butter on the bread slices, then reassemble and wrap in aluminum foil.

✳ **DIVA DO-AHEAD:** At this point, you can refrigerate for up to 24 hours.

**4.** Preheat the oven to 350°F. Bake the bread until heated through, 20 to 25 minutes. Serve hot.

# Basic Dinner Rolls

Makes about 20 rolls

Rich with egg and milk, these are the quintessentially comforting soft rolls that you love to serve with Thanksgiving dinner or slather with apple butter for breakfast.

**¾ cup warm milk (105°F)**

**1 package active dry yeast**

**⅓ cup sugar**

**1½ teaspoons salt**

**½ cup (1 stick) unsalted butter, melted**

**2 large eggs**

**1 large egg yolk**

**4¼ cups unbleached all-purpose flour**

**1.** In a 4-cup measure, stir together the milk, yeast, and 1 tablespoon of the sugar. Set aside until the mixture begins to bubble, about 10 minutes.

**2.** In a large bowl, combine the remaining sugar, the salt, melted butter, whole eggs, and yolk. Add the yeast mixture and stir to combine. Add 3 cups of the flour and stir until the mixture begins to come together. Add another ¾ cup of flour and stir until the dough pulls away from the sides of the bowl and begins to form a ball. Place on a lightly floured work surface and knead, adding more flour as needed, until the dough is smooth and elastic. (You can also do this in a stand mixer fitted with a dough hook.) Transfer the dough to a buttered bowl, cover, and let rise in a warm, draft-free spot until doubled in bulk, 45 minutes to 1 hour.

**3.** Coat two 9-inch round cake pans with nonstick cooking spray. Punch down the dough, then break off 1-inch pieces and roll them into balls. Place the balls in the prepared pans.

✳ **DIVA DO-AHEAD:** At this point, you can cover and freeze for up to 6 weeks. Defrost overnight in the refrigerator before continuing.

Cover the dough and let rise again until doubled in bulk, about 30 minutes.

**4.** Preheat the oven to 375°F. Bake the rolls until golden brown, 17 to 22 minutes. Serve warm.

✳ **DIVA DO-AHEAD:** At this point you can let cool, then store in zipper-top plastic bags at room temperature for 2 days or freeze for up to 6 weeks. Defrost if necessary and rewarm the rolls before serving.

# DRESSING UP BROWN-AND-SERVE ROLLS

**Brown-and-serve rolls** are the ones in the bread aisle that look like raw bread dough wrapped in plastic wrap. Sprinkle these premade rolls with a few simple ingredients and no one will ever know that it was store-bought bread. Here are a few of my favorite "dress-ups" for these rolls.

## Blue Cheese Brown-and-Serve Rolls

Makes 12 rolls

- ¼ cup (½ stick) unsalted butter, melted
- 1 tablespoon olive oil
- ½ cup finely crumbled mild blue cheese, such as Gorgonzola or Maytag
- ½ teaspoon Worcestershire sauce
- 4 shakes of Tabasco sauce
- One 11-ounce package brown-and-serve rolls

In a small bowl, combine the butter, oil, blue cheese, Worcestershire, and Tabasco, stirring to blend. Drizzle over the rolls and bake according to the package directions.

## Cheesy Chipotle Brown-and-Serve Rolls

Makes 12 rolls

- ¼ cup (½ stick) unsalted butter, melted
- 1 tablespoon olive oil
- ⅛ teaspoon chipotle chile powder
- ⅛ teaspoon dried oregano, crumbled
- One 11-ounce package brown-and-serve rolls
- ½ cup finely shredded Monterey Jack, pepper Jack, cheddar, or queso fresco cheese

In a small bowl, combine the butter, oil, chipotle powder, and oregano. Brush over the rolls, then sprinkle with the cheese. Bake according to the package instructions.

## Garlic-Parmesan Brown-and-Serve Rolls

Makes 12 rolls

- ¼ cup (½ stick) unsalted butter, melted
- 1 tablespoon olive oil
- 1 teaspoon garlic powder
- 1 teaspoon sweet paprika
- One 11-ounce package brown-and-serve rolls
- ¼ cup freshly grated Parmesan cheese

In a small bowl, combine the butter, oil, garlic powder, and paprika. Brush over the rolls, then sprinkle with the Parmesan. Bake as directed on the package.

# Pita Chips

Makes about 48 chips

Pita chips are sold at your grocer for an exorbitant amount of money, but you can bake and freeze these great dippers for next to nothing. I like to make a slew of them at one go, then store them in zipper-top freezer bags, so I can pull out what I need about 1 hour before serving. They are terrific with hummus, white bean dip, or any other dip that you might care to choose. I like to top these with kosher or coarse sea salt, but you can leave them plain or sprinkle them with your choice of dried herbs.

**1 bag 6-inch round pita breads (there should be 6 to 8 in the bag)**

**½ cup (1 stick) unsalted butter, melted**

**2 tablespoons olive oil**

**¼ cup kosher salt**

**1.** Preheat the oven to 350°F and line 2 baking sheets with silicone liners, parchment paper, or aluminum foil.

**2.** For thick chips, quarter each pita bread with a chef's knife, cutting through both layers. For a more delicate chip, cut each wedge into 2 triangles, separating the top of the bread from the bottom. Lay the bread on the prepared baking sheets.

**3.** Combine the butter and oil and brush over the pita. Sprinkle with the salt and bake until crisp and golden brown, about 15 minutes.

**4.** Remove from the oven and let chips cool completely.

✳ **DIVA DO-AHEAD:** At this point, you can store in zipper-top plastic bags at room temperature for up to 3 days or freeze for up to 2 months.

## Diva Variations

Omit the salt and sprinkle the chips with any of these flavorings:

- Garlic salt
- Dried *herbes de Provence*
- Dried *fines herbes*
- Dried rosemary
- Dried oregano
- Cinnamon sugar (for sweet chips)
- Freshly grated Parmesan or Romano cheese
- Chipotle or another chile powder

# Heavenly Scones

Makes 16 to 20 scones

My friend Lora Brody's scones are absolutely the best and are especially delicious with Lemon or Lime Curd (see page 587) and Mock Clotted Cream (see below).

**3 ¾ cups unbleached all-purpose flour**

**1 ½ tablespoons baking powder**

**½ teaspoon salt**

**⅓ cup sugar**

**2 ½ cups heavy cream**

**2 large egg yolks**

**2 tablespoons milk or heavy cream**

**3 tablespoons sugar**

**1.** Line a baking sheet with a silicone liner, aluminum foil, or parchment paper.

**2.** Whisk together the flour, baking powder, salt, and sugar in a large bowl. Stir in the heavy cream and continue stirring until the dough begins to form a rough mass. Turn out the dough onto a lightly floured work surface and knead until smooth, about 6 times. Divide in half and shape into two disks about ¾ inch thick. Cut the disks into 8 or 10 wedges each and transfer to the prepared baking sheet.

✳ **DIVA DO-AHEAD:** At this point, you can freeze the cut scones. Once they are frozen, transfer to a zipper-top plastic bag, where they will keep for 1 month. Defrost for 30 minutes before continuing.

**3.** Preheat the oven to 400°F.

**4.** Whisk together the egg yolks and milk, brush over the tops of the scones, and sprinkle with the sugar. Bake until golden brown, about 20 minutes. Serve warm.

## Diva Variations

**Heavenly Cranberry Scones:** Toss ½ cup of unsweetened dried cranberries (or blueberries or cherries) into the flour mixture before adding the cream.

**Heavenly Ginger Scones:** Toss ½ cup of finely chopped crystallized ginger into the flour mixture before adding the cream.

**Heavenly Chocolate Chip Scones:** Toss ½ cup of semisweet chocolate chips into the flour mixture before adding the cream.

**Heavenly Lemon Scones:** Toss in 1 tablespoon of finely grated lemon zest with the flour, add 1 teaspoon of lemon oil or 2 teaspoons of lemon extract to the cream, and proceed as directed.

## Mock Clotted Cream

You can approximate clotted cream, the traditional accompaniment for scones in England, very easily. Simply beat 1 cup of heavy cream until it is so stiff your spatula will stand up in it. The cream will keep in the refrigerator for up to 4 days. Rewhip before serving.

# Cranberry-Oat Scones

Makes about 16 scones

These hearty scones aren't quite as elegant as Heavenly Scones (left), but they are another terrific do-ahead bread. If you like dried blueberries or cherries, feel free to substitute them for the cranberries. These are great served with Mock Clotted Cream (see left).

1½ cups old-fashioned rolled oats

1⅓ cups unbleached all-purpose flour

2 teaspoons baking powder

½ cup granulated sugar

1½ cups unsweetened dried cranberries

½ cup (1 stick) cold unsalted butter, cut into small bits

½ cup heavy cream

¼ cup whole milk

¼ cup firmly packed light brown sugar

**1.** Line a baking sheet with a silicone liner, aluminum foil, or parchment paper.

**2.** In a large bowl, combine the oats, flour, baking powder, granulated sugar, and cranberries, stirring to mix. Add the butter and combine, using your fingertips to break up the butter until the mixture resembles coarse meal. Drizzle in the cream, stirring with a wooden spoon until the dough begins to form. Turn out the dough onto a floured work surface and, with a rolling pin, roll into a disk about ¾ inch thick. Cut into 16 wedges and place on the prepared baking sheet.

✳ **DIVA DO-AHEAD:** At this point, you can freeze the scones. Once frozen, transfer to a zipper-top plastic bag and store in the freezer for up to 6 weeks. Defrost for 30 minutes before continuing.

**3.** Preheat the oven to 350°F.

**4.** Brush the tops of the scones with the milk and sprinkle with the brown sugar. Bake until golden brown, 15 to 20 minutes. Serve immediately.

### Freezing Scones

Baked scones can be frozen for about 1 month in zipper-top plastic bags, but they lose something when they are reheated.

However, if freezing the baked scones is the way you want to go, defrost them overnight, place them on a baking sheet lined with aluminum foil, parchment paper, or a silicone liner, and preheat the oven to 350°F. Place a pan of boiling water on the bottom rack of the oven and warm the scones for about 10 minutes, until heated through. The water will provide moisture and the scones should turn out nicely.

# Pineapple–Cream Cheese Muffins

Makes 12 muffins

My favorite Hawaiian flavors are combined in these yummy muffins, which have a surprise filling of cream cheese and pineapple, surrounded by a tender cake studded with macadamia nuts. These will really make your guests sit up and take notice when you serve brunch!

One 8-ounce package cream cheese, softened

One 4-ounce can pineapple chunks in syrup, thoroughly drained

1 cup plus 1 tablespoon sugar

10 tablespoons (1¼ sticks) unsalted butter, softened and cut into chunks

2 large eggs

¼ cup whole milk

2 cups cake flour

½ cup chopped macadamia nuts

¼ teaspoon baking powder

**1.** Preheat the oven to 400°F. Line 12 muffin cups with paper liners or coat with nonstick cooking spray.

**2.** In a medium-size bowl, cream together the cream cheese, pineapple, and 1 tablespoon of the sugar.

**3.** With an electric mixer, cream together the butter and remaining 1 cup of sugar in a large bowl. Add the eggs and milk and beat until thoroughly combined. Add the flour, nuts, and baking powder and continue to beat until the batter is blended. (It will be stiff.) Spoon 1 heaping tablespoon of batter into each of the prepared muffin cups. Top with 1 tablespoon of cream cheese filling and spoon another tablespoon of batter over the filling. Bake for 15 minutes, then reduce the oven temperature to 350°F and bake until golden and a skewer inserted in the center comes out clean, another 10 minutes. Serve warm.

❋ **DIVA DO-AHEAD:** You can let cool and refrigerate overnight or freeze for up to 6 weeks. Defrost for 24 hours and rewarm in a 350°F oven for 5 to 10 minutes.

# Coffee Cake Muffins

Makes 12 muffins

Anyone who has ever been addicted to the yellow cake and crumbly topping of packaged crumb coffee cake will love these muffins. The cake is moist and dense, the topping suitably crumbly, and the whole shebang takes about 5 minutes to put together in the food processor, so you have no reason to go out and buy those packaged cakes.

## Topping

½ cup firmly packed light brown sugar

½ cup unbleached all-purpose flour

½ teaspoon ground cinnamon

¼ cup (½ stick) cold unsalted butter, cut into bits

## Muffins

1½ cups unbleached all-purpose flour

1 teaspoon baking powder

⅛ teaspoon baking soda

1 cup granulated sugar

½ cup (1 stick) unsalted butter, softened and cut into small bits

2 large eggs

½ cup sour cream (low-fat is okay, but you'll need to add another 2 to 3 minutes to the baking time)

1 teaspoon vanilla extract

**1.** To make the topping, put the brown sugar, flour, and cinnamon in a food processor, and pulse to combine. Drop the butter on top and pulse until the mixture begins to form small, pebble-like nuggets. If you don't have a food processor, combine the dry ingredients in a small bowl and cut the butter into the flour with two knives or a pastry blender or use your fingertips.

❊ **DIVA DO-AHEAD:** At this point, you can store in a zipper-top plastic bag in the refrigerator for up to 5 days or freeze for up to 2 months.

**2.** Preheat the oven to 400°F. Line 12 muffin cups with paper liners or coat with non-stick cooking spray.

**3.** To make the muffins, in a food processor, combine the flour, baking powder, baking soda, and sugar and pulse 2 or 3 times. Sprinkle the butter over the dry ingredients and pulse until the mixture is the size of small peas. Add the eggs, sour cream, and vanilla and process for 30 seconds. Scrape down the sides of the work bowl and pulse until the batter is blended. Scoop ¼ cup of the batter into each muffin cup and top with 1 tablespoon of the streusel topping. Bake until golden and a skewer inserted into the center comes out clean, 15 to 17 minutes. Serve warm.

❊ **DIVA DO-AHEAD:** You can let cool and refrigerate overnight or freeze for up to 6 weeks.

# Blueberry Streusel Muffins

Makes 12 muffins

These scrumptious blueberry muffins are made even better by the crispy brown sugar streusel sprinkled over the top. I love to serve these on a buffet table for brunch with another bread choice; they are usually gone in a few minutes, so plan to make extras. The finished muffins freeze for only 3 weeks because of the water content in the blueberries.

### Topping

½ cup firmly packed light brown sugar

½ cup unbleached all-purpose flour

½ teaspoon ground cinnamon

¼ cup (½ stick) cold unsalted butter, cut into bits

### Muffins

½ cup (1 stick) unsalted butter, softened

¾ cup granulated sugar

1 large egg

⅔ cup buttermilk

1 teaspoon vanilla extract

2 cups unbleached all-purpose flour

2 teaspoons baking powder

1 cup individually frozen (not packed in syrup; see The Diva Says) or fresh blueberries, picked over for stems

**1.** To make the topping, put the brown sugar, flour, and cinnamon in a food processor, and pulse to combine. Drop the butter on top and pulse until the mixture begins to form small, pebble-like nuggets. If you don't have a food processor, combine the dry ingredients in a small bowl and cut the butter into the flour with two knives or a pastry blender or just use your fingertips. Set aside.

**DIVA DO-AHEAD:** At this point, you can store in a zipper-top plastic bag in the refrigerator for up to 5 days or freeze for up to 2 months.

**2.** Preheat the oven to 400°F. Line 12 muffin tins with paper liners or coat with nonstick cooking spray.

**3.** To make the muffins, with an electric mixer, cream together the butter and sugar in a large bowl until fluffy. Blend in the egg, buttermilk, and vanilla. Sift in the flour and baking powder, then drop the blueberries on top of the dry ingredients and stir until just blended, being careful not to break up the blueberries too much.

**4.** Spoon ¼ cup of batter into each muffin cup and top with 1 tablespoon of the streusel topping. Bake until golden brown and a skewer inserted into the center comes out clean, 17 to 20 minutes.

✳ **DIVA DO-AHEAD:** At this point, you can let cool and freeze the muffins for up to 3 weeks.

Serve warm.

The Diva Says:

Do not defrost the frozen blueberries. Using frozen berries instead of fresh will add about 3 minutes to the cooking time.

# Apple Muffins

Makes 12 muffins

With all the flavors of an apple pie, but not the work, these muffins will have your guests wanting a slice of cheese or some vanilla ice cream on the side. They are dense with apples and nuts, and they freeze beautifully. I actually like to make them the day before I serve them. Serve them with pork at lunch or dinner, or at a breakfast or brunch buffet.

¾ cup vegetable oil

1 cup sugar

1 large egg

1 teaspoon vanilla extract

2 cups unbleached all-purpose flour

½ teaspoon baking soda

½ teaspoon ground cinnamon

⅛ teaspoon ground nutmeg

2 medium-size Granny Smith apples, peeled, cored, and finely chopped

½ cup golden raisins (optional)

½ cup chopped pecans or walnuts (optional)

**1.** Preheat the oven to 350°F. Line 12 muffin cups with paper liners or coat with nonstick cooking spray.

**2.** In a large bowl, stir together the oil, sugar, egg, and vanilla until blended. Add the flour, baking soda, cinnamon, and nutmeg and stir until the mixture begins to come together. Add the apples and, if using, the raisins and nuts, and continue to mix until incorporated into the batter. Scoop ⅓ cup of the batter into each muffin cup. Bake until golden and a skewer inserted into the center comes out clean or with a few crumbs adhering to it, 20 to 25 minutes. Serve warm.

✳ **DIVA DO-AHEAD:** You can let cool and refrigerate for up to 3 days or freeze for up to 6 weeks.

# All-Purpose Muffin Mix for Diva-Like Entertaining

Makes 12 muffins

This is your emergency kit, ready on a moment's notice to give you freshly baked muffins with the addition of an egg, some milk, and a little melted butter. Toss in a few fresh or frozen berries or some dried cranberries or chopped apples, and you'll have your guests wondering how you pulled it off.

### Ready-and-Waiting Muffin Mix

**2 cups self-rising flour**

**½ cup sugar**

**¼ cup firmly packed light brown sugar**

**1 teaspoon ground cinnamon**

**⅛ teaspoon ground nutmeg**

### To make muffins

**1 large egg, beaten**

**¾ cup whole milk**

**¼ cup (½ stick) unsalted butter, melted**

### Diva Variations

When the muffins are done, dip the tops in melted butter and cinnamon sugar.

Add 1 cup of berries (fresh or frozen) to the batter and bake as directed, adding 3 extra minutes for frozen berries.

Add 1 cup of chopped pecans or walnuts to the batter and bake as directed.

**1.** In a zipper-top plastic bag, combine the mix ingredients and seal the bag.

✳ **DIVA DO-AHEAD:** You can keep at room temperature for about 3 months or freeze for up to 1 year. When ready to use, let sit at room temperature for about 30 minutes to warm up.

**2.** To make the muffins, preheat the oven to 400°F and coat 12 muffin cups with non-stick cooking spray or insert paper liners.

**3.** Transfer the muffin mix to a large bowl, stir in the egg, milk, and melted butter, and continue stirring until moistened and smooth. Spoon ¼ cup of batter into each muffin cup. Bake until golden brown and a skewer inserted into the center comes out clean, 15 to 18 minutes.

# The Diva's Biscuit Mix

Makes about twelve 2-inch biscuits

Another pantry secret, this mix can be stored at room temperature for a few months, or in the freezer for an even longer period. This makes light and tender biscuits, which I love to serve with fried chicken, roasted pork, or any brunch dish.

Ready-and-Waiting Biscuit Mix

**3 cups all-purpose flour**

**2 teaspoons baking powder**

**½ teaspoon baking soda**

**5 tablespoons Saco dry buttermilk powder (see The Diva Says)**

**1 teaspoon salt**

To make biscuits

**¾ cup (1½ sticks) cold unsalted butter, cut into bits**

**1¼ cups water**

**1 large egg**

**1.** To make the mix, in a zipper-top plastic bag, stir together the ingredients and seal the bag.

✳ **DIVA DO-AHEAD:** The mix will keep at room temperature for up to 3 months and in the freezer for up to 6 months.

**2.** To make the biscuits, preheat the oven to 400°F and line a baking sheet with parchment paper, aluminum foil, or a silicone liner.

**3.** Transfer the biscuit mix to a large bowl and, using your fingertips, work in the butter until the mixture is the size of peas. Gradually stir in the water and egg and continue stirring until the mixture begins to leave the sides of the bowl and forms a rough mass. Add more water if the dough is dry.

**4.** Turn out the dough onto a floured work surface, knead once or twice, then pat it into a rectangle about ¾ inch thick. Cut into 2-inch biscuits, using a floured biscuit cutter or drinking glass. Reroll the scraps and cut out additional biscuits until the dough is used up. Transfer to the baking sheet and bake until light brown on top, 12 to 15 minutes. Remove from the oven and serve immediately.

The Diva Says:

Saco brand buttermilk powder is a terrific pantry staple to keep around when you need buttermilk in your recipes.

Diva Variation

**Cheesy Biscuits:** Add 1 cup of shredded cheddar, Swiss, Parmesan, or crumbled blue cheese to the dough.

# Pizza Dough

Makes two 8-inch or one 14- to 16-inch crust

Pizza is a great buffet food because it can be served at room temperature. One of my favorite buffets is a build-your-own-pizza party, where you pair guests who might not know each other and have them build their own pie for dinner. It's a great way to get conversation going and your guests will love being involved in the process. Most grocery stores sell fresh pizza dough, but if yours doesn't, this recipe is simple and the dough freezes well. You can also use large pita breads (12 to 14 inches) or Boboli brand pizza shells.

---

1 package active dry yeast

1 teaspoon sugar

1 cup warm water (105°F)

3¼ cups unbleached all-purpose flour

1½ teaspoons salt

2 tablespoons olive oil, or as needed

---

**1.** In a 4-cup measuring cup, combine the yeast, sugar, and water and let stand until the mixture begins to bubble, about 10 minutes.

**2.** In a large bowl, stir together the flour and salt. Add the proofed yeast mixture and 1 tablespoon of the olive oil. Stir until the mixture comes together, then transfer to a lightly floured work surface and knead until the dough is smooth and elastic, adding more water if the dough is too dry or more flour if the dough is sticky. (This can also be done in a stand mixer fitted with a dough hook.) Brush a bowl with some of the remaining olive oil and turn the dough into the bowl. Cover and let rise until it is doubled in bulk, about 1 hour.

✳ **DIVA DO-AHEAD:** At this point, you can cover and freeze for up to 3 months. Defrost in the refrigerator before continuing.

**3.** Punch down the risen dough and turn out onto a floured work surface. Press with your fingertips to spread it out and pop any air bubbles. Roll out with a floured rolling pin into two 8-inch circles or one 14- to 16-inch round. If the pizza recipe you are using calls for an unbaked crust, the dough is ready for the toppings (skip step 4). If the recipe calls for a baked crust, preheat oven to 425°F and brush a baking sheet with the remaining olive oil.

**4.** Transfer the dough to the prepared pan, prick the dough with a fork, and drizzle with a bit more oil. Bake until golden brown, 12 to 14 minutes. Let cool for about 10 minutes, then remove from the pan. If not using immediately, cool completely and cover the crust with aluminum foil or plastic wrap until ready to use.

# Pesto and Shrimp Pizza

Serves 10

Gloriously green, with a topping of pink shrimp and lovely cheese, this pizza goes together in no time and it's always a winner. You can have all the ingredients prepped and ready to go and then assemble right before serving, or you can assemble the entire pizza up to 2 hours ahead of time.

One 14- to 16-inch baked pizza crust, homemade (left) or store-bought

¼ cup mascarpone cheese

½ cup Basil Pesto, homemade (page 97) or store-bought

½ cup chopped oil-packed sun-dried tomatoes, drained, oil reserved

½ cup pine nuts, toasted (see page 83)

10 large shrimp, cooked in boiling water just until pink, drained, cooled, peeled, and cut in half crosswise

⅓ cup shredded Parmesan cheese

## Diva Variations

Substitute Tapenade, homemade (page 84) or store-bought, for the pesto, and feta cheese for the Parmesan.

Use Sun-Dried Tomato Pesto (page 97), omit the sun-dried tomatoes, and garnish with chopped fresh basil.

Use Cilantro Pesto (page 472) and substitute shredded Monterey or pepper Jack cheese for the Parmesan.

Substitute 3 coarsely chopped roasted red peppers for the pesto, and feta cheese for the Parmesan.

**1.** Set the pizza crust on a serving platter.

**2.** In a small bowl, combine the mascarpone and pesto until blended. Spread the mixture evenly over the pizza crust. Sprinkle the tomatoes and pine nuts evenly over the pesto. In a small bowl, toss the shrimp with the reserved oil from the tomatoes and distribute the shrimp over the pizza. Sprinkle the pizza with the cheese.

**3.** Slice the pizza into small squares or bite-sized pieces.

✳ **DIVA DO-AHEAD:** At this point, you can cover and refrigerate for up to 2 hours. Let come to room temperature before serving.

# Pizza Margherita

Serves 10

The colors of the Italian flag are represented well in this version of the classic pizza, named for the queen of Italy who, at the end of the nineteenth century, asked to eat what the common people ate. Containing nothing more than fresh tomatoes, mozzarella, and basil (representative of the Italian flag), this pizza is delightful served on a buffet table.

---

**Two 12-inch round pita breads, or 1 large Boboli brand shell, or one 16-inch freshly baked pizza crust (see page 536)**

**¼ cup olive oil**

**1 pound fresh mozzarella cheese, thinly sliced or torn into rough shreds**

**3 cups cherry tomatoes, cut in half**

**1 teaspoon salt**

**½ teaspoon freshly ground black pepper**

**½ cup packed fresh basil leaves, cut into chiffonade (see The Diva Says)**

---

✳ **DIVA DO-AHEAD:** The mozzarella can be sliced or shredded and ready to go, and the tomatoes can be tossed with the salt, pepper, basil, and oil and kept at room temperature for several hours before assembling the pizza.

**1.** Brush each crust with some of the oil and arrange the mozzarella on top.

**2.** In a medium-size bowl, toss together the tomatoes, salt, pepper, basil, and the remaining oil until combined. Spread evenly over each pizza, then cut into serving pieces.

## The Diva Says:

To cut basil or any herb into chiffonade, stack the leaves, then roll them up like a cigar. With a chef's knife, cut the basil into fine shreds. This helps release the oils in the basil, resulting in an even more intense flavor.

# Caramelized Pear and Gorgonzola Pizza

Serves 10

This decadently rich pizza is one I serve as part of an antipasto platter in my entertaining classes, and everyone loves it. The sweet pears and sharp blue cheese combine on a crispy crust to give you one delicious bite after another. The pears should be almost ripe, but still firm; fully ripe pears are too juicy.

**3 medium-size almost ripe but firm pears, peeled, cored, and cut into ¼-inch wedges**

**⅓ cup firmly packed light brown sugar**

**1 unbaked pizza crust, homemade (see page 536) or store-bought**

**1½ cups crumbled Gorgonzola cheese**

**2 tablespoons extra virgin olive oil**

**1.** Preheat the oven to 375°F. Line a baking sheet with aluminum foil or a silicone liner.

**2.** Arrange the pears on the baking sheet in a single layer and sprinkle with the brown sugar. Bake until golden brown, 30 to 35 minutes.

✳ **DIVA DO-AHEAD:** At this point, you can cool, cover, and refrigerate for up to 3 days or freeze for up to 1 month. If previously frozen, toss defrosted pears in a hot skillet to reheat and evaporate any moisture.

**3.** Preheat the oven to 400°F. Arrange the pears over the pizza crust, then sprinkle the Gorgonzola evenly over the pears. Drizzle with the olive oil, and bake until the crust is crisp and the cheese is melted and beginning to bubble and turn golden, 20 to 25 minutes.

✳ **DIVA DO-AHEAD:** Make this only a few hours or less before you want to serve it, since it's great warm or at room temperature.

# Smoked Salmon Pizza

Serves 10

This rather unusual pizza is terrific to serve at a brunch buffet or as part of a pizza buffet. All the components can be readied the night before, so it's just a matter of assembling it before serving.

Three 4-ounce containers whipped cream cheese, softened

4 scallions (white and tender green parts), finely chopped

One 14-inch baked pizza crust, homemade (see page 536) or store-bought

½ pound thinly sliced smoked salmon

¼ cup finely chopped red onion

¼ cup capers, drained and chopped

**1.** In a small bowl, stir together the cream cheese and scallions until blended. Spread the cream cheese evenly over the pizza crust, top with the smoked salmon, and sprinkle with the red onion and capers.

✻ **DIVA DO-AHEAD:** At this point, you can refrigerate for up to 6 hours. Remove from the refrigerator 30 minutes before serving.

**2.** Slice the pizza into portions and serve.

# Simply Pizza

This is the pizza I serve at home or for parties when I just want a little bit of Italy in the mix. It takes well to a variety of toppings (see variations below), and you can substitute your favorite cheeses, if you'd like. The pizza is delicious warm or at room temperature. All the components can be waiting in the fridge, and you can put it together right before baking.

**One 14- to 16-inch unbaked pizza crust, homemade (see page 536) or store-bought**

**²/₃ cup Pizza Sauce, homemade (page 482) or store-bought**

**6 ounces Munster cheese, thinly sliced**

**½ cup freshly grated Parmesan cheese**

**2 teaspoons dried oregano, crumbled**

**1 to 2 tablespoons extra virgin olive oil**

**1.** Preheat oven to 400°F. Line a baking sheet with aluminum foil or a silicone liner.

**2.** Roll out the dough to a ½-inch thickness and place on the prepared baking sheet.

**3.** Spread a thin layer of sauce over the crust, then arrange the Munster slices evenly over the sauce. Sprinkle with the Parmesan and oregano and drizzle with the oil. Bake until the bottom of the crust is crispy and the cheeses have melted and turned golden brown, 15 to 20 minutes.

**4.** Remove the pizza from the oven and let rest for 10 minutes before slicing.

✳ **DIVA DO-AHEAD:** At this point, you can let cool, cover and refrigerate for up to 2 days or freeze for up to 1 month. Reheat on a baking sheet in a 350°F oven for 10 to 15 minutes.

The Diva Says:

If you have a pizza stone, by all means use it instead of the baking sheet.

## Diva Variations

Add any of the following toppings:

• ³/₄ pound Italian sausage, cooked and cut into ½-inch-thick rounds

• 2 cups cut-up meatballs (about 5 regular size or 10 minis)

• 2 or 3 roasted red peppers, coarsely chopped

• One 14.5-ounce can artichoke hearts, drained and coarsely chopped

• ½ medium-size red onion, sliced ½ inch thick and separated into rings

• ½ pound sautéed sliced mushrooms (You need to cook mushrooms before putting them on pizza, otherwise they will be watery and the crust won't crisp up.)

• 12 thin slices pepperoni, or to your taste

• ½ cup chopped capocollo (Italian smoked ham—I like to use the hot version)

# Pizza Primavera

Serves 10

This pizza is inspired by one my husband ordered at a little trattoria in Rome. It was a warm pizza topped with greens, tomatoes, and fresh mozzarella tossed with a little olive oil and balsamic vinegar. Even in March, it had the taste of spring, and we loved the mingling of the crisp crust, vinaigrette, greens, and smooth mozzarella. For this version, you can use a baked shell and top it with the salad.

One 14-inch baked pizza crust, homemade (see page 536) or store-bought

1 cup cherry tomatoes, cut in half

1 cup bocconcini (small fresh mozzarella balls), drained and cut in half (see The Diva Says)

1 teaspoon salt

½ teaspoon freshly ground black pepper

⅓ cup extra virgin olive oil

3 tablespoons balsamic vinegar

2 cups mixed field greens

**1.** Place the pizza crust on a serving plate.

**2.** In a large bowl, combine the tomatoes, mozzarella, salt, and pepper. Sprinkle with the oil and vinegar and toss together. Taste for vinegar, salt, and pepper and add more if necessary.

✳ **DIVA DO-AHEAD:** At this point, the tomato and mozzarella salad can be stored in the refrigerator for 1 day.

**3.** Toss the tomato salad with the field greens and spread the salad over the crust. Cut into serving pieces.

✳ **DIVA DO-AHEAD:** The pizza can sit at room temperature for up to 2 hours.

The Diva Says:
If bocconcini aren't available, use one 8-ounce fresh mozzarella ball, cut into ½-inch dice.

# Wrap 'n' Rollers

Serves 12

These wrapped sandwiches will disappear fast on your buffet table, so make sure you have lots on hand in different flavors. They should be made up to 24 hours ahead of time to give the bread time to soften. Thirty minutes before serving, cut with a serrated knife and arrange on platters. These are relatively inexpensive to make and when you compare the cost and taste to those from your local deli, you'll be glad you're making your own. If you are unable to find lavash, large flour tortillas will work just fine.

**Two 16 x 12-inch sheets lavash bread**

**Two 8-ounce packages cream cheese, softened**

**1 clove garlic, minced**

**1 teaspoon Worcestershire sauce**

**1 cup Basil Pesto, homemade (page 97) or store-bought**

**¼ pound thinly sliced prosciutto, cut into matchsticks**

**1½ cups shredded provolone cheese**

**½ cup pine nuts**

**1 cup oil-packed sun-dried tomatoes, drained and cut into matchsticks**

**Chopped fresh basil for garnish**

**Chopped fresh parsley for garnish**

**1.** Spread 2 large pieces of plastic wrap or aluminum foil on a flat work surface and arrange a lavash in the center of each one.

**2.** With an electric mixer, beat together the cream cheese, garlic, and Worcestershire in a medium-size bowl until smooth.

Spread a thin layer of the cream cheese over a lavash. Spread half the pesto over the cream cheese and sprinkle evenly with half the prosciutto, provolone, pine nuts, and tomatoes. Roll up the lavash and wrap in the plastic or foil. Repeat with the second lavash.

❋ **DIVA DO-AHEAD:** At this point, refrigerate for at least 6 hours or overnight.

**3.** Thirty minutes before serving, slice the rollers into 1-inch-thick rounds, arrange on a serving platter, and garnish with basil and parsley.

## The Diva Says:

Some supermarkets carry large flour tortillas and lavash in flavors, such as cilantro-spinach and tomato-basil. Their colors will add interest to your buffet table, so I encourage you to use any of these in your sandwiches.

# South of the Border Roll-Ups

Serves 12

Filled with chiles, cheese, chopped turkey, and cilantro, these roll-ups are a great appetizer or snack to serve when watching your favorite sports teams on TV. I like to serve guacamole and fresh salsa on the side to dollop on top.

**Twelve 10-inch flour tortillas**

**One 8-ounce package cream cheese, softened**

**1 cup sour cream**

**½ teaspoon chili powder**

**¼ pound thinly sliced roast or smoked turkey, cut into matchsticks**

**1½ cups shredded mild cheddar cheese (or half cheddar and half pepper Jack)**

**½ cup pickled jalapeño peppers, drained and finely chopped**

**½ cup pitted black olives, drained and chopped**

**6 scallions (white and tender green parts), thinly sliced**

**½ cup seeded and finely chopped red bell pepper**

**¼ cup chopped fresh cilantro for garnish**

**1 recipe Guacamole Olé (page 88) for serving**

**1 recipe Salsa Fresca (page 90) for serving**

**1.** Lay 4 pieces of plastic wrap or aluminum foil on a flat work surface and arrange a tortilla in the center of each.

**2.** In a medium-size bowl, cream together the cream cheese, sour cream, and chili powder. Spread one-third of the mixture in a thin layer over the 4 tortillas. Sprinkle one-third of the turkey, cheese, olives, scallions, bell pepper, and cilantro over the tortillas, roll up, and wrap in the plastic or foil.

**3.** Repeat the process 2 more times with the remaining 8 tortillas.

✳ **DIVA DO-AHEAD:** At this point, refrigerate for at least 6 hours or overnight.

**4.** Thirty minutes before serving, cut the tortillas with a serrated knife into 1-inch-thick rounds. Arrange on a platter, garnish with cilantro, and serve with guacamole and salsa on the side.

# Creamy Horseradish and Roast Beef Roll-Ups

Serves 12

These elegant and delicious sandwiches filled with roast beef, horseradish, and marinated red onions are perfect for a New Year's buffet, a Super Bowl party, or an appetizer spread. Use leftover roast beef or flank steak, or buy it thinly sliced at the deli. Make sure you take these out of the fridge about 45 minutes before serving to soften the onions.

**Two 16 x 12-inch sheets lavash bread**

**1 cup sour cream**

**2 tablespoons prepared horseradish**

**1 tablespoon Dijon mustard**

**⅓ pound thinly sliced roast beef**

**1 recipe Marinated Red Onions (page 165), drained**

## Diva Variations

**Beefy Blue Cheese Wraps:** Substitute 1 cup of crumbled blue cheese for the horseradish, omit the mustard, and proceed as directed.

**Club Wrap:** Omit the sour cream, horseradish, roast beef, and onions and spread the lavash with mayonnaise. Sprinkle with chopped turkey or chicken, finely diced tomatoes, crumbled crisply fried bacon, and finely shredded lettuce.

**1.** Spread 2 large pieces of plastic wrap or aluminum foil on a flat work surface and arrange a lavash in the center of each one.

**2.** In a small bowl, stir together the sour cream, horseradish, and Dijon. Spread a layer over a lavash, then top with half the roast beef and drained onions. Roll up and wrap in plastic or foil. Repeat with the second lavash.

❋ **DIVA DO-AHEAD:** At this point, refrigerate for at least 4 hours or overnight.

**3.** Thirty minutes before serving, slice the rolls into 1-inch-thick rounds with a serrated knife and arrange on a large serving platter.

# The Basic Hero

Serves 10

This Italian sandwich is filled with a tomato, artichoke, and olive salad and then piled high with Italian meats and cheeses. Perfect for a picnic or tailgate, or as part of a grazing menu, the sandwich should be made at least 4 hours ahead of time.

One 1-pound loaf Italian bread, cut in half lengthwise

1 cup cherry tomatoes (optional), quartered

½ cup pitted Kalamata olives, drained and coarsely chopped

One 4.5-ounce jar marinated artichoke hearts, drained, reserving the marinade, and coarsely chopped

2 roasted red peppers, coarsely chopped

¼ pound thinly sliced soppressata

¼ pound thinly sliced mortadella

¼ pound thinly sliced prosciutto

¼ pound thinly sliced capocollo

1½ cups finely shredded lettuce

1 cup thinly shredded provolone cheese

Olives for serving

Pickles for serving

**1.** Hollow out the bottom half of the bread, leaving a ¾-inch-thick shell.

**2.** In a small bowl, toss together the tomatoes, if using, and the olives, artichokes, and red peppers. Taste for seasoning and add a little of the reserved marinade if needed. Pile into the bottom of the bread and layer with the sliced meats. Top with the lettuce and cheese and sprinkle with some of the marinade. Cover with the top half of the bread and wrap in aluminum foil or plastic wrap.

✳ **DIVA DO-AHEAD:** At this point, refrigerate for at least 4 and up to 12 hours. Bring to room temperature before continuing.

**3.** Cut the sandwich into 1-inch-thick slices and secure each one with a toothpick. Put a bowl of olives and another with pickles in the center of a platter and surround with the sliced sandwiches.

## The Diva and Her Garnishes

My deli garnishes hero sandwiches with long frilled toothpicks threaded with large black olives, green pimento-stuffed olives, and dill pickle chunks. This is a great way to serve your guests that little extra something with the sandwich, and it looks really cool.

## Diva Variation

If you would like, you can also make this with 2 unsliced round Italian bread loaves. When ready to serve, cut the rounds into wedges.

# The Guacamole Club

Serves 12

This beautiful sandwich makes a real statement for lunch or a light supper or as part of a grazing menu. You can vary the type of bread you use; buy challah or another kind of egg bread or use a soft-crusted Italian loaf. You can't go wrong; everyone loves a club sandwich.

**One 1-pound loaf egg bread, such as challah, or a soft-crusted Italian bread**

**¾ cup guacamole**

**½ cup mayonnaise**

**1½ cups finely shredded lettuce**

**2 medium-size ripe tomatoes, thinly sliced**

**Salt and freshly ground black pepper to taste**

**1 pound sliced bacon, cooked until crisp, drained on paper towels, and crumbled**

**¾ pound thinly sliced roast turkey**

### The Foot-and-a-Half Sandwich

These sandwiches fall into the no-brainer category. You pile on the fillings, slam the bread halves together, refrigerate to let the flavors mellow, then slice and serve. They are best served at room temperature and are a really nice addition to your buffet table. You will want a long loaf of bread at least 3 inches wide; that way you can slice neat, narrow sandwiches out of it. I don't recommend baguettes, which don't hold as much filling. A bread with a softer crust, such as an Italian loaf, is a better choice.

**1.** Lay a large piece of plastic wrap or aluminum foil on a flat work surface. Split the loaf in half lengthwise and hollow out the bottom half, leaving a ¾-inch-thick shell. Center the hollowed-out bread on the foil or plastic wrap.

**2.** Spread the guacamole on the bottom half and top with the mayonnaise, so it seals in the guacamole. Top with the lettuce and tomatoes, seasoning the tomatoes with salt and pepper. Sprinkle with the bacon and top with the turkey slices. Cover with the top half of the bread and wrap in the plastic or aluminum foil.

✳ **DIVA DO-AHEAD:** At this point, you can refrigerate for up to 8 hours. Bring to room temperature before continuing.

**3.** Slice the sandwich with a serrated knife into 1-inch-thick slices, secure the slices with toothpicks, arrange on a serving platter, and serve.

# The Cubano

Serves 12

This savory sandwich combines melted Swiss cheese and succulent roast pork; it's a great way to recycle leftovers. Cuban sandwiches are usually grilled, but this one is delicious heated in the oven; serve it warm or at room temperature.

**One 1-pound loaf soft-crusted Italian bread**

**½ cup mayonnaise**

**2 canned chipotle chiles in adobo sauce**

**Salt to taste (optional)**

**2 scallions (white and tender green parts), chopped**

**4 cups sliced or shredded roast pork shoulder (see page 422)**

**2 cups shredded imported Swiss cheese**

**4 to 6 small dill pickles, thinly sliced lengthwise, plus extra for serving**

**1.** Place a large piece of aluminum foil on a flat work surface. Cut the bread in half lengthwise and lay the bottom in the center of the foil. Hollow it out a bit, leaving a ¾-inch-thick shell.

**2.** In a food processor, process the mayonnaise and chiles together until smooth. Season with salt if necessary and stir in the scallions. Spread over the bottom of the bread and top with the pork, cheese, and pickles. Cover with the top half of the bread, and wrap in the foil.

✳ **DIVA DO-AHEAD:** At this point, you can refrigerate for up to 24 hours. Bring to room temperature before continuing.

**3.** Preheat the oven to 350°F. Place the sandwich on a baking sheet and bake, still in the foil, for 45 minutes. The cheese will be melted and the sandwich hot throughout.

**4.** Remove from the oven and let rest for about 10 minutes. Remove the foil, cut into 1-inch-thick slices, and secure the slices with toothpicks. Arrange on a serving platter with additional dill pickles.

## The Diva Says:

I find the small dill pickles are nicer to slice and taste better than the large ones. I buy the fresh pickles that are sold in the refrigerator case near the hot dogs.

# Ultimate Roast Beef Sandwich

Serves 10

This sandwich is so delicious, I actually dream about it! Layered with roast beef, caramelized onions, and horseradish spread, it's a carnivore's delight. I like to serve this warm, but you can certainly put it on a buffet table at room temperature. If you don't want to make a large sandwich, the filling is also delicious on a little Parker House type of roll; pile a bunch of them on a platter—trust me, they won't be there long!

**One 1-pound loaf soft-crusted Italian bread**

**½ to ¾ cup Horseradish Sauce (page 493)**

**1 recipe Perfectly Caramelized Onions (page 244), at room temperature**

**¾ pound thinly sliced roast beef**

### Diva Variation

**Blue Heaven Roast Beef Sandwich:**
Substitute Old-Fashioned Blue Cheese Dressing (page 215) for the Horseradish Sauce and proceed as directed.

**1.** Place a large piece of aluminum foil on a flat work surface. Cut the bread in half lengthwise and place the bottom half in the center of the foil. Hollow it out a bit, leaving a ¾-inch-thick shell.

**2.** Spread the Horseradish Sauce on the bottom half and top with the onions, then the roast beef. Cover with the top half of the bread and wrap in the foil.

✳ **DIVA DO-AHEAD:** At this point, you can refrigerate for up to 24 hours. Bring to room temperature before continuing.

**3.** Preheat the oven to 350°F. Place the sandwich on a baking sheet and bake until warm, about 25 minutes.

**4.** Remove from the oven and let rest for 10 minutes. Cut into 1-inch-thick slices, secure with toothpicks, and arrange on a serving platter.

# Breakfast and Brunch

**A late morning or early afternoon meal,** brunch is a little lunch and a little breakfast, served anywhere from about 10:00 A.M. to 2:00 P.M. The dishes in this chapter will help you put on a brunch that people will talk about for weeks afterward. If you are hosting a special brunch around a holiday or occasion, plan on serving the food about 45 minutes after the stated time on your invitation, which will give you time to serve drinks as your guests arrive. If there are any latecomers, they will have to catch up on the Bloody Marys or mimosas.

For a brunch, I recommend that you brew coffee and store it in thermal carafes or, if you have a large coffee urn, brew it in the urn (see page 41), then serve it from thermal carafes. Set out sugar, sweetener, and creamer for the coffee. You may also want to fill a thermal carafe with hot water for tea and set out an assortment of tea bags as well as lemon slices. Chilled juices are also expected at brunch, with or without the addition of alcohol. Warmed spiced cider is nice during the holidays, and mulled wine can be served during the colder months.

If you are serving breakfast or brunch to overnight guests, it's a good idea to assemble the dishes the day before and refrigerate them. In the morning, take them out of the fridge for 30 minutes to bring them to room temperature and then bake them. To keep my guests well supplied with coffee, I use a coffeemaker with a timer. Once I've emptied a freshly made pot into a thermal carafe, I can refill the coffeemaker with premeasured packages of ground coffee, which I've ground myself and frozen, and fresh water. Make the menu simple: Buy already cut up fruit to serve and precook the bacon or sausages the day before so you just need to reheat them in the microwave on 50 percent power until warmed. The smells of breakfast will have your guests out of bed in no time!

When entertaining at breakfast or brunch, I suggest you serve one sweet and one savory entrée and fresh fruit or a baked fruit compote to round out the meal. Breakfast meats, such as ham, bacon, sausage, and smoked turkey, also make a nice addition if you are serving lots of people.

Each recipe in this chapter is simple to prepare and most should be made the day before, then heated through just before serving. I've taken all the guesswork out of making brunch easy and stress-free. These recipes are perfect for a family breakfast, an Easter brunch, a Christmas breakfast, or feeding the kids the day after the prom.

## GARNITURE BAR

**Since your guests** will be serving themselves, it's nice to set up a little garniture bar at the end of the table, so they can garnish their entrées with their choice of toppings, whether it's sour cream and guacamole on top of chili, or onions, capers, and sour cream on the smoked salmon strata.

Set out small bowls filled with garnishes and make sure each dish has its own serving spoon or small tongs to make it simple to transfer to plates.

Check the garnishes during the party to make sure you don't run out, and always have extras ready in zipper-top plastic bags or bowls in the refrigerator for quick refills. Keep capers, onions, and lemon wedges in bags, but refrigerate extra sour cream in a serving dish, to swap our for empties during the party.

To keep the garnishes cool on the table, place them in a shallow tray or bowl and surround with cracked ice.

# Overnight French Toast

Serves 10 to 12

The horrifying thought of flipping mountains of French toast on the griddle for guests inspired me to come up with this simple but elegant way to make French toast, and everyone loves it. A takeoff on bread pudding, the bread is soaked overnight, then baked the next morning. You can bake the mixture in muffin cups for individual portions (see French Toast Muffins on page 557) or serve it family style in a 13 x 9-inch baking dish. Either way is terrific for serving French toast to an army.

**1 pound bread (see below), crust removed if hard**

**1 cup sugar**

**2 teaspoons ground cinnamon**

**8 large eggs**

**2 cups heavy cream**

**1.** Tear the bread into 1-inch pieces and put in a large bowl (you will have about 9 cups of bread).

**2.** In a small bowl, mix together the sugar and cinnamon.

## What Kind of Bread?

When making bread puddings or French toast, I buy breads with a soft crust and use the entire loaf, crust and all. If I have leftover crusty bread, I remove the crust, then tear the bread apart. Crusty breads absorb all the liquid and are still quite chewy after cooking, which isn't the texture you want. Croissants, brioches, and even leftover doughnuts all work well in French toast batters.

**3.** In another large bowl, whisk together the eggs, cream, and ¾ cup of the cinnamon sugar, then pour over the bread, stirring until coated.

✳ **DIVA DO-AHEAD:** At this point, cover and refrigerate for at least 2 hours or overnight.

**4.** Preheat the oven to 350°F. Coat a 13 x 9-inch baking dish with nonstick cooking spray. Spread the batter in the prepared dish and sprinkle the top with the remaining cinnamon sugar. Bake until puffed and golden brown, 35 to 40 minutes.

**5.** Remove from the oven and serve with warm maple syrup.

## The Diva Says:

If you would like to lower the fat in this dish, use an egg substitute product and whole milk.

### Diva Variation

**Holiday French Toast:** At Christmastime, to use up eggnog I substitute 2 cups of eggnog for the heavy cream, use only 6 large eggs, and sprinkle the finished dish with a little ground nutmeg.

# Amaretto-Peach French Toast 🥃🥤🍷🍸

Serves 10

This elegant dish is like a peach French toast cobbler. Soak the bread briefly, combine it with the peaches, and let the fruit macerate overnight. Then give the dish a crunchy sweet topping and bake. I don't recommend that you freeze this toast, but you can put it together so quickly before serving that I think you'll be making this again and again, to rave reviews.

**French Toast**

**6 large eggs**

**⅔ cup milk**

**1 tablespoon amaretto liqueur**

**1 tablespoon baking powder**

**2 tablespoons granulated sugar**

**½ teaspoon ground cinnamon**

**One 8-ounce loaf French bread, cut into ½-inch-thick slices**

**Fruit**

**8 cups sliced ripe peaches, or two 16-ounce bags frozen sliced peaches, defrosted**

**½ cup granulated sugar**

**1 teaspoon ground cinnamon**

**Pinch of ground nutmeg**

**1 teaspoon cornstarch**

**Topping**

**1 cup granulated sugar**

**2 teaspoons ground cinnamon**

**½ cup slivered almonds**

**3 tablespoons unsalted butter, melted**

**Confectioners' sugar**

**1.** Coat a 13 x 9-inch baking dish with non-stick cooking spray.

**2.** To begin the French toast, in a medium-size bowl, whisk together the eggs, milk, amaretto, baking powder, sugar, and cinnamon. Put the bread on a rimmed baking sheet in a single layer. Slowly pour the egg mixture over the bread and turn the slices until they are totally soaked.

**3.** To prepare the fruit, put the peaches, granulated sugar, cinnamon, nutmeg, and cornstarch in the prepared baking dish, stir to coat the peaches, and cover with the soaked bread, wedging it in to fit.

✳ **DIVA DO-AHEAD:** Cover and refrigerate for at least 2 hours or overnight.

**4.** Preheat the oven to 375°F.

**5.** To make the topping, in a small bowl, mix together the sugar and cinnamon. Sprinkle evenly over the bread and top with the almonds. Brush with some or all of the melted butter and bake until golden and the peaches are bubbling around the sides of the dish, 20 to 25 minutes.

**6.** Remove from the oven and sift confectioners' sugar over the top. To serve, lift out the toast with a spatula or tongs, place on individual plates, and spoon the fruit sauce on top.

### Diva Variations

Substitute 2 pints of fresh blueberries or two 16-ounce bags of frozen blueberries for the peaches, or use a combination of blueberries and peaches. Raspberries and peaches are also wonderful, and so are mixed berries.

## Freezing French Toast

If you would like to bake any of the French toast or stuffed French toast recipes in this chapter and then freeze them, reduce the cooking time by about 10 minutes. Remove the dish from the oven, allow to cool to room temperature, cover tightly with aluminum foil or plastic wrap, and freeze for up to 1 month. If you're freezing French toast muffins, after cooling them, pop them out of the tin, transfer to a zipper-top plastic bag, seal, and freeze. Defrost any of these dishes for 24 hours in the refrigerator. Remove from the refrigerator an hour before baking, and preheat oven to 350°F. Cover with aluminum foil and bake the French toast or stuffed French toast in the oven for 20 minutes. Heat the muffins, covered, on a baking sheet for about 15 minutes.

# Cottage Garden Stuffed French Toast 🥤🍺🍷🍾

Serves 10

Every time I eat out, my family makes fun of me because I'm always thinking about recipes. I first had stuffed French toast at a small restaurant called the Cottage in the village of La Jolla. The French toast was stuffed with mascarpone cheese and fresh strawberries and covered with a delicious strawberry sauce and whipped cream. I like to use an egg bread for this, but you can also use cinnamon swirl bread or raisin bread. If fresh berries are out of season, use frozen whole berries (not in syrup), defrosted, drained, and then sliced.

**24 slices good quality egg bread, such as challah, or another bread of your choice, crust removed**

**1½ cups mascarpone cheese**

**⅓ cup granulated sugar**

**1 cup sliced strawberries**

**8 large eggs**

**1 cup heavy cream**

**2 teaspoons vanilla extract**

**⅓ cup unsalted butter, melted**

**½ cup cinnamon sugar (see The Diva Says)**

**Confectioners' sugar for garnish; or Strawberry Sauce (page 640), whipped cream, and sliced fresh strawberries**

**1.** Coat two 13 x 9-inch baking dishes with nonstick cooking spray.

**2.** Lay 12 slices of the bread on a work surface, setting aside the other 12 slices.

**3.** In a large bowl, cream together the mascarpone, granulated sugar, and strawberries until blended. Spread some of the mixture evenly over each piece of bread. Cover the filling with the remaining 12 bread slices and transfer to the prepared pans, stacking the sandwiches to fit. You should have 2 or 3 layers.

**4.** In a large bowl, whisk together the eggs, cream, and vanilla until blended. Carefully pour over the stuffed bread, tilting the pan to coat the bread thoroughly.

❋ **DIVA DO-AHEAD:** At this point, cover and refrigerate for at least 2 hours or overnight.

**5.** Preheat oven to 350°F. Brush the tops of the stuffed bread with the melted butter and sprinkle with the cinnamon sugar. Bake until puffed and golden brown, 25 to 35 minutes.

❋ **DIVA DO-AHEAD:** At this point, you can cool completely, cover, and freeze for 1 month. Defrost overnight in the refrigerator, and bake, covered, in a preheated 350°F oven for 20 minutes, or until heated through.

**6.** Cut into squares and sift confectioners' sugar over the top, or garnish with Strawberry Sauce, whipped cream, and sliced berries.

## The Diva Says:

I always have a jar of cinnamon sugar in my pantry for sprinkling on French toast, pancakes, and waffles. Simply mix 1 cup of sugar with 2 teaspoons of ground cinnamon and stir to blend. Store in an airtight container.

## French Toast Muffins

Individual French toast muffins can be made from any of these recipes. Soak the bread in the batter in a bowl or in zipper-top plastic bags overnight. Remove from the refrigerator 30 minutes before baking. Coat a 12-cup muffin tin with nonstick cooking spray. With a $1/2$-cup ice cream scoop, drop the French toast mixture into the muffin cups and sprinkle with cinnamon sugar. Bake at 350°F until golden brown, 20 to 25 minutes. Remove from the muffin cups and serve.

## Diva Variations

**Apricot and Cheese Stuffed French Toast:** Replace the mascarpone, sugar, and strawberries with a mixture of two 8-ounce packages of cream cheese, softened, $2/3$ cup of apricot preserves, 2 teaspoons of grated lemon zest, and 1 tablespoon of amaretto liqueur.

**Cappuccino Stuffed French Toast:** Replace the mascarpone, granulated sugar, and strawberries with a mixture of 1 cup of ricotta cheese, one 8-ounce package of cream cheese, softened, 2 tablespoons of strong brewed coffee, 8 ounces of semi-sweet chocolate, grated, and $1/2$ teaspoon of ground cinnamon.

**Almond Stuffed French Toast:** Omit the mascarpone, granulated sugar, and strawberries and replace them with a mixture of 2 cups of almond paste and one 8-ounce package of cream cheese, softened.

**Honey Cream Cheese Stuffed French Toast:** For the mascarpone, granulated sugar, and strawberries substitute a mixture of two 8-ounce packages of cream cheese, softened, $1/3$ cup of honey, 2 tablespoons of orange juice, and 2 teaspoons of grated orange zest.

**Maple Pecan Stuffed French Toast:** Replace the mascarpone, granulated sugar, and strawberries with a mixture of two 8-ounce packages of cream cheese, softened, $1/4$ cup of pure maple syrup, and $3/4$ cup of chopped pecans.

**Lemon Ginger Stuffed French Toast:** Omit the mascarpone, granulated sugar, and strawberries and replace them with a mixture of 1 cup of ricotta cheese, 1 cup of mascarpone cheese, $1/2$ cup of granulated sugar, 1 teaspoon of lemon extract, 2 teaspoons of grated lemon zest, and $1/2$ teaspoon of ground ginger.

# Praline Apple French Toast

Serves 10

The molten caramel pecan sauce that bakes underneath the apple French toast makes this a very special brunch dish. If you would like a spectacular presentation, I recommend baking it in 2 round pie pans, so that you can turn them upside down to reveal the prettier side. If you serve it in a 13 x 9-inch dish, however, your guests will find a lovely surprise when they scoop into the dish. I like to use a softer cooking apple such as Golden Delicious in this dish, rather than a Granny Smith, but it's fine to use your favorite cooking apple.

¾ cup (1½ sticks) unsalted butter, melted

½ cup granulated sugar

⅔ cup firmly packed light brown sugar

2 cups pecan halves

6 cups torn egg bread or good quality white bread

3 Golden Delicious apples, peeled, cored, and chopped into ½-inch pieces

6 large eggs

2 cups heavy cream

2 teaspoons ground cinnamon

¼ cup sugar

1 tablespoon vanilla extract

1. Coat with nonstick cooking spray two 9-inch round pie pans, 2½ inches deep, or a 13 x 9-inch baking dish.

2. Combine the melted butter and both sugars in a medium-size bowl. Pour into the prepared pan(s), tilt to cover the bot-tom evenly, then arrange the pecans over the bottom. Cover and refrigerate until ready to use.

3. Put the bread and apples in a large bowl.

4. In a medium-size bowl, beat together the eggs, cream, cinnamon, sugar, and vanilla. Pour over the bread and apples and mix well.

✳ **DIVA DO-AHEAD:** At this point, cover and refrigerate for at least 2 hours or overnight.

5. Preheat the oven to 350°F. Pour the bat-ter into the prepared pan(s) and bake until puffed and golden, 45 to 55 minutes.

✳ **DIVA DO-AHEAD:** See Freezing French Toast on page 555.

6. Let rest for 5 minutes, then turn out onto serving platters if you used pie pans.

# Crustless Quiche Lorraine

Serves 10

I've never been very fond of traditional quiche because even when the crust is prebaked, it becomes soggy on the bottom. To fix the problem, I've developed a very satisfying crustless quiche that's a snap to put together. If you'd like, you can make this quiche in greased muffin tins for individual servings; in this case, bake for 25 minutes.

**8 large eggs**

**2 cups heavy cream**

**1 teaspoon salt**

**½ teaspoon freshly ground black pepper**

**6 shakes of Tabasco sauce**

**2 scallions (white and tender green parts), finely chopped**

**8 strips bacon, cooked until crisp, drained on paper towels, and crumbled**

**3 cups finely shredded Swiss cheese**

**1.** In a large bowl, whisk together the eggs, cream, salt, pepper, and Tabasco. Stir in the scallions, bacon, and cheese, whisking until blended.

**❋ DIVA DO-AHEAD:** At this point, you can cover and refrigerate overnight.

**2.** Preheat the oven to 350°F. Coat a 10-inch pie pan with nonstick cooking spray.

**3.** Pour the quiche batter into the prepared pan and bake until a knife inserted into the center comes out clean and the quiche has puffed up above the rim of the baking dish, 40 to 50 minutes.

**❋ DIVA DO-AHEAD:** At this point, you can let cool, cover, and refrigerate overnight or freeze for up to 6 weeks. Defrost and bring to room temperature. Reheat in a 350°F oven for 20 minutes.

Serve warm or at room temperature.

## Diva Variations

Feel free to experiment with this basic recipe by trying some of the suggestions below.

● Substitute Gouda cheese for the Swiss and 1 cup of diced cooked chicken (½-inch dice) for the bacon.

● Substitute mild cheddar for the Swiss and ½ pound of smoked sausage (such as chorizo, andouille, or kielbasa), cut into ½-inch dice, for the bacon.

● Substitute Havarti with dill cheese for the Swiss and 1 cup of tiny bay shrimp for the bacon.

● You can use a lower fat cheese, whole milk instead of the heavy cream, and egg substitute in this dish—the quiche won't be quite as fluffy, but it will work.

# Spinach-Boursin Quiche

Serves 10

A beautifully colored and deliciously spiced quiche, this one gets its character from garlicky Boursin cheese.

**2 tablespoons unsalted butter**

**Two 16-ounce bags frozen chopped spinach, defrosted and squeezed dry**

**1 teaspoon salt**

**½ teaspoon freshly ground black pepper**

**⅛ teaspoon ground nutmeg**

**8 large eggs**

**2 cups heavy cream**

**Two 3.5-ounce packages Boursin cheese, softened**

### If You're Going Low-Fat

Regular cheese (full fat) was used in testing the egg dishes in this chapter, but low-fat (please don't use nonfat) cheeses can be substituted. Just remember that low-fat cheese will add a bit more liquid to the mix, and therefore you'll need to bake them a little longer. Also, they won't puff up as much.

**1.** In a large skillet over medium heat, melt the butter; add the spinach and cook, stirring, for 1 minute, breaking up the spinach. Add the salt, pepper, and nutmeg, stirring to blend. Cook, stirring, until the liquid in the pan has evaporated, another 4 minutes. Taste the spinach for salt and pepper and add more if needed.

**2.** In a large bowl, whisk together the eggs, cream, and Boursin until blended. Add the spinach and stir until mixed together.

❋ **DIVA DO-AHEAD:** At this point, you can cover and refrigerate overnight.

**3.** Preheat the oven to 350°F. Coat a 10-inch pie pan with nonstick cooking spray.

**4.** Pour the egg mixture into the prepared pan and bake until puffed and golden, 40 to 50 minutes.

❋ **DIVA DO-AHEAD:** At this point, you can let cool, cover, and refrigerate overnight or freeze for up to 6 weeks. Defrost if necessary and let come to room temperature. Reheat in a 350°F oven for 20 minutes.

Let the quiche rest for 5 to 10 minutes before cutting.

# Huevos Rancheros Casserole

Serves 10

Traditional huevos rancheros are tortillas covered with Ranchero Sauce, eggs over easy, and cheese. This casserole is a great imitation, and the best way to serve this classic dish to a crowd. The Ranchero Sauce can be made ahead and frozen, and the whole casserole should be assembled the day before, then baked in the morning.

**8 large eggs**

**¾ cup chunky salsa, drained if liquidy**

**¾ cup chopped scallions (white and tender green parts)**

**1½ cups shredded cheddar cheese**

**1 cup sour cream, plus extra for serving**

**Twelve 6-inch soft corn tortillas, torn into small pieces**

**2 cups Ranchero Sauce (page 562), kept warm**

**1 cup shredded Monterey Jack cheese**

**1 recipe Guacamole Olé (page 88) for serving**

**1.** Coat a 13 x 9-inch baking dish with non-stick cooking spray.

**2.** In a large bowl, beat together the eggs, salsa, scallions, cheddar, and sour cream. Stir in the tortilla pieces and pour into the prepared pan.

✳ **DIVA DO-AHEAD:** At this point, you can cover and refrigerate overnight. Bring to room temperature before continuing.

**3.** Preheat the oven to 350°F. Spread 1 cup of Ranchero Sauce over the casserole, top with the Monterey Jack, and bake until puffed and the cheese is golden, 35 to 45 minutes.

**4.** Let rest for 5 minutes, then serve with the remaining warm Ranchero Sauce, sour cream, and guacamole.

# Ranchero Sauce

Makes about 4 cups

Traditionally served over enchiladas, huevos rancheros, and quesadillas, this sauce is a winner served on the side with grilled meats and poultry, or spooned over other egg dishes.

2 tablespoons vegetable oil

2 large onions, thinly sliced

2 cloves garlic, minced

1 medium-size green bell pepper, seeded and cut into thin strips

1 medium-size red bell pepper, seeded and cut into thin strips

1 teaspoon ground cumin

1 teaspoon salt

⅛ teaspoon chili powder

2 tablespoons tequila

4 cups tomato puree (see The Diva Says)

1. Heat the oil in a large, deep skillet over medium-high heat, add the onion, and cook, stirring, until softened, about 3 minutes. Add the garlic, peppers, cumin, salt, and chili powder and cook for 4 to 6 min-utes, stirring to prevent the vegetables and spices from sticking or burning. Reduce the heat and sauté for another 5 minutes, until the vegetables are soft and the garlic and onions are almost translucent.

2. Add the tequila and allow it to evapo-rate. Add the tomato puree and bring to a boil. Reduce heat to low and simmer until the sauce is thickened, about 30 minutes.

✳ **DIVA DO-AHEAD:** At this point, you can let cool, cover, and refrigerate for up to 5 days or freeze for up to 2 months.

Serve warm or at room temperature.

## The Diva Says:

If you like a chunky tomato sauce, use two 15.5-ounce cans of whole plum tomatoes instead of the puree and crush the tomatoes in your hand before adding them and their juice.

# Hash Brown Sausage Casserole

Serves 10

This simple do-ahead entrée is a terrific dish to serve at brunch. The casserole can be made the night before or you can throw it all together right before baking. There are lots of varia-tions on this theme, and I highly recommend each one of them!

1 pound bulk pork sausage

1 large onion, chopped

8 large eggs, beaten

3 tablespoons all-purpose flour

1 cup sour cream (low-fat is okay)

6 scallions (white and tender green parts), chopped

1 teaspoon dried sage

1 teaspoon dried thyme

½ teaspoon lemon pepper seasoning

½ cup milk

2 cups (half of a 1-pound bag) frozen shredded hash brown potatoes, defrosted

1½ cups shredded mild cheddar cheese

**1.** Coat a 13 x 9-inch baking dish or a 12-cup muffin pan with nonstick cooking spray.

**2.** In a large skillet, cook the sausage and onion together, stirring and breaking apart the meat, until the sausage is no longer pink. Drain in a colander and let cool.

**3.** In a large bowl, beat together the eggs, flour, sour cream, scallions, sage, thyme, lemon pepper, and milk until blended. Fold in the cooled sausage mixture, potatoes, and 1 cup of the cheese. Pour into the prepared pan or divide equally among the muffin cups. Sprinkle with the remaining ½ cup of cheese.

✳ **DIVA DO-AHEAD:** At this point, you can cover and refrigerate overnight. Bring to room temperature before continuing.

**4.** Preheat oven to 325°F. Bake until puffed and golden brown, 25 to 35 minutes for the casserole, 15 to 20 minutes for muffins.

The Diva Says:

Frozen shredded hash brown potatoes (in the frozen vegetable section of your market) are gold in your freezer if you want to put together a quick frittata or another breakfast dish. They defrost quickly (a zap in the microwave for about 30 seconds per cup), absorb flavors well, and provide a nice base to build a dish around. Make sure you use the shredded variety of hash browns, rather than the chunky kind.

**Diva Variations**

**Southwestern Hash Brown Sausage Casserole:** Substitute chorizo for the bulk sausage and Monterey Jack cheese for the cheddar. Add ¼ cup of canned chopped green chiles, rinsed and drained, to the onion while sautéing. Omit the sage, thyme, and lemon pepper and replace with ½ teaspoon of chili powder and ½ teaspoon of ground cumin. Serve garnished with sour cream and chunky salsa.

**Mediterranean Hash Brown Sausage Casserole:** Substitute Italian sweet sausage for the bulk sausage and mozzarella for the cheddar. Omit the sage, thyme, and lemon pepper and substitute 1 teaspoon of dried oregano and ½ teaspoon of dried basil. Sprinkle 2 to 3 tablespoons of freshly grated Parmesan over the top before baking.

**Ham and Gruyère Hash Brown Casserole:** Substitute 2 cups of cubed ham (½-inch cubes) for the sausage and Gruyère for the cheddar.

# Strata

Serves 10

A strata is just cheese, bread, and egg custard, layered together and baked, but there are so many ways to make this easy brunch dish that I'm including this basic recipe and several variations (see pages 565 to 569). Recipes for strata vary from one cookbook to the next. Some will tell you to dice the bread before layering it in the casserole dish, while others say to use slices of bread—it is, in the end, a matter of personal taste. I have found that sandwich bread works best laid in the pan in slices, while baguettes and other irregularly shaped loaves are best torn into pieces. Since all loaves are not created equal, you may have a little bread left over; just make bread crumbs out of it for use another day.

8 large eggs

2 cups whole or 2% milk

1 teaspoon salt

6 shakes of Tabasco sauce

1 teaspoon dry mustard

One 1-pound loaf good quality sliced white bread, crust removed, or 1 baguette, crust removed and torn into ½-inch pieces

¼ cup (½ stick) unsalted butter, melted

3 cups shredded cheddar cheese

**1.** Coat a 13 x 9-inch baking dish with non-stick cooking spray.

**2.** In a large bowl, whisk together the eggs, milk, salt, Tabasco, and mustard until blended.

**3.** Arrange as much of the bread as you can in a single layer in the bottom of the prepared dish, wedging it in to fit. Brush with some of the melted butter and sprinkle with 1½ cups of the cheese. Arrange the remaining bread over the cheese, brush with the butter, and pour over the egg mixture, tilting the pan to get the batter into the bottom of the dish. Sprinkle with the remaining 1½ cups of cheese.

✳ **DIVA DO-AHEAD:** At this point, cover and refrigerate overnight. Bring to room temperature before continuing.

**4.** Preheat the oven to 350°F. Bake the strata until puffed and golden, 30 to 40 minutes. Let rest for 5 to 10 minutes before serving.

### Strata Muffins

If you'd like to make any of the strata recipes in this book in muffin tins, tear the bread into small pieces or chop in a food processor. Coat the cups and the upper surface of standard-size muffin tins with nonstick cooking spray and layer the bread and other ingredients in the cups. Cover and refrigerate overnight, then bring to room temperature. Bake the strata muffins in a preheated 350°F oven until puffed and golden, 20 to 25 minutes. Let rest for 5 minutes before removing from the pans and serving.

# Mushroom and Asparagus Strata

Serves 10

A vegetarian entrée for your buffet, this strata is simple and elegant, with its bright green asparagus set against the lemon-yellow egg batter. Although I've suggested button mushrooms, you can substitute cremini if you like.

8 large eggs

2 cups whole or 2% milk

6 shakes of Tabasco sauce

2 teaspoons salt

1 teaspoon dry mustard

½ cup (1 stick) unsalted butter

½ pound button mushrooms, sliced

½ teaspoon freshly ground black pepper

½ pound asparagus, trimmed of tough stem ends and cut into 1-inch pieces

One 1-pound loaf good quality sliced white bread, crust removed, or 1 baguette, crust removed and torn into ½-inch pieces

2 cups shredded Gruyère cheese

½ cup freshly grated Parmesan cheese

1. Coat a 13 x 9-inch baking dish with non-stick cooking spray.

2. In a large bowl, whisk together the eggs, milk, Tabasco, 1 teaspoon of the salt, and the mustard until blended.

3. Melt 2 tablespoons of the butter in a large skillet over high heat, add the mushrooms, and cook, stirring, for 2 minutes. Sprinkle with ½ teaspoon of the remaining salt and ¼ teaspoon of the pepper and continue to cook until the liquid in the pan has evaporated and the mushrooms begin to turn golden brown, about 8 minutes. Remove from the pan and set aside.

4. Melt another 2 tablespoons of butter in the same skillet over medium heat, add the asparagus, and sprinkle with the remaining ½ teaspoon of salt and ¼ teaspoon of pepper. Cook the asparagus, stirring, until coated with the butter and just beginning to soften, about 3 minutes. Set aside. Melt the remaining ¼ cup (½ stick) of butter.

5. Arrange as much of the bread as you can in a single layer in the prepared dish, wedging it in to fit. Brush with the melted butter and spread the mushrooms and asparagus evenly over it. Sprinkle with 1½ cups of the Gruyère and cover with the remaining bread. Brush with butter, then pour over the egg mixture, tilting the pan to make sure the eggs are soaking the bread. Sprinkle the top with the remaining ½ cup of Gruyère and the Parmesan.

✳ **DIVA DO-AHEAD:** At this point, cover and refrigerate overnight. Bring to room temperature before continuing.

6. Preheat the oven to 350°F. Bake the strata until puffed and golden, 30 to 40 minutes. Let rest for 5 to 10 minutes before serving.

## So, How Much Cheese Is That?

For every 2 ounces of a soft cheese such as mozzarella, cheddar, or Monterey Jack, you will get ½ cup of loosely packed shredded cheese. So, for 1 cup of shredded cheese, you'll need 4 ounces, or ¼ pound, of cheese.

For Parmesan and other hard cheeses, ½ ounce of cheese will give you ¼ cup of lightly packed finely grated cheese, so for 1 cup of grated cheese, you'll need 2 ounces of cheese, or ⅛ pound.

Remember, though, that because cheese is a natural substance, there will be variations in moisture content, which will affect these quantities a bit one way or the other—I always buy more cheese than I think I need, just in case.

# Monte Cristo Strata

Serves 10

A Monte Cristo is a deep-fried ham, turkey, and Swiss cheese sandwich, which happens to be one of my daughter's favorite indulgences. This strata combines all those flavors in one fabulous brunch offering. I like to serve it with sliced strawberries on the side.

**8 large eggs**

**2 cups whole or 2% milk**

**6 shakes of Tabasco sauce**

**1 teaspoon dry mustard**

**One 1-pound loaf good quality sliced white bread, or 1 baguette, crust removed and torn into ½-inch pieces**

**¼ cup (½ stick) unsalted butter, melted**

**½ pound sliced turkey, cut into matchsticks**

**½ pound sliced Black Forest ham, cut into matchsticks**

**3 cups shredded Swiss cheese**

### Freezing Egg Dishes

Egg dishes freeze well after baking. I generally decrease the baking time by about 10 minutes; the center will still be a little soft. After the dish is removed from the oven, it will continue to cook as it rests. Defrost the frozen dish in the refrigerator, then cover and bake in a 350°F oven for 20 minutes. The dish will still have some moisture, so it can be reheated without becoming dried out.

**1.** Coat a 13 x 9-inch baking dish with non-stick cooking spray.

**2.** In a large bowl, whisk together the eggs, milk, Tabasco, and mustard until blended.

**3.** Arrange as much of the bread as you can in a single layer in the prepared dish, wedging it in to fit. Brush with some of the melted butter and top, in layers, with the turkey, ham, and 1½ cups of the Swiss. Top with the remaining bread, brush with the remaining butter, and pour the egg mixture over everything, tilting the pan to make sure the bread is coated. Sprinkle with the remaining 1½ cups of Swiss cheese.

✳ **DIVA DO-AHEAD:** Cover and refrigerate overnight. Bring to room temperature before continuing.

**4.** Preheat the oven to 350°F. Bake the strata until puffed and golden, 30 to 40 minutes. Let rest for 5 to 10 minutes before serving.

# Crab Cake Strata

Serves 10

I love crab cakes, and this dish has my favorite crustacean wrapped up in an elegant brunch entrée. It is terrific with a side of Roasted Asparagus (page 226) and fresh fruit.

**8 large eggs**

**1 cup whole or low-fat milk**

**1 cup mayonnaise (low-fat is okay)**

**2 teaspoons Old Bay seasoning**

**1 tablespoon Worcestershire sauce**

**¼ cup chopped fresh Italian parsley**

**1 teaspoon Dijon mustard**

**1 pound lump crabmeat, picked over for shells and cartilage**

**9 cups soft Italian or French bread cubes, hard crusts removed (about one 1-pound loaf)**

**½ cup freshly grated Parmesan cheese**

**Lemon wedges for garnish**

## Diva Variations

Substitute 1 pound of medium-size cooked shrimp or 3 cups of cooked diced chicken or turkey for the crab.

You can also make this strata as muffins. In step 2, pour the mixture into 18 muffin cups, sprinkle with cheese over the top, and bake for 20 to 22 minutes. Makes 18 muffins.

**1.** Coat a 13 x 9-inch baking dish with nonstick cooking spray.

**2.** In a large bowl, whisk together the eggs, milk, mayonnaise, Old Bay, Worcestershire, parsley, and Dijon until blended. Stir in the crabmeat and bread until well combined. Pour into the prepared dish and sprinkle the cheese over the top.

✳ **DIVA DO-AHEAD:** Cover and refrigerate overnight. Bring to room temperature before continuing.

**3.** Preheat the oven to 350°F. Bake the strata until puffed and golden brown, 45 to 55 minutes. Let rest for 5 minutes and serve with lemon wedges on the side for garnish.

# Smoked Salmon and Bagel Strata

Serves 10

This elegant strata, beautifully colored with pink salmon and bright green dill, is perfect for a New Year's brunch or any other special midday meal. It's a delicious solution to the problem of what to do with leftover bagels. Garnish the strata with chopped red onion, capers, and additional sour cream for a truly spectacular presentation.

**8 large eggs**

**1½ cups whole or 2% milk**

**1 cup sour cream (low-fat is okay), plus extra for serving**

**¾ pound smoked salmon, cut into matchsticks**

**¼ cup chopped fresh dill**

**2 teaspoons grated lemon zest**

**½ teaspoon freshly ground white pepper**

**6 plain or egg bagels, cut into ½-inch pieces**

**Sprigs fresh dill for garnish**

**½ cup finely chopped red onion for serving**

**½ cup drained and chopped capers for serving**

**Lemon wedges for serving**

**1.** Coat the inside of 13 x 9-inch baking dish with nonstick cooking spray.

**2.** In a large bowl, whisk together the eggs, milk, and sour cream until blended. Stir in the salmon, dill, lemon zest, and white pepper until combined. Stir in the bagel cubes, pushing down to soak them in the batter. Transfer to the prepared dish.

✳ **DIVA DO-AHEAD:** Cover and refrigerate overnight. Bring to room temperature before continuing.

**3.** Preheat the oven to 350°F. Bake the strata until puffed and golden, 45 to 55 minutes. Let rest for 5 minutes. Garnish with the dill sprigs and serve with the chopped onion, capers, sour cream, and lemon wedges on the side.

# Ham and Potato Frittata

Serves 10

Frittatas are great vehicles for using up leftovers, and for serving eggs to the masses for breakfast or brunch. You can have the components ready a day ahead of time, then combine and bake in the oven. You will need a pan that can be used on the stove top and then placed in the oven. A cast-iron skillet works well, and so does a braiser pan, which is deep, with a handle on each side (available from Calphalon and All-Clad).

2 tablespoons unsalted butter

1 tablespoon vegetable oil

½ cup finely chopped yellow onion

4 cups diced cooked red potatoes
(½-inch dice; 4 large or 6 medium-size potatoes)

1 teaspoon salt

½ teaspoon freshly ground black pepper

1 cup finely diced ham

8 large eggs

¼ cup milk

6 shakes of Tabasco sauce

1½ cups shredded mild cheddar or your choice of cheese

**1.** In a 12-inch-wide, 2-inch-deep, stove-to-oven skillet, heat the butter and oil together. When the butter has melted, add the onion and cook for 1 minute, stirring. Add the potatoes, sprinkle with the salt and pepper, and cook until the potatoes begin to color, turning them often, about 5 minutes. Add the ham and cook for another 2 minutes.

✳ **DIVA DO-AHEAD:** At this point, you can let cool, transfer to a storage container, and refrigerate overnight. Reheat, tossing the potatoes and ham in the same skillet over medium heat, before continuing.

**2.** Preheat the oven to 350°F.

**3.** In a large bowl, whisk together the eggs, milk, and Tabasco and pour the mixture over the potatoes in the pan. Lift the potatoes off the bottom of the pan and stir and lift the eggs, so they do not stick. Push the cooked egg toward the center of the pan and tilt it so the uncooked egg runs toward the edge. When the eggs are partially cooked, sprinkle them with the cheese and place in the oven. Bake until the cheese is melted and the eggs are done, about 15 minutes.

✳ **DIVA DO-AHEAD:** At this point, you can let cool, cover, and refrigerate overnight. Serve the frittata cold or at room temperature, or reheat, covered with aluminum foil, in a 350°F oven for 15 minutes.

# Pesto and Tomato Frittata

Serves 10

This tasty buffet dish will please your vegetarian guests (there is always one in the crowd) and it will satisfy the carnivores as well. Pesto is beaten into the eggs so that it flavors the entire dish. Sun-dried tomatoes and a little extra cheese round out this delicious frittata.

**8 large eggs**

**½ cup milk**

**1½ cups shredded mozzarella cheese**

**½ cup pesto of your choice, homemade (page 97, 472, or 473), or store-bought**

**½ cup oil-packed sun-dried tomatoes, drained and cut into matchsticks**

**½ cup freshly grated Parmesan cheese**

**1.** Coat a 10-inch round baking dish with nonstick cooking spray.

**2.** In a large bowl, whisk together the eggs and milk until blended. Stir in 1 cup of the mozzarella, the pesto, and the sun-dried tomatoes. Pour into the prepared dish and top with the remaining ½ cup of mozzarella and the Parmesan.

✳ **DIVA DO-AHEAD:** At this point, you can cover and refrigerate overnight.

**3.** Preheat the oven to 350°F. Bake the frittata until puffed, golden, and set in the center, 35 to 40 minutes.

✳ **DIVA DO-AHEAD:** At this point, you can let cool, cover, and refrigerate overnight. Serve the frittata cold or at room temperature, or reheat, covered with aluminum foil, in a 350°F oven for 15 minutes.

# Cheesy Ham and Grits Casserole

Serves 10

This rich grits casserole is just the thing to serve at a buffet brunch, and it's a great way to recycle leftover ham.

2 cups whole or 2% milk

1 cup water

1 teaspoon salt

¾ cup quick-cooking grits

¼ cup (½ stick) unsalted butter

2 cups shredded mild cheddar cheese

2 cups diced ham (½-inch dice)

8 large eggs

**1.** Coat a 13 x 9-inch baking dish with nonstick cooking spray.

**2.** In a 3-quart saucepan, bring the milk, water, and salt to a boil. Add the grits and stir until they thicken and begin to boil. Remove from the heat and transfer to a large bowl. Stir in the butter, cheese, ham, and eggs, then transfer to the prepared dish.

**DIVA DO-AHEAD:** At this point, you can cover and refrigerate overnight. Bring to room temperature before continuing.

**3.** Preheat the oven to 350°F. Bake the casserole until puffed and golden brown, about 45 minutes.

**DIVA DO-AHEAD:** You can let cool, cover, and refrigerate overnight or freeze for up to 1 month. Defrost overnight in the refrigerator and bring to room temperature. Reheat in a 350°F oven, covered with aluminum foil, for 15 minutes.

# Bacon for a Crowd

Serves 10

It is tough to cook bacon on the stove top for a large group and get it nice and crisp, but your oven can be your friend. Baked on rimmed baking sheets, the bacon comes out crisp and evenly cooked. You can sprinkle a little light brown sugar over it halfway through cooking to give it a sweet taste, if you'd like.

**2 pounds sliced bacon**

**1.** Preheat the oven to 400°F. Line 2 rimmed baking sheets with a silicone liner or aluminum foil. (Make sure they're rimmed, or you will have bacon grease everywhere!)

**2.** Separate the bacon into slices and lay them out on the baking sheets. It's okay if slices touch their neighbors; they will shrink during cooking. Cook the bacon until crisp and browned, 10 to 15 minutes. If you are cooking 2 sheets at once, you will need to swap racks in the middle of the cooking time so the bacon cooks evenly.

**3.** When the bacon is cooked and crisp, transfer it to paper towels to drain.

✳ **DIVA DO-AHEAD:** At this point, you can let cool, place in zipper-top plastic bags, and refrigerate for 4 to 5 days. To reheat the bacon, place it on paper towels on rimmed baking sheets and bake in a preheated 300°F oven until warm, about 10 minutes.

## The Diva Says:

Already cooked bacon is available in vacuum-sealed bags at your supermarket. Warm it in a 350°F oven for 5 minutes.

### Diva Variation

**Maple Bacon:** Two or 3 minutes before the bacon is crisp, drain off the fat and drizzle the bacon with maple syrup. Cook until crisp.

# Desserts

**Desserts are the last thing that your guests will eat,** so each dessert you serve should be simple but scrumptious. I always tell my students to splurge on dessert, but to keep it simple. I mean, who doesn't love a hot fudge sundae? Jazzing that up with crushed Oreos, chocolate-covered espresso beans, whipped cream, and a cherry on top gives it that extra something special. All of the desserts in this chapter can be made ahead of time, most can be frozen, and they are all four-star endings for your meals. I can always rely on the dessert to propel an ordinary dinner into the stratosphere.

*Cookies* are great buffet items because they can be picked up and walked around with, plus your guests won't feel as if they have eaten a ton of dessert—after all, they're just cookies, right? Drop cookies freeze well, and you can even freeze the dough if you want to bake them fresh the day of the party. Bar cookies and brownies are also great buffet items because you can make a lot without tons of work. They can also be frozen and taken out of the freezer the day of the party.

*Frosted layer cakes* make a big impression at festive meals celebrating birthdays, anniversaries, and other special occasions. The layers can be frozen months ahead of time in standard gallon-size zipper-top plastic bags, then taken from the freezer, thawed, and frosted the day before serving. Generally, a layer cake will serve 12 to 14 people.

*Cupcakes* are great for buffets; many cake recipes in this chapter provide tips for converting them into cupcakes. They freeze well (frosted or unfrosted) and are the perfect two- to three-bite dessert after a meal, requiring no plate and no fork.

*Majestic tube* or *bundt cakes* are terrific for parties because they slice easily and you can feed a lot of people—one recipe that I was given said "feeds an army" in the serving suggestion! These cakes all freeze well, so that you can make them ahead of time and have them on hand.

*Sweet cheesecakes* are a wonderful ending to a meal and they have to be made a day or two ahead or even frozen. Whether you make them in a springform pan, individual mini-cakes, or bars, cheesecakes are a luxurious way to end your meal.

*Trifles* are layered desserts featuring liqueur-soaked cake, fruit, and a cream filling. The beauty of this dessert is that it goes together quickly if you use frozen pound cake (remember, "Nobody doesn't like Sara Lee") and you have to make it a day or two ahead of time for the flavors to marry. The availability of frozen fruit makes trifle a winner year-round, and it looks spectacular on a buffet table, whether you make it in a trifle bowl or a 13 x 9-inch baking dish.

*Pies, tarts, cobblers,* and *crumbles* are terrific desserts to serve because the crusts and fillings can be made ahead of time. Most can be baked ahead and stored in the refrigerator or at room temperature for at least a day before serving. Another reason these desserts are so appealing is that they take advantage of seasonal flavors—if it's summer, make a tart with fresh blueberries, or a cobbler with local blackberries, or a pie with fresh peaches.

*Bread puddings* are nothing more than jazzed-up French toast, but they are terrific vehicles for entertaining. They need to be prepared at least 24 hours ahead of time, and they take advantage of what you have on hand—stale bread, eggs, milk or cream, and some flavorings. You can serve them as a part of breakfast or as dessert, and they can be baked individually in cupcake tins or in a large casserole dish.

*Sauces* are the finishing touch to make your desserts sparkle with color and flavor. A little pool of raspberry sauce can transform a brownie into a four-star dessert. Most sauces can be made up to a week ahead and refrigerated or frozen.

I love making dessert in 13 x 9-inch baking dishes because they can be cut easily into squares and you can even serve from the pan if you'd rather not arrange the dessert on a platter. Desserts made in a 13 x 9-inch pan will yield about twenty-four 2-inch squares, but you may want to cut some into 1-inch squares because they are so rich. Jelly roll or 15 x 12-inch sheet pans will yield about fifty-six 2-inch squares, and even more if you cut them into triangles. This means one jelly roll pan will feed the masses for dessert.

Springform pans are terrific for molded desserts and cheesecakes. Once the dessert is baked and/or refrigerated, the ring comes off, and you have a beautiful cake to display on a cake stand or platter.

## Where's the Coffee?

Serving hot fresh coffee to guests, whether for dessert or for brunch, is essential. Make sure you grind the coffee a few days ahead, premeasure it for your pot, and seal it in plastic bags. Freeze the coffee until ready to use. If you have a large 45-cup coffee urn (these are relatively inexpensive investments), you will need two 8-ounce cups of ground coffee to brew 45 cups. Keep the coffee hot in thermal carafes for serving, or allow your guests to help themselves.

My only warning before you begin this chapter is that baking is science. Each recipe has been tested so that you can get a perfect result. Please don't think that if you substitute skim milk for whole milk you will have the same cake; yours may fall or it may just taste awful. Changing pan sizes will also affect the way the dessert turns out. Make sure you read the directions all the way through and use the correct ingredients. Substitutions probably won't work unless I've suggested them in the recipe. When I cook on the stove top, I always improvise, but when I bake, I follow the recipe, and I recommend that you do the same!

## Ingredients

*Unbleached all-purpose flour:* This is the workhorse flour in the kitchen, suitable for cookies, brownies, cakes, and some breads. I prefer King Arthur and Pillsbury, which are available in most grocery stores.

*Cake flour:* Cake flour is specifically formulated to adhere to the wet molecules in the cake batter, which ends up producing a fine crumb. You'll find it used in several recipes in this chapter.

*Key lime juice:* Sweet Key limes, which are much smaller and softer than regular limes, are delicious in cakes and pies, and are becoming more common in gourmet markets and supermarkets. Bottled Key lime juice is sold in most gourmet stores (see Sources, page 669). I recommend using the bottled juice or fresh Key limes instead of juicing those hard, regular limes.

*Dried fruits:* Raisins aren't the only dried fruit on the grocer's shelf anymore. Dried cranberries, blueberries, apples, apricots, and pineapple are just a few that are now available. Make sure you store these in zipper-top plastic bags and discard after about 6 months.

*Butter:* For baking I recommend unsalted butter, but when margarine is an acceptable substitute, I note this in the recipe. If all you have is salted butter, then omit the salt in the recipe and proceed as directed. Sometimes the salted butter will sweat some water, which will add a bit to the baking time and affect the end result. (Remember, substitutions can make a difference in baking.)

*Sour cream:* All the recipes containing sour cream were tested with full-fat sour cream, but you can substitute low-fat (*not* nonfat). Keep in mind, however, that when the fat is taken out, water is whipped in. As a result, your baking times will be a little longer and cakes won't rise as dramatically because of the difference in the water content.

*Cream cheese:* All the recipes containing cream cheese were tested with Kraft Philadelphia brand cream cheese, the big daddy of them all. If you like, you can use low-fat cream cheese (often sold as Neufchâtel), but, like sour cream, there is extra water in the lower-fat version, so the baking time will probably need to be extended to deal with the extra moisture.

*Nonstick cooking spray:* This product makes clean-up a breeze and helps get your baked good out of the pan quickly without leaving half of it on the bottom. I recommend Baker's Joy, which is a combination of oil and flour, so that your baking dish is greased and floured in one spray!

*Eggs:* Buy the freshest eggs possible; check the date on the end of the carton to find out when they expire. Grade AA large eggs are what I used for testing. Egg substitute can be used in the recipes, too. If you are concerned about using raw eggs because of the danger of food-borne illness, namely salmonella, then I recommend that you use a pasteurized egg product in recipes calling for uncooked eggs.

*Milk:* When a recipe calls for milk, it was tested with whole milk. If a lower-fat milk is an acceptable substitute, I will note that in the recipe. The fat in whole milk may be necessary for the dessert to bake properly, so please don't alter the recipe unless I've told you it's okay.

*Buttermilk:* Fresh buttermilk or buttermilk powder reconstituted with water are both acceptable to use in recipes calling for buttermilk. If you can't locate either, for every cup of buttermilk called for, use 1 cup of whole milk mixed with 1 teaspoon of distilled white vinegar.

*Vanilla:* Tahitian vanilla is the most fragrant and delicious of the vanillas, but its flavor tends to disappear when it is baked. I recommend you use Tahitian vanilla for fresh presentations, such as stirring into cooled custards and whipped creams. For baking, you can use vanilla powder or Madagascar-Bourbon vanilla extract or vanilla paste (see Sources, page 669). Make sure it's a pure vanilla extract and not an imitation vanilla flavor.

*Orange and lemon oils:* Oil essences have become more widely available (see Sources, page 669) and they impart an incredibly deep flavor to baked goods. I recommend that you try them, especially with the Cranberry Bliss Bars (page 631). You will want to use half the amount of an extract if you are substituting a flavored oil.

*Ghirardelli ground chocolate:* A ground chocolate powder, rather than an unsweetened cocoa, this powder makes a delicious chocolate cake, frosting, brownies, and incredible hot chocolate!

*Cocoa powder:* Unsweetened cocoa powder comes in Dutch-process and regular (such as Hershey's versions). The Dutch-process is darker, but has a lighter flavor than that of regular cocoa. You can use either for these recipes unless the type of cocoa is specified.

*Bar chocolates:* Unsweetened chocolate is usually sold in boxes of 1-inch squares. These squares need to be melted (usually with fat such as butter or vegetable oil) before baking. Bittersweet, semisweet, and milk chocolates are sweetened chocolates that come in bar and chip form.

## Chocolate Shavings

A swivel peeler is a great tool for getting long curls of chocolate for garnishing your desserts. If you want grated chocolate, a microplane works very well and so does a grater. The chocolate will become soft when it comes in direct contact with your skin, so I advise you to hold the chocolate with a paper towel to keep this from happening.

*White chocolate:* White chocolate is basically cocoa butter; it comes in bar and chip form. For melting, I recommend white chocolate in bar form, because the chips are not designed to melt. White chips can be substituted for milk chocolate or semisweet chocolate in your chocolate chip cookie recipes. If you would like the chocolate to melt in your cookies, then chop a bar of white chocolate and use that instead. I recommend Lindt or Baker's white chocolate bars; any brand of white chocolate chips is fine for the recipes in this chapter.

**Vegetable oil:** Use light, neutral-tasting oil for desserts. I tested all the recipes with canola oil, which I recommend.

**Nutmeg:** Use whole nutmeg berries and grate them on a microplane or a nutmeg grater.

**Nuts:** Fresh nuts add a lot of flavor and texture to baked goods. Make sure you store them in the freezer so that they don't get rancid.

# Ryan's Happy Birthday Yellow Cake with Chocolate Sour Cream Frosting

Makes one 2-layer 9-inch cake; serves 12 to 14

My friend Lora Brody's wonderful book *Basic Baking* (Morrow, 2000) included a new technique for blending cake batters, which I have used over and over again. Instead of creaming the butter and sugar together, you add the butter in small bits to the flour, sugar, and leavening, as you would for a pie dough. The resulting cake is tender, light, and delicious. I decided to try it in the food processor with my son Ryan's favorite cake. This recipe is almost quicker than a box cake mix and 100 times more delicious. It will become your favorite all-purpose vanilla cake to make for a special occasion. It is also delicious split into 4 layers and spread with various fillings.

**2 cups cake flour**

**1 teaspoon baking powder**

**½ teaspoon salt**

**½ teaspoon baking soda**

**1¾ cups sugar**

**¾ cup (1½ sticks) unsalted butter, softened and cut into ½-inch bits**

**1 cup buttermilk**

**4 large eggs**

**1 tablespoon vanilla extract**

**1 recipe Chocolate Sour Cream Frosting (page 584)**

**1.** Preheat the oven to 375°F. Coat two 9-inch round baking pans with nonstick cooking spray, preferably Baker's Joy (see page 579).

**2.** In a food processor, combine the flour, baking powder, salt, baking soda, and sugar and pulse 2 or 3 times. Distribute the butter over the flour mixture and pulse until the flour resembles small peas.

**3.** Pour the buttermilk into a 2-cup measuring cup, add the eggs and vanilla, and beat with a fork to break up the eggs. With the food processor running, add this through the feed tube and process for about 45 seconds. Scrape down the sides, then process again for another 30 to 45 seconds, until blended.

**4.** Divide the batter equally between the 2 prepared pans. Smooth the tops, without pressing down on the batter. Bake until golden and a skewer inserted into the center comes out clean, 25 to 30 minutes. Transfer the pans to a rack and let the cakes cool for about 10 minutes. Remove from the pans, return to the rack, and let cool completely.

✳ **DIVA DO-AHEAD:** At this point, you can cover with plastic wrap or put in zipper-top plastic bags and refrigerate for 2 days or freeze for up to 2 months. Defrost before continuing.

**5.** When the cake has cooled, lay 2½-inch-wide strips of waxed or parchment paper around the outside of the cake platter to catch the drips of icing (you can remove them later). If the layers have domed centers, meaning they're not quite level, use a serrated knife to level the tops. Place a layer, bottom side up, over the strips and spread 1 cup of the frosting from the center of the cake out toward the edge. Place the other layer, bottom side up, over the frosted layer and spread another cup of frosting from the center to the edge. With an offset spatula, spread frosting around the outside of the cake in an even layer. If you wish, use a spoon or the tip of the spatula to make indentations in the top layer of frosting and swirl them in a decorative pattern. Or spread the frosting as evenly and smoothly as possible, then decorate the top with chopped nuts, Chocolate Leaves (page 585), or fresh berries. (If using berries, do this no more than 1 hour before serving.) Remove the paper strips and discard.

## Diva Variations

This cake can also be baked in a 15 x 12-inch jelly roll pan for 12 to 15 minutes, cooled, and cut into strips to use for trifle or for layering in parfaits. Here are some other things you can do:

**Here Comes Peter Cottontail Cake:** Every Easter I make a bunny cake for my (now adult) children. To make your own, bake 2 round layers, then cut one of them into 2 ears and a bow tie. (Cut the sides into 2 equal tapered ovals, leaving the center as the bow tie.) Place the round cake in the center of a baking sheet covered with aluminum foil or a large serving dish. Place the bow tie underneath the round, and position the ears on either side of the round. Frost the cake, then decorate with coconut, and use licorice for whiskers and jellybeans for eyes and a mouth.

**Oh Christmas Tree Cake:** Pour the batter into a 13 x 9-inch baking pan and increase the baking time to 45 minutes. Cut the long sides so that you have a triangular shape, and cut the trimmed-away portions into a trunk for the bottom. Decorate with white frosting and red and green sprinkles.

**Lemon Cake:** Process the grated zest of 1 lemon with the dry ingredients. Omit the vanilla, and add 2 teaspoons of lemon oil or 1 teaspoon of lemon extract. Bake as directed.

**Marble Cake:** Before beginning the recipe, process 8 ounces of German's Sweet Chocolate or semisweet chocolate in the food processor until finely chopped, about 2 minutes. Remove from the work bowl, clean out the bowl, and proceed with the recipe. When you pour the batter into the layer pans, reserve ½ cup of batter in the work bowl. Add the reserved chocolate and 2 teaspoons of Dutch-process unsweetened cocoa powder and process for 2 seconds. Spoon dollops of the chocolate batter on top of the vanilla batter, then cut through the batters with a knife to create a marble pattern. Bake as directed.

**Maple-Pecan Cake:** Toast 1 cup of chopped pecans until golden and fragrant (see page 83). Omit the vanilla, add 1 tablespoon of pure maple syrup, and stir in the pecans once the batter is blended. Bake as directed.

**Cupcakes:** Minicupcakes make the perfect addition to the buffet table—one bite and they are gone. The master recipe will make about 90 minicupcakes; if you don't want to make that many, bake 48 (four 12-cup mini-muffin tins) and one 8- or 9-inch cake layer. The minicupcakes will bake more quickly than the cake layer, about 15 minutes. Or use the master recipe to make 48 standard-size cupcakes, and bake for 20 to 25 minutes.

# Chocolate Sour Cream Frosting

Makes about 4 cups, enough to frost one 2-layer 9-inch cake or 48 cupcakes

This luxurious frosting is terrific on vanilla or chocolate cakes. The sour cream gives it a nice tangy flavor, and since the frosting is not overly sweet, the chocolate flavor is deep and satisfying.

**3 cups confectioners' sugar**

**¼ cup unsweetened cocoa powder**

**2 teaspoons vanilla extract**

**6 tablespoons (¾ stick) unsalted butter, softened**

**¼ cup sour cream, plus extra to thin the frosting if needed**

Stir together the sugar and cocoa in the bowl of a stand mixer or a large mixing bowl. In a stand mixer fitted with a paddle or a hand-held mixer with beaters, add the vanilla, butter, and sour cream and beat on medium-high speed until the mixture reaches a spreading consistency. Add more sour cream if the frosting is too thick.

✳ **DIVA DO-AHEAD:** At this point, you can cover and refrigerate for up to 1 week or freeze for up to 2 months. If refrigerated or frozen, bring to room temperature before using, because it will be difficult to spread when taken directly from the refrigerator. Beat to soften; you may need to add a bit of sour cream.

# Chocolate Leaves

Makes 10 to 20 leaves depending on leaf size

Making chocolate decorations for your cakes is simple and fun. Make sure the leaves you use are not toxic and that they have been washed and dried thoroughly. Camellia leaves are good choices and so are citrus leaves (orange, lemon, or lime).

**Leaves for use as molds (see headnote)**

**1 cup chopped semisweet chocolate (about 6 ounces)**

**1 tablespoon unsalted butter**

**1.** Line a baking sheet with aluminum foil or waxed paper and place the leaves on the baking sheet upside down.

**2.** In a small saucepan over low heat, melt the chocolate and butter together, stirring until smooth. Remove from the heat.

**3.** With a small spatula, spread the chocolate on the underside of the leaves and set aside for 3 to 5 minutes. Place the baking sheet in the freezer until the chocolate is set, about 5 minutes.

**4.** Peel the leaves off the chocolate.

✳ **DIVA DO-AHEAD:** At this point, you can freeze the chocolate leaves in an airtight container for up to 3 months.

# Lemon Icebox Cake

Makes one 4-layer 9-inch cake; serves 12 to 14

This is a light and airy dessert to serve after a heavy meal. The tart lemon filling is offset by the whipped cream and cake. You could also make this with lime curd instead of lemon curd.

**1 recipe Ryan's Happy Birthday Yellow Cake (page 582), baked in two 9-inch round pans and cooled**

**3 cups heavy cream**

**½ cup confectioners' sugar**

**1 recipe Lemon Curd (recipe follows)**

**1 cup sliced almonds (optional), toasted (see page 83)**

**1.** Split the cake layers in half horizontally, and line the edge of a serving platter with waxed or parchment paper strips.

**2.** With an electric mixer, whip the cream in a large bowl until soft peaks form, then add the confectioners' sugar and beat until stiff peaks form.

**3.** Lay a cake layer over the paper strips and spread a ½-inch-thick layer of lemon curd over it. Top with some of the whipped cream, and continue in this way, adding two more of the cake layers and using up the lemon curd. Top with the fourth cake layer and spread the remaining whipped cream over the top and sides of the cake. Press almonds into the sides of the cake if using. Remove the waxed paper strips.

✳ **DIVA DO-AHEAD:** At this point, cover and refrigerate for at least 6 and up to 24 hours.

# Lemon Curd

Makes about 4 cups

---

**1 cup sugar**

**6 large eggs**

**½ to ⅔ cup fresh lemon juice**

**½ cup (1 stick) butter, cut into ½-inch cubes**

---

In a 2-quart saucepan, combine the sugar, eggs, and ½ cup of the lemon juice and whisk until smooth. Set over medium heat and continue to whisk until the mixture begins to thicken and bubble, about 5 minutes. Stir in the butter cubes, a bit at a time, lower the heat, and continue to cook, stirring constantly, until the curd is thickened. Taste and add the remaining lemon juice if you would like it more tart. Remove from the heat, press a piece of plastic wrap directly against the surface to keep a skin from forming, and let cool to room temperature.

✳ **DIVA DO-AHEAD:** At this point, you can refrigerate for up to 1 week or freeze for up to 2 months. Defrost before continuing.

### Diva Variation

**Lime Curd:** Substitute lime juice for the lemon juice to make lime curd.

# Strawberry Shortcake Layer Cake

Makes one 4-layer 9-inch cake; serves 12 to 14

Many people prefer the biscuit type of shortcake, but this cake is so delicious and looks so spectacular on the serving table, you may just forget about those hard little shortcakes.

1 recipe Ryan's Happy Birthday Yellow Cake (page 582) or The Arlene Dahl Chocolate Cake (page 590), baked in two 9-inch round pans and cooled

4 pints fresh strawberries

½ to 1 cup granulated sugar (depending upon the sweetness of the berries)

1 tablespoon liqueur, such as Grand Marnier or amaretto (optional)

3 cups heavy cream

½ cup confectioners' sugar

**1.** Set aside 1 pint of strawberries for garnish. Hull the remaining 3 pints of strawberries, slice ½ inch thick, and put in a large bowl.

**2.** Split the 2 cake layers in half horizontally with a serrated knife. Arrange strips of waxed or parchment paper around the edge of a serving platter.

**3.** Sprinkle the sliced strawberries with the granulated sugar and liqueur, if using, stirring to blend. Taste the berries while you are stirring to make sure they are sweet enough.

**4.** With an electric mixer, whip the cream in another large bowl until soft peaks form, then add the confectioners' sugar and continue to beat until stiff peaks form.

**5.** Place one cake layer on the waxed paper strips, top with a thin layer of about a third of the sliced strawberries, then a thin layer of whipped cream. Continue in this way, adding two more of the cake layers and using up the sliced berries. Top with the fourth cake layer and spread the remaining whipped cream over the top and sides of the cake. Garnish the top with the whole berries, or cut them in half and arrange in a chevron pattern from the center. Remove the waxed paper strips.

✳ **DIVA DO-AHEAD:** At this point, cover and refrigerate for at least 6 and up to 24 hours.

# Nancy Kelly's Two-Day Memphis Coconut Cake

Makes one 4-layer 9-inch cake; serves 12 to 16

My cooking buddy Nancy Kelly at the Viking Culinary Arts Center told me that Southerners are very particular about their coconut cakes. Then she proceeded to give me this recipe for what I term a "marinated" coconut cake because it needs to sit for at least 2 days before you serve it. This is very popular in the South and there are lots of versions, but I like this one the best. It makes quite a spectacle on the buffet table, garnished with sliced fresh strawberries, bananas, and pineapple.

**Two 9-inch yellow cake layers, homemade (see page 582) or store-bought**

**3 cups heavy cream**

**Three 7-ounce packages Baker's Angel Flake coconut**

**2 cups sour cream**

**2 cups sugar**

**4 cups sliced fresh fruit (berries, pineapple, kiwis, and bananas) for garnish**

## Cutting Cake

Serving cake to a multitude can sometimes be a headache. The way caterers do it at weddings is to cut a 1½-inch circle in the middle of the cake, then cut the wedges from the edge of the cake to the circle. Then they cut up the circle. This approach will give you even slices. A 9-inch layer cake can actually serve up to 20 people when cut this way.

**1.** Split each cake layer in half horizontally with a serrated knife. Place strips of waxed or parchment paper around the edge of a serving plate, and center a cake layer on the plate.

**2.** With an electric mixer, beat the cream in a large bowl until stiff peaks form.

**3.** In another large bowl, combine 2 cups of the coconut, the sour cream, sugar, and whipped cream. Spread some of the filling and frosting mixture over the cake and repeat the layers, ending with the cake. Frost the top and sides of the cake with the remaining frosting. Sprinkle the cake with the remaining coconut.

✳ **DIVA DO-AHEAD:** At this point, cover lightly with plastic wrap and refrigerate for 2 days before serving.

**4.** Garnish with the fruit before serving.

# The Arlene Dahl Chocolate Cake ⬤⬤⬤⬤

Makes twenty-four 2-inch squares or 24 cupcakes

Several years ago, the actor Lorenzo Lamas rented the home of a friend of mine to film a television series that he was starring in. On days when they were filming, my friend could not "use" the house or the kitchen. On her son's birthday, I made this cake to bring over and met Lorenzo's mother, Arlene Dahl, while I was there. She couldn't resist a piece of it and pronounced it "mahvelous!" This is the cake my daughter, Carrie, requests for her birthday. It's a homespun chocolate cake made with Ghirardelli ground chocolate (not unsweetened cocoa). The cake has a dense texture like an old-fashioned chocolate cake but with a lighter chocolate flavor, and it is covered with a cream cheese frosting.

**3 cups unbleached all-purpose flour**

**2 cups sugar**

**1 cup Ghirardelli ground chocolate**

**2 teaspoons baking soda**

**1 cup vegetable oil, such as canola**

**1 cup buttermilk**

**2 large eggs**

**¾ cup plus 2 tablespoons boiling water**

**1 teaspoon vanilla extract**

**1 recipe Cream Cheese Frosting (page 597; optional)**

**1 recipe World's Best Hot Fudge Sauce (page 501; optional)**

**1.** Preheat the oven to 350°F. Coat a 13 x 9-inch baking pan with nonstick cooking spray.

**2.** In a large bowl, whisk together the flour, sugar, chocolate, and baking soda. Stir in the oil, buttermilk, eggs, water, and vanilla. With an electric mixer, blend on low speed until smooth, about 3 minutes. Pour into the prepared pan and bake until a skewer inserted into the center comes out clean, 40 to 50 minutes.

**3.** Place the cake on a rack and let cool completely, then remove it from the pan if you plan to serve the cake on a platter (otherwise, keep it in the pan).

**DIVA DO-AHEAD:** At this point, you can cover with plastic wrap and refrigerate for up to 2 days or freeze for up to 2 months. Defrost before continuing.

**4.** Frost the cake or serve plain with vanilla ice cream and the hot fudge sauce.

**DIVA DO-AHEAD:** At this point, the frosted cake can be frozen for up to 2 months.

### Diva Variations

This cake can also be prepared in two 9-inch round pans and baked for 30 to 35 minutes. Let the cake cool in the pans for 15 minutes, then transfer to a wire rack to cool completely. Or bake the cake in a jelly roll pan lined with a silicone liner, aluminum foil, or parchment paper for 17 to 22 minutes.

## EDIBLE FLOWERS

**Flowers make beautiful garnishes** for cakes and other desserts. Although all these plants are edible, I don't recommend eating them. Use whole blossoms or their petals to garnish desserts for added color and dramatic effect.

- Carnation
- Chrysanthemum
- Citrus blossoms
- Daylily
- English daisy
- Fuchsia
- Gardenia
- Gladiola
- Hibiscus
- Jasmine
- Lavender
- Lilac
- Nasturtium
- Pansy
- Petunia
- Orchid
- Rose
- Rose geranium
- Tulip
- Violet

# Black Forest Cake

Makes one 4-layer 9-inch cake; serves 12 to 14

Filled with cherries and whipped cream, this is a spectacular cake to serve for a special party or as part of a dessert buffet.

1 recipe The Arlene Dahl Chocolate Cake (page 590) or Quick Chocolate Cake (see page 594), baked in two 9-inch round pans and cooled

2 cups cherry preserves

1 cup fresh or frozen sweet cherries, defrosted if necessary, pitted, and coarsely chopped

½ cup kirsch (cherry brandy)

2 tablespoons water

3 cups heavy cream

½ cup sugar

**1.** Split the cake layers in half horizontally with a serrated knife. Place strips of waxed or parchment paper around the edges of a serving plate.

**2.** In a medium-size bowl, combine the preserves, chopped cherries, and 2 tablespoons of the kirsch. Combine the remaining 6 tablespoons of kirsch and the water.

**3.** With an electric mixer, beat the cream in a large bowl until soft peaks form, then add the sugar and beat until stiff peaks form.

**4.** Center a cake layer on the serving plate and brush with about one-third of the diluted kirsch. Spread with about one-third of the preserves mixture, in a thin layer, then top with some of the whipped cream. Continue in this way, adding 2 more cake layers and using up the kirsch and the preserves mixture. Cover with the fourth layer of cake and spread the top and sides of the cake with the remaining whipped cream. Remove the paper strips from the serving plate.

✳ **DIVA DO-AHEAD:** At this point, cover and refrigerate for at least 6 and up to 36 hours.

### Diva Variation

Substitute apricot preserves for the cherry preserves and brush the layers with amaretto mixed with water instead of the kirsch. Decorated the top of the cake with Chocolate-Dipped Apricots (page 657).

# Chocolate-Coconut Cake

Makes one 4-layer 9-inch cake; serves 12 to 14

This gorgeous dark cake with creamy white frosting and toasted coconut is simple to put together and makes a real statement on the table.

1 recipe The Arlene Dahl Chocolate Cake (page 590) or Quick Chocolate Cake (see page 594), baked in two 9-inch round pans and cooled

One 7-ounce package Baker's Angel Flake coconut, toasted (see below)

2 cups Vanilla Custard (page 641)

2 cups heavy cream

¼ cup sugar

## Toasting Coconut

If you need to toast more than 1 cup of coconut, scatter it on a baking sheet lined with a silicone baking liner or a sheet of parchment paper and bake at 350°F until it begins to turn golden, 7 to 10 minutes. Remove from the oven and transfer to a bowl to keep it from browning any further.

If you need to toast 1 cup or less, you can put the coconut in a nonstick skillet over medium heat and toss until it begins to turn golden in color. Remove the coconut from the skillet immediately.

**1.** Split the cake layers in half horizontally with a serrated knife. Place strips of waxed or parchment paper around the edges of a serving plate, and center a cake layer on the plate.

**2.** In a medium-size bowl, stir together 1 cup of the coconut and the Vanilla Custard. Spread a ½-inch-thick layer of the coconut custard over the cake, about one-third of the mixture. Top with another cake layer and half of the remaining filling. Repeat the layers once more, using up all of the filling and then top with the fourth cake layer.

**3.** With an electric mixer, beat the cream in another medium-size bowl until soft peaks form, then add the sugar and beat until stiff peaks form. Frost the top and sides of the cake with the cream, then sprinkle the top and sides with the remaining 1 cup of coconut. Remove the paper strips.

✳ **DIVA DO-AHEAD:** At this point, cover and refrigerate for at least 4 hours or overnight.

# Chocolate Tiramisu Cake

Makes one 2-layer 9-inch cake; serves 12 to 14

Tiramisu became all the rage a few years back, but I felt that there was something lacking. I decided to try it with chocolate cake instead of the traditional ladyfingers; the difference is incredible. Students who take my Do-Ahead Christmas class love this simple and delicious twist on the classic. The whole dessert has to be made a few days ahead of time to let the flavors develop.

## Quick Chocolate Cake

- 2 cups granulated sugar
- 1¾ cups unbleached all-purpose flour
- ¾ cup Dutch-process unsweetened cocoa powder
- 1½ teaspoons baking powder
- 1½ teaspoons baking soda
- 1 teaspoon salt
- 2 large eggs
- 1 cup whole milk
- ½ cup vegetable oil
- 2 teaspoons vanilla extract
- 1 cup boiling water

## Brushing Liquid

- ¾ cup brewed espresso
- ¼ cup dark crème de cacao or Kahlúa

## Mascarpone Filling

- 2½ cups mascarpone cheese
- ½ cup granulated sugar
- ¼ to ⅓ cup heavy cream
- ¼ teaspoon ground cinnamon

## For Dusting

- ½ cup Dutch-process unsweetened cocoa powder
- 1 cup confectioners' sugar

**1.** Preheat the oven to 350°F. Coat two 9-inch round baking pans with nonstick cooking spray.

**2.** To make the chocolate cake, in a large bowl, whisk together the granulated sugar, flour, cocoa, baking powder and soda, and salt. Stir in the eggs, milk, oil, and vanilla. With an electric mixer, beat on medium speed for 2 minutes. Stir in the boiling water and mix until blended, about 2 more minutes. Divide the batter equally between the prepared pans and bake until a skewer inserted into the center comes out clean, 30 to 35 minutes.

**3.** Place the pans on a rack and let cool for 10 minutes. Remove the cakes from the pans and let cool completely on the racks.

**4.** Split each layer in half horizontally with a serrated knife. Line the inside of a 9-inch springform pan with plastic wrap.

**5.** To make the brushing liquid, in a 2-cup measuring cup, combine the espresso and crème de cacao.

**6.** To make the filling, in a large bowl, beat together the cheese, ¼ cup of the espresso mixture, the granulated sugar, ¼ cup of the heavy cream, and the cinnamon until smooth. If the mixture is thick, thin it with the remaining heavy cream.

**7.** For dusting the cake, sift together the cocoa and confectioners' sugar in a medium-size bowl.

**8.** Place a cake layer in the bottom of the prepared pan, cutting to fit if necessary. Brush some of the remaining espresso mixture liberally over the cake, then spread a thin layer of the mascarpone filling over the espresso-soaked cake. Continue in this way, adding a layer, brushing it, and covering it with the fill-ing, ending with the fourth cake layer. Brush the final layer with the espresso mixture, and spread with the remaining mascarpone filling.

**9.** When ready to serve, remove the ring from the springform pan and serve the cake, dusted with the cocoa and sugar mixture.

## The Diva Says:

Some of my students have been known to make this with a cake mix, and I say that necessity is the mother of invention, but I urge you to try the homemade chocolate cake—it's almost as fast.

### A Better Brush

A silicone pastry brush goes right into the dishwasher after it's used, and comes out clean, without any annoying bristles coming off on your food, as with the natural bristle brushes. These new brushes come in small sizes for indoor cooking and larger sizes for outdoor barbecuing.

# Absolutely the Best
# Carrot Cake

Makes one 13 x 9-inch cake or 30 cupcakes; serves 12 to 15

Everyone has a favorite version of this moist cake topped with cream cheese frosting. This one benefits from the addition of pineapple, which gives the cake extra moisture and flavor.

- 1½ cups canola oil
- 2 cups sugar
- 3 large eggs
- 2 teaspoons vanilla extract
- 3 cups grated carrots
- One 8-ounce can crushed pineapple (do not drain)
- ½ cup chopped nuts of your choice
- 3 cups unbleached all-purpose flour
- 2 teaspoons baking soda
- 2 teaspoons ground cinnamon
- 1 recipe Cream Cheese Frosting (recipe follows)

1. Preheat the oven to 350°F. Coat a 13 x 9-inch baking pan with nonstick cooking spray or place liners in 30 muffin cups.

2. In a large bowl, beat together the oil, sugar, eggs, and vanilla. Add the carrots, pineapple and juice, and nuts, stirring until blended. Add the flour, baking soda, and cinnamon and stir to combine. Pour the batter into the prepared pan or cups and bake until a skewer inserted into the center comes out clean, 40 to 50 minutes for cake or 15 to 17 minutes for cupcakes.

3. Place the pan or muffin tins on a rack and let cool completely. Spread the top of the cake or cupcakes with the cream cheese frosting.

✳ **DIVA DO-AHEAD:** At this point, you can cover and refrigerate for up to 4 days or freeze for up to 2 months.

## The Diva Says:

The food processor will make short work of grating the carrots, but some grocers carry already grated carrots. These are a little drier than freshly grated carrots, so if you're using them, add an extra ½ cup to the batter to make up for the lack of moisture.

I generally leave a 13 x 9-inch cake in the pan rather than removing it to frost it. The cake slices into nice serving pieces and most people don't have a serving platter large enough to hold a 13 x 9-inch cake. If you do, then by all means transfer the cooled cake to a serving platter, then frost the top and sides.

# Cream Cheese Frosting

Makes 6 cups, enough to frost two 9-inch layers, one 13 x 9-inch cake, or 48 cupcakes

This luxurious frosting is not too sweet and has a nice tangy flavor, thanks to the cream cheese and lemon extract.

**One 3-ounce package cream cheese, softened**

**½ cup (1 stick) unsalted butter or margarine**

**5 cups confectioners' sugar**

**½ teaspoon lemon extract**

**1 teaspoon vanilla extract**

**Milk, as needed**

Using an electric mixer, beat together the cream cheese and butter in a medium-size bowl. Add the confectioners' sugar and extracts and beat until the mixture is a spreadable consistency. If the frosting is too thick, beat in some milk, ½ teaspoon at a time, until the desired consistency is reached.

✳ **DIVA DO-AHEAD:** At this point, you can cover and refrigerate for up to 5 days or freeze for up to 6 months. I recommend you soften it at room temperature after it has been refrigerated, so it's easy to spread.

## BUNDT AND TUBE PANS

**Bundt and tube pans** (or angel food cake pans) are generally 10 inches in diameter and hold up to 12 cups of batter. Both have a tube in the center, giving you a cake with a hole in the middle. The tube pan bottom is sometimes removable, and sometimes the pan is one solid piece. For these recipes it isn't critical to have a removable bottom.

Unlike a straight-sided tube pan, a bundt pan is fluted, so your cake will have an attractive design when it is unmolded from the pan. You can substitute a tube pan for all of the cakes in this chapter that call for a bundt pan. If your bundt pan has an intricate design, make sure that you spray all the nooks and crannies with a nonstick cooking spray such as Baker's Joy before transferring the batter to the pan. This will ensure your lovely cake pops right out of the pan.

# Donna's Anise Pound Cake

Makes one 10-inch tube or bundt cake; serves about 20

My cousin Donna is not only a wonderful hostess but also an amazing baker. She decided that she would try and replicate my grandmother's anise cake, and I think hers is actually better! The cake really needs to sit overnight to develop its flavors.

### Cake

**3 cups unbleached all-purpose flour**

**1½ cups granulated sugar**

**1 teaspoon baking soda**

**2 teaspoons baking powder**

**1 teaspoon salt**

**1¼ cups whole milk**

**1 cup (2 sticks) unsalted butter, softened**

**4 large eggs**

**Two 1-ounce bottles anise extract**

### Glaze

**One 1-pound box confectioners' sugar**

**¼ cup milk**

**½ cup sprinkles**

**1.** Preheat the oven to 350°F. Coat a 10-inch tube or bundt pan with nonstick cooking spray.

**2.** To make the cake, in a large bowl, whisk together the flour, granulated sugar, baking soda and powder, and salt. With an electric mixer, beat in the milk and butter on low speed, raise the speed to medium, and beat for 2 minutes. Scrape down the bowl and add the eggs, one at a time, beating after each addition. Add the anise extract and beat for another minute. Scrape into the prepared pan and bake until a skewer inserted into the center comes out clean, about 1 hour.

**3.** Place the pan on a rack and let cool for 25 minutes, then remove the cake from the pan. Return to the rack and let cool completely.

✳ **DIVA DO-AHEAD:** At this point, you can cover and freeze for up to 6 weeks. Defrost before continuing.

**4.** To make the glaze, with an electric mixer, beat together the confectioners' sugar and milk in a large bowl until creamy. Spread over the cooled cake and let it drip down the sides. Grandma always sprinkled hers with red and blue sprinkles, but you can use whatever you'd like to give this cake a festive air.

# Vanilla Citrus Pound Cake

Makes one 10-inch tube or bundt cake; serves about 20

This pound cake would be a blue ribbon winner at the county fair. I make it when I want something plain to serve with berries or with a cup of tea. It is flavored with lemon, orange, and vanilla, which give it a distinctive taste. The cake tastes best when it is made a day or two ahead to let the flavors develop.

2⅔ cups sugar

1 cup (2 sticks) unsalted butter or margarine

6 large eggs

2¾ cups unbleached all-purpose flour

½ teaspoon salt

¼ teaspoon baking soda

½ teaspoon vanilla extract

¼ teaspoon orange oil, or ½ teaspoon orange extract

¼ teaspoon lemon oil, or ½ teaspoon lemon extract

1 cup sour cream

## Keeping the Moisture In

Standard 1-gallon zipper-top plastic bags will hold 9-inch layer cakes and bundt cakes easily. I recommend them for storing your cakes in the refrigerator or freezer because they will keep out moisture and prevent the cakes from spoiling.

**1.** Preheat the oven to 350°F. Coat a 10-inch tube or bundt pan with nonstick cooking spray.

**2.** With an electric mixer, beat together the sugar, butter, and eggs in a large bowl until light and fluffy, about 3 minutes. Add the flour, salt, and baking soda, mixing on low speed to blend. Add the vanilla, oils, and sour cream and beat until smooth and blended. Scrape into the prepared pan and bake until a skewer inserted into the center comes out clean, 60 to 70 minutes.

**3.** Place the pan on a rack and let cool for 25 minutes, then remove the cake from the pan and let cool completely on the rack.

✳ **DIVA DO-AHEAD:** At this point, you can cover and freeze for up to 2 months.

## The Diva Says:

I usually don't frost this cake, but you can use the glaze from Donna's Anise Pound Cake (left) or just dust it with confectioners' sugar.

# Chocolate Fudge Pound Cake

Makes one 10-inch tube or bundt cake; serves 20

You can serve this fudgy cake all by itself, dusted with confectioners' sugar, or frost it or glaze it. If you like, serve it with a scoop of coffee ice cream and cover the ice cream and cake with hot fudge sauce, or accompany it with a few fresh raspberries or strawberries. Any way you serve it, it's an impressive dessert.

¾ cup (1½ sticks) unsalted butter or margarine

3 cups sugar

5 large eggs

1 cup whole milk

2 teaspoons vanilla extract

3 cups unbleached all-purpose flour

1 teaspoon salt

1 teaspoon baking soda

¾ cup unsweetened cocoa powder

**1.** Preheat the oven to 350°F. Coat a 10-inch tube or bundt pan with nonstick cooking spray.

**2.** With an electric mixer, beat the butter and sugar together in a large bowl until fluffy, about 2 minutes. Add the eggs, one at a time, beating well after each. Add the milk and vanilla and beat until blended. Add the flour, salt, baking soda, and cocoa and beat on low speed until the flour disappears into the batter. Transfer to the prepared pan and smooth the top. Bake until a skewer inserted into the center comes out clean, about 1 hour.

**3.** Place the pan on a rack and let cool for 25 minutes, then remove the cake from the pan and let cool completely on the rack.

✻ **DIVA DO-AHEAD:** At this point, you can cover tightly and store at room temperature for up to 4 days or freeze for up to 2 months.

# Warm Thanksgiving Apple Cake

Makes one 11 x 15-inch cake; serves 24

I have been teaching this simple cake to my Do-Ahead Thanksgiving students for over a decade and it is always a big hit. This makes a lot of cake, but trust me when I say there won't be many leftovers, and if there are, you can refreeze them without any problem. At Thanksgiving, I serve the cake with vanilla ice cream and Toasted Pecan Sauce (page 501), but it's also terrific with Cream Cheese Frosting (page 597).

**1 pound (4 sticks) unsalted butter, softened**

**2 cups sugar**

**4 large eggs**

**3 cups unbleached all-purpose flour**

**2 teaspoons baking soda**

**2 teaspoons ground cinnamon**

**½ teaspoon ground nutmeg**

**5 medium-size Granny Smith apples, peeled, cored, and finely chopped**

**1 cup chopped pecans**

**1 tablespoon vanilla extract**

**1.** Preheat the oven to 350°F. Coat an 11 x 15-inch jelly roll pan with nonstick cooking spray.

**2.** With an electric mixer, beat the butter and sugar together in a large bowl until light and fluffy. Beat in the eggs, one at a time, and continue beating until blended. Add the flour, baking soda, and spices and beat until just incorporated. Stir in the apples, nuts, and vanilla. Scrape into the prepared pan. Bake until a skewer inserted into the center comes out with just a few crumbs attached to it, 35 to 40 minutes.

**3.** Set the pan on a rack to cool for 10 minutes, cut into squares, and serve.

✳ **DIVA DO-AHEAD:** At this point, you can cool completely, cover, and refrigerate for up to 2 days or freeze for up to 6 weeks. Before serving, reheat the chilled or defrosted cake, covered with aluminum foil, in a 350°F oven for 10 minutes.

# Key Lime Cheesecake

Makes one 9-inch cake; serves 12 to 16

The clean flavor of Key limes and a crunchy macadamia nut crust make this cheesecake a great addition to any buffet table. It is beautiful topped with fresh sliced strawberries, but if they are not in season, serve it in a pool of Strawberry or Raspberry Sauce (pages 640 and 503). You can find bottled Key lime juice in most gourmet stores. Key limes are showing up in gourmet stores and supermarkets with increasing frequency. If you can't find either, you can substitute half lime juice and half lemon juice.

### Macadamia Crust

**1½ cups graham cracker crumbs (about 18 crackers)**

**½ cup chopped macadamia nuts**

**2 tablespoons sugar**

**½ cup (1 stick) unsalted butter, melted**

### Filling

**Three 8-ounce packages cream cheese, softened**

**1¾ cups sugar**

**1 cup sour cream**

**3 tablespoons unbleached all-purpose flour**

**3 large eggs**

**⅔ cup Key lime juice, or more to taste**

**1 teaspoon vanilla extract**

**3 cups strawberries (optional), hulled and cut in half, for garnish**

**Strawberry Sauce (page 640) or Raspberry Sauce (page 503) for serving (optional)**

**1.** Line a springform pan with aluminum foil and coat with nonstick cooking spray.

**2.** To make the crust, in a medium-size bowl, stir together the ingredients until they begin to come together. Press into the bottom of the prepared pan and about 1 inch up the side.

✳ **DIVA DO-AHEAD:** At this point, you can cover and freeze for up to 2 months.

**3.** Preheat the oven to 350°F.

**4.** To make the filling, with an electric mixer, beat together the cream cheese and sugar in a large bowl until smooth, about 2 minutes. Blend in the sour cream and flour, beating until smooth. Add the eggs, one at a time, beating well after each addition. Add the lime juice and vanilla and beat until just blended. (At this point, you may want to taste the batter and see whether it needs more lime juice. Some people like theirs with a strong lime flavor, others want just a hint; this recipe is somewhere in between.) Scrape the filling into the prepared pan and bake until the center is just about set, about 1 hour and 15 minutes. Turn off the oven, leave the cake inside, and leave the door ajar for 1 hour. (This helps the cheesecake cool evenly and prevents cracking.)

**5.** Remove the pan from the oven, place on a rack, and let cool completely.

✳ **DIVA DO-AHEAD:** At this point, while the cheesecake is still in the pan, cover and refrigerate for at least 6 hours and up to 4 days or freeze for up to 2 months. Defrost before continuing.

**6.** To unmold the cheesecake, remove from the refrigerator, take off the outer ring of the springform pan, and peel the foil away from the rim of the cake. Run a long or offset spatula underneath the cake to loosen it from the foil and slide the cake onto a serving platter. Decorate the top with the sliced strawberries, if using; otherwise, serve with Strawberry or Raspberry Sauce.

## The Diva Says:

Graham cracker crumbs are sold in the supermarket in the baking aisle. They are a little pricey, so you may just want to buy graham crackers and crush them yourself in the food processor or in a sealed plastic bag with a rolling pin. Once the crackers have been crushed, you can store them in a zipper-top plastic bag in the freezer for up to 6 months.

## Refrigerating or Freezing Cheesecake

It is not necessary to take the cheesecake out of the pan before refrigerating or freezing it. If you will need your springform pan for another use, refrigerate or freeze the cheesecake in the pan until firm or frozen. Remove the pan, and refrigerate or freeze the cake in a 2-gallon zipper-top plastic bag, or wrap it tightly in plastic wrap. Defrost the cheesecake, if necessary, peel away the foil that lined the pan, and with a long, wide spatula, slide the cake onto a serving plate.

## Cutting Cheesecake

Wide unflavored, unwaxed dental floss makes a great cutting tool for cheesecakes. Cut a piece of floss about 6 inches longer than the diameter of the cheesecake, hold it tautly over the cheesecake, and slice through, keeping the floss taut. You can make some preliminary marks on the top of the cheesecake before cutting to make this easier.

When using a knife to cut a cheesecake, always rinse it in hot water after each cut to remove any excess cheesecake that adheres to the knife.

# Piña Colada Cheesecake

Makes one 9-inch cake; serves 10 to 12

Tropical flavors from the islands make this cheesecake a delicious choice to serve after Asian or grilled entrées for a cooling end to the meal. The crunchy macadamia nuts in the crust highlight nuggets of pineapple, dark rum, and creamy coconut in the filling. This is best made a day or two ahead.

### Macadamia Crust

**1½ cups crushed graham crackers (about 18) or vanilla wafers (about 40)**

**½ cup (1 stick) unsalted butter, melted**

**¼ cup sugar**

**½ cup chopped macadamia nuts**

### Filling

**Four 8-ounce packages cream cheese, softened**

**1 cup sugar**

**4 large eggs**

**2 large egg yolks**

**2 tablespoons dark rum**

**Two 4-ounce cans crushed pineapple, thoroughly drained (about ¾ cup)**

**1 cup canned cream of coconut, such as Coco Lopez or Goya**

**1.** Line a 9-inch springform pan with aluminum foil and coat with nonstick cooking spray.

**2.** To make the crust, in a medium-size bowl, stir together the ingredients until well blended. Press into the bottom and up the sides of the prepared pan.

✳ **DIVA DO-AHEAD:** At this point, you can cover and freeze for up to 2 months.

**3.** Preheat the oven to 350°F.

**4.** To make the filling, with an electric mixer, cream together the cream cheese and sugar in a large bowl until smooth and light. Add the whole eggs and yolks, one at a time, beating after each addition. Add the rum, pineapple, and cream of coconut, blending on low speed just to combine. Scrape into the prepared crust and bake until the center is set, 45 to 55 minutes. Turn oven off and leave cheesecake in the oven with the door slightly ajar for 1 hour.

**5.** Remove the cheesecake from the oven, place it on a rack, and let cool completely.

✳ **DIVA DO-AHEAD:** At this point, you can cover and refrigerate for up to 2 days or freeze for up to 2 months. Defrost before continuing.

**6.** To unmold cheesecake, remove the outer ring of the pan and peel the foil away from sides of the cake. Run a long or offset spatula under the cake to loosen it from the foil and slide cake onto a serving platter.

# Petite Cheesecakes with Fruit Toppings

Makes 24 petite cheesecakes; serves 12

These jewel-like bites of cheesecake are so simple to make. The crust is a whole vanilla wafer and the cheesecakes are made in standard muffin cups, so you can use pretty decorative liners to match the season, orange in fall, for example, and red at Christmastime. Make the cheesecakes at least a day ahead of time.

24 vanilla wafers

Two 8-ounce packages cream cheese, softened

¾ cup sugar

2 large eggs

1 teaspoon fresh lemon juice

1 teaspoon vanilla extract

1½ to 3 cups fruit toppings (see The Diva Says)

**1.** Preheat the oven to 350°F. Line two 12-cup cupcake tins with paper or foil liners. Place a vanilla wafer in each, right side up, and set aside.

**2.** With an electric mixer, beat together the cream cheese and sugar in a large bowl until light and fluffy, about 3 minutes. Add the eggs, one at a time, beating after each addition. Stir in the lemon juice and vanilla and beat until smooth.

**3.** Spoon the filling into the cupcake tins, filling each cup two-thirds full. Bake until set, 20 to 25 minutes. Let cool to room temperature.

**DIVA DO-AHEAD:** At this point, cover and refrigerate for at least 8 hours and up to 2 days or freeze for up to 2 months. Defrost before continuing.

**4.** Twenty-four hours before serving, top each cheesecake with 1 to 2 tablespoons of fruit topping.

## The Diva Says:

The easiest way to top these cheesecakes is to use canned cherry, blueberry, or apple pie filling. That being said, sliced fresh strawberries, kiwis, raspberries, and blueberries all make better-tasting toppings and are a lot lighter, without the gluey sauce that the canned fillings have. I have also topped these with apricot, strawberry, or raspberry jam, or with chopped fresh pineapple and toasted coconut.

# Mom's Apple Pie Cake

Makes one 13 x 9-inch cake; serves 10

My mother shared this recipe with me years ago and I've been making it for my family ever since. The apples bake under a crunchy crust, while the cake-like interior absorbs the juices and flavorings from the baking apples. You can bake the cake on the morning of the day you want to serve it, then give it a quick warm-up in a preheated 350°F oven for about 10 minutes. It is delicious served warm, but it can sit at room temperature; we like it for breakfast at my house!

### Apple Mixture

**10 medium-size Granny Smith apples, cored, peeled, and sliced**

**2 teaspoons ground cinnamon**

**2 tablespoons sugar**

**2 teaspoons fresh lemon juice**

### Batter

**1½ cups (3 sticks) unsalted butter or margarine, melted**

**2 cups unbleached all-purpose flour**

**2 cups sugar**

**2 large eggs**

**1½ cups pecan halves**

**1.** To make the apple mixture, toss together the apples, cinnamon, sugar, and lemon juice in a large bowl.

✳ **DIVA DO-AHEAD:** At this point, you can store in a zipper-top plastic bag in the refrigerator overnight.

**2.** Preheat the oven to 375°F. Coat a 13 x 9-inch baking pan with nonstick cooking spray. Transfer the apples to the prepared pan.

**3.** To make the batter, combine the melted butter, flour, sugar, eggs, and pecans, stirring until blended. Pour over the apples and bake until the top is crisp and golden and the apples are bubbling underneath, 45 minutes to 1 hour.

**4.** Serve the cake warm or at room temperature with unsweetened whipped cream or vanilla ice cream.

# Sinful Chocolate Pecan Pie

Makes one 9-inch pie; serves 10

This decadent pie borders on sin! The chocolate chips melt in the caramel filling and end up surrounding the pecans, giving you a turtle pie of sorts. Very thin slivers of this should be served with unsweetened whipped cream or vanilla ice cream. I like to make this pie with bourbon, but you can omit it or use Kahlúa for a mocha-flavored pie; Scotch whiskey is also nice. If you like, substitute walnuts for the pecans.

2 cups pecan halves

1 cup semisweet chocolate chips

One unbaked 9-inch pie shell (see page 608 or 609)

4 large eggs

½ cup (1 stick) unsalted butter, melted

1 cup light corn syrup

1 cup firmly packed light brown sugar

¼ cup bourbon

**1.** Preheat the oven to 400°F.

**2.** Scatter the pecans and chocolate chips over the bottom of the prepared piecrust.

**3.** In a large bowl, whisk together the eggs, melted butter, corn syrup, brown sugar, and bourbon until well blended. Pour over the pecans and chips. Place the pie on a baking sheet lined with a silicone liner or aluminum foil and bake for 15 minutes.

**4.** Reduce the oven temperature to 350°F and bake until the filling is set and golden brown, about another 25 minutes. (Insert a knife into the center; it should come out with a bit of filling on it, but it should not be runny.) Remove the pie from the oven and let cool.

✳ **DIVA DO-AHEAD:** At this point, you can cover and refrigerate overnight or freeze for up to 1 month.

Serve warm or at room temperature.

# PASTRY CRUST

**Here's where the rubber** meets the road when it comes to making dessert. Piecrust is a problem for a lot of people, so when I was testing recipes for this chapter, I needed to come up with pastry crusts that were flavorful and simple to reproduce in home kitchens. I scoured books and Web sites and talked with bakers I admire, and it all came down to two inviolate principles:

**1.** The ingredients must be cold.

**2.** Shortening is necessary for flakiness, butter for flavor, and ice water to bind it all together.

After that, I was on my own as to which was the best way to mix the ingredients together and roll out the crust. The pixie dust factor is all the things that contribute to disaster in a kitchen: The ingredients are wrong; it's a dry day and the dough needs more water; it's a humid day and the dough doesn't need any water at all; the kitchen is so hot, it's warming up the cold ingredients.

So, dear reader, these are the piecrusts I make in my kitchen: One is solid butter and doesn't need to rest before rolling, while the other is half shortening and half butter, which will need to rest before you roll it. I keep the shortening and butter in the fridge until I'm ready to use them, cut the cold unsalted butter into tiny cubes (cut each 1/4-pound stick in half lengthwise and then in half again lengthwise, and cut each skinny rod of butter into about 8 pieces), and keep a measuring cup with ice water on the counter. Both recipes are enough for two 9-inch crusts or one double crust. The piecrust freezes well for about 2 months, so even if you only need one crust, why not make both and freeze one? The recipe is easy to cut in half, however, if you'd prefer to make just one crust.

## Flaky Pastry Crust

Makes two 9-inch piecrusts

**2½ cups all-purpose flour**

**½ teaspoon salt**

**1 teaspoon sugar (omit if the crust is for a savory pie, such as a quiche)**

**½ cup solid vegetable shortening (I prefer Crisco)**

**½ cup (1 stick) cold unsalted butter**

**3 to 5 tablespoons ice water, as needed**

**1.** Combine the flour, salt, and sugar in a food processor and pulse 5 times to distribute the ingredients. Put the shortening on top of the flour mixture and pulse to break it up. Add the butter cubes and pulse 8 to 10 times, until the mixture begins to resemble crumbs and works its way up the sides of the work bowl. Scrape down the work bowl and pulse 2 more times. Sprinkle 3 tablespoons of the ice water over the dough and pulse 4 or 5 times, until the mixture begins to come together. If you feel you need more water, add 2 more tablespoons and pulse again. The mixture should not come together in a ball, but rather still be crumbly.

**2.** Place half of the crumbly dough in the center of a large sheet of plastic wrap or waxed paper and, using the wrap, knead the dough into a round disk about ½ inch thick. Repeat this procedure with the remaining dough, and wrap each disk in plastic wrap.

✳ **DIVA DO-AHEAD:** At this point, refrigerate for at least 1 hour and up to 4 days or freeze for up to 2 months. Or refrigerate one crust and freeze the other. If frozen, defrost the crust in the refrigerator; take the crust out 10 to 15 minutes before rolling.

**3.** With a rolling pin and a floured work surface, roll out one of the chilled disks into a 12-inch circle. Coat a pie pan with nonstick cooking spray, roll the pastry over the rolling pin, and transfer it to the pie pan. Gently nudge the pastry into the pan with your knuckles, being careful not to tear it, and trim the top edges, either folding under some of the pie dough and making a decorative rim or using a pastry wheel to make a decorative edge. If you tear the dough, don't panic—just patch it with another piece of dough.

✳ **DIVA DO-AHEAD:** At this point, if you are going to bake the filling in the pie shell, you can cover and refrigerate for up to 2 days or freeze for up to 2 months. Defrost in the refrigerator before continuing.

**4.** If you wish to prebake the pie shell, prick the bottom and sides of the shell, fit a piece of buttered aluminum foil into the pie shell with the buttered side facing the pastry, then cover the foil with pie weights or dried beans to help keep the pastry from rising in the oven. Bake in a preheated 425°F oven

for 10 to 12 minutes, then remove the pie weights or beans and the foil and bake the crust until golden, another 7 to 10 minutes. Let cool before filling.

## All Butter Piecrust

Makes two 9-inch piecrusts

When I was searching for the best piecrust recipes, this one fell out of an old cookbook of my mom's. It was written on a card that was yellowed and worn, but my mother's comment was all I needed to read—"makes the best piecrust."

- **2 cups unbleached all-purpose flour**
- **2 tablespoons sugar**
- **½ teaspoon salt**
- **1 cup (2 sticks) cold unsalted butter, cut into bits**
- **¼ cup ice water**

**1.** Butter two 9-inch pie pans.

**2.** Put the flour, sugar, and salt into a food processor and pulse to blend. Put the butter on top of the dry ingredients and pulse 6 to 8 times, until the mixture is crumbly and the butter has been incorporated. With the machine running, add the water, 1 tablespoon at a time, until the mixture begins to come together.

**3.** Transfer the dough to a floured work surface, gather it into a rough disk, and cut it into 2 pieces. Pat each half into a disk and flatten slightly. Roll out each disk with a lightly floured rolling pin into a 12-inch circle. Roll the dough over the rolling pin and transfer to a prepared pie pan. Gently nudge the pastry into the pan with your knuckles, being careful not to tear it, and trim the top edges, either folding under some of the pie dough and making a decorative rim or using a pastry wheel to make a decorative edge. If you tear the dough, don't panic—just patch it with another piece of dough.

✳ **DIVA DO-AHEAD:** At this point, if you are going to bake the filling in the pie shell, you can cover and refrigerate for up to 2 days or freeze for up to 2 months. Defrost before continuing.

**4.** If you wish to prebake the pie shell, prick the bottom and sides of the shell, fit a piece of buttered aluminum foil into the pie shell with the buttered side facing the pastry, then cover the foil with pie weights or dried beans to help keep the pastry from rising in the oven. Bake in a preheated 425°F oven for 10 to 12 minutes, then remove the pie weights or beans and the foil and bake the crust until golden, another 7 to 10 minutes. Let cool before filling.

## The Diva Says:

If you have trouble rolling out doughs, buy one of the new silicone rolling pins. They are fantastic for rolling out *any* dough.

## When Homemade Piecrust Isn't an Option

Your supermarket carries frozen and fresh pastry crust that you can use if you are in a crunch for time. The fresh pastry is found in the same section as the tubes of dough for crescent rolls and biscuits. It just needs to be placed in a pie pan, then baked as directed. Marie Callender's frozen deep-dish piecrusts are a good brand to buy in a pinch. Follow the baking directions on the package.

Crumb crusts, both graham cracker and chocolate cookie crusts, are available in the baking section of your supermarket. These are shallow piecrusts, so if you have a lot of filling, you may need to use 2 purchased crumb crusts for some of the recipes in this section. I'm not fond of these crusts because I think they have a distinct aftertaste. But, as I said, if you are in a hurry, these can save you. I would use them for frozen ice cream pies but not for pudding or fruit-filled pies.

# Chocolate-Raspberry Tart

Makes one 9-inch tart; serves 10

This luxurious combination of flaky pastry, raspberry jam, and chocolate ganache is simple to put together and you can refrigerate or freeze the tart until you are ready to serve.

½ cup seedless raspberry jam

¼ cup Chambord, amaretto, or Grand Marnier

One 9-inch pie shell (see page 608 or 609), prebaked and cooled

1½ cups heavy cream

One 12-ounce bag semisweet chocolate chips

1 cup heavy cream (optional), whipped until stiff peaks form, for garnish

1 cup fresh raspberries (optional) for garnish

**1.** In a small bowl, blend together the jam and 2 tablespoons of the liqueur. Spread over the bottom of the pie shell.

**2.** In a small saucepan, heat the cream and chocolate chips, stirring, over medium-low heat until the chocolate is melted. Reduce the heat to low and stir until the mixture thickens a bit. Remove from the heat and let cool completely, about 1 hour.

**3.** Add the remaining 2 tablespoons of liqueur to the chocolate mixture. With an electric mixer, beat until smooth and creamy. Spread over the jam in the pie shell and smooth the top.

✳ **DIVA DO-AHEAD:** At this point, cover and refrigerate for at least 4 hours and up to 2 days or freeze for up to 1 month.

**4.** If you like, garnish each slice of the tart with a dollop or rosette of whipped cream, and arrange a few berries on the plate.

The Diva Says:

This pie does not freeze rock solid, so you can actually serve it straight out of the freezer—it's delicious refrigerated or frozen.

## To Get on a Roll

One thing I can't be without in my kitchen is a large silicone pastry mat, on which I roll out piecrusts. This sheet is a generous 16 by 24 inches, giving me plenty of room to roll. Other chefs prefer to roll their pastry on marble (which can be chilled), and still others prefer a cloth pastry sheet. I find that the silicone is easy to use and simple to clean. You can find these mats at www.discountcooking.com or www.kingarthurflour.com.

# Blueberry–Lemon Curd Tart

Makes one 10-inch tart; serves 10 to 12

Fresh blueberries are a delightful taste of summer. The tart lemon curd in this pie is a perfect foil for the sweet berries, as are the toasted almonds in the crust. For a different flavor, try Vanilla Custard (page 641) under the berries rather than the lemon curd.

**1½ cups unbleached all-purpose flour**

**⅔ cup sugar**

**½ teaspoon salt**

**½ cup sliced almonds**

**1 cup (2 sticks) cold unsalted butter, cut into small bits**

**2 cups Lemon Curd (page 587)**

**1 quart fresh blueberries, picked over for stems**

**½ cup blueberry jelly**

**2 cups heavy cream, whipped until stiff peaks form**

**1.** Preheat the oven to 375°F. Coat a 10-inch tart pan with a removable bottom with nonstick cooking spray.

**2.** Combine the flour, sugar, salt, and almonds in a food processor and pulse 2 or 3 times to mix. Scatter the butter evenly over the top and pulse 6 or 7 times, until the mixture becomes crumbly. Press the crust evenly into the prepared pan, using your knuckles to press down; the crust should go all the way up the sides. Bake until lightly browned, about 20 minutes. Remove from the oven and let cool completely. Remove the outer ring from the pan.

✳ **DIVA DO-AHEAD:** At this point, you can slip the crust, still on the bottom of the pan, into a 2-gallon zipper-top plastic bag and seal. Store at room temperature overnight or freeze for up to 2 months. Defrost before continuing.

**3.** With a long spatula, separate the shell from the bottom of the pan and transfer it to a serving plate. With an offset spatula, spread the lemon curd over the bottom of the tart, smoothing to level the filling. Arrange the blueberries on top so they cover the surface.

**4.** Dissolve the blueberry jelly in a small, heavy saucepan over medium heat and let cool slightly. Brush over the tart, covering the blueberries.

✳ **DIVA DO-AHEAD:** At this point, you can cover and refrigerate for up to 4 hours.

**5.** Before serving, garnish the tart with whipped cream.

# Mixed Fruit Tart with Glaze

Makes one 10-inch tart; serves 10 to 12

Make sure you use fruits that are in season and complement each other in taste and texture. The finished tart can be refrigerated for up to 8 hours; after that, the pastry will get a bit soggy and the fruit will begin to look a little peaked.

### Press-In Lemon Crust

**2 cups unbleached all-purpose flour**

**⅔ cup sugar**

**½ teaspoon salt**

**¾ cup (1½ sticks) cold unsalted butter, cut into bits**

**1 large egg yolk**

**Grated zest of 1 lemon**

### Filling

**Two 8-ounce packages cream cheese, softened**

**½ cup sugar**

**2 teaspoons lemon juice**

**2 tablespoons milk, or more as needed**

**4 cups cut-up fresh fruit of your choice, such as berries, mangoes, kiwis, cherries, oranges, and pineapple**

### Glaze

**1 cup fruit juice, such as cranberry juice cocktail, orange juice, or apricot**

**¼ cup sugar**

**1 tablespoon cornstarch**

**1 tablespoon unsalted butter**

**1.** Preheat the oven to 375°F. Coat a 10-inch tart pan with a removable bottom with nonstick cooking spray.

**2.** To make the crust, in a food processor, combine the flour, sugar, and salt, pulsing a few times to blend. Scatter the butter on top and pulse 5 or 6 times, until the mixture begins to look coarse. With the machine running, add the egg yolk and lemon zest and process until the crust begins to come together. Press the dough evenly into the prepared pan, using your knuckles to press down; the crust should go all the way up the sides. Bake until golden brown, about 20 minutes. Remove from the oven and let cool completely. Remove the outer ring from the pan.

❋ **DIVA DO-AHEAD:** At this point, you can slip the crust, still on the bottom of the pan, into a 2-gallon zipper-top plastic bag and seal. Store at room temperature overnight or freeze for up to 2 months. Defrost before continuing.

**3.** To make the filling, in the food processor, combine the cream cheese, sugar, lemon juice, and milk and process until it reaches a spreadable consistency.

**DIVA DO-AHEAD:** At this point, you can cover and refrigerate for up to 5 days.

**4.** With a long spatula, separate the shell from the bottom of the pan and transfer it to a serving plate. Spread the cream cheese mixture over the prepared crust and smooth it out. Top the cream cheese mixture with the fruit, arranging it in a decorative pattern.

**5.** To make the glaze, heat the juice in a small nonreactive saucepan over medium heat, add the sugar and cornstarch, and stir until the mixture begins to thicken and bubbles. Remove from the heat and whisk in the butter. Let cool to room temperature, then brush over the fruit tart.

**DIVA DO-AHEAD:** At this point, cover and refrigerate for at least 1 hour and up to 4 hours before serving.

## The Diva Says:

You can also use hot apricot preserves or marmalade or melted jelly to glaze fruit tarts. If the preserves seem a little thick, thin them with water, lemon juice, or an appropriate liqueur.

# Cool and Creamy Margaritaville Pie with Macadamia Nut Crust and Triple Sec Crème

Makes one 10-inch pie; serves 10

Take yourself to sunny Mexico by serving this frozen confection, based on a margarita, after a summertime barbecue.

Press-in Macadamia Nut Crust

**2 cups unbleached all-purpose flour**

**¾ cup sugar**

**1 cup (2 sticks) cold unsalted butter, cut into bits**

**¾ cup chopped macadamia nuts**

Tequila-Spiked Lime Cream Filling

**3 cups Lime Curd (see page 587)**

**¼ cup gold tequila**

**2 cups heavy cream, whipped until stiff peaks form**

Triple Sec Crème

**1½ cups heavy cream**

**¼ cup sugar**

**3 tablespoons Triple Sec**

**1 lime, thinly sliced, for garnish**

**12 fresh strawberries, hulled, for garnish**

**1.** Preheat the oven to 375°F. Coat a 10-inch deep-dish pie pan with nonstick cooking spray.

**2.** To make the crust, put the flour and sugar in a food processor and process just to combine. Scatter the butter on top and pulse until the mixture begins to look crumbly. Add the nuts and pulse again until the mixture is crumbly but coming together. Press evenly into the bottom and up the sides of the pie pan, using your knuckles to press down. Bake until golden, 10 to 15 minutes. Let cool on a rack.

**3.** To make the filling, in a large bowl, whisk together the Lime Curd and tequila. Fold in the whipped cream, and then pour into the cooled piecrust.

❋ **DIVA DO-AHEAD:** At this point, cover and freeze for at least 6 hours and up to 1 month.

**4.** To make the crème, with an electric mixer, beat the heavy cream in a large bowl until soft peaks form. With the mixer running, gradually add the sugar and Triple Sec and beat until the cream forms stiff peaks.

❋ **DIVA DO-AHEAD:** At this point, you can cover and refrigerate for up to 4 hours. Rewhip with a whisk before continuing.

**5.** Remove the pie from the freezer 20 minutes before serving and spread the crème over the top. Serve, garnished with lime slices and strawberries.

# Mud Pie

Makes one 13 x 9-inch pie or two 9-inch pies; serves 12

There are lots of variations on mud pie, but this one is my favorite. It's made in a 13 x 9-inch baking dish so that you can cut it into squares to serve the masses. There is fudge sauce swirled through the coffee ice cream, and I serve additional warm fudge sauce, which I keep warm in a fondue pot, over each serving. Be sure to have lots of whipped cream and toasted almonds on hand for garnishing. If you prefer, you can make this recipe in two 9-inch pie pans.

### Oreo Cookie Crust

**5 cups crushed Oreo cookies (about 50 cookies)**

**6 tablespoons (¾ stick) unsalted butter, melted**

### Filling

**½ gallon good quality coffee ice cream, softened**

**2 cups World's Best Hot Fudge Sauce (page 501), cooled completely, or one 16-ounce jar Hershey's Hot Fudge Chocolate Shoppe Topping**

**1½ cups sliced almonds, toasted (see page 83)**

**2 cups heavy cream**

**1.** Preheat the oven to 325°F. Coat one 13 x 9-inch baking dish or two 9-inch pie pans with nonstick cooking spray.

**2.** To make the crust, in a large bowl, blend together the cookies and butter until they begin to stick together when pinched between two fingers. Press evenly into the bottom and up the sides of the prepared baking dish or pie pans. Bake until crisp, 6 to 8 minutes. Remove from the oven and let cool completely.

✳ **DIVA DO-AHEAD:** At this point, you can cover and store at room temperature for up to 12 hours, refrigerate for up to 5 days, or freeze for up to 1 month.

**3.** To make the filling, smooth half of the ice cream into the pie shell, then drizzle with one-third of the fudge sauce, and sprinkle with half of the almonds. Cover with the remaining ice cream and drizzle with half of the remaining fudge sauce.

✳ **DIVA DO-AHEAD:** At this point, cover and freeze until firm, about 4 hours, and up to 1 month.

**4.** With an electric mixer, whip the heavy cream in a medium-size bowl until stiff peaks form.

✳ **DIVA DO-AHEAD:** At this point, you can cover and refrigerate for up to 4 hours. Rewhip with a whisk before using.

**5.** Remove the pie from the freezer about 20 minutes before serving. Heat the remaining fudge sauce. Cut the pie into serving portions with a sharp knife, dipping the knife into hot water before each cut. Drizzle some of the hot fudge over each portion, sprinkle with the remaining almonds, and top with dollops of the whipped cream.

### Diva Variation

Here's a way to make this pie with the lowest amount of fat possible. The crust will merely be crumbs in the pan, rather than a real crust, but it does work. Substitute low-fat Oreos for the regular Oreos and omit the butter. Sprinkle the crumbs over the bottom of the pie pans or baking dish, then use nonfat coffee ice cream and nonfat hot fudge sauce for the pie. Nonfat ice cream does not freeze rock solid, so you won't need to take it from the freezer in advance of serving it; just serve it right from the freezer.

# Banana Split Pie

Makes one 13 x 9-inch pie or two 9-inch pies; serves 12

All my favorite flavors are here, wrapped up in one pie to serve on a summer night. Serve this for your Fourth of July party or as dessert for a special birthday or another celebration.

### Vanilla Wafer Crust

**5 cups crushed vanilla wafers (about 2 boxes, or 100 wafers)**

**6 tablespoons (¾ stick) unsalted butter, melted**

**½ cup sugar**

### Filling

**4 ripe bananas, peeled and sliced ½ inch thick**

**1 pint vanilla ice cream, softened**

**1 pint chocolate ice cream, softened**

**1 pint strawberry ice cream, softened**

**2 cups World's Best Hot Fudge Sauce (page 501), cooled completely, or one 16-ounce jar Hershey's Hot Fudge Chocolate Shoppe Topping, plus extra for serving (optional)**

**1½ cups Strawberry Sauce (page 640)**

**One 8-ounce can crushed pineapple, thoroughly drained**

**2 cups heavy cream**

**1 cup chopped dry-roasted peanuts**

**1.** Preheat the oven to 325°F. Coat one 13 x 9-inch baking dish or two 9-inch pie pans with nonstick cooking spray.

**2.** To make the crust, in a large bowl, stir together the cookie crumbs, melted butter, and sugar until well combined. Press into the prepared pie pans or baking dish and bake until the crust is beginning to look crisp, 6 to 8 minutes. Remove from the oven and let cool completely.

❋ **DIVA DO-AHEAD:** At this point, you can cover and store at room temperature for up to 12 hours, refrigerate for up to 2 days, or freeze for up to 1 month.

**3.** To make the filling, cover the bottom of the crust with a layer of sliced bananas. Place alternating scoops of vanilla, chocolate, and strawberry ice creams, tightly packed next to each other, into the prepared crust. Smooth out the ice cream, pushing down gently, so you don't have any empty spaces. Drizzle with half of the hot fudge sauce and strawberry sauce, and spread with half of the pineapple. Top this layer with the remaining bananas. Repeat the layer of ice creams, then the sauces and pineapple.

✳ **DIVA DO-AHEAD:** At this point, cover and freeze until firm, at least 4 hours and up to 1 month.

**4.** With an electric mixer, whip the heavy cream in a medium-size bowl until stiff peaks form.

✳ **DIVA DO-AHEAD:** At this point, you can cover and refrigerate for up to 4 hours. Rewhip with a whisk before continuing.

**5.** Remove the pie from the freezer about 20 minutes before serving, then cut into serving portions with a sharp knife, dipping it into hot water after each cut. Garnish each slice with the chopped peanuts and whipped cream. You can also serve warmed fudge sauce on the side, if desired.

## More Ice Cream Pie Ideas

**Butter Pecan Praline Pie:** Using 2 cups of Toasted Pecan Sauce (page 501) at room temperature and 3 pints of butter pecan ice cream, slightly softened, cover the bottom of a prebaked Vanilla Wafer Crust (see page 617) with a thick layer of the sauce, then half the ice cream. Repeat the layers, ending with the remainder of the sauce.

✳ **DIVA DO-AHEAD:** At this point, cover and freeze until firm, at least 4 hours and up to 2 months.

Top the pie with 1½ cups of heavy cream that has been whipped with an electric mixer until stiff peaks form.

**Peanut Butter Chocolate Pie:** Using 2 cups of chopped Reese's Peanut Butter Cups (about 6 large or 20 small cups), 3 pints of slightly softened vanilla ice cream, and 2 cups of World's Best Hot Fudge Sauce (page 501) or one 16-ounce jar Hershey's Hot Fudge Chocolate Shoppe Topping, at room temperature, sprinkle one-third of the candy over the bottom of a prebaked Oreo Cookie Crust (see page 616). Top with half the ice cream, and spread with half the fudge sauce. Repeat the layers, ending with the remaining fudge sauce.

✳ **DIVA DO-AHEAD:** At this point, cover and freeze until firm, at least 4 hours and up to 2 months.

Top the pie with 1½ cups of heavy cream that has been whipped with an electric mixer until stiff peaks form.

**Cherry-Chocolate Ice Cream Pie:** Using 2 cups of fresh or frozen sweet cherries, defrosted, pitted, and coarsely chopped, 3 pints of slightly softened Ben & Jerry's Cherry Garcia ice cream, and 2 cups of World's Best Hot Fudge Sauce (page 501) or one 16-ounce jar Hershey's Hot Fudge Chocolate Shoppe Topping at room temperature, spread one-third of the cherries in the bottom of a prebaked Oreo Cookie Crust (see page 616). Top with half the ice cream, then half the fudge sauce. Repeat the layers, ending with fudge sauce.

✳ **DIVA DO-AHEAD:** At this point, cover and freeze until firm, at least 4 hours and up to 2 months.

Top the pie with 1½ cups of heavy cream that has been whipped with an electric mixer until stiff peaks form.

**Gorilla Pie:** To begin, you will need 3 medium-size medium-ripe bananas, peeled and sliced into ½-inch-thick rounds, 2 cups of World's Best Hot Fudge Sauce (page 501) or one 16-ounce jar Hershey's Hot Fudge Chocolate Shoppe Topping at room temperature, 1½ cups of chopped dry-roasted peanuts, and 3 pints of slightly softened vanilla ice cream. Distribute half the bananas over a prebaked Oreo Cookie Crust (see page 616). Cover with half the fudge sauce and half the ice cream. Sprinkle evenly with half the peanuts and repeat the layers, ending with the remaining peanuts.

✳ **DIVA DO-AHEAD:** At this point, cover and freeze until firm, at least 4 hours and up to 2 months.

Top the pie with 1½ cups of heavy cream that has been whipped with an electric mixer until stiff peaks form.

**Chocolate Mint Pie:** To begin, you will need 3 pints of softened mint chocolate chip ice cream, 20 coarsely chopped Andes Mints, and 2 cups of World's Best Hot Fudge Sauce (page 501) or one 16-ounce jar Hershey's Hot Fudge Chocolate Shoppe Topping at room temperature. Spread 1 pint of the ice cream over the bottom of a prebaked Oreo Cookie Crust (see page 616), cover with one-third of the fudge sauce, and sprinkle with half the chopped mints. Repeat the layers two more times, ending with fudge sauce.

✳ **DIVA DO-AHEAD:** At this point, cover and freeze until firm, at least 4 hours and up to 2 months.

Top the pie with 1½ cups heavy cream that has been whipped with an electric mixer until stiff peaks form.

**Straw-Anna Pie:** To begin, you will need 2 pints of strawberries, hulled, sliced ½ inch thick, and tossed with ¼ cup sugar; 3 medium-size, medium-ripe bananas, peeled and cut into ½-inch-thick rounds; and 3 pints of slightly softened vanilla ice cream. Spread half the strawberries in the bottom of a prebaked Vanilla Wafer Crust (see page 617) top with half the bananas, and spread with half the ice cream. Repeat the layers, ending with the ice cream.

✳ **DIVA DO-AHEAD:** At this point, cover and freeze until firm, at least 4 hours and up to 2 months.

Top the pie with 1½ cups of heavy cream that has been whipped with an electric mixer until stiff peaks form. Sprinkle with ¾ cup of toasted slivered almonds (see page 83).

**Raspberry and Cream Pie:** To begin, you will need 2 cups of Raspberry Sauce (page 503) combined with 1 cup of fresh or individually frozen raspberries, defrosted, and 3 pints of slightly softened vanilla ice cream. Spread one-third of the raspberry mixture over the bottom of a prebaked Vanilla Wafer Crust (see page 617) and top with 1 pint of the ice cream. Repeat the layers two more times.

✳ **DIVA DO-AHEAD:** At this point, cover and freeze until firm, at least 4 hours and up to 2 months.

Top the pie with 1½ cups of heavy cream that has been whipped with an electric mixer until stiff peaks form.

# Pumpkin Ice Cream Pie

Makes one 9-inch pie; serves 10 to 12

Here's another dessert you can serve for Thanksgiving. I call this the pie for people who don't like pumpkin pie. The pumpkin is lightened by mixing it with vanilla ice cream, which gives it an ethereal quality that most people love. This is divine with warmed Butterscotch Sauce (page 502).

### Graham Cracker Crust

**6 tablespoons (¾ stick) unsalted butter, melted**

**3 cups graham cracker crumbs (30 to 36 whole graham crackers)**

**6 tablespoons granulated sugar**

**½ teaspoon ground cinnamon**

### Filling

**One 16-ounce can pumpkin puree (2 cups)**

**⅔ cup firmly packed light brown sugar**

**1 teaspoon ground cinnamon**

**1 teaspoon ground ginger**

**¾ teaspoon ground nutmeg**

**⅛ teaspoon ground cloves**

**3 pints vanilla ice cream, softened**

**1.** Preheat the oven to 375°F. Coat the inside of a 9-inch springform pan with nonstick cooking spray. To make the crust, blend the crust ingredients together in a large bowl and press evenly into the bottom and up the sides of the prepared pan. Bake for 6 to 8 minutes, until crisp. Allow to cool completely.

**DIVA DO-AHEAD:** At this point, freeze the crust while you make the filling, or up to 2 months. Do not defrost.

**2.** To make the filling, in a 3-quart saucepan over low heat, combine the pumpkin, brown sugar, and spices and cook, stirring, until the sugar dissolves and the puree thickens, about 5 minutes. Refrigerate until cool.

**3.** Beat together the ice cream and cooled pumpkin mixture, and spread this evenly in the frozen piecrust.

**DIVA DO-AHEAD:** At this point, cover and freeze until firm, at least 4 hours and up to 6 weeks.

**4.** Remove the pie from the freezer 15 minutes before serving. Remove the ring from the pan. To serve, cut the pie with a sharp knife, dipping the knife into hot water after each cut.

# Crispy Rice Bars

Makes twenty-four 2-inch bars

Everyone wants to be a kid some of the time, and these treats will bring out the kid in all of your guests. Easy to put together and fun to eat, these treats won't last long and they are terrific at a barbecue buffet. One of my friends even had her wedding cake made out of these crispy treats.

**5 tablespoons unsalted butter**

**Two 10.5-ounce bags miniature marshmallows**

**One 7-ounce jar marshmallow creme, such as Marshmallow Fluff**

**9 cups crispy rice cereal**

**1.** Line a 15 x 12-inch baking sheet with a silicone liner, parchment or waxed paper, or aluminum foil and coat with nonstick cooking spray.

**2.** In a large saucepan, melt the butter over medium-low heat, add the marshmallows and marshmallow creme, and stir until the marshmallows are melted. Gently stir in the cereal and continue stirring to coat. Pour into the prepared pan, spreading it to the sides of the pan.

**3.** Let the mixture cool completely. Cut into twenty-four 2-inch bars or squares and serve.

✳ **DIVA DO-AHEAD:** At this point, you can cover with plastic wrap and store at room temperature for up to 24 hours.

## Diva Variations

Children love to eat these bars. For added color and even more kid appeal, add 2 cups of small candies, such as Jelly Bellies, mini-chocolate chips, or small gummy bears, when you stir in the cereal.

**Chocolate-Covered Crispy Rice Bars:** If you would like to gild the lily, melt 1 cup of semi-sweet chocolate chips and drizzle over the squares or dip one side of each of the bars into the chocolate; if you dip them, set them on a wire rack to let the chocolate harden.

**Crispy Rice Cake:** To make your rice bars into a cake, I recommend making a double batch in two 9-inch and two 8-inch cake pans. When the bars have cooled, arrange them on a serving platter in tiers beginning with the 9-inch layers. You can then cover the entire "cake" in a rolled fondant icing for the full wedding cake effect. Fondant can be purchased at craft or gourmet shops. Roll it out to a size that will cover the top and sides of your squares, and wrap the fondant around them. If you like, decorate the fondant with roses, leaves, or other piped decorations.

# Belafonte Bars

Makes twenty-four 2-inch squares

Named after the Harry Belafonte song about the witch doctor who put the lime in the coconut, these will cure whatever is ailing you. A riff on lemon squares, these have a cleaner flavor from the lime juice, and the macadamias and coconut give the crust an interesting taste.

### Crust

**2 cups unbleached all-purpose flour**

**½ cup confectioners' sugar**

**1 cup (2 sticks) cold unsalted butter**

**1 cup Baker's Angel Flake coconut**

**½ cup chopped macadamia nuts**

### Filling

**1½ cups granulated sugar**

**½ cup fresh lime juice**

**¼ cup unbleached all-purpose flour**

**1 teaspoon baking powder**

**4 large eggs**

**Confectioners' sugar for dusting**

**1.** Preheat the oven to 350°F. Coat a 13 x 9-inch baking pan with nonstick cooking spray.

**2.** To make the crust, combine the ingredients in a food processor and pulse until the mixture resembles small peas. Press into the bottom of the prepared pan, using your knuckles to press down. Bake until browned, about 20 minutes. Remove from the oven and let cool for 10 minutes.

**3.** To make the filling, combine the ingredients in the food processor and process until smooth. Pour over the baked crust and bake until the filling is set, another 20 minutes.

**4.** Let cool completely, then cut into twenty-four 2-inch squares and dust with confectioners' sugar.

✳ **DIVA DO-AHEAD:** At this point, you can cover and refrigerate for up to 2 days or freeze for up to 2 months.

## The Diva Says:

You can make a double batch in a 15 x 12-inch jelly roll pan; the baking time will be the same.

An easy way to press a crust into a baking pan is to cut a piece of plastic wrap 4 inches longer than the pan. Use the plastic to help press in the crust.

### From Baking Pan to Freezer

Freezing large pans might seem cumbersome if you don't have a lot of freezer space, but you can always remove the cakes or bars from their baking pans and stack them in smaller plastic boxes, separated by plastic wrap.

# World's Greatest Cream Cheese Brownies

Makes twenty-four 2-inch squares

It will be hard for you to have just one of these decadently rich brownies swirled with cream cheese filling and topped with a luxurious chocolate frosting. They freeze well and are a terrific dessert to bring to someone's house; just make sure you bring along a copy of the recipe because you are bound to get requests.

### Filling

**One 8-ounce package cream cheese, softened**

**⅓ cup sugar**

**1 large egg**

**½ teaspoon vanilla extract**

### Brownie Batter

**1 cup (2 sticks) unsalted butter, softened and cut into chunks**

**2 cups sugar**

**4 large eggs**

**1 cup unsweetened cocoa powder**

**1 cup unbleached all-purpose flour**

### Frosting

**1 cup sugar**

**5 tablespoons unsalted butter**

**⅓ cup milk**

**One 6-ounce package semisweet chocolate chips**

**1.** To make the filling, put the ingredients in a food processor and process until smooth. Remove from the work bowl and set aside.

**2.** Preheat the oven to 350°F. Coat a 13 x 9-inch baking pan with nonstick cooking spray.

**3.** To make the batter, combine the butter, sugar, and eggs in the food processor and process until smooth. Add the cocoa and pulse 4 or 5 times. Add the flour and pulse until it disappears into the mixture.

**4.** Spread half the chocolate batter over the bottom of the prepared pan; dot with the cream cheese filling, then top with the remaining chocolate batter, and swirl the batter and filling with a spatula. Bake until a skewer inserted into the center comes out with some crumbs adhering to it, 35 to 40 minutes.

**5.** To make the frosting, in a small saucepan, combine the sugar, butter, and milk.

Bring to a boil and continue boiling for 1 minute, stirring constantly. Remove from the heat and stir in the chocolate pieces until smooth. Pour over the warm brownies. Let cool on a rack for 10 minutes and, while still warm, cut into twenty-four 2-inch squares.

✳ **DIVA DO-AHEAD:** At this point, you can cool completely, cover, and refrigerate for up to 2 days or freeze for up to 2 months. Defrost in the refrigerator, if necessary, and remove 1 hour before serving to bring to room temperature for the best flavor and texture.

### Diva Variations

**World's Greatest Mint Cream Cheese Brownies:** Add 2 tablespoons of green crème de menthe or 2 teaspoons of peppermint extract to the cream cheese filling.

**World's Greatest Mocha Cream Cheese Brownies:** Add 1 tablespoon of espresso powder to the cream cheese filling and 1 tablespoon of espresso powder to the frosting. Decorate the finished and frosted brownies with chocolate-covered espresso beans.

### Diva Brownie Multiplication

You can double the recipe and bake in a 15 x 12-inch jelly roll pan; the baking time will be the same.

### Cutting the World's Greatest Brownies

I recommend you cut these while they are still warm. If you wait, the cream cheese will set up and make it more difficult to cut even, pretty squares. Make sure you wipe the knife before each cut so your cuts are clean.

# Crème de Menthe Layered Brownies

Makes twenty-four 2-inch squares

There is something soothing about the combination of mint and chocolate. These chewy chocolate brownies, frosted with a cool mint frosting and drizzled with a bittersweet chocolate glaze, make a fabulous ending to any meal. I recommend you make them a day or two in advance.

### Brownies

**1 cup (2 sticks) unsalted butter**

**4 ounces unsweetened chocolate**

**2 cups granulated sugar**

**4 large eggs**

**1 cup unbleached all-purpose flour**

**2 teaspoons white crème de menthe or peppermint extract**

### Crème de Menthe Frosting

**¼ cup (½ stick) unsalted butter or margarine, softened**

**2 cups confectioners' sugar**

**1 teaspoon white crème de menthe or peppermint extract**

**1 tablespoon milk, as needed**

### Chocolate Glaze

**6 ounces bittersweet or semisweet chocolate, coarsely chopped**

**3 tablespoons unsalted butter**

**1.** Preheat the oven to 350°F. Coat a 13 x 9-inch baking pan with nonstick cooking spray.

**2.** To make the brownies, in a large microwaveable bowl, melt the butter and chocolate on High for 2 minutes, stirring to melt the chocolate. (Alternatively, melt the chocolate and butter in a small, heavy saucepan over low heat on the stove top and transfer to a large bowl.) Add the granulated sugar and eggs, stirring to combine. Add the flour and crème de menthe and beat until smooth. Pour into the prepared pan and bake until a skewer inserted into the center comes out with a few crumbs clinging to it, 25 to 30 minutes. Remove from the oven and let cool completely in the pan on a rack.

**3.** To make the frosting, in a large bowl, with an electric mixer, beat together the butter, confectioners' sugar, and crème de menthe until smooth. Add the milk if the frosting needs thinning. Spread the frosting evenly over the cooled brownies.

**4.** To make the glaze, in a small microwaveable bowl, melt the chocolate and butter together on High for 1 to 2 minutes. (Alternatively, melt them together in a small, heavy saucepan over low heat on the stove top.) With an offset spatula, spread the glaze evenly over the frosting. Chill the brownies for 1 hour, then cut into twenty-four 2-inch squares.

✳ **DIVA DO-AHEAD:** At this point, you can cover and refrigerate for up to 2 days or freeze for up to 6 weeks. Defrost before serving.

### Shaving Chocolate

If you have a bar of chocolate that is too thick to chop, shave the chocolate off the bar with a serrated knife.

# Peanut Butter Brownie Squares

Makes twenty-four 2-inch bars

The combination of peanut butter and chocolate is a classic, and these brownies disappear fast whenever I make them. Simple yet elegant, with a drizzle of chocolate and a shower of chopped peanuts, these will be a favorite with your guests.

### Brownies

1 cup (2 sticks) unsalted butter

4 ounces unsweetened chocolate

2 cups granulated sugar

4 large eggs

1 cup unbleached all-purpose flour

### Peanut Butter Frosting

1 cup creamy peanut butter (don't use natural)

½ cup (1 stick) unsalted butter

3 cups confectioners' sugar

2 to 3 tablespoons milk, as needed

### Chocolate Drizzle

½ cup semisweet chocolate chips

1 teaspoon unsalted butter or margarine

½ cup chopped honey-roasted peanuts

**1.** Preheat the oven to 350°F. Line a 15 x 10-inch jelly roll pan with a silicone liner, parchment paper, or aluminum foil and coat with nonstick cooking spray.

**2.** To make the brownies, in a large microwaveable bowl, melt the butter and chocolate together in the microwave on High for 2 minutes, stirring to melt the chocolate. (Alternatively, melt them together in a large, heavy saucepan over low heat on the stove top.) Stir in the granulated sugar, eggs, and flour, beating until smooth. Pour into the prepared pan and bake until a skewer inserted into the center comes out with some crumbs adhering to it, 14 to 16 minutes. Remove from the oven and let cool completely in the pan on a rack.

✳ **DIVA DO-AHEAD:** At this point, you can cover and refrigerate for up to 3 days or freeze for up to 2 months. Defrost before continuing.

**3.** To make the frosting, with an electric mixer, cream together the peanut butter and butter in a large bowl until smooth. Add the confectioners' sugar and beat on low speed until the mixture begins to come together. Gradually add the milk and beat at medium speed until the frosting reaches a spreadable consistency. Spread over the cooled brownies.

**4.** To make the drizzle, in a small microwaveable bowl, melt the chocolate and butter together on High for 1 minute, stirring to melt the chocolate. (Alternatively, melt them together in a small, heavy saucepan over low heat on the stove top.) Drizzle over the peanut butter frosting in a pretty design. Sprinkle the brownies with the peanuts and refrigerate until the chocolate is firm, about 2 hours.

**5.** Cut the brownies into twenty-four 2-inch bars.

✳ **DIVA DO-AHEAD:** At this point, you can cover and refrigerate for up to 3 days or freeze for up to 2 months. They're great right from the freezer!

## DRIZZLE, DRIZZLE EVERYWHERE

**Drizzles are the professional** chef's trick for making dishes visually appealing. You can create a little of this magic in your own kitchen, but you will need a large space around the dish you are drizzling so that the drizzle actually begins and ends off the plate. Begin by laying some plastic wrap or paper towels around the dish to create a 6-inch border for catching the drips. To drizzle the Peanut Butter Brownie Squares with chocolate, dip a large rubber spatula into the melted chocolate mixture. Holding the spatula 4 to 6 inches above the dish, begin drizzling at the far end of the plastic wrap, continuing across the dish in a diagonal or another decorative pattern—it's very much like flicking paint off a brush. Instead of using a spatula, you can also put the chocolate in a squeeze bottle (the chef's best friend) or a plastic bag with a corner snipped off and drizzle with that.

# Caramel-Pecan Turtle Brownies

Makes twenty-four 2-inch squares

Chocolate-covered caramel-and-pecan candies are called "turtles," and these brownies are another example of how decadently divine chocolate and caramel are together. The caramel layer remains a bit soft at room temperature, but you can refrigerate before serving if you want a less oozy presentation.

1 cup (2 sticks) cold unsalted butter, cut into bits

2 cups sugar

4 large eggs

1 cup unsweetened cocoa powder

1 cup unbleached all-purpose flour

One 14-ounce bag Kraft caramels

2 tablespoons milk

2 cups pecan halves

**1.** Preheat the oven to 350°F. Coat a 13 x 9-inch baking pan with nonstick cooking spray.

**2.** Combine the butter, sugar, and eggs in a food processor and process until smooth. Add the cocoa and pulse 4 or 5 times. Add the flour and pulse until it disappears into the mixture.

**3.** Remove the wrappers from the caramels and place in a heavy saucepan over medium heat. Add the milk and stir until the caramels are melted.

**4.** Spread half the chocolate batter over the bottom of the prepared pan, then pour the caramel over that, keeping it away from the edges of the pan. (The caramel can seep out and stick to the bottom of the pan, making it difficult to remove the cooled brownies.) Top the caramel with half the pecans, then the remaining chocolate batter. It is easiest to dot the top of the caramel layer with blobs of the chocolate batter, rather than to try and spread out the batter in an even layer. The chocolate batter may not totally cover the caramel layer—that's okay. Sprinkle the remaining pecans evenly over the top and bake until a skewer inserted into the center comes out with some crumbs and caramel on it, 30 to 35 minutes.

**5.** Remove from the oven, cut the brownies into squares, and leave them in the pan on a rack to cool completely.

✳ **DIVA DO-AHEAD:** At this point, you can cover and refrigerate for up to 2 days or freeze for up to 6 weeks.

# Sour Cream Cheesecake Squares

Makes thirty-six 1½-inch squares

I have been making these cheesecake squares for longer than I care to remember. They are a delicious alternative to making a large cheesecake in a springform pan, and you can garnish the top of each square with fruit, crumbled espresso beans, chocolate drizzle, or a fruit sauce. I advise you to make these at least 1 or 2 days before serving.

### Graham Cracker Crust

**1½ cups graham cracker crumbs (about 18 whole crackers)**

**½ cup (1 stick) unsalted butter, melted**

**½ cup sugar**

### Cream Cheese Filling

**Three 8-ounce packages cream cheese, softened**

**1 cup sugar**

**5 large eggs**

**1½ teaspoons vanilla extract**

### Sour Cream Topping

**2 cups sour cream**

**¼ cup sugar**

**1 teaspoon vanilla extract**

**1.** Preheat the oven to 325°F. Coat a 13 x 9-inch baking pan with nonstick cooking spray.

**2.** To make the crust, in a large bowl, combine the ingredients and press into the bottom and halfway up the sides of the prepared pan. Set aside.

**3.** To make the filling, with an electric mixer, cream together the cream cheese and sugar in a large bowl until light and fluffy, about 4 minutes. Add the eggs, one at a time, beating after each addition. Add the vanilla and beat until the filling is smooth. Pour into the crust and bake until set, 35 to 40 minutes.

**4.** Meanwhile, make the topping. In a small bowl, stir together the sour cream, sugar, and vanilla.

**5.** When the cheesecake is done, remove from the oven and increase the oven temperature to 450°F. Spread the sour cream mixture over the hot cheesecake and return to the oven for 5 minutes.

**6.** Remove from the oven and immediately cut into squares. Let cool completely in the pan on a rack.

✳ **DIVA DO-AHEAD:** At this point, cover and refrigerate for at least 6 hours and up to 2 days or freeze for up to 2 months.

# Peter's Pumpkin Bars

Makes about forty 2-inch bars

Remember Peter, Peter, pumpkin eater from the nursery rhyme? The story went that he had a wife and couldn't keep her, but if he'd made her these delectable bars, he'd have been much more successful! Ginger-and-clove-spiced pumpkin cake is frosted with orange cream cheese frosting for a spicy sweet treat in the fall or anytime. I recommend using canned pumpkin because you are adding so much flavoring that you won't be able to tell the difference between fresh and canned.

Bars

**4 large eggs**

**1⅔ cups granulated sugar**

**1 cup canola oil**

**One 16-ounce can pumpkin puree (2 cups)**

**2 cups unbleached all-purpose flour**

**2 teaspoons baking powder**

**1 teaspoon baking soda**

**2 teaspoons pumpkin pie spice**

Orange Cream Cheese Frosting

**One 3-ounce package cream cheese, softened**

**½ cup (1 stick) unsalted butter or margarine, softened**

**1 teaspoon orange oil, or 2 teaspoons orange extract**

**2 cups confectioners' sugar**

**1 to 2 tablespoons milk, as needed**

**1.** Preheat the oven to 350°F. Line a 15 x 10-inch jelly roll pan with a silicone liner, aluminum foil, or parchment paper. If you are using foil or parchment, coat with non-stick cooking spray.

**2.** To make the bars, in a large bowl, beat together the eggs, granulated sugar, and canola oil until blended. Add the pumpkin puree and mix until smooth. Stir in the flour, baking powder, baking soda, and pumpkin pie spice and continue stirring until smooth. Pour into the prepared pan and bake until a skewer inserted into the center comes out clean, 20 to 25 minutes.

**3.** Remove from the oven and let cool completely in the pan on a rack.

**4.** To make the frosting, with an electric mixer, beat the cream cheese, butter, and orange oil in a large bowl until blended, or process in a food processor until smooth. Add the confectioners' sugar and beat or process until the mixture reaches a spreadable consistency. Sometimes the butter or cream cheese will have excess water in it and you will need to add a bit more sugar. Or the mixture may seem dry; in that case, add a bit of milk to thin it. Spread the frosting over the cooled cake.

✳ **DIVA DO-AHEAD:** At this point, you can cover and refrigerate for up to 2 days or freeze for up to 6 weeks. Defrost before serving.

**5.** Cut into forty 2-inch bars.

# Cranberry Bliss Bars

Makes about forty 2-inch bars

Every fall, Starbucks makes these delectable treats, and I bought close to 50 of them while trying to figure out how they're made. This is very close to the original, but I like it a little better because I have added orange oil to the batter and frosting. A dense bar flecked with dried cranberries and white chocolate bits, it freezes beautifully.

Bars

1 cup (2 sticks) unsalted butter, melted

1½ cups firmly packed light brown sugar

½ cup granulated sugar

4 large eggs

1 teaspoon orange oil, or 2 teaspoons orange extract

2½ cups unbleached all-purpose flour

2 teaspoons baking powder

½ teaspoon ground ginger

½ teaspoon pumpkin pie spice

¾ cup unsweetened dried cranberries

¾ cup white chocolate chips

### Creamy Orange Frosting

**One 3-ounce package cream cheese, softened**

**6 tablespoons (¾ stick) unsalted butter or margarine**

**2 cups confectioners' sugar**

**½ teaspoon orange oil, or 1 teaspoon orange extract**

### Garnish

**¼ cup unsweetened dried cranberries**

**¼ cup white chocolate chips**

**2 tablespoons grated orange zest**

### Drizzle

**8 ounces white chocolate, chopped**

**2 tablespoons unsalted butter**

**1.** Preheat the oven to 350°F. Line a 15 x 10-inch jelly roll pan with a silicone liner, aluminum foil, or parchment paper. If you are using foil or parchment, coat it with nonstick cooking spray.

**2.** To make the bars, with an electric mixer, beat together the butter, brown and granulated sugars, eggs, and orange oil in a large bowl until combined. Add the flour, baking powder, and spices and beat until the flour begins to blend into the batter, 45 seconds to 1 minute. Add the cranberries and chips, stirring just to blend and being careful not to overmix. Spread in the prepared pan and bake until a skewer inserted into the center comes out with a few crumbs adhering to it, 15 to 17 minutes. Remove from the oven and let cool completely in the pan on a rack.

**3.** To make the frosting, with an electric mixer, cream together the cream cheese and butter in a large bowl until fluffy, or

process them in a food processor. Add the confectioners' sugar and orange oil and beat or process until the frosting reaches a spreadable consistency. Spread it evenly over the cooled bars.

※ **DIVA DO-AHEAD:** The frosting can be refrigerated for up to 3 days or frozen for up to 2 months.

**4.** For the garnish, sprinkle the frosted bars with the cranberries and white chocolate chips.

**5.** To make the drizzle, in the top of a double boiler set over simmering water, melt the chopped white chocolate with the butter, stirring until smooth. Drizzle over the frosting in a decorative pattern and garnish with the orange zest.

※ **DIVA DO-AHEAD:** At this point, you can cover and refrigerate for up to 3 days or freeze for up to 6 weeks.

# Amaretto Shortbread Bars

Makes about forty 2-inch squares

These crisp and crunchy shortbreads are a favorite with all my guests. Serve them with fresh berries and Vanilla Custard (page 641) and you've got yourself one heck of an easy dessert.

> 1 cup sugar, plus extra for sprinkling
>
> 2 cups unbleached all-purpose flour
>
> 1 large egg, separated
>
> ¼ cup amaretto
>
> 1 cup (2 sticks) cold unsalted butter, cut into bits
>
> ¾ cup sliced almonds

**1.** Preheat the oven to 325°F. Coat a 13 x 9-inch baking pan with nonstick cooking spray.

**2.** Put the sugar and flour in a food processor and pulse to combine.

**3.** In a small bowl, stir the egg yolk together with 2 tablespoons of the amaretto.

**4.** Put the butter on top of the flour-and-sugar mixture and pulse until crumbly. With the machine running, add the yolk mixture through the feed tube and turn the machine off as soon as the mixture begins to come together (this should not take too long). Spread in the prepared pan, pressing down the dough to make it about ½ inch thick. Make sure the layer is compact and doesn't appear crumbly.

**5.** Beat together the egg white and remaining 2 tablespoons of amaretto in a small bowl and brush over the shortbread. Sprinkle the top with the almonds, then sprinkle with sugar. Bake until the almonds are golden brown, about 40 minutes. Remove from the oven and let cool in the pan for 10 minutes.

**6.** Cut the shortbread into 2-inch squares with a sharp knife and let cool completely in the pan.

✳ **DIVA DO-AHEAD:** At this point, you can store in an airtight container for up to 3 days or freeze for up to 2 months.

# Faye's Fabulous Sugar Cookies

Makes about forty-eight 3-inch cookies

Faye Volkman is a lovely woman who works at CooksWares in Cincinnati, where I am privileged to teach. When the recipe for these cookies appeared in their newsletter, I headed straight to the kitchen to try them. They were the best sugar cookies I had ever made. Simple to put together, they do need to chill before you roll them out. Then you can decorate them with sprinkles, cinnamon sugar, maple sugar (divine!), or frosting. However you decide to top them, I guarantee you'll keep this recipe and make it again and again.

1½ cups (3 sticks) unsalted butter, softened

1⅓ cups granulated sugar

2 teaspoons vanilla extract

2 large eggs

3 cups unbleached all-purpose flour

½ teaspoon baking soda

1 teaspoon cream of tartar

¼ cup milk

Colored sprinkles, sugar, cinnamon sugar, or maple sugar for decorating the cookies

**1.** With an electric mixer, cream together the butter and granulated sugar in a large bowl until fluffy. Add the vanilla and eggs, one at a time, beating after each addition.

## Ready to Roll

Cookie doughs need to be kept cold until you're ready to roll. Once on the counter, they will soften within 10 minutes.

Add the flour, baking soda, and cream of tartar and beat on low speed until the dough comes together, about 2 minutes. Turn out onto a large sheet of plastic wrap and flatten into a 1-inch-thick square.

✳ **DIVA DO-AHEAD:** At this point, refrigerate for at least 2 hours and up to 2 days or freeze for up to 2 months. Defrost before proceeding.

**2.** Preheat the oven to 375°F. Line 2 baking sheets with a silicone liner, parchment paper, or aluminum foil.

**3.** Working with one-quarter of the dough at a time, roll it out onto a floured surface with a floured rolling pin to about ¼-inch thickness. Cut with the cookie cutters of your choice and place on the prepared baking sheets. When you have used up all the dough, brush each cookie with a little bit of milk and sprinkle with colored sprinkles or sugar. Bake until lightly browned around the edges, 10 to 12 minutes.

**4.** Let the cookies cool on the baking sheets for 3 to 4 minutes before transferring to a rack to cool completely.

**✳ DIVA DO-AHEAD:** At this point, you can store in an airtight container at room temperature for up to 4 days or freeze for up to 2 months.

### Diva Variation

If you would like to make frosted cookies, brush them with milk, but omit the sugar or sprinkles. When the cookies are cooled, decorate with your choice of frosting.

### Keeping the Kids Busy

Having a party and inviting children? Bake a batch of Faye's Fabulous Sugar Cookies (left), make up pots of frosting (or purchase canned frosting), and buy lots of sprinkles and decorations appropriate to the season. Let the kids use small butter knives to decorate the cookies, which they can take home after the party. If there are very young children, then I recommend giving them graham crackers to decorate, rather than the cookies. Since this might get messy, tape black plastic garbage bags onto the floor underneath the cookie table. Tape butcher paper to the table and, when the kids are finished, just roll up the paper and plastic and toss them away.

# Ryan's Milk Chocolate Chip Cookies 🥤🥛🍸

Makes about thirty-six 2-inch cookies

I don't know any other food that has so much nostalgia associated with it; for some reason, a chocolate chip cookie can just help make the day go better. My son, Ryan, loves milk chocolate chips in his cookies, but you can certainly substitute your favorite chips, whether semisweet, white, or any of the flavored chips on the market. I'm including this recipe so that some lucky woman (a smart cookie) can make these for Ryan!

| | |
|---|---|
| 1 cup (2 sticks) unsalted butter, softened | 2⅓ cups unbleached all-purpose flour |
| 1 cup firmly packed light brown sugar | 1 teaspoon salt |
| ½ cup granulated sugar | 1 teaspoon baking soda |
| 2 large eggs | One 12-ounce bag milk chocolate chips |
| 2 teaspoons vanilla extract | |

**1.** Preheat the oven to 375°F. Line 2 baking sheets with a silicone liner, aluminum foil, or parchment paper.

**2.** With an electric mixer, cream together the butter and both sugars in a large bowl until light and fluffy, about 2 minutes. Add the eggs and vanilla and beat until combined. Add the flour, salt, and baking soda and beat until the flour disappears into the dough, about 1½ minutes. Stir in the chips.

**3.** Using a small scoop (about 2 tablespoons), drop mounds of dough 1½ inches apart on the prepared sheets. Wet your hands and press down a bit to flatten them. Bake until golden brown around the edges but still a bit soft in the center, 12 to 14 minutes.

**4.** Let cool for 5 minutes on the baking sheets, remove the cookies from the sheets, and let cool completely on the rack.

✳ **DIVA DO-AHEAD:** At this point, store in an airtight container at room temperature for up to 4 days or freeze for up to 2 months.

## Diva Variations

Although Ryan likes these cookies as is, here are some add-ins that are favorites with the other members of my family:

- One 12-ounce package of semisweet chocolate chips and 1 cup of chopped pecans or walnuts

- One 12-ounce package of white chocolate chips and 1 cup of chopped macadamia nuts

- One 12-ounce package of peanut butter chips and 1 cup of chopped honey-roasted peanuts

- 1 cup of peanut butter chips and 1 cup of milk chocolate or semisweet chocolate chips

- One 12-ounce package of mint chocolate chips

- 2 cups of your favorite candy bars, coarsely chopped (about 12 ounces), such as Baby Ruth, Snickers, or Nestlé Crunch bars

- 2 cups of plain M&M's candies

- 2 cups of chopped Reese's Peanut Butter Cups (You can also use the Reese's chips if you like, but the chopped peanut butter cups are awesome.)

## Cookies as Gifts

I dedicate the week after Thanksgiving to baking two different types of cookies per day to give to friends for Christmas gifts. I usually make bar cookies, which have a great yield, and freeze them. Then the week before Christmas I defrost them, arrange them on pretty holiday-themed paper plates, and cover with holiday-themed plastic wrap. They are much appreciated during that last week before Christmas, when everyone is too busy to think, let alone bake!

# Black and White Chocolate Chip Cookies

Makes 3 to 4 dozen cookies

These decadently delicious chocolate cookies are a bit delicate, but well worth the extra care required to make them. They freeze well, but I don't think you'll have many leftovers.

1½ cups (3 sticks) unsalted butter, softened

1½ cups firmly packed light brown sugar

1 cup granulated sugar

2 teaspoons vanilla extract

3 large eggs

1 cup Dutch-process unsweetened cocoa powder

3 cups unbleached all-purpose flour

1½ teaspoons baking soda

One 12-ounce bag white chocolate chips

One 6-ounce bag semisweet chocolate chips

**1.** Preheat the oven to 350°F. Line 2 baking sheets with a silicone liner, aluminum foil, or parchment paper.

**2.** With an electric mixer, cream the butter and both sugars together in a large bowl until light and fluffy. Add the vanilla and the eggs, one at a time, blending well after each addition. Add the cocoa, flour, baking soda, and both chips, beating until just blended. Make sure you scrape the bottom of the bowl and reblend if there is excess butter or sugar on the bottom.

**3.** With a small scoop (about 2 tablespoons—I like to use an ice cream scoop), drop mounds of dough onto the baking sheets about 2 inches apart. Wet your hands and press down on the cookies to flatten them just a little. Bake for 10 to 12 minutes. The tops will look set, but the cookies will be very soft.

**4.** Remove from the oven, let cool on the sheets for 7 to 10 minutes, then transfer the cookies to racks to cool completely.

✳ **DIVA DO-AHEAD:** At this point, you can store in an airtight container at room temperature for up to 4 days or freeze for up to 2 months.

## Freezing Cookie Dough

The dough for drop cookies freezes well. Scoop it onto baking sheets and freeze until firm, then remove the frozen dough from the sheets and store in zipper-top plastic bags for up to 2 months. When you're ready to bake, take the unbaked cookies out of the freezer and put them on the baking sheet while you preheat the oven. Then pop them in and add 2 to 3 minutes to the baking time.

# Macadamia, White Chocolate, and Coconut Cookies

Makes about thirty-six 2-inch cookies

You can find a similar cookie at stores in your local mall, but I think this version is a knock-out. If you don't like coconut, you can certainly leave it out, but it gives the cookies extra moistness and makes them chewier. These are great to take to a barbecue or picnic or make into ice cream sandwiches.

1 cup (2 sticks) unsalted butter, softened

½ cup granulated sugar

1 cup firmly packed light brown sugar

2 large eggs

2 teaspoons vanilla extract

2¼ cups unbleached all-purpose flour

1 teaspoon baking soda

One 12-ounce bag white chocolate chips

2 cups chopped macadamia nuts

One 10-ounce bag sweetened angel flake coconut

## Hot Baking Sheets and Cool Cookies

When baking soft or chewy cookies, remove them from the oven when the edges begin to brown but the center is still a bit soft. The cookies will continue to cook on the hot baking sheet before they actually cool, becoming crisp around the edges but remaining chewy in the middle. And they won't burn or overcook.

**1.** Preheat the oven to 350°F. Line 2 baking sheets with a silicone liner, aluminum foil, or parchment paper.

**2.** With an electric mixer, cream the butter and both sugars together in a large bowl until fluffy. Add the eggs and vanilla, beating until well combined. With the mixer on low speed, beat in the flour, baking soda, chocolate chips, nuts, and coconut, and continue beating until well blended. Drop the dough onto the prepared sheets in rounded tablespoonfuls, spacing them 1 inch apart. Wet your hands and flatten each ball of dough. Bake until the tops look dry and are beginning to brown, 10 to 12 minutes.

**3.** Remove the cookies from the oven and let cool on the sheets for 10 minutes, then transfer to a rack to cool completely.

✳ **DIVA DO-AHEAD:** At this point, you can store in an airtight container at room temperature for up to 3 days or freeze for up to 2 months.

# Strawberry Cannoli

Makes about 16 cannoli

Crispy cookies replace the deep-fried dough normally used for cannoli. I prefer to make this with fresh strawberries because they don't contain as much liquid as frozen berries, but frozen will work in a pinch. Just make sure you drain them well before stirring them into the filling. If you are serving these on individual plates, pool some Strawberry Sauce (page 640) on each plate, set a cannoli on top, and dust with confectioners' sugar.

## Cannoli Cookies

**½ cup (1 stick) unsalted butter, softened**

**⅔ cup granulated sugar**

**4 large egg whites**

**1 cup unbleached all-purpose flour**

**1 teaspoon grated orange zest**

**½ teaspoon orange extract or ¼ teaspoon orange oil**

## Strawberry Cannoli Filling

**1½ cups heavy cream**

**2 cups mascarpone cheese**

**⅔ cup granulated sugar**

**½ teaspoon orange extract**

**2 cups hulled and finely diced fresh strawberries**

**⅔ cup finely chopped pistachios for garnish**

**Confectioners' sugar for dusting**

**1.** Preheat the oven to 375°F. Line 2 baking sheets with a silicone liner, aluminum foil, or parchment paper.

**2.** To make the cookies, with an electric mixer, beat together the butter and sugar in a medium-size bowl until light and fluffy. Add the egg whites and beat until well combined. On low speed, beat in the flour, orange zest, and extract until smooth.

**3.** Drop 1 tablespoonful of batter onto the baking sheet for each cannoli and spread it with a small offset spatula into a 4-inch circle. You should be able to get 3 or 4 cookies on a sheet. Bake until the edges are golden brown and the center of each cookie is beginning to turn from yellow to gold, 7 to 8 minutes.

**4.** Remove from the oven and, using a large offset spatula, wrap each cookie around a 1-inch dowel or tube, shaping the cookie into a tube. Let cool until crisp, about 3 minutes.

※ **DIVA DO-AHEAD:** At this point, you can let cool and store in an airtight container at room temperature for up to 2 days.

**5.** To make the filling, with an electric mixer, whip the cream in a large bowl until stiff peaks form. Add the mascarpone, sugar, and extract and beat until combined. Fold in the strawberries.

※ **DIVA DO-AHEAD:** At this point, you can cover and refrigerate for up to 24 hours.

**6.** Stir the filling and, using a piping bag fitted with a large plain tip, pipe into the cannoli cookies or use an offset spatula to fill them. Dip the end of the filled cannoli into the pistachios, arrange on a platter, and dust with confectioners' sugar.

※ **DIVA DO-AHEAD:** At this point, you can cover and refrigerate for up to 2 hours.

### The Diva Says:

Traditional cannoli are tube shaped, but you can also shape these cookies into bowls by draping them, hot from the oven, on overturned custard cups, teacups, or small bowls. To serve, pool some sauce on a plate, top with a cannoli "bowl," and fill the bowl with the mascarpone mixture. Garnish with additional sliced berries if desired.

### Diva Variation

If you would like to make chocolate cannoli, substitute unsweetened cocoa powder for ½ cup of the flour.

# Strawberry Sauce

Makes 4 cups

I don't strain this sauce as I do Raspberry Sauce (page 503); I like to leave in chunks of berries. This is a simple sauce to put together. Make it during strawberry season and freeze it for use later in the year.

> 4 pints fresh strawberries, hulled and halved
>
> 1 to 1½ cups sugar, depending on the sweetness of the berries
>
> 2 tablespoons fresh lemon juice

In a 2-quart saucepan, combine the strawberries, sugar, and lemon juice, stirring to dissolve the sugar. Warm over medium heat, stirring, until it begins to simmer gently, then cook over low heat until the berries are softened and the sauce is thickened, about 10 minutes.

※ **DIVA DO-AHEAD:** At this point, you can let cool, cover, and refrigerate for up to 4 days or freeze for up to 2 months.

Serve warm or cold.

# Vanilla Custard

Makes 4 cups; serves 10 to 12

Prepared on the stove top like a cooked pudding, this custard is super simple to make and is a great base for myriad flavors. Used as a dessert sauce, it transforms ordinary cake or cookies into delectable desserts. The custard is thickened with cornstarch, which reduces the chances that the eggs will scramble and gives you a nice, stable custard to work with. If you think it's too thick, thin it with a bit of heavy cream or a flavored liqueur. If you prefer a different flavor, substitute your favorite extract or liqueur for the vanilla; try coconut, orange, lemon, brandy, rum, or whatever strikes your fancy.

⅓ cup sugar

¼ cup cornstarch

3 cups whole milk

6 large egg yolks

2 teaspoons vanilla paste (see The Diva Says), vanilla extract, or an extract or liqueur of your choice

**1.** In a 2-quart saucepan, whisk together the sugar, cornstarch, milk, and egg yolks until smooth. Place over medium-high heat and whisk until the mixture thickens and comes to a boil, 4 to 5 minutes.

**2.** Remove from the heat and stir in the vanilla. Transfer to a glass bowl and press plastic wrap against the surface to keep a skin from forming.

✳ **DIVA DO-AHEAD:** At this point, refrigerate for at least 4 hours and up to 4 days, or freeze for up to 1 month.

The Diva Says:

Vanilla paste is relatively new to the market, but you can find it in gourmet stores. It is fabulous for custards and other desserts in which the alcohol in the vanilla extract will cook off, taking some of the flavor with it. Vanilla paste is made from the tiny seeds of the vanilla bean. It is more convenient to use than a vanilla bean, and the flavor is far superior to that of vanilla extract. Substitute it in equal amounts for extract.

## Saving Your Custard

Sometimes, even if you are very careful, you may end up with scrambled eggs in your custard. When you see this starting to happen, remove the pan from the heat and continue to stir until the custard is thickened. Then strain the custard through a fine-mesh sieve and let cool. That should remove the scrambled eggs from the pudding, and you are the only one to know!

# Chocolate Custard

Makes 4 cups; serves 10 to 12

Great to serve with shortbread cookies for dessert, slathered between layers of cake, or layered with other goodies for parfaits, this recipe will make you look like a star!

⅔ cup sugar

¼ cup cornstarch

½ cup Dutch-process unsweetened cocoa powder

3 cups whole milk

6 large egg yolks

2 teaspoons vanilla extract

## The Proof's in the Pudding

A lot of us don't have time to make our own custard when we entertain on the fly. I usually have some Bird's Dessert Mix in my pantry, a British mix that makes an awesome custard—most people can't tell it's store-bought. You have to cook the custard, then cool it, so it's a bit like making your own, except the eggs and other ingredients are in the mix; you just add milk. Jell-O brand also makes an instant pudding that you can use in a pinch; keep a box on hand, just in case. To change the flavor dramatically, substitute heavy cream for the milk and stir in your favorite extract: vanilla, almond, orange, brandy, or coconut. That should take away the processed flavor and give you a nice dessert.

**1.** In a 2-quart saucepan, whisk together the sugar, cornstarch, cocoa, milk, and egg yolks until smooth. Place the pan over medium heat and whisk until the mixture begins to thicken and comes to a boil, 4 to 5 minutes.

**2.** Remove from the heat and stir in the vanilla. Transfer to a glass bowl and press plastic wrap directly onto the surface to keep a skin from forming.

✳ **DIVA DO-AHEAD:** At this point, refrigerate for at least 4 hours and up to 4 days, or freeze for up to 1 month.

# Chocolate Banana-Rama Pudding Parfaits

Makes 12 parfaits

This dessert features layers of crunchy vanilla wafers, bananas, and vanilla and chocolate custard. Serve it for a terrific ending to a barbecue or casual dinner on the patio. Make sure you cover the bananas completely with the custard, so they don't discolor.

> **3 cups Vanilla Custard (page 641)**
>
> **16 vanilla wafers, crushed**
>
> **1½ cups Chocolate Custard (left)**
>
> **4 small ripe bananas, sliced ½ inch thick**
>
> **½ cup grated chocolate of your choice**
>
> **2 cups heavy cream**
>
> **¼ to ⅓ cup sugar, to your taste**

**1.** Place 2 tablespoons of vanilla custard in the bottom of each 6-ounce parfait glass. Top with a sprinkle of the wafers, 2 tablespoons of chocolate custard, a layer of sliced bananas, and another layer of vanilla custard. Sprinkle the top of each parfait with some grated chocolate.

✳ **DIVA DO-AHEAD:** At this point, cover and refrigerate for at least 2 hours and up to 2 days.

**2.** With an electric mixer, beat the cream in a medium-size bowl until it forms soft peaks, then add the sugar and beat until stiff peaks form.

✳ **DIVA DO-AHEAD:** At this point, you can cover and refrigerate for up to 4 hours. Rewhip with a whisk before using.

**3.** Top each parfait with whipped cream and serve immediately.

## Pudding Parfaits

Pudding parfaits—layers of pudding, cake or crumbled cookies, nuts, and/or fruit—make simple and elegant desserts that you can assemble ahead and bring to the table when you are ready. These look swell in martini and margarita glasses; for casual affairs, clear straight-sided plastic cups are a great option. You can also mix and match the parfaits if you would like to have more than one selection.

## The Diva Says:

Your container will determine how many layers you will have. If you have tall, dramatic parfait glasses, you may have more layers, and that's fine; this isn't an exact science, it's a parfait.

### Diva Variation

You can also make this with only the Vanilla Custard (4½ cups), omitting the chocolate altogether.

# Butterscotch Pudding Parfaits 🥛🥛

Makes 12

All of these layered confections are named for the French word for "perfect"—*parfait*. The butterscotch flavor featured here is *parfait* for those who don't like chocolate.

> 1 recipe Vanilla Custard (page 641)
>
> 24 vanilla wafers, crushed
>
> 1 cup Butterscotch Sauce, homemade (page 502) or store-bought
>
> 2 cups heavy cream
>
> ½ to ⅓ cup sugar, to your taste

**1.** Spoon 2 tablespoons of vanilla custard in the bottom of each 6-ounce parfait glass. Top with a sprinkle of the wafers and then 1 tablespoon of the butterscotch sauce, and repeat the layers.

❋ **DIVA DO-AHEAD:** At this point, cover and refrigerate for at least 4 hours and up to 2 days.

**2.** With an electric mixer, beat the cream until it forms soft peaks. Add the sugar and beat until stiff peaks form.

❋ **DIVA DO-AHEAD:** At this point, you can cover and refrigerate for up to 4 hours. Rewhip with a whisk before using.

**3.** Garnish the parfaits with the whipped cream and serve immediately.

## PERFECT PARFAIT IDEAS

- Fresh fruit makes a great layer between puddings. For twelve 6-ounce servings, you will need 4 cups of custard and 2 cups of chopped or sliced fruits. Some especially good choices are chopped pineapple (try it layered with Vanilla Custard [page 641] and garnished with toasted coconut), sliced fresh strawberries, blackberries, blueberries, raspberries, peeled and chopped kiwi, chopped sweet cherries, mandarin orange segments, and seedless red grapes, cut in half.

- Dried fruits such as chopped apricots, cherries, and cranberries also make a nice layer; you will need 1 to 1½ cups for 12 servings.

- Minimarshmallows layered with Chocolate Custard (page 642) and crushed graham crackers will give you a nice s'mores parfait.

- Crumbled or cut-up cake or ladyfingers and crumbled cookies make great layers; try cubes of angel food cake or pound cake (about 2 cups for 12 servings) or leftover brownies. To spice things up, brush the cake with a little liqueur, rum, or brandy.

# Peach Melba Trifle

Serves 10

Trifle is a traditional English dessert made with ladyfingers or pound cake soaked in a liqueur or sherry, then layered with custard and fruit. This one takes its flavor cues from Peach Melba, the classic poached peach and raspberry dessert, layering them for an amazingly simple but scrumptious confection. You will need a deep, straight-sided dish for a spectacular presentation. A trifle bowl is an inexpensive investment and you can use it for all kinds of other dishes, such as layered vegetable salads or fresh fruit salads. Trifle should be made at least a day ahead of time to let the flavors develop.

**6 cups peeled and thinly sliced fresh peaches or frozen sliced peaches, defrosted**

**½ cup sugar**

**2 tablespoons fresh orange juice**

**Grated zest of 1 orange**

**⅛ teaspoon ground nutmeg**

**¼ cup Grand Marnier or another orange liqueur**

**2 tablespoons Chambord or another raspberry liqueur or water**

**1½ cups seedless raspberry jam**

**One 16-ounce frozen pound cake, defrosted and cut into ½-inch-thick slices**

**¼ cup water**

**1 recipe Vanilla Custard (page 641) flavored with ¼ cup Grand Marnier or another orange liqueur**

**2 cups heavy cream**

**Sliced almonds, toasted (see page 83), for garnish**

**1.** In a large bowl, combine the peaches, sugar, orange juice and zest, nutmeg, and 2 tablespoons of the Grand Marnier, stirring to coat the peaches. Set aside.

**2.** Combine the Chambord and raspberry jam and set aside.

**3.** Cover the bottom of a large glass bowl with a single layer of pound cake slices, cutting them to fit if necessary. Dilute the remaining 2 tablespoons of the Grand Marnier with the water and brush the cake with it. Spread the slices with some of the jam mixture, then cover with a thin layer of custard and some of the peaches. They will have accumulated a lot of juice, so I recommend you use a slotted spoon to transfer them to the serving bowl as you layer them in. (The leftover peach juice is delicious boiled down for about 10 minutes and used as a syrup over ice cream or waffles.) Continue layering in this manner, making sure you spread the ingredients all the way to the sides of the bowl, so they show on the outside. End with a layer of pound cake.

**4.** With an electric mixer, whip the cream in a medium-size bowl until it forms stiff peaks. Spread the cream over the trifle.

✳ **DIVA DO-AHEAD:** At this point, cover and refrigerate for at least 8 and up to 36 hours.

**5.** Sprinkle the almonds over the trifle just before serving.

### Trifle for a Hungry Crowd
To double or triple a trifle recipe for a huge group, layer it in 13 x 9-inch baking dishes and cut it into squares for easier serving.

# Strawberry-Amaretto Trifle 🥤🥛🍷🍸

Serves 12 to 14

This is the trifle I serve for dessert for Christmas dinner when I'm not making Chocolate Tiramisu Cake (page 594), and sometimes I make both. Since strawberries aren't in season in December, I have used individually frozen strawberries with great success. The crushed amaretti cookies are a crunchy surprise, and they give the trifle another layer of flavor.

One 16-ounce frozen pound cake, defrosted and cut into ½-inch-thick slices

½ cup amaretto

1 recipe Vanilla Custard (page 641)

2 tablespoons water

3 cups sliced fresh strawberries, or individually frozen whole strawberries, defrosted and cut in half

1½ cups crushed amaretti cookies (about 14)

2 cups heavy cream, whipped until stiff peaks form

1 cup sliced almonds, toasted (see page 83), for garnish

**1.** Cover the bottom of a large glass bowl or trifle bowl with a single layer of pound cake slices, cutting them to fit if necessary.

**2.** Combine 3 tablespoons of the amaretto with the custard and stir to blend.

**3.** Add the water to the remaining 5 tablespoons of amaretto and brush the pound cake slices in the bowl with some of this. Spread a layer of the custard over the cake, top with a layer of strawberries, and sprinkle with the amaretti cookies. Repeat the layers, ending with strawberries and amaretti. Spread the whipped cream over the top of the trifle and, using the back of a spoon, make the cream stand up in peaks for a little drama.

✳ **DIVA DO-AHEAD:** At this point, you can cover and refrigerate for at least 24 hours and up to 2 days.

**4.** Just before serving, sprinkle with the almonds.

> ## Stabilizing Whipped Cream
>
> To help whipped cream keep its loft, add a package of whipped cream stabilizer before beating it. The cream will stay fluffy for up to 8 hours. You can also make your whipped cream in a $CO_2$-charged canister and pipe it onto your dessert right before serving.

# Strawberry, Pineapple, and Coconut Trifle

Serves 12 to 14

This tropical confection is a delicious ending to a meal and looks divine, with its rum-soaked pound cake, layers of golden pineapple and red strawberries, and shower of toasted coconut on top. Make this when strawberries are in season. For the fresh pineapple, try to find a Maui Gold or Jet Express; these are a bit more expensive, but they taste freshly picked.

**One 16-ounce frozen pound cake, defrosted and cut into ½-inch-thick slices**

**½ cup dark rum, such as Meyer's**

**1 recipe Vanilla Custard (page 641)**

**2 tablespoons water**

**1 medium-size pineapple, peeled, cored, and cut into ½-inch-thick slices**

**3 cups sliced fresh strawberries**

**2 cups heavy cream, whipped until stiff peaks form**

**2 cups Baker's Angel Flake coconut, toasted (see page 593)**

**1.** Cover the bottom of a large glass bowl or trifle bowl with a single layer of pound cake slices, cutting them to fit if necessary.

**2.** Stir 3 tablespoons of the rum into the custard.

**3.** Stir the water into the remaining 5 tablespoons of rum and brush the cake layer with some of this. Spread a layer of custard over the cake and top with a layer of pineapple slices, and then a layer of strawberries. Repeat the layers, ending with the strawberries. Spread the top with the whipped cream.

**✳ DIVA DO-AHEAD:** At this point, you can cover and refrigerate for at least 24 hours and up to 2 days.

**4.** Right before serving, sprinkle the trifle liberally with the toasted coconut.

## The Diva Says:

Fresh pineapple can be quite expensive. If it's out of your budget, I recommend using canned sliced Hawaiian pineapple, though the flavor won't compare. Make sure you drain it well. If you open your fresh pineapple and discover that it has no flavor, marinate it in some confectioners' sugar and a bit of rum to sweeten it up.

## Picking a Fresh Pineapple

Pineapples are picked when they are ripe. Don't buy a pineapple and leave it on the counter, thinking it will ripen there, because it's as ripe as it is going to get and may begin to ferment if you leave it for a few days. (It may even begin to hiss at you!) When selecting a pineapple, pick it up and inspect it for any soft spots—if it has one, don't buy it. The color of pineapples can vary, but I usually look for one that is golden. Although the color doesn't ensure that the pineapple is ripe, it's a good indicator of freshness. Sniff the pineapple at the base of the leaves; if it smells like pineapple, that's your pick. Some people pull out one of the leaves; if it pulls out easily, the pineapple is supposed to be a good one.

# Peach Praline Crumble

Serves 12 to 14

I love crumbles because there is no bottom piecrust to get soggy, just a crumbly, buttery topping that absorbs the flavors of the fruit while staying crisp. Crumbles work well on the buffet table and will please your guests; people love homey, comforting desserts. This is delicious with vanilla ice cream or unsweetened whipped cream.

### Peach Mixture

**8 cups peeled and sliced (½-inch thick) fresh peaches or frozen sliced peaches, defrosted**

**2 teaspoons fresh lemon juice (if you are using fresh peaches)**

**1¼ cups granulated sugar**

**2 tablespoons cornstarch**

**¼ teaspoon ground nutmeg**

### Crumble Topping

**1½ cups firmly packed light brown sugar**

**1½ cups unbleached all-purpose flour**

**1 cup (2 sticks) cold unsalted butter, cut into bits**

**1½ cups chopped pecans**

**1.** To make the peach mixture, in a large bowl, combine the peaches, lemon juice if using (this will prevent the fresh peaches from discoloring), granulated sugar, cornstarch, and nutmeg, stirring to dissolve the sugar.

✳ **DIVA DO-AHEAD:** At this point, you can store in a zipper-top plastic bag and refrigerate for up to 2 days.

**2.** To make the crumble topping, in a food processor, combine the brown sugar and flour and pulse 3 times to blend well. Scatter the butter evenly over the top and pulse 6 to 8 times, until the mixture forms crumbs but doesn't hold together.

✳ **DIVA DO-AHEAD:** At this point, you can store in a zipper-top plastic bag and refrigerate for up to 3 days or freeze for up to 2 months. Bring to room temperature before continuing.

**3.** Preheat the oven to 400°F.

**4.** Transfer the peach mixture to a 13 x 9-inch baking dish, sprinkle the crumble over the top, and scatter the pecans evenly over the crumble. Bake for 10 minutes, reduce the oven temperature to 350°F, and bake until the topping is golden brown and the peaches are bubbling, another 20 to 25 minutes. Let rest for 10 minutes before serving.

### The Diva Says:

Frozen peaches are actually more reliably flavorful than fresh peaches, unless it is the peak of the season. I recommend that you use frozen peaches unless store-bought peaches are at their best.

Frozen peaches may "drool" a lot of liquid when mixed with the sugar and cornstarch, so use a slotted spoon to transfer them to the baking dish and discard most of the accumulated liquid in the bowl or boil it down for a quick peachy sauce that's awfully nice over ice cream or waffles. (The sauce can be frozen for up to 3 months.)

### Diva Variations

Crumble toppings are delicious on apples, berries, pears, and plums. You may need to increase the baking time for firmer fruits such as pears and apples.

# Old-Fashioned Berry Cobbler

Serves 12

Brilliant berries are nestled under a biscuit-like crust to make a dessert that your guests will love, especially when served with sweetened whipped cream or ice cream. This is the dish to take to a picnic in the park or a barbecue. If you'd like, you can use frozen berries, which you don't need to defrost, though you will have to add about 10 minutes to the cooking time. The cobbler should be served the day it's made. You can rewarm it in a low oven or on a covered barbecue (use a disposable aluminum pan because the bottom will discolor on the barbecue).

---

**8 cups berries (see The Diva Says)**

**2 cups sugar**

**⅛ teaspoon ground nutmeg**

**1½ tablespoons cornstarch**

**2 cups Bisquick baking mix**

**1 cup whole milk**

**½ teaspoon ground cinnamon**

**¼ cup (½ stick) unsalted butter, melted**

---

**1.** In a large bowl, combine the berries, 1¼ cups of the sugar, the nutmeg, and cornstarch, stirring to blend. Pour into a 13 x 9-inch baking dish.

✳ **DIVA DO-AHEAD:** At this point, you can cover and refrigerate overnight.

**2.** Preheat the oven to 400°F.

**3.** In a medium-size bowl, blend together the Bisquick, ½ cup of the remaining sugar, and the milk. Spread over the berries.

**4.** In small bowl, combine the remaining ¼ cup of sugar and the cinnamon. Brush the top of the dough with the melted butter and sprinkle with the cinnamon sugar. Bake the cobbler until the top is golden brown and the berries are bubbling, about 30 minutes. Let rest for 10 minutes before serving.

## The Diva Says:

Use a mixture of your favorites berries, or all just one type. Blueberries, blackberries, boysenberries, and Marionberries are all great by themselves, but if you wish, you can add raspberries and/or strawberries.

# Traditional Bread Pudding

Serves 12

I first had bread pudding in New Orleans and thought it was the most sinful dessert I had ever eaten. When I learned it was made from leftover bread and pantry ingredients, I decided it was the Diva's best friend for dessert. It is assembled at least 12 hours in advance and can bake right before serving—another virtue. Saucing this creation is optional; I love Vanilla Custard (page 641) or berry sauces with it.

---

**9 cups torn bread with crust removed**

**1 cup sugar**

**2 teaspoons flavoring of your choice, such as cinnamon or vanilla extract**

**8 large eggs**

**2 cups heavy cream or milk**

---

**1.** Put the bread in a large bowl.

**2.** In another large bowl, whisk together the sugar, flavoring, eggs, and heavy cream until blended. Pour over the bread, stirring to blend well.

✳ **DIVA DO-AHEAD:** At this point, cover and refrigerate for at least 12 and up to 36 hours. Bring to room temperature before continuing.

**3.** Preheat the oven to 350°F. Coat a 13 x 9-inch baking dish or a 12-cup muffin tin with nonstick cooking spray. Spoon the bread pudding mixture into the prepared baking dish or use an ice cream scoop to scoop it into the muffin cups. Bake until puffed and golden brown, 35 to 40 minutes for the large pudding, 22 to 25 minutes for the muffin size. Remove the bread pudding from the oven and let rest for 10 minutes.

✳ **DIVA DO-AHEAD:** See page 652 for instructions on freezing.

# BREAD PUDDINGS

**Bread puddings are perfect** examples of a master recipe that has led to lots of delicious side trips. The beauty of bread pudding is that it must be made the day before, and needs just 45 minutes of baking right before serving. Bread pudding is simply French toast taken on a culinary wild ride, with the addition of your favorite sweet or savory combinations. You can use these sweet bread puddings for dessert or serve them for a breakfast or brunch buffet. You will need a 13 x 9-inch baking dish, or you can use muffin cups to make individual bread puddings. Whichever way you decide to serve them will work beautifully.

If you would like to freeze the bread pudding, bake it for 15 minutes less than the suggested time, remove it from the oven, and let cool to room temperature (this will allow it to cook while retaining some moisture). Cover with plastic wrap and freeze for up to 1 month. Defrost the pudding overnight in the refrigerator, then leave it out at room temperature for about 45 minutes before baking. Cover the pudding loosely with aluminum foil and reheat in a preheated 350°F oven for 20 minutes. Make sure you use an instant-read thermometer to test the internal temperature of the pudding; it should be 145°F. (It's a good idea to check the temperature because the center may still be a little frozen when you reheat the pudding, and it will not cook as fast as the rest of the pudding.) If you have made cupcake-size puddings, rewarm the defrosted cupcakes by placing them on a baking sheet, covering with foil, and baking for 15 to 20 minutes.

## The Diva Says:

Your mom always told you to eat your bread crusts so you'd have curly hair, but for bread puddings, I recommend that you remove them on particularly crusty bread, such as a French loaf. You want the bread practically to dissolve in the egg custard.

Bread puddings are usually served with a sauce and I've recommended several in this chapter, but feel free to make your own choices. You may even decide to serve fresh fruit with your bread pudding instead of a sauce. The puddings are generally served warm, but are perfectly fine at room temperature, too. I recommend that you let them rest for about 10 minutes before serving.

# Chocolate Croissant Bread Pudding 🥛🍺🍷🥂

Serves 12

This decadently rich bread pudding transforms leftover stale croissants into a dessert that will have people waiting in line! I often freeze day-old croissants and when I have enough, I make this for brunch or dessert. If you don't have croissants, this recipe also works well with challah, brioche, donuts, or any other egg-based bread. The pudding is very nice served with Vanilla Custard (page 641) or Raspberry Sauce (page 503).

> **9 cups torn croissants (about 10 large ones)**
>
> **2 cups semisweet chocolate chips or chunks**
>
> **1 cup sugar**
>
> **2 teaspoons white crème de cacao or vanilla extract**
>
> **8 large eggs**
>
> **2 cups heavy cream**

**1.** Put the croissants and chocolate chips in a large bowl.

**2.** In another large bowl, whisk together the sugar, crème de cacao, eggs, and heavy cream until blended. Pour over the croissants and chocolate, stirring to blend.

✳ **DIVA DO-AHEAD:** At this point, cover and refrigerate for at least 12 and up to 36 hours. Bring to room temperature before continuing.

**3.** Preheat the oven to 350°F. Coat a 13 x 9-inch baking dish or a 12-cup muffin tin with nonstick cooking spray. Pour the bread pudding into the prepared baking dish or use an ice cream scoop to fill the muffin cups. Bake until puffed and golden brown, 35 to 40 minutes for the large pudding, 22 to 25 minutes for the muffin size. Remove from the oven and let rest for 10 minutes.

✳ **DIVA DO-AHEAD:** See box at left for instructions on freezing.

# Berry Pudding with Macadamia-Caramel Sauce

Serves 12

This home-style dessert comes from a lovely restaurant named Tuscany. It was served in individual ramekins, but you can make it for a crowd in a 13 x 9-inch baking dish. I like to serve this with vanilla ice cream and caramel sauce, but it's also scrumptious with a berry sauce and sweetened whipped cream.

**8 cups crumbled cornbread, homemade or from a mix (2 boxes of Jiffy cornbread work just fine)**

**3 cups mixed fresh berries, such as blueberries, raspberries, and blackberries, or individually frozen berries, defrosted**

**2 cups heavy cream**

**8 large egg yolks**

**1 cup plus 2 tablespoons sugar**

**2 tablespoons vanilla extract or ¼ cup amaretto**

**1 to 2 tablespoons cold unsalted butter, cut into bits**

**1 recipe Macadamia-Caramel Sauce (recipe follows)**

**1.** Coat a 13 x 9-inch baking dish with non-stick cooking spray.

**2.** Combine the crumbled cornbread and berries in a large bowl.

**3.** In another large bowl, whisk together the cream, egg yolks, 1 cup of sugar, and the vanilla. Pour the mixture over the cornbread and berries and stir well to combine and coat. Let soak for a few minutes, until some of the liquid is absorbed, then transfer to the prepared dish. Sprinkle the top with the remaining 2 tablespoons of sugar and dot with the butter.

❋ **DIVA DO-AHEAD:** At this point, cover and refrigerate for at least 8 and up to 24 hours. Bring pudding to room temperature before continuing.

**4.** Preheat the oven to 350°F. Bake the pudding until puffed and pale golden brown, 40 to 55 minutes. Let rest for 10 minutes.

❋ **DIVA DO-AHEAD:** See page 652 for instructions on freezing.

Serve warm with the caramel sauce.

# Macadamia-Caramel Sauce

Makes about 3½ cups

This buttery caramel sauce studded with chopped macadamia nuts is delicious over bread pudding, ice cream, or plain chocolate cake.

¼ cup (½ stick) unsalted butter

1 cup chopped macadamia nuts

1 cup firmly packed light brown sugar

1 cup heavy cream

Melt the butter in a large saucepan over medium heat. Add the nuts and toast in the butter for 2 to 3 minutes, stirring. Add the brown sugar and stir until melted. Add the heavy cream, bring to a boil, and remove from the heat.

✳ **DIVA DO-AHEAD:** At this point, you can let cool, cover, and refrigerate for up to 1 week or freeze for up to 2 months.

Serve warm.

# Piña Colada Bread Pudding with Macadamia Nuts

Serves 12

Although this seems like a taste of the tropics, the original idea came from a demonstration at the New Orleans School of Cooking, where a wild and crazy Cajun chef was cooking up bread puddings of all flavors for an adoring crowd.

8 cups torn bread (I love using Hawaiian sweet bread, but you can use challah, croissants, or egg bread)

2 cups liquid piña colada mix (see The Diva Says)

6 large eggs

1 cup heavy cream

One 8-ounce can crushed pineapple

¼ teaspoon grated nutmeg

1 cup Baker's Angel Flake coconut

1½ cups finely chopped macadamia nuts

¼ cup (½ stick) unsalted butter, melted

**1.** Coat a 13 x 9-inch baking dish with non-stick cooking spray.

**2.** Place the bread in a large bowl.

**3.** In another large bowl, whisk together the piña colada mix, eggs, heavy cream, pineapple (and its juice), and nutmeg, stirring to blend. Pour over the bread and stir to blend. Transfer to the prepared dish, sprinkle with the coconut and macadamia nuts, and drizzle with the butter.

✳ **DIVA DO-AHEAD:** At this point, cover and refrigerate for at least 8 and up to 24 hours. Bring to room temperature before continuing.

**4.** Preheat the oven to 350°F. Bake the pudding until it is puffed and golden brown, 40 to 50 minutes. Let rest for 10 minutes.

✳ **DIVA DO-AHEAD:** See page 652 for instructions on freezing.

Serve with Macadamia-Caramel Sauce (see page 655).

## The Diva Says:

The piña colada mix has rum in it, so if you prefer to make the pudding nonalcoholic, replace with pineapple-coconut juice.

# Chocolate-Dipped Apricots

Makes about 40 apricots

Every year the Neiman Marcus catalogue sells these delicious confections at an outrageous price, but you can make them in your own kitchen in no time. I like to serve these on a buffet table as part of the dessert offerings, or use as decorations on a cake or cheesecake.

**2 tablespoons unsalted butter**

**One 12-ounce bag semisweet chocolate chips**

**1 pound dried apricots**

### Diva Variation

**Double Chocolate–Dipped Apricots:** In addition to the semisweet chocolate, melt 12 ounces of chopped white chocolate (not chips) with 2 tablespoons of unsalted butter in another small saucepan. Dip the apricots into the dark chocolate as directed. When the chocolate is set, dip the other side of each apricot into the melted white chocolate and let the chocolate set before storing.

**1.** Line a baking sheet with parchment or waxed paper, a silicone liner, or aluminum foil.

**2.** In a small saucepan over low heat, melt the butter and chocolate together, stirring until smooth.

**3.** Remove from the heat and, using a long skewer, dip half of each apricot into the chocolate, then place on the prepared baking sheet to let the chocolate set.

✳ **DIVA DO-AHEAD:** At this point, you can store in an airtight container for up to 2 days or freeze for up to 2 months.

# Bittersweet Chocolate Fondue

Makes about 3 cups; serves 10 to 12

This rich fondue is perfect to serve as dessert for a casual dinner. Make sure you have lots of long skewers and a variety of dippers for your guests.

**¾ cup heavy cream**

**12 ounces bittersweet chocolate, broken into small pieces**

**2 teaspoons liqueur, such as amaretto, Grand Marnier, Frangelico, or brandy (optional)**

**1.** In a 2-quart saucepan over medium heat, bring the cream to a boil. Add the chocolate, remove from the heat, and allow the chocolate to melt into the cream. Whisk until smooth, then stir in the liqueur if using.

✳ **DIVA DO-AHEAD:** At this point, you can let cool, cover, and refrigerate for up to 3 days. Rewarm over low heat.

**2.** Transfer to a slow cooker or fondue pot and serve warm.

## Diva Variations

**Mexican Chocolate Fondue:** This variation is inspired by the hot chocolate sold in Mexico. Add ½ teaspoon ground cinnamon and 1 tablespoon espresso granules to the cream and proceed as directed.

**Mocha Fondue:** This chocolate and coffee combination can't be beat. Add 2 table-spoons of espresso granules to the cream while it is boiling and proceed as directed.

**Instant Chocolate Fondue:** A 16-ounce can of Hershey's Hot Fudge Chocolate Shoppe Topping heated in a fondue pot is a Diva's best friend—there's even a nonfat version.

## Fruity Fondue Dippers

- Dried apricots
- Dried pineapple, cut into bite-size pieces
- Whole strawberries with stems left on
- Bananas, peeled, cut into ½-inch chunks, and brushed with lemon juice
- to prevent discoloration (I usually don't cut them until right before serving)
- Apples, sliced into ¼-inch wedges, seeded section cut off, and brushed with lemon juice
- Orange segments
- Melon balls (for Nonnie's Amaretto Fondue, right)

# Nonnie's Amaretto Fondue

Makes 4 cups; serves 10 to 12

This delicious sauce is a great dip for fresh fruit and small pieces of cake. My friend Nonnie and I have been known to use instant vanilla pudding in a pinch in place of the custard. You can also substitute Grand Marnier for the amaretto if you'd like an orange-flavored sauce. If you would prefer to leave out the alcohol, replace it with ½ teaspoon of almond extract for almond-flavored fondue or 1 teaspoon of orange extract for an orange-flavored crème.

> **2 cups chilled Vanilla Custard (page 641)**
>
> **2 cups heavy cream, whipped until stiff peaks form**
>
> **¼ cup amaretto**

Put the custard in a large bowl and fold in the whipped cream and amaretto.

✳ **DIVA DO-AHEAD:** At this point, cover and refrigerate for at least 4 hours and up to 2 days, or freeze for up to 1 month. Defrost at room temperature and rewhip with a whisk before serving.

# Toblerone Fondue

Makes about 3 cups; serves 10 to 12

Toblerone, those wonderful milk chocolate and hazelnut candy bars, make an outrageously delicious fondue. Because milk chocolate is a little finicky, make sure you chop the bars finely so they melt in the boiling cream quickly.

> **1 cup heavy cream**
>
> **Three 6-ounce Toblerone Milk Chocolate bars, finely chopped**

**1.** In a 2-quart saucepan, heat the cream to boiling. Remove from the heat, add the chocolate, and whisk until melted.

✳ **DIVA DO-AHEAD:** At this point, you can let cool, cover, and refrigerate for up to 3 days. Rewarm over low heat.

**2.** Transfer to a slow cooker or fondue pot and serve warm.

> ## More Fondue Dippers
> - Pound cake or angel food cake, cut into cubes
> - Biscotti
> - Pretzel sticks or small twisted pretzels (for chocolate fondue only)
> - Shortbread cookies
> - Macaroons, cut into bite-size pieces

# Tuxedo Strawberries

*Makes 24 strawberries*

This simple way to dip strawberries is fun, and the end result makes you look like a genius! The strawberries are dipped in white chocolate, then bittersweet chocolate, and for a final touch, they each get a little bow tie and buttons. Serve them as a garnish for ice cream, pudding, cakes, or other desserts, or on a plate by themselves.

¼ cup heavy cream

12 ounces white chocolate, finely chopped

12 ounces bittersweet or semisweet chocolate, finely chopped

24 perfect 2-inch strawberries with stems, washed and patted dry

**1.** Line a baking sheet with waxed or parchment paper or aluminum foil.

**2.** In a small, heavy saucepan, heat 2 tablespoons of the cream over low heat, then add the white chocolate and stir until melted and smooth. In another small, heavy saucepan, repeat the procedure with the dark chocolate and the remaining 2 tablespoons of cream. Remove both saucepans from the heat.

**3.** Holding each strawberry by the stem, either dip it into the white chocolate or, using a spoon, drizzle it with white choco-late to coat the berry all the way up to the stem. Lay the berries on the baking sheet until the chocolate is set.

**4.** When the white chocolate is set, line the baking sheet with fresh paper or foil. Dip each strawberry into the dark choco-late, creating a V shape in the front of the berry (it will look like the opening of a tuxedo jacket). Lay the berries on the baking sheet.

**5.** With a toothpick, place 3 tiny dots of dark chocolate down the front of the V shape for buttons and draw a small bow tie in dark chocolate. Allow the chocolate to set for about 15 minutes.

❋ **DIVA DO-AHEAD:** At this point, you can store at room temperature for up to 3 hours or refrigerate for up to 8 hours. Refrigeration will cause the chocolate to sweat when it comes to room temperature, so wipe the berries carefully with a paper towel if this happens.

# Chocolate Truffles

Makes about thirty 1-inch truffles

Seductive and deeply flavored, truffles are simple to make. They should be served at room temperature, so be sure to bring them out of the refrigerator about 45 minutes before serving. What you choose to roll the truffles in is up to you, whether it's unsweetened cocoa powder, melted chocolate, finely chopped nuts, or confectioners' sugar.

¾ **cup heavy cream**

12 **ounces semisweet chocolate, finely chopped**

2 **tablespoons alcoholic flavoring of your choice, such as amaretto, bourbon, Grand Marnier, Cointreau, Chambord, dark rum, or Kahlúa; or 1 teaspoon vanilla extract**

½ **cup coating, such as sifted cocoa powder, sifted confectioners' sugar, or chopped nuts**

**1.** In a small saucepan, heat the cream to boiling and remove from the heat. Add the chocolate and stir until melted and smooth. Stir in the flavoring, let cool, cover, and set aside at room temperature for 2 hours.

**2.** Line a baking sheet with parchment or waxed paper, a silicone liner, or aluminum foil.

**3.** Using a small scoop or a tablespoon, scoop out balls of the chocolate and roll them between the palms of your hands to make them round. Place on the baking sheet. Spread the coating on another baking sheet and roll the truffles in it, covering them evenly, and then return them to the lined baking sheet. Serve immediately or store.

✳ **DIVA DO-AHEAD:** At this point, you can place in an airtight container and refrigerate for up to 2 weeks or freeze for up to 6 months. Defrost overnight in the refrigerator and bring to room temperature for 45 minutes before serving.

# Suggested Menus for Stress-Free Entertaining

All of these menus are for 12 people; for a larger group, you will need to increase the ingredients in each recipe (please refer to the chart on page 24), and you may also want to add more dishes.

## Casual Brunch

**Little Diva's Favorite Bloody Mary** (page 46) station

**Field Greens with Basil Vinaigrette** (page 173)

**Apple Muffins** (page 533) *or* **Blueberry Streusel Muffins** (page 532)

**Overnight French Toast** (page 553)

**Hash Brown Sausage Casserole** (page 562)

**Fresh fruit with Nonnie's Amaretto Fondue** (page 659)

## Informal Brunch I

**Mimosas** (page 43) **and Little Diva's Favorite Bloody Mary** (page 46) **station**

**Field Greens with Basil Vinaigrette** (page 173)

**Amaretto-Peach French Toast** (page 554)

**Spinach-Boursin Quiche** (page 560)

**Bacon for a Crowd** (page 573)

**Heavenly Scones** (page 528)

## Informal Brunch II

**Mimosas** (page 43) **and Little Diva's Favorite Bloody Mary** (page 46) **station**

**Cottage Garden Stuffed French Toast** (page 556)

**Smoked Salmon and Bagel Strata** (page 569)

**Baked Rhubarb** (page 269)

**Spinach Salad with Strawberries and Raspberry Vinaigrette** (page 170)

**Coffee Cake Muffins** (page 531)

## Formal Brunch

**Sangria** (page 48 or 49) *or* **Mimosas** (page 43) **and Little Diva's Favorite Bloody Mary** (page 46) **station**

**Spicy Nuts** (page 143)

**Glazed Ham** (page 449)

**Mushroom and Asparagus Strata** (page 565)

**Stuffed Tomatoes** (page 263)

**Neapolitan Potato Cake** (page 248) *or* **Cranberry-Oat Scones** (page 529)

**Fresh fruit layered with Nonnie's Amaretto Fondue** (page 659)

**Praline Apple French Toast** (page 558)

## Casual Lunch I

**Brewski Cheddar Dip** (page 75) **with Pretzels**

**Pigs in a Blanket** (page 130)

**Buffalo Chicken Cutlets for Sandwiches** (page 314)

**Marinated Orange Salad** (page 167)

**Diane's Original Chopped Salad** (page 179)

**Cool and Creamy Margaritaville Pie with Macadamia Nut Crust and Triple Sec Crème** (page 614) *or* **World's Greatest Cream Cheese Brownies** (page 623) **and Belafonte Bars** (page 622)

## Casual Lunch II

**White Peach Sangria** (page 48)

**Crudités with dip of your choice** (pages 74–91)

**Crab Louis Chopped Salad** (page 181)

**New-Fashioned Chicken Waldorf Salad** (page 208)

**Dilly Bread** (page 520)

**Mixed Fruit Tart with Glaze** (page 613) *or* **Petite Cheesecakes with Fruit Toppings** (page 605)

## Informal Lunch I

**Mimosas** (page 43)

**Sangria** (page 48 or 49)

**Marinated Goat Cheese with crackers** (page 102)

**All New Dijon Dilly Dip with crudités** (page 79)

**Curried Chicken Salad** (page 207) **over spinach salad** *or* **The Diva's Shrimp Salad** (page 209) **over Field Greens with Basil Vinaigrette** (page 173)

**Heavenly Scones** (page 528) *or* **Dilly Bread** (page 520)

**Strawberry Shortcake Layer Cake** (page 588) *or* **Peach Melba Trifle** (page 645)

## Informal Lunch II

**Mexican Beer and Margaritas** (pages 50 and 51)

**Chipotle Corn Dip** (page 85) **with tortilla chips or crudités**

**South of the Border Roll-Ups** (page 544)

**The Cubano** (page 548)

**Southwestern Chopped Salad** (page 185)

**Southwestern Cornbread** (page 519)

**Key Lime Cheesecake** (page 602) *or* **Belafonte Bars** (page 622), **garnished with fresh strawberries**

## Formal Lunch

**Pear Bellinis** (page 57)

**Spicy Nuts** (page 143)

**Field Greens with Basil Vinaigrette** (page 173)

**Honey Mustard–Glazed Salmon** (page 351) *or* **'Shroom Stuffed Chicken Breasts** (page 306)

**Roasted Asparagus** (page 226)

**Heavenly Scones** (page 528) *or* **Garlic-Parmesan Bread** (page 524)

**Black Forest Cake** (page 592) *or* **Chocolate-Raspberry Tart** (page 611)

## Casual Grazing Party

**Tequila Sunrise** (page 44) *or* **Mama D's Easy Margarita** (page 50)

**Chipotle Wings** (page 297)

**Creamy Cilantro Dip** (page 78) **with crudités**

**Black Bean, Corn, and Salsa Dip** (page 86) **with chips**

**Chipotle Corn Dip** (page 85) **with chips**

**Pigs in a Blanket** (page 130)

**Deviled Southwestern Eggs** (see page 142)

**Spicy Nuts** (page 143)

**South of the Border Roll-Ups** (page 544) *or* **The Guacamole Club** (page 547)

**Pizza Margherita** (page 538)

**Peel and Eat Shrimp** (page 373) **with Bloody Mary Shrimp Cocktail Sauce** (see page 110)

**Black and White Chocolate Chip Cookies** (page 637)

**Belafonte Bars** (page 622)

## Formal Grazing Party I

**Cosmopolitan Cocktails** (page 53) *or* **Sgroppinos** (page 58) **or your favorite martini**

**All New Dijon Dilly Dip** (page 79) **with fresh vegetable dippers**

**Red, White, and Green Pesto Torte** (page 95) **with baguette or crackers**

**Baked Brie with Apricots and Dried Cranberries** (page 101) **with baguette or crackers**

**Mediterranean Wings** (page 296)

**Marinated Shrimp** (page 108)

**Devilishly Good Deviled Eggs** (page 141)

**Bacon-Wrapped Dates with Parmesan** (page 140)

**Pesto and Shrimp Pizza** (page 537)

**Stuffed Mushrooms** (page 139)

**Cheese platter**

**Tuxedo Strawberries** (page 660) *or* **fresh fruit skewers with Nonnie's Amaretto Fondue** (page 659)

**World's Greatest Cream Cheese Brownies** (page 623) *or* **Amaretto Shortbread Bars** (page 633)

## Formal Grazing Party II

**Full bar with Champagne**

**Smoky Blue Dip** (page 74) **with potato chips**

**Cranberry-Walnut Cheese Ball** (page 93)

**Fresh Herb Ranch Dip** (page 78) **with crudités**

**Boiled Shrimp** (page 109) **with dipping sauces**

**Garlic-Stuffed Clams** (page 117)

**Bacon-Wrapped Dates with Parmesan** (page 140)

**Puffed Mushroom Delights** (page 138)

**Devilishly Good Deviled Eggs** (page 141)

**Smoked Salmon Spread** (page 80) *or* **Whole Hog Sausage Rolls** (page 132)

**Warm Olives** (page 121)

## Casual Outdoor Dinner

**Vodka Slush** (page 43) *or* **Old-Fashioned Lemonade** (page 63) *or* **Shirley's Old-Fashioned Ice Tea** (page 64)

**Smoky Blue Dip** (page 74) **with Pita Chips** (page 527), **potato chips, or crudités**

**Fresh Herb Ranch Dip** (page 78) **with crudités and crackers** *or* **Party Mix** (page 145)

**Layered Vegetable Salad** (pages 157 and 158)

**Crispy Fried Chicken** (page 318) *or* **Oven-Fried Chicken** (page 317)

**Dilly Red Potato Salad** (page 193)

**Perfect Corn on the Cob** (page 237) *or* **Grilled Vegetables** (page 266)

**Dijon, Bacon, and Swiss Bread** (page 523)

**Banana Split Pie** (page 617) *or* **Caramel-Pecan Turtle Brownies** (page 628) **with vanilla ice cream and World's Best Hot Fudge Sauce** (page 501)

## Informal Dinner I

**Red Sangria** (page 49)

**Rosemary White Bean Spread** (page 90) **with Pita Chips** (page 527)

**Antipasto with Napa-Style Marinated Parmesan** (page 122), **Fresh Herb Tortellini-and–Olive Skewers** (page 123), **and Tarragon-Marinated Mushrooms** (page 125)

**Ryan's Creamy Caesar Salad** (page 174)

**Caprese Salad** (page 176)

**Breaded Chicken Cutlets Italian Style** (page 312)

**Zucchini Parmesan** (page 260)

**Lemon Icebox Cake** (page 586) *or* **Strawberry Cannoli** (page 639)

## Informal Dinner II

**Kir Royales** (page 56)

**Tapenade** (page 84) **with Pita Chips** (page 527)

**Mock Boursin Cheese** (page 91) **stuffed into celery**

**Roasted Wild Mushroom Salad** (page 163)

(continued on next page)

**Quick Simply Baked Fish** (page 338) *or*
**Lemon Chicken Oreganata** (page 319)
*or* **Garlic and Herb Stuffed Leg of Lamb**
(page 461)

**Green Bean and Smoked Mozzarella Salad**
(page 161)

**Stuffed Tomatoes à la Française** (page 263)

**Peperonata** (page 231)

**Salad dressed with Cabernet Vinaigrette**
(page 212)

**Chocolate-Raspberry Tart** (page 611) *or*
**Chocolate Tiramisu Cake** (page 594)

## Formal Dinner

**Champagne** *or* **Cosmopolitan Cocktails**
(page 53)

**Chesapeake Bay Seafood Cheesecake**
(page 99)

**Sausage-Stuffed Clams** (page 116)

**Cranberry–Blue Cheese Field Greens Salad**
(page 172)

**Roast Beef Tenderloin** (page 385) **with
Brandied Triple Mushroom Sauté** (page 243)

**Make-Ahead Garlic Mashed Potatoes** (see
page 247) *or* **French Onion Bread Pudding**
(see page 282)

**Spinach Parmesan Casserole** (page 257)

**Honey-Thyme Carrots** (page 236)

**Chocolate Tiramisu Cake** (page 594) *or*
**Black Forest Cake** (page 592)

## Thanksgiving Dinner

This is the menu that I teach to my students, and it's also the menu that I serve on Thanksgiving to my family. I've suggested some substitutions here as well.

**Warm Spiced Cider** (page 61) *or* **Mulled Wine**
(page 60)

**Dried Herb Ranch Dip** (page 77) **with
crudités** *or* **Rosemary Walnuts** (page 144)

**Traditional Thanksgiving Turkey** (page 332)

**Make-Ahead Cheesy Mashed Potatoes**
(page 246)

**Gulliver's Corn** (page 238)

**Sweet Potato–Apple Gratin** (page 262)

**Green Beans with Sherried Onion and
Mushroom Sauce** (page 230) *or* **Roasted
Brussels Sprouts with Pancetta** (page 232)

**Cranberry Chutney** (page 480)

**Warm Thanksgiving Apple Cake** (page
601) **with Toasted Pecan Sauce** (page 501)
*or* **Sinful Chocolate Pecan Pie** (page 607)
*or* **Mom's Apple Pie Cake** (page 606) *or*
**Pumpkin Ice Cream Pie** (page 620) **with
Butterscotch Sauce** (page 502)

## Traditional Easter Dinner

This Easter dinner showcases a beautifully glazed ham and all the traditional trimmings.

White or Blush Sangria (page 49)

Carrie's Chutney Cheese Ball (page 92) with crackers

Cheesy Sticks (page 136)

Layered Vegetable Salad with Creamy Dill and Chive Dressing (page 157)

Roasted Asparagus (page 226)

Cheesy Potato Gratin (page 253)

Glazed Ham (page 449)

Old-Fashioned California Cornbread (page 517)

Strawberry Shortcake Layer Cake (page 588) *or* Strawberry, Pineapple, and Coconut Trifle (page 647) *or* Nancy Kelly's Two-Day Memphis Coconut Cake (page 589)

## Alternative Easter Dinner

Mediterranean flavors make this dinner a winner when you want to depart from the traditional ham.

Red Sangria (page 49)

Marinated Goat Cheese (page 102) with crackers

Warm Olives (page 121)

Field Greens with Basil Vinaigrette (page 173)

Rolled Boneless Leg of Lamb (page 457) *or* Roasted Rack of Lamb (page 466)

Pastitsio (page 415)

Roasted Asparagus (page 226)

Artisan bread of your choice from a local bakery

Lemon Icebox Cake (page 586) *or* Nancy Kelly's Two-Day Memphis Coconut Cake (page 589) *or* Petite Cheesecakes with Fruit Toppings (page 605)

## Passover Dinner

Kir Royales (page 56) and kosher wine

All New Dijon Dilly Dip (page 79) with crudités

Roasted Garlic-Eggplant Dip (page 89) with matzoh

Marinated Orange Salad (page 167)

Roasted Roots (page 264)

Grilled Vegetables (page 266)

Mom's Sunday Roast Chicken (page 330) *or* The Very Best Brisket (page 400)

Matzoh

Chocolate Dipped Apricots (page 657), Tuxedo Strawberries (page 660), and Chocolate Truffles (page 661)

## Christmas Dinner

This dinner is elegant but simple enough so that all you will need to do in the hours before the meal is roast the beef and reheat your sides.

Kir Royales (page 56) *or* Champagne

Baked Brie with Apricots and Dried Cranberries (page 101) and baguette *or* Cheesy Pesto Pinwheels (see page 135)

Field Greens with Basil Vinaigrette (page 173) *or* Cranberry–Blue Cheese Field Greens Salad (page 172)

Roast Beef Tenderloin (page 385) *or* New York Strip Roast (page 387)

Make-Ahead Cheesy Mashed Potatoes (page 246) *or* Savory Bread Pudding (page 281)

Spinach Parmesan Casserole (page 257)

Honey-Thyme Carrots (page 236)

Basic Dinner Rolls (page 525)

Chocolate Tiramisu Cake (page 594) *or* Strawberry-Amaretto Trifle (page 646)

## Christmas Eve Dinner

If your night-before dinner is also a celebration, though a lesser one than on Christmas Day, I recommend this simple meal.

Antipasto platter with marinated mushrooms, assorted meats and cheeses, and baguette

Ryan's Creamy Caesar Salad (page 174)

Seafood Lasagna (page 360) *or* Pastitsio (page 415) *or* Lemon Chicken Oreganata (page 319)

Lemon Icebox Cake (page 586) *or* Chocolate Tiramisu Cake (page 594)

## New Year's Eve Dinner

Champagne

Baked Brie (page 101), with topping of your choice

Boiled Shrimp (page 109) with dipping sauces *or* a Raw Bar (see page 118)

Field greens with Spicy Nuts (page 143) and Sherry Vinaigrette (page 214)

Chicken Stuffed with Prosciutto and Fontina (page 299) *or* Seafood Florentine (page 354) *or* Chicken Florentine (see page 354)

Stuffed Tomatoes (page 263)

Florentine Rice Casserole (page 277, to accompany the stuffed chicken) *or* Pilaf Milanese (page 276, to accompany seafood)

Cousin Nella's Umbrian Easter Bread (page 515)

Chocolate-Coconut Cake (page 593) *or* Tuxedo Strawberries (page 660), Chocolate-Dipped Apricots (page 657), and Chocolate Truffles (page 661)

# Sources

**The GadgetSource.com**
Calvert Retail, LP
P.O. Box 302
Montchanin, DE 19710
(800) 458-2616
www.thegadgetsource.com

Ice cube bags.

**Great News! Discount
Cookware and Cooking
School**
1788 Garnet Avenue
San Diego, CA 92109
(888) 478-2433
www.discountcooking.com

Cookware (All-Clad, Emile Henry), gadgets (microplanes, spatulas, silicone liners), and ingredients in my hometown.

**King Arthur Flour
The Baker's Catalogue**
135 Route 5 South
P.O. Box 1010
Norwich, VT 05055
(800) 827-6836
www.kingarthurflour.com

Catalogue and online site with baking ingredients (chocolate, Nielsen-Massey vanilla, Key lime juice, citrus oils) and equipment.

**The Kitchen Shoppe**
101 Shady Lane
Carlisle, PA 17013
(800) 391-2665
www.kitchenshoppe.com

Shell canapé baking dishes, kitchen equipment, and ingredients (vanilla paste and Bourbon vanilla).

**Nellie & Joe's**
P.O. Box 2368
Key West, FL 33045
(800) LIME-PIE
www.keylimejuice.com

Key lime juice.

**Superior Touch
Better than Bouillon**
2355 E. Francis Street
Ontario, CA 91761
(909) 923-4733
www.superiortouch.com

Soup bases and lobster stock.

**Sur La Table**
5701 6th Avenue #486
Seattle, WA 98108
(800) 243-0852
www.surlatable.com

National chain that carries cookware, gadgets, ingredients, linens, and tableware at their stores as well as online.

**Williams-Sonoma, Inc.**
3250 Van Ness Avenue
San Francisco, CA 94109
(877) 812-6235
www.williams-sonoma.com

National chain with cookware, gadgets, ingredients, linens, and tableware, available at their stores and online.

# Measurement Equivalents

Please note that all conversions are approximate.

## Liquid Conversions

| U.S. | Metric |
|------|--------|
| 1 tsp | 5 ml |
| 1 tbs | 15 ml |
| 2 tbs | 30 ml |
| 3 tbs | 45 ml |
| 1/4 cup | 60 ml |
| 1/3 cup | 75 ml |
| 1/3 cup + 1 tbs | 90 ml |
| 1/3 cup + 2 tbs | 100 ml |
| 1/2 cup | 120 ml |
| 2/3 cup | 150 ml |
| 3/4 cup | 180 ml |
| 3/4 cup + 2 tbs | 200 ml |
| 1 cup | 240 ml |
| 1 cup + 2 tbs | 275 ml |
| 1 1/4 cups | 300 ml |
| 1 1/3 cups | 325 ml |
| 1 1/2 cups | 350 ml |
| 1 2/3 cups | 375 ml |
| 1 3/4 cups | 400 ml |
| 1 3/4 cups + 2 tbs | 450 ml |
| 2 cups (1 pint) | 475 ml |
| 2 1/2 cups | 600 ml |
| 3 cups | 720 ml |
| 4 cups (1 quart) | 945 ml |
| | (1,000 ml is 1 liter) |

## Weight Conversions

| U.S./U.K. | Metric |
|-----------|--------|
| 1/2 oz | 14 g |
| 1 oz | 28 g |
| 1 1/2 oz | 43 g |
| 2 oz | 57 g |
| 2 1/2 oz | 71 g |
| 3 oz | 85 g |
| 3 1/2 oz | 100 g |
| 4 oz | 113 g |
| 5 oz | 142 g |
| 6 oz | 170 g |
| 7 oz | 200 g |
| 8 oz | 227 g |
| 9 oz | 255 g |
| 10 oz | 284 g |
| 11 oz | 312 g |
| 12 oz | 340 g |
| 13 oz | 368 g |
| 14 oz | 400 g |
| 15 oz | 425 g |
| 1 lb | 454 g |

## Oven Temperatures

| °F | Gas Mark | °C |
|-----|----------|-----|
| 250 | 1/2 | 120 |
| 275 | 1 | 140 |
| 300 | 2 | 150 |
| 325 | 3 | 165 |
| 350 | 4 | 180 |
| 375 | 5 | 190 |
| 400 | 6 | 200 |
| 425 | 7 | 220 |
| 450 | 8 | 230 |
| 475 | 9 | 240 |
| 500 | 10 | 260 |
| 550 | Broil | 290 |

# Index